Leiths

MEAT BIBLE

Also in the Leiths series

Leiths Cookery Bible
Leiths Techniques Bible
Leiths Vegetarian Bible
Leiths Fish Bible
Leiths Baking Bible
Leiths Simple Cookery

Leiths
MEAT BIBLE

**MAX CLARK &
SUSAN SPAULL**

BLOOMSBURY

LONDON · BERLIN · NEW YORK · SYDNEY

First published in Great Britain 2010
This paperback edition published 2012

Copyright © 2010 by Leiths School of Food and Wine

The moral right of the authors has been asserted

Bloomsbury Publishing Plc, 50 Bedford Square, London WC1B 3DP

A CIP catalogue record for this book is available from the British Library

ISBN 978 1 4088 3352 0

Photography by William Lingwood
Home economy by Lucy Mckelvie
Props styling by Jo Harris
Illustrations by Kate Simunek
Book design by Here + There
Typseset by China by C&C Offset Printing Co, Ltd

10 9 8 7 6 5 4 3 2 1

www.bloomsbury.com

Contents

Acknowledgements

Writing a book is a team effort and there were so many people on the team for the *Meat Bible* we hope we can convey our deepest gratitude to all.

First and foremost we wish to thank Leiths School of Food and Wine for making this book possible, for the inspiring food environment and a great group of co-workers who have always been ready to test, re-test and taste all our recipes.

We would also like to thank our editor at Bloomsbury, Natalie Hunt, who has been steadfast and focused throughout the project. Thanks also to William Lingwood, the photographer, who created these superb photographs along with home economist Lucy Mckelvie. Thank you both for these beautiful, delicious photos. Thank you too to Trish Burgess, our copyeditor, for her keen eye for detail and organisation.

Max is deeply grateful to her dear, late, much loved and missed friend Ed Mann, for his encouragement, support and never-ending faith in her, and without whom she may not have pursued her interest in food writing.

She would also like to thank the staff at Billfields, in particular Darren and Joe North and Paul Quinn, for sourcing and supplying the highest quality meat, poultry and game for both the recipe testing and photography, and for their incredible patience, help and advice on all aspects of butchery.

Susan would like to give special thanks to Robert and Rebecca, John and Kerry at La Muse, France, Jonathan and Caroline Compton, Tess Backhouse and Trevor Underwood for their unwavering support and enthusiasm.

Foreword

This book is definitely one for carnivores. Max Clark has been writing recipes for Leiths for many years, but this is her first Leiths Bible. Her passion for meat is unbounded. Susan Spaull has written several Bibles and is a very experienced chef. Their combined talents have produced a truly wonderful book.

The recipes range from the humble Shepherd's Pie to the vastly complicated Beef en Gelée. They make use of simple meats such as pork chops, but also very exotic ones such as kangaroo and alligator.

This is a cookbook for amateurs and professionals alike. Although full of creative and tempting recipes, it is also a practical and theoretical manual. There is information about all the different methods of cooking meat, and why to choose one method over another. There are helpful charts that cover everything from roasting times to cuts of meat, and there is advice on how to carve, slice and chop.

Understanding a little of the theory behind cooking can make the task so much simpler and less stressful. For example, I don't know many home cooks who are not liable to panic when serving up a roast because everything seems to need last-minute attention. In fact, the key to a perfectly roast piece of meat is in allowing it to rest for 20 minutes before it is carved. Having learnt that simple rule, the gravy-making can become a joy rather than a pain. This book is filled with useful advice of the kind that will remind you that good cooking is rewarding and also fun.

I hope that you will enjoy cooking from this book, that it will encourage you to try new and unusual recipes, and that it will become an invaluable manual in your kitchen.

Caroline Waldegrave OBE

Introduction

Meat has been a favourite part of man's diet for more than two million years. Some anthropologists believe that the consumption of meat, and in particular cooked meat, enabled the brains of our early ancestors to increase in size, thereby – over time – producing a more intelligent species. Whatever our beliefs about the evolutionary process, we do know that the protein from meat is of primary importance to modern man for developing and maintaining brain function and muscle mass and, as such, is a key part of our diet.

Although the supply of meat was infrequent and intermittent prior to the domestication of animals, dedicated hunting by our ancestors produced a great variety of small animals and birds for the ancient table. The skilful hunter was prized for his ability and was justly honoured by the community. This can be observed in the tradition of feast days with their centrepiece of large joints of roasted meat and the ritual of carving the meat at the table by the head of the group. These traditions were part of the pattern of life of our ancestral tribes. Today, the Sunday roast remains synonymous with the gathering of family and friends – our tribe.

With the domestication of many animals, meat is now readily available in a huge variety of forms. In the last fifty to one hundred years, cooking methods have become more sophisticated as our kitchen equipment has become more reliable and more affordable. Although families are now smaller and large joints of meat are not cooked as frequently as they were in the past, the consumption of meat remains very popular throughout the world.

Leiths Meat Bible provides detailed information about each type of meat, poultry and game. Here is everything today's cook needs to know, from how to choose each cut of meat to selecting the best cooking method. The *Meat Bible* enables the cook to learn about the structure of meat and what happens to it when it is heated, what causes a piece of meat to be tough or tender and which flavours will enhance the particular meat.

There are simple step-by-step instructions on various aspects of butchery, such as how to joint a chicken, trim a rack of lamb and bone a duck, through to how to construct an impressive crown roast of lamb or prepare a pig's trotter. The recipes in this book include traditional favourites and modern restaurant-style creations. They are organised into sections, each dedicated to a specific type of meat, poultry, game or exotic animal, along with their relevant preparation techniques and cooking methods. Every category begins with recipes using the largest joints of meat or whole birds and progresses through to individual portions, minced meat and offal. And for every roast there are detailed carving directions.

There is a section of supplementary recipes which covers pastry, pasta, stocks, sauces and vegetables. The content of this section is by no means exhaustive, but aims to provide the cook with the most frequently needed and favourite accompaniments to the meat recipes. After all, what would roast beef be without Yorkshire pudding?

We hope that *Leiths Meat Bible* will encourage and inspire cooks of all skill levels to try new ideas, from the simple to the technically challenging.

Max Clark and Susan Spaull

Notes for Using this Book

Unless stated otherwise:
- All spoon measures are level.
- All eggs are medium, weighing approximately 60 g in the shell.
- Onions, carrots, ginger and garlic are peeled before use.

Oil and Cooking Fats

Many meat recipes require the meat to be browned in oil or other fat. If the type of fat is not specified in the recipe, use your favourite oil or fat, or an all-purpose salad oil, such as sunflower oil, corn oil or vegetable oil.

Butter, although delicious in flavour, burns at low temperatures. Unsalted butter has fewer impurities than salted butter, so it will reach a slightly higher temperature. Clarified butter and ghee are butter in which the milk solids and salt have been removed, making it possible to heat them to a high temperature without smoking and burning.

There are three methods for making clarified butter. The first is to put the butter into a saucepan with a cupful of water and heat until melted and frothy. Allow to cool and set solid, then lift the butter, now clarified, off the top of the liquid. The second method is to heat the butter until foaming. Continue to heat until the milk solids begin to sizzle but without allowing them to burn. Pour it through fine muslin or a double layer of clean J-cloth. The third method is to melt the butter in a heavy-based saucepan and skim off the froth with a slotted spoon. Pout the clear butter into a bowl, leaving behind the white solids. Note that clarified butter will act as a seal on pâtés or potted meats, and is useful for frying as it will withstand great heat before burning.

Using a combination of light olive oil and unsalted butter together for browning meat means that a high temperature can be achieved, with the added benefit of extra flavour from the butter. Alternatively, the meat can be browned in corn or seed oil, then a little butter added to the pan near the end of the cooking process. This creates a very deep and shiny colour on the meat, and will thicken the pan juices slightly.

Goose and duck fat can be bought in jars and tins, and are good for roasting meats, especially those low in natural fats. They are also excellent for roasting potatoes, producing a very light and crisp result.

Olive oil comes in different strengths and qualities, from light to extra virgin. In general, the more expensive the oil, the stronger the flavour and the better its overall quality. Olive oil doesn't heat well because its structure begins to denature at relatively low temperatures and this has a detrimental effect on the flavour. Given that it cannot reach the same temperatures as corn or seed oils, it can be difficult to brown meat in it successfully, particularly if a good, dark brown colour is desired. Extra virgin olive oil is probably best kept for use in salad dressings, or for drizzling over a cooked dish for extra flavour and shine, or wherever it is not adversely affected by heating, in order to enjoy its distinct and fresh fruity qualities.

Salad oil is an all-purpose seed or vegetable oil (e.g. sunflower, corn, safflower) that is tasteless and has a high smoke point (232°C/450°F for sunflower oil, 266°C/510°F for safflower oil), so it can be heated to the appropriate temperature when cooking, or used as a neutral medium to carry other flavours, as in dressings.

Salt

Salt is an important ingredient in cooking, not just to enhance the flavour of food, but as a preservative in a dry cure or brine solution. It is important not to apply salt to raw meat until you are ready to cook it because the salt will draw the moisture from the meat whilst it is waiting to be cooked and the moist surface will not brown readily.

Many recipes in this book recommend a particular type of salt, such as flaky sea salt or rock salt. It is by no means essential to the recipe to use the type suggested, but doing so will give the best results. There are many different types of salt available, and they vary in their quality and uses. The type of salt used should be specific for the job.

All-purpose table salt has a particularly abrasive texture and strong flavour that can dominate the flavour of a delicate dish. It is best used for salting water for cooking vegetables, pasta and rice, or added to dishes where its flavour will be cooked out, as in casseroles.

Coarse sea salt gives a crunchy texture and has a slightly 'softer', more complex flavour than table salt due to the variety of minerals present in addition to sodium chloride. It is excellent for seasoning roast potatoes, adding to the crunchy texture of their exterior. It will also help to produce good crackling on roast pork.

Flaky sea salt is the best choice of salt when it is to be eaten 'raw', such as in a salad or very lightly cooked dishes. This is also the salt to use when cooking delicately flavoured ingredients so that their taste isn't overwhelmed by the flavour of salt.

Natural, unbleached salts are increasingly popular and come either as a chunk, rather like a large, semi-precious stone, or as clumps of smaller crystals, which have a soft, moist texture. Their natural pink and grey colours can look rather unappetizing as most of us are used to using bleached, pure white salt, but they are well worth trying as they are delicate and quite delicious. The cost, though, might make them prohibitive for general daily use.

Understanding Meat

The French word for meat is *viande*, derived from the Latin *vivenda*, meaning 'that which gives life', and is particularly accurate as meat is rich in protein, minerals and vitamins. It is relatively expensive and in the past was eaten in smaller quantities than it is today.

Rituals and customs have surrounded the slaughter of animals and consumption of meat throughout history. Today these customs are still evident in the tradition of eating roasts for religious celebrations, such as Christmas and Easter. For many families in Britain, the Sunday roast remains an important weekly occasion.

Certain religions have customs specifying the method by which animals are slaughtered. Orthodox Jewish people can eat meat only from animals that have cloven hooves and chew the cud. These animals must be ritually slaughtered and prepared to render the meat kosher (literally 'proper') by a special butcher. Some Muslims eat only meat that has been killed by a licensed *halal* (literally 'lawful') butcher according to Islamic law.

The Structure of Meat

Muscle tissue is composed of three basic materials: water, protein and fat. Meat contains 43–65 per cent water, depending upon the age of the animal (a younger animal will contain more water and less fat), 12–30 per cent protein and 5–45 per cent fat.

Meat contains no carbohydrate, as any present in the form of glycogen is broken down into lactic acid when the animal is slaughtered and hung. This chemical reaction is vital in the maturing process as the lactic acid tenderizes the muscle fibres. The texture and flavour of cooked meat depends on the proportion of water to fat in the meat, the structure of the muscle proteins and the quantity of connective tissue binding the muscle tissue together.

Muscle Fibres

Meat is composed of long, thin cells called filaments that can be as long as the muscle itself. The filaments are bound together to form muscle fibres, which are in turn bound together with connective tissue in bundles. In a young animal, the muscle fibres are fine, but as the animal matures and exercises more, each muscle fibre coarsens and enlarges in diameter due to an increase in the number of muscle filaments. In turn, each bundle increases in width, causing the overall muscle to enlarge. The muscle fibre bundles are aligned in groups to form an individual muscle, which is contained and connected to the bone by tough connective tissue.

The Grain of Meat

The grain of meat is formed by the groups of muscle fibres running the length of the muscle. It is easier to chew meat along the length of these fibres than across them. For this reason, meat is carved across the grain so that it can be chewed with the grain.

Connective Tissue

Connective tissue is an integral part of muscle as it surrounds the individual muscle fibres and each muscle fibre bundle, and sheaths the entire muscle, as well as tying the muscle to the bone. Connective tissue varies in structure and distribution with each tissue type. Muscles that get a lot of exercise, as in the neck and shoulders of grazing animals, contain tough, thick membranes that run between each muscle section, but these are not as rubbery as the gristly connective tissue that surrounds arteries or forms the tendons that attach muscle to bone. By contrast, muscles that receive little exercise or come from very young animals have small amounts of very fine connective tissue.

Connective tissue is made up of the proteins elastin, reticulin and collagen. Elastin, as its name suggests, has elastic properties and is an important structural component of blood vessel walls and ligaments. Reticulin is a fibrous protein, found between muscle cells and the muscles themselves. It also forms a large part of the initial bone structure in young animals, before the bones calcify and harden. Elastin and reticulin are both very tough to eat and are not broken down or tenderized by cooking.

Collagen is a structural protein found in the skin and the tendons and between muscle cells and muscles. It is also present in large quantities in the bones of young animals. Collagen breaks down into gelatine when cooked slowly in water. Meat containing a large quantity of collagen becomes very tender and improves in flavour as it breaks down and the muscle fibres separate, making the meat easier to chew.

The quality and price of a cut of meat are largely determined by the quantity, distribution and type of connective tissue. Cuts for quick-cooking methods and roasting are the most expensive as they are tender, containing very little connective tissue. Cuts for slow roasting, braising and stewing have a moderate amount of connective tissue and require long, slow cooking in liquid to break it down. The cheapest cuts of meat are rich in connective tissue and require cooking for a long period of time.

Fat

Fat is distributed through and around muscle in the form of adipose fatty tissue, as well as under the skin in the form of deposit fatty tissue. Thin streaks and flecks of adipose fat running between muscle fibre bundles are known as 'marbling'. Marbling is a desirable quality, especially in beef, as the fat tenderizes and enhances the meat's flavour when cooked.

The quantity, distribution and nature of the fat in meat greatly affect its texture, flavour and keeping qualities, and determine the way it is prepared for cooking. Fat makes meat succulent by separating the muscle fibres as it melts during cooking, and oils the tissue, making it easier to chew and cut. Very lean meat has a tendency to toughen and dry out when cooked because the fibres shrink and pack closely together, squeezing out much of the water in the meat. Deposit fat on the surface of muscles does not tenderize meat in the same way, but protects it from excessive moisture loss during cooking.

Fat is present in meat in two different forms: saturated and unsaturated. Unsaturated fat tends to be soft at room temperature, as it does not pack as evenly or densely as saturated fat, which tends to be hard. Pork, poultry and lamb fat contain a higher proportion of unsaturated fat than beef and are therefore much softer, even just out of the refrigerator.

The Colour of Meat

The colour of meat depends upon the following:

- The quality of the myoglobin, a bright red protein in the muscle tissue that holds the oxygen carried to the blood.
- The amount of exercise the muscle has had; the more exercise, the darker the meat.
- The age of the animal; the younger the animal, the paler the meat.
- The species of the animal.
- The diet of the animal.
- The length of time the animal has been hung; the longer the hanging, the darker the meat.
- If the meat is packaged in an oxygen-flushed container, the colour will be brighter than meat that has not been flushed.

Hanging Meat

Immediately after slaughter the still-warm meat is soft but very tough. It is hung for a period of time to allow the structure of the meat to change and improve its flavour and texture. Much of the structural change in meat is caused by the accumulation of lactic acid, which lowers the pH, causing a proportion of the protein present in the muscle fibres to denature and unravel. This process, occurring several hours after the animal is slaughtered, is the first stage in partially breaking down or tenderizing the muscles so that the meat is easier to cut and eat. The accumulating lactic acid also brings on rigor mortis by activating the proteins responsible for contracting the muscle. The contracting muscle becomes extremely stiff, making the meat too tough to eat even after prolonged cooking. Rigor mortis lasts for up to a day in beef and for approximately six hours in pork and chicken. The muscle then begins to relax as the meat proteins continue to change chemically and structurally.

Meat benefits from a period of ageing before it is eaten because it continues to tenderize and develops more flavour. The connective tissue is not affected by the accumulation of lactic acid or enzyme activity in the time taken to tenderize meat and therefore remains unchanged.

The hanging time of meat is often limited by the degradation of fat. Fat is susceptible to bacterial growth and becomes rancid quite quickly. Saturated fat is harder and more stable and takes longer to spoil than unsaturated fat. This is one of the main reasons why beef can be hung longer than meats containing a high proportion of unsaturated fats, such as poultry, pork and lamb.

Storage of Meat During Hanging

To allow the meat to age with the minimum growth of bacteria, it is stored in the dark at very cold temperatures: 1–3°C/34–38°F. The enzymes that degrade components of the meat are also retarded at low temperatures. Cheap cuts of meat are hung for a minimal amount of time, which may be only as long as it takes to transport the carcass from the abattoir to the butcher's shop.

See also Factors Affecting the Tenderness of Meat, page 6.

Choosing Meat

Although the most expensive cuts of meat are tender, they do not have the strength of flavour of tougher cuts. Provided that tougher cuts have been hung for long enough and are cooked correctly, they can be as pleasing to eat as meat from the fillet or loin. For more information see individual types of meat, but in general look for the following:

- The meat should not be too fatty or contain too much gristle.
- The joints should be reasonably small, and any exposed bones should be pinkish-blue in colour, indicating a young animal.
- The meat should have a firm, close texture.
- The meat should never be slimy.
- The meat should not smell.
- The fat should be pale creamy-coloured, not yellow.

Meat Storage and Hygiene

Before the animal is slaughtered most micro-organisms are present only on its skin and hair; they are present in the muscle only if the animal is diseased. The bacteria responsible for meat spoilage are transferred from the skin to the flesh as the meat is cut into portions.

Although meat is usually washed before packaging, a good many bacteria remain on its surface. The concentration of bacteria present on the skin and flesh varies between animals. A piece of pork may have a few hundred bacteria per square centimetre, whereas chicken may harbour many thousands over the same area. As a result, chicken tends to spoil more quickly.

Hygiene when Handling Raw Meat

Due to the high concentration of bacteria present on the surface of raw meat, it is important to prepare it on a work surface that can be washed thoroughly with hot, soapy water.

Once the meat has been prepared, first rinse your hands, knives, any other utensils and the chopping board in cold water to remove any loose fragments of protein. If equipment used to prepare meat is immediately dipped into hot water, the protein cooks on to their surfaces, making it harder to remove. Once the equipment has been rinsed in cold water, transfer it to hot, soapy water and wash and dry thoroughly.

Storing Uncooked Meat

In the refrigerator

Bacteria thrive on most meat unless it is kept below 4°C/40°F in the refrigerator. Cold temperatures reduce the rate at which bacteria multiply and the rate at which enzymes degrade the meat protein. Nevertheless, the bacteria are still partially active and will spoil the meat if it is stored for too long.

Uncooked meat must be stored separately from cooked meat and food that will not be heated before it is eaten. Raw meat loses fluid and blood, containing bacteria, while it is stored, and this could drip on to and contaminate other food stored nearby, resulting in food poisoning. For this reason, it should always be stored at the bottom of the refrigerator.

To preserve its freshness and colour, meat must be allowed to breathe. If it comes tightly wrapped, pierce the cling film or rewrap in oxygen-permeable cling film or paper and refrigerate for no longer than 2 or 3 days. Meat bought in oxygen-flushed sealed containers at a supermarket is best left intact as this packaging is designed to keep meat fresh as long as possible. Some cuts of meat are vacuum-packed, which will keep the meat fresh for several weeks. However, many chefs feel that vacuum-packing is detrimental to the texture of meat.

In the freezer

Meat can be kept for much longer if it is stored in the freezer at -18°C/0°F. Most bacteria responsible for meat spoilage require water and warmer temperatures to work actively and are therefore inhibited as long as the meat is frozen. However, meat can still oxidize when frozen, which is why thawed meat is often dull in colour. It is important to wrap the meat tightly before storing it in the freezer, to prevent the surface of the meat drying out, which would affect its taste and texture.

Although meat freezes well, when defrosted it will be of lower quality than fresh if ice crystals that might have formed damage the muscle cell walls. When the meat is defrosted, liquid or water contained in the cells sometimes drains away to form a pool of fluid. The loss of fluid results in tougher, drier cooked meat. Meats containing a high proportion of unsaturated fats, such as lamb, pork and poultry, should be eaten within a few months of freezing, as the fats may become rancid. Beef may be frozen for 9 months as its fat is saturated and is less likely to deteriorate.

Storing Cooked Meat

Although cooking meat usually makes it safe to eat, airborne bacteria soon colonize and multiply on its surface. It is therefore important to keep cooked meat well wrapped and chilled to reduce the rate of deterioration.

The flavour of cooked meat deteriorates rapidly in the refrigerator in a matter of hours. This is because during cooking the fat molecules become unstable, and, once cool, become highly vulnerable to oxidation and bacteria. Meat containing high proportions of unsaturated fat is more vulnerable to flavour deterioration than meat containing saturated fat. To slow the rate of flavour spoilage, reduce the chances of oxidation by wrapping the cooked meat well in cling film, making sure that any air bubbles are eliminated. It is also recommended that meat be eaten within 2 days unless it is cured, in which case it can be kept for up to 1 week without its flavour being impaired.

Factors Affecting the Tenderness of Meat

The tenderness of meat depends not only on the way it is cooked, but on the structure of the muscles making up the cut or joint. If the muscle fibres are coarse and there is a high density of connective tissue, the meat will be tougher than if it has a fine grain and the meat is lean.

Age of the Animal

The younger the animal and the less exercise it has taken, the more tender its meat will be as the muscle fibres are fine, and the more delicate its flavour. As the animal matures and exercises, the muscle fibres coarsen, making the meat tougher to cut and chew.

Amount of Exercise

Meat from older animals will remain finer-grained and tender if the animal is not allowed to exercise. The most tender cuts of meat are from muscles that are least used. The fillet, for example, is extremely tender as it runs along the back of the animal and gets little exercise. By contrast, the neck, shoulders, chest and legs are used constantly for supporting the head while grazing, walking and standing, so meat from these areas is relatively tough.

Method of Rearing

This refers to the general conditions in which the animal lives, the quality of the feed it is given and whether the animal is able to exercise. These factors are important in determining the flavour and texture of meat. A cheap cut, such as stewing steak, from a high-quality animal will taste delicious if cooked properly in a casserole. An expensive cut, such as sirloin steak, from a low-quality animal will be flavourless and tough. A good butcher will choose meat from reputable suppliers who will know how the animals have been reared. Organic meat should have a better flavour than a non-organic, but will not necessarily be more tender. Organic meat is higher in price because of the labour costs incurred during production. The state of the animal prior to slaughter can also affect the tenderness of the meat; for example, if it is relaxed and peaceful, the meat is likely to be more tender.

Storage Time before Cooking

The carcass should be hung at temperatures no higher than 2°C/35°F for the appropriate amount of time. At this temperature the meat will become increasingly tender as enzymes that partially break down the structure of the proteins are active, while bacterial activity responsible for meat spoilage is retarded.

Distribution of Fat in Meat

Prime beef, for example, must have a certain amount of marbling to provide flavour, tenderness and succulence when eaten.

Presence of Connective Tissue

The larger the amount of connective tissue present, the tougher the meat will be.

Freezing

Freezing results in the formation of ice crystals, which can damage the meat cells and partially break down the structure (see Storing Uncooked Meat, page 5). Freezing can also cause a loss of moisture in the meat.

Method of Cooking

This is probably the most important factor that affects the ultimate tenderness of meat. The method of cooking should be chosen to suit a particular cut of meat, taking into account the coarseness of muscle fibres and the quantity and distribution of fat and connective tissue. These factors are largely determined by where a particular cut is found on the animal.

The most tender, and therefore expensive, cuts of meat containing very little fat and connective tissue are mainly from the back part of the animal. These cuts are suitable for grilling, pan-frying and roasting. Tender cuts are usually cooked until pink in the centre so that the muscle fibres are only partially affected by the heat, and remain soft and moist. If tender meat is cooked thoroughly to the centre, it becomes hard, tough and dry because the muscle fibres shrink in the heat, squeezing out the juices. This explains why it is almost impossible to produce a tender well-done grilled steak.

Methods of Tenderizing Meat

Tough cuts of meat can be tenderized in three ways:
• Long, slow cooking.
• Pounding, cutting or mincing, to break down the structure of the meat physically.
• Marinating, to break down the structure of the meat chemically.

Long, Slow Cooking

Although tender cuts are best eaten pink, tougher cuts, containing a high proportion of connective tissue, must be cooked for longer at low temperatures. With gentle, prolonged cooking in liquid heated to just below boiling (100°C/212°F) the collagen in connective tissue is broken down into gelatine, a soft-textured substance that is sticky when heated. Also, due to the breakdown of collagen, the muscle fibres are no longer held firmly together and fall apart. As a result of this disintegration of collagen and the formation of gelatine, tough meat becomes moist, extremely tender and meltingly easy to eat.

Less expensive cuts containing a small proportion of fat and connective tissue from around the forelegs are suitable for slow-cooking methods using very little liquid, such as braising and pot-roasting. The cheapest cuts (neck, knuckle, breast and tail) contain a high proportion of connective tissue and must be stewed in liquid for a long time to break the connective tissue down into gelatine.

Mincing Meat

Tougher cuts of meat, especially beef, veal and pork, are minced to break down the tough muscle fibres and connective tissue. Top-quality mince is obtained from leaner cuts and can contain as little as 5 per cent fat. It is minced coarsely to retain its flavour and juices. Lower-quality mince is from tougher cuts, contains more connective tissue and fat, and is often ground very finely as a result. Mince is used in burgers and meat sauces.

Marinating Meat

Meat is marinated to give it flavour and to soften its texture slightly. A marinade is a combination of acidic ingredients, such as wine or lemon juice, oil and aromatic ingredients, such as onions, garlic, herbs and peppercorns. The acidic ingredients will soften the proteins on the exposed surface of the meat.

Aromatic spices and herbs in marinades should be used in moderation as their flavour can become overpowering. The marinade should cover the meat. If the quantity of marinade seems insufficient to do so, place the meat and marinade in a plastic bag and tie it to draw the liquid around the meat.

The longer the meat is left in the marinade, the more pronounced the effect. Tender cuts of meat, such as fillet steak or chicken breast, should be marinated for no longer than a couple of hours. If the meat is left in the marinade for too long, the marinade could overpower the flavour or even break down the structure of the meat, giving it a pasty texture. Tougher cuts of meat, such as chuck steak for a stew or shoulder of venison for a casserole, can be marinated for as long as 2 or 3 days provided they are stored at below 4°C/40°F.

Meat steeped in marinades should be drained well and wiped dry before browning because the wet surface of the meat will prevent browning taking place.

Marinades may be used as the liquid constituent in braised dishes and stews, or to baste roasting meat. Do not use a marinade that has been in contact with raw meat as a sauce unless it is boiled first to destroy any bacteria.

For examples of marinade recipes, see Fried Beef with Sichuan Peppercorns (see page 60), Coq au Vin (page 286) and Venison Casserole (page 422).

Brining Meat

Brining, a popular preparation for meat and fish in Scandinavia, has become a widely used treatment to make meat more tender and juicy. This is achieved by soaking the meat in a brine solution of 2–4 tablespoons salt mixed into 1 litre water for a period of time ranging from 1 hour to 48 hours. Sugar can also be added to a brine solution, if desired. Add 1–2 tablespoons of sugar to 1 litre of water.

Most cuts of meat can be brined, with the smaller, thinner pieces of meat taking the least amount of time, and large roasts, such as a turkey, taking up to 2 days. The meat should be totally immersed in the brine and kept refrigerated during the brining period.

The salt causes the meat proteins to disarray and soften, which allows them to absorb some of the water. When the meat is cooked, water content will still be lost, but as it has been increased by the brining, the final water content after cooking will be as much as 10 per cent greater than it would have been if the meat had not been treated.

Some meat producers and supermarkets will brine their cuts of meat to increase the weight of the meat as well as its juiciness. This 'added water' should be noted on the label.

As brining obviously makes the meat saltier to eat, this factor needs to be taken into consideration both from a dietary standpoint and when choosing how to serve it. Meats that have been brined before cooking are often served with a fruit-based sauce so that the sweetness counter-balances the salt (see Barbecued Chicken Breasts with Peach and Mint Salsa, page 299).

Methods of Cooking Meat

Cooking methods can be divided into two main categories: fast, dry methods (roasting, frying, grilling and barbecuing) and slow, moist methods (poaching, pot-roasting, braising and stewing).

The important difference between fast, dry and slow, moist cooking methods is not the amount of moisture involved but the temperature and rate of heating at which they are typically cooked. Dry cooking methods generally use temperatures of 180°C/350°F/gas mark 4, well above the boiling point of water, to cook the meat by conduction, whereas moist cooking methods are limited to the boiling point of water (100°C/212°F), but are usually carried out at temperatures just below boiling point, thereby cooking the meat slowly and gently. As a result, dry cooking methods are suited to tender cuts of meat and moist cooking methods are generally better for cooking tougher cuts containing a larger quantity of connective tissue.

When meat is heated the proteins start to denature at 38°C/100°F, slowly unravelling and coagulating with each other. This effect is visible: when meat is placed in a hot pan the surface of the meat loses its translucency within moments, to become opaque and then dry. Juices from the meat may also accumulate in the base of the pan as the coagulating, shrinking protein squeezes the juices out of the meat. As the meat reaches an internal temperature of 55°C/130°F the muscle fibres shrink considerably in both width and length. Due to the shrinkage of muscle fibres, the coagulation of proteins and the resulting loss of liquid, meat shrinks on cooking. By 77°C/170°F the fibres have shrunk as much as they can and start to separate from each other along their length, and the coagulated proteins have squeezed out most of the liquid contained in the meat, causing it to become firm and dry. This is why rare meat is so juicy and moist to eat and well done meat is tough and dry.

The colour of meat is also affected by cooking, due to the denaturing of the protein myoglobin, the red pigment in muscle. Myoglobin remains red up to 55°C/130°F, but from 60°C/140°F it starts to become lighter pink, fading to brown at 77°C/170°F. Thus raw meat is bright red, rare meat is pinkish-red, and well-done meat becomes greyish-brown as it increases in temperature.

Fast, dry methods

The following fast, dry methods are used to cook tender cuts of meat.

Roasting: In the oven, either on a spit or in a roasting pan

Frying: Including sautéing and stir-frying.

Grilling or barbecuing: Including chargrilling.

Slow, moist methods

Poaching: The raw meat is submerged in barely simmering water or flavoured cooking liquor until it is cooked through.

Pot-roasting: The meat is browned first, then cooked with very little liquid in a pot with a tightly fitting lid, either in the oven or on the hob.

Braising: As for pot-roasting, but slightly more liquid is used.

Stewing: The meat is usually browned, then immersed in liquid. The meat is simmered in a pot with a tightly fitting lid for a prolonged period of time, 2–3 hours, or until tender.

In many of these moist cooking methods, it is important to brown the meat first for reasons of taste and appearance.

Browning

Meat may be browned at a high temperature in the initial stages of cooking, not to seal in the juices, as used to be believed, but to brown the surface of the meat to enhance its flavour and colour. Meat is either seared in hot oil or fat in a pan or, for larger cuts, in a very hot oven preheated to 200–220°C/400–425°F/gas mark 6–7 for a short amount of time (15–20 minutes). Browned meat will taste more flavourful than poached meat because the surface moisture is boiled off quickly, enabling a crust of concentrated proteins to develop. As these proteins are heated to the temperature of the pan or grill, they start to caramelize or brown to a characteristic golden colour, enhancing both the flavour and appearance of the meat. This browning is called the Maillard reaction, after the scientist who first described it. (See also Points to Remember about Frying and Browning, page 17.)

Fast, Dry Cooking Methods

Roasting

Oven-roasting means cooking in an oven with no other liquid than fat. Although roasting and grilling used to be virtually the same process carried out in front of an open fire, where both large and small cuts of meat were spit-roasted, today roasting is actually baking. Provided that the meat was of a uniform shape and thickness, spit-roasting ensured that no part of the meat dried out because the fat and meat juices ran over the surface as it rotated. Today's ovens dispense with the long and arduous job of turning a spit, and some ovens or grills have electrically operated spits (rotisseries) built into them.

In modern well-insulated and thermostatically controlled ovens, even without rotisseries, roasts need little attention other than occasional basting to prevent the upper part of the meat from drying out and to enhance their flavour. If the meat has a top layer of fat, basting may not even be necessary. Once the meat is roasted, a simple pan gravy (see page 463) can be made with the meat juices that collect in the pan during roasting. The gravy can be made while the meat 'rests' before carving.

Roasting is used mostly to cook tender joints of meat where the heat will take a relatively long time to reach the centre. The meat may be placed in a very hot oven for a short period of time to initiate the browning process (see Browning, opposite). The oven temperature is then lowered to ensure that the meat does not dry out or cook too quickly.

Both the cooking time and the roasting temperature are determined by the amount of connective tissue in a cut of meat. A rib roast (see page 32) is a tender cut of meat with very little connective tissue, and is roasted for a relatively short period of time. Cheaper cuts of meat containing coarser meat fibres and more connective tissue, such as chump or rump (see page 35), are roasted at a lower temperature. Slow-roasted meat has a tendency to dry out due to the prolonged cooking time, and is often moister if pot-roasted with a little liquid to retain moisture (see Slow, Moist Cooking Methods, page 21).

Points to Remember about Roasting Meat

- Bones are good conductors of heat and will transfer it into the centre of the joint. This should be taken into account when calculating the roasting time, as meat on the bone will cook more quickly than meat off the bone.
- A long thin piece of meat weighing 2.3 kg will take less time to cook than a round piece of the same weight, so the times given in the roasting tables are intended only as a guide.
- Lean joints should be basted with fat during roasting to help preserve the meat's moisture, as well as to form a crisp, browned crust. Alternatively, a layer of pork fat or bacon can be tied around the joint to protect the lean meat beneath, a technique known as 'barding'; or fat can be threaded through the meat, a technique known as 'larding'.
- Stuffed meats should be cooked at around 180°C/350°F/gas mark 4, giving the stuffed joint long enough to cook through without drying out, but not long enough to enable bacteria in the stuffing to flourish.
- When using a fan (convection) oven, reduce cooking times by 10 per cent, or lower the oven temperature by 10°C/50°F.
- A joint needs to be roasted for a short time at a high temperature to brown the meat for colour and flavour. After that, turn the oven down to a lower temperature for the remainder of the roasting time to avoid excessive shrinkage. For specific roasting times, see the relevant meat sections.

Method for roasting meat

1 Weigh the joint and establish the length of cooking time (see pages 33, 193, 377).
2 Heat the oven (electric ovens take longer to heat up than gas ovens).
3 Prepare the joint for roasting (see individual types of meat).

4 Heat some dripping in a roasting pan and, if the joint is lean, brown it over direct heat so that it is well coloured. Pork and lamb rarely need this treatment, but many cuts of beef and veal do.

5 Place the joint in a roasting pan, on a rack if you have one available, as this aids the circulation of hot air and prevents the meat from frying in its own fat.

6 Roast for the time calculated, checking the meat halfway through. Turn it over if it is well browned on top, and baste with the melted fat and juices that have collected in the bottom of the pan.

7 When the joint of meat is cooked (see Testing Roast Meat for Doneness, below), stand the roast on a warm serving platter and if the meat will be standing for more than 30 minutes, cover loosely with foil.

Testing roast meat for doneness

The essential point is that the meat must reach an internal temperature of 52°C/125°F to be rare, 60°C/140°F to be medium (pink) and 70°C/160°F to be well done. A meat thermometer inserted into the thickest part of the meat and left there during cooking eliminates guesswork. Do not let the thermometer touch the bone.

The skewer test: This is a crude but reliable alternative to using a meat thermometer to test the doneness of larger joints of meat.

1 Insert a skewer into the centre of the thickest part of the joint.
2 Leave it there for 10 seconds.
3 Draw the skewer from the meat and rest the tip of the skewer on the sensitive skin on the inside of your wrist.

- If the skewer is cool, the meat is still not done and requires more cooking.
- If the skewer is warm but bearable on the skin, the meat is cooked rare.
- If the skewer is unbearably hot and cannot be held on the skin for a fraction of a second, the meat is well done.

Resting roast meat

Let the roast sit on a warmed serving platter after removing it from the oven. Unless the meat will be standing for longer than 30 minutes, it is not necessary to cover it or place it in a warming oven. If it is going to stand for longer than 30 minutes, cover it loosely with foil or place it in a warming oven no higher than 70°C/150°F/gas mark ¼.

The resting time:

- Allows intense heat present in the outer layers of meat to penetrate the centre of the joint to cook it more evenly.
- Allows the hot juices to redistribute themselves more evenly throughout the joint. In a large roast, the heat drives the juices into the centre, and resting it allows these juices some time to seep back into the outer layers, giving an even colour and juiciness throughout.
- Allows the protein strands to relax, making the meat easier to carve and more tender to eat.

Carving Meat

Carving is a skill that takes practice and patience to master. Some people like to carve the meat in the kitchen, placing it on a warmed platter ready to bring to the table. Others prefer the theatre of carving the meat at the table. Wherever you feel most comfortable, the methods and tips below will make the task much easier.

- Before a joint of meat is carved it needs to be well rested. This means that it has been allowed to stand outside the oven for about 20 minutes before carving. This is necessary for the fibres in the meat to relax, enabling them to reabsorb the juices and soften to allow easier carving.
- The fibres of each muscle run beside each other in a particular direction, rather like the grain in a piece of wood. Before carving the meat it is important to determine the direction of the grain so that you slice across it. If the meat is carved in this manner, your teeth will chew with the grain, making the meat seem more tender.
- Start by placing the joint on a chopping board or serving plate so that the fibres run from left to right. Make sure you are using a board or plate that will collect any juice that runs out of the meat: these can be added to your gravy.
- Use a carving knife with a thin, sharp blade and a fork with long tines and a finger guard. Cut from far away towards you and back again, using a sawing motion with long, smooth strokes to give you slices of meat cut across the grain.

Note: Instructions for carving specific types of meat can be found after the first relevant recipe. For example, carving a fore rib of beef appears after English Roast Beef.

Roasting Meat: What has gone wrong when...

The meat is under-browned.
- The initial oven temperature was too low for the surface of the meat to brown. Leaner and smaller joints should be browned first by shallow frying before roasting in the oven.
- The meat was not cooked long enough at the initial higher roasting temperature.

The meat has cooked more quickly than expected.
- Either the oven temperature is too hot or the joint is long and thin and/or is on the bone.

The meat is dry.
- The joint was not basted regularly during roasting. Lean cuts must be basted very regularly, or protected by tying on a layer of fat.
- The meat is overcooked.

The meat is tough.
- The meat is overcooked. Alternatively, a cheap cut has been roasted that would have been better pot-roasted.

Spit-roasting

Chicken, lamb, pork, kid and goat can be spit-roasted. To spit-roast meat it is important to distribute its weight evenly along the length of the spit, with the limbs tied against the body or on the spit to prevent them from catching and burning. In order to brown the surface of the meat, first brush it with oil and place the spit a short distance from the burning embers. Once an even brown crust has formed, move the meat further away from the heat so that it cooks slowly and evenly in the centre. Baste the surface of the meat periodically with oil to help protect it from drying out.

Frying

Frying, sometimes referred to as 'shallow-frying', and sautéing are both quick cooking methods, suitable for small, not too thick, tender pieces of meat cut into steaks, strips, dice and medallions. The difference between the two methods is the amount of fat used in cooking. For sautéing, an almost dry pan with no more than a tablespoon of fat is used; for frying, food is cooked in up to 6 mm of fat.

When meat is fried, some of the fat in which it was cooked is eaten with it. For this reason the flavour of the fat – or lack of it – will affect the taste of the dish. Olive oil, butter, bacon dripping, lard and beef dripping all give distinctive flavour to fried foods, while corn, safflower, peanut and most other vegetable oils have little or no flavour.

Choosing fat for frying

When choosing fat for frying, remember that some fats can be heated to much higher temperatures than others before they break down and start to burn. For example, clarified butter, which is butter with all its milk solids removed (see page xii), can be heated to higher temperatures than whole butter. Pure bacon dripping, lard, beef dripping and solid frying fat can withstand more heat than margarine, butter or vegetable oil.

It is unwise to fry meat in pure butter unless the meat is sliced very thinly, is extremely tender (veal escalopes, for example – see page 115) or requires little cooking, as butter contains milk proteins that are likely to burn before thick slices of meat are cooked. A little butter, however, is often added to vegetable oil for frying to enrich its flavour. The oil and butter mixture is sufficiently hot for frying when the butter begins to foam. Extra virgin olive oil is not suitable for frying as it has a low smoke point and its characteristic flavour is lost when it is heated to high temperatures.

Points to Remember about Frying and Browning

- Fry in a wide, uncovered pan. A lid traps the vapours, causing the meat to stew or steam rather than fry crisply.
- Heat the fat. If the fat is cool when the meat is put in, it will not brown, will lack flavour, look unattractive and may even absorb some of the cool fat and become greasy. Before adding the meat to the pan, test the temperature of the oil with one piece of meat. If the meat sizzles, the remaining meat can be added, otherwise wait for a few moments before testing the oil temperature again. Carefully regulate the temperature of the pan to prevent the meat from overbrowning.
- If the fat begins to smoke before the meat is added, allow the pan to cool a little, as the meat is likely to scorch. If the fat is smoking, remove the pan from the heat and drain the fat into a metal container as it will taste burnt and spoil the flavour of the meat.
- Fry a little meat at a time spaced out evenly over the base of the pan. Adding too much meat at once to hot fat lowers the temperature and again hinders the browning. The meat is also liable to steam in its own juices, becoming grey and unappetizing.
- When the meat is added to the hot pan, it will usually stick to the base. As the surface of the meat browns and dries, it slowly releases itself from the pan and at this point is ready to be flipped over to brown on the other side. It is important not to disturb the meat or prise it from the base of the pan whilst it is browning as the surface of the meat is likely to tear and the browning process will be incomplete. Turn the meat only when it is fully released.
- The side of the meat that is browned first when frying is the presentation side because it will have the most appealing appearance. Moisture collects on the second side to be fried, and damp meat does not brown as well as dry meat.
- The meat should be fried until it is evenly browned on all sides. Once the meat is browned, it can be transferred to a casserole for stewing or braising, to a hot oven for roasting, or the heat may be reduced to medium-low to complete the cooking in the pan.

Sautéing

Sautéing is used mainly to brown small cubes, slices or strips of meat, often before they are added to a stew or sauce, which is frequently made in the same pan (see Beef Stroganoff, page 46). Meats such as pork chops or chicken pieces may be given an initial browning (see Points to Remember about Frying and Browning, above) and then cooked with added ingredients that will eventually form a sauce.

Method for sautéing

1 Brown the meat all over in minimal fat. Remove from the pan and keep warm.
2 Deglaze the pan with liquid, such as water, stock, cream or wine.
3 Add the flavourings for a sauce.
4 If the initial browning has cooked the main ingredients sufficiently, reduce the sauce by rapid boiling and pour it over the dish. Garnish and serve immediately.
5 If the meat needs further cooking, return it to the pan and simmer it in the sauce until tender, then proceed as above.

Stir-frying

The meat is cut into dice, strips or thin slices and fried quickly in a small quantity of hot oil, in a wok or large frying pan over a high heat. To cook and brown the small pieces of meat evenly, they are moved constantly with a wooden spoon or ladle until cooked through. Stir-frying is a fast cooking method and is suited to tender cuts of meat, such as poultry breast (see Stir-fried Chicken with Cashew Nuts, page 307), fillet of beef and pork fillet.

Grilling

Intense heat is the secret of successful grilling. Although this method requires active attention from the cook, the food cooks quickly and the charred surface gives great flavour. To produce succulent, perfectly grilled meat that is crisp brown outside and pink and juicy inside, it is absolutely essential to heat the grill to its highest setting. It may take 10 or even 20 minutes for the grill on a good domestic cooker to come to the right temperature. Under a cooler grill, the surface of the meat will not brown, in which case it is best to fry the meat instead.

Grilling will not tenderize meat, so only tender cuts should be grilled. Ideally, the cuts should be no thicker than 5 cm, or the centre of the meat will remain cold and raw when the outside is black. A thicker piece of meat will need to finish cooking in the oven after grilling. Unless the cut is fairly thin, once the meat browns it must be moved further away from the heat source so that the interior can cook before the surface burns. Basting with the pan juices, olive oil or butter adds flavour and gloss. Turning the meat is necessary for even cooking and should be done halfway through the cooking time, when the first surface is attractively brown.

Points to Remember about Grilling

- Brush the meat with butter, oil or a mixture of the two to keep it moist and to speed up the browning process.
- Do not salt meat in advance as salt draws out moisture. Salt immediately before grilling.
- Avoid piercing the meat, which will allow the juices to escape, so turn it during grilling with tongs or spoons rather than a sharp instrument, such as a fork.
- Serve immediately. Grilled meat loses moisture, dries up and toughens if kept hot for any length of time.
- The second side to be grilled is the presentation side because this will have a freshly caramelized and shiny surface, whereas the first side will have sat on the baking sheet or roasting pan in a pool of fat and meat juices.

Chargrilling

The meat is cooked quickly on a ridged, cast-iron griddle pan or skillet heated on a hob, or on a grill heated by red-hot coals. The griddle, skillet or grill rack should be heated over a strong flame, then brushed with oil before the meat is arranged on it. Chargrilled meat blackens where it touches the raised ridges on the griddle or the bars of the grill, to produce a striped effect. The blackened areas give the meat its characteristic chargrilled flavour and appearance.

Lean meat, such as poultry, is often marinated in a liquid containing oil before being chargrilled to protect it from drying out (see Methods of Tenderizing Meat, page 7). Alternatively, brush the surface of the meat with oil as it cooks. Use oil with a high smoke point, such as vegetable oil. Chargrilled meat that can be served pink is best served medium-rare, but pork and poultry must be cooked through.

Thin portions of poultry such as the breasts, beef steaks, lamb cutlets and medallions of pork fillet/tenderloin are most suited to being chargrilled as the heat can penetrate the meat quickly. Small chickens may also be chargrilled if flattened and spatchcocked (see Spatchcocked Chutney-grilled Poussins, page 319). Larger, thicker pieces of meat may be marked on the grill (see below), then transferred to a hot oven to finish cooking.

Points to Remember about Chargrilling

- Brush the chargrill with a flavourless oil with a high smoke point before cooking.
- Heat the chargrill until it just starts to smoke.
- Place the meat to be chargrilled at an angle across the ridges. To produce a diamond pattern, first place the end of the meat at 10 o'clock, then, after 1 minute, turn the end of the meat to 2 o'clock.
- Do not move the meat until it has released itself after 1 or 2 minutes of cooking as this would tear the surface of the meat.
- Turn the meat with tongs rather than a fork, which would pierce the meat and allow juices to escape.
- The first side to be chargrilled is the presentation side.

Marking meat on a ridged cast-iron griddle

Diagonal lines: To produce diagonal blackened lines on the meat, place the meat on the heated, oiled griddle at an angle of 45° and grill until it releases itself. Turn the meat over so that it lies at the same angle and cook until the meat releases from the grill, by which time it should be sufficiently cooked or ready to transfer to a hot oven to finish cooking.

Cross-hatching: To form cross-hatch markings on the meat, place it on the griddle at an angle, as above. As soon as the meat releases itself, swing the portion of meat to rest diagonally in the opposite direction at the same angle and leave long enough for the meat to be marked in a pronounced cross-hatched pattern. Turn the meat over and repeat. As it takes some time to create the markings, it is best to use this technique for thick slices of meat, such as beef steak, which are less likely to overcook (see Grilled Steak, page 49).

Factors determining grilling time for tender cuts of meat
The cooking time for steak varies according to the thickness, density and fat content of the meat, as well as the intensity of the heat source, whether that be the base of the pan or a grill. When grilling meat, the distance of the meat from the grill will also determine the

rate at which the meat browns and cooks. Open-textured steak, such as sirloin, will cook faster than the same thickness and weight of closer-textured rump. Cooking a steak under the grill will also take longer than in a frying pan or griddle pan as the meat is not in direct contact with the heat source (see cooking times for fillet and sirloin steak, pages 34–35).

Testing grilled and fried meat for doneness

All grilled and fried meats should be well browned on the surface. However, the best guide to whether meat is done is its texture. Feel the meat by pressing it firmly with a finger. Rare meat feels soft, almost raw; medium-done meat is firmer, with some resilience to it; and well-done steak feels firm (see The test of the thumb, below). With practice, there should be no need to cut into the meat to check if it is cooked to the degree desired. Try not to cut into the meat until you are fairly sure that it is ready as with every cut juices are lost.

The test of the thumb

A less intrusive method for checking the doneness of small portions of meat is the thumb test, where the cook presses the surface of the meat with the tips of the fingers and compares the texture of the meat to that of the fleshy base of the thumb, held in turn against each finger of the same hand, to discern how well the meat is cooked. Although this method is very accurate, practice is required in order to recognize the changes in texture as the meat cooks from uncooked to rare to medium to well done.

When the thumb is relaxed the base of the thumb feels soft and flabby, like the texture of uncooked meat. When the thumb is held against the base of the index finger, the fleshy area becomes softly springy and represents the texture of rare cooked meat. If the tip of the thumb is moved to the middle finger the fleshy area becomes firmer and more like the texture of medium-rare meat. If the tip of the thumb is moved to the ring finger, the fleshy area firms a little more and feels more springy to the touch, like the texture of medium meat. Finally, on moving the thumb to touch the little finger, the fleshy area becomes firm and loses its spring, to represent the texture of well-done meat.

With practice the thumb test can reliably inform the cook of the stage a small joint or sliced portion of meat has reached in cooking without the use of a meat thermometer. The thumb test is not suitable for large joints of meat because the outer layers may be quite well cooked whilst the centre may still be rare. Under these circumstances it is best to use a meat thermometer or the skewer test (see Roasting Times, pages 33, 193, 377 and Testing Roast Meat for Doneness, page 14).

The test of the thumb for checking doneness of meat

Barbecuing

This is an outdoor cooking method dating back to ancient times, whereby meat is effectively grilled or spit-roasted over burning charcoal or a gas flame. If using coals, they may take as long as 2 hours to reach the point where the embers are flameless yet burn with the necessary intensity. When ready for barbecuing, charcoal glows bright red in the dark and has an ashy-grey appearance in daylight. Due to the intense cooking temperatures involved, barbecued meat will cook quickly – a small lamb cutlet, for example, will be cooked perfectly in 2 minutes. Tender cuts of meat, such as beef, pork or lamb steaks and poultry breasts, are ideal for barbecuing.

To barbecue portions of meat over charcoal, first brush with oil or clarified butter to prevent them from sticking to the grill and to protect them from drying out. The grill is placed on a rack above the charcoal, normally distanced from the embers so that the food can initially be held just above the heat until browned, then moved to a higher position to continue cooking more slowly until it is cooked through. It is very important to ensure that pork and poultry in particular are cooked thoroughly to avoid any danger of food poisoning. Small chickens may be grilled on the barbecue if they are flattened and spatchcocked beforehand (see Spatchcocked Chutney-grilled Poussins, page 319). Meat and poultry are often marinated before barbecuing to tenderize the meat and enhance its flavour (see Methods of Tenderizing Meat, page 7).

Points to Remember about Barbecuing

- Heat the barbecue until it is very hot.
- If using charcoal, let the coals burn down until they are ashy-grey on the surface.
- Never squirt lighter fluid on to an open fire.
- Brush the meat, rather than the grill, with oil.
- Do not turn the meat until it has cooked sufficiently to be self-releasing, usually 1–2 minutes.
- Do not use a fork to turn the meat as it will pierce the surface and result in juices being lost.
- Do not turn the meat over more than once, as frequent turning causes the meat to dry out.
- Ensure poultry is cooked thoroughly.

Slow, Moist Cooking Methods

The following methods are ideal for cooking tough cuts of meat because the application of heat for a prolonged period of time will cause the collagen in the meat to soften and become sticky. The moisture will help keep the meat from becoming too dry.

The tender-tough-tender principle

These methods of cooking illustrate the tender-tough-tender principle of meat cookery: that is, when meat is rare, it is tender. As it cooks the muscle fibres tighten and the meat becomes tough. With further cooking the connective tissue gelatinizes and the muscle fibres start to separate, giving the meat a tender texture.

The following methods can also be used for tender cuts of meat, but cooking should be stopped when the meat is still pink, or just cooked in the case of chicken, or it is likely to become tough and dry due to the lack of collagen.

Poaching or Boiling

Poaching is a method of cooking meat by immersing it in liquid, then heating the liquid until the occasional bubble rises to the surface. This method is used for Turkey Tonnato (see page 348).

Although the term 'boiling' is sometimes used in reference to cooking meat, any meat cooked by this method is actually poached. This way it cooks gently. Meat that is allowed to boil for a prolonged period of time will become fibrous and dry and will be very hard to slice. The meat fibres will shrink to the extent that almost all the juices in the meat will be squeezed out into the surrounding liquid. When meat is poached, most of its nutrients enrich the surrounding liquid in which it is cooked. As a result, the liquid usually forms a major part of the meal, usually as a broth served either before or with the meat.

Poaching is suited to both tender and tough cuts of meat. Following the tender-tough-tender rule, tender cuts of meat are poached very gently until just cooked to prevent them from becoming tough (see Chicken Breasts Stuffed with Red Pepper Mousseline, page 282). However, meat containing a great deal of connective tissue is cooked in barely trembling water for as long as 3–4 hours, until it falls off the bone as the connective tissue is breaking down. The connective tissue gelatinizes and becomes meltingly tender.

Poaching can take place either on the hob or in the oven at 150°C/300°F/gas mark 2. A ham or large piece of bacon is cooked when the meat has shrunk back from the bone or, if boneless, when it has visibly shrunk in size by about one-fifth. The rind or skin will peel off easily and a skewer will penetrate the meat with little pressure.

Points to Remember about Poaching

- Do not allow the poaching liquid to boil. This will cause the meat to toughen.
- If possible allow the meat to cool in the poaching liquid by placing the pot in a sink full of cold water. Change the water frequently to keep the water cold.

Poaching Meat: What has gone wrong when...

The meat is dry and tough.

- The meat has been boiled.
- The wrong cut of meat was used.
- The meat has been overcooked.

• The meat has been overcooked.

Pot-roasting

Pot-roasting is not really roasting but rather baking in a pot, either in the oven or over a low heat on the hob. It involves cooking meat in its own juices and might better be called a simpler version of braising. It is an old, economical method of cooking that was much used to cook tough cuts of meat, with plenty of connective tissue, in the days before there were many domestic ovens.

Traditionally, very little liquid is added to a pot-roast, other than the fat needed for browning, as moisture from the meat provides most of the liquid during cooking. With poultry, a few spoons of liquid are usually added after browning.

A casserole with a tightly fitting lid creates a small oven. Steam is formed inside the pot from the moisture given off by the added liquid or by the meat itself, and this tenderizes and cooks it. If the lid does not fit tightly, the steam can escape. To make sure the lid does fit tightly, cover the top of the casserole or pan with a piece of greaseproof paper and place the lid on top, jamming it down firmly. If the casserole or pan is too big, the liquid spreads over a large area and is more likely to boil away, so choose one into which the meat will fit snugly.

A flameproof casserole can be used both on the hob and in the oven, first for browning the meat, then for pot-roasting. Otherwise, brown the meat in a frying pan and transfer it with all the pan juices to a casserole for pot-roasting.

A traditional tip when pot-roasting is to cook the browned meat on a piece of pork rind. This adds flavour and prevents the meat scorching. A *mirepoix* of diced vegetables, such as carrot, onion and celery, is sometimes placed under the meat for the same reason. This can be either raw or browned in the same fat as the meat, though the meat should be removed from the pan while the vegetables are browning. Once cooked, they can be served with the meat or used as the basis of a sauce.

Pot-roasted meat can be tenderized by marinating before cooking (see Methods of Tenderizing Meat, page 7) or made more succulent by larding it (see Veal Fricandeau, page 110). This is especially important with lean joints. As the meat cooks, the fat partially melts, making the meat juicy and adding flavour and richness to the sauce. As long as the meat cooks slowly, the liquid in the pan is not likely to boil or, more importantly, to evaporate. This liquid becomes a richly flavoured sauce for the meat after cooking. Any vegetables cooked with the meat will help to thicken it.

Transfer the pot-roasted joint to a warmed serving dish or board for carving, and remove any strings or skewers. If there is too much liquid left in the pan, simply reduce it by boiling, or thicken it with beurre manié (see Cookery Terms and Kitchen French, page 512).

Pot-roasting: What has gone wrong when...

The meat and pot are dry.

• The lid did not fit tightly enough, allowing the moisture to escape as steam during cooking.
• The pot may have been too big for the joint or recipe, causing juices to spread and dry up on the base of the pot.

The meat and accompanying juices look grey and unappetizing.

• The meat was not browned thoroughly and evenly before pot-roasting.

Braising

Braising, in the true sense of the word, is a method of cooking meat slowly on a *mirepoix*, a thick bed of diced vegetables, with the addition of strong stock (see Braised Haunch of Venison, page 421). In practice, the term 'braising' is often confused with pot-roasting as in both methods food is cooked slowly in a pan with a tightly fitting lid. The main difference is that pot-roasted food is cooked with little, if any, liquid other than the fat used from browning the ingredients, while braising involves some liquid and at least some chopped vegetables to add moisture to the pan, even if a true *mirepoix* is not used. A pot-roast should taste roasted and be decidedly fattier than a braise, which is closer to a stew, and for flavour depends more on juices and stocks than on fat.

Meat for braising should be fairly lean and contain a reasonable quantity of connective tissue as this cooking method is ideal for breaking the tissue down into gelatine, which is very important for the final rich flavour and sticky texture of a braised dish. Any fat that melts into the stock should be skimmed off before serving. Poultry may be braised, unless it is old and tough, when stewing or poaching are more suitable cooking methods because all the flesh is submerged in liquid.

The vegetables for the *mirepoix* should be browned quickly in hot fat and stirred constantly to ensure even colouring, then transferred to a heavy casserole dish or pan. The meat can be browned in the same fat before it is placed on top of the vegetables and stock is added. As the vegetables cook, they will disintegrate, helping to thicken the stock. Making a strong, reduced, well-flavoured stock is time-consuming, but is one of the key factors in good braising (see Brown Stock, page 452).

As with pot-roasting, meat may be marinated overnight in the refrigerator, and large pieces of exceptionally lean meat may be larded to ensure that they remain moist. Dry the meat well before browning it.

Points to Remember about Braising

- Fry the *mirepoix* of vegetables and a few tablespoons of diced salt pork or bacon slowly in oil and butter, shaking the pan and stirring until the vegetables are evenly browned all over.
- Brown the meat on all sides and place it on top of the vegetables in a heavy casserole.
- Add stock and cover the meat. (If the stock is not rich enough and does not set solid with gelatine when cold, the braise will not have the correct melting, sticky texture.) Stew, without basting, until half-cooked.
- Lift out the meat, strain the stock and discard the *mirepoix*, which by now will have imparted its flavour. Return the meat to the casserole and, in a separate pan, reduce the stock by rapid boiling until it is thick and syrupy, then pour it over the meat.
- There will no longer be enough stock to cover the meat and there is a danger, even in a covered pan, of the exposed top drying out, so turn the meat every 15 minutes and baste it with the stock. By the end of the cooking time, when the meat is tender, the stock should be reduced sufficiently to provide a shiny coating that will not run off the meat. It will penetrate the flesh, moistening it and giving it the slightly glutinous texture of perfectly braised meat.

Braising Meat: What has gone wrong when...

The braised dish looks grey and unappetizing.
- The ingredients were insufficiently browned before the liquid was added.

The braised dish looks very dark and tastes burnt.
- The ingredients were overbrowned.

The sauce is thin in flavour and consistency.
- The meat contained too little connective tissue.
- The stock was not sufficiently gelatinous and strongly flavoured.

The dish is fatty.
- The fat that melts in the cooking liquor was not skimmed off before serving or reducing the sauce to a syrupy consistency.

The meat is tough.
- The meat requires more cooking, slowly at a low temperature.

Stewing

A stew essentially consists of small pieces of meat that have been cooked slowly and gently in plenty of liquid. Examples include Family Beef Stew and Navarin of Lamb (see pages 63 and 175). Many stews require preliminary frying of the meat, and sometimes of onions, shallots, carrots or mushrooms as well. This browning gives a richer flavour to the stew and adds colour and flavour to the sauce, which will be made using the browned sediment and dried-on juices sticking to the pan after frying. These are called browned stews. White stews, such as Blanquette de Veau (see page 114), are usually made without the preliminary browning and are less rich, milder in flavour and easier to digest. Both brown and white stews are served in their cooking liquid, which is usually thickened to a syrupy sauce.

Deglazing the browning pan

The principles of browning (see page 12) apply to the preliminary frying for a brown stew. If the sauce is not to taste insipid or be pale in colour, you must start with a good, even colour on the meat. Deglaze the pan as often as necessary by adding several tablespoonfuls of cold water, stock or wine from the recipe to the hot pan. Allow the liquid to boil whilst scraping the brown colour from the pan with a wooden spoon. Pour this *deglaçage* into a bowl and reserve to add to the casserole or sauce. Wipe the pan with kitchen paper and add more oil and heat to continue browning. Deglazing serves three essential purposes: it prevents the stuck sediment in the pan from burning; it allows the flavour of the sediment to be captured and incorporated into the sauce; and it cleans the pan ready for the next batch of meat.

Due to the large quantity of liquid used to cook the meat, the accompanying sauce may be thin in flavour and texture and might need to be reduced to a syrupy consistency once the meat is tender. The cooking liquor is strained into a clean, wide pan and boiled until it is thick enough to coat the meat and other ingredients lightly.

The meat can be simmered on the hob or cooked in the oven at 150°C/300°F/gas mark 2 until tender. If the meat is a tender cut, as used in Chicken Sauté Normande (see page 287), it will usually be done within 1 hour. If a tougher cut is stewed, as in Lamb Daube (see page 169), it will need at least 1½ hours, or even up to 3 hours, until it becomes tender.

Points to Remember about Stewing

- If making a brown stew, ensure the meat is well-browned before adding any liquid.
- Do not cut the meat into cubes smaller than 3 cm or it is likely to dry out.
- The stewing pan should be tightly covered.
- Ensure the meat is covered by the liquid so that it does not dry out.
- Do not allow the meat to boil.
- Ensure the meat has cooked long enough to become tender again, at least 1½ hours.

Stewing Meat: What has gone wrong when...

The meat is tough.
- The stew has not been cooked for long enough.
- The stew has been allowed to boil.

The meat is dry.
- The stew has been allowed to boil.
- A cut of meat without much connective tissue or marbled fat was used.
- The meat was cut too small.

The stew looks grey and unappetizing.
- The ingredients were insufficiently browned before the liquid was added. Each surface of sliced or diced meat and vegetables should be evenly browned before adding the liquid. Also make sure that the *déglaçage* from the base of the pan is used in the stew to add its colour and flavour.

The stew looks very dark and tastes burnt.
- The ingredients were overbrowned, or the sediment collecting in the base of the pan during browning was not deglazed regularly enough, causing it to burn and taint the flavour of the finished dish.

The sauce is thin in flavour and consistency.
- The sauce was not reduced to a syrupy consistency and seasoned sufficiently before serving the stew.

The stew is fatty.
- The fat that melts into the cooking liquor was not skimmed off before serving or reducing the sauce to a syrupy consistency.

The meat has collapsed into shreds.
- The meat was stewed for too long. It should be cooked until it is tender and the fibres are just beginning to fall apart.
- The meat may have been cut too small.

The meat is tough.
- The meat requires more cooking, slowly at a low temperature.

Beef

Beef is the most popular red meat in the UK, and is enjoyed in many forms, from the Sunday roast served with Yorkshire pudding and lots of gravy, to the fillet steak for special occasions and the ubiquitous fast-food hamburger. The pastures of the UK are ideal for producing top-quality beef, and grass-fed animals are considered to make some of the best beef in the world.

History

Cattle were amongst the animals domesticated by Neolithic man, and remains have been found in Turkey dating beyond 6500 BC. The word 'cattle' is derived from the Anglo-French *chattel*, meaning 'possession'. All cattle can be traced back to a single ancestor, the auroch. However, the last of the auroch breed is reported to have died in Poland in the 1600s. By that time cattle were living in most parts of the world: the Romans recorded seeing red-coloured cattle in the southern part of Britain about 55 BC, and later European explorers took cattle to the New World, where they have thrived. Today the main producers of beef worldwide are the USA, Argentina, Brazil and Australia.

Common Breeds

The most common breeds in the UK are the Aberdeen Angus, the Hereford, the Belted Galloway and the shorthorn. Most of the cattle that are used for beef comes from bullocks, castrated male animals aged 18–24 months. The females, called heifers, are kept for breeding. A herd of cattle raised for their meat is called a suckler herd. This is because they are allowed to suckle their mother for about six months, in contrast to dairy herds, where the calves are taken away soon after birth.

The suckler herd can be fed grass or grain, or a combination of the two. Grass-fed cattle are often 'finished' in a feedlot, where they are fed grain to get their weight up before slaughter. The meat is tender, and cattle are now bred to be much leaner than they were in the past. Grass-fed beef is considered to have a better flavour than beef that is solely grain-fed; however, flavour is also influenced by the method and period of hanging.

Once their best days of milk production have passed at approximately 12–18 months old, dairy cattle are also sold for meat. They are then 'finished' to fatten them for slaughter, although the common dairy breed, the Holstein, is not one that develops good-quality muscle. Unless you are buying your beef from an independent butcher or farmer, you are unlikely to know if your beef has come from a suckler herd or from a dairy cow, but sometimes the breed of a joint is marked on the label.

Although per capita consumption of beef in the UK declined during the 1980s and 1990s because of dietary concerns and crises in the beef industry, such as BSE, it has since risen.

In the USA per capita consumption of beef is nearly twice as much as in the UK, and consumption is even higher in South American cattle-rearing countries, such as Argentina and Brazil. It is less popular in Asian countries where Hinduism is practised, because eating beef is forbidden for religious reasons.

In Japan the Wagyu breed is used to produce several types of beef, of which the most well known in the West is Kobe beef. This beef is produced by a labour-intensive process that involves feeding the cattle on beer and massaging them to keep them relaxed. It is designed to develop an intensely marbled meat that is well flavoured and extremely tender. Due to the production method, Kobe beef is extremely expensive.

Hanging Beef

Hanging is a particularly important factor in determining the tenderness and flavour of beef. The meat needs to be hung in a fan-cooled air-store for at least 2 weeks, preferably longer, in order for the muscles to relax and the flesh to soften. During this time the flavour also develops, becoming stronger and more complex.

The carcass is hung at the abattoir for a short period before being sold to the butcher or supermarket, where it should be hung for a longer period, usually 2–3 weeks. During hanging, the carcass loses weight through evaporation, so there is a trade-off between flavour and profit. For this reason, meat that has been hung for a long period will often cost more than meat that has been hung for a shorter time. After hanging, the carcass is cut down for selling to the consumer.

There is an increasing trend for supermarkets to pack their meat in vacuum-sealed packaging. This vacuum-packed meat is then kept for a week or two before being sold. Although vacuum-packing increases the length of time the meat can be stored, many people feel that it adversely affects the flavour and texture.

Choosing Beef

- Choose deep or dull red meat rather than a bright orange-red (see The Colour of Meat, page 3). The dull colour suggests that the meat has been hung for a sufficient time to tenderize it. This is difficult in the supermarket because managers assume that their customers want 'bright' meat, so there is much use of clever lighting and oxygen-flushed packaging to prolong the bright red colour of the pigment myoglobin.
- The meat should have a slightly moist, shiny appearance, but bloody juices should not have collected in the packaging.
- The meat should be firm and springy to the touch and have a sweet, light scent.
- Avoid meat that is soft, spongy or has a slimy appearance.
- Fat should be a pale creamy colour and firm in texture. Tender cuts will be even more succulent when cooked if they contain 'marbling' – a fine network of fat running through the meat. Yellow-coloured fat indicates an older animal.
- Bones should be pink, sometimes with a blue tinge, and shiny to indicate a young animal.

- There should be few or no tough lines of the connective tissue known as gristle. A strip of gristle running between the fat and lean layers usually indicates an old animal (see Factors Affecting the Tenderness of Meat, page 6).

Storing Beef

- Remove any plastic packaging from the beef. Joints of beef should be placed on a plate, then covered loosely with greaseproof paper or foil. Store in the lower part of the refrigerator for up to 4 days. To freeze, double-wrap, label and freeze for up to 9 months.
- Beef cut into steaks or stewing meat should be stored in the same way as joints of beef, but should be used within 48 hours. Double-wrap and freeze for up to 3 months.
- Minced beef and offal can be left in the wrapper from the supermarket or butcher and stored in the lower part of the refrigerator for 24 hours. Freeze mince for up to 3 months or offal for up to 1 month.

Cuts of Beef

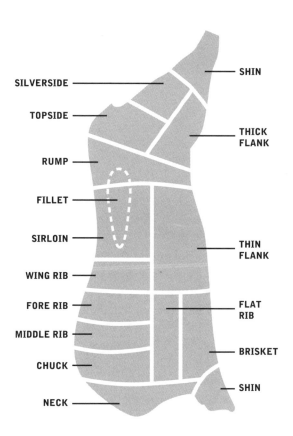

Cut	Recommended Cooking Methods	Recipe Reference
Brisket/Thick flank	Pot-roasting	Pot-au-feu (page 78)
	Stewing	Family Beef Stew (page 63)
	Braising	Braised Silverside (page 78)
	Pies	Steak and Mushroom Pie (page 76)
Chuck/Middle rib	Stewing	Family Beef Stew (page 63)
	Braising	
	Pies	Steak and Mushroom Pie (page 76)
Fillet	Roasting	Fillet of Beef en Croûte (page 40)
	Frying	Fried Steak (page 49)
	Sautéing	Beef Stroganoff (page 46)
	Grilling	Grilled Steak (page 49)
Neck	Stewing	Family Beef Stew (page 63)
	Braising	
Rump steak	Grilling	Grilled Steak (see page 49)
	Stewing	Family Beef Stew (page 63)
Whole sirloin/Fore rib/ Wing rib	Roasting	English Roast Beef (page 38)
Topside/Silverside Flat rib	Pot-roasting	Pot-au-feu (page 78)
	Stewing	Family Beef Stew (page 63)
	Braising	Braised Silverside (page 78)
Shin/Thin flank	Stewing	Family Beef Stew (page 63)
	Pies	Steak and Mushroom Pie (page 76)

Methods of Cooking Beef

Roasting

Beef is generally roasted at a high oven temperature for 20 minutes to brown the meat, or it may be browned in fat on the hob before being transferred to the oven. Whichever the method of browning, calculate the cooking time after the browning has been done, using the Beef Roasting Table opposite. Roast beef should be served pink and a little bloody to retain its tender succulence.

Below are listed the best cuts of beef for roasting. Allow 225 g of meat on the bone per person, or 170 g off the bone.

- **Fillet:** One of the most expensive cuts of beef, as it is extremely tender and requires little preparation before cooking. A whole fillet can be roasted on its own or encased in puff pastry and baked to make Fillet of Beef en Croûte (see page 40).
- **Fore rib:** One of the larger roasting joints, sold on the bone, or boned and rolled.
- **Sirloin:** The most expensive roasting joint, sold on the bone, or boned and rolled. It is sometimes sold with the fillet attached, and this can be cut off and served separately.

- **Wing rib:** A large cut close to the sirloin and fillet, and one of the most expensive joints of beef as it is the most tender end of the rib.

There are two types of thermometer that can be used to test the temperature of meat. One type is inserted into the thickest part of the meat, not touching the bone, and left there throughout the cooking time. Another type, sometimes called an instant-read thermometer, is inserted when required into the thickest part of the meat to take the temperature reading, then removed. See the relevant roasting chart (below and on pages 193 and 377) for the temperature required.

Beef Roasting Table*

	Oven temperature			Cooking time	Internal temperature	
	C°	F°	Gas mark		C°	F°
Brown	220°	425°	7	20 mins, plus . . .	—	—
Rare	190°	375°	5	30 mins per kg	52°	125°
Medium	190°	375°	5	40 mins per kg	60°	140°
Well done	190°	375°	5	50 mins per kg	70°	160°

  ★ This table also applies to veal, lamb and venison.

Grilling and Frying

Tender beef, containing very little connective tissue, is cut mainly from the hindquarter. This includes the fillet, sirloin, rump, topside and rib of beef, all of which are suitable for roasting or slicing into steaks for grilling or frying.

Steaks are slices of meat of varying thickness cut from the fillet, rump or sirloin. They are lean, contain very little connective tissue or fat, and must therefore be cooked quickly by grilling or pan-frying to retain their moist, tender texture. Before cooking, any membranes or excess fat around the edge should be trimmed away.

Timings and cookery methods for different cuts of beef are given on pages 34 and 35. It is very useful, however, to be familiar with the Test of the Thumb (see page 20) when cooking steak. Cooking times will vary depending on the thickness and the temperature of the meat, and the temperature of the grill or pan.

- Blue steak will be dark red with the fibres only just beginning to set, and just hot.

- Rare steak will be dark red with muscle fibres just set, and the juices running freely.

- Medium-rare steak will be a deep pink and well set with fewer free-flowing juices.

- Medium steak is pale pink in the centre with very few free-flowing juices.

- **Well-done steak** will have no trace of pinkness and the meat will be firmly set, brownish-grey in colour but still moist.

Fillet steak

Fillet of beef is a long, lean, boneless cut of meat that runs along the back of the animal. It is subjected to very little activity and therefore contains almost no connective tissue, is finely grained, very lean and extremely tender. It is often roasted whole (see Fillet of Beef en Croûte, page 40) or is sliced either diagonally or across into steaks of varying thickness for grilling or frying.

Due to the tenderness of the meat, the fillet and steaks cut from it should be cooked rare to medium-rare to prevent the meat from drying out. When choosing fillet steak for grilling, look for meat finely flecked with fat as this will help to keep the steak moist. Fillet beef may also be cut across the grain, into strips no thicker than a finger, for sautéing in hot fat to make dishes such as Beef Stroganoff (see page 46).

- **Tournedos**, cut across the tail of the trimmed fillet into neat 3 cm slices, weighing 100–125 g.

- **Chateaubriand**, cut from the thick end or centre of the fillet into a neat piece weighing approximately 500–675 g, and serving 2–3 people. Due to its size, it may be grilled, spit-roasted or oven-roasted (see Browning, page 12 and Roasting, page 12), or pan-fried to brown, then roasted in the oven to finish cooking.

- **Medallions** are neat slices about 1 cm thick, cut diagonally across the ends of the fillet or across the thicker centre. As they are relatively thin, they must be fried quickly in hot fat (see Frying, page 16).

Grilling times for fillet steaks approximately 3.5 cm thick

(These suggestions for cooking times, assuming a good, hot grill, should be regarded only as guidelines.)

Blue steak	2¼ mins per side
Rare steak	3¼ mins per side
Medium-rare steak	4¼ mins per side
Medium steak	5 mins per side

Frying times for fillet steaks approximately 3.5 cm thick

(These suggestions for cooking times, assuming a good, hot pan, should be regarded only as guidelines.)

Blue steak	1½ mins per side
Rare steak	2¼ mins per side
Medium-rare steak	3¼ mins per side
Medium steak	4½ mins per side

Sirloin steak

Sirloin steak is cut from the upper side of the true sirloin, wing rib and fore rib.

• Entrecôte is the eye of the sirloin, cut into individual steaks.

• T-bone steaks include the bone. The sirloin is on one side and the fillet on the other. This is the largest steak and can serve two people.

• Porterhouse is a double-sized T-bone cut from the wing rib.

Grilling times for sirloin steaks approximately 2 cm thick
(Sirloin steak is cut slightly thinner than fillet and therefore requires less grilling time.)

Blue steak	1¼ mins per side
Rare steak	1¾ mins per side
Medium-rare steak	2¼ mins per side
Medium steak	2¾ mins per side

Frying times for sirloin steaks approximately 2 cm thick
(Sirloin steak is cut slightly thinner than fillet and therefore requires less frying time.)

Blue steak	1 min per side
Rare steak	1½ mins per side
Medium-rare steak	2 mins per side
Medium steak	2¼ mins per side

Rump steak

Steaks cut from the rump are large slices about 2 cm thick, cut across the grain. For individual servings the steaks are cut into 2–3 smaller neat pieces. Minute steaks, made by flattening individual portions of rump steak, are large and thin, and best fried quickly in hot fat. Rump steak is thinly marbled with fat, which gives it a moist, succulent texture and an excellent flavour when grilled or pan-fried. It is probably the most flavourful of the steaks, but is tougher than sirloin or fillet steak. Cook as for sirloin or use for stewing.

Rib-eye steak

A boneless rib-eye steak is cut from the prime part of the muscle that runs between the ribs through the top loin and sirloin, which undoubtedly makes it one of the juiciest, most tender (and expensive) cuts of beef. It is also called a prime rib steak, a Delmonico steak, a Spencer steak and a market or beauty steak, and in Australia and New Zealand is known as the Scotch fillet. It is well marbled with soft fat and therefore best served medium-rare or medium in order to ensure that the fat melts during the cooking process.

A rib-eye steak is sometimes confused with the bone-in French entrecôte steak, which is cut further down from the rib roast. Other terms for bone-in cuts are bone-in rib-eye, or cowboy rib-eye, again cut from the rib, meaning there will be a higher percentage of fat throughout the meat. The advantage of the bone still being attached, as with all cuts of meat, is that there will be fat alongside the bone, thus adding to the overall flavour and succulence of the steak.

Frying and Sautéing Beef: What has gone wrong when...

The meat starts to boil rather than fry when added to the pan.
- The pan and oil are not hot enough when the meat is added, causing it to stew slowly as the meat shrinks and loses most of its juices.
- Too much meat has been added at one time, causing the pan to cool down.

The meat is sticking and catching to the bottom of the pan.
- The pan is too dry; add more oil or fat.
- The meat was turned too soon.

The fat appears to be smoking and burning before the meat is cooking.
- You are using fat, probably whole butter, that burns when subjected to high temperatures for more than a few minutes. Use whole butter to fry only very thin, tender cuts of meat.
- The temperature of the pan is too high.

The surface of the meat is overbrowned before the centre is cooked.
- The pan and the oil are too hot. Remove the pan from the heat briefly to allow it to cool a little before adding more meat. If the oil or fat is smoking, clean the pan and start again as it might taint the flavour of the fried food.

The meat looks greasy and under-browned.
- The meat was added to the pan when the oil was still too cool.

The meat has become tough and dry.
- The meat is overcooked. Once the surface of the meat is evenly browned, turn the heat down to medium so that the centre of the meat can cook more slowly and gently.

Making Mince

Minced meat can be made at home by using a mincer or by chopping the meat with two knives (see diagram below).

Cross-chopping using 2 knives

Beef mince is usually made from the tougher cuts of meat, such as silverside or stewing beef from the neck. The meat should be reasonably lean or have most of the fat removed before being minced. Although mincing physically breaks down the meat fibres and connective tissue, minced meat requires at least 45 minutes' cooking to tenderize it. Beef mince is used to make Shepherd's Pie (see page 80), meat sauces, such as bolognese sauce, or packed together to make burgers or Italian Meatballs (see page 88).

Minced meat carries a high risk of food poisoning, from *E. coli* in particular. This is because the many surfaces on the mince can harbour bacteria, which thrive at low temperatures. To avoid possible food poisoning, always cook minced beef until well done. The interior of a burger should be grey and have reached a temperature of 70°C/160°F. If, however, you mince your own prime cuts of beef, you can then have a rare burger.

Best beef cuts for long-cooking mince
- Chuck
- Blade (fairly lean)
- Skirt
- Shin
- Silverside
- Neck

Best beef cuts for rare/medium-rare burgers
- Rump
- Sirloin

These cuts can be mixed with 50 per cent chuck.

English Roast Beef and Yorkshire Pudding

Traditionally, roast beef is served with roast potatoes, Yorkshire pudding, gravy and horseradish sauce.

SERVES 10

2.3 kg sirloin or rib of beef

a little dry English mustard

salt and freshly ground black pepper

To serve

Yorkshire Pudding (see page 496)

Roast Potatoes (see page 493)

Horseradish sauce

1 Weigh the beef and calculate the cooking time according to the Beef Roasting Table, page 33.
2 Heat the oven to 220°C/425°F/gas mark 7.
3 Season the beef with a little mustard, salt and plenty of pepper, then place in a roasting pan. Do not season the meat in the pan as this could result in over-seasoned gravy.
4 Roast for 20 minutes to brown the surface of the meat.
5 Turn the oven temperature down to 170°C/325°F/gas mark 3 and roast for the calculated cooking time.
6 Allow the roast to stand at room temperature for 20 minutes, then carve as described opposite.

NOTE: The beef may be served simply with 'God's gravy', the juices that run from the meat before and during carving. If thickened gravy is required, see page 463.

Carving a large fore rib of beef

1 Place the meat on its side and make a 5 cm cut along the length of the rib to release the meat from the bone.

2 Stand the meat up, rib-side down. Carve slices from the joint, as shown below, then lift off and place on a warmed platter.

Carving a small fore rib of beef

1 Cut between the bone and the meat to remove the bone.

2 Place the meat on its side and cut across the width into short, vertical slices.

Carving a sirloin on the bone

This is tackled from the top and bottom – the slices cut as thinly as possible on the top, whilst the undercut or fillet slices are carved more thickly. Each diner should be given a slice or two from both top and bottom.

Wine: Dry reds, medium- and full-bodied, from Bordeaux to Australian Shiraz, depending on taste

Fillet of Beef en Croûte

As the fillet is so lean, it should be served pink or rare to ensure that it remains succulent and tender.

This dish may be prepared a day in advance up to step 8. In this case, it is important that the mushrooms and pâté should be completely cold before mixing together. The pastry-covered fillet should be left ready for the oven on the baking sheet, loosely covered with cling film or foil to prevent the egg glaze from sticking.

SERVES 8

1.8 kg thick piece of fillet

freshly ground black pepper

Worcestershire sauce (optional)

15 g beef dripping or 1 tablespoon oil

340 g flour quantity Puff Pastry (see page 480)

flour, for rolling

30 g butter

115 g flat mushrooms, very finely chopped

115 g Chicken Liver Pâté (see page 364)

beaten egg, to glaze

1 Heat the oven to 230°C/450°F/gas mark 8.

2 Skin and trim the fillet and season with pepper and Worcestershire sauce, if using. Heat the dripping or oil in a roasting pan and, when hot, add the meat and brown on all sides. Transfer to the oven and roast for 20 minutes. This recipe assumes that rare beef is desired, but longer cooking at this stage, without the pastry, will ensure a more well-done fillet. For medium beef, cook for a further 10 minutes and for well-done beef a further 15 minutes.

3 Remove the fillet from the roasting pan and allow to cool.

4 Take one-third of the pastry and roll it on a floured surface until it is a little more than the length and breadth of the fillet. Place it on a damp baking sheet, prick all over with a fork and bake in the oven for about 20 minutes, until golden brown. Place the pastry on a wire rack and leave to cool. Turn the oven off.

5 Melt the butter in a frying pan and quickly fry the mushrooms, then leave to cool. Place the pastry base on a baking sheet. Mix the cold mushrooms with the pâté and spread the mixture over the cooked pastry base. Place the cold fillet on top of this and use a sharp knife to cut away any pastry that is not covered by the fillet.

6 On a floured surface roll the remaining pastry large enough to cover the fillet generously. Lift up this 'blanket' and lay it gently over the fillet. Using a sharp knife, cut off the corners of the blanket and reserve these trimmings.

7 Lift one length of the blanket and brush the underside with beaten egg. Using a palette knife, lift the base and tuck the blanket neatly underneath it. Repeat with the other 3 sides.

8 Shape the pastry trimmings into leaves. Brush the pastry-covered fillet with beaten egg. Decorate with the pastry leaves and brush again with beaten egg. Refrigerate until the pastry is firm to the touch.

9 Heat the oven to 200°C/400°F/gas mark 6.

10 Bake the fillet in the heated oven for 20 minutes, or until the pastry is golden brown and shiny. To check that the beef is cooked, insert a skewer through the pastry into the centre of the meat and leave there for 10 seconds or so, then withdraw it. If the skewer

is hot to the touch, the meat is done (see Skewer Test, page 14).

11 Serve hot or cold. If served hot, the fillet should be carved at the table or the juices will be lost and the meat may become grey and unappetizing in appearance.

Wine: Dry reds, such as Rioja or Burgundy, because of their naturally higher acidity

Beef en Croûte: What has gone wrong when...

The meat is dry.

- The fillet may have been fried for too long before roasting. Fry in very hot oil to brown its surface as quickly as possible to avoid overcooking.
- The meat was roasted for too long and is overcooked.

The pastry base is soggy.

- The base was undercooked. Ensure the bottom of the base is crisp and an even golden brown colour before removing from the oven.
- The pastry base was too thick.

The pastry melted before it started to bake.

- The fillet may still have been warm when the pastry was laid over it.
- The oven was too cool when the Beef en Croûte was placed in it.
- The pastry was not chilled sufficiently before baking.

Fillet of Beef Carpaccio

Unlike bresaola (page 47), which is aged and cured, carpaccio is made from fresh raw beef. However, it is served in a similar way.

SERVES 6

675 g fillet steak, cut across the grain into thin slices

½ teaspoon horseradish cream
lemon juice
salt and freshly ground black pepper

For the sauce

3 tablespoons plain yoghurt
3 tablespoons double cream
3 tablespoons Mayonnaise (see page 466)
1 tablespoon made English mustard

To garnish

rocket leaves
shavings of Parmesan cheese

1 Flatten the slices of beef between 2 sheets of cling film or dampened greaseproof paper using a mallet or rolling pin. Carefully remove all the sinews.

2 When the slices are as thin as possible, spread them over plates without letting them overlap.

3 Mix together the first 4 sauce ingredients.

4 Flavour to taste with the remaining ingredients.

5 Garnish with the rocket and Parmesan shavings. Serve the sauce separately.

Wine: Red Burgundy or Cru Beaujolais (Fleurie, Brouilly); or German Riesling Kabinett or Fiano di Avellino

Fillet of Beef with Salmoriglio

Salmoriglio is a southern Italian sauce used with both meat and fish. The beef it accompanies here must be top quality, as it is eaten raw. The charring on the outside forms a tasty crust, which is a delicious contrast to the raw, sweet meat inside. Chilling the beef before carving makes it easier to slice.

SERVES 10–12

1 tablespoon oil
1.35 kg fillet of beef, trimmed
flaky sea salt and freshly ground black pepper

For the salmoriglio

2 tablespoons lemon thyme, roughly chopped
2 tablespoons oregano, roughly chopped
1 teaspoon flaky sea salt
2 tablespoons lemon juice

100 ml extra virgin olive oil

For the salad

50 g watercress, washed and picked over
50 g lambs' lettuce, washed and picked over

For the dressing

75 ml olive oil
2½ tablespoons balsamic vinegar

1 Heat the oil in a heavy-based frying pan. Season the beef fillet with salt and black pepper and brown very well on all sides until charred on the outside but still raw in the centre. Remove from the pan and allow to cool. Refrigerate for 1 hour.

2 To make the salmoriglio pound the herbs and salt together using a pestle and mortar. Add the lemon juice and oil, and season with black pepper.

3 Slice the beef fillet into 1 cm slices. Lay the slices between sheets of cling film and beat lightly with a rolling pin or saucepan to flatten. Remove the cling film and arrange the slices on a serving plate. Spoon over the salmoriglio.

4 Put the watercress and lambs' lettuce into a bowl. Combine the olive oil and balsamic vinegar. Season with salt and black pepper. Pour over the salad leaves and toss well. Serve with the beef fillet.

Wine: Dry, medium-bodied reds, such as Chianti Classico or Barolo

Steak Tartare

The beef in this recipe is served raw, so it is essential that it is top quality and very fresh.

SERVES 4

450 g fillet steak	about 1 tablespoon finely chopped green pepper
about 4 tablespoons salad oil	about 1 tablespoon chopped fresh parsley
3 egg yolks	salt and freshly ground black pepper
Worcestershire sauce (optional)	crisp lettuce, to garnish
about 3 tablespoons finely chopped onion	

1 Chop or mince the steak finely and mix with all the other ingredients.

2 Shape into 4 rounds and arrange on a serving dish. Garnish with the lettuce.

NOTES: To cater for varying tastes, restaurants often mix this dish to the customer's requirements at the table. The meat is presented in a hamburger shape on the plate, with the egg yolk in a half shell sitting on top of it, and surrounded by the prepared chopped vegetables. The waiter then proceeds to beat the flavourings, oil and yolk into the meat with a fork.

Steak tartare is sometimes garnished with anchovy fillets or even caviar.

Hot potatoes, rather than a salad, are surprisingly good with steak tartare. Chips or matchstick potatoes are best.

Wine: Full-bodied red, such as Australian Shiraz; or Champagne, Riesling Kabinett, or dry French rosé

Beef en Gelée

This recipe has been adapted from a Cordon Bleu recipe.

SERVES 4

450 g centre piece of beef fillet

1 tablespoon oil

50 g butter, softened

170 g good-quality duck liver pâté

¼ teaspoon Dijon mustard

2 teaspoons dry sherry

4 slices of very good-quality cooked ham

850 ml Aspic (see page 458)

salt and freshly ground black pepper

To garnish

2 tomatoes, blanched, peeled and deseeded

4 sprigs of fresh chervil

1 Heat the oven to 200°C/400°F/gas mark 6.

2 Tie the beef fillet into a neat shape. Season with salt and pepper. Heat the oil in a roasting pan. Add the fillet and brown lightly all over, then roast in the hot oven for 30 minutes.

3 Remove from the oven and leave to get completely cold.

4 Beat the butter into the pâté a little at a time. Add the mustard and sherry and season to taste with salt and pepper. Set aside.

5 Cut the cold beef fillet into 4 even-sized steaks about 1 cm thick. Spread a layer of pâté on top of each steak. Lay a slice of ham over the layer of pâté and press down lightly. Trim the edges neatly.

6 Put the steaks into a dish and carefully spoon in just enough liquid but cold aspic to cover them. Leave to set in the refrigerator.

7 Meanwhile, prepare the garnish: cut the tomato flesh into small diamond shapes and pick over the chervil.

8 Arrange the garnish on top of the steaks and coat again, very carefully, with a little cold aspic. Leave to set in the refrigerator.

9 Pour any remaining aspic into a shallow tray and chill until firm, then dice.

10 To serve, cut around the steaks with a circular or oval cutter. Place on individual plates and garnish with the diced aspic.

Wine: Dry rosé or a light red, such as Valpolicella

Roast Sirloin with Rocket and Roasted Vegetable Salad

SERVES 4

500 g sirloin or fillet in one piece

1 tablespoon coriander seeds

1 small bunch of rosemary

2 tablespoons olive oil

For the salad

1 small aubergine, sliced thickly

2 Portobello mushrooms

1 red pepper, deseeded and quartered

100 g rocket, watercress and spinach salad

1 tablespoon balsamic vinegar

3 tablespoons olive oil

salt and freshly ground black pepper

For the sauce

2 tablespoons Mayonnaise (see page 466)

2 tablespoons crème fraîche

½ tablespoon horseradish sauce

1 teaspoon wholegrain mustard

1 Trim all the fat and membrane from the beef.

2 Grind together the coriander and rosemary, then press on to the surface of the beef. Grind over some black pepper. Wrap in cling film and chill.

3 Mix together the ingredients for the sauce, season with freshly ground black pepper and set aside.

4 Grill the aubergine, mushrooms and red pepper. Slice into finger-sized strips and set aside.

5 Heat the oven to 180°C/350°F/gas mark 4. Heat the grill or barbecue.

6 Pat the meat with the 2 tablespoons of oil, then grill or barbecue it on all sides.

7 Place in a roasting pan and finish cooking in the oven to the desired degree of doneness. A meat thermometer should register 52°C/125°F for rare, 60°C/140°F for medium, and 70°C/160°F for well done (see Testing the Temperature of Meat, page 33). Let stand at room temperature for 10 minutes or longer to rest.

8 Toss the salad leaves with the balsamic vinegar and 3 tablespoons of oil. Season with salt and pepper. Divide between 4 plates.

9 Scatter over the aubergine, mushrooms and peppers.

10 Slice the beef thinly and arrange over the salad. Drizzle with the sauce and serve.

Wine: Full-bodied red, such as Australian Cabernet

Beef Stroganoff

The instructions given below for sautéing strips of fillet beef also apply to other tender cuts of meat cut into small pieces and cooked by the same method.

The essence of a perfect Beef Stroganoff is the speed at which the beef strips are cooked. If using tougher meat than fillet, however, the beef must be stewed gently (after adding the mushrooms and stock) until tender. This alternative method can produce very good results.

SERVES 4

450 g fillet of beef
50 g butter
1 medium onion, thinly sliced
225 g mushrooms
100 ml dry white wine

150 ml Brown Stock (see page 452)
1 tablespoon oil
2 tablespoons brandy
4 tablespoons crème fraîche
salt and freshly ground black pepper

1 Cut the beef into 5 cm strips the thickness of a finger.
2 Melt half the butter in a frying pan and cook the onion over a low heat until soft and transparent. Add the mushrooms and toss over the heat for 1 minute. Add the wine and stock. Boil rapidly to reduce to about 2 tablespoons. Stir well, then pour into a bowl, scraping the pan.
3 Heat the oil and the remaining butter in the pan. Once the fat is sufficiently hot to cause a strip of beef to sizzle vigorously, add some of the beef strips. Do not overcrowd the pan. Fry over a high heat to brown the surface without overcooking the middle. Transfer the strips to a plate as they are browned.
4 Reduce the heat, pour the brandy into the hot pan and set it alight. As soon as the flames subside, pour in the mushroom and stock mixture. Return the beef strips to the pan and stir in half the crème fraîche. Season the sauce to taste with salt and pepper. If the sauce is too thin, remove the beef strips and boil rapidly to reduce to a syrupy consistency.
5 Reheat, then tip into a warmed serving dish and roughly fork in the remaining crème fraîche. If the crème fraîche is very thick, it can be diluted with a little water.

Wine: Medium-bodied dry red, such as Saint-Emilion, Rioja or Côtes-du-Rhône

Bresaola

Originally from Valtellina in northern Italy, bresaola is cured, air-dried meat that is aged for up to three months. During the ageing process, the meat becomes dehydrated, hard and very intense in colour, turning almost purple.

There are many methods used to make bresaola. Some require the meat to be marinated in wine before the spicing and drying process, whilst others just use a dry rub of spices. Juniper berries, cinnamon and nutmeg are the most commonly used spices, and these are mixed with salt before being rubbed into the surface of the meat. The meat is then wrapped in muslin and hung up to dry. The length of the drying process depends on the size of the meat, so varies between 2 and 12 weeks. A water loss of up to 40 per cent can be expected during the curing time.

Whatever method of preparation is employed, it is essential that a good cut of meat is used for this curing process and that it is well trimmed of fat and sinews. The resulting meat is very soft and tender, and is usually sliced paper thin.

SERVES 16–20

1 × 3.5 kg silverside of beef, trimmed of all fat

For the marinade

1 bottle of red burgundy
1 carrot, roughly chopped
1 onion, cut into quarters
3 cloves of garlic, crushed
900 g coarse sea salt
6 large sprigs of rosemary
6 large sprigs of thyme
5 bay leaves
12 cloves

15 black peppercorns, roughly crushed
1 teaspoon dried chilli flakes
finely pared zest of ½ an orange
finely pared zest of ½ a lemon

To serve

olive oil
shavings of Parmesan cheese
rocket
lemon wedges
hot crusty bread

1 Place the meat in a large non-metallic bowl. Add the marinade ingredients and mix well. The meat should be completely covered with the marinade.

2 Cover the bowl and place in the refrigerator for 1 week, turning occasionally, until the meat feels quite firm.

3 Remove the meat from the marinade, pat dry with kitchen paper and wrap in a double layer of butter muslin. Hang the meat in a cool place to dry for 10–14 days. It should be quite hard to the touch.

4 Unwrap the bresaola and scrub the outside well with vinegar (it is quite normal for a white mould to appear on the outside). Rub the bresaola with olive oil, wrap in greaseproof paper and keep in the refrigerator until needed.

5 To serve, slice the bresaola wafer thin and arrange in overlapping slices on a large plate. Drizzle with good olive oil and top with shavings of Parmesan. Serve with a bowl of rocket, some lemon wedges and hot crusty bread.

Wine: Light red (Beaujolais-style) or a less aromatic dry white

Bresaola with Figs, Rocket and Goat's Cheese Dressing

It is important to use a fresh, light goat's cheese, which will combine easily with the oil and vinegar to create a creamy dressing. If the cheese is too strong or dense in texture, the flavour will be too powerful and the dressing too thick and 'dry'.

Semi-dried or mi-cuit figs are moist and chewy, and readily available from most supermarkets and healthfood stores. Fully dried figs may be used instead, but will benefit considerably from being soaked for 5–10 minutes in boiling water or hot tea, such as fragrant Earl Grey, to plump them up. Drain them and pat dry after soaking, then use as instructed. Fresh figs are a little too soft and juicy for this recipe and do not have the concentrated sweetness required to balance the flavours of this dish.

SERVES 4

50 g fresh goat's cheese

2 tablespoons sherry vinegar

5 tablespoons olive oil

85 g rocket

juice of ½ a lemon

85 g semi-dried figs, roughly chopped

225 g sliced Bresaola (see page 47)

flaky sea salt and freshly ground black pepper

1 Put the goat's cheese in a small bowl and mash to a smooth paste.
2 Beat in the vinegar and oil. Season with salt and pepper.
3 Toss the rocket in the lemon juice, season with salt and pepper and stir in the chopped figs.
4 Lay the slices of bresaola on a flat work surface and divide the rocket and fig mixture between them, Roll up to enclose the mixture. There should be some rocket exposed at either end.
5 Arrange the rolls on a serving plate and drizzle the goat's cheese dressing over them. Serve immediately.

Wine: Fruity, aromatic white, such as Riesling

Grilled Steak

This recipe can be used with fillet, sirloin or rump steak, but the grilling times will differ. Serve each steak topped with a slice of Maître d'Hôtel Butter or Béarnaise Sauce (see page 474 or 472).

SERVES 4

4 fillet, sirloin or rump steaks, 170–200 g each
butter, melted

salt and freshly ground black pepper

1 Heat the grill to its highest setting. Do not start cooking until the maximum temperature is reached. Brush the grill rack and the steaks with a little melted butter.
2 Season the steaks with pepper. Sprinkle lightly with salt just before cooking to prevent loss of juices from the surface of the meat.
3 Grill the steak quickly on both sides, approximately 5 cm from the heat source (see pages 34 and 35 for grilling times). For a blue or rare steak, keep the heat fierce for the whole cooking time. For well-done steaks, lower the temperature to medium after the initial browning.
4 Allow the meat to stand for 5 minutes before serving to allow the fibres to reabsorb the free-running juices.

Wine: Dry reds, medium- and full-bodied, such as Argentinian Malbec or Australian Shiraz/Cabernet

Fried Steak

This recipe can be used with fillet, sirloin or rump steak, although the frying times will differ, depending on the thickness of the steak. If a ridged griddle pan is used, the steak can be marked with cross-hatching (see page 19).

SERVES 4

4 fillet steaks, cut 3.5 cm thick, or 4 sirloin
  or rump steaks, cut 2 cm thick
oil or dripping, for frying
salt and freshly ground black pepper

To serve

Maître d'Hôtel Butter or Béarnaise Sauce
  (see page 474 or 472)

1 Season the steaks with pepper. Sprinkle lightly with salt just before cooking.
2 Brush the frying pan with a little oil or dripping and place over a medium heat until hot.
3 Cook the steaks on both sides until they are evenly browned (see pages 34 and 35 for frying times). For a blue or rare steak, keep the heat fierce for the whole cooking time. For better-done steaks, lower the temperature to medium after the initial browning.
4 Serve each steak topped with a slice of Maître d'Hôtel Butter or a spoonful of Béarnaise Sauce.

Wine: Dry reds, medium- and full-bodied, such as Argentinian Malbec or Australian Shiraz/Cabernet

Steak Wellington

SERVES 4

4 × 170 g fillet steaks

Worcestershire sauce

30 g beef dripping or 2 tablespoons oil

50 g flat mushrooms, chopped

85 g Chicken Liver Pâté (see page 364)

1 quantity Rough Puff Pastry (see page 479) or
  500 g bought puff pastry

beaten egg, to glaze

salt and freshly ground black pepper

watercress, to garnish

To serve

300 ml Wild Mushroom Sauce (see page 468)

1 Trim any fat or membranes from the steaks. Season with pepper and a few drops of Worcestershire sauce.

2 Heat the dripping or oil in a frying pan and brown the steaks quickly on both sides. The outside should be brown, the middle absolutely raw. Reserve the frying pan unwashed. Leave the meat to cool on a wire rack (this is to allow the fat to drip off the steaks rather than cooling and congealing them).

3 Cook the mushrooms in the frying pan, then tip them into a bowl to cool.

4 Beat the pâté into the mushrooms. Check the seasoning. Spread one side of each steak with the pâté mixture. Roll out the pastry until it is about the thickness of a £1 coin. Cut into 4 × 18 cm squares.

5 Place each steak, pâté side down, on a piece of pastry. Brush the edges with water and draw them together over the steak, making a neat and well-sealed parcel. Place them on a damp baking sheet, pâté side up, and brush with the beaten egg. Make a small slit in the top of each parcel so that the steam can escape. Decorate with leaves made from the pastry trimmings. Brush these with egg too. Place in the refrigerator for 10 minutes to allow the pastry to firm.

6 Meanwhile, heat the oven to 230°C/450°F/gas mark 8.

7 Brush the steak parcels with a little more beaten egg. Bake in the hot oven for 15 minutes, or until the pastry is golden brown. The meat will be pink. Meanwhile, reheat the sauce.

8 Arrange the steaks on a warmed serving plate. Garnish with watercress and serve the sauce separately.

Wine: Dry reds, such as Rioja, Burgundy or Chianti Classico, because of their naturally higher acidity

Sirloin Stir-fry with Noodles

The cooking time for this recipe is very short, so prepare all the ingredients before starting to cook.

SERVES 4

340 g sirloin steak, trimmed and cut into
   5 mm strips
1 teaspoon caster sugar
¼ teaspoon ground coriander
¼ teaspoon ground cumin
2 tablespoons dark soy sauce
150 g baby sweetcorn
100 g mangetout
2 tablespoons groundnut oil
1 clove of garlic, sliced
1 cm piece of fresh root ginger, peeled and sliced
1 red pepper, deseeded and cut into strips
100 g chestnut mushrooms, sliced

For the sauce

1 tablespoon groundnut oil
1 clove of garlic, crushed
1 cm piece of fresh root ginger,
   peeled and finely grated
225 ml Brown Stock (see page 452)
1 tablespoon dark soy sauce
1–2 teaspoons hot chilli sauce
1 tablespoon cornflour
3 sections of medium egg noodles
2 tablespoons sesame oil

To serve

2 tablespoons coriander leaves, chopped
3 spring onions, trimmed and finely chopped

1 Place the steak in a bowl and sprinkle over the sugar, coriander, cumin and soy sauce. Stir to coat the steak.
2 Blanch the baby corn in boiling water then add the mangetout and cook for 30 seconds. Drain and refresh in cold water. Place on kitchen paper to dry.
3 Heat the oil in a wok or frying pan. Add the sliced garlic and ginger, cook for 30 seconds to flavour the oil, then discard.
4 Fry the red pepper for 1 minute, then add the mushrooms. Remove and set aside.
5 Boil a pan of water for the noodles.
6 Fry the steak in batches over a high heat to brown. Remove and keep warm.
7 For the sauce, heat the oil in the wok or frying pan, add the crushed garlic and grated ginger and cook for 30 seconds.
8 Add the beef stock, soy sauce and chilli sauce to the pan. Scrape the bottom to remove the browned bits. Mix the cornflour with 2 tablespoons cold water and pour into the stock. Boil to thicken.
9 Return the meat and vegetables to the sauce and heat through.
10 In the meantime, cook the noodles in the boiling water until tender, about 2 minutes.
11 Drain the noodles and toss with the sesame oil.
12 Place the noodles in a serving dish and top with the stir-fry. Sprinkle over the coriander and spring onions and serve.

Wine: Light or medium-bodied, fruity red (Beaujolais-style) or an aromatic, fruity white

Rib-eye Steaks with Home-made Chips and Aïoli

SERVES 4

675 g Maris Piper or other floury potatoes

2 × 340 g cans goose fat

½ tablespoon oil

1 clove of garlic, bruised

4 × 250 g rib-eye steaks

flaky sea salt and freshly ground black pepper

sprigs of chervil, to garnish

To serve

1 quantity Aïoli (see page 466)

1 Peel the potatoes and cut them into slices 1 cm thick. Cut the slices lengthwise into chips 2 cm wide. Rinse under cold running water and dry well. Lay the chips on a clean tea towel.

2 Heat the goose fat in a heavy-based, medium-sized saucepan to 120°C/250°F (see Warning opposite). Place about a quarter of the chips in a chip basket and lower them carefully into the hot fat. Cook for about 5 minutes, or until tender but not coloured.

3 Lift the chips out of the pan and leave to drain on crumpled kitchen paper. Repeat this process with the remaining chipped potatoes.

4 Heat the oil in a frying pan, add the garlic and cook over a gentle heat for 2–3 minutes. Remove the garlic and discard.

5 Place the pan over a medium-high heat until it is beginning to smoke. Season the steaks and brown quickly on both sides. Lower the temperature and continue to cook the steaks for a further 2–4 minutes (see Grilling and Frying, page 33).

6 Meanwhile, increase the temperature of the goose fat to 190°C/375°F and finish cooking the chips in batches, for a further 2 minutes or until crisp and golden brown. Drain on kitchen paper and sprinkle with plenty of salt.

7 Place the steaks on warmed plates with a pile of the chips and garnish with sprigs of chervil. Serve with the aïoli handed separately.

Wine: Full-bodied dry red, such as Malbec from Argentina, Merlot from Australia or Châteauneuf-du-Pape

WARNING: DEEP-FRYING

Deep-frying can be dangerous, so bear in mind the following safety tips:
- Do not overfill a pan or deep-fryer with oil: it should never be more than half full.
- Never leave hot fat unattended.
- Do not allow oil to overheat. If it starts to smoke, turn off the heat and add a large chunk of bread.
- Never move a pan of hot oil.
- Have a lid to hand to cover the pan in case it bursts into flames.
- Dry food thoroughly before frying.
- Always lower food gently into hot fat so that it doesn't splash.
- Do not allow any water to come in contact with the hot oil as it will make the oil splutter.

Rib-eye Steaks with Field Mushrooms in Sage Butter

SERVES 4

60 g unsalted butter

8 large field mushrooms, peeled and thickly sliced

12 large sage leaves, shredded

1 teaspoon lemon juice

1 tablespoon horseradish sauce

1 tablespoon vegetable oil

4 × 225–250 g rib-eye steaks

salt and freshly ground black pepper

1 Melt the butter in a large frying pan and fry the mushrooms briskly for 1–2 minutes or until well browned.

2 Reduce the heat, stir in the shredded sage and season with salt and pepper. Stir in the lemon juice and horseradish sauce and continue to cook for a further minute. Remove from the pan and keep warm.

3 Season the steaks on both sides with salt and pepper.

4 Wipe the pan with kitchen paper, add the oil and heat until very hot. Fry the steaks, browning well on both sides, then reduce the heat and cook for a further 2–3 minutes.

5 To serve, put a steak on each serving plate, garnish with mushrooms, and pour over the hot sage butter. Serve immediately.

Wine: Full-bodied dry red, such as Malbec from Argentina, Merlot from Australia or Châteauneuf-du-Pape

Grilled Rib-eye Steak with Caponata

This is an impressive and easy recipe for entertaining. Ask the butcher to cut the steak about 5 cm thick to give you plenty for four people.

SERVES 4

1 rib-eye steak, 5 cm thick (about 750 g)

300 ml fruity red wine

1 large onion, coarsely chopped

2 cloves of garlic, crushed

1 tablespoon balsamic vinegar

1 tablespoon soft dark brown sugar

1 tablespoon olive oil, for barbecuing/griddling

salt and freshly ground black pepper

For the caponata

1 medium aubergine

1 teaspoon salt

3 tablespoons olive oil, for frying

2 sticks of celery, cut into 1.5 cm dice

1 red pepper, deseeded and cut into 1.5 cm dice

100 g raisins

50 g black olives, pitted and halved

150 g passata (thick tomato sauce)

flaky sea salt

For the salad

100 g rocket

1 tablespoon olive oil

sprinkle of balsamic vinegar

1 Place the steak in a close-fitting non-corrosive container or large plastic bag. Season with freshly ground black pepper.

2 Combine the wine, onion, garlic, balsamic vinegar and brown sugar. Pour over the steak. Marinate for 4 hours or overnight.

3 To make the caponata, cut the aubergine into 1.5 cm dice. Place in a colander, sprinkle with the salt and leave to drain over a plate for 30 minutes. Rinse and pat dry with kitchen paper.

4 Place half the oil in a sauté pan and fry the aubergine, celery and red pepper in batches on all sides to brown lightly. Add the remaining oil if the pan gets too dry. Transfer the vegetables to a plate and set aside.

5 Remove the steak from the marinade and pat dry with kitchen paper.

6 Heat the oven to 190°C/375°F/gas mark 5.

7 Place the marinade, including the onion and garlic, in a small saucepan. Add the raisins. Boil until syrupy, then fry to caramelize the onions. Stir in the reserved vegetables, the olives and passata. Season with sea salt and freshly ground black pepper to balance the sweet/salty flavour. Set aside to serve at room temperature.

8 Heat a barbecue or griddle pan until very hot. Brush the steak with the oil and season with salt and pepper. Cook the steak until well browned, about 2 minutes per side.

9 If the steak needs further cooking, place it in a roasting pan and put into the oven for 10–30 minutes (rare to well done) until cooked to the desired doneness (see page 14). Leave to rest at room temperature for 10 minutes.

10 Toss the rocket leaves with the oil and balsamic vinegar. Season.

11 Slice the beef 3 cm thick. Add any pan juices to the caponata. To serve, arrange on plates with the rocket salad and caponata.

Wine: Southern Italian red, such as Aglianico, Primitivo or Salice Salentino

Pan-fried Sesame Steaks with Shallots and Creamed Spinach

SERVES 4

4 × 170 g fillet steaks

4 tablespoons sesame seeds

1 tablespoon oil

salt and freshly ground black pepper

For the shallots and spinach

4 banana shallots, blanched, peeled
   and halved lengthwise

75 g unsalted butter

1 tablespoon olive oil

2 bay leaves

150 ml dry white wine

finely grated zest of 1 lemon

4 tablespoons mascarpone cheese

1 tablespoon wholegrain mustard

675 g baby leaf spinach

1 Heat the oven to 180°C/350°G/gas mark 4.

2 Season the steaks with salt and pepper and press the sesame seeds on to both sides. Chill well.

3 Meanwhile, arrange the shallots, cut-side up, in a single layer in a large, shallow flameproof casserole. Dot with 45 g of the butter and drizzle over the olive oil.

4 Add the bay leaves and season with salt and pepper. Roast in the centre of the oven for 45–60 minutes, until the shallots are very tender.

5 About 10 minutes before the shallots are ready, heat the oil for the steaks in a heavy-based frying pan. Fry the steaks on both sides over a low heat until the sesame seeds are golden brown. Transfer to a roasting pan and place in the oven for 5 minutes.

6 Meanwhile, remove the shallots from the oven. Place the casserole over a direct heat, pour in the wine and bring to the boil, scraping the bottom of the pan to remove any sediment. Boil for 2–3 minutes or until syrupy. Place the shallots in a bowl, pour over the juices and keep warm. Discard the bay leaves.

7 Return the dish to the heat and add the remaining 30 g butter. Stir in the lemon zest and cook over a very low heat for a few seconds. Stir in the mascarpone and mustard and cook gently for 30 seconds.

8 Add the spinach and toss quickly to coat with the sauce. Season to taste with salt and pepper and pile on to a warmed serving dish. Top with the shallots and pour over the juices. Serve with the sesame steaks.

Wine: Full-bodied red with sweetness, such as a New Zealand Pinot Noir

Steak and Mustard Butter Sandwiches

Any type of good bread roll or thickly sliced loaf can be used as a base for these sandwiches. However, the open texture of ciabatta ensures that plenty of the hot, sweet mustard butter soaks into the surface, making it deliciously moist and tasty, and not just a medium to carry a topping, as with many open sandwiches. Using a roll also provides a crisper base, which adds to the overall texture.

The mustard and honey are beaten into the butter before being spread on the bread in order to distribute the flavours evenly. Wholegrain mustard and a blended, clear honey have been used here to create a balance that suits most palates, but any combination of mustard and honey can be used, depending on how hot or sweet a flavour is required. English mustard can be rather powerful and fiery, and some types of honey may be too 'flowery' for some tastes.

Sirloin, rump or fillet steaks can all be used, depending on the occasion and budget.

SERVES 4

55 g unsalted butter, softened

1½ tablespoons wholegrain mustard

1 tablespoon clear honey

2 ciabatta rolls, cut in half horizontally

4 × 140 g sirloin steaks, trimmed

1 tablespoon oil

1½ tablespoons water

1 tablespoon balsamic vinegar

1 bunch of watercress, washed and trimmed

salt and freshly ground black pepper

1 Heat the oven to 180°C/350°F/gas mark 4.

2 Put the butter, mustard and honey in a small bowl and beat well. Season with salt and pepper.

3 Spread the cut sides of the bread with the mustard butter. Place in the oven on a baking sheet to warm through and melt the butter whilst you cook the steaks.

4 Season the steaks with salt and pepper. Heat the oil in a heavy-based frying pan and, when very hot, brown the steaks well on both sides. Reduce the heat and continue cooking until done to your liking (see pages 34 and 35 for timings). Remove the steaks from the pan and keep warm.

5 Pour the water and vinegar into the pan and bring to the boil, scraping the bottom to remove any sediment.

6 Divide the watercress between the warm, buttered bread. Slice the steaks thickly and place them on top of the watercress. Pour over the pan juices and serve immediately.

Wine: Medium-bodied red, such as Côtes-du-Rhône, Minervois or Corbières

Mixed Grill

Grilling times depend on the thickness of the ingredients and the temperature of the grill. The suggestions below should be regarded as guidelines only. A mixed grill is traditionally served with chips or straw potatoes.

SERVES 1

110 g rump or sirloin steak
oil, for brushing
50 g calves' liver
1 chipolata sausage
1 lamb's kidney

1 rasher of back bacon
1 whole tomato
2 large flat mushrooms
salt and freshly ground black pepper
sprigs of watercress, to garnish

When preparing a mixed grill, begin by grilling the meat that will take the longest time to cook and then gradually add the other ingredients so that everything is ready at the same time.

Steak: Flatten the steak slightly, brush it with oil and season with pepper. It should be salted just before cooking.

Liver: Remove the membrane that surrounds the liver. Cut the remaining meat into thin pieces, brush with oil and season with pepper.

Chipolata sausages: Do not prick or add any extra fat.

Kidney: Skin and halve the kidney, snipping out the core. Brush with oil and season with pepper.

Bacon: Cut off the rind. Put the bacon on a board and use the back of a knife to stretch it: this helps to prevent shrinking and curling during grilling.

Tomato: Cut in half, brush with a little oil and season with salt and pepper.

Mushrooms: Peel the mushrooms, cut the stalk to 1 cm, brush with oil and season with salt and pepper.

1 Heat the grill to its highest setting.
2 When very hot, place the chipolata sausage under it.
3 After 1 minute, add the liver and the kidney.
4 After 1 further minute, add the steak and bacon. Grill for 1 minute.
5 Turn over the sausage and steak and grill for 1 further minute.
6 Add the tomato halves and mushrooms and grill for a further 2 minutes or so, turning over the tomato halves and turning the sausage if necessary.
7 As the items are ready, put them on a warmed serving platter, carefully draining the fat from the sausage and bacon. Just before serving, garnish with sprigs of watercress.

Wine: Full-bodied red, such as Châteauneuf-du-Pape, Hermitage or Aglianico

Thai Stir-fried Beef with Red Peppers and Beansprouts

SERVES 4

675 g sirloin of beef, trimmed

2½ tablespoons fish sauce

3 tablespoons oyster sauce

2 tablespoons cornflour

2 tablespoons oil

1 clove of garlic, crushed

5 cm piece of fresh root ginger, peeled and grated

1 large red pepper, deseeded and cut into 5 mm strips

2 large red chillies, deseeded and very finely chopped

1 large or 2 small heads bok choi, cut into quarters

110 g beansprouts

1½ tablespoons clear honey

2 tablespoons water

85 g glass noodles, soaked in boiling water for
   4 minutes and drained

1 small bunch of Thai holy basil, shredded

salt and freshly ground black pepper

1 lime, cut into wedges, to serve

1 Shred the beef as finely as possible, and put into a large non-metallic bowl with 1½ tablespoons of the fish sauce and 1½ tablespoons of the oyster sauce. Cover and leave in a cool place for 1–1½ hours.

2 Remove the beef from the marinade and pat dry. Mix the beef with the cornflour and season with salt and pepper.

3 Heat 1 tablespoon of the oil in a work or very large frying pan and fry the beef in batches until well browned. Remove from the pan and keep warm.

4 Heat the remaining oil, add the garlic and ginger and fry for 30 seconds.

5 Add the red pepper and chillies and fry for a further 30 seconds.

6 Stir in the bok choi, beansprouts, the remaining fish sauce and oyster sauce, the honey and water. Return the beef to the pan and add the prepared noodles. Heat thoroughly, stirring occasionally.

7 Transfer to a warmed serving dish and sprinkle over the holy basil.

8 Serve on a warmed dish with the lime wedges to squeeze over.

Wine: Light or medium-bodied fruity red (Beaujolais-style) or an aromatic, fruity white

Oriental Beef Salad

The components of this salad can be prepared in advance and assembled at the last minute. The salad can be served either hot or cold, making it ideal for the English summer.

SERVES 4–6

450 g sirloin steak

oil, for frying

2 cloves of garlic, crushed

225 g button mushrooms

225 g mangetout, blanched and refreshed

For the marinade

2 onions, thinly sliced

5 tablespoons dry sherry

5 tablespoons light soy sauce

2 tablespoons sesame oil

freshly ground black pepper

For the dressing

6 tablespoons grapeseed or sunflower oil

3 tablespoons white wine vinegar

1 tablespoon Dijon mustard

1 teaspoon clear honey

To serve

450 g new potatoes, boiled

1 bunch of coriander, chopped

2 tablespoons toasted sesame seeds

1 Trim the steak of fat. Mix together the marinade ingredients. Add the steak and leave to marinate overnight in the refrigerator.

2 Remove the steak and pat dry, reserving the marinade.

3 Heat the oil in a frying pan over a medium heat and fry the steak on both sides to the desired doneness (see page 35 for timings). Set aside at room temperature.

4 Strain the onions from the marinade, then fry in a little oil until well browned and caramelized. Add the garlic and cook for a further minute.

5 In the meantime, whisk the dressing ingredients together.

6 When the onions are done add them to the dressing.

7 Place the mushrooms and marinade in the frying pan and cook until syrupy. Add to the dressing, then leave to cool.

8 To serve, cut the steak into strips. Layer the potatoes, mangetout, meat and onion/mushroom mixture on a large serving dish. Sprinkle with the coriander and the sesame seeds. Serve immediately.

Wine: Strong, savoury red from southern Italy or an Australian Shiraz

Fried Beef with Sichuan Peppercorns

SERVES 4–6

450 g lean beef, such as rump steak

85–110 g carrots, cut into julienne strips

3–4 sticks of celery, cut into julienne strips

½ teaspoon salt

600 ml oil, for deep-frying, plus 2 tablespoons

1 teaspoon cornflour

2–3 dried red chillies, halved and deseeded

½ teaspoon ground roasted Sichuan peppercorns

1 teaspoon sesame oil

For the marinade

2 tablespoons light soy sauce

2 teaspoons sugar

1 tablespoon Shaoxing wine or dry sherry

1 teaspoon sesame oil

½ teaspoon ground roasted Sichuan peppercorns

For the thickening

1–1½ teaspoons cornflour

scant 1 teaspoon sugar

4 tablespoons water

1 Shred the beef across the grain into thread-like strips 7.5 cm long. Put into a bowl.

2 Add all the marinade ingredients and combine well. Allow to stand at room temperature for 45–60 minutes so that the marinade permeates every sliver of beef.

3 Put the carrots and celery into a bowl and add a pinch of salt to draw out the water. Leave for 20–30 minutes, then drain. Pat dry, if necessary.

4 Mix the ingredients for the thickening in a small bowl and set aside.

5 Heat the oil in a wok until very hot (see Warning, page 53). Remove the beef from the marinade and coat evenly with the cornflour. Tip the beef gently into the oil and deep-fry for 2–3 minutes, or until crisp. Turn off the heat, remove the beef with a large, hand-held strainer and drain on kitchen paper. Wash and dry the wok.

6 Reheat the wok over a medium heat until hot. Add 2 tablespoons oil and swirl it around. Tip in the chillies, fry until dark in colour, then remove and discard them. Add the carrots and celery. Stir for a few minutes until dry before adding the beef. Continue to stir over a low heat for a further 1–2 minutes, or until everything is quite dry and crisp. Add the thickening gradually and stir until the beef is coated.

7 Sprinkle with the ground Sichuan peppercorns and sesame oil before serving.

Wine: Full-bodied red or white, such as Zinfandel or New World Chardonnay

Teriyaki Beef with Mushrooms and Noodles

Teriyaki, a Japanese method of cooking, translates as 'shiny and grilled'. This method is popular for chicken and beef.

SERVES 4–6

4 × 170 g sirloin steaks, trimmed of fat

150 ml teriyaki sauce

3 tablespoons medium-dry sherry

3 tablespoons dark soy sauce

oil, for frying

2 onions, finely sliced

450 g oyster mushrooms, pulled into pieces

450 g chestnut mushrooms, sliced

4 sheets of thick egg noodles

220 g frozen petits pois

salt

steamed bok choi, to serve

1   Place the steaks in a shallow dish, add the teriyaki sauce, sherry and soy sauce and marinate for 30 minutes.

2   Meanwhile, heat 2 tablespoons of the oil and fry the onions over a low heat until soft but not coloured.

3   Add the mushrooms, stir well and cover with a lid, stirring occasionally until the mushrooms have released some liquid. Remove the lid and increase the heat, stirring, until the onions and mushrooms are browned. Transfer the mixture to a plate and set aside.

4   Remove the steaks from the dish and scrape off any marinade clinging to them. Reserve the marinade. Wipe the frying pan and heat 1 tablespoon of oil.

5   When the pan is very hot, fry the steaks until brown on both sides (about 1 minute per side). Reduce the heat and continue to fry the steaks for about 1½–2 minutes each side or until rare. Leave them to rest on a chopping board, then cut into slices approximately 5 mm thick.

6   Place the noodles and peas in a pan of vigorously boiling salted water. Cook according to the instructions on the noodle packet. Drain.

7   Return the mushroom mixture to the frying pan and place over the heat. When sizzling, add the marinade and 5 tablespoons water. Bring to the boil, then stir in the noodles and peas. Remove from the heat and stir in the sliced steak.

8   Pile on to plates and serve with steamed bok choi.

VARIATIONS: Any type of mushroom can be used in this recipe, and sugar snap peas or mangetout can be substituted for the petits pois. Sliced bok choi or a handful of beansprouts could also be added to the mushrooms at step 7.

Wine: Full-bodied red, such as Australian Shiraz, or an adventurous choice – Guinness

Ropa Vieja

This dish of braised beef is popular in Cuba and the Caribbean, where it is served with saffron rice and black beans. The Spanish name means 'old clothes', a reference to the colourful shreds in this dish, which supposedly resemble rags.

SERVES 4

700 g beef brisket or flank steak in one piece

For the braising liquid

1 onion, sliced
1 large carrot, sliced
2 stalks of celery, sliced
3 cloves of garlic, crushed
½ teaspoon cumin seeds
½ teaspoon dried oregano
1 teaspoon salt
juice of 1 lime
½ teaspoon black peppercorns

For the sauce

4 tablespoons olive oil
1 red onion, sliced
1 red pepper, deseeded and sliced
1 green pepper, deseeded and sliced
2 cloves of garlic, crushed
2 red chillies, deseeded and diced
1 teaspoon ground cumin
pinch of ground cinnamon
1 × 400 g can chopped tomatoes
1 tablespoon tomato purée
2 tablespoons chopped fresh coriander, to garnish

1 Place the beef in a large, heavy-based pan.
2 Add the ingredients for the braising liquid plus enough cold water to cover. Bring to the boil slowly, skimming any fat or scum from the surface.
3 Turn the heat down so that the liquid barely trembles. Cover and cook for 1½–2 hours, or until the meat is tender.
4 Allow the beef to cool in the liquid for 30 minutes, then transfer to a board.
5 Retain the liquid, but discard the vegetables in it. Boil the liquid until reduced to 600 ml.
6 Meanwhile, shred the beef into fine strips and chill until required.
7 To make the sauce, heat the oil in a frying pan and soften the onion. Add the peppers and cook until soft.
8 Add the garlic and chillies and cook for a further minute, then add the cumin and cinnamon. Cook for 30 seconds, stirring continuously, then add the tomatoes, tomato purée and reduced poaching liquid.
9 Simmer the sauce for 1 hour, until it has the thickness of Italian tomato sauce.
10 To serve, stir in the meat and heat thoroughly. Garnish with the coriander.

Wine: Flavoursome red, such as Zinfandel, or Chilean and Argentinian reds

To Prepare Meat for Stewing

Remove the gristle but not all the fat, as it will add moisture and flavour. Cut the meat into pieces no smaller than 3.5 cm. Pieces that are cut too small will fall apart into shreds or become dry and tough during prolonged cooking.

Family Beef Stew

The flavour of this stew improves if kept for a day before eating, and the barley swells up even more to thicken the sauce.

SERVES 4

675 g chuck steak, trimmed (see above)
dripping or oil
600 ml Brown Stock (see page 452)
2 mild onions, sliced
3 medium carrots, cubed

1 bay leaf
2 parsley stalks
pinch of chopped fresh thyme
30 g pearl barley
salt and freshly ground black pepper

1 Heat the oven to 150°C/300°F/gas mark 2.
2 Cut the steak into 4 cm cubes.
3 Melt a little of the dripping in a sauté pan. Brown the beef cubes on all sides, a few at a time, then transfer to a heatproof casserole. After browning each batch of meat, deglaze the pan with a little stock, scraping up the sediment. Reserve this liquid (*déglaçage*). When all the meat has been browned and transferred to the casserole, taste the *déglaçage*. If it does not taste burnt, add it to the casserole dish.
4 Heat a little more dripping or oil and fry the onions and carrots until golden brown. Place them in the casserole dish.
5 Pour the remaining stock into the pan and bring to the boil, scraping any remaining sediment from the bottom. Stir in the seasoning, bay leaf, parsley stalks, thyme and barley and pour over the meat. Bring to a simmer.
6 Cover the casserole and cook in the oven for 2–2½ hours, or until the meat is tender enough to cut with a fork. Skim off any excess fat.

Wine: Medium- to full-bodied red, such as Côtes-du-Rhône, a New World red blend, or Rioja

Beef Bourguignon

This stew can be cooked on top of the cooker, over a low heat, for 1½–2 hours, but slow oven-cooking produces a better result. The meat becomes as soft as butter, but not shredded or falling apart, and there is no danger of it 'catching' on the bottom.

SERVES 4

675 g chuck steak

1 tablespoon beef dripping or oil

12 small button onions or shallots

30 g butter

1 clove of garlic, crushed

2 teaspoons plain flour

300 ml red wine

300 ml Brown Stock (see page 452)

1 bouquet garni (see page 512)

50 g piece of fatty bacon, diced

115 g button mushrooms

salt and freshly ground black pepper

chopped fresh parsley, to garnish

1 Cut the beef into 4 cm cubes, discarding any fat and gristle.

2 Heat half the dripping or oil in a flameproof casserole and brown the beef cubes very well, a few at a time. They must be brown on all sides. Transfer them to a bowl as they are done. When the bottom of the pan becomes brown, add a little water, swishing it about and scraping up the sediment. Reserve this *déglaçage*, then heat up a little more dripping or oil and continue to brown the meat. When it has all been browned and transferred to the bowl, deglaze the pan one last time and pour all the *déglaçage* over the meat.

3 Heat the oven to 150°C/300°F/gas mark 2.

4 Immerse the button onions in boiling water for 30 seconds, then immerse in cold water. Peel off the skins. Dry them and fry in half the butter until well browned.

5 Add the garlic and stir in the flour. Cook, stirring, for 1 minute.

6 Pour in the wine and stock. Stir until boiling, again scraping the bottom of the pan.

7 Put the meat and sauce in the casserole and add the bouquet garni. Season with salt and pepper. Cover and cook in the hot oven for 2–3 hours, or until the meat is very tender.

8 Meanwhile, cut the bacon into 1 cm cubes and blanch in boiling water for 1 minute. Refresh and drain well.

9 Wipe the mushrooms but do not peel or remove the stalks. Cut into quarters if large.

10 Melt the remaining butter in a frying pan and, when foaming, add the bacon and mushrooms and cook fairly fast until golden brown. Lift them out and add to the beef when it has been cooking for 1 hour. Return to the oven for a further hour, until the meat is tender.

11 When the meat is tender, use a slotted spoon to lift the meat, bacon and vegetables into a clean casserole. Remove the bouquet garni and check the seasoning. Boil the sauce fast to reduce to a syrupy consistency. If the sauce is too salty, thicken it with a little beurre manié (see page 512) rather than reducing it.

12 Pour the sauce over the beef and serve sprinkled with parsley.

Wine: Red Burgundy

Caribbean Spiced Beef Casserole

SERVES 6

1.35 kg stewing beef

3 tablespoons vegetable oil

1 tablespoon soft brown sugar

600 ml Brown Stock (see page 452)

2 onions, sliced

1 clove of garlic, crushed

2 green chillies, chopped

chopped fresh coriander, to garnish

For the marinade

1 onion, grated 2 cloves of garlic, chopped

2 teaspoons ground allspice

1 teaspoon chopped fresh thyme

1 teaspoon ground coriander

½ teaspoon ground cumin

freshly ground black pepper

To serve

Boiled Rice (see page 494)

1 Trim the meat of fat and cut into 5 cm cubes.

2 Combine the marinade ingredients in a bowl, add the meat and mix well. Refrigerate for 2 hours or overnight.

3 Scrape the marinade off the meat. Heat a little oil in a sauté pan and brown the meat in batches. As each batch is browning, sprinkle with a little of the sugar to caramelize. Deglaze the pan with some of the stock in between batches. Reserve the *déglaçage*.

4 Heat the oven to 150°C/300°F/gas mark 2.

5 Heat the remaining oil and fry the onions until golden brown. Add the garlic and chillies and cook for a further minute. Place in an ovenproof casserole. Top with the beef, the remaining stock and the reserved *déglaçage*.

6 Cover the casserole and place in the oven for 2–3 hours, or until the meat is tender.

7 Remove the meat from the dish and keep warm. Purée the contents of the casserole (boil to reduce if too thin) and pour over the meat.

8 Garnish with the coriander and serve with boiled rice.

Wine: Red wine with good fruit, such as New Zealand or Chilean Pinot Noir

Carbonnade of Beef

This classic Belgian casserole uses ale to enrich the sauce and tenderize the meat. It's delicious with new potatoes and glazed carrots with orange and nutmeg.

SERVES 6–8

4 tablespoons oil

450 g onions, thinly sliced

1.35 kg chuck steak

2 cloves of garlic, crushed

1 tablespoon soft brown sugar

1 tablespoon plain flour

425 ml brown ale

425 ml Brown Stock (see page 452)

1 teaspoon chopped fresh thyme

1 bay leaf

2 teaspoons wine vinegar

8 slices French bread

8 tablespoons wholegrain mustard

salt and freshly ground black pepper

1 Heat 2 tablespoons of the oil in a saucepan and stir in the onions. Cover with a piece of dampened greaseproof paper and a lid and cook over a low heat until softened, about 15 minutes.

2 Heat the oven to 150°C/300°F/gas mark 2. Cut the beef into 4 pieces each measuring about 7 × 5 cm.

3 Heat the remaining oil in a large frying pan and brown the beef over a medium heat a few pieces at a time. Transfer to an ovenproof casserole dish. Pour in a little water into the frying pan between batches and scrape up any sediment. Reserve this *déglaçage*.

4 Remove the lid and paper from the onions. Add the garlic and sugar, and cook for 1 minute. Stir in the flour, then continue to cook until lightly browned. Add the ale, stock and reserved *déglaçage*. Simmer, stirring, for 2 minutes. Add the herbs, vinegar and seasoning.

5 Pour the stock mixture over the meat in the casserole, cover and cook in the oven for 2½ hours.

6 To serve, increase the oven temperature to 190°C/375°F/gas mark 5. Remove the bay leaf from the casserole and discard. Spread the bread slices with the mustard and place, mustard-side up, on top of the casserole. Cook uncovered for 15 minutes until the bread is crisp.

Wine: Full-bodied red with high acidity – Rioja Reserva, Aglianico, or a southern Italian red

Beef Short Ribs Braised with Cider

Although cider seems an odd combination with beef, the fruitiness is delicious with the slow-cooked meat.

SERVES 4

800 g meaty short ribs, cut into 10 cm pieces

3 tablespoons olive oil

1 large onion, sliced

1 medium carrot, diced

250 ml dry cider

250 ml Brown Stock (see page 452)

2 bay leaves

6 sprigs of thyme

30 g softened butter

20 g plain flour

salt and freshly ground black pepper

2 tablespoons chopped fresh parsley, to garnish

To serve

Mashed Potatoes or Soft Polenta
(see page 491 or 495)

1 Season the ribs with salt and pepper. Heat the oil in an ovenproof casserole, then brown the short ribs on all sides. Remove from the pan and set aside.

2 Turn the heat to low and cook the onion and carrot until softened and slightly browned. If the pan is too dry, add a little more oil.

3 Heat the oven to 170°C/325°F/gas mark 3.

4 Add the cider to the hot pan and bring to a simmer, scraping up the browned bits from the bottom. Add the stock, bay leaves and thyme.

5 Return the short ribs to the pan. The liquid should just cover them; if not, add water to do so. Bring to a simmer.

6 Cover the pan and place in the oven for 2½–3 hours, or until the meat is falling from the bone. The dish can be made ahead up to this point and cooled.

7 Remove any fat from the surface of the liquid, then warm over a medium heat. When the meat is heated through, remove it from the liquid and keep warm.

8 Mix the softened butter and the flour to a paste (beurre manié).

9 Bring the beef liquid to the boil, then skim any fat from the surface. Boil rapidly to reduce until the flavour has concentrated. There should be about 700 ml liquid.

10 Whisk the beurre manié into the boiling liquid and boil to thicken. Pour over the beef ribs. Serve garnished with the chopped parsley, and with mashed potatoes or soft polenta.

Wine: Light to medium-bodied red, such as Saumur-Champigny, Saint-Emilion or Cru Beaujolais

Oxtail Stew with Horseradish Mash and Caramelized Shallots

2 oxtails, cut into 3 cm lengths, total
  weight about 1.35 kg

seasoned plain flour

30 g beef dripping or oil

340 g carrots, thickly sliced

225 g onions, sliced

150 ml red wine

600 ml water or stock

1 teaspoon chopped fresh thyme

½ teaspoon sugar

1 teaspoon tomato purée

juice of ½ a lemon

salt and freshly ground black pepper

2 tablespoons chopped fresh parsley, to garnish

To serve

Caramelized Shallots (see page 499)

Horseradish Mash (see below)

1 Wash and dry the oxtails. Trim off any excess fat and toss in seasoned flour.
2 Melt the dripping in a heavy saucepan, add the oxtail, a few pieces at a time, and brown evenly on all sides. Transfer to a plate as they are done.
3 Brown the carrots and onions in the same pan.
4 Replace the oxtail. Pour over the wine and water or stock and add the thyme and sugar, and season. Bring to the boil, then simmer for 2 hours.
5 Heat the oven to 150°C/300°F/gas mark 2.
6 Using a slotted spoon, transfer the vegetables and pieces of meat to a casserole.
7 With a small ladle or spoon, skim off the fat that rises to the top of the remaining liquid. Add the tomato purée and lemon juice and bring to the boil.
8 Pour this liquid over the oxtail, cover with a lid and cook in the oven for about 3 hours, or until the meat is almost falling off the bone. Sprinkle with parsley before serving with horseradish mash and caramelized shallots.

NOTES: If the sauce is too thin, transfer the meat and vegetables to a warmed serving dish and boil the sauce rapidly until reduced to the desired consistency.

When buying oxtail, choose short, fat tails with a good proportion of meat on them. Long, stringy, thin tails are poor value – poor in flavour and short on meat.

Oxtail is very good served with dumplings (see page 486).

HORSERADISH MASH

675 g potatoes, peeled and cut into even-sized
  chunks

2 tablespoons crème fraîche

50 g butter

3 tablespoons creamed horseradish sauce

salt and freshly ground black pepper

1 Cook the potatoes in boiling salted water until tender. Drain thoroughly.
2 Push the potatoes through a sieve or mouli. Return them to the dry pan.

3 Place the pan on the hob and add the crème fraîche, butter and creamed horseradish. Beat well and season to taste with salt and pepper.

Wine: A rich red, such as New Zealand or Californian Pinot Noir, or Châteauneuf-du-Pape

Tsimmes

There are many variations of this traditional dish for Rosh Hashanah (Jewish New Year). A sweet and spicy flavour, produced by honey, cinnamon and carrots, is the most usual. The meat is cooked long and slowly, so start it a day in advance. Serve with noodles.

SERVES 6–8

2 kg beef brisket

1 teaspoon sweet Hungarian paprika

½ teaspoon ground cinnamon

¼ teaspoon ground cayenne

4 tablespoons vegetable oil

2 large onions, finely chopped

3 cloves of garlic, crushed

1 × 400 g can chopped tomatoes

900 ml Brown Stock (see page 452)

500 g carrots, sliced

1 tablespoon orange flower honey

salt and freshly ground black pepper

4 tablespoons chopped fresh parsley, to garnish

1 Trim any fat from the brisket.

2 Combine the paprika, cinnamon and cayenne and rub into the meat.

3 Heat the oven to 170°C/325°F/gas mark 3.

4 Heat the oil in an ovenproof casserole dish. Season the meat with salt and pepper, then brown it over a low heat. Set aside on a plate.

5 Add the onions to the casserole and sweat, covered with a piece of dampened greaseproof paper and a lid, until soft and transparent. Stir in the garlic and cook for a further minute.

6 Return the beef to the casserole, then add the tomatoes and stock. The liquid should just cover the meat. If necessary, add water.

7 Bring to a simmer, then cover and place in the oven for 3 hours.

8 Add the carrots and honey to the casserole and cook for a further hour.

9 Remove the meat from the sauce and keep warm. Boil the sauce to concentrate to a good flavour. Strain into a warmed gravy boat to serve.

10 Serve the meat sliced into thin strips and garnished with the parsley.

Wine: Côtes-du-Rhône, Beaujolais or Montepulciano d'Abruzzo

Hungarian Goulash with Soured Cream and Chive Dumplings

SERVES 4

1 kg beef stewing steak

3 tablespoons vegetable oil

1 large onion, chopped

2 sticks of celery, chopped

600 ml Brown Stock (see page 452)

2 tablespoons sweet Hungarian paprika

1 tablespoon tomato purée

2 sprigs of thyme

1 bay leaf

salt and freshly ground black pepper

To serve

Soured Cream and Chive Dumplings (see page 486)

1 Cut the beef into 5 cm cubes, removing any gristle. Set aside.

2 Heat 1 tablespoon of the oil in a small saucepan and stir in the onion and the celery. Cover with a dampened piece of greaseproof paper and a lid. Cook over a low heat until softened.

3 Heat the oven to 150°C/300°F/gas mark 2.

4 Heat 1 tablespoon of the oil in a large sauté pan. Season the meat with salt and pepper, then brown in batches on all sides. As each piece is done, place in an ovenproof casserole dish.

5 Deglaze the pan with some of the stock in between batches and add the *déglaçage* to the casserole dish.

6 When all the meat has been browned and added to the casserole, stir the paprika into the remaining oil in the sauté pan and cook over a low heat for 30 seconds. Add the remaining stock to the sauté pan. Stir in the tomato purée. Add the contents of the sauté pan to the casserole dish.

7 Place the thyme sprigs and the bay leaf in the casserole and cover with a tight-fitting lid. Bring to a simmer, then place in the oven for 2 hours, or until the meat is tender. The recipe can be made ahead to this point.

8 About 20 minutes before the end of the cooking time, remove the thyme and bay leaf. Float the dumplings in the liquid, then re-cover the casserole and cook for the remaining time.

Wine: Blended red, such as Saint-Emilion, Rioja, Rhône or Australian Shiraz/Cabernet

Beef in Ale with Pickled Walnuts and Cranberries

SERVES 4

3 tablespoons vegetable oil

1 Spanish onion, sliced

900 g beef stewing steak, cut into 4 cm pieces

440 ml light ale

1 tablespoon dark muscovado sugar

600 ml Brown Stock (see page 452)

4 pickled walnuts

100 g fresh or frozen cranberries

2 tablespoons plain flour

½ teaspoon dry English mustard

30 g softened butter

salt and freshly ground black pepper

2 tablespoons chopped fresh parsley, to garnish

To serve

Mashed Potatoes or Baked Potato with Soured Cream and Chives (see page 491 or 492).

1 Place half the oil in a small saucepan over a low heat.

2 Stir in the onion and cover with a piece of dampened greaseproof paper and a lid. Cook until translucent and softened. Set aside.

3 Heat the oven to 150°C/300°F/gas mark 2.

4 In a sauté pan heat the remaining oil over a medium heat.

5 Season the meat with salt and pepper, then brown in batches on all sides. Deglaze the pan with some of the ale in between batches, reserving the *déglaçage*.

6 Place the onion and the browned meat in an ovenproof casserole dish. Pour in the *déglaçage* and any remaining ale. Stir in the sugar and add just enough stock to cover the meat. Place in the oven and cook for 1½ hours.

7 Skin the pickled walnuts, then drain on kitchen paper. Stir into the casserole along with the cranberries.

8 Return to the oven and cook for a further 30 minutes, or until the meat is tender and the cranberries are starting to split.

9 Strain the contents of the casserole through a sieve, pouring the liquid into a sauté pan. Transfer the solids to a warmed serving dish.

10 Bring the liquid to the boil. Mix the flour and mustard with the butter, then whisk into the boiling liquid bit by bit until it has thickened to coating consistency. Adjust the seasoning to taste, then strain the sauce over the meat.

11 Garnish with the parsley and serve with mashed or baked potatoes.

Wine: Full-bodied red, such as Argentinian Malbec, or Newcastle Brown Ale

Sauté of Beef with Green Peppercorns

SERVES 4

675 g skirt of beef
1 tablespoon oil
1 tablespoon brandy
450 ml Demi-glace Sauce (see page 464)

4 tablespoons double cream (optional)
2 teaspoons canned green peppercorns,
  well rinsed and drained
salt and freshly ground black pepper

1 Cut the beef into 5 cm cubes, discarding any fat.

2 Heat the oil in a heavy-based frying pan and brown the beef very well on all sides a few pieces at a time. Transfer them to a bowl as they are done, deglazing the pan with a little water between batches.

3 Tip off any excess fat from the pan, put back the meat, add the brandy and set alight with a match. When the flames subside, pour in the demi-glace sauce, cover and simmer very gently until the meat is tender. This will take at least 45 minutes, depending on the quality of the meat.

4 Add the cream, if using, and the peppercorns, and adjust the seasoning to taste.

Wine: A weighty red, such as Châteauneuf-du-Pape, Primitivo or Zinfandel

Gaeng Ped Nua (Spicy Red Beef)

The ingredients needed for this recipe are available in Thai food shops.

SERVES 6–8

3 tablespoons oil

2 tablespoons Thai red curry paste

1.35 kg braising steak, cut into strips

1 stalk of lemon grass, cut into strips

a few makrut (citrus) leaves

340 g creamed coconut

2 tablespoons nam pla (Thai fish sauce)

½ teaspoon sugar

2 red peppers, deseeded and cut into strips

1 bunch of fresh Thai basil, leaves only

To serve

Boiled Rice (see page 494)

1 Heat the oil in a large wok or frying pan and fry the curry paste for 1 minute. Add the strips of beef and stir-fry, ensuring that the curry paste coats the meat. Cover with water and add the lemon grass and broken-up makrut leaves.

2 Simmer until the beef is tender (about 1½ hours). Remove the meat and keep warm before reducing the sauce.

3 Mix the creamed coconut with 600 ml water and add it to the pan. Reduce until the sauce is thick.

4 Add the nam pla, sugar and red peppers and simmer until the peppers are just cooked.

5 Stir in the basil leaves and serve with boiled rice.

NOTE: If the sauce curdles (which it often does), it can be brought back together with vigorous whisking.

Drink: Chilled lager to offset the heat

Beef Curry with Almonds

This is an adaptation of a recipe by Josceline Dimbleby. As with many recipes that include a large variety of dried spices, it doesn't matter if you don't have them all – just use a little extra of the ones you do have. The cumin and coriander, however, are essential.

SERVES 4

675 g chuck steak

3–4 tablespoons sunflower oil

85 g blanched almonds

1 teaspoon ground cardamom

½ teaspoon ground cloves

2 teaspoons freshly ground black pepper

2 teaspoons ground cumin

1 tablespoon ground coriander

½ teaspoon ground turmeric

2 onions, sliced

3 cm piece of fresh root ginger, peeled and very finely chopped

2 cloves of garlic, crushed

1 × 400 g can tomatoes

salt

2 tablespoons Greek yoghurt

fresh coriander leaves, to garnish

1 Trim the beef of as much fat and gristle as possible and cut into 3.5 cm cubes.

2 Put 1 tablespoon of the oil into a frying pan and heat gently. Add the almonds and fry until golden brown. Set aside.

3 Heat a little more oil in the pan, add the dry spices and cook slowly for 1 minute.

4 Put the spices and almonds into a blender with 150 ml water and whizz to a smooth purée.

5 Heat the oven to 170°C/325°F/gas mark 3.

6 Wipe the frying pan clean: it is important to prevent the final curry having bits of burnt spices in it. Add 1 tablespoon oil, heat well and brown the beef cubes on all sides a few at a time. Transfer to a flameproof casserole. If the bottom of the pan becomes too brown and sticky, pour in a little water between batches and swish it about, scraping up the sediment. Pour this *déglaçage* into the casserole. Add a little more oil to the frying pan and continue browning the meat until all is transferred to the casserole.

7 Deglaze the pan again and heat a little oil. Add the onions and fry slowly until they are a deep golden brown. Add the ginger and garlic and simmer for a further minute. Add the almond purée and the tomatoes. Stir well, bring to the boil and simmer for 1 minute. Season to taste with salt, then pour over the meat. Place the casserole on the hob and bring back to the boil. Cover and transfer to the oven for 2–3 hours, or until the meat is very tender.

8 Check the curry 2 or 3 times during the cooking process, and if it is becoming too dry, add a little water.

9 Just before serving, stir the yoghurt into the curry and reheat on the hob without boiling. Pour into a warm serving dish and garnish with the coriander leaves.

Wine: A red southern Italian wine or Rioja

Slow-cooked Leg of Beef with Honey Parsnip Crisps

This dish takes three days to complete, as marinating and long, slow cooking of the meat are required to produce the soft, sticky texture of the finished dish, but it is worth the time and effort. The meat must have a good proportion of fat to create a gelatinous finish, so do not overtrim it.

It is essential to use claret or a similar medium-bodied wine as a more powerful, tannic wine will produce a purple-tinted sauce.

SERVES 6

1 × 3 kg leg of beef, butterfly-boned, sinews removed (see page 138)
350 ml claret
150 ml Madeira
2 bay leaves
4 sprigs of thyme
1 handful of parsley stalks, bruised
2 blades of mace
1 small clove of garlic, crushed
3 tablespoons oil

6 banana shallots, each cut lengthwise into 6 wedges
2 carrots, cut into 3 cm diagonal slices
2 sticks of celery, finely sliced on the diagonal
2 teaspoons plain flour
½ tablespoon tomato purée
600 ml Veal Stock (see page 454)
salt and freshly ground black pepper

To serve

Honey Parsnip Crisps (see opposite)

1 Open out the leg of beef and place cut-side up in a shallow, non-metallic dish. Pour over the wine and Madeira. Add the bay leaves, thyme, parsley stalks, mace and crushed garlic. Season well with just black pepper.

2 Cover and leave to marinate for 24 hours in the refrigerator, turning occasionally.

3 Remove the meat from the marinade and pat dry. Reserve the marinade. Heat 1 tablespoon of the oil in a very large flameproof casserole and brown the meat well on all sides. Remove from the pan and set aside.

4 Add the remaining oil to the casserole and brown the shallots, carrots and celery. Sprinkle over the flour and brown lightly.

5 Stir in the tomato purée, then pour in the reserved marinade and the stock, scraping any sediment from the bottom of the pan. Return the meat to the casserole and bring to the boil. Season with salt, cover with a lid and simmer very gently for 3½–4 hours, skimming occasionally. Allow to cool completely, then refrigerate overnight.

6 Using a slotted spoon, remove the solidified fat from the surface of the liquid. (This can be stored in the refrigerator and used for roasting potatoes.)

7 Return the casserole to the heat and bring to the boil. Reduce the heat and simmer gently for a further 1–1½ hours, skimming off any fat.

8 Remove the meat from the casserole. It should be very tender and just breaking up. Shred it into large pieces and set aside. Strain the liquid and add the vegetables to the meat.

9 Return the liquid to the casserole and boil rapidly until it is reduced by half, looks glossy and has a strong flavour.

10 Return the meat and vegetables to the sauce and reheat gently. Season to taste. Serve with Honey Parsnip Crisps (see opposite).

HONEY PARSNIP CRISPS

SERVES 6

2 large parsnips

oil, for deep-frying

2 tablespoons clear honey

flaky sea salt

1 Top and tail and peel the parsnips. Using a vegetable peeler, cut them into thin strips along the length.

2 Half-fill a saucepan with oil and heat until a cube of bread sizzles and browns in 30 seconds (see Warning, page 53).

3 Drop the strips into the hot oil a few at a time and cook until golden brown. Drain on kitchen paper and sprinkle with a little salt.

4 Warm the honey in a small pan. Place the parsnip crisps on a baking sheet and drizzle the honey over them. Toss gently and serve immediately.

Wine: Full-bodied red, either New World or Mediterranean, or a South African Merlot

Steak and Mushroom Pie

The beef in the recipe is trimmed, chopped and browned in the same way as stewing beef (see Family Beef Stew, page 63). It is then cooked very gently and slowly for at least 2 hours to break down the connective tissue. The meat mixture must be cold before topping with the pastry. Once the pie is assembled, it is baked for 30 minutes to cook the pastry and to tenderize the meat further.

SERVES 4

675 g chuck steak

oil or dripping, for frying

1 onion, finely chopped

225 g brown cap mushrooms

30 g plain flour

425 ml Brown Stock (see page 452)

1 tablespoon chopped fresh parsley

salt and freshly ground black pepper

1 quantity Rough Puff Pastry
   (see page 479) or 500 g bought puff pastry

beaten egg, to glaze

1 Trim away the excess fat from the steak and cut the meat into 3 cm cubes.

2 Heat the oil or dripping in a frying pan and fry a few beef cubes at a time until browned all over. Transfer them to a heatproof casserole as they are done.

3 Fry the onion in the same fat until soft and brown. Add the mushrooms and cook for 5 minutes, until soft.

4 Stir in the flour and cook for 1 minute. Gradually add the stock, stirring continuously and scraping any sediment from the bottom of the pan. Bring to the boil, then simmer for 1 minute. Pour over the meat in the casserole, season with salt and pepper and simmer slowly until the meat is tender (about 2 hours).

5 If the sauce is too greasy, skim off the fat; if it is too thin, transfer the meat to a pie dish and boil the sauce rapidly until syrupy. Pour the sauce over the meat, add the parsley and leave until completely cold.

6 Roll the pastry out to the thickness of a £1 coin. Cut a long strip just wider than the rim of the pie dish, brush the lip of the dish with water and press the strip down along it.

7 Brush the strip with water, then lay the sheet of pastry over the dish. Press it down firmly and cut away any excess.

8 Cut a 1 cm hole in the centre of the pie to allow steam to escape, and half-cover with a leaf-shaped piece of pastry made from the pastry trimmings.

9 Decorate the top of the pie with more pastry leaves. Brush all over with beaten egg. Refrigerate until the pastry is firm.

10 Heat the oven to 200°C/400°F/gas mark 6.

11 Bake the pie in the oven for 30 minutes, or until the pastry is well risen and golden brown.

Wine: Medium- or full-bodied red, such as Syrah/Shiraz, or stout

Cornish Pasties

SERVES 4

1½ quantity Shortcrust Pastry (see page 476) or
   375 g bought shortcrust pastry
110 g chuck steak, very finely diced
1 large onion, finely chopped

1 large potato, finely chopped
2 tablespoons water
salt and freshly ground black pepper
beaten egg, to glaze

1 Chill the pastry in the refrigerator.
2 Prepare the filling by mixing together the meat, onion and potato. Add the water, season with salt and pepper and mix thoroughly.
3 Heat the oven to 200°C/400°F/gas mark 6.
4 Divide the chilled pastry into 4 equal pieces and roll out to the thickness of a £1 coin. Place a 20 cm plate on the pastry and cut around it to make a circle.
5 Spoon the meat and vegetable mixture into the centre of each circle. Brush around the edge with water. Carefully bring the sides up and over the filling, pressing them together so that the pasties look like closed purses. Using floured fingers, crimp the edges. Place on a baking sheet, brush with beaten egg and chill in the refrigerator until firm.
6 Brush the pasties again with beaten egg, then bake near the top of the oven for 10–15 minutes. Turn the temperature down to 180°C/350°F/gas mark 4 and bake for a further 45–50 minutes. Check occasionally, and if the pasties show signs of overbrowning, move to a lower shelf and cover loosely with foil.

Drink: Rhône, Corbières or Beaujolais, or a good IPA (Indian Pale Ale)

Braised Silverside with Dumplings

This recipe uses salt beef, which is beef that has been cured in a dry mixture of salt and spices. In the USA it is called corned beef.

SERVES 6

1.35 kg piece of salt silverside or brisket

1 bouquet garni (see page 512)

6 medium onions

4 large carrots, quartered

12 Dumplings (see page 486)

chopped fresh parsley, to garnish

1 Soak the beef in cold, unsalted water for about 3 hours to soften the meat.

2 Put the beef into a large saucepan of fresh unsalted water and bring slowly to the boil, skimming as the scum rises to the surface.

3 When the water is simmering, add the bouquet garni and half-cover the pan to prevent the water from evaporating too quickly, but avoid boiling. Simmer for 3 hours. Remove the bouquet garni and skim off any fat.

4 Now add the vegetables and simmer for a further hour, or until the meat and vegetables are tender.

5 Meanwhile, cook the dumplings: if there is room in the saucepan, float them in the liquid 20 minutes before the end of the cooking time. If not, remove some of the stock from the pan (topping up with boiling water if necessary) and simmer the dumplings in a separate saucepan.

6 Place the beef on a large warmed serving dish. Surround it with the vegetables and the dumplings. Cover and keep warm.

7 Taste the stock. If insipid, reduce by rapid boiling to concentrate the flavour. Skim if necessary.

8 Pour a ladleful or so of hot liquid over the meat and vegetables, sprinkle with parsley and serve immediately. Serve the remaining hot liquid separately in a warmed sauceboat.

Wine: Medium-bodied red, such as a Médoc from Bordeaux

Pot-au-feu Ordinaire

SERVES 4–6

1 kg beef bones, sawn into 5–7.5 cm pieces

1 kg silverside or topside of beef, tied compactly

2.25 litres water

15 g salt

200 g carrots

110 g turnips

200 g leeks

3 onions, 1 stuck with 2 cloves

30 g parsnip

30 g celery

1 Place the bones in a large saucepan and put the meat on top. Add the water and salt. Place over a very low heat so that you can skim the liquid when it boils. It should take about 30 minutes to come to the boil and must be skimmed constantly to make a very clear broth.

2 When the liquid boils, splash on 3 tablespoons cold water and skim again. When the liquid returns to the boil, add another 3 tablespoons cold water. This produces a third lot of scum, this time almost white. Skim again. When the liquid starts to boil once more, add a further 3 tablespoons cold water. The little scum that rises this time should be perfectly white and clean. Skim it. Now add the vegetables and skim off any scum that rises. With a damp cloth, carefully wipe the inside edges of the saucepan so that no traces of scum remain.

3 Simmer very slowly for 3 hours. (It can also be cooked in a low oven or, ideally, in the slow oven of an Aga.) Keep checking for scum, and remove it with a slotted spoon.

4 Using a slotted spoon, remove the vegetables from the broth and divide between soup bowls. Ladle the broth over them.

5 Remove the meat and place on a chopping board. Slice thinly to serve. Accompany with a selection of pickled gherkins, coarse salt, horseradish sauce, capers, mustard and French dressing.

Wine: Medium-bodied, blended red, such as Côtes-du-Rhône, Languedoc or Chianti Classico

Hot Salt Beef Sandwiches with Dill Pickles

SERVES 4

8 thick slices sourdough or rye bread

4 heaped teaspoons Mayonnaise (see page 466)

4 teaspoons creamed horseradish

8 large slices (about 340 g) hot salt beef (see page 78)

4–6 large dill pickles, rinsed, dried and thickly sliced

shredded iceberg lettuce

flaky sea salt and freshly ground black pepper

1 Heat the oven to 200°C/400°F/gas mark 6. Wrap the bread loosely in foil and place in the centre of the oven for 5 minutes.

2 Unwrap the bread and lay the slices on a board. Mix the mayonnaise and creamed horseradish together and spread over the warm bread.

3 Place the hot salt beef on 4 of the bread slices, top with the sliced dill pickles and lettuce, and season with pepper and more salt if you wish.

4 Cover with the remaining slices of bread, cut each sandwich in half, and serve.

Drink: A good English bitter or dry cider

Shepherd's Pie

Shepherd's pie is technically made with minced lamb, but at Leiths we make it with beef.

SERVES 4–5

oil, for frying

675 g minced beef

1 onion, finely chopped

1 carrot, finely chopped

1 stick of celery, finely chopped

2 teaspoons plain flour

600 ml Brown Stock (see page 452)

1 bay leaf

1 teaspoon Worcestershire Sauce (optional)

1 teaspoon tomato purée

salt and freshly ground black pepper

900 g Mashed Potatoes, for the topping
 (see page 491)

1 Heat a little oil in a large frying pan over a medium/high heat and fry half the mince. Brown well all over, stirring periodically with a wooden spoon or spatula. Remove with a slotted spoon and place in a sieve over a bowl to catch the fat. Repeat with the remaining mince. Transfer all the meat to a saucepan.

2 Heat a little more oil in the frying pan and fry the onion, carrot and celery until just beginning to brown.

3 Add the flour to the fat in the frying pan and cook until brown.

4 Add the stock and bring slowly to the boil, stirring continuously.

5 Now add the bay leaf, Worcestershire sauce (if using), tomato purée, salt and pepper. Pour into the saucepan containing the browned mince and mix well.

6 Set the saucepan over a medium heat to simmer. Cover and leave to cook for 45 minutes. Check the pan every so often and add extra water if the mixture becomes too dry.

7 Heat the oven to 200°C/400°F/gas mark 6.

8 Remove the bay leaf from the mince and tip the meat mixture into a pie dish, spooning off some of the liquid if the mixture is too runny.

9 When slightly cooled, spread the mashed potato over the top. If making in advance, allow the filling to cool completely before topping with the potato.

10 Fork the potato up to leave the surface rough, or draw the fork over the surface to mark with a pattern.

11 Place in the oven for 20–30 minutes, or until the potato is brown and crisp.

Wine: Most dry reds work well, especially Bordeaux

Shepherd's Pie: What has gone wrong when...

The mince is not browned sufficiently.

- Too much meat at a time was placed in the pan, so it has boiled in its own liquid rather than fried in hot fat.
- The pan and oil were not sufficiently hot to brown the mince.
- The mince was not browned for long enough.

Souffléd Shepherd's Pies

SERVES 4

4 baking potatoes, scrubbed

oil, for greasing

flaky sea salt

2 eggs, separated

2 tablespoons double cream

1 small bunch of chives, snipped

85 g Parmesan cheese, freshly grated

freshly ground black pepper

½ quantity Shepherd's Pie filling (see opposite)

1 Heat the oven to 200°C/400°F/gas mark 6.

2 Rub the potatoes with a little oil and sprinkle over a little salt. Bake for 1¼ hours, or until very tender.

3 Cut the potatoes in half lengthwise. Scoop out the flesh without damaging the skin, and place in a large mixing bowl. Set the skins aside.

4 Add the egg yolks, cream, chives and half the Parmesan to the cooked potato. Season with salt and pepper and mix well.

5 In a separate bowl, whisk the egg whites until medium peaks are formed. Fold them into the potato mixture.

6 Divide the pie filling between the potato skins, and pile the potato mixture on top.

7 Sprinkle over the remaining Parmesan and return the potatoes to the oven for 15 minutes, or until hot, risen and golden brown. Serve immediately.

Wine: Medium-bodied red, such as Bordeaux, or an Alsace Riesling

Spaghetti Bolognese

SERVES 4

340 g spaghetti

For the sauce

85 g unsmoked bacon

2 tablespoons olive oil

340 g lean minced beef

1 medium onion, finely diced

1 stick of celery, chopped

1 clove of garlic, crushed

110 g mushrooms, sliced

100 ml red wine

300 ml Brown Stock (see page 452)

1 × 400 g can chopped tomatoes

1 teaspoon tomato purée

1 teaspoon dried basil

1 teaspoon chopped fresh marjoram or oregano

salt and freshly ground black pepper

4 tablespoons freshly grated Parmesan cheese,
   to serve

1 Dice the bacon, place in a large frying pan and fry slowly in its own fat until lightly browned. Remove from the pan and set aside.

2 Add a little oil to the pan if necessary and fry the mince until well browned all over.

3 Using a slotted spoon, transfer the mince to a saucepan.

4 Place 1 tablespoon of the oil in the frying pan. Add the onion and celery. Cook over a low heat, stirring occasionally, until soft and lightly coloured. Add the garlic and mushrooms and cook for 5 minutes. Tip into the pan of meat. Add the bacon.

5 Pour the wine into the frying pan and bring to the boil, scraping up any sediment. Stir in the stock, tomatoes and tomato purée. Pour on to the meat in the saucepan. Add the herbs and season to taste. Cover and simmer for 1–1½ hours, or until the meat is tender. If greasy, skim off as much of the fat as possible.

6 While the sauce is cooking, boil the spaghetti according to the manufacturer's instructions. Tip into a colander and drain briefly, leaving a little water clinging to it.

7 Return the spaghetti to the pan and pour over the hot bolognese sauce. Toss gently, turning carefully with a wooden spoon.

8 Place the spaghetti in a warmed serving dish. Serve with the Parmesan sprinkled on top, or hand separately.

Wine: Hearty Italian red, such as Barbera d'Alba, Montepulciano d'Abruzzo or Rosso Conero

English Roast Beef and Yorkshire Pudding, page 38.

Carving a joint of beef

Cutting the joint along the ribs.

Carving thin slices.

Mixed Grill, page 57.

Thai Stir-fried Beef with Red Peppers and Beansprouts, page 58.

Steak and Mushroom Pie, page 76.

Hot Salt Beef Sandwiches with Dill Pickles, page 79.

Veal Medallions and Grilled Vegetables with Aïoli, page 120.

Venison Casserole with Chestnuts and Cranberries, page 422.

Lasagne Verdi Bolognese

SERVES 4

For the meat sauce

about 3 tablespoons olive oil

1 onion, finely chopped

4 cloves of garlic, chopped

340 g lean minced beef

100 ml dry white wine

30 g plain flour

300 ml Brown Stock (see page 452)

1 tablespoon chopped fresh parsley

1 teaspoon chopped fresh marjoram

pinch of ground cinnamon

1 tablespoon tomato purée

salt and freshly ground black pepper

For the cream sauce

45 g butter

40 g plain flour

1 bay leaf

600 ml full-fat milk

salt and freshly ground black pepper

pinch of freshly grated nutmeg

For the pasta

140 g Green Pasta (see page 489) or 8 leaves of
     bought green lasagne sheets

3 tablespoons freshly grated Parmesan cheese

1 To make the meat sauce, heat the oil in a small pan. Stir in the onion, cover with a piece of greaseproof paper and a lid and cook gently until softened, about 10 minutes. Remove the lid and the paper, stir in the garlic and cook for a further minute. Set aside.

2 In a sauté pan heat enough oil to cover the bottom thinly. Brown the minced beef in two or three batches, deglazing with the wine in between batches.

3 Return the browned meat to the sauté pan and sprinkle over the flour. Cook, stirring over medium heat, for a couple of minutes to cook the flour.

4 Stir in the stock, *deglaçage*, parsley, marjoram, cinnamon and tomato purée. Season, then turn the heat down so that the mixture just simmers. Cover with a lid and cook for 1 hour, or until the meat is tender. Allow to cool to room temperature.

5 To make the cream sauce, melt the butter in a saucepan. Remove from the heat and stir in the flour to make a smooth paste. Add the bay leaf then return to the heat and cook, stirring, for 1 minute. Remove from the heat.

6 Gradually stir in the milk to make a smooth sauce then return to the heat. Bring to the boil, stirring continuously. Simmer for 2 minutes. Season to taste with salt, pepper and nutmeg. Remove the bay leaf. If the lasagne is being prepared in advance, allow to cool to room temperature.

7 Cook the pasta, if required, according the manufacturer's instructions. Otherwise, roll out the fresh pasta and cut into rectangles measuring about 20 × 10 cm.

8 Place a thin layer of the meat sauce in an ovenproof lasagne dish. Cover with a layer of pasta then spoon over a layer of meat sauce. Cover with a layer of cream sauce. Continue layering in this order finishing with a layer of pasta, then cream sauce. Sprinkle over the Parmesan.

9 To bake, heat the oven to 190°C/375°F/gas mark 5. Bake for about 30 minutes or until bubbling and well browned on top.

Wine: Italian red, such as Barbera d'Alba, Montepulciano d'Abruzzo, Rosso Conero or Salice Salentino

Hamburgers

SERVES 4

675 g minced lean beef steak

1 small onion, grated (optional)

2 tablespoons chopped fresh parsley or mixed herbs

1 teaspoon Worcestershire sauce (optional)

salt and freshly ground black pepper

1 Heat the grill.

2 Mix all the ingredients together with a fork. Check the seasoning.

3 With wet hands, divide the mixture into 4 equal pieces and shape into flattish rounds. Make a slight dip in the centre because the burgers will shrink and thicken as they cook.

4 Grill steadily, turning once. Allow 3 minutes per side for rare burgers, 5 minutes for well done.

5 Serve on a warmed dish or in burger buns.

Wine: Everyday red, such as Zinfandel, Chilean red or Argentinian Malbec

Italian-style Meatloaf

Meatloaf is delicious served hot with Mashed Potatoes and Red Onion Gravy (see pages 491 and 463), or cold in a crusty baguette with salad.

SERVES 4–6

500 g best-quality minced beef

250 g pork mince

1 medium red onion, very finely chopped

2 cloves of garlic, crushed

2 eggs, beaten

100 g fresh breadcrumbs

2 teaspoons salt

2 teaspoons dried oregano

30 g finely grated Parmesan or Cheddar cheese

150 ml tomato ketchup

freshly ground black pepper

1 Heat the oven to 190°C/375°F/gas mark 5.

2 Place the beef and pork mince in a large bowl. Add the rest of the ingredients, reserving 50 ml ketchup for the top. Mix well using a fork or clean hands.

3 Form into an oval loaf shape and place in a shallow ovenproof dish.

4 Spread the reserved ketchup over the meatloaf.

5 Bake in the centre of the oven for 1 hour, or until cooked through. A probe will register 70°C/160°F when it's done.

6 Lift on to a serving platter. Cut into 1.5 cm slices to serve.

Wine: Montepulciano d'Abruzzo or Australian Shiraz/Cabernet

Kibbeh

This recipe for stuffed cracked wheat shells has been adapted from one by Claudia Roden in her book *Middle Eastern Food*. Kibbeh are popular as part of a *meze* – a collection of small dishes served as a first course.

SERVES 4

225 g bulghar or cracked wheat
450 g minced beef
1 small onion, roughly chopped
salt and freshly ground black pepper

For the filling

2 tablespoons sunflower oil
1 onion, finely chopped
50 g pine nuts
285 g minced beef

1 teaspoon ground cinnamon
½ teaspoon ground allspice
1 tablespoon chopped fresh parsley
1 tablespoon chopped fresh mint
sunflower oil, for deep-frying
sprigs of coriander, to garnish

To serve

natural yoghurt
sesame oil

1 Soak the bulghar in cold water for 20 minutes.
2 Meanwhile, mix together the mince, onion and salt and pepper in a food processor.
3 Drain the bulghar and process, in batches, with the beef mixture, until very soft. Knead well by hand, then set aside.
4 To make the filling, heat the oil in a frying pan and fry the onion until soft but not brown. Add the pine nuts and fry until golden. Add the mince and fry until lightly browned all over. Add the cinnamon, allspice, parsley, mint and season with salt and pepper.
5 With wet hands, take a small egg-sized portion of the kneaded shell mixture and roll into a ball. Make a deep dent in the centre and shape into a thin-walled 'pot' with a pointed bottom by turning and pressing it in your palm.
6 Put some stuffing inside the dent and pinch the top of the pot together to seal it. Shape the top to a point. Repeat with the rest of the mixture, wetting your hands frequently.
7 Heat the oil in a deep-fryer (see Warning, page 53) until a cube of bread sizzles, and fry 4–5 kibbeh at a time until golden brown. Drain well on kitchen paper.
8 Flavour the yoghurt with sesame oil.
9 Arrange the kibbeh on a warmed serving plate, garnish with coriander and hand the yoghurt sauce separately.

Wine: Cabernet Sauvignon from the Middle East

Stuffed Peppers

SERVES 4

4 large green or red peppers

2 tablespoons olive oil

1 medium onion, chopped

1 clove of garlic, crushed

1 green or red chilli, deseeded and finely diced

400 g good-quality minced beef

110 g long-grain white rice

300 ml Brown Stock (see page 452)

300 ml Tomato Sauce I (see page 469)

pinch of cinnamon

2 teaspoons chopped fresh rosemary

30 g raisins

salt and freshly ground black pepper

1 tablespoon chopped fresh parsley, to garnish

1 Cut the tops off the peppers and discard. Scoop out the seeds and place the peppers in a shallow ovenproof dish that will hold the peppers tightly upright.

2 Heat the oil in a sauté pan and cook the onion until translucent. Add the garlic and chilli and cook for a further minute. Transfer to a plate.

3 Brown the mince in batches, adding a little more oil if the pan is dry. Return all the meat to the pan and season with salt and pepper.

4 Add the rice and cook for 2 minutes, stirring constantly.

5 Add the stock, tomato sauce, cinnamon, rosemary and raisins. Cover and cook for 30 minutes.

6 About 10 minutes before the end of the cooking time, heat the oven to 190°C/375°F/ gas mark 5.

7 When the rice is cooked, divide the mixture between the peppers.

8 Pour over the tomato mixture. Cover with foil and bake for 30 minutes, or until the peppers are soft.

9 Sprinkle with the parsley and serve.

Wine: A southern Italian red or an adventurous sparkling red Shiraz from Australia

Baked Stuffed Aubergines

SERVES 4

2 medium aubergines

oil, for frying

285 g lean minced beef

1 onion, finely chopped

½ green pepper, deseeded and chopped

50 g mushrooms, chopped

1 clove of garlic, crushed

1 teaspoon plain flour

300 ml Brown Stock (see page 452)

1 bay leaf

2 teaspoons tomato purée

1 teaspoon chopped fresh parsley

lemon juice

15 g butter, melted

grated Gruyère or strong Cheddar cheese

dried breadcrumbs

salt and freshly ground black pepper

To serve

300 ml Tomato Sauce II (see page 469)

1 Cut the aubergines in half lengthwise and scoop out the centre, leaving the shells with about 5 mm of flesh attached. Sprinkle lightly with salt and leave upside down to drain.

2 Chop the aubergine flesh, place in a sieve and sprinkle lightly with salt. Leave to drain for 20 minutes.

3 Heat a little oil in a saucepan and fry the mince until evenly brown.

4 Rinse and dry the aubergine flesh. Add to the mince along with the onion, green pepper, mushrooms and garlic and cook for a further 3–4 minutes.

5 Stir in the flour. Cook for 1 minute, then add the stock, bay leaf, tomato purée, parsley, freshly ground black pepper and lemon juice. Bring to the boil, stirring continuously, then cover and simmer for 20–25 minutes. Remove the bay leaf.

6 Heat the oven to 200°C/400°F/gas mark 6.

7 Wash and dry the aubergine shells, brush with the melted butter and fill with the mince mixture. Sprinkle over the grated cheese and breadcrumbs.

8 Bake in the hot oven for 30 minutes, or until the aubergine shells are tender and the cheese well browned. Serve with the tomato sauce.

Wine: A rich Italian red from the south, perhaps Sicily or Sardinia

Italian Meatballs

The meat in meatballs is tenderized by mincing rather than long cooking. To ensure maximum tenderness and flavour, ask the butcher for minced rump steak. You can season the meat as you wish, perhaps with a mixture of parsley, basil, rosemary, oregano, sage and/or thyme.

SERVES 4

550 g good-quality minced beef

50 g fresh breadcrumbs

1 egg, beaten

1 clove of garlic, crushed

2 tablespoons chopped fresh mixed herbs
  or 2 teaspoons dried herbs

1 teaspoon salt

freshly ground black pepper

2 tablespoons olive oil

2 quantities Tomato Sauce II (see page 469)

340 g spaghetti, to serve

1 Place the meat, breadcrumbs, egg, garlic, herbs and salt in a bowl. Season with pepper and mix together with a fork.
2 Divide the mixture into 20 equal-sized pieces and shape into balls using dampened hands.
3 Heat the oil in a sauté pan over a medium heat and brown the meatballs in batches on all sides.
4 Place the meatballs in the sauce and simmer for 30 minutes to cook through.
5 Cook the spaghetti in boiling salted water until al dente, then drain and serve with the meatballs.

Wine: Medium-bodied Italian red, such as Montepulciano d'Abruzzo or Vino Nobile di Montepulciano

Swedish Meatballs

These small meatballs in a rich, soured cream sauce make delicious canapés. They can also be served as a main course with boiled rice.

MAKES 40 AS CANAPÉS
SERVES 6–8 AS A MAIN COURSE

30 g butter

1 onion, finely chopped

75 g white breadcrumbs

100 ml milk

500 g minced beef

400 g minced pork or veal

1 teaspoon salt

½ teaspoon ground black pepper

¼ teaspoon freshly grated nutmeg

2 tablespoons oil, for frying

For the sauce

30 g butter

1 clove of garlic, crushed

30 g plain flour

425 ml Brown Stock (see page 452)

200 ml soured cream

2 teaspoons cornflour

1 teaspoon tomato purée

1 teaspoon Bovril

2 tablespoons chopped fresh dill

salt and freshly ground black pepper

1 Melt the butter in a small saucepan and stir in the onion. Cover with a piece of dampened greaseproof paper and a lid. Cook over a low heat, stirring occasionally, until very soft and translucent. Transfer to a plate and allow to cool.

2 In the meantime, place the breadcrumbs in a small bowl with the milk. Allow to stand for 10 minutes.

3 Place the meat, salt, pepper and nutmeg in a large bowl. Add the cooled onion and the soaked breadcrumbs.

4 Using clean hands, squeeze the mixture together to combine evenly.

5 To shape the meatballs, dampen your hands and shape into 3 cm balls, placing them on a tray or plate in a single layer as you work.

6 Heat the oil in a large frying pan. Fry the meatballs until browned on all sides (see Points to Remember about Frying and Browning, page 17). Transfer to an ovenproof casserole dish. Do not wash the frying pan as the brown glaze will add flavour to the sauce.

7 Heat the oven to 180°C/375°F/gas mark 5.

8 To make the sauce, melt the butter in the unwashed frying pan.

9 Add the garlic and cook for 30 seconds, stirring.

10 Stir in the flour and cook for a further 30 seconds. Remove from the heat.

11 Gradually stir in the stock to make a smooth sauce. Return to the hob and cook over a medium heat, stirring. Bring to the boil and boil for 1 minute.

12 Place the soured cream in a large bowl and stir in the cornflour. Stir the hot sauce gradually into the soured cream.

13 Stir in the tomato purée and the Bovril. Add salt and pepper as needed. Pour the sauce over the meatballs.

14 Cover the casserole dish and bake in the oven for 25 minutes, or until the meatballs are cooked through. Stir in the dill and serve.

Wine: Medium-bodied red, such as Chianti Classico

Meatballs: What has gone wrong when...

The meatballs fall apart when they are fried.

• The meat was not squeezed firmly enough when the meatballs were shaped.

Empanadas

These Spanish and Mexican pastries are similar to Cornish pasties, but have a spicy filling.

MAKES 8

1½ quantity Shortcrust Pastry
  (see page 476) or 500 g bought shortcrust
  pastry
1 teaspoon paprika
2 tablespoons vegetable oil
1 small onion, finely chopped
1 clove of garlic, crushed
450 g minced beef

150 ml water
1 teaspoon Cajun spice
pinch of ground cinnamon
pinch of ground cayenne
200 g chopped tomatoes
salt and freshly ground black pepper
1 egg, beaten, to glaze

1 Make the shortcrust pastry according to the directions on page 476, but add the paprika to the flour. Divide the dough into 8 equal pieces and roll each into a 15 cm round. Wrap with cling film and chill.

2 To make the filling, place half the oil in a sauté pan and stir in the onion. Cover with a piece of dampened greaseproof paper and cook over a low heat until softened, about 10–15 minutes. Remove the paper and turn up the heat slightly to brown the onions. Stir in the garlic and cook for a further 30 seconds. Remove from the pan and set aside.

3 Place the remaining oil in the sauté pan and brown the beef over a medium heat. Using a slotted spoon, transfer the meat to a sieve set over a bowl and allow any excess fat to drain away. Remove any excess fat from the pan.

4 Add some of the water to the hot pan and scrape up any sediment. Return the meat to the pan, stir in the spices and cook for 1 minute. Add the tomatoes and the remaining water, then stir in the onions and garlic.

5 Transfer the mixture to a saucepan and cook at a low simmer for 1 hour, or until the meat is tender and the sauce is no longer watery. Season with salt and pepper. Allow to cool.

6 Lay the pastry circles on the work surface in a single layer. Brush 1 cm of the edges with the beaten egg.

7 Divide the filling between the pastry rounds, then fold over to make half-moon shapes. Crimp the edges. Lightly grease 2 baking sheets.

8 Brush the pastries with the egg glaze. Chill until the pastry is firm.

9 Meanwhile, heat the oven to 200°C/400°F/gas mark 6.

10 Brush the pastries again with the egg glaze, place on the prepared baking sheets and bake for 25 minutes, or until golden brown. Serve warm.

Wine: Full-bodied Spanish red – Ribera del Duero, Priorato or Montsant – or a Douro red from Portugal

Beef Consommé

This is an elegant and sophisticated soup. Time and care are needed to complete the fiddly clearing process, but the effort is worthwhile.

1¾ litres well-flavoured Beef Bouillon
   (see page 453)

5 tablespoons sherry or Madeira
whites of 3 eggs plus shells

1 Pour the bouillon and sherry or Madeira into a large, clean metal saucepan. Place over a gentle heat.
2 Crush the eggshells and place in a bowl with the egg whites. Whisk until frothy. Pour into the bouillon. Whisk with a balloon whisk until the mixture boils and rises. Stop whisking immediately and take the pan off the heat. Allow the mixture to subside. Take care not to break the crust formed by the egg white.
3 Bring the consommé up to the boil again and then allow to subside. Repeat this once more. (The egg white will trap the sediment and clear the stock.) Allow to cool for 10 minutes.
4 Fix a double layer of fine muslin over a clean basin and carefully strain the consommé through it, taking care to hold back the egg-white crust. When all the liquid is through allow the crust to slip into the muslin. Strain the consommé again, this time through both egg-white crust and cloth. Do not try to hurry the process by squeezing the cloth as this will produce a murky consommé: it must be allowed to drip through at its own pace. The consommé is now ready for serving.

NOTE: To serve the consommé *en gelée* (jellied), pour the liquid into a shallow pan or tray to cool, then refrigerate until set. Chop roughly with a knife, then spoon into ice-cold soup cups. Serve with a wedge of lemon and toast.

Wine: Dry sherry

Calves' Liver

After poultry livers, calves' liver is the most popular type of liver, followed by lambs' liver. Calves' liver is rich in flavour and has little, if any, wastage, so 100 g per serving is usually sufficient. Liver is traditionally served with sautéd onions, as in the recipe opposite.

Choosing liver

- The liver should not have a strong smell.
- It should be bright red rather than brown and shiny.
- Choose pieces of liver that have few tubes running through them.

Storing liver

- Keep in the bottom of the refrigerator for not more than 24 hours: liver deteriorates rapidly.
- Freeze for up to 1 month.

Using liver

- Pull the thin membrane from the outside of the liver and cut out any noticeable tubes.
- Cut into slices about 5 mm thick.
- It is important not to overcook liver or it will become tough. It should be pink on the inside, but not bloody, when served.
- Frying is the best way to cook liver so that it is browned on the outside and pink on the inside. It can also be grilled, but it is rather more difficult to get it nicely browned without being overcooked.

Liver and Bacon

SERVES 4

50 g butter

1 onion, thinly sliced

8 rashers of rindless streaky bacon

450 g calves' or lambs' liver, skinned and sliced (see opposite)

seasoned plain flour

300 ml Brown Stock (see page 452)

2 tablespoons sherry (optional)

1 small bunch of watercress, to garnish

1 Heat half the butter in a frying pan and fry the onion slowly until soft and brown. Tip the onion into a saucer.

2 Heat the grill. Place the bacon under it and cook until crisp and brown but not brittle. Turn off the grill and leave the bacon under it to keep warm.

3 Remove any large tubes from the liver. Dip the slices in seasoned flour and keep well separated on a plate.

4 Heat the remaining butter in the frying pan and fry the liver slices, a few at a time, adding more butter if necessary. Note that liver is easily spoiled by overcooking. Arrange the slices on a warmed shallow platter and keep warm.

5 Put the onion and any of its fat back into the pan and add a sprinkling of the seasoned flour – just enough to absorb the fat. Cook for 1 minute. Pour in the stock and stir well as it comes to the boil. Add the sherry, if using.

6 Boil the sauce rapidly to reduce and thicken it. This will also give a richer appearance and concentrate the flavour. Taste and season as necessary.

7 Pour the sauce over the liver, top with the bacon and garnish with watercress. Serve at once as liver toughens on standing.

Wine: Full-bodied red, such as a Rhône or New World Shiraz/Syrah

Calves' Liver: What has gone wrong when...

The liver is tough and rubbery.

• It has been overcooked.

The sauce is pale.

• The liver was not browned sufficiently during cooking.

Calves' Liver Lyonnaise

SERVES 4

50 g unsalted butter

1 large onion, thinly sliced

450 g calves' liver, skinned and sliced into
  4 pieces (see page 92)

seasoned plain flour

300 ml Brown Stock (see page 452)

1 tablespoon fresh orange juice

1 tablespoon mixed fresh herbs, such as
  rosemary, thyme and sage

salt and freshly ground black pepper

1 Heat half the butter in a frying pan and slowly cook the onion until golden brown. This will take up to 40 minutes. Place in an ovenproof dish and keep warm.
2 Dip the liver into the seasoned flour, shaking off any excess.
3 Heat the remaining butter in a sauté pan over a medium heat until foaming.
4 Fry the liver for about 2 minutes on each side, until golden brown. Place on top of the onions and keep warm. Add a teaspoon of the seasoned flour to the pan and cook until brown. Stir in the stock and orange juice. Boil for 2 minutes.
5 Add the herbs and season with salt and pepper. Pour over the liver and serve.

Wine: Medium-bodied red, such as Burgundy, Cru Beaujolais, Rioja or Chianti Classico

Pan-fried Calves' Liver with Balsamic Vinegar and Crème Fraîche Sauce

Calves' liver works well with creamy sauces because of its delicate flavour and soft texture. Sometimes, however, a sauce can be overwhelmingly creamy and in need of something with a little 'bite', such as lemon juice or vinegar. Here the natural sweetness of balsamic vinegar results in a softer, well-rounded finish.

SERVES 4

1 tablespoon oil

15 g unsalted butter

4 × 170 g slices calves' liver, skinned (see page 92)

1 tablespoon water

50 ml balsamic vinegar

50 ml crème fraîche

salt and freshly ground black pepper

To serve

Wilted Spinach (see page 497)

1 Heat the oil and butter in a large frying pan. Season the liver slices with salt and pepper and fry for about 2 minutes on each side, until nicely browned but still pink in the middle. Remove from the pan and keep warm.
2 Pour the water and the balsamic vinegar into the pan and scrape up any sediment. Add the crème fraîche and bring to the boil, stirring well. Taste and season with salt and pepper.
3 Divide the spinach between 4 warmed serving plates, top with a slice of liver and pour over the balsamic vinegar and crème fraîche sauce. Serve immediately.

Drink: New World Merlot or a quality dry cider

Ox and Calves' Kidneys

Choosing Kidneys

The kidneys from oxes and calves are multi-lobed, resembling a bunch of grapes. They are sold either ready-prepared or still encased in their white fat (suet). The best are from the youngest animals. Kidneys should be plump and a deep red-brown colour. Due to their powerful flavour, they are usually served with a strong sauce, such as mustard sauce.

Storing Kidneys

Kidneys are best eaten as fresh as possible, and should be consumed within a day or two of purchase. They should be kept in the refrigerator, loosely wrapped in greaseproof paper.

If they are purchased from a supermarket, do not open the package until ready to cook.

Using Kidneys

Remove the suet, then peel away the thin membrane. Halve or cut into bite-sized pieces, discarding the central core. Ox kidneys are used for Steak and Kidney Pie (see page 96).

Sautéd Kidneys

12 lambs' kidneys

50 g Clarified Butter (see page xii)

3 tablespoons dry sherry

2 tablespoons chopped fresh parsley

salt and freshly ground black pepper

1 Skin, halve and core the kidneys with kitchen scissors.
2 Melt the butter in a frying pan and brown the kidneys quickly all over. Transfer to a sieve set over a bowl and discard the juices. Return the kidneys to the pan.
3 Pour in the sherry and cook briskly for 1 minute. Season, stir in the parsley and serve.

Drink: Chilled fino sherry

Sautéd Kidneys: What has gone wrong when...

The kidneys are tough and rubbery.
• The kidneys are overcooked.

The sauce tastes bitter.
• The kidney juices were used in the sauce.
• The kidneys were not drained.

Steak and Kidney Pie

SERVES 4

675 g chuck steak

225 g ox kidney

oil or dripping, for frying

1 onion, finely chopped

30 g plain flour

425 ml Brown Stock (see page 452)

1 tablespoon chopped fresh parsley

salt and freshly ground black pepper

1 quantity Rough Puff Pastry

   (see page 479) or 500 g bought puff pastry

beaten egg, to glaze

1 Trim away the excess fat from the steak and cut the meat into cubes about 3 cm square. Cut the kidney into cubes, discarding any core.

2 Heat the oil or dripping in a frying pan and fry a few steak cubes at a time until browned all over. Transfer them to a flameproof casserole as they are done.

3 Fry the onion in the same fat until soft and brown. Stir in the flour and cook for 1 minute. Gradually add the stock, stirring continuously and scraping any sediment from the bottom of the pan. Bring to the boil, then simmer for 1 minute. Pour over the meat in the casserole, season with salt and pepper and simmer slowly until the meat is tender (about 2 hours).

4 If the sauce is too greasy, skim off the fat; if it is too thin, transfer the meat to a pie dish and boil the sauce rapidly until syrupy. Add the parsley, then pour the sauce over the meat and leave until completely cold.

5 Heat the oven to 200°C/400°F/gas mark 6.

6 Roll out the pastry to the thickness of a £1 coin. Cut a long strip just wider than the rim of the pie dish. Brush the lip of the dish with water and press the pastry strip along it.

7 Brush the strip with water, then lay the sheet of pastry over the dish. Press it down firmly around the rim. Cut away any excess pastry.

8 Cut a 1 cm hole in the centre of the pie to allow steam to escape and half-cover with a leaf-shaped piece of pastry made from the pastry trimmings.

9 Decorate the top with more pastry leaves. Brush all over with beaten egg. Leave in the refrigerator to chill until firm.

10 Bake in the oven for 30 minutes, or until the pastry is well risen and golden brown.

Wine: A classic match for Rhône reds and New World Shiraz/Syrah

Steak and Kidney Pudding

Traditionally, steak and kidney puddings served straight from the bowl are presented wrapped in a white linen napkin.

SERVES 4

675 g chuck steak

225 g ox kidney

plain flour, for dusting

1 quantity Suet Pastry (see page 483)

butter, for greasing

2 teaspoons very finely chopped onion

2 teaspoons chopped fresh parsley

salt and freshly ground black pepper

1 Cut the steak into 3 cm cubes.
2 Cut the kidney into cubes, discarding the core.
3 Place the steak and kidney in a large sieve, add some flour and shake until the meat is lightly coated.
4 Lightly grease a 1 kg pudding basin.
5 On a floured surface, roll out two-thirds of the pastry into a circle about 1 cm thick. Lightly flour the surface of it, then fold it over to form a half-moon shape. With the straight side away from you, roll it out lightly so that the straight side becomes curved and you again have a circle of pastry. Now separate the layers (the flour will have stopped them sticking together when folded over), and the pastry will resemble a bag. Use it to line the prepared basin, easing the pastry where necessary to fit, and trimming off the top so that 1 cm sticks up over the edge.
6 Fill the lined basin with layers of meat, sprinkling plenty of salt, pepper, onion and parsley in between the layers.
7 Add water to come three-quarters of the way up the meat.
8 Roll the remaining third of suet pastry into a circle 5 mm thick and just large enough to cover the pudding filling. Put in place, wet the edges and press them together securely.
9 Cover the pudding with a double piece of greaseproof paper, pleated down the centre to allow room for the pastry to expand, and a similarly pleated piece of foil. Tie in place with string.
10 Put the basin in a steamer or a saucepan of boiling water with a tightly fitting lid for 5–6 hours, taking care to top up with boiling water occasionally so as not to boil dry.
11 Remove the paper and foil and serve the pudding from the bowl.

NOTE: As the filling of the pudding can dry out somewhat during the long cooking time, it is worth having a gravy boat of hot Brown Stock (see page 452) to moisten the meat when serving.

VARIATION: A small can of smoked oysters makes a delicious addition to the meat filling.

Wine: A classic match for Rhône reds and New World Shiraz/Syrah

Brains

Calves' brains are darker in colour than those of lambs and sheep, but the flavour is very mild. Lambs' brains are pale with a creamy texture and delicate flavour, and are the most prized by connoisseurs. Sheep brains are a little darker than those of lambs, but similar in flavour. Beef and pork brains are darker and firmer than other types, and have a higher percentage of veins. It is unlikely that either of these would be used for human consumption.

Choosing and Preparing Brains

- When buying brains, you should look for a pale, pinky-grey colour, and they should be free of any blemishes or blood clots.
- Prior to cooking, the brains need to be soaked in several changes of cold water to remove as much of the blood as possible.
- After soaking and rinsing, brains should be blanched briefly in a pan of boiling, acidulated water. Drain and rinse them under cool running water. Carefully pick off the fine membrane that covers the brain, handling the brain very carefully. Pat dry with kitchen paper.
- Brains can be poached in a court-bouillon, stewed, or sautéd.
- Poaching and stewing takes 10 minutes for lamb and sheep brains, and 15 minutes for calves' brains. They are usually cooked whole. When done, they should feel springy but not rubbery when pressed with a fingertip. If they do feel rubbery, they are overcooked.
- To serve fried, slice the prepared, clean brains thickly. Dust them with seasoned flour and fry in a little vegetable oil for 2–3 minutes. Alternatively, coat the slices in beaten egg and breadcrumbs and deep-fry for 1–2 minutes (see Warning, page 53).

Brains with Brown Butter

SERVES 4

4 calves' brains	1 handful of fresh parsley
Court-bouillon (see page 457)	50 g butter
about 3 gherkins	3 tablespoons lemon juice
about 10 capers	salt and freshly ground black pepper

1 Wash the brains well and soak in cold water for 2–3 hours. Drain them.
2 Bring the court-bouillon to the boil, add the brains and poach for 15 minutes. Remove and drain thoroughly.
3 Cut the brains into slices, removing any membranes. Transfer to a warm serving dish, season with salt and pepper and keep warm.
4 Chop the gherkins, capers and parsley.
5 Heat the butter in a pan until just turning brown. Immediately add the gherkins, capers, parsley and lemon juice. Bring to the boil, then pour over the brains and serve.

Wine: A light red, such as Saumur-Champigny, or a European white, such as Alsace Pinot Gris

Ox Cheek Daube

The word *daube* means 'stew' or 'casserole'. If a tight-fitting lid is not available, a paste of flour and water (called *repère* or luting paste) can be placed around the edge of the dish to create a seal. It is chipped off and discarded when the stew is ready.

SERVES 4

900 g ox cheek or veal cheek, cut into large
   pieces, excess sinews removed
1 bottle of red wine
2 tablespoons oil
2 onions, finely sliced
2 carrots, cut into 3 cm chunks
2 sticks of celery, finely sliced
6 shallots, quartered
600 ml Brown Stock (see page 452)
1 small handful of parsley stalks

6 sprigs of fresh thyme
1 tablespoon tomato purée
1 tablespoon cider vinegar
½ tablespoon soft dark brown sugar
salt and freshly ground black pepper

To serve

Horseradish Mash (see page 68)
Caramelized Shallots (see page 499)

1 Put the cheek meat into a large, non-metallic bowl and pour over the red wine. Leave to marinate for 24 hours.

2 Drain the meat, reserving the wine.

3 Heat 1 tablespoon of the oil in a large, flameproof casserole and brown the meat a few pieces at a time. Transfer to a plate and set aside.

4 Add the remaining oil to the pan and brown the onions, carrots, celery and shallots. Pour in the reserved wine and the stock and bring to the boil.

5 Return the meat to the pan and add the parsley stalks, thyme, tomato purée, vinegar and sugar. Season with salt and pepper. Cover the pan with a tight-fitting lid and simmer very gently for 3–4 hours, or until the meat is very tender and falling apart.

6 Using a slotted spoon, transfer the meat to a warmed serving dish and keep warm. Strain the liquid and discard the vegetables.

7 Return the liquid to the pan and boil rapidly until it is reduced by two-thirds, tastes strong and looks glossy. Season to taste and pour the sauce over the meat. Serve with the mash and shallots.

Wine: Châteauneuf-du-Pape, New World Pinot Noir or Merlot

Tongue

Ox, sheep's and lambs' tongues are the most readily available. Tongue is usually salted, pressed and served cold accompanied by a piquant sauce.

Pressed Ox Tongue

SERVES 4

1 ox tongue, fresh or salted

salt

6 black peppercorns

1 bouquet garni (see page 512)

2 onions, sliced

2 carrots, sliced

1 stick of celery, sliced

425 ml Aspic, made from brown stock (see page 458)

1 If the tongue is salted, soak it in fresh water for 4 hours. If the tongue is fresh, soak it in brine (salty water, see page 9) for 1–2 hours.

2 Place it in a saucepan and pour in enough water to cover completely. Add salt if the tongue is fresh. Add the peppercorns, bouquet garni, onions, carrots and celery.

3 Bring gently to the boil, skimming off any scum. Cover tightly and simmer for 3–4 hours, or until tender when pierced with a skewer. Remove from the heat and leave to cool for 1 hour in the liquid.

4 Take out the tongue. Remove the bones from the root and peel off the skin.

5 Curl the warm tongue tightly and fit it into a deep round cake tin or tongue press. Cool.

6 Pour a little cool jellied stock or aspic into the tin.

7 Place a plate that just fits inside the tin on top of the tongue. Stand a heavy weight (about 4 kg) on the plate and leave overnight in the refrigerator.

8 To carve, unmould the tongue and slice thinly across the top of the round.

NOTE: The stock in which the tongue is cooked is suitable for use in making the jellied stock, provided it is not too salty.

Wine: Medium red, such as Bordeaux

Pressed Ox Lips

Although they are rarely available, ox lips are well worth the time and effort involved in cooking them. The flavour and texture are much like those of both ox tongue and cheek. Some parts are quite meaty and fibrous, while others are very soft and fatty. Long, slow cooking tenderizes the meat, with the fattier parts becoming soft and gelatinous. After cooking, the tough outer skin needs to be removed. This can be done either by cutting it off with a small, sharp knife, or peeling it, rather as you would for ox or lambs' tongues. The meat should then be shredded or cut into fairly even-sized chunks to ensure a good distribution of the two different textures throughout the finished dish.

As ox lips are not easy to come by, a specific weight of meat has not been given in the recipe that follows. Simply adjust the amount of vegetables to suit the amount of meat available – roughly 1 small onion, 1 small carrot and 1 stick of celery per 340 g of meat – and add enough water to cover. However, due to the lengthy preparation and cooking process, it is probably not worth making the recipe with less than 675 g–1 kg of meat.

Ox lips freeze very well and will keep for up to 3 months. Defrost them thoroughly before cooking.

SERVES 6–8

ox lips	1 large bouquet garni (see page 512)
onions, roughly chopped	a few whole cloves
carrots, roughly chopped	lots of freshly chopped parsley
celery, roughly chopped	salt and freshly ground black pepper

1 Place the ox lips in a large saucepan with the vegetables, bouquet garni, cloves and seasoning. Cover with water and bring to the boil, skimming occasionally.

2 Reduce the heat and cover the pan with a lid. Simmer gently until the meat is tender when pierced with a skewer (1.35 kg of meat will take approximately 3 hours).

3 Allow the meat to cool for 1 hour in the liquid. When cool enough to handle, lift it from the stock with a slotted spoon. Peel the skin away from the meat, or cut it off with a sharp knife.

4 Roughly shred the meat and place it in a bowl. Stir in the parsley and adjust the seasoning.

5 Turn the mixture into a suitably sized terrine or loaf tin, pressing it down lightly and keeping it 1 cm from the top.

6 Pour a little of the cool stock into the terrine and allow it to settle, repeating the process until the terrine is completely full.

7 Place a piece of card wrapped in cling film on top of the terrine. Stand a small weight on top of the card and leave overnight in the refrigerator.

8 Unmould the terrine and serve carved into thick slices.

Wine: A light red or a dry rosé from Tavel, Provence or Navarra

Tripe

Tripe is the stomach lining of cows, sheep, pigs, goats and deer. Beef tripe is the most commonly available, and usually comes from the first three of the four chambers in a cow's stomach. It varies in texture, depending on which part of the stomach it comes from. The rumen produces a flat, smooth-textured tripe, which is sometimes called blanket tripe. The reticulum produces honeycomb or pocket tripe, so named because of its pocked nature. And the omasum produces book or leaf tripe.

The abomasum, which produces abomasum or reed tripe, is rarely seen because it is not fit for human consumption. It contains the very last of the stomach's contents and is greenish-grey in colour (because of the chlorophyll from undigested grass), so is also known as unwashed or green tripe. Dogs find it particularly appetizing, and it is frequently found in commercially prepared dog food.

Using Tripe

Tripe requires a considerable amount of preparation before cooking, and most butchers sell 'prepared' or 'white' tripe. It needs to be scraped and blanched or boiled before the cooking process can begin. The blanching softens the tripe somewhat, but the actual cooking time is still lengthy because of its tough texture.

Tripe can be braised very slowly on a bed of vegetables to create a moist, steamy environment, or immersed in liquid and simmered very gently. This will result in a meltingly soft and delicately flavoured meat that is a good medium for either a spicy tomato sauce or sharp accompaniments, such as lemon, capers and cornichons.

Deep-fried Tripe and Onions

SERVES 4

2 large onions
675 g tripe
2 bay leaves
1 parsley stalk
2 carrots, sliced
6 black peppercorns

300 ml Fritter Batter (see opposite)
oil, for deep-frying
salt

To serve
Tartare Sauce (see opposite)

1 Slice 1 onion thickly and put it with the tripe in a large pan of cold water. Add the bay leaves, parsley stalk, carrots and peppercorns. Season with salt.
2 Bring to the boil. Cover and simmer for as long as necessary to produce tender tripe (usually about 1½ hours).
3 Meanwhile, make up the fritter batter, but do not add or whisk the egg white.
4 Drain the tripe and allow to cool slightly. Cut into equal-sized thin strips.
5 Slice the remaining onion carefully and separate into rings.
6 Whisk the egg white and fold it into the batter mixture.

7 Fill a large saucepan two-thirds full with oil and heat until a cube of bread sizzles and browns (see Warning, page 53).

8 Coat the tripe with the batter. Lower the strips, a few at a time, into the hot oil and cook until well browned. Drain on kitchen paper and sprinkle with salt.

9 Coat the onion rings in the batter. Fry them like the tripe strips in step 8, draining well.

10 Serve the tripe as soon after frying as possible, topped with the onion rings.

NOTES: Tripe is usually sold blanched and par-boiled. The additional cooking time needed can range from 30 minutes to 2 hours.

Tomato Sauce I or II (see page 469) are also good with deep-fried tripe.

FRITTER BATTER

MAKES 300 ML

125 g plain flour
pinch of salt
2 eggs

300 ml milk
1 tablespoon oil

1 Sift the flour with the salt into a bowl.

2 Make a well in the centre, exposing the bottom of the bowl.

3 Put 1 whole egg and 1 yolk into the well and mix with a wooden spoon or whisk until smooth, gradually incorporating the surrounding flour. Pour in the milk and continue whisking. The mixture should have a thick, creamy consistency.

4 Add the oil and allow the batter to rest in the refrigerator for 30 minutes.

5 When ready to use the batter, whisk the egg white until stiff but not dry. Fold into the mixture with a metal spoon. Use the batter immediately.

TARTARE SAUCE

Although this sauce usually accompanies fish, it's also very good with the tripe recipe above.

SERVES 4

150 ml Mayonnaise (see page 466)
1 tablespoon chopped capers, rinsed
1 tablespoon chopped gherkins, rinsed
1 tablespoon chopped fresh parsley

1 shallot, finely chopped
a squeeze of lemon juice
salt and freshly ground black pepper

1 Mix together all the ingredients. Check the seasoning.

Wine: White Burgundy

Veal

Veal is the meat of a calf that is reared for slaughter when weaned at 4–5 months old, much the same age as lambs and pigs. Milk-fed veal is pale and creamy in colour, with a delicate, bland flavour. It is considered a luxury meat and, compared to other types of meat, it is expensive. A veal calf will yield a relatively small amount of meat compared to a steer, so the quantity available for sale is limited. Much of it is sold to restaurants.

History

Historically, veal is produced from the dairy calves that are not needed to replenish the milking herd. Every dairy cow needs to have a calf each year to maintain her milk production, so more calves are born than are required for the herd. In the past these animals were kept in crates, fed milk-based food and not allowed to take exercise. The Dutch in particular were well known for this practice. However, the crate-rearing process is now banned in most countries.

As with all meat, the quality of veal is directly related to its age, diet and the amount of exercise it is allowed. These factors are particularly noticeable in veal, however, because once the calf is old enough to consume food other than milk, or if it has taken exercise, the meat becomes pinker due to the haemoglobin formed in the muscles. When this occurs the meat is called 'rose veal'. Although the meat will be tougher and have lost its 'milky' flavour, many people prefer it as the animal has lived a more natural life.

Common Types

Veal is particularly popular in Europe, where the Dutch have been renowned for their milk-fed veal for many years, and there are many regional specialities. The French use the stewing cuts for Blanquette de Veau, a creamy white stew, and the Italians use the shin for Osso Bucco and the fillet for Vitello Tonnato, a poached joint of veal served in a creamy tuna and caper sauce. The fillet is the best cut for roasting. It is often tied with string into a round shape, called a 'cushion', before roasting.

Choosing Veal

- The flesh should be pale pink, soft but not flabby, and finely grained.
- Veal should never look bloody or really red as this suggests the animal is much older than 4 months.
- There should be a very little white creamy fat.

- Do not worry if there is a lot of gelatinous tissue around the meat as this is a natural characteristic of a very immature animal. However, it should be removed before cooking unless the meat is to be braised or stewed, in which case it will break down and help to enrich the flavour and consistency of the cooking liquor.
- Avoid meat that is dark in colour or has a slimy appearance.
- Veal will not have a marbled appearance because the animal is too young to have developed fat.

Storing Veal

Discard any plastic packaging. Place the meat on a plate and cover with cling film. Store in the bottom of the refrigerator for up to 2 days. Freeze up to 3 months.

Cuts of Veal

Veal cuts are similar to those of beef, but are smaller in size.

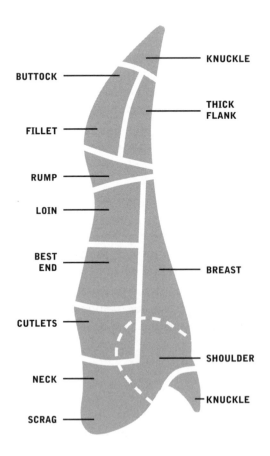

Cut	Recommended Cooking Methods	Recipe Reference
Best end Best end cutlets	Roasting Frying	Roast Loin of Veal (page 109) see Lamb, Frying (page 135)
Breast	Braising Stewing	Veal Fricandeau (page 110) Blanquette de Veau (page 114)
Buttock	Stewing	Blanquette de Veau (page 114)
Escalopes	Frying Roasting	Veal Escalopes with Rosemary (page 115)
Feet	Stock	see Brown Stock (page 452)
Fillet (cushion)	Frying	see Beef, Grilling and Frying (page 33)
Knuckle	Braising Stewing	Mediterranean Veal Knuckle Stew (page 112) Blanquette de Veau (page 114)
Leg	Roasting Braising Stewing	Roast Loin of Veal (page 109) Veal Fricandeau (page 110) Blanquette de Veau (page 114)
Loin Loin chops	Roasting Braising Frying	Roast Loin of Veal (page 109) Veal Fricandeau (page 110) see Beef, Frying (page 35)
Rump	Frying Braising	see Beef, Frying (page 35) Veal Fricandeau (page 110)
Scrag	Stewing	Blanquette de Veau (page 114)
Shoulder	Braising Stewing Pies	Veal Fricandeau (page 110) Blanquette de Veau (page 114) Veal and Ham Raised Pie (page 121)

Methods of Cooking Veal

Veal lends itself to most methods of cooking meat because it is very tender. However, it is seldom grilled because its absence of fat means that it becomes too dry. As there is little fat on a calf and a high proportion of water in the meat, care must be taken to moisten veal frequently during cooking to prevent it from excessive moisture loss, shrinkage and dryness. Due to the immaturity of the meat, veal tends to be bland, so is usually seasoned well and served with sauces or stuffing. Cuts containing a larger quantity of connective tissue, such as the leg, shoulder and neck, may be cooked slowly and gently by poaching, braising or stewing (see The Tender-tough-tender Principle, page 21).

Roasting

The best joints for roasting are:
- Loin
- Fillet

Roasting fillet of veal

As veal fillet is so lean and tender it must either be larded (see below) or protected by a layer of fat tied around it (see page 13). First brown the veal in hot fat over direct heat, or roast in the oven for 20 minutes at 200°C/400°F/gas mark 6, then roast, allowing 20 minutes per 450 g at 180°C/350°F/gas mark 4.

Roasting other cuts of veal

Veal cuts other than fillet can be roasted in the same way as beef; for timings see Beef Roasting Table, page 33.

Larding or braising

Veal, like other very lean meat, should be larded before roasting. This promotes tenderness and adds flavour. The technique is most commonly used for slow-roasted dishes. A special larding needle is used, which has a clamp at the opposite end from the point to grip the fat. As the meat cooks, the fat partially melts, making the meat juicy and adding flavour and richness to the sauce.

To lard a joint, cut the larding fat (usually rindless back pork fat) into thin strips longer than the joint or other piece of meat you are cooking and put one of them into the tunnel of the needle, clamping down the hinge to hold it in place. The fat should extend a little way out of the needle. Thread the strip all the way through the meat at 1 cm intervals, twisting the needle gently to prevent the fat from pulling off. Then release the clamp and trim the two ends of fat close to the meat. Repeat with the remaining strips throughout the lean meat, keeping them 3 cm apart.

Braising

Leg, shoulder, breast and knuckle of veal are the cuts recommended for braising. As veal contains very little fat, the joint is larded with pork fat to moisten it while it cooks. Veal contains gelatinous proteins that break down on slow cooking to enrich the flavour and consistency of the sauce.

Frying

The fillet, known as the 'cushion', is found at the top of the hind leg and is most frequently sliced into escalopes. These are cut with the grain into thin slices not more than 6 mm thick. The fillet contains very little fat or connective tissue, so is extremely tender and therefore expensive. The tender cuts from the forequarter of a top-quality, milk-fed calf may also be boned out and sliced for escalopes.

Roast Loin of Veal

SERVES 6

1 × 1 kg boneless loin of veal, in one piece	1 tablespoon vegetable oil
30 g butter	1 teaspoon plain flour
2 teaspoons Dijon mustard	300 ml Brown Stock (see page 452)
chopped fresh mixed herbs	salt and freshly ground black pepper

1 Heat the oven to 180°C/350°F/gas mark 4. Weigh the veal and calculate the cooking time at 20 minutes per 450 g.

2 Using a sharp knife, cut away the rind and most of the fat from the loin, leaving a layer of fat about 1 cm thick. Make criss-cross incisions in the fat layer.

3 Spread the butter and half the mustard over the lean side of the joint. Spread the remaining mustard on the fat side, making sure that it penetrates the incisions well. Sprinkle with the herbs, then season with salt and pepper. Roll and tie up securely with string.

4 Heat the oil in a roasting pan. When it is hot, put the joint into it and brown the surface evenly. (As the veal is roasted at a moderate temperature for a relatively short time, it might not brown sufficiently in the oven, see page 12).

5 Place the pan in the oven and roast for the calculated cooking time.

6 Transfer the joint to a warmed serving dish. Skim the excess fat from the pan. With a whisk or wooden spoon, scrape the bottom of the pan, then stir in the flour and cook until the roux is golden brown. Add the stock, stir until boiling, then simmer for 2 minutes.

7 Check the seasoning and pour into a warmed sauceboat. Serve with the joint.

Wine: Light red, perhaps Dolcetto, or a dry rosé

Veal Fricandeau

The term *fricandeau* is used for veal that is braised and glazed with its own juices. Joints of veal that are to be braised or roasted are often larded with strips of pork fat in order to supply the meat with an internal system of basting. As the fat renders down during cooking, it moistens the meat from within, keeping it juicy. Without this, the natural low fat content of young animals can lead to the meat drying out during cooking.

SERVES 8

200 g long strips of pork fat
1 × 1.35 kg piece rump or loin of veal, cut
   lengthwise along the grain
45 g unsalted butter
2 onions, thinly sliced
2 carrots, thinly sliced

600 ml Veal Stock (see page 454)
200 ml dry white wine
salt and freshly ground black pepper

To serve
Wilted Spinach (see page 497)

1 Season the pork fat with salt and pepper.
2 Take a strip of pork fat and press into the tunnel of a larding needle. Push the needle right through the meat. Gently turn the needle so that the fat does not come loose. When the fat is through the length of the meat, pull the needle away, leaving the fat embedded in the meat. Repeat this 10–12 times, making sure that there is an equal distance between the strips. Leave the little ends of the pork fat sticking out of the veal flesh.
3 Heat the oven to 180°/350°F/gas mark 4.
4 Melt the butter in a flameproof casserole. Add the onions and carrots and cook until just beginning to soften. Remove the vegetables and reserve. Add the veal and brown it lightly all over. Season with salt and pepper. Return the vegetables to the pan.
5 Add 5 tablespoons each of the stock and wine. Bring to the boil, then reduce the heat and simmer until the liquid has just evaporated. Add the remaining stock and wine. Bring to the boil, then cover with a piece of buttered greaseproof paper and a lid and cook in the oven for 1 hour.
6 Using a ladle, transfer half the braising liquid to a saucepan. Reduce by boiling rapidly until syrupy. Use this to baste over the fricandeau as it cooks. The surface of the meat should become brown and sticky.
7 Increase the oven temperature to 190°C/375°F/gas mark 5 and remove the covering paper and lid. Baste the veal frequently with the braising juices. Cook for 1 further hour, uncovered, to brown the meat.
8 Remove the veal from the casserole. Cover and leave to stand in the turned-off oven while you make the sauce.
9 Strain all the meat juices into a saucepan. Bring to the boil, then add a dash of cold water. (This will help to bring the scum to the surface.) Skim off all the scum. Repeat this process if necessary.
10 Meanwhile, cook the spinach and arrange on a large, warmed serving dish. Place the veal on top of the spinach and hand the sauce separately.

Wine: White Burgundy

Osso Bucco

This is a substantial peasant dish seasoned with a last-minute scattering of chopped parsley and grated lemon zest (gremolata). The sauce may be sieved to make it smooth, but the dish is quite often served without doing so.

SERVES 4

3 tablespoons good-quality olive oil

1 large or 2 small onions, finely chopped

1 large carrot, finely chopped

2 cloves of garlic, crushed

4 large, meaty pieces of knuckle of veal, cut crossways with the bone and marrow in the centre

2 teaspoons plain flour

2 teaspoons tomato purée

340 g ripe tomatoes, blanched, peeled and chopped

150 ml dry white wine

300 ml Veal Stock (see page 454)

1 bouquet garni (see page 512)

salt and freshly ground black pepper

To garnish

1 tablespoon chopped fresh parsley

grated zest of 1 lemon

1 Put 1 tablespoon of the oil into a saucepan, add the onion, carrot and garlic and cover with a tight-fitting lid. Cook over a low heat without browning.

2 Heat the remaining oil in a large saucepan and brown the meat, one or two pieces at a time, on all sides. Transfer to a plate as they are browned.

3 When they are all done, sprinkle the flour into the pan and stir well. Add the tomato purée, cooked vegetables, tomatoes, wine, stock, salt and pepper and bring to the boil.

4 Replace the veal, immerse the bouquet garni in the liquid and cover the pan. Simmer for 1 hour, or until the veal is very tender but not quite falling off the bone.

5 Take the veal out and place on a warmed serving platter with a fairly deep lip. Cover with kitchen foil and keep warm while you boil the sauce rapidly until thick. Stir frequently and watch that it does not catch and burn at the bottom.

6 Remove the bouquet garni. Push the sauce through a sieve, then pour over the meat. Sprinkle with the parsley and grated lemon zest.

Wine: Classic Italian red, such as Chianti Classico or Vino Nobile di Montepulciano

Mediterranean Veal Knuckle Stew

SERVES 4–6

1.35 kg veal knuckle, sawn into 8 cm pieces
seasoned flour
3 tablespoons oil
3 red onions, thickly sliced
2 cloves of garlic, crushed
450 g plum tomatoes, blanched, peeled and
  roughly chopped
300 ml red wine

300 ml Veal Stock (see page 454)
1 bouquet garni (see page 512)
2 anchovies, rinsed and drained
100 g pitted black olives
2 tablespoons freshly chopped marjoram
salt and freshly ground black pepper
hot crusty bread, to serve

1 Dip the pieces of veal knuckle in the seasoned flour and shake off the excess.
2 Heat 1 tablespoon of the oil in a flameproof casserole and brown the veal pieces, a few at a time, until well coloured, adding more oil as necessary. Deglaze the pan between batches with a little water, reserving the *déglaçage*.
3 Remove the browned veal from the pan and set aside.
4 Heat the remaining oil in the casserole and brown the onions well. Add the garlic and cook for a further minute. Add the tomatoes, wine, stock, bouquet garni and *déglaçage*, season with salt and pepper and bring to the boil.
5 Add the veal knuckle to the pan, return to the boil and reduce to a simmer. Cover the pan with a tight-fitting lid and simmer on a very low heat for 2–2¼ hours, or until the meat falls from the bone. It may be necessary to top up with a little water from time to time.
6 Remove the pieces of meat from the pan with a slotted spoon and set aside. Discard the bouquet garni. Skim any fat from the surface of the pan and bring the sauce to the boil.
7 Mash the anchovies with a fork and stir into the sauce. Stir in the olives and marjoram. Return the veal to the pan and heat through. Serve with the crusty bread.

Wine: Côtes-du-Rhône

Veal Knuckle and Black-eyed Bean Stew

SERVES 4

225 g black-eyed beans

4 × 170 g veal knuckles, untrimmed

2 tablespoons extra virgin olive oil

30 g butter

2 red onions, finely chopped

4 cloves of garlic, crushed

50 g prosciutto, diced

5 tablespoons red wine

300 ml Veal Stock or White Chicken Stock
  (see page 454 or 451)

10 plum tomatoes, blanched, skinned,
  deseeded and chopped

1 tablespoon chopped fresh parsley

1 tablespoon chopped fresh basil

3 tablespoons fresh white breadcrumbs

2 tablespoons freshly grated Parmesan cheese

salt and freshly ground black pepper

1 Soak the beans in cold water overnight. The following day, drain and cover with fresh water. Bring to the boil, then lower the heat and simmer for 1–1½ hours, or until tender. Drain the beans and set aside.

2 Heat the oven to 150°C/300°F/gas mark 2.

3 Season the veal knuckles with salt and pepper.

4 Heat the oil and butter together in a flameproof casserole. Brown the veal well on all sides, then remove and keep warm.

5 Add the onions to the casserole and cook for 10–12 minutes, or until very soft. Add the garlic and prosciutto and cook for a further 2–3 minutes.

6 Add the wine and stock and bring to the boil, then add the beans, tomatoes and herbs. Return the veal to the casserole, cover and cook in the oven for 1–1½ hours, or until the veal is tender. Add more water if the beans begin to dry out.

7 When the veal is cooked, lift on to a plate and keep warm. Reduce the liquid in the casserole if necessary by boiling rapidly. Return the veal to the casserole, sprinkle the top with the breadcrumbs and Parmesan, and cook, uncovered, in the oven for a further 10 minutes. Serve very hot.

Wine: Pinot Noir

Blanquette de Veau

This recipe is made with cheaper cuts of veal suitable for stewing, such as shoulder and leg, often known as 'pie veal'. Blanquette de Veau is a white stew, which means that the ingredients are not browned before simmering in stock or water. Once the meat is cooked, the cooking liquor is thickened with an egg and cream liaison just before the dish is served.

SERVES 4

900 g pie veal

1 slice of lemon

1 bouquet garni (see page 512)

2 carrots, cut into sticks

2 onions, sliced

1 teaspoon cornflour

1 egg yolk, or 2 for a rich sauce

150 ml double cream

salt and freshly ground black pepper

chopped fresh parsley, to garnish

1 Trim the fat from the veal, but do not worry about the gristle as much of it will convert to gelatine as it cooks. Put the veal into a saucepan of cold water with the lemon slice. Bring slowly to the boil, skimming thoroughly. Add the bouquet garni and a little salt. Remove the lemon slice and continue to simmer gently for 30 minutes.

2 Add the carrots and onions and continue to simmer until the meat is very tender and the vegetables are cooked, a further 30–40 minutes.

3 Strain the liquid into a jug and skim off any fat. There should be 300 ml liquid. Should there be less, add water. If there is more, return the liquid to the pan and reduce by boiling rapidly. Pick over the meat, removing any fat or gristle, then put the meat and vegetables into an ovenproof serving dish. Discard the bouquet garni.

4 Mix the cornflour in a cup with 2 tablespoonfuls of cold water. Stir the mixture into the liquid in the pan and continue to stir while bringing to the boil. You should now have a sauce that is very slightly thickened, about the consistency of single cream. If it is still too thin, do not add more cornflour, but boil rapidly until reduced to the correct consistency. Season to taste with salt and pepper.

5 Mix the egg yolk and cream together in a bowl. Add some of the sauce, mix well and return to the pan. Reheat gently, stirring constantly, until the egg yolks have thickened the sauce to the consistency of double cream. Do not allow the sauce to boil or the eggs will curdle. Pour the sauce over the meat and vegetables.

6 Serve garnished with chopped parsley.

Wine: Red Burgundy or Rioja, or a dry white, such as a Condrieu

Veal Marsala

Marsala, a fortified wine from Sicily, adds a touch of sweetness to this classic recipe. Substitute medium sherry if Marsala is not available.

SERVES 4

4 × 140 g veal escalopes
30 g Clarified Butter (see page xii)
2 tablespoons Marsala

4 tablespoons double cream
squeeze of lemon juice
salt and freshly ground black pepper

1 Put the veal escalopes between 2 sheets of dampened greaseproof paper or cling film and beat lightly with a meat mallet, rolling pin or heavy-based saucepan until thin. Season with salt and pepper.
2 Melt the butter in a frying pan and, when it is foaming, fry the escalopes briskly to brown them lightly (1–2 minutes per side). Transfer to a warmed plate and keep warm.
3 Pour off any fat in the pan. Add 4 tablespoons water and the Marsala, swish it about and bring to the boil. Add the cream and season well with salt, pepper and a squeeze of lemon juice. Return the veal to the pan to heat through gently.

Wine: A southern Italian red, such as Salice Salentino

Veal Escalopes with Rosemary

SERVES 4

4 × 140 g veal escalopes
30 g Clarified Butter (see page xii)
1 teaspoon chopped rosemary
4 tablespoons dry white wine mixed with
  4 tablespoons water

2 tablespoons double cream or crème fraîche
a few drops of lemon juice
salt and freshly ground black pepper

1 If the escalopes are not very thin, place them between 2 sheets of dampened greaseproof paper or cling film and beat gently with a meat mallet, rolling pin or heavy-based saucepan to a thickness of 5 mm. Season with salt and pepper.
2 Melt the butter with the rosemary in a frying pan over a medium heat. When the butter is foaming, fry the escalopes (one or two at a time if they won't fit in the pan together) for 1–2 minutes on each side until a very pale brown (be careful not to overcook them). Remove the veal with a slotted spoon or fish slice and keep warm in a very low oven. Pour any excess fat from the pan.
3 Add the diluted wine to the hot pan and heat, scraping up any sediment with a wooden spoon. Boil to reduce by half, then add the cream and a few drops of lemon juice. Check the seasoning. Pour over the veal and serve immediately.

Wine: Light red Burgundy (Macon, Givry, Mercurey) or an Italian Merlot

Veal Martini

SERVES 4

4 × 170 g veal escalopes

30 g unsalted butter

1 tablespoon finely chopped sage

2 tablespoons dry white vermouth

4 tablespoons double cream

salt and freshly ground black pepper

watercress, to garnish

1 Trim the veal carefully and season with salt and pepper.

2 Heat the butter in a large frying pan until just turning brown. Add the veal, in batches if necessary, and fry for about 1 minute an each side, until lightly browned and just cooked. Do not overcook. Transfer the escalopes to a warmed serving dish.

3 Tip off all the fat from the pan. Wipe out the pan if at all burnt. Add 4 tablespoons water, the sage and vermouth. Bring to the boil and reduce to half the original quantity by boiling rapidly.

4 Scrape any sediment from the bottom of the pan. Add the cream and bring to the boil, then reduce the heat and simmer until thickened slightly. Season with salt and pepper and pour over the veal. Garnish with bouquets of watercress and serve immediately.

Wine: Dry white, such as Gavi

Veal Piccata

SERVES 4

4 veal escalopes (about 675 g in total)

seasoned flour

100 g unsalted butter

juice of 1 lemon mixed with 2 tablespoons water

4 tablespoons small capers, rinsed

2 tablespoons chopped fresh parsley

salt and freshly ground black pepper

To serve

tagliatelle or rice

green salad

1 Place the escalopes between 2 pieces of dampened greaseproof paper. Beat with a heavy-based saucepan to a thickness of 5 mm.

2 Dredge the escalopes with the seasoned flour, shaking off the excess. Place in a single layer on a plate.

3 Melt half the butter in a large frying pan over a medium–high heat until it becomes frothy.

4 Add the escalopes, in batches if necessary, and fry for 2 minutes per side, or until golden brown and cooked through. Transfer to a serving plate and keep warm.

5 Clean the frying pan, then heat the remaining butter until it turns golden brown.

6 Pour in the lemon juice and water, stirring to make a light emulsion.

7 Stir in the capers and parsley.

8 Pour the sauce over the escalopes and serve immediately with tagliatelle or rice and a green salad.

Wine: Sangiovese chilled rosé

Veal Escalopes with Ragoût Fin

Meaning 'fine stew' in French, *ragoût fin* is a roux-thickened stew or sauce flavoured with either lemon or vinegar.

SERVES 4

110 g calves' sweetbreads

20 g butter, plus extra for frying

1 small onion, finely chopped

30 g bacon, diced

50 g button mushrooms, sliced

1 tablespoon chopped fresh parsley

7 g plain flour

150 ml Veal Stock (see page 454)

4 × 140 g veal escalopes

squeeze of lemon juice

salt and freshly ground black pepper

To garnish

sprigs of watercress

lemon wedges

1 Soak the sweetbreads in cold water for 4 hours, changing the water every time it becomes pink, probably 4 times. There should be no blood at all when the sweetbreads are ready for cooking.

2 Place them in a saucepan of cold water and bring to boiling point, but do not allow to boil. Simmer for 2 minutes. Rinse under cold running water and dry well.

3 Pick over the sweetbreads, removing all the skin and membrane. Chop them coarsely.

4 Melt the butter and add the onion. Cook slowly until soft but not coloured. Add the bacon and sweetbreads and cook for 3 minutes. Stir in the mushrooms and parsley and leave over a low heat for 1 minute.

5 Mix in the flour and cook for 1 minute. Remove from the heat and stir in the stock. Return to the heat and bring slowly to the boil, stirring continuously. Season with salt and pepper. Simmer for 1 minute, then set aside to cool and solidify.

6 Place the veal escalopes between 2 pieces of dampened greaseproof paper or cling film and beat them lightly with a meat mallet, rolling pin or heavy-based saucepan until quite thin.

7 Divide the sweetbread mixture between the escalopes and fold them in half.

8 Melt some butter in a large frying pan and, when foaming, add the escalopes. Brown lightly on both sides. Reduce the temperature and cook slowly for 4–5 minutes. Lift out the escalopes on to a warm serving plate.

9 Increase the heat under the frying pan and brown the butter. Remove from the heat and add a squeeze of lemon juice. Pour over the escalopes and serve garnished with watercress and lemon wedges.

Wine: Light red Burgundy or Cru Beaujolais

Veal Florentine

The word 'Florentine' denotes the presence of spinach in a recipe. Here strips of succulent veal are layered with soft spinach. This makes an excellent supper dish because it can be made in advance and reheated.

SERVES 4

50 g butter

1 clove of garlic, crushed

6 tomatoes, blanched, peeled and sliced

900 g spinach, cooked and chopped

pinch of freshly grated nutmeg

4 × 140 g veal escalopes

600 ml Mornay Sauce (see page 461)

1 tablespoon grated Cheddar or Parmesan cheese

1 tablespoon dried breadcrumbs

salt and freshly ground black pepper

1 Heat the oven to 180°C/350°F/gas mark 4.

2 Melt a quarter of the butter and fry the garlic quickly. Add the tomatoes and cook for 30 seconds. Place them in a dish big enough to hold the veal in one layer.

3 Melt another quarter of the butter in the pan, then toss the spinach in it. Season with salt, pepper and nutmeg. Spread the spinach on top of the tomatoes.

4 Put the veal between 2 pieces of dampened greaseproof paper or cling film and flatten by beating evenly with a meat mallet, rolling pin or heavy-based saucepan. Cut across the grain into strips.

5 Heat the remaining butter in a large frying pan and fry the veal strips until lightly browned all over. Put them on top of the spinach and season with salt and pepper.

6 Heat the mornay sauce and pour evenly over the veal and spinach. Sprinkle with the grated cheese and breadcrumbs.

7 Bake in the oven for 15 minutes, or until bubbly and hot, then grill to brown the top.

NOTE: Chicken Florentine can be made in the same way, using strips of poached chicken in place of veal.

Wine: Medium-bodied Italian red, such as Barbera d'Alba or Chianti Classico

Veal Medallions with Wild Mushrooms

SERVES 4

170 g unsalted butter, chilled and diced

4 × 140 g veal medallions

110 g mixed wild mushrooms, sliced

425 ml Brown Stock (see page 452)

100 ml dry white wine

salt and freshly ground black pepper

1 Melt 15 g of the butter in a frying pan. When it is foaming, brown the veal lightly on both sides (2–3 minutes per side). Transfer the meat to a warmed plate.

2 Add the mushrooms to the pan and fry until tender. Remove with a slotted spoon and arrange around the veal.

3 Add the stock and wine and bring to the boil, scraping up any sediment from the bottom of the pan. Boil until reduced to 5 tablespoons.

4 Allow the stock to cool slightly. Whisking vigorously and continuously with a wire whisk, add the rest of the butter. This should take about 2 minutes and the sauce should thicken. Taste, season and pour over the veal.

NOTE: Veal cutlets may be used instead of medallions.

Wine: Amarone or Zinfandel

Hungarian Veal Medallions with Aubergine

SERVES 4

1 large aubergine	1 teaspoon paprika
30 g seasoned plain flour	3 tablespoons dry white wine
4 × 140 g veal medallions	150 ml single cream
110 g larding pork, cut into 4 strips, or 4 thin,	300 ml Mornay Sauce (see page 461)
rindless rashers of streaky bacon	1 tablespoon grated Parmesan cheese
oil, for frying	1 tablespoon dried white breadcrumbs
30 g Clarified Butter (see page xii)	salt and freshly ground black pepper
1 shallot, finely chopped	

1 Heat the oven to 130°C/250°F/gas mark 1.

2 Cut the aubergine into slices 1 cm thick. Sprinkle with salt and leave in a colander for 20 minutes to extract the bitter juices (degorge). Rinse well, pat dry and dip in the seasoned flour.

3 Wrap the veal medallions carefully in the pork fat strips or the streaky bacon. Tie with string.

4 Heat the oil in a frying pan and fry the aubergine until golden brown and tender. Remove from the pan, drain on kitchen paper and keep warm in the oven.

5 Dust the medallions with seasoned flour. Heat the butter in the pan and fry the veal for 3–4 minutes on each side, or until just cooked. Remove and keep warm in the oven.

6 Add the shallot to the pan and cook slowly for 2 minutes, then add the paprika and continue cooking for a further 2 minutes. Pour on the wine and boil to reduce by half. Cool slightly, pour in the cream and season with salt and pepper. Reheat, boil to reduce if a little thin, then set aside.

7 Heat the grill to its highest setting. Meanwhile, reheat the mornay sauce.

8 Lay the aubergine slices in a large ovenproof dish. Remove the strings from the veal and lay the medallions on top of the aubergines. Coat with the mornay sauce. Sprinkle with the cheese and crumbs and brown under the grill. Reheat the paprika sauce and trickle it around the dish.

Wine: A rich red, such as Chilean Merlot or Australian Shiraz

Veal Medallions and Grilled Vegetables with Aïoli

SERVES 8

8 × 140 g veal medallions
olive oil
salt and freshly ground black pepper

For the vegetables

2 aubergines, cut in lengthwise slices
olive oil
3 large red peppers, halved and deseeded
6 medium courgettes, cut into thin diagonal slices
4 onions, sliced

6 tomatoes, blanched, peeled, quartered and
  deseeded
balsamic vinegar
finely chopped fresh mint
finely chopped fresh basil

To serve

1 quantity Aïoli (see page 466)

1 Salt the aubergines and leave in a colander for 20 minutes to extract the bitter juices.
2 Heat the grill to its highest setting.
3 Rinse the aubergine slices and pat dry with kitchen paper. Paint each side of the slices lightly with oil and grill until dark brown but not burnt.
4 Grill the peppers, skin-side up, until they are charred and blistered. Place in a plastic bag to cool. Remove the skin and cut the flesh into strips.
5 Lightly oil the courgettes and grill until just cooked.
6 Sauté the onions in a little oil until light brown.
7 Layer the vegetables, including the tomatoes, in a bowl, sprinkling each layer with balsamic vinegar, chopped mint and basil. Marinate for 1 hour.
8 Brush both sides of the veal with oil and sprinkle with salt and pepper. Grill under a hot grill for 3–4 minutes on each side, depending on the thickness of the meat.
9 Place the cooked veal and some of the marinated vegetables on warmed dinner plates. Serve a spoonful of aïoli beside the vegetables.

NOTE: Veal cutlets can be used in place of medallions.

Wine: Amarone or Zinfandel

Veal and Ham Raised Pie

In the UK meat terrines that are covered in pastry are called 'raised pies'. The pastry is raised around the meat to cover and encase it. Originally, the pastry was used as a container and was not meant to be eaten; today, however, it is eaten along with the meat. A sturdy paste called hot watercrust pastry is the type that is most frequently used for raised pies. The gelatinous quality of veal makes it very good for raised pies and terrines.

The pastry case in this recipe should be made at least an hour in advance of the filling. The finished pie must be left overnight for the aspic to set.

SERVES 4

450 g flour quantity Hot Watercrust Pastry
  (see page 485)
675 g boned shoulder of veal
115 g ham
1 onion, chopped

2 tablespoons chopped fresh parsley
1 egg, beaten
300 ml Aspic, flavoured with tarragon
  (see page 458)
salt and freshly ground black pepper

1 Make the pastry and mould the pastry case (see illustration, page 485).

2 Heat the oven to 190°C/375°F/gas mark 5.

3 Cut the veal and ham into cubes. Trim away most of the fat and all the skin and gristle. Season with salt and pepper, then combine with the onion and parsley.

4 Fill the pastry case with the meat mixture, pressing it firmly into the corners, then cover with the remaining pastry. Press the edges together. Make a neat hole in the middle of the lid. Place a lightly buttered piece of doubled greaseproof paper around the pie and secure with a paper clip.

5 Bake for 15 minutes. Reduce the oven temperature to 170°C/325°F/gas mark 3 and bake for a further hour. Thirty minutes before the pie is due to come out of the oven, remove the paper 'collar' and brush the pastry evenly all over with beaten egg. Remove the pie from the oven and allow to get cold.

6 Warm the aspic enough to make it just liquid but not hot. Using a funnel, pour the aspic into the pie. Allow to set slightly, then add more aspic until you are sure that the pie is completely full. This will take some time. Leave in the refrigerator for the jelly to reset.

NOTE: This is the classic English pie, but a pâte à pâte crust (see page 486) can be used for a richer, more tender casing.

Wine: Fruity red, such as Beaujolais, or a dry white, such as Alsace, Austrian or Australian Riesling

Veal Spring Rolls

MAKES 16

16 spring roll wrappers

For the filling

50 g beansprouts

50 g French beans

50 g carrots, cut into julienne strips

1 stick of celery, trimmed and cut into julienne
   strips

1 courgette, cut into julienne strips

110 g lean veal, cut into fine julienne strips

1 tablespoon oil

1 cm piece of fresh root ginger, peeled and sliced

1 clove of garlic, sliced

1 tablespoon soy sauce

1 lightly beaten egg white

oil, for deep-frying (see Warning,
   page 53)

salt and freshly ground black pepper

1 First make the filling. Blanch the beansprouts for 15 seconds. Drain and refresh under cold running water. Top and tail the French beans and cut them in half lengthwise. Mix the sprouts and beans with the carrots, celery and courgette. Mix in the veal.

2 Heat the oil in a wok or frying pan, add the ginger and garlic and cook over a low heat for 2 minutes to infuse the flavours. Remove the ginger and garlic.

3 Turn up the heat and quickly stir-fry the meat and vegetables. Season with the soy sauce, salt and pepper. Remove from the heat and leave to cool.

4 Divide the filling between the spring roll wrappers, placing it in the centre of each one. Fold the 2 opposite corners of the wrappers on top of the filling, then roll up from one exposed corner to the other to form rolls. Brush with the egg white.

5 Heat the oil in a deep-fat fryer until a cube of bread will sizzle vigorously in it. Add the spring rolls and fry until golden brown. Drain well on kitchen paper. Sprinkle with salt and serve.

Wine: Gewürztraminer or Viognier

Sweetbreads

Sweetbreads are the thymus and pancreas glands of calves and lambs. Thymus sweetbreads are long and irregular in shape, while those from the pancreas are spherical. Calves' sweetbreads are superior to lambs'. Sweetbreads are blanched to whiten them, then poached, braised or sautéd.

- Choose pale sweetbreads with only a small amount of connective tissue. Avoid any that look bloody.
- Store in the coldest part of the refrigerator and use within 24 hours. Freezing is not recommended.

Pan-fried Sweetbreads on Toasted Brioche with Sour Lemon Glaze

Mirin is sweet rice wine vinegar that can be found in most supermarkets and Japanese speciality shops. If unavailable, dry vermouth or cider or sherry vinegar can be used in its place.

SERVES 4

500 g veal sweetbreads	4 thick slices of Savoury Brioche, toasted
45 g unsalted butter	(see page 487)
finely grated zest of 1 lemon	salt and freshly ground black pepper
juice of 2 lemons	sprigs of chervil, to garnish
1 tablespoon mirin	

1 Soak the sweetbreads in cold water for 4 hours. Change the water every time it becomes pink (probably 4 times). There should be no blood at all when the sweetbreads are ready for cooking.
2 Place them in a saucepan of cold water and bring to the boil. Reduce the heat and poach for 2 minutes.
3 Drain the sweetbreads and rinse under cold running water. Dry well and pick them over, removing all skin and membrane, and cut into small, bite-sized pieces.
4 Melt 30 g of the butter in a frying pan and fry the sweetbreads until lightly browned. Reduce the heat and continue to cook for a further 1–2 minutes, or until just cooked through. Remove from the pan with a slotted spoon and keep warm.
5 Add the remaining butter to the pan and, when foaming, add the lemon zest, lemon juice and mirin. Bring to the boil and reduce to about 2 tablespoons. Return the sweetbreads to the pan, season with salt and pepper and stir to coat with the glaze.
6 Spoon the sweetbreads on to the warm, toasted brioche and serve garnished with sprigs of chervil.

Wine: Medium-bodied red, such as a Burgundy or Brunello di Montalcino

Chicken and Sweetbread Ravioli with Chervil and Crème Fraîche Sauce

SERVES 4

1 quantity Egg Pasta (see page 488)

oil, for frying

1 shallot, diced

450 g veal sweetbreads, soaked in cold water

170 g chicken breast, skinned and chopped

pinch of ground mace

½ egg

150 ml double cream

salt

paprika

lemon juice

1 teaspoon chopped fresh chervil

For the sauce

75 ml white port

2 tablespoons Marsala

300 ml Veal Stock (see page 454)

sprig of thyme

200 ml crème fraîche

1 teaspoon chopped fresh chervil

salt and freshly ground black pepper

1 Wrap the pasta in cling film and set aside to relax.

2 Heat a little oil in a pan and sweat the shallot gently until soft and translucent.

3 Put the sweetbreads into a saucepan of cold water, bring to the boil and poach for 2 minutes. Drain and refresh under cold running water, then remove the membrane. Cut the sweetbreads into small cubes and fry these in very hot oil in a large frying pan until they are golden brown. Allow to cool.

4 Put the chicken breast and mace into a food processor and whizz for 1 minute.

5 Add the egg and process the mixture for another minute. Chill for 15 minutes in the refrigerator. Force the mixture through a sieve to ensure a velvety texture.

6 Transfer to a cold bowl set in an ice bath. Gradually beat in the cream. Stir in the shallot and sweetbreads and season well with salt, paprika and lemon juice. Stir in the chervil.

7 Roll out the pasta as thinly as possible, using a pasta machine or a rolling pin, to form a strip approximately 15 × 32 cm. Brush the edges lightly with water.

8 Place teaspoonfuls of the filling in even rows at intervals of 4 cm over half the pasta. Fold the other half of the pasta over filling. Press together, firming around each mound and making sure that all the air is excluded. Cut between the mounds, making sure that the edges of the ravioli are sealed. Place on a wire rack or silicon paper while you make the sauce. Do not cover.

9 To make the sauce, put the port and Marsala into a saucepan and boil rapidly until reduced by one-third. Add the stock and thyme and boil again until reduced by half.

10 Add the crème fraîche and reduce again by half, or until the sauce is of a coating consistency. Remove the sprig of thyme. Add the chervil and season to taste with salt and pepper.

11 Cook the pasta in a large saucepan of boiling salted water until tender (about 3–4 minutes).

12 To serve, drain the pasta well, arrange on 4 warmed individual serving plates and pour over the sauce.

Wine: Dry Riesling from Austria, Alsace or Germany, preferably with a bit of age

Sweetbread Terrine with Warm Caramelized Radicchio Salad

SERVES 6–8

675 g veal sweetbreads, soaked in several
   changes of cold water

225 g very lean minced pork

1 egg, beaten

30 g fresh white breadcrumbs

1 tablespoon white port

about 6 sage leaves, very finely chopped

salt

paprika

1 large sheet of pig's caul, soaked in water
   (see page 513)

crusty bread, to serve

For the radicchio salad

1 small head radicchio

3 tablespoons sunflower oil

1 tablespoon raspberry vinegar

1 teaspoon soft light brown sugar

salt and freshly ground black pepper

1 Put the sweetbreads into a saucepan of cold water, bring to the boil and poach for 2 minutes. Drain and refresh under cold running water, then remove the membranes and cut them into large, even-sized pieces.

2 In a large bowl, mix together the minced pork, egg, breadcrumbs, port and chopped sage. Season with salt and paprika.

3 Heat the oven to 170°C/325°F/gas mark 3.

4 Line a 1 kg loaf tin with a large sheet of the caul, cutting it with scissors to fit. Spread a quarter of the pork mixture over the bottom of the tin. Push a third of the sweetbreads down well into the pork. Repeat with the remaining ingredients, finishing with a layer of the pork mixture. Wrap the loose ends of the caul over the top and press down well.

5 Cover the mixture with a piece of greased greaseproof paper, then cover with foil.

6 Stand the loaf tin in a roasting pan half-filled with hot water (a bain-marie) and bake in the middle of the oven for 1¼–1½ hours. When done, the terrine should feel firm to the touch and be shrinking away from the sides of the tin. Remove from the pan of water and place a small weight on top. Allow to cool, then refrigerate overnight.

7 To make the salad, heat the grill to its highest setting.

8 Cut the radicchio in half and remove the core. Cut each half into 5–6 wedges and place them in a bowl.

9 Whisk together the oil, vinegar and sugar and season with salt and pepper. Pour the dressing over the radicchio and toss lightly. Transfer to a baking sheet.

10 Place under the grill for 30–45 seconds, or until beginning to brown.

11 Turn the terrine on to a plate and cut into 2 cm slices. Serve with the warm radicchio salad and crusty bread.

Wine: European Chardonnay, perhaps from Italy or southern Burgundy – Saint-Véran or Pouilly-Fuissé

Veal Offal Stew

Any combination of offal can be used in this stew, but it is best to keep to one type of animal in order to appreciate the flavour. For instance, if pig's liver were to be used with veal kidneys, the flavour of the liver would be very dominant and overwhelm the flavour of the delicate veal offal.

SERVES 4

2 tablespoons oil

110 g piece of green streaky bacon (see page 222), rined removed and cut into lardons

2 banana shallots, very finely sliced lengthwise

2 sticks of celery, finely sliced on the diagonal

1 teaspoon flour

2 teaspoons tomato purée

150 ml white wine

150 ml Madeira

300 ml Veal Stock (see page 454)

1½ tablespoons rowanberry jelly

2 large sprigs of thyme

225 g veal sweetbreads, blanched, refreshed and picked over, cut into 2 cm pieces (see page 123)

225 g veal kidney, core removed and cut into 2 cm pieces

225 g calves' liver, cut into 2 cm pieces

seasoned flour

1 bunch of baby carrots, cooked

340 g baby new potatoes, cooked

30 g unsalted butter, chilled and cut into small cubes

1 tablespoon chervil, freshly chopped

salt and freshly ground black pepper

sprigs of chervil, to garnish

1 Heat 1½ tablespoons of the oil in a heavy-based casserole and fry the lardons until well browned. Remove from the pan with a slotted spoon, drain on kitchen paper and set aside.

2 Add the shallots and celery to the pan and cook until lightly browned. Add the flour and tomato purée and cook for 1 minute. Pour in the wine and Madeira and flambé. When the flames subside, add the stock, rowanberry jelly and thyme. Return the bacon to the pan and season with salt and pepper. Simmer gently for 30 minutes, uncovered.

3 Dip the sweetbreads, kidney and liver pieces into the seasoned flour and shake off the excess.

4 Heat the remaining oil in a frying pan and fry the sweetbreads on all sides until golden brown. Transfer to a colander. Fry the kidney and liver pieces in the same way and add to the sweetbreads. Allow to drain for 5 minutes before adding to the casserole along with the carrots and potatoes, then cook very gently for 5–7 minutes.

5 Stir the cold butter into the sauce bit by bit until incorporated. Season with salt and pepper. Add the chopped chervil.

6 Serve on warmed plates garnished with fresh chervil.

NOTE: If rowanberry jelly is not available, redcurrant jelly may be used instead.

Wine: Côtes-du-Rhône or Australian Shiraz/Cabernet

Veal Kidneys with Wholegrain Mustard and Leek Cream

SERVES 4

60 g unsalted butter

2 large leeks, white parts only

1 tablespoon wholegrain mustard

150 ml crème fraîche

500 g veal kidneys

2 tablespoons Pernod

lemon juice

salt and freshly ground black pepper

1 Melt 30 g of the butter in a sauté pan and add the leeks. Cook over a low heat for about 15 minutes, or until the leeks have softened.
2 Add the mustard and crème fraîche and cook until the juices have evaporated.
3 Remove the membranes and cores from the kidneys and cut into chunks.
4 Melt the remaining butter in a frying pan and fry a handful of kidney pieces at a time, shaking the pan until the kidneys are brown but still pale inside. Transfer to a sieve set over a bowl and discard the juices.
5 Pour the Pernod into the hot pan. Set it alight. As soon as the flames subside, pour in the leek cream mixture. Return the kidneys to the pan to reheat. Season with lemon juice, salt and pepper and turn into a warmed serving dish.

Wine: Bold red, such as Douro, Ribera del Duero or New World Merlot

Veal Kidneys Robert

SERVES 2–3

150 ml dry white wine

450 g veal kidneys

45 g unsalted butter

1 teaspoon Dijon mustard

2 teaspoons chopped fresh parsley

squeeze of lemon juice

2 tablespoons double cream

salt and freshly ground black pepper

1 Put the wine into a saucepan and boil until reduced by half.
2 Remove the membranes and cores from the kidneys, and slice them quite thinly.
3 Melt the butter in a frying pan, then fry the kidney slices a handful at a time, shaking the pan until they are brown but still pale inside. Transfer to a sieve set over a bowl and discard the juices.
4 Add the mustard, reduced wine, half the parsley, the lemon juice, salt and pepper to the pan. Bring to the boil, stirring continuously. Stir in the cream, then check the seasoning. Simmer until syrupy. Stir in the kidneys.
5 Turn into a warmed serving dish and sprinkle with the remaining parsley.

Wine: Rich red from the Rhône, Languedoc, Australia or Argentina

Veal Kidney Feuilletées

A feuilletée case is a container made from puff pastry and used to hold savoury fillings or fresh fruit. For this recipe, if ceps, chanterelles or morels are not available, use oyster or small button mushrooms instead.

SERVES 4

1 quantity Puff Pastry (see page 480) or
   500g bought puff pastry
1 beaten egg, to glaze

For the filling
150 ml dry white wine
340 g veal kidneys
50 g butter

50 g ceps, sliced
50 g small chanterelles
50 g small morels
2 teaspoons Dijon mustard
1 tablespoon chopped fresh parsley
6 tablespoons double cream
salt and freshly ground black pepper

1 Flour the work surface, then roll the pastry into a large rectangle 1 cm thick. Cut it into 4 diamonds, each side of them measuring 10 cm. Place the diamonds on a baking tray and brush with beaten egg. Using a sharp knife, score a line about 1 cm from the edge of each diamond without cutting all the way through the pastry. The interior diamond will form a 'hat' for the pastry case. Make a design inside this diamond with the knife. Flour the blade of the knife and use it to 'knock up' the sides of pastry. Chill for 15 minutes.

2 Heat the oven to 220°C/425°F/gas mark 7.

3 Bake the diamonds in the hot oven for 20 minutes or until puffed up and brown. With a knife, outline and remove the 'hats' and scoop out any uncooked dough inside. Return the cases to the oven to dry out for 5 minutes. Transfer to a wire rack to cool. Reduce the oven temperature to 180°C/350°F/gas mark 4.

4 Meanwhile, prepare the filling. Put the wine into a saucepan. Boil until reduced by half.

5 Remove the membranes and cores from the kidneys and cut into chunks.

6 Melt a little of the butter in a frying pan and fry all the mushrooms over a very low heat for about 3 minutes. Set aside.

7 Fry the kidney pieces, a small handful at a time, in the remaining butter over a high heat. Transfer to a sieve set over a bowl. Bitter juices will run out of the kidneys and these should be discarded.

8 Return the pastry cases to the oven for 4 minutes to reheat.

9 Put the reduced wine, mustard, parsley and cream into the frying pan. Season with salt and pepper. Bring to the boil and reduce by boiling rapidly for 1 minute or until syrupy. Add the kidneys and mushrooms to the sauce.

10 Divide the filling between the 4 pastry cases. Put on the hats and serve immediately.

Wine: Rioja, Bairrada, Burgundy or Bourgueil

Marrow

The best marrow yield comes from the long veal shinbones. It is rich and fatty, and can be used to thicken stocks and sauces where meat is cooked on the bone, such as in Osso Bucco (see page 111). During the cooking process, the marrow becomes soft and liquid, and seeps into the sauce or stock. Alternatively, it can be extracted and eaten in its own right. All bones in any animal contain marrow, and this will intensify the flavour of any dish, but the marrow from veal bones is the only one to be eaten in this way because it has the most delicate flavour.

Marrow on Toast with French Radish Salad

Ask your butcher to saw the veal bones into chunks for roasting. The cooked marrow can either be removed and served piled on to crusty bread or toast, or the bones can be served whole for diners to scoop out the marrow for themselves. In this case, a marrow spoon, or similar long-handled utensil, must be provided in order to extract all of the rich, sticky content of the bones. Either way, serve a sharp, salty accompaniment, such as capers or cornichons, to cut through the richness of the marrow and provide a contrasting texture. Here, the bones are served whole with a refreshing, crunchy radish salad.

SERVES 4

12 x 7–10 cm pieces veal marrow bone
warm crusty bread or hot toast, to serve

For the salad
1 small shallot, very finely diced
1 tablespoon oil

1 tablespoon lemon juice
1 bunch of French breakfast radishes
½ tablespoon capers, rinsed and chopped
½ tablespoon cornichons, rinsed and chopped
1 large handful of flat leaf parsley, roughly chopped
flaky sea salt and freshly ground black pepper

1 Heat the oven to 200°C/400°F/gas mark 6.
2 Put the bones into a large roasting pan and roast for 20 minutes, or until the marrow begins to loosen. Take care not to overcook or it will become liquid.
3 Meanwhile, place the shallot in a small bowl with the oil, lemon juice and a good pinch of salt flakes. Cover and leave to stand for 10–15 minutes.
4 Wash and trim the radishes, keeping some of leafy green bits on top. Cut in half lengthwise and pile them on to a serving dish.
5 Stir the capers, cornichons and parsley into the shallots and season with black pepper. Pour the dressing over the radishes.
6 Remove the bones from the oven and put 3 pieces on each of 4 serving plates. Serve with the radish salad, crusty bread or toast and a small bowl of sea salt flakes to sprinkle over the extracted marrow.

Drink: Alsace Pinot Gris or a glass of bitter

Lamb

Lamb is consumed throughout the world and is particularly popular in the Middle East, where any reference to 'meat' means lamb. Young lamb is sweet and almost flowery in taste, especially when cooked pink.

Most lambs are slaughtered between the ages of 4 and 6 months. Milk-fed baby lamb is available in the late spring. It has a pale pink colour and is very tender and sweet. Older lamb that is sold in March or April will have come from animals that were artificially encouraged to lamb before Christmas, usually by feeding the sheep with high-protein cereal pellets.

By the time a lamb is a year old it will be called a hogget. From its second spring or summer it will be classified as mutton. Although hogget can be cooked pink, mutton needs long, slow cooking in order to tenderize the connective fibres that have grown tough during the animal's longer life. Older lamb can be strongly flavoured, and sheep that are stressed during slaughter produce tough, unpleasantly flavoured meat.

History

Sheep belong to the same family as cattle, Bovidae. Like cattle, they are ruminants and eat only grass. Sheep were domesticated about the same time as cattle, before 6500 BC. They are well suited to living in hilly and/or rocky areas where it is not possible to graze cattle. They can also be herded easily, an attribute that aids domestication.

An important part of every culture, the sheep is valued for its wool and milk, as well as its meat. It is part of many religious festivals throughout the world, both on the table and, in the past, as a sacrifice. Although lamb is not as popular as beef in the UK, the animals thrive throughout the country.

Breeds

While sheep have been cross-bred since the 1600s in order to develop better wool and meat, they have largely avoided being intensively farmed because they can survive on land that is otherwise unproductive.

The most popular breeds in the UK are the Texel, Romney and Cromedale. The lamb will have a different flavour depending on the breed and where they have been living (either in the hills or lowland) and what they have been eating.

In France a highly prized young lamb from the salt marshes is called *pré-salé* (salt-marsh) lamb. A similar meat comes from the Romney marshes in southern England.

Salt-marsh Lamb

The subtle flavour and texture of salt-marsh lamb is derived from the herbal grasses that grow around the coastal marshes on which the sheep graze. The marshes or 'sea meadows' are abundant with samphire, sea lavender and thrift, which make the meat light and sweet.

The coastal estuaries of Britain are regularly washed by the sea, and the salty water kills a large number of parasites and bacteria that can be harmful to sheep. This reduces the need for antibiotics and chemicals.

L'agneau pré-salé, from the salt marshes of Normandy, has long been considered a delicacy by the French.

Pyrenean Milk-fed Lamb

Milk-fed lamb is reared by specialist Pyrenees farmers. The meat is usually available only to the restaurant trade, but may be sourced from online suppliers that specialize in artisan produce (see page 529).

The pale, exceptionally tender and sweet meat is a result of the lambs having only ever suckled on their mother's milk. The unweaned lambs are brought down from the mountains and slaughtered when aged 45–48 days old.

As the lambs are slaughtered so early, the remaining ewes' milk is used to make local cheese. Given that the grazing pastures are high up in the mountains, the ewes' diet is completely natural and of a high quality, and this is reflected in the milk and resulting delicate flavour of the cheese.

Hanging Lamb

Lamb does not benefit from as long a hanging time as beef; 3–7 days is long enough. Much of the lamb from New Zealand is vacuum-packed before being shipped around the world, either fresh or frozen.

Lamb that is chilled too quickly can suffer from 'cold-shortening', which causes the muscle to shrink and tighten, resulting in tough meat. The cost of the meat should reflect the quality, but the best way to ensure it is good is to buy from a reputable supplier.

Lamb from the UK is highly sought after and generally more expensive than New Zealand lamb. New Zealand lamb is imported in three qualities, which will be reflected in the price.

Choosing Lamb

- Lamb should be brownish-pink, but not bloody. The colour of the meat varies with the age and breed of the lamb (see The Colour of Meat page 3).
- Young lamb will be pinker than older lamb, which will be more red in colour.
- The meat should be fine grained and not hard.
- The fat should be creamy white and not oily.

- Look for a joint that is meaty and short rather than long and thin.
- Avoid lamb that looks slimy, grey or has blood spots.
- The pink membrane on the outside of the fat, called the bark or fell, should be pliable, not hard and wrinkled.
- The bones should be white and moist-looking.

Choosing Mutton

- Mutton will be dark in colour, similar to beef, but with a brownish tinge.
- The fat and bones should be white.
- It should not be bloody.
- It will have a 'sheepy' odour.

Storing Lamb

Lamb should be stored in the same way as beef (see page 31).

Cuts of Lamb

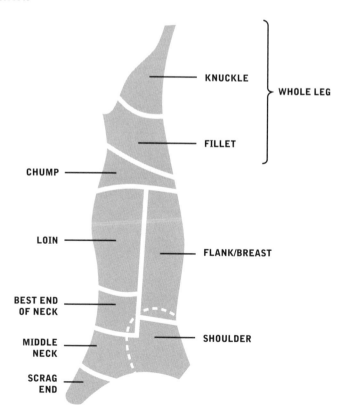

KNUCKLE

WHOLE LEG

FILLET

CHUMP

LOIN

FLANK/BREAST

BEST END OF NECK

MIDDLE NECK

SHOULDER

SCRAG END

Cut	Recommended Cooking Methods	Recipe Reference
Chump/Chops	Braising	Leg of Lamb Braised with Garlic and Baby Vegetables (page 147)
	Grilling	see Grilled Steak (page 49)
	Frying	see Fried Steak (page 49)
Collops	Grilling	see Grilled Steak (page 49)
	Frying	see Fried Steak (page 49)
Cutlets/Noisettes	Frying	Lamb Noisettes with Onion and Mint Purée (page 160)
Fillet end of leg/ Lamb steaks	Grilling	Lamb Steak à la Catalane with Lentils (page 162)
	Frying	see Fried Steak (page 49)
Knuckle	Braising	Lamb Shanks with Italian Mushroom Sauce (page 167)
	Stewing	Lamb Daube (page 144)
Leg	Roasting	Roast Leg of Lamb (page 144)
	Braising	Leg of Lamb Braised with Garlic and Baby Vegetables (page 147)
	Stewing	Lamb Daube (page 169)
	Barbecuing/Grilling	Butterflied Leg of Lamb (page 148)
Loin, whole	Roasting	Rack of Lamb (page 156)
Loin chops/ Cutlets	Grilling	see Grilled Steak (page 49)
	Frying	see Fried Steak (page 49)
Rack	Roasting	Rack of Lamb with Mustard and Breadcrumbs (page 156) Crown Roast of Lamb with Couscous and Apricot Stuffing (page 155) Guard of Honour (page 142)
Saddle	Roasting	Roast Saddle of Lamb (page 152)
Scrag and Middle neck	Stewing	Lamb Daube (page 169)
Shoulder	Roasting	Shoulder of Lamb 'en Ballon' Stuffed with Feta (page 151)
	Stewing	Lamb Daube (page 169)

Methods of Cooking Lamb

Roasting

The best lamb cuts for roasting are:

- **Leg**
- **Loin**
- **Rack of lamb**, cut from between the middle neck and loin.
- **Shoulder**, from the foreleg cut. Shoulder is cheaper than other roasting joints, such as leg, as it contains a higher proportion of fat and is more difficult to carve on the bone.
- **Saddle** consists of both loins of lamb, left attached at the backbone. It is cut from the best end to the end of the loins and includes the kidneys. A saddle weighs 2–4.5 kg and feeds approximately 6–8 people.

To prepare lamb for roasting remove the pink membrane (bark) if present and cut away any inspection stamps.

Lamb is roasted in the same way as beef. For roasting times, see the Beef Roasting Table (page 33). If lamb without a trace of pinkness is desired, allow an extra 20 minutes after the calculated time is up.

Grilling and Frying

The best cuts of lamb for grilling and frying are:

- **Best end cutlets**
- **Loin chops**
- **Chump chops**
- **Steaks from fillet end of leg**

Braising

The best cuts of lamb for braising are:

- **Chump**
- **Chops**
- **Loin**
- **Leg**
- **Shoulder**
- **Knuckle**

Stewing

Best cuts of lamb for stewing are:

- **Knuckle**
- **Scrag and middle neck**
- **Leg**
- **Shoulder**

Lamb stews are mostly made with middle neck of lamb from between the shoulders, and the scrag end. These cuts have large proportions of connective tissue, fat and bone, and must be trimmed well.

Cooking Minced Lamb

The best lamb cuts for making mince are:

- **Scrag**
- **Middle neck**
- **Breast**

Cooked lamb left over from a roast is also very good when minced and used to make hot dishes such as traditional shepherd's pie. However, minced beef can be used instead (see page 80).

Preparing Lamb

Open-boning a Leg of Lamb

1 Cut neatly along the bones on the non-fleshy side of the leg from the tapered bony knuckle end to the hip joint at the fillet end. (a)
2 Gradually work out the bones by cutting and scraping away the meat. (b)

Cutting along the bone (a)

Removing the bone (b)

Points to Remember about Open-boning

- Use a boning knife designed specifically for the purpose: it has a long, rigid blade and pointed tip.
- Hold the knife firmly like a dagger, with the tip pointing down.
- Always cut away from the hands and body to prevent injury if the knife slips.
- Keep the knife as sharp as possible. Blunt knives need more pressure to wield and are therefore more inclined to slip.

Open-boning a Shoulder of Lamb

As shoulder joints are difficult to carve, they are often open-boned, then rolled or stuffed and tied to look like a balloon (*ballon*).

1 Position the joint with the wide blade bone sideways on to you. (a)
2 Insert the tip of the knife into the shoulder just above and below the blade bone. Scrape the meat away from the flat bone. (b)
3 Scrape around the ridge of the blade bone, taking care not to cut through the bark. (c) Continue to scrape the meat from the bone.
4 Starting from the leg end of the bone, cut through the bark where it is attached to the bone on the underside of the shoulder. Scrape the meat from the bone until the 'elbow' is reached. (d) The bone should now be released from the meat. Remove it by pulling from the blade end.

Bone position in shoulder joint (a)

Scraping around the blade bone (b)

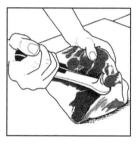

Working around the ridge (c)

Removing the bone beyond the 'elbow' by scraping away the connective tissues and meat (d)

Tunnel-boning a Leg of Lamb

Both leg and shoulder of lamb can be tunnel-boned. Tunnel-boning means to remove the bone without opening out the meat. It is rather more difficult than open-boning, but it is a useful method as a stuffing can be inserted where the bone was removed so that the meat can be easily carved across its width.

1 Loosen the bark and any flesh from the tapered bony knuckle end of the leg.
2 Inserting the knife between the loosened bark and the bone, scrape and cut the flesh away from the bone as far up the knuckle as possible, being careful not to pierce the surface of the meat.
3 Turn the leg around and insert the knife between the fillet end and the bone. Again, loosen the meat slowly and carefully away from the bone with a combination of scraping and cutting, keeping the knife as close to the bone as possible and making every effort to keep the meat intact. Fold the loosened meat down and away from the bone as you go so that you can see the course the three bones take through the meat, but being especially careful at each joint, until you meet the loosened flesh at the knuckle end.
4 Pull the three bones out of the joint. Take care to remove any glands from inside the meat. These look like translucent grey nodules about the size of a hazelnut.
5 The meat can then be stuffed and sewn at each end before roasting.

Making a Butterfly Joint

Butterfly-boning is an open-boning technique used to flatten a thick piece of meat, usually the leg, to an even thickness so it can be grilled or barbecued.

1 Bone the joint as described in Open-boning a Leg of Lamb on page 136, then open out the meat so it resembles a pair of butterfly wings.
2 Remove the grey gland, which will be about the size of a hazelnut. (a)
3 Slash the thicker section of meat to allow heat to penetrate inside so the joint will cook evenly. (b)

Removing the gland (a)

Slashing the meat (b)

Stuffing a Boned Shoulder of Lamb

1　To stuff a boned shoulder, season the joint inside with salt and pepper and spoon in the stuffing. (a)
2　Tie the joint with string to shape into a round (*ballon*). To do this, turn the shoulder over, skin-side up. Tie the end of a 3-metre piece of string firmly around the shoulder, making a knot in the middle at the top. (b) Take the string around again, but this time at right angles to the first line, again tying at the first knot.
3　Continue this tying process until the ballon is trussed about 8 times. (c) The indentations made by the string should resemble the grooves in a melon or the lines between the segments of a beach ball. Tuck in any loose flaps of meat or bark.

Stuffing the shoulder (a)　　　Making the first tie (b)　　　The tied balloon shape (c)

Preparing a Saddle of Lamb

1　Trim off any excess fat from underneath the saddle.
2　Remove the bark by lifting at one corner with a sharp knife and hold it tightly in a tea towel to prevent it slipping out of your grip. Give a sharp tug and pull off all the bark in one piece. (a)
3　Trim away all but 3 cm of the two flaps. Trim off any very large pieces of the fat from the edges of the saddle, but leave the back fat. Tuck the flaps under the saddle.
4　Cut out the kidneys but keep them (they can be brushed with butter and attached to the end of the saddle with wooden skewers 30 minutes before the end of the roasting time).
5　Using a sharp knife, score the back fat all over in a fine criss-cross pattern. (b)
6　The pelvic or aitchbone, protruding slightly from one end of the saddle, can be removed if you wish. If left in place, it can be covered with a ham frill (see page 225) when the saddle is served.

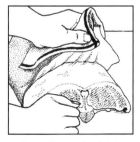
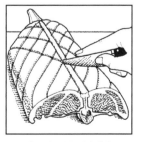

Removing the bark (a)　　　Scoring the fat (b)

Preparing a Rack of Lamb

Rack of lamb, also known as best end of neck, is extremely tender and sweet, and is best roasted either on the bone or boned and rolled. Before a whole best end is roasted, both the outer bark and chine bone are removed, and the ends of the bones are exposed for presentation by trimming off the fat and meat. A best end can be prepared with an English trim, in which the bones are cleaned 3 cm from the ends, or with the French trim, in which the bones are exposed down almost to the 'eye' of the meat.

An English-trimmed best end of neck can be roasted whole, separated into cutlets by cutting between the bones and grilled or fried, or used to make a crown roast or a guard of honour (see page 142).

1 To trim the rack: lift a corner of the bark from the neck end with a small knife, hold it firmly, using a cloth to get a good grip, and peel it off. (a)
2 Chine the lamb if the butcher has not already done so. This involves sawing carefully through the rib bones just where they meet the chine bone (spine). Take care not to saw into the eye of the meat. Now, using a sharp knife, remove the chine bone completely. (b)
3 Remove the half-moon-shaped piece of flexible cartilage found buried between the layers of fat and meat at the thinner end of the best end. This is the tip of the shoulder blade. It is simple to work out with the knife and your fingers. (c)
4 Remove the rubbery, cream-coloured tendon, known as the 'paddywack', found between the fat and meat at the edge of the eye. (d)
5 Chop off the cutlet bones so that the length of the remaining bones is not more than twice the length of the eye of the meat.
6 Make a vertical cut through the fat (e) to the rib bones, just below the line of the meat for a French trim, or 3 cm from the tips of the bones for an English trim.
7 Remove the fat below this line to expose the rib bones. (f) Now cut away the meat between the bones down to the horizontal line to produce a crenellated effect.
8 Using a small sharp knife, scrape the exposed bones clean to remove all traces of meat, fat and connective tissue. (g) (Any remaining tissue on the bones will cause them to blacken when the rack is roasted.)
9 Now trim the fat covering the eye of the meat until it is no more than 2 mm thick, taking care not to cut into the meat. (h)

Preparing a rack of lamb

Skinning the rack of lamb (a)

Removing the chine bone (b)

Removing the shoulder blade (c)

Removing the paddywack (d)

Cutting through the fat (e)

Exposing the bones (f)

Scraping the bones (g)

Trimming the fat (h)

Preparing French-trimmed Cutlets

French-trimmed best end cutlets are cut from the skinned, chined and trimmed rack of lamb following the instructions opposite.

To cut the cutlets from the prepared rack:

1 If thin, small cutlets are required, cut between each pair of bones as evenly as possible, splitting the rack into 6–7 small cutlets.
2 If fattier cutlets are required, carefully ease out every other rib bone. Then cut between the remaining bones into thick cutlets.
3 Now trim the fat from the thick end of each cutlet. Cutlets are suitable for grilling and frying, and 2–3 cutlets should be served per person.

Preparing a Crown Roast of Lamb

A crown roast of lamb is assembled using two or three large best ends. Once the best ends are trimmed (see page 141):

1   Bend each best end into a semi-circle, with the fatty side of the ribs inside. To facilitate this it might be necessary to cut through the sinew between each pair of cutlets from the thick end to a depth of about 3 cm. Take care not to cut into the eye of the meat.
2   Sew the ends of the racks together to make a circle, with the meaty part forming the base of the crown.
3   Tie a piece of string around the 'waist' of the crown.
4   Stuff the crown: a crown roast is traditionally stuffed with a non-meat stuffing.
5   Roast as recipe on page 155.
6   Remove the string. To carve, cut down between each pair of bones.

Preparing a crown roast

Preparing a Guard of Honour

English-trim two best end racks of lamb as described on pages 140–1.

1   Hold the two best ends, one in each hand, facing each other on a board, with the meaty part of the racks on the board, and the fatty sides on the outside.
2   Jiggle them so that the rib bones interlock and cross at the top.
3   Sew or tie the bases together at intervals.
4   Stuff the arch, if required.
5   Roast as for rack of lamb, above.
6   Remove the string. Carve by slicing between each pair of bones.

Preparing a guard of honour

Preparing Noisettes of Lamb

Noisettes are boneless cutlets tied into a neat round shape with string. They are made from the loin or best end and are suitable for grilling or frying (see page 160).

1 Remove the bark from the meat (see Preparing a Rack of Lamb, pages 140–1).
2 Remove the chine bone, then all the rib bones, easing them out with a short, sharp knife. (a)
3 Remove the half-moon-shaped piece of flexible cartilage found buried between the layers of fat and meat at the thinner end of the best end.
4 Remove the 'paddywack', the tendon found between the fat and the meat at the edge of the eye.
5 Trim off any excess fat from the meat, leaving a very thin layer of fat. Roll it up tightly, starting at the thick meaty side and working towards the thin flap.
6 Tie the roll neatly with separate pieces of string at 4 cm intervals.
7 Trim any ragged ends of the roll to neaten them.
8 Now slice the roll into pieces, cutting accurately between each pair of pieces of string. (b)
9 The average seven-bone best end will give 4–6 noisettes.
10 Remove the string from the noisettes after cooking.

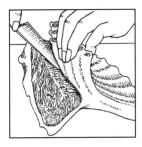

Removing the rib bones (a)

Cutting noisettes of lamb (b)

Roast Leg of Lamb

An average-sized leg of lamb weighs between 1.35–2.5 kg and is relatively lean and easy to carve. It is also available boned and rolled.

SERVES 6–8

1 × 1.8 kg leg of lamb
3 large sprigs of fresh rosemary
200 ml red wine
salt and freshly ground black pepper

For the gravy
2 tablespoons plain flour

300 ml Brown Stock, made with lamb bones
(see page 452)
1 teaspoon redcurrant jelly

To serve
Mint Sauce (see below)

1 Heat the oven to 200°C/400°F/gas mark 6.
2 Weigh the joint and calculate the cooking time (see page 33). Wipe the meat, season with salt and pepper and place in a roasting pan with the sprigs of rosemary on top.
3 Roast in the oven for the calculated cooking time. Thirty minutes before the end of cooking, pour the wine over the lamb.
4 When the lamb is cooked, remove the joint from the oven and place it on a warmed serving dish.
5 To make the gravy, carefully pour off all but 2 tablespoons of fat from the roasting pan. Reserve the meat juices.
6 Add the flour to the fat remaining in the pan and, using a wire whisk or wooden spoon, stir it over a low heat until a deep brown. Remove from the heat and stir in the stock, meat juices and redcurrant jelly. Return to the heat, stirring all the time, and simmer for 2 minutes.
7 Check the seasoning and strain into a warmed gravy boat.
8 Carve the leg of lamb as shown opposite.

MINT SAUCE

1 large handful of fresh mint
2 tablespoons caster sugar

2 tablespoons hot water
2 tablespoons wine vinegar

1 Wash the mint and shake it dry. Remove the stalks and chop the leaves finely. Place in a bowl with the sugar.
2 Pour on the hot water and leave for 5 minutes to dissolve the sugar. Add the vinegar and leave to soak for 1–2 hours.

Legs of lamb, pork, bacon (gammon or ham), veal and venison are carved similarly. Put the leg, meaty-side up, on a chopping board or serving plate and grasp the knuckle bone with one hand, or pierce the joint firmly with a carving fork. Cut a small shallow 'v'. Carve slices of meat from both sides of the 'v', then turn the leg over and take horizontal slices from the other side.

Carving a leg of lamb by cutting slices of meat from both sides of the 'v'

Carving a leg of lamb by cutting diagonally from the knuckle end

Wine: Cabernet Sauvignon-based wines from Bordeaux, California, Australia, South Africa or South America

Gigot of Lamb with Stuffed Artichoke Hearts

If you wish, you can serve the artichoke leaves with a vinaigrette dressing as a first course.

SERVES 4–5

1 small leg of lamb
1 clove of garlic, cut into slivers (optional)
large pinch of fresh rosemary leaves
2 teaspoons dripping
8 globe artichokes or 8 canned artichoke hearts
225 g celeriac
110 g Mashed Potatoes (see page 491)
30 g butter
2 teaspoons plain flour

150 ml Brown Stock, made with lamb bones
  (see page 452)
1 teaspoon redcurrant jelly
salt and freshly ground black pepper
1 small bunch of watercress, to garnish

To serve
Vinaigrette (optional, see page 474)

1 Heat the oven to 200°C/400°F/gas mark 6.
2 Wipe the lamb. Season with salt and pepper. If liked, spike thin slivers of garlic into the meat near the bone. Sprinkle with rosemary. Weigh the lamb and calculate the cooking time (15 minutes per 450 g and 15 minutes over).
3 Heat the dripping in a roasting pan, add the lamb, baste well and put in the hot oven for the calculated time.
4 To prepare the artichokes, wash them and cook in a pan of boiling salted water for about 45 minutes, or until the leaves will pull away easily from the whole. Peel away all the leaves, keeping them to serve with a vinaigrette dressing as a first course. Using a teaspoon, scrape out the prickly choke of each artichoke, then trim the base with a sharp knife so that it will stand steady.
5 While the artichokes are cooking, peel the celeriac and boil in salted water until quite tender. Drain well. Push the flesh through a sieve. Beat in the mashed potato, half the butter, and salt and pepper to taste.
6 Pile this mixture into the artichoke bottoms. Brush with the remaining butter and place on a greased baking sheet.
7 When the lamb is tender, remove from the oven. Turn the heat down to 150°C/300°F/gas mark 2 and put the artichokes into the oven to warm as it is cooling down.
8 Place the lamb on a warm serving dish.
9 Carefully pour off all but 1 tablespoon of fat from the roasting pan while retaining any meat juices.
10 Add the flour to the remaining liquid in the pan and, using a wire whisk or wooden spoon, stir it over a gentle heat until a delicate brown. Remove from the heat and stir in the stock and redcurrant jelly. Return to the heat, stirring all the time, and simmer for 2 minutes.
11 Season with salt and pepper as necessary, then strain into a warm gravy boat. Surround the lamb with the artichokes and garnish with watercress.

Wine: Bordeaux, Rioja or Coonawarra Cabernet Sauvignon from Australia

Marrow on Toast with French Radish Salad, page 129.

Pan-fried Sweetbreads on Toasted Brioche with Sour Lemon Glaze, page 123.

Braised Lamb Shanks with Flageolet Beans, page 168.

Roast Leg of Lamb, page 144.

Cutting a 'v' slice.

Taking slices from the sides of the 'v'.

Preparing a rack of lamb

1 Removing the chine bone.

2 Removing the bark and excess fat.

3 Cutting through the fat to the rib bones.

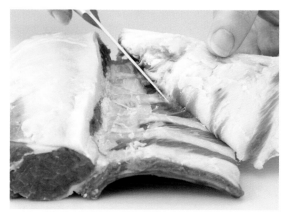

4 Removing the fat to expose the rib bones.

5 Scraping the bones clean.

6 Trimming the fat from the meat.

Rack of Lamb with Mustard and Breadcrumbs, page 156.

Mu-shu Pork on Little Gem Leaves, page 216.

Leg of Lamb Braised with Garlic and Baby Vegetables

Braising the lamb will produce well-done, meltingly tender meat.

SERVES 6

1 × 2 kg leg of lamb
50 g butter
2 cloves of garlic, crushed
300 ml dry white wine
300 ml Brown Stock (see page 452)
675 g small new potatoes
340 g baby carrots, scraped

200 g defrosted or fresh petits pois
2 tablespoons butter, softened
2 tablespoons plain flour
4 tablespoons double cream
salt and freshly ground black pepper
2 tablespoons chopped mint, to garnish

1 Trim the lamb of all membrane and fat. Season with salt and pepper.
2 Mix together the 50 g butter and garlic and spread all over the lamb. Leave to stand for 30 minutes.
3 Heat the oven to 180°C/350°F/gas mark 4.
4 Place a flameproof casserole dish over a medium heat and brown the lamb on all sides.
5 Add the wine and stock and bring to the boil.
6 Add the potatoes and cover with a lid. Cook in the oven for 1½ hours, then add the carrots.
7 After a further 30 minutes add the peas.
8 When the vegetables are cooked, transfer the lamb and vegetables to a large warmed platter and cover with foil to keep warm.
9 Put the casserole dish over direct heat and bring the juices to the boil.
10 Mix together the softened butter and flour and whisk bit by bit into the sauce. Boil for 2 minutes. Adjust to a coating consistency by boiling further or by adding water.
11 Pass the sauce through a sieve. Stir in the cream, then pour over the lamb and vegetables. Sprinkle with the mint and serve.

Wine: Crisp, young red, such as Chinon, St Nicolas de Bourgueil, Minervois or Barbera d'Alba

Butterflied Leg of Lamb

SERVES 6–8

1 × 2.7 kg leg of lamb, butterfly-boned
  (see page 138)

2 tablespoons soy sauce

½ onion, sliced

4 sprigs of fresh thyme

2 bay leaves

3 cloves of garlic, sliced

2 tablespoons good-quality olive oil

salt and freshly ground black pepper

1 small bunch of watercress, to garnish

1 Weigh the boned leg of lamb and calculate the cooking time at 8 minutes per 450 g plus 20 minutes.

2 Open the leg of lamb and place it fat-side down on a large plate. Sprinkle over the soy sauce, onion, thyme, bay leaves, garlic, oil and freshly ground pepper. Fold the 3 'butterfly' ends inwards to encase the flavourings, then cover and leave to marinate overnight in the refrigerator.

3 Heat the oven to 230°C/450°F/gas mark 8.

4 Open out the boned leg and lay it flesh-side down in a roasting pan. Sprinkle the fatty side fairly liberally with salt and roast in the oven for 20 minutes. Turn the oven down to 200°C/400°F/gas mark 6 and roast for a further 8 minutes per 450 g. For example, 1.8 kg leg (boned weight) will require about 50 minutes' cooking.

5 If you prefer, heat the barbecue or grill until very hot (see page 18). Grill the meat fat-side down first, then turn over and grill the other side. The time for each side will depend on the thickness of the meat (see Grilled Steak, page 49). To test for doneness see page 20. Leave to rest for 10 minutes.

6 Carve the lamb by slicing thinly across the grain. Garnish with watercress to serve.

Wine: Médoc – Cru Classé or Cru Bourgeois

Roast Butterflied Leg of Lamb with Three Beans

SERVES 6

1 leg of lamb, butterfly-boned (see page 138)

1 × 400 g can borlotti beans, rinsed and drained

1 × 400 g jar large butter beans, rinsed and
  drained

1 heaped tablespoon sun-dried tomato paste

1 tablespoon finely chopped thyme leaves

200 ml Brown Stock, made with lamb bones
  (see page 452)

15 g unsalted butter

140 g French beans, topped and tailed

1 tablespoon lemon juice

salt and freshly ground black pepper

1 large bunch of watercress, to garnish

1 Heat the oven to 220°C/425°F/gas mark 7.

2 Season the lamb with salt and pepper on both sides, and place fat-side up on a wire rack set over a roasting pan. Roast for 45 minutes.

3 Reduce the heat to 200°C/400°F/gas mark 6. Remove the lamb from the roasting pan and set aside. Spoon the borlotti beans and butter beans into the roasting pan, add the sun-dried tomato paste, thyme, stock and butter and mix with the lamb juices.

4 Replace the lamb on the rack over the beans and return to the oven for a further 30–35 minutes, or until the lamb is crisp and brown on the outside and pink and juicy in the middle.

5 Remove the lamb from the oven and leave to rest for 10 minutes.

6 Bring a large pan of salted water to the boil and cook the French beans for 2 minutes. Drain and add to the roasting pan. Mix all of the beans together, stir in the lemon juice and season with salt and pepper. Transfer to a warmed serving plate.

7 Carve the lamb thickly and arrange in overlapping slices on top of the beans. Garnish with watercress and serve immediately.

Wine: Médoc – Cru Classé or Cru Bourgeois

Salt-marsh Lamb with Samphire Salad

Samphire is the collective name for various sea vegetables found on coastal cliffs and marshlands. It includes rock samphire, golden samphire and marsh samphire. The name is derived from Sampierre, a corruption of the French words Saint Pierre (St Peter), the patron saint of fishermen. Sometimes referred to as 'poor man's asparagus', samphire is very fleshy and succulent and has a distinctive 'ozone' flavour. It can be eaten raw, blanched or steamed, and is also very good pickled. Fishmongers sell samphire when in season – between May and June. There is an affinity between salt-marsh lamb and samphire as both of them come from the same region, and the samphire has formed part of the sheep's natural grazing pasture.

SERVES 6–8

1 leg of salt-marsh lamb, butterfly-boned
  (see page 138)
1 tablespoon olive oil
flaky sea salt and freshly ground black pepper

For the salad

3 tablespoons olive oil
juice of 1 lemon
1 small shallot, very finely chopped
500 g rock samphire, washed and trimmed of woody ends

1 Heat the oven to 220°C/425°F/gas mark 7.

2 Flatten out the lamb completely and place it fat-side up in a roasting pan. Rub the fat with the oil and season with plenty of flaky sea salt and black pepper. Place on the top shelf of the oven and roast for 30 minutes.

3 Reduce the heat to 150°C/300°F/gas mark 2 and continue to cook for a further 15 minutes. The lamb should be very pink. Turn off the oven and allow the meat to rest in the warm oven while you make the salad.

4 Put the oil and lemon juice into a small bowl, add the shallot and season with salt and pepper.

5 Bring a large pan of salted water to the boil and plunge in the samphire. Drain immediately.

6 Pour the dressing over the warm samphire and toss together. Pile into a serving dish.

7 Slice the lamb thickly and arrange it on top of the samphire. Pour the pan juices over the meat and serve.

Wine: Pauillac from Bordeaux

Slow-roast Lamb Shoulder with Rosemary

SERVES 6

1 × 1.7 kg lamb shoulder

2 onions, thickly sliced

3 cloves of garlic, bruised

3 sprigs of rosemary

300 ml red wine

salt and freshly ground black pepper

For the sauce

20 g plain flour

300 ml Brown Stock (see page 452)

1 Heat the oven to 150°C/300°F/gas mark 2.

2 Remove any bark and stamps from the lamb by paring thinly with a sharp knife. Season with salt and pepper.

3 Place the onions in a flameproof roasting pan and top with the garlic, rosemary and lamb.

4 Pour the wine around the lamb, then cover the entire roasting pan with foil.

5 Place in the oven for 2 hours.

6 Remove the lamb from the oven and discard the foil. Increase the oven temperature to 190°C/375°F/gas mark 5.

7 Place the lamb in a second roasting pan and return it to the oven, uncovered, for a further 45–60 minutes to brown.

8 Meanwhile, make the sauce. Place the first roasting pan and its contents over a medium heat. Cook, stirring, until the juices have evaporated and the onions are starting to fry.

9 Stir in the flour and cook for a further 2 minutes. Gradually stir in the stock. Bring to the boil, then lower the heat so that the sauce just simmers. Cook for 5 minutes. The sauce should be of a light coating consistency (like single cream). Add water if it is too thick, or continue to simmer if it is too thin.

10 Sieve into a small saucepan and keep warm. Serve in a warmed gravy boat.

11 When the lamb is browned place it on a warmed platter to rest for about 10 minutes before carving.

Carving a shoulder of lamb

Cut into thick slices from the centre to the edge until the bone is exposed along one side. Cut small horizontal slices from the top and bottom of the bone.

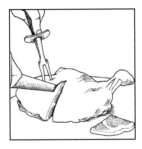

Wine: Malbec

Shoulder of Lamb 'en Ballon' Stuffed with Feta

Tying the boned and stuffed joint in the way required here makes for a uniform shape. The meat cooks evenly and it is easy to carve.

SERVES 6

1 × 1.8 kg boned whole shoulder of lamb
  (see page 137)
85 ml red wine
20 g plain flour

For the stuffing

225 g feta cheese, cut into 1 cm cubes
2 teaspoons green peppercorns, rinsed

1 shallot, finely chopped
85 g fresh white breadcrumbs
2 tablespoons thinly sliced sun-dried tomatoes
1 tablespoon fresh thyme leaves
1 egg, beaten
salt and freshly ground black pepper
sprigs of watercress, to garnish

1 Heat the oven to 200°C/400°F/gas mark 6.

2 Trim the lamb of excess fat, leaving a thin layer on the outside to keep the meat moist while cooking.

3 Mix together the stuffing ingredients, beat lightly and season carefully with salt and pepper (the feta can be very salty).

4 Season the inside of the lamb and spread with the stuffing. If the shoulder has been tunnel-boned, push the stuffing into the lamb.

5 Using thin string, tie the lamb into a balloon shape (see page 139).

6 Weigh the lamb and calculate the cooking time. For pink lamb, allow 20 minutes per 450 g plus 20 minutes. For well-done lamb, cook for a further 30 minutes.

7 Put the lamb into a roasting pan and roast in the oven for the calculated time.

8 Thirty minutes before the lamb is ready, pour the wine over the joint.

9 When the lamb is cooked, remove it from the oven and place in a warm place to rest for 10 minutes.

10 Pour off all but 1 tablespoon of fat from the roasting pan, place the pan on the hob and stir in the flour. Cook, stirring, for 1 minute. Add some water and bring to the boil, then simmer for 5 minutes.

11 Just before serving, remove the string from the lamb. Carve by cutting wedges from the centre to the edge, like a cake.

12 Garnish with small sprigs of watercress. Serve with the gravy.

Wine: Dry red from southern Italy or Greece – Aglianico or Naoussa

Roast Saddle of Lamb

SERVES 6–8

1 saddle of lamb
1 clove of garlic, cut into slivers (optional)
sprigs of fresh rosemary
dripping or oil
salt and freshly ground black pepper

For the gravy

1 tablespoon flour
425 ml Brown Stock, made with lamb bones
  (see page 452)

1 Heat the oven to 200°C/400°F/gas mark 6.
2 Prepare the saddle of lamb as described on page 143. If desired, stick a few slivers of garlic into the saddle near the bone. Season with salt and pepper and a scattering of rosemary. Weigh the joint and calculate the cooking time (see page 33). The saddle cooks in less time than shoulder or leg of lamb because of its shallow shape and large proportion of bone, which acts as an efficient heat conductor.
3 Heat 2 tablespoons of dripping in a roasting pan. When it is hot, add the saddle of lamb, tucking the flaps underneath and basting well.
4 Roast for the calculated time. If the saddle is very large, it should be covered with dampened greaseproof paper halfway through roasting to prevent it from becoming too brown.
5 Lift the meat on to a warmed serving platter. Pour away all but 2 tablespoons of fat from the pan while retaining the juices. Stir the flour into the pan to absorb the fat. Cook over the heat, stirring, until russet brown. Add the stock slowly to make a smooth sauce. Stir until boiling, taking care to scrape up any sediment stuck to the bottom of the pan. Simmer for 2 minutes, then season to taste with salt and pepper.
6 Carve the saddle as described below.

Carving a saddle of lamb

The chump end of the saddle is cut in thin slices across the grain of the meat, at right angles to the backbone. But the main part of the saddle, lying either side of the backbone, is cut in thin strips or narrow slices down the length of the saddle. This can be done on the bone, but it is easier if you lift off the whole side of the saddle in one piece and cut into long slices.

Redcurrant-glazed Roast Loin of Lamb Stuffed with Kidneys and Herbs

SERVES 4

50 g flat leaf parsley

1 small bunch of chives

6 large sage leaves

30 g pine nuts, lightly toasted

1 small eating apple, peeled, cored and
  roughly chopped

1 teaspoon Dijon mustard

finely grated zest of 1 small lemon

juice of ½ a lemon

1 teaspoon extra virgin lemon olive oil

900 g loin of lamb, boned

3 lamb's kidneys, skinned and inner cores removed

75 ml red wine

150 ml Brown Stock, made with lamb bones
  (see page 452)

2 tablespoons redcurrant jelly

20 g unsalted butter, cut into small cubes and
  chilled

salt and freshly ground black pepper

1 bunch of watercress, to garnish

1 Heat the oven to 230°C/450°F/gas mark 8.

2 Chop the herbs roughly and place in the small bowl of a food processor. Add the pine nuts, apple, mustard, lemon zest and juice and the oil, and process until fairly smooth. Season with salt and pepper.

3 Lay the meat on a flat surface, fat-side down and trim off any excess fat. Season well with salt and pepper. Spread the herb paste down the centre of the meat.

4 Lay the kidneys on top of the paste and season with a little more salt and pepper. Wrap the lamb around the kidneys and tie neatly with string at intervals along the length of the meat.

5 Place the lamb in a roasting pan and put into the middle of the oven for 15 minutes, then reduce the heat to 200°C/400°F/gas mark 6. Pour the wine and stock into the roasting pan and return to the oven for 25 minutes.

6 Place the redcurrant jelly in a small saucepan and heat very gently until melted. Spread the warm jelly over the lamb and cook for a further 10 minutes.

7 Remove the lamb from the roasting pan and allow to rest in a warm place.

8 Skim the fat from the juices in the roasting pan and place the roasting pan over a direct heat. Bring to the boil, scraping the bottom of the pan to release the sediment. Simmer for 5 minutes, or until the sauce has reduced by half, then beat in the cold butter. Check the seasoning.

9 Slice the meat thickly and arrange on a warmed serving plate. Pour over the sauce and garnish with watercress.

Wine: Sweeter style of Cabernet Sauvignon from Margaret River (Western Australia), Chile or California

Spiced Loin of Lamb

SERVES 4

2 × 6–7 bone racks of lamb

2 tablespoons vegetable oil

1 tablespoon flour

300 ml Brown Stock, made with lamb bones
  (see page 452)

1 teaspoon black peppercorns

½ teaspoon chilli flakes

1 teaspoon mild/sweet chilli powder

2 teaspoons flaky sea salt

2 teaspoons ground cinnamon

For the spice rub

1 tablespoon fennel seeds

1 teaspoon coriander seeds

To serve

Lemon Buttered Couscous (see page 495)

1 Start by making the rub. Toast the fennel, coriander and peppercorns in a small pan over a medium heat. As soon as the fennel turns light brown, add the chilli flakes (make sure your extractor fan is on). Toss quickly, then turn on to a plate to cool. Put in a grinder or blender with the chilli powder, salt and cinnamon and grind to a fine powder. Store in a glass jar.

2 Remove the eye of the meat from the bones or ask your butcher to do this.

3 Season the meat with 3 tablespoons of the spice rub and set aside for 1 hour, or store overnight in the refrigerator.

4 Heat the oven to 200°C/400°F/gas mark 6.

5 Scrape any excess rub from the meat. Heat the oil in a frying pan and brown the meat on all sides. (The recipe can be made in advance up to this point.)

6 Place the meat in a roasting pan and roast until it feels slightly firm to the touch. If the meat was at room temperature, this will be in 12–15 minutes. If it has been chilled after browning, it will take about 20 minutes.

7 Remove the meat from the oven and place on a chopping board. Allow to stand for 10–15 minutes.

8 In the meantime, make the sauce by stirring the flour into the pan that the meat was browned in, adding a bit more oil if the pan is dry. Cook over a medium heat until brown. Whisk in the stock and bring to the boil to make a thin sauce.

9 Carve the meat into thin slices and serve with the couscous.

Wine: Merlot-based wine from Saint-Emilion, Pomerol, South Africa or California

Crown Roast of Lamb with Couscous and Apricot Stuffing

SERVES 4–6

1 crown roast or 2 × 7-bone matching
  racks of lamb, chined
50 g butter
1 large sprig of fresh rosemary, bruised
1 bunch of watercress

50 g dried apricots, chopped
½ bunch of spring onions, finely chopped
2 tablespoons chopped fresh parsley
50 g pine nuts, toasted
salt and freshly ground black pepper

For the stuffing

300 ml Brown Stock, made with lamb bones
  (see page 452)
½ teaspoon saffron strands
170 g uncooked couscous
2 tablespoons olive oil

For the gravy

15 g plain flour
300 ml Brown Stock, made with lamb bones
  (see page 452)

1 If the butcher has not trimmed and tied the meat into a crown, follow the instructions on pages 140–2.

2 To make the stuffing, heat the chicken stock in a small saucepan with the saffron. Allow to stand for 10 minutes.

3 Place the coucous in a large heatproof bowl and pour over the warm stock. Using a fork, stir in the olive oil. Allow to stand until the couscous has absorbed the stock, about 10 minutes.

4 Stir in the apricots, spring onions, parsley and pine nuts. Season to taste with salt and freshly ground black pepper. Allow to cool completely.

5 Fill the centre of the crown roast with the cold stuffing. Weigh the lamb and calculate the cooking time according to the chart on page 33.

6 Heat the oven to 200°C/400°F/gas mark 6. Melt the butter in a roasting pan. Add the rosemary and put in the crown of lamb. Wrap the ends of the bones with wet brown paper, then with foil to prevent them from burning. It is easier to cover a few bones at a time than to cover the whole crown. Brush over the melted butter.

7 Roast the lamb for the calculated cooking time. Lift out the crown.

8 Pour off the contents of the roasting pan. Skim off 2 tablespoons fat and return to the pan. Stir in the flour, scraping up any sediment from the bottom of the pan. Cook over a medium heat until brown. Add the stock and stir until boiling. Simmer for 2 minutes. Season to taste with salt and pepper

9 Garnish the crown with sprigs of watercress in the centre. Hand the gravy separately in a warmed gravy boat.

Wine: Chilean or Australian Merlot

Rack of Lamb with Mustard and Breadcrumbs

SERVES 2

1 rack (best end) of lamb, chined and French-trimmed
(see pages 140–1)

2 teaspoons Dijon mustard

1 tablespoon fresh white breadcrumbs

1 tablespoon chopped mixed herbs, such as mint,
chives, parsley, thyme

2 teaspoons unsalted butter

salt and freshly ground black pepper

1 Trim off as much fat as possible from the meat.
2 Mix together the mustard, breadcrumbs, herbs, salt, pepper and butter. Press a thin layer of this mixture over the rounded side of the rack of lamb. Refrigerate for 30 minutes.
3 Heat the oven to 220°C/425°F/gas mark 7.
4 Place the lamb, crumbed-side up, in a roasting pan and roast for 25 minutes for a 7-bone rack, less for a smaller one.
5 To carve, cut down between the individual bones. Serve with the butter and juices from the pan poured over the top.

NOTE: If preparing an English-trimmed rack, double the quantity of topping.

Wine: Languedoc red from Pic Saint Loup/Minervois or a Ribera del Duero

Lamb Wrapped in Rosemary and Pancetta

SERVES 4

2 × 7-bone racks of lamb

12 slices of pancetta

3 tablespoons finely chopped rosemary

oil, for baking and sautéing

salt and freshly ground black pepper

For the sauce

bones and any trimmings from the lamb

1 onion, cut into eighths

1 small carrot

1 stick of celery

2 sprigs of rosemary

1 bay leaf

300 ml red wine

2 tablespoons oil, for the roux

2 tablespoons flour

1 teaspoon redcurrant jelly

1 Remove the eye of the meat from the bones, reserving the bones and trimmings for step 5. Season with salt and pepper, then roll in the chopped rosemary.
2 Place 2 large pieces of cling film side by side on the work surface. Arrange 6 slices of pancetta, slightly overlapping, on each sheet, then cover with another 2 sheets of cling film. Beat gently with a heavy-based saucepan to join the pancetta slices together.
3 Remove the top sheets of cling film, then place a piece of lamb on each area of pancetta. Roll up and chill to firm for at least 1 hour, or overnight.
4 Heat the oven to 200°C/400°F/gas mark 6.

5 To make the sauce, place the bones, trimmings, onion, carrot and celery in a roasting pan. Pour in a little oil and bake until brown, about 1 hour. Set aside and turn off the oven.

6 Place the bones, vegetables, rosemary and bay leaf in a saucepan and cover with 600 ml cold water and the wine. Bring to the boil and skim. Turn down the heat and leave to steam for 2–3 hours. Strain the stock, discarding the vegetables and bones.

7 Heat 2 tablespoons oil in a saucepan. Stir in the flour and cook until dark brown. Off the heat gradually add the stock, then return to the heat and cook until thickened. Stir in the redcurrant jelly, then sieve the sauce and keep warm.

8 Reheat the oven to 200°C/400°F/gas mark 6.

9 Heat 4 tablespoons oil in a sauté pan. Brown the pancetta-wrapped lamb all over, then place on a wire rack over a roasting pan. Bake in the oven for 10 minutes.

10 Leave to stand for 10 minutes, then slice each fillet into 6.

Wine: Dry red, such as Médoc, Saint-Emilion or Brunello di Montalcino

Roast Rack of Lamb with a Redcurrant Glaze and Hot Redcurrant Chutney

If using fresh redcurrants, use a fork to strip them off the stem. Top and tail them, pick over and wash before use. The chutney can be made a day or two ahead, then reheated before serving.

SERVES 4

2 × 6–7 bone racks of lamb, chined, trimmed and skinned (see pages 140–1)

For the chutney
1 tablespoon oil
2 onions, finely chopped
4 tablespoons balsamic vinegar
3 tablespoons soft light brown sugar

450 g fresh or frozen redcurrants
1 large sprig of fresh thyme
1 bay leaf
salt and freshly ground black pepper

For the glaze
4 teaspoons redcurrant jelly, warmed
1 teaspoon balsamic vinegar

1 Start by making the chutney. Heat the oil in a saucepan, then add the onions. Cover with a dampened piece of greaseproof paper and a lid, and cook until soft but not coloured.

2 Stir in the balsamic vinegar and sugar. Add the redcurrants, sprig of thyme and bay leaf and bring to the boil. Simmer for 20–25 minutes, or until thick and syrupy. Discard the thyme and bay leaf and season with salt and pepper. Set aside.

3 Heat the oven to 220°C/425°F/gas mark 7.

4 Trim about half the fat from the meat. Using a sharp knife, score the remaining fat with a criss-cross pattern and season with salt and pepper. Place in a roasting pan and roast for 20 minutes.

5 Mix the warmed redcurrant jelly and balsamic vinegar together, then use a pastry brush to brush it over the meat. Return to the oven for a further 5 minutes, or until bubbling and caramelized. Gently reheat the chutney and serve with the lamb.

Wine: Cabernet Sauvignon from Margaret River (Western Australia), Chile or California

Mediterranean Lamb

SERVES 4

2 × 6-bone lamb racks, chined (see pages 140–1)

flaky sea salt

1 large clove of garlic, crushed

1 × 400 g can pimientos, rinsed, drained and
  thickly sliced

85 g sun-blushed tomatoes, very well drained
  and roughly chopped

1 tablespoon vermouth

1 tablespoon Brown Stock (see page 452) or water

170 g green beans, topped and tailed, blanched
  and refreshed

85 g Kalamata olives, pitted

½ tablespoon finely chopped oregano

1 tablespoon roughly chopped basil

freshly ground black pepper

torn basil leaves, to garnish

1 Heat the oven to 220°C/425°F/gas mark 7.

2 Remove the bark and excess fat from the lamb. Using a sharp knife, score a criss–cross
  pattern into the remaining fat. Season with the sea salt.

3 Put the lamb in a roasting pan and place on the top shelf of the oven. Roast for 15
  minutes. Reduce the heat to 200°C/400°F/gas mark 6.

4 Pour off the excess fat from the pan and add the garlic, pimientos, sun-blushed tomatoes,
  vermouth, and stock or water to the lamb. Stir gently and return to the oven for a
  further 10 minutes, or until the lamb is crisp on the outside and pink in the middle.

5 Remove the lamb from the roasting pan and allow to rest. Place the pan over a direct
  heat and add the beans, olives and oregano to the vegetables. Cook for 1 minute, or
  until the beans are hot.

6 Stir in the chopped basil, taste and season.

7 Carve the lamb into cutlets and place on a warmed serving dish with the vegetables
  spooned around.

8 Garnish with the torn basil and serve immediately.

Wine: Dry red from Languedoc, Roussillon, Aglianico or Salice Salentino

Lamb Cutlets Grilled with Herbs

SERVES 4

30 g butter, melted

1 tablespoon oil

12 French-trimmed lamb cutlets (see page 141)

mixed chopped fresh herbs, such as thyme, basil,
mint, parsley, marjoram, rosemary

salt and freshly ground black pepper

1 Heat the grill to its highest setting.
2 Combine the melted butter and oil, then brush over the cutlets. Sprinkle over half the herbs and season with salt and pepper.
3 Place the cutlets under the grill, about 8 cm from the heat (see page 19) and cook for 3–4 minutes (3 minutes per side should give a succulent pink cutlet, 4 minutes a well-done cutlet).
4 Turn the cutlets over, baste with the fat from the bottom of the pan and sprinkle with the remaining herbs.
5 Grill for 3–4 minutes.
6 Arrange the cutlets on a warmed serving dish and pour over the pan juices. Serve immediately.

Wine: Red Bordeaux, Rioja or red Languedoc

Greek-style Lamb Cutlets

SERVES 4

12 lamb loin cutlets, trimmed of fat

olive oil

grated zest and juice of 1 lemon

1–2 tablespoons chopped fresh oregano

salt and freshly ground black pepper

1 Coat the lamb chops with a little olive oil and the grated lemon zest.
2 Heat a barbecue or griddle pan until very hot.
3 Season the chops with salt and freshly ground black pepper.
4 Cook the chops for about 3 minutes per side for meat that is just pink. Transfer to a serving plate.
5 Combine the oregano with the lemon juice and 4 tablespoons olive oil. Pour over the warm chops. Allow to stand for 10 minutes before serving.

Wine: Dry red from Italy, such as Cannonau, or from Greece, such as Naoussa

Lamb Noisettes with Onion and Mint Purée

SERVES 4

2 × 6–7-bone racks of lamb, chined
unsalted butter and vegetable oil, for frying
salt and freshly ground black pepper

1 large Spanish onion, very finely chopped
pinch of caster sugar
2 tablespoons chopped fresh mint
1 small bunch of watercress, to garnish

For the onion and mint purée

50 g butter

1 Remove the eye of the meat from the bones. Season with salt and pepper, then roll up each best end in a sheet of cling film and chill to firm for at least 1 hour, or overnight. Unwrap and slice each roll into 4 noisettes.
2 Press the noisettes between 2 plates, ideally for 1 hour, and refrigerate.
3 Meanwhile, make the onion purée. Melt the butter in a frying pan, add the onion and cook slowly, covered with a piece of dampened greaseproof paper and a lid, until completely soft (this might take 45 minutes). Sprinkle with the sugar, increase the heat and cook until the onions are a very pale brown. Transfer to a liquidizer and blend to a purée, then push through a sieve. Stir in the mint.
4 Season the noisettes, then fry in butter and oil for 5 minutes per side, then remove the string and arrange on a warmed serving plate. Garnish with watercress and hand the warm onion and mint purée separately.

Wine: Dry red from Languedoc or New World Merlot

Lamb Noisettes with Pistachio and Apricot Stuffing

SERVES 4

2 × 7-bone racks of lamb
2 tablespoons oil

50 g shelled pistachios, roughly chopped
115 g wholewheat breadcrumbs
1 tablespoon chopped fresh thyme
beaten egg, to bind
salt and freshly ground black pepper

For the stuffing

50 g dried apricots, diced

1 Remove the bones from the meat.
2 Mix together the stuffing ingredients, then place a long log of stuffing on each boned rack, on the fat of the meat, next to the eye.
3 Roll up the meat to enclose the stuffing. Tie the 2 rolls at intervals with string.
4 Heat the oil in a frying pan and brown the meat on all sides. (The lamb can be prepared ahead up to this point.)
5 Heat the oven to 200°C/400°F/gas mark 6.
6 Place the lamb on a wire rack over a roasting pan.

7 Bake in the centre of the oven for 15–20 minutes if cooking immediately after browning, or for 30–35 minutes if cooking from chilled.

8 Allow the lamb to stand for 10 minutes, then remove the string and cut each roll into 6 noisettes.

Wine: Cabernet- or Merlot-based wine from the New World

Lamb Steaks with Roast Butter Beans and Tomatoes

Placing the lamb on top of the beans allows the juices to be soaked up by the starchy beans. They become soft, creamy and very savoury. Most types of canned beans work well in this dish, and even lentils can be used.

SERVES 4

2 tablespoons extra virgin olive oil

2 × 400 g cans butter beans, rinsed and drained

4 ripe plum tomatoes, quartered

1 tablespoon sunflower oil

4 × 170 g thick-cut lamb leg steaks, trimmed

1 tablespoon sun-dried tomato paste

1½ tablespoons balsamic vinegar

50 g coriander leaves, roughly chopped

salt and freshly ground black pepper

coriander leaves, to garnish

1 Heat the oven to 200°C/400°F/gas mark 6.

2 In a large roasting pan heat the olive oil, stir in the butter beans and tomatoes and place in the oven for 5 minutes.

3 Meanwhile, heat the sunflower oil in a large frying pan, season the lamb steaks and brown them on both sides.

4 Remove the beans and tomatoes from the oven and stir in the sun-dried tomato paste and balsamic vinegar. Lay the lamb steaks and any pan juices on top and cook for a further 5–7 minutes, or until the lamb is pink in the middle.

5 Remove the lamb from the roasting pan and stir in the chopped coriander. Divide the beans between 4 warmed serving plates and put a lamb steak on top of each pile. Garnish with coriander leaves and serve.

Wine: Red with fresh acidity, such as Cru Beaujolais or Barbera d'Alba

Lamb Steak à la Catalane with Lentils

Like beefsteaks, lamb steaks, cut from the upper leg, can be eaten cooked blue to well done, but if overcooked, they will become tough. The meat is at its most succulent when cooked until pink in the middle.

SERVES 4

4 lamb steaks, 1 cm thick, cut across the
    upper leg, bones removed
1 bunch of watercress, to garnish

For the marinade

150 ml olive oil
6 cloves of garlic, crushed
2 tablespoons chopped fresh thyme
1 large onion, sliced
24 black peppercorns, slightly crushed
salt

For the lentils

olive oil, for frying
4 onions, finely chopped
4 cloves of garlic, crushed
225 g (raw weight) green or brown lentils, cooked
2 tablespoons tomato purée
4 tablespoons chopped mixed herbs
salt and freshly ground black pepper
sesame oil

1 Lay the lamb steaks in a shallow dish. Pour over the oil and add all the other marinade ingredients. Leave the steaks to marinate in the refrigerator for at least 8 hours, preferably 24 hours, turning them over 2 or 3 times.

2 To prepare the lentils, heat a little oil and sweat the onions and garlic until completely soft and transparent.

3 Add the lentils, tomato purée and herbs and season with salt, pepper and a little sesame oil to taste. Keep warm.

4 Meanwhile, heat a heavy frying pan or griddle until really hot, or heat the grill for at least 10 minutes.

5 Remove most of the oil from the lamb steaks and put them in the hot pan or under the heated grill. Fry or grill, turning once, until both sides are a rich brown. Garnish with watercress to serve.

Wine: Medium-bodied dry red from Rioja, Navarra or the Douro

Fillet of Lamb with Artichoke Hearts, Peas and Pistou

Although lamb fillet is fairly expensive, the dish is, overall, a rustic one, and good served in deep bowls with the lamb sliced and piled on top of the vegetables. Lamb leg steaks can be used as a cheaper alternative to fillet. Hot crusty bread, to mop up the pistou and wipe the bowl, would be a good addition.

SERVES 4–6

2 tablespoons oil

2 lamb loin fillets, trimmed

1 clove of garlic, crushed

1 × 400 g can artichoke hearts, drained and
  quartered

225 g frozen peas

150 ml Brown Stock (see page 452)

50 g unsalted butter, chilled and cut into cubes

salt and freshly ground black pepper

To serve

1 quantity Pistou (see below)

1 Heat the oven to 200°C/400°F/gas mark 6.
2 Heat 1 tablespoon of the oil in a heavy-based frying pan. Season the lamb fillets and brown well on all sides. Transfer to a roasting pan and place in the oven for 12–15 minutes.
3 Meanwhile, heat the remaining oil in the frying pan and sweat the garlic gently until soft but not browned.
4 Add the artichokes and peas to the garlic, pour over the stock and bring to the boil. Reduce the heat and simmer gently for 2–3 minutes, or until the artichokes and peas are heated through.
5 Remove the lamb from the oven and allow to rest for 5 minutes. Add any pan juices to the artichokes and peas.
6 Stir the butter into the frying pan bit by bit until incorporated and the sauce is slightly thickened and shiny. Season with salt and black pepper.
7 Slice the lamb fillets thickly and arrange in overlapping slices on a warmed serving dish. Arrange the artichokes and peas around the lamb, and pour the sauce over the top. Top with the pistou and serve immediately.

PISTOU

This Mediterranean herb paste resembles pesto, but is a lighter alternative.

SERVES 4

4 cloves of garlic

4 tablespoons chopped fresh basil

3 tablespoons olive oil

1 Put the garlic and basil into a mortar or blender and pound or whizz to a paste.
2 Add the oil drop by drop (as when making mayonnaise), mixing all the time, to form an emulsion. Use as required.

Wine: Dry red from southern France, such as Côtes-du-Rhône, Minervois or Corbières

Moroccan Sauté of Lamb with Chickpeas

This spiced dish uses *ras al hanout*, meaning 'top of the shop', a blend of more than twenty spices (see Suppliers, page 529). Every shop has its own blend, but if you cannot find it, substitute 1 teaspoon ground cumin plus ½ teaspoon each ground cinnamon, ground cayenne pepper, ground black pepper and ground ginger. Serve this quickly cooked dish with rice or couscous (see page 494 or 495).

SERVES 4

750 g lamb leg steaks

1 tablespoon *ras al hanout* spice

3 tablespoons dark soy sauce

2 tablespoons tomato ketchup

3 tablespoons vegetable oil

sea salt

2 × 400 g cans chopped tomatoes

1 × 400 g can chickpeas, drained and rinsed

½ teaspoon caster sugar

To serve

4 tablespoons toasted pine nuts

2 tablespoons chopped fresh coriander

1 Trim the fat from the lamb steaks, then cut the meat into 2 cm pieces.
2 Place the lamb in a non-corrosive dish and sprinkle over the *ras al hanout*.
3 Stir in the soy sauce and ketchup. Cover and chill for 1 hour or overnight.
4 Heat the oil in a sauté pan. Season the meat with salt, then brown in batches, removing each batch as it is browned. Return all the meat to the pan.
5 Add the tomatoes, chickpeas and sugar to the sauté pan and cook over a medium heat until the tomatoes have broken down and are no longer watery, about 10 minutes.
6 Serve over rice or couscous sprinkled with the pine nuts and coriander.

Wine: Full-bodied Merlot from Australia, South Africa, Chile or California; or a dry white, such as Viognier

Minted Lamb Kebabs with Tzatziki

This is an easy way to serve lamb. If using wooden skewers, be sure to soak them in water for 20 minutes before use.

SERVES 4

600 g boneless leg of lamb

4 tablespoons dark soy sauce

6 tablespoons tomato ketchup

4 tablespoons chopped fresh mint

salt and freshly ground black pepper

½ iceberg lettuce, shredded, to serve

For the tzatziki

½ cucumber, deseeded and coarsely grated

½ teaspoon salt

200 ml Greek yoghurt

1 small clove of garlic, crushed

1 Cut the lamb into 2 cm cubes. Place in a non-corrosive dish. Season with salt and pepper.
2 Sprinkle over the soy sauce, then add the tomato ketchup and mint. Stir to combine.
3 Cover with cling film and chill for 1 hour or overnight.

4 Make the tzatziki by placing the cucumber in a sieve set over a bowl. Mix in the salt and leave to stand for 30 minutes.

5 Rinse the cucumber with cold water, then pat dry on kitchen paper.

6 Mix the cucumber with the yoghurt and garlic. Chill until required.

7 Thread the lamb chunks on to skewers.

8 Heat the grill or barbecue until very hot.

9 Grill the lamb for about 2 minutes on each side, or until browned on the outside and still pink in the middle.

10 Serve on a bed of the lettuce with the tzatziki on the side.

Wine: High-acidity red, such as Chianti Classico or the Greek speciality Xinomavro

Indonesian Mixed Meat Kebabs

If using wooden skewers for this recipe, be sure to soak them in water for 20 minutes before use.

SERVES 4

225 g lean lamb, cut into 1 cm cubes

225 g lean pork, cut into 1 cm cubes

2 medium onions, blanched and quartered

1 green pepper, blanched, deseeded and cut into 8

1 red pepper, blanched, deseeded and cut into 8

110 g button mushrooms

1 small bunch of coriander, to garnish

For the marinade

140 g low-fat natural yoghurt

1 teaspoon ground ginger

1 clove of garlic, crushed

pinch of ground cumin

pinch of ground coriander

grated zest and juice of ½ a lemon

salt and freshly ground black pepper

1 Mix the marinade ingredients in a bowl. Add the lamb and pork, stirring to coat well. Cover and leave for several hours in a cool place, turning occasionally.

2 Heat the grill to its highest setting.

3 Thread the meat, onion, peppers and mushrooms on to 4 skewers and baste with any extra marinade.

4 Place under the grill and cook for 5 minutes on each side. Garnish with sprigs of coriander.

Wine: Pinot Noir (red) or Pinot Gris (white) from New Zealand or Australia

Lamb Tagine with Prunes and Almonds

This popular Moroccan dish has many variations, but the flavours of cinnamon, ginger and saffron combined with fruit, such as prunes or apricots, are ubiquitous. Serve with rice or couscous (see page 494 or 495).

SERVES 4

800 g boneless neck fillet of lamb
1 large red onion, finely chopped
2 cloves of garlic, crushed
1 teaspoon ground cinnamon
½ teaspoon ground ginger
pinch of saffron strands

1 tablespoon clear honey
12 pitted prunes
4 tablespoons chopped fresh parsley
flaky sea salt and freshly ground black pepper
2 tablespoons browned flaked almonds, to garnish

1 Heat the oven to 170°C/325°F/gas mark 3.
2 Remove most of the fat from the lamb, then cut the fillets into 2 cm chunks.
3 Place in an ovenproof casserole dish. Season with salt and lots of pepper.
4 Add the onion, garlic, cinnamon, ginger, saffron and honey to the casserole dish. Pour over enough cold water to cover.
5 Bring to a simmer on the hob, then cover and place in the oven for 1½–2 hours, or until the lamb is very tender.
6 After 1 hour, add the prunes.
7 If desired, the lamb can be removed from the casserole and the sauce boiled to thicken it; otherwise add the parsley and stir well. Garnish with the almonds and serve.

Wine: Dry red from Languedoc, Roussillon or Châteauneuf-du-Pape

Breast of Lamb with Rosemary Potatoes

SERVES 4

900 g breast of lamb, boned
1 tablespoon oil
250 g button onions, blanched, peeled and trimmed
1 small clove of garlic, crushed
300 ml Brown Stock, made with lamb bones
   (see page 452)
1 teaspoon very finely chopped rosemary
1 tablespoon very finely chopped lemon thyme

1 tablespoon roughly chopped flat leaf parsley
finely grated zest of 1 small lemon
salt and freshly ground black pepper

For the potatoes
675 g floury potatoes, cut into 3 cm cubes
½ tablespoon very finely chopped rosemary
15 g unsalted butter, melted

1 Season the meat on both sides with salt and pepper.
2 Heat the oil in a large shallow flameproof casserole and brown the lamb well on both sides. Pour off all but 1 tablespoon of the fat and reduce the heat.

3 Add the onions and fry very gently until they are a deep, golden brown. Add the garlic and cook for a further minute.

4 Pour the stock over the lamb and onions, add the 3 lots of herbs and the lemon zest and bring to the boil. Reduce the heat, then cover with a lid and simmer very gently for 1¾ hours, skimming occasionally.

5 Bring a large pan of salted water to the boil and cook the potatoes for 10–15 minutes, or until tender. Drain in a colander and shake roughly to fluff up the edges. Season with salt and black pepper and stir in the ½ tablespoon rosemary.

6 When the lamb is cooked heat the grill.

7 Skim any excess fat from the surface of the casserole and place the potatoes around the lamb, pushing them down into the liquid. Brush with the melted butter.

8 Place the casserole under the grill and cook until the potatoes and lamb are well browned and crisp.

Wine: Red Bordeaux, red Burgundy or Barolo

Lamb Shanks with Italian Mushroom Sauce

SERVES 4

6 tablespoons olive oil

4 meaty lamb shanks

250 g chestnut mushrooms, roughly chopped

2 medium onions, coarsely chopped

1 carrot, diced

1 stalk of celery, diced

2 cloves of garlic, crushed

250 ml full-bodied red wine

1 bay leaf

500 ml Brown Stock, made with lamb bones
 (see page 452)

2 × 400 g cans chopped tomatoes

2 tablespoons shredded basil

1 tablespoon chopped fresh oregano

salt and freshly ground black pepper

400 g pappardelle pasta, to serve

1 Heat half the oil in an ovenproof casserole. Season the lamb shanks, then brown well on all sides. Remove from the pan.

2 Add the mushrooms and brown over a medium-high heat. Remove and set aside.

3 Add the remaining oil to the pan and cook the onions, carrot and celery over a medium-low heat until browned. Add the garlic and cook for a further minute.

4 Add the wine and the bay leaf. Boil over a high heat until reduced by half.

5 Heat the oven to 150°C/300°F/gas mark 2.

6 Add the stock and the tomatoes to the casserole and bring to a simmer.

7 Return the lamb to the casserole, then cover and place in the oven.

8 After 2 hours, stir the mushrooms and herbs into the sauce. Cook for a further hour, or until the lamb is tender.

9 If necessary, boil the sauce to thicken it. Discard the bay leaf.

10 Cook the pasta according to the manufacturer's instructions. Drain and serve with the sauce.

Wine: Barolo, Barbaresco or a mature red Burgundy

Braised Lamb Shanks with Flageolet Beans

SERVES 4

4 × 450g lamb shanks

2 cloves of garlic, peeled and sliced

2 onions, 1 roughly chopped, 1 sliced

1 bouquet garni (see page 512)

1 bottle of Côtes du Rhône or other full-bodied red
   wine

250g dried flageolet beans

4 tablespoons vegetable oil

100g smoked streaky bacon, diced

600 ml Brown Stock (see page 452)

30g butter

2 tablespoons plain flour

salt and freshly ground black pepper

1 Remove any bark and fat from the lamb shanks. Put the lamb shanks into a large non-metallic bowl with the garlic, roughly chopped onion and bouquet garni. Pour over the wine. Refrigerate for 24 hours.

2 Cover the flageolet beans with water and leave to stand overnight.

3 Heat the oven to 170°C/325°F/gas mark 3.

4 Heat half the oil in a heavy sauté pan, add the sliced onion and cook until soft. Add the bacon and cook until lightly browned. Set aside.

5 Remove the lamb shanks, onion, and bouquet garni from the wine and pat the meat dry. Reserve the wine. Discard the onion and bouquet garni.

6 Heat the remaining oil in a large flameproof casserole dish. Brown the lamb shanks on all sides and add the bacon and sliced onion. Add the wine to the sauté pan and scrape to remove any sediment. Add the stock, bring to the boil and boil for 2 minutes.

7 Pour the wine mixture over the lamb shanks in the casserole. Cover and cook in the oven for 2½–3 hours, or until the meat will come away from the bone easily.

8 Meanwhile, drain the flageolet beans and place in a saucepan. Cover with water and bring to the boil. Boil hard for 10 minutes, then lower the heat and simmer until tender. Drain.

9 Turn the oven temperature down to 100°C/200°F/gas mark 1.

10 Transfer the lamb, bacon and onion to a warmed serving dish. Place the beans around the meat. Cover with foil and return to the oven.

11 Skim off as much of the fat as possible from the wine mixture in the casserole. Boil to reduce to approximately 600 ml. Mix the butter and flour to a paste, then whisk it into the boiling sauce a little at a time to thicken it. Season to taste with salt and pepper and strain over the meat. Serve immediately.

Wine: Full Red

Lamb Daube

This recipe uses shoulder meat, but leg or middle neck can be used instead.

SERVES 4

900 g boned shoulder of lamb

1 tablespoon oil

115 g streaky bacon, diced

1 onion, chopped

150 ml Brown Stock, made with lamb bones
(see page 452)

1 bouquet garni (see page 512)

55 g plain flour

For the marinade

300 ml red wine

1 medium onion, cut into thick slices

1 clove of garlic, bruised

3 whole allspice berries

1 Trim the lamb and cut it into large pieces measuring 3 × 5 cm.

2 Mix all the marinade ingredients together. Lay the pieces of lamb in it and refrigerate overnight.

3 Heat the oven to 170°C/325°F/gas mark 3.

4 Remove the meat from the dish, reserving the marinade.

5 Heat the oil in a heavy-based frying pan and brown the bacon and onion. Lift out with a slotted spoon and place in a casserole.

6 Brown the lamb in the same pan, a few pieces at a time. Lay them on top of the bacon and onion.

7 Strain the marinade into the empty pan. Add the stock. Bring to the boil, scraping the bottom of the pan to loosen any sediment. Pour over the meat.

8 Immerse the bouquet garni in the liquid in the casserole.

9 Add enough water to the flour to make a stiff dough (luting paste). Cover the casserole with the lid and press a band of the dough around it to seal completely.

10 Cook in the oven for 1½ hours, then chip off and discard the luting paste and remove the bouquet garni.

11 Lift the meat out and place on a warmed serving dish. Keep warm.

12 Boil the sauce to reduce to a syrupy consistency and pour over the meat.

Wine: Dry European red, such as Bordeaux, Burgundy or Rioja

Lamb with Dill Sauce

SERVES 4

900 g boneless lamb, cut into large chunks

1 onion, sliced

1 carrot, cut into sticks

1 tablespoon dill seeds, crushed, or 3–4 sprigs
  of fresh dill

1 bay leaf

12 black peppercorns

½ teaspoon salt

720 ml White Chicken Stock (see page 451)

30 g butter

1 tablespoon plain flour

1 egg yolk

3 tablespoons double cream

2 teaspoons lemon juice

salt and freshly ground black pepper

1 Put the meat, onion, carrot, dill seeds or stalks, but not the fresh leaves, bay leaf, peppercorns and ½ teaspoon salt into a saucepan.

2 Cover with the stock and bring slowly to the boil. Turn down the heat and cook as slowly as possible for 2–2½ hours, or until the meat is tender.

3 Lift out the meat, discarding the bay leaf and dill stalks, and place in a casserole or serving dish. Cover to prevent drying out, and keep warm.

4 Strain the stock and skim off all the fat. Measure the remaining liquid and make up to 425 ml with water if necessary. Return to the saucepan.

5 Mix the butter and flour together to a smooth paste. Whisk this gradually into the hot stock, and continue whisking steadily until the sauce is smooth. Bring to the boil, then simmer for 2 minutes.

6 Mix the egg yolk and cream in a bowl. Mix a little of the hot sauce into the cream mixture, then stir this back into the sauce. Be careful not to boil the sauce now or the yolk will scramble. Flavour the sauce with the lemon juice and season to taste with salt and pepper. Chop the dill leaves if you have them, and stir in. Pour over the meat and serve immediately.

Wine: Red Bordeaux, or a white Alsace Pinot Gris or Grüner Veltliner

Ragout of Lamb with Borlotti Beans

If using canned beans, rinse thoroughly and add 10 minutes before serving to heat through.

SERVES 4

1.35 kg boneless lamb, preferably
  from the shoulder
2 tablespoons oil
2 onions, finely chopped
1 clove of garlic, crushed
30 g plain flour
300 ml brown ale
300 ml Brown Stock, made with lamb bones
  (see page 452)

1 tablespoon tomato purée
1 tablespoon soft light brown sugar
3 anchovies, finely chopped
3 large sprigs of rosemary
3 large sprigs of thyme
220 g fresh borlotti beans, podded weight
salt and freshly ground black pepper

1 Trim the lamb and cut into large pieces.

2 Heat 1 tablespoon of the oil in a large casserole and brown the meat on all sides. Transfer to a plate.

3 Heat the remaining oil and fry the onions slowly. When brown, add the garlic and cook for a further minute.

4 Stir in the flour and cook, stirring, for 1 minute. Remove from the heat and pour in the ale and stock.

5 Return to the heat and bring slowly to the boil, then simmer for 2 minutes, stirring continuously. Add the tomato purée, sugar, anchovies, rosemary and thyme.

6 Return the meat to the casserole, season with salt and pepper and cover with a tight-fitting lid. Simmer very gently for 1¼ hours.

7 Add the beans to the pan and continue to cook for a further 15 minutes, uncovered, or until the beans are cooked through and the meat is very tender.

Wine: Dry red from Languedoc-Roussillon, the Rhône or Australia

Lamb and Chickpea Curry

SERVES 4

2 teaspoons cumin seeds

2 teaspoons coriander seeds

1 teaspoon fennel seeds

2 tablespoons vegetable oil or ghee

1 large onion, finely chopped

2 cloves of garlic, crushed

1 teaspoon ground turmeric

½ teaspoon chilli powder

675 g boneless leg or shoulder of lamb

1 × 400 g can chopped tomatoes

1 × 400 g can chickpeas, drained and rinsed

salt and freshly ground black pepper

2 tablespoons chopped fresh coriander, to garnish

To serve

Basmati Rice (see page 494)

1 Toast the cumin, coriander and fennel seeds in a small, dry frying pan over a medium heat, stirring continuously for 2 minutes. Set aside to cool.

2 Heat the oil or ghee in a pan, then cook the onion over a low heat until softened. Turn up the heat to medium and cook until turning golden.

3 Add the garlic and cook for a further minute. Remove from the heat.

4 Grind the cooled seeds in a spice grinder or with a mortar and pestle. Combine with the turmeric, and chilli powder.

5 Heat the oven to 150°C/300°F/gas mark 2.

6 Cut the lamb into 3 cm pieces, removing any fat or gristle.

7 Place the onions and garlic in an ovenproof casserole dish over a medium heat. Stir in the spices and cook for 30 seconds. Add the meat and cook for 2 minutes, stirring to coat in the spices.

8 Add the tomatoes and chickpeas and just enough water to cover the meat. Season with salt and pepper. Bring to a simmer, then cover and place in the oven.

9 Check the curry after 1 hour: if it is too dry, add additional water. Cook in total for 1½ hours, or until the meat in tender enough to cut with a spoon.

10 Garnish with coriander and serve with basmati rice.

Wine: Merlot from Australia, Chile, California or Washington State

Rogan Josh

SERVES 4

675 g boned leg of lamb, cut into 3 cm cubes

4 tablespoons oil

4 bay leaves

6 cardamom pods

5 cm cinnamon stick

6 cloves

1 onion, chopped

1 teaspoon fennel seeds

2 teaspoons ground cumin

2 teaspoons ground coriander

1 teaspoon chilli powder

4 cloves of garlic

5 cm piece of fresh root ginger, peeled and grated

150 ml natural yoghurt

200 ml water

salt

½ teaspoon garam masala

4 teaspoons paprika

1 Trim the lamb of fat. Heat the oil in a frying pan and brown the lamb in batches. Remove from the pan and reserve.

2 Add the bay leaves, cardamom pods, cinnamon stick, cloves and onion to the pan. Fry until the onion is lightly browned.

3 Grind the fennel seeds to a powder and mix with the cumin, coriander and chilli. Put the garlic, ginger and yoghurt in a blender and whizz together. Add both the spices and the yoghurt mix to the onion along with the meat.

4 Pour in the water and add salt to taste. Simmer until the lamb is tender, about 1–1½ hours.

5 Just before serving add the garam masala and the paprika.

Wine: Côtes-du-Rhône Villages or Pinot Noir from Chile or New Zealand

Lancashire Hotpot

SERVES 4

900 g middle neck of mutton or lamb chops

3 lambs' kidneys (optional)

900 g potatoes

50 g melted butter, plus extra for greasing

1 teaspoon chopped fresh thyme or pinch of
   dried thyme

2 large onions, thinly sliced

2 carrots, sliced

1 bay leaf

600 ml Brown Stock, made with lamb bones
   (see page 452)

salt and freshly ground black pepper

1 Heat the oven to 180°C/350°F/gas mark 4.

2 If necessary, cut the meat into chops, trimming away most of the fat.

3 Skin, split, core and quarter the kidneys, if using.

4 Wash and peel the potatoes, discard any eyes and cut into slices about 5 mm thick.

5 Butter a casserole dish and line it with a layer of potatoes. Season well with salt, pepper and thyme.

6 Layer the chops, onions, carrots and kidneys on top of the potatoes, seasoning well with salt, pepper and thyme, and adding the bay leaf when the casserole is half full. Finish with a neat layer of potatoes overlapping each other.

7 Pour in enough stock to come to the bottom of the top layer of potatoes.

8 Brush the surface with plenty of melted butter and season well with salt and pepper.

9 Cover the casserole and bake in the oven for about 2 hours.

10 Remove the lid and continue to cook for a further 30–40 minutes, until the potatoes are brown and crisp and the meat is completely tender.

Wine: Medium-bodied red blend, such as Corbières, Fitou or Côtes-du-Rhône

Navarin of Lamb

Sometimes said to take its name from the Battle of Navarino in 1827, this dish – a lamb stew – long precedes that date and is more likely to have been named after the *navet* (turnip) it contains.

SERVES 4

900 g middle neck of lamb

2 tablespoons dripping or oil

1 tablespoon plain flour

1 litre Brown Stock, made with lamb bones
  (see page 452)

1 clove of garlic, crushed

1 tablespoon tomato purée

1 bouquet garni (see page 512)

12 button onions, blanched and peeled

pinch of caster sugar

1 turnip, cut into sticks

3 carrots, cut into sticks

3 potatoes, cut into chunks

salt and freshly ground black pepper

1 Cut the lamb into 3 cm pieces and season with salt and pepper.

2 Heat 1 tablespoon of the dripping or oil in a heavy-based saucepan and brown the meat on all sides. Pour off the fat into a frying pan. Sprinkle the meat with the flour. Cook for 1 minute, then stir in the stock, garlic and tomato purée. Add the bouquet garni. Stir until boiling, then simmer for 1 hour. Skim off any surface fat.

3 Heat 1 tablespoon of the dripping or oil in the frying pan and cook the onions with the sugar until brown. Add the turnip, carrots and potatoes, adding more dripping as needed and fry these until browned.

4 Add the browned vegetables to the meat stew, cover tightly and continue cooking over a low heat, or in a moderate oven (170°C/325°F/gas mark 3) for a further 30–40 minutes, or until the meat is tender. Taste for seasoning.

5 Remove the bouquet garni. Allow the navarin to stand for 5 minutes, then skim off the surface fat and spoon the stew into a warmed serving dish.

NOTE: Fresh peas or beans are sometimes added to the navarin after the final skimming. The stew must then be cooked further until they are just tender.

Wine: Côtes-du-Rhône

Moussaka

Moussaka is a traditional dish found in every village in Greece. There are as many different variations as there are cooks, but the universal ingredients are tomatoes, onions, garlic and aubergines.

SERVES 4

340 g aubergine
6 tablespoons olive oil
1 large onion, finely chopped
675 g minced lamb or beef
150 ml white wine
150 ml water
1 clove of garlic, crushed
1 × 400 g can tomatoes, or 3 large tomatoes,
  blanched, peeled and chopped
2 tablespoons chopped fresh parsley

2 teaspoons chopped fresh oregano or
  1 teaspoon dried oregano
pinch of ground cinnamon
225 g floury potatoes
salt and freshly ground black pepper

For the topping

200 ml Greek yoghurt
1 egg, beaten
4 tablespoons grated Parmesan cheese

1 Remove the stalk, then cut the aubergine into slices 6 mm thick. Salt the slices on both sides, then leave in a colander for 30 minutes for some of the juices to drain out.
2 Place 2 tablespoons of the oil in a small saucepan and sweat the onion over a low heat until soft.
3 Heat 2 tablespoons of the remaining oil in a sauté pan and brown the mince in batches, taking care not to overcrowd the pan. Place the browned mince in a sieve over a bowl to drain away the excess fat.
4 Mix together the wine and water and use a little to deglaze the pan in between batches of meat. Reserve the *déglaçage*.
5 Add the garlic to the onion and cook for 1 minute.
6 Combine the onion, garlic, browned meat, tomatoes, remaining wine/water, parsley, oregano and cinnamon in a large saucepan and simmer for 45 minutes.
7 Boil the potatoes until tender. Drain, cool and cut into slices 6 mm thick.
8 Heat the grill. Rinse the aubergine slices and pat dry on kitchen paper.
9 Brush the aubergines on both sides with the remaining oil and grill until browned.
10 Heat the oven to 180°C/350°F/gas mark 4.
11 Place a thin layer of the meat in a shallow ovenproof dish. Arrange a layer of aubergine slices on top, then add a thin layer of meat sauce followed by a layer of potato. Continue layering, finishing with a layer of meat.
12 Mix together the yoghurt, egg and cheese. Spread over the moussaka. (The dish can be made up to this point one day in advance and refrigerated until needed.)
13 Bake for 45 minutes until golden brown on top and hot in the centre.

Wine: Dry, Greek red, such as Naoussa

Babotie

A traditional South African dish, babotie was originally made with leftovers flavoured with spices from Indonesia. The name comes from the Indonesian word *bobotok*.

SERVES 4

1 slice of white bread
150 ml milk
30 g butter, plus extra for greasing
1 onion, chopped
1 small eating apple, chopped
1 tablespoon curry powder
450 g cooked lamb, minced
50 g blanched almonds, roughly chopped
1 tablespoon chutney

a few raisins
1 tablespoon vinegar or lemon juice
salt and freshly ground black pepper

For the topping
2 eggs, beaten
300 ml Greek yoghurt
1 tablespoon flaked almonds

1 Soak the bread in the milk.
2 Grease an ovenproof dish and heat the oven to 180°C/350°F/gas mark 4.
3 Melt the butter in a saucepan, add the onion and apple and cook over a low heat until soft but not coloured. Add the curry powder and cook for 1 further minute.
4 Combine the onion mixture with the lamb, almonds, chutney, raisins and vinegar or lemon juice. Fork the bread into the meat. Season with salt and pepper and pile into the prepared dish.
5 To make the topping, mix the eggs with the yoghurt. Season with salt and pepper.
6 Pour this over the meat mixture, place the almonds on top and bake in the oven for 30–35 minutes, until the topping has set and browned.

Wine: Pinotage, Cabernet Sauvignon or Syrah from the Cape

Mutton Stew with Garlic Mash

Lamb from an animal over 2 years old is referred to as 'mutton'. It has a much more intense flavour, and the texture and colour of the meat is generally coarser and darker than that of lamb. It is particularly good for making pies and casseroles, where the meat will soften and tenderize, and its depth of flavour will intensify even further. Consequently, this rich, full flavour will be best appreciated with robust accompaniments so that their flavour isn't overwhelmed by that of the meat. Garlic is a popular addition to many lamb dishes, and is used here in the mashed potato. The amount can be adjusted according to taste.

SERVES 4

900 g mutton, trimmed and cut into 3 cm cubes
seasoned flour
3 tablespoons oil
1 large onion, finely sliced
3 tablespoons port
3 tablespoons Madeira
425 ml Brown Stock (see page 452)
2 teaspoons tomato purée
1 bouquet garni (see page 512)

1 large sprig of rosemary, bruised
salt and freshly ground black pepper

For the garlic mash
675 g potatoes, cut into chunks
100 ml double cream
1 tablespoon mascarpone cheese
30 g unsalted butter
2 cloves of garlic, crushed

1 Place the meat in a large bowl and toss in the seasoned flour. Shake off the excess.
2 Heat 2 tablespoons of the oil in a large, heavy-based frying pan and fry the meat in batches until well browned. Remove with a slotted spoon and transfer to a casserole.
3 Heat the remaining oil in the pan and fry the onion gently until golden brown. Add to the meat.
4 Pour the port, Madeira and stock into the pan. Stir in the tomato purée and scrape the bottom to remove any sediment. Bring to the boil, season with salt and pepper and pour this *déglaçage* over the meat and onions. Add the bouquet garni and rosemary, then cover with a lid and simmer very gently for 1¾–2 hours, skimming occasionally.
5 About 30 minutes before the end of the cooking time, place the potatoes in a large pan of boiling, salted water and cook until tender. Pass the potatoes through a vegetable mouli or a sieve and return to the pan.
6 Heat the oven to 200°C/400°F/gas mark 6.
7 Pour the cream into a small saucepan, add the mascarpone, butter and crushed garlic, bring to a simmer and pour the mixture over the mashed potatoes. Stir well and season with salt and pepper.
8 Remove the bouquet garni and rosemary from the casserole, then transfer the meat mixture to a large ovenproof dish.
9 Pipe or spoon the mash over the meat and place the dish in the oven for 15–20 minutes, or until the potato is brown and crisp and the meat is piping hot.

Wine: Côtes-du-Rhône or Crozes-Hermitage from France; Priorato from Spain; or Douro red from Portugal

Mutton Pies with Herb Scone Crusts

SERVES 4

	For the scone topping
900 g mutton, trimmed and cut into 3 cm cubes	225g self-raising flour
seasoned flour	½ teaspoon salt
3 tablespoons oil	50 g butter, cut into small dice
1 large onion, finely sliced	1 teaspoon finely chopped fresh thyme
3 tablespoons port	1 teaspoon finely chopped fresh flat leaf parsley
3 tablespoons Madeira	finely grated zest of ½ a lemon
425 ml Brown Stock (see page 452)	150 ml buttermilk
2 teaspoons tomato purée	1 egg, beaten
1 bouquet garni (see page 512)	
1 large sprig of rosemary, bruised	
salt and freshly ground black pepper	

1 Place the meat in a large bowl and toss in the seasoned flour. Shake off the excess.

2 Heat 2 tablespoons of the oil in a large, heavy-based frying pan and fry the meat in batches until well browned. Remove with a slotted spoon and transfer to a casserole.

3 Heat the remaining oil in the pan and fry the onion gently until golden brown. Add to the meat.

4 Pour the port, Madeira and stock into the pan. Stir in the tomato purée and scrape the bottom of the pan to remove any sediment. Bring to the boil, season with salt and pepper and pour this *déglaçage* over the meat and onions. Add the bouquet garni and rosemary, then cover with a lid and simmer very gently for 1¾–2 hours, skimming occasionally.

5 Remove the bouquet garni and rosemary from the pan and divide the meat between four 10cm ovenproof dishes.

6 Heat the oven to 200°C/400°F/gas mark 6.

7 To make the scone crust, sieve the flour and salt into a large bowl. Rub in the butter until the mixture resembles breadcrumbs. Stir in the herbs and lemon zest. Make a large well in the centre, pour in the buttermilk and mix to a soft, spongy dough with a knife. On a floured surface, knead the dough very lightly until just smooth. Roll or press the dough out to about 4 cm thick and stamp out four 10 cm rounds with a pastry cutter.

8 Place a scone on top of each of the dishes and brush with beaten egg. Put the dishes on a baking sheet and place on the top shelf of the oven for 15 minutes or until the scones are well-risen and golden brown and the meat is piping hot.

Wine: Côtes-du-Rhône or Crozes-Hermitage from France; Priorato from Spain; or Douro red from Portugal

Mutton with Black Beans

If using dried beans, start soaking them the night before. The dish will improve with standing for a day.

SERVES 4

100 g dried black beans or 1 × 400 g can
black beans, drained
4 tablespoons vegetable oil
450 g neck of mutton or lamb, cut into
3 cm cubes
150 ml water or Brown Stock, made with lamb
bones (see page 452)
1 large onion, chopped
1 green pepper, deseeded and chopped
2 cloves of garlic, crushed
2 teaspoons ground coriander
1 teaspoon ground hot chilli pepper

1 × 400 g can chopped tomatoes
2 tablespoons tomato purée
2 teaspoons Worcestershire sauce
salt and freshly ground black pepper

To garnish

4 tablespoons soured cream
4 tablespoons chopped fresh coriander

To serve

Boiled Rice (see page 494)

1 If using dried beans, soak them in plenty of cold water overnight. Drain, cover with fresh water and cook until tender.

2 Heat enough oil in a sauté pan to coat the bottom. Season the mutton and brown in batches, adding more oil as required. Place the browned meat in an ovenproof casserole dish.

3 Deglaze the pan with the water or stock, scraping the bottom to remove any sediment. Reserve the *déglaçage*.

4 Heat the oven to 150°C/300°F/gas mark 2.

5 Heat 1 tablespoon oil in a saucepan, add the onion and cover with a piece of dampened greaseproof paper and a lid. Leave to sweat over a low heat for 10 minutes, stirring occasionally. Add the green pepper and cook until starting to soften.

6 Stir in the garlic, coriander and chilli powder and cook for a further minute.

7 Add the onion mixture to the meat along with the reserved *déglaçage*, the chopped tomatoes, tomato purée, Worcestershire sauce and beans.

8 The meat should be covered by the liquid. If not, add just enough water to cover.

9 Cover the casserole dish, then place in the oven and cook for 2 hours, stirring once or twice. If the meat begins to looks too dry, add more water.

10 When the meat is tender, remove from the casserole dish and keep warm.

11 Adjust the sauce to a thick coating consistency either by adding water or boiling to reduce. Stir the meat into the sauce.

12 Garnish with soured cream and chopped fresh coriander. Serve with the rice.

Wine: A tannic red, such as Madiran or Cahors from southwest France

Curried Goat

This goat recipe is included here in the lamb section because the meat is similar in texture and flavour to mutton.

SERVES 4

1.35 kg goat meat, from the leg, boned

1 teaspoon salt

1 teaspoon freshly ground black pepper

1½ tablespoons curry powder

2 teaspoons flour

3 tablespoons oil

2 onions, finely sliced

1 large red chilli, finely chopped

600 ml Brown Stock (see page 452)

2 teaspoons tomato purée

500 g floury potatoes, cut into 3 cm cubes

1 Trim the goat meat of excess fat, then cut into 3 cm cubes and place in a large bowl.

2 Mix the salt, pepper and curry powder together and add to the bowl. Rub the mixture into the meat. Cover and refrigerate for 1 hour.

3 Dust the meat with the flour.

4 Heat 2 tablespoons of the oil in a large, heavy-based frying pan. Fry the meat in batches until well browned on all sides. Using a slotted spoon, transfer the meat to a large flameproof casserole.

5 Heat the remaining tablespoon of oil in the frying pan and add the onion. Cook gently over a low heat for 10–12 minutes, or until soft and golden brown. Add the chilli and cook for a further 30 seconds.

6 Stir in the stock and tomato purée and bring to the boil, scraping the bottom of the pan to release the sediment.

7 Pour the sauce over the meat, then cover with a close-fitting lid and simmer gently for 2–2½ hours.

8 Add the potatoes to the casserole and continue to cook, uncovered, for 30 minutes, or until the meat is very tender, the potatoes are just beginning to break up and the sauce is syrupy.

9 Taste and season if necessary. Serve immediately in warmed bowls.

Wine: Chilean Merlot or Pinot Noir, or Languedoc from France

Glazed Lambs' Tongues with Creamed Puy Lentils

SERVES 4

2 tablespoons dripping or oil

8 lambs' tongues, blanched and skinned
  (see page 100)

1 onion, finely sliced

1 carrot, roughly chopped

1 stick of celery, roughly chopped

½ tablespoon white wine vinegar

75 ml dry white wine

300 ml Veal Stock or Brown Chicken Stock
  (see page 454)

1 bouquet garni (see page 512)

salt and freshly ground black pepper

sprigs of flat leaf parsley, to garnish

For the lentils

170 g Puy lentils

110 g piece of smoked streaky bacon, chopped

1 onion, cut into quarters, studded with 4 cloves

2 large sprigs of thyme

grated zest of ½ a lemon

4 tablespoons mascarpone cheese

2 tablespoons finely chopped flat leaf parsley

1 Heat the oven to 150°C/300°F/gas mark 2.

2 Heat 1 tablespoon of the dripping or oil in a heavy-based casserole and fry the tongues, a few at a time, until lightly browned. Remove from the pan and set aside.

3 Heat the remaining dripping or oil, add the onion, carrot and celery and brown well.

4 Arrange the lambs' tongues on top of the vegetables in a single layer and pour over the vinegar, wine and stock. Add the bouquet garni and season with salt and pepper.

5 Bring to the boil, then cover the casserole with a lid. Place in the oven for 2 hours, basting occasionally.

6 Put the lentils into a large saucepan and cover with cold water. Add the bacon, onion, thyme and lemon zest and bring to the boil. Reduce the heat and simmer very gently for 12–15 minutes, or until al dente.

7 Drain the lentils and discard the onion, bacon and thyme. Return the lentils to the hot pan, add the mascarpone and simmer very gently for 2–3 minutes, stirring occasionally. Season with salt and pepper and stir in the parsley.

8 Remove the lambs' tongues from the casserole and slice thickly. Strain the sauce into a clean saucepan and boil rapidly until reduced to about 4 tablespoons.

9 Place the lentils in a deep serving dish, put the lambs' tongues on top and spoon over the glaze. Garnish with sprigs of flat leaf parsley.

Wine: Lightly chilled Beaujolais, or dry Riesling from Alsace, Germany or Austria

Lambs' Kidneys

Lambs' kidneys are shaped like kidney beans, but are about 5 cm long. They are often sold covered in the whole fat (suet). Store as described on page 95.

Lambs' kidneys are highly regarded and are often served grilled. Peel away the suet and the thin membrane, then cut in half. Use kitchen scissors to remove the fatty core and blood vessels. The kidneys should be cooked just enough to become brown on the outside whilst remaining pink on the inside or they will be tough and rubbery. Thread on to a skewer to grill (see Grilling, page 15). They can also be braised.

Lambs' Kidneys with Wild Mushrooms in Brioche Buns

4 small Savoury Brioche buns
  (see page 487)
30 g unsalted butter
8 lambs' kidneys, cores and sinews removed,
  and cut into thin slices
170 g mixed wild mushrooms, roughly torn

1 teaspoon Dijon mustard
4 tablespoons double cream
2 teaspoons finely chopped tarragon
lemon juice
salt and freshly ground black pepper

1 Heat the oven to 200°C/400°F/gas mark 6.
2 Cut the tops off the brioche buns, retaining them for use as 'lids'. Hollow out the buns slightly, then place on a baking sheet and put into the middle of the oven to warm through.
3 Heat the butter in a frying pan and, when foaming, add the kidneys. Fry briskly on both sides until well browned. Reduce the heat and cook gently for a further minute, or until pink in the middle. Remove from the pan with a slotted spoon and keep warm.
4 Add the mushrooms to the pan and fry for 1–2 minutes. Stir in the mustard, double cream and tarragon and bring to the boil.
5 Return the kidneys to the pan, season with lemon juice, salt and pepper and stir gently to coat with the sauce.
6 Remove the warm buns from the oven and divide the mixture between them. Replace the lids and serve immediately.

Wine: Rioja Reserva, Barolo or Côte-Rôtie from the Rhône

Kidneys Turbigo

This dish is named after a French town in Lombardy. Classic turbigo does not include soured cream, but it's a delicious addition.

SERVES 4

9 lambs' kidneys
60 g butter
225 g small pork sausages
12 baby onions or shallots
225 g button mushrooms
2 tablespoons dry sherry

425 ml Brown Stock (see page 452)
1 bouquet garni (see page 512)
30 g plain flour
150 ml soured cream
salt and freshly ground black pepper
sprigs of fresh parsley, to garnish

1 Skin the kidneys, halve them and remove the cores with kitchen scissors.
2 Heat half the butter in a frying pan, then brown the kidneys quickly, a few at a time, on both sides. They should cook fast enough to go brown rather than grey. Transfer them to a sieve set over a bowl as you go.
3 Now fry the sausages, then the onions, and finally the mushrooms. As each is cooked, put on a plate.
4 Put everything back into the pan, except for the kidney juice in the bowl (the blood can be very bitter). Pour over the sherry and stock and immerse the bouquet garni in the liquid. Add salt and pepper and cover with a lid.
5 Cook over a very low heat for about 1 hour, or until the kidneys and onions are tender. Make sure that the kidneys are submerged during cooking.
6 Lift the meat and vegetables on to a warmed serving dish, discarding the bouquet garni. Reduce the liquid by boiling rapidly to half the original quantity.
7 Put the remaining butter and the flour in a bowl and work together to a paste (beurre manié). Drop about half of it into the sauce and whisk or stir briskly while bringing slowly to the boil. If the sauce is still on the thin side, add the remaining butter and flour mixture in the same way, whisking out the lumps. Boil for 1 minute.
8 Mix half the soured cream with some of the hot liquid. Add to the pan, stir, but do not boil, and pour over the dish. Serve the remaining soured cream separately. Garnish the dish with sprigs of parsley.

Wine: Pinot Noir from Oregon, California or South Africa.

Lambs' Kidneys with Mushrooms in Mustard Sauce

SERVES 2

6 lambs' kidneys

30 g Clarified Butter (see page xii)

115 g large flat mushrooms, cut into thick slices

4 tablespoons double cream

2 teaspoons Dijon mustard

lemon juice

salt and freshly ground black pepper

1 tablespoon chopped fresh parsley, to garnish

1 Prepare the kidneys as described opposite, then cut into 2 cm chunks.

2 Melt the butter in a frying pan until foaming, then fry the kidneys over a high heat to brown on all sides. Place in a sieve to drain. Discard the juices.

3 Cook the mushrooms in the pan for 3 minutes, then return the kidneys and cook for about 2 minutes, until pale pink on the inside.

4 Stir in the cream and mustard. Taste and season with lemon juice, salt and pepper. Garnish with the parsley.

Wine: Pinot Noir from Oregon, California or South Africa

Haggis

Even in Scotland, haggis is seldom made at home today, mainly because a sheep's pluck, consisting of the liver, heart and lights (lungs), makes too much haggis for a modern-sized family, and cleaning the stomach of the sheep (which forms the skin of the haggis) is a tedious and messy business, requiring much washing and careful scraping. This recipe is for a simplified haggis, cooked in a pudding basin instead of a sheep's stomach.

SERVES 4

2 onions

2 sheep's hearts

450 g lamb's liver

50 g oatmeal

85 g chopped beef suet

1 teaspoon chopped fresh sage

pinch of ground allspice

butter, for greasing

salt and freshly ground black pepper

1 Peel the onions and put them, with the cleaned hearts and liver, into a saucepan of water. Boil for 40 minutes, then lift them out of the liquid.
2 Mince the hearts, liver and onions and mix with the oatmeal, suet, sage, allspice and plenty of salt and pepper. Add enough of the cooking liquid to give a soft dropping consistency.
3 Grease a pudding basin and fill with the mixture. Cover with greaseproof paper and kitchen foil and tie with string.
4 Steam for 2 hours. Serve hot.

NOTE: Very good haggis can be bought in reliable shops. Do not prick haggis before boiling or baking – it might burst. A haggis should be boiled for 30 minutes per 450 g, but for a minimum of 1 hour. It can also be baked, wrapped in kitchen foil, at 180°C/350°F/gas mark 4 for 30 minutes per 450 g, but for a minimum of 1 hour. Place the wrapped haggis in a casserole, add a little water and cover tightly.

Drink: Syrah/Shiraz, whisky or beer

Stuffed Lambs' Hearts

SERVES 4

4 lambs' hearts, tubes and sinews removed
100 ml light red wine
300 ml Brown Stock (see page 452)
1 bouquet garni (see page 512)
salt and freshly ground black pepper
1 bunch of watercress, to garnish

For the stuffing

2 tablespoons oil
1 onion, finely chopped
1 stick of celery, finely diced
85 g fresh white breadcrumbs
8 large sage leaves, finely chopped
15 g flat leaf parsley, finely chopped
1 small eating apple, peeled and coarsely grated
50 g unsalted butter, melted

1 Rinse the hearts under cold running water and pat dry. Season lightly with salt and pepper.

2 Heat 1 tablespoon of the oil in a heavy-based frying pan and sweat the onion and celery until soft. Transfer to a bowl and stir in the breadcrumbs, herbs, grated apple and melted butter. Season with salt and pepper.

3 Heat the oven to 180°C/350°F/gas mark 4.

4 Push the stuffing down into the hearts and secure with a metal skewer. Heat the remaining oil in a casserole and brown them well on all sides.

5 Pour the wine and stock over the hearts, add the bouquet garni and bring to the boil. Cover and place in the oven for 1½ hours, skimming occasionally.

6 Transfer the hearts to a warm dish and keep warm in the turned-off oven.

7 Strain the sauce into a saucepan. Skim off any fat, then reduce by boiling rapidly, until syrupy.

8 Remove the skewers from the hearts and cut each of them in half. Place 2 halves on each serving plate and pour the sauce over them. Garnish with sprigs of watercress.

Wine: Châteauneuf-du-Pape or a Shiraz from Australia or South Africa

Pork

Pork is a very versatile meat, which may be eaten fresh, cured, salted or smoked. There is very little of the pig that cannot be eaten: even the ears can be used in various ways.

Fresh pork has a mild, sweet, almost nutty flavour that marries well with pungent herbs, spices, fruit and vegetables. Traditionally, pork is flavoured with sage, but the herbs thyme, rosemary and fresh coriander also go well with it. Tart fruits, such as apples and apricots, and strong-tasting vegetables, such as red cabbage, cauliflower and beetroot, are commonly served alongside. These vegetables are often acidulated with vinegar to help cut through the meat's rich flavour.

History

The origins of the wild boar, the ancestor of today's domestic pig, can be traced back to the Far East up to 16,000 years ago. As the wild boar is omnivorous, it was easily domesticated. Traces of domesticated pigs, which had originated in the Far East, have been found in Europe dating back 9000 years. The cave paintings in Lascaux, France, illustrate the importance of this animal in the life of early man. The Roman cookery writer Apicius gave many recipes for pork, both fresh and cured.

Pork is eaten all around the world, with the exception of Jewish and Islamic cultures. As pigs are unable to sweat, and are therefore very sensitive to heat and will die if it is too hot, it is unlikely that they found the Middle Eastern climate hospitable. In addition, pigs are scavengers, making consumption of their meat forbidden by Jewish dietary law.

Pork consumption has been on the increase for many years. The Chinese are the largest producers, followed closely by the Americans and Europeans. Today pigs for the fresh meat market are bred for low fat content. The pork that is now produced industrially is more than 50 per cent lower in fat than it was 50 years ago. There is very little intra-muscular fat in pork. Much of the fat can be found in a layer around the outside of the muscles, and this can be easily removed. Pork has a high amount of B vitamins, in addition to iron, zinc, and potassium.

Industrially produced pigs are fed on a diet of cereal flours until they weigh 90–100 kg at around 6 or 7 months old. The meat from animals slaughtered at this age is generally tender and mild in flavour. Bacon pigs are older when slaughtered, so the comparable cuts of bacon contain more fat than those of fresh pork.

Common Breeds

The most common breeds for industrial production are the Landrace, the Large White and the Duroc. Rare breed pigs, such as the Gloucester Old Spot and the Saddleback, raised as free-range animals, are becoming increasingly popular because of their more intense flavour. Wild boar meat can also be found on sale now, having been scarce because of the animal's near extinction in the UK.

Some pigs are sold as suckling pigs when they are 4–6 weeks old. At this age their flesh is extremely tender and has a very mild, delicate flavour. Weaned piglets older than 6 weeks are called 'porkers'. Suckling pig is a traditional dish at Easter celebrations in many southern European countries.

Whole suckling pig is ideally roasted on a spit, but if this is not possible, it can be roasted in a very large oven. During Elizabethan times suckling pig was often served boned and stuffed as a chaudfroid, a preparation of cold meat coated with aspic-mayonnaise. Today suckling pig is traditionally served hot with the head on, with an apple or orange between the jaws.

Choosing Pork

- Pork is not hung, so this information is not given at the retail level.
- The meat should be pale pink, not red or dark, which would suggest an older animal. However, rare breed animals and those that have been raised free range will have a darker colour than industrially produced meat.
- The meat should be close-grained and firm to the touch.
- The meat should be evenly covered with a layer of fat no more than 1 cm thick. The fat should be firm and white, not oily, and without a greyish tinge.
- The bones should be small and bluish-pink in colour, indicating that the meat is from a young animal.
- The skin should be thin, pliable, and free of hair. Older pigs have coarse, thick skin.

Storing Pork

Fresh pork should be stored in the refrigerator for up to 2 days. It can be frozen double-wrapped for up to 6 months. Pork mince should be cooked and consumed within 24 hours. If frozen, it will keep for up to 3 months.

Cuts of Pork

Most of the fresh pork sold in Britain is cut from the back, leg and shoulder of the pig. The more unusual cuts will need to be ordered from the butcher.

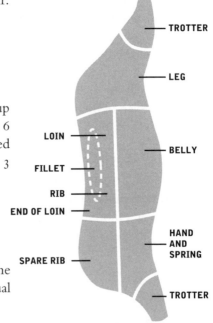

TROTTER

LEG

LOIN

BELLY

FILLET

RIB

END OF LOIN

HAND
AND
SPRING

SPARE RIB

TROTTER

Cut	Recommended Cooking Methods	Recipe Reference
Baby back ribs Spare ribs	Barbecuing/Roasting/Baking	Five-spice Barbecue Pork Ribs (page 213) Chinese Spare Ribs (page 211)
Belly	Roasting	Slow-roast Belly Pork (page 199)
	Braising	Braised Loin of Pork with Prunes (page 201)
	Pies	Pork Pie (page 220)
	Sausages	Classic Pork Sausages (page 239) Boudin Blanc (page 241)
Fillet/tenderloin	Roasting Grilling	Pork Fillet with Bramley Crushed Potatoes (page 207)
	Frying	Thai Basil Pork (page 206)
Hand and spring	Stewing/Braising	Hot Sweet Potato and Sausage Stew (page 245)
	Pies	Pork Pie (page 220)
Leg	Roasting	Roast Pork (page 194)
	Stewing	Java Pork (see page 205)
	Braising	Braised Loin of Pork with Prunes (page 201)
	Pies	Pork Pie (page 220)
Loin	Roasting	Roast Pork (page 194)
Loin chops	Grilling	Grilled Pork Chops with Caramelized Apples (page 203)
	Frying	See frying times for beef steaks (page 35)
Trotter	Braising	Pigs' Trotters and Porcini Mushrooms (page 215)

Methods of Cooking Pork

Pork comes from young, relatively lean animals, so can be cooked by any cooking method (see Methods of Cooking Meat, page 11). Pork is traditionally cooked until it is no longer pink, as historically pigs have been associated with eating waste and used to be prone to trichinosis worms. These days it is unlikely that good-quality pork would be a health risk when eaten pink, but it is still usually cooked until well done. However, because of its low fat content and negligible amount of marbling in the meat, pork risks being dry and tough if overcooked. Most chefs recommend cooking to 65°C/150°F interior temperature.

Roasting

The best cuts for roasting as a Sunday joint are the loin and leg, but the belly can also be roasted successfully. A suckling pig is roasted whole, either on a spit or in the oven.
• **Belly:** This is cut from the rear end of the belly and is quite fatty. Slow roasting is the best method of cooking it because the fat keeps the meat moist. Choose a cut from the thick end as it has a higher proportion of meat. Belly pork may be eaten fresh or salted. When eaten fresh, it is often boned, stuffed and rolled before roasting.
• **Fillet/Tenderloin:** Can be trimmed of its membrane and roasted whole. Care must be taken not to overcook it or it will become very dry.

- **Leg:** Sold as a large joint weighing 4.5–6.75 kg, or cut into upper fillet and lower knuckle.
- **Loin:** This is considered to be superior to leg and is more expensive. A loin roast with the bones in and part of the fillet still attached is particularly good because the bones give extra flavour and the meat becomes meltingly tender. The loin is a large joint that is sold either whole or cut into fore loin and hind loin joints. The loin can also be boned, stuffed (if desired) and rolled.

Making crackling

Crackling is the skin of the pig that has been roasted until it is brown and crisp. Liberally sprinkled with salt, it is often the favourite part of a roasted joint of pork. The best crackling comes from large roasts that have spent a long time, at least 2 hours, in the oven. Scoring the skin allows the heat to penetrate more easily into the layer of fat below the skin and makes the crackling easier to cut once roasted. Ask the butcher to score the skin for you, or do it yourself with a small, very sharp knife. Rub the skin with oil and sprinkle generously with sea salt just before roasting.

Grilling and Frying

Pork is bred to be lean, so if especially tender cuts, such as loin chops and fillet, are overcooked, the meat will be dry and tough. This presents a challenge to the cook. It is difficult to cook the meat until it is no longer pink but still moist and juicy. Pork chops benefit from brining (see page 9). Also read Testing Roast Meat for Doneness (page 14) before cooking the recipes for loin chops and fillet/tenderloin.

Chops are sliced from the loin or spare rib joints, and are generally 2 cm thick. Loin chops are usually cut from either end of the fore loin and have a thick layer of fat running along the outer edge. They are trimmed of rind, and the fat should be snipped or cut across (from the outside towards the meat) at 1 cm intervals because the fat shrinks during cooking, and this tends to make the chops curl out of shape. Chump chops are cut from the hind loin and have a bone at their centre. Spare-rib chops are cut from just behind the head. They contain less fat and bone than loin and chump chops, and are usually cut more thinly.

Stewing and Pies

Any of the cuts of pork are suitable for stewing or making into pies, but it makes economic sense to use less expensive cuts, such as the shoulder.

Preparing a Pork Fillet/Tenderloin

The fillet (or tenderloin) lies along the back of the pig next to the loin. It is the leanest and most tender pork cut. A pork fillet weighs about 340 g and will serve two generously.

1   Remove and discard the small 'false fillet' that is sometimes found running the length of the fillet. Using a boning knife or thin fish filleting knife, trim the silver membrane from the fillet.

Removing the membrane
from pork fillet

2 To prepare medallions, cut the fillet across the length, slightly on the diagonal, into 3 cm slices.

3 Place the slices in a single layer between two sheets of cling film, then beat with a small heavy saucepan or frying pan to flatten to half their thickness. This helps to tenderize the pork and allows it to cook more quickly.

Preparing Feet and Trotters

Although the feet of calves, sheep and lambs are available, pigs' trotters are the most widely used for cooking. Calves' feet are generally split and used for stock (see page 449).

Pigs' trotters are purchased scalded, dehaired and dehoofed. Sometimes they are brined, and in ethnic markets they can be coloured a vibrant red. They can be cooked whole, stewed in a well-flavoured stock, grilled or braised. They can also be boned and stuffed with forcemeat before roasting, braising or crumbling and frying. Pigs trotters' contain a large quantity of connective tissue and are often boiled to make jellied stock and brawns. Hot pigs' trotters are traditionally served with mustard sauce; when cold, they're often accompanied with vinaigrette.

1 Buy blanched pigs' trotters. Singe off any remaining hairs.

2 Place in a large pan and cover with water and aromatic vegetables. Bring to a simmer and cook for 4 hours, or until tender.

3 Weight the trotter under a chopping board to press out excess water.

4 Slit the underside of each trotter, starting at the ankle end.

5 Using a sharp knife, cut the main tendon, then start to work off the skin by cutting around it close to the bone. (a)

6 Pull the skin right down and cut through the knuckle joint at the first set of toes. Snap and twist off the bones and discard. (b)

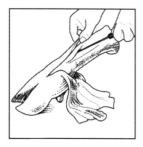

Working off the skin (a)

Cutting the main tendon (b)

Pork Roasting Table

	Oven temperature			Cooking time	Internal temperature	
	°C	°F	Gas mark		°C	°F
Brown	220°C	425°F	7	30 mins plus . . .	—	—
Then cook until well done	190°C	375°F	5	+ 50 mins per kg	70°	160°

Roast Pork with Apple Sauce

SERVES 4–6

1 × 2 kg loin or leg of pork, skin intact
oil
salt
1 small bunch of watercress, to garnish

For the gravy

20 g plain flour
300 ml Brown Stock (see page 452)
freshly ground pepper

To serve

Apple Sauce (see below)

1 Heat the oven to 220°C/425°F/gas mark 7.
2 If you want crackling, use a sharp knife to score through the rind evenly at 6 mm intervals. Rub with oil and salt.
3 Place the pork in a roasting pan and roast at the top of the oven for 2½ hours. After 30 minutes turn the temperature down to 190°C/375°F/gas mark 5. (The initial high temperature is important to promote crisp crackling.)
4 Once the pork is cooked, place it on a serving dish and allow to stand, uncovered, in a warm place.
5 To make the gravy, tip out all but 2 tablespoons of fat from the roasting pan, reserving as much of the meat juices as possible.
6 Add the flour and stir over a medium heat until well browned.
7 Remove from the heat, add the stock gradually and mix well with a wire whisk or wooden spoon. Return to the heat and bring slowly to the boil, stirring all the time. Simmer for a few minutes until the gravy is shiny. Season to taste with salt and pepper. Strain into a warmed gravy boat.
8 Garnish the pork with watercress and serve with the gravy and apple sauce.

APPLE SAUCE

450 g Bramley apples
grated zest of ¼ lemon

3 tablespoons water
2 teaspoons sugar

1 Peel, quarter, core and chop the apples.
2 Place in a heavy saucepan with the lemon zest, water and sugar. Cover and cook over a very low heat until the apples are soft, stirring occasionally. Add extra sugar if required.

Loin and best end of pork, veal and lamb are often roasted on the bone to prevent shrinkage, but to carve them it is easier to remove the meat from the ribcage and slice to the desired thickness. To carve a loin of pork, the crackling can be removed in one piece. The meat is then sliced and the crackling can be cut, with scissors, into the same number of pieces as there are slices of meat. If boned, the meat is cut similarly, but in thinner slices, about 5 mm thick.

To carve a loin of pork, remove the bones and crackling before slicing

Wine: Aromatic, fruity white, especially from Germany or Alsace

Pork: What has gone wrong when...

The crackling is not crisp enough.
- The pork roast was not cooked for long enough.
- The skin was not scored through to the fat layer.
- The pork roast was cooked at too low a temperature.
- The pork roast was covered.
- The skin was insufficiently salted before roasting.

Roast Suckling Pig with Coriander

Whole spit-roasted pigs, either suckling or fully grown, form the centrepiece of feasts around the world. A roast suckling pig should be cooked to the point where it is just cooked inside, with a crisp, brown skin. It can be eaten hot or cold.

SERVES 8–10

1 × 6 kg suckling pig
18 cloves of garlic
grated zest and juice of 3 limes
4 tablespoons chopped fresh coriander
2 tablespoons capers, rinsed and chopped
4 tablespoons olive oil
1 teaspoon salt
1 teaspoon finely grated black pepper

1 teaspoon curry powder
1 bunch of coriander, stalks removed
2 tablespoons sunflower oil

To garnish

1 bunch of watercress
1 small apple

1 Using a sharp knife, cut 2 cm incisions all over the body, but not the head, of the pig. Slice 5 cloves of garlic thinly and tuck into the incisions.

2 Crush the remaining cloves of garlic and mix with the lime zest and juice, chopped coriander, capers, olive oil, salt, pepper and curry powder.

3 Rub half the mixture around the cavity of the pig and the remainder over the outside.

4 Place the coriander leaves inside the body cavity. Leave to marinate in the refrigerator for 24 hours.

5 Heat the oven to 200°C/400°F/gas mark 6.

6 Place the pig in a large roasting pan with the back facing upwards. Cover the ears and snout with foil to prevent them from burning.

7 Brush with sunflower oil and rub salt over the skin. Roast for 30 minutes, basting regularly to prevent the skin from cracking.

8 Turn the oven down to 180°/350°F/gas mark 4 and continue to roast for 1½ hours, or until the juices run clear when the thigh meat is pierced with a skewer.

9 Let the pig stand for 20 minutes before serving garnished with the watercress and the apple placed in the jaws.

NOTE: If you roast the pig on a wire rack, the skin will crisp all over as the heat of the oven circulates freely around the pig.

Wine: Aromatic dry or fruity white, such as Australian Riesling

Boned Loin of Pork Roast with Sour Cherry, Lime and Sage Stuffing

SERVES 4–6

1 × 1.4 kg boned loin of pork
1 small onion, sliced
1 tablespoon olive oil
sea salt

For the stuffing
100 g dried sour cherries
2 tablespoons brandy
1 tablespoon butter

1 small onion, finely chopped
100 g fresh breadcrumbs
zest of 1 orange
juice of ½ lime
2 tablespoons chopped fresh parsley
1 tablespoon chopped fresh purple sage
½ egg, beaten
salt and freshly ground black pepper

1 Open out the pork loin on a chopping board cut-side up. Remove any fat from the interior. Place the sliced onion in the bottom of a large roasting pan.

2 Heat the oven to 200°C/400°F/gas mark 6.

3 Meanwhile, make the stuffing. Chop the cherries roughly and soak in the brandy for 10 minutes. The brandy can be heated a little if the cherries are very dry.

4 Melt the butter in a small saucepan and sweat the chopped onion, covered with a dampened piece of greaseproof paper and a lid, until softened.

5 Stir the onion into the breadcrumbs.

6 Mix the cherries into the breadcrumbs along with the orange zest, lime juice, parsley and sage.

7 Add enough egg to lightly bind the stuffing. Season with salt and freshly ground black pepper.

8 Place the stuffing along the inside of the meat. Roll the meat up and tie with string at 3 cm intervals. Rub the skin of the pork with the oil, then sprinkle with sea salt.

9 Place the pork, stuffing-side down, on the onions in the roasting pan and roast in the centre of the oven for 50 minutes per 1 kg. Allow to stand for 20 minutes before removing the string and carving into thick slices.

Wine: Either a fruity red (Beaujolais style) or an aromatic dry white (Riesling)

Pork Chop Roast with Sticky Toffee Pears

This recipe uses a pork loin, which is roasted on the bone before being carved into chops for serving. Cooking meat in a large piece on its bone helps keep the meat moist and succulent. The pork loin is French-trimmed, as per a lamb rack, which gives an elegant finish to the dish. It looks particularly impressive when carved at the table.

The accompanying pears are cooked in brown sugar and honey, giving them a soft and sticky toffee-like coating. The addition of Poire William liqueur, whilst a little extravagant, is delicious. Calvados, cognac and brandy are all good substitutes.

SERVES 4

1 × 4-bone pork loin, French-trimmed
   (see page 141)
oil
coarse sea salt
600 ml medium dry cider
300 ml Brown Chicken Stock (see page 454)
salt and freshly ground black pepper
1 small bunch of watercress, to garnish

For the sticky toffee pears

2 large ripe Conference pears, peeled,
   quartered and cored
85 g unsalted butter
1½ tablespoons soft dark brown sugar
1 tablespoon Poire William liqueur
1 tablespoon clear honey
4 small sage leaves, finely shredded

1 Heat the oven to 220°C/425°F/gas mark 7.
2 Using a sharp knife, score the skin at intervals about 5mm apart, cutting through the skin but not right through the fat.
3 Pour a kettleful of boiling water over the meat, then pat dry with kitchen paper. Brush the skin lightly with oil and sprinkle with sea salt to help create a crisp crackling.
4 Place the pork in a roasting pan and roast for 30 minutes.
5 Reduce the heat to 180°C/350°F/gas mark 4. Pour the cider and stock into the pan and continue to roast for a further 45 minutes, or until the juices run clear when the meat is pierced with a skewer. Remove the pork from the pan and allow to rest in a warm place.
6 Meanwhile, cut each pear quarter in half lengthwise.
7 Melt the butter in a shallow frying pan and sprinkle with the sugar. Stir over a low heat until the sugar has melted.
8 Add the pears to the pan and cook over a gentle heat until soft.
9 Increase the heat under the pears and pour over the Poire William and honey. Cook briskly until the pears are a good golden brown colour.
10 Stir in the shredded sage leaves and keep warm.
11 Meanwhile, make the gravy. Skim the fat out of the roasting pan and bring the remaining liquid to the boil. Boil vigorously until syrupy and reduced to about 200 ml. Season with salt and pepper.
12 Carve the pork between the bones into 4 thick chops, place on a warmed serving dish and pour over the gravy. Serve with the sticky pears and garnish with the watercress.

Drink: Aromatic fruity white or a good cider

Slow-roast Belly Pork with Caramelized Quinces

Pork belly is a very fatty cut of meat. When cooked slowly most of the fat renders down and becomes liquid, basting the meat from within. Increasing the oven temperature towards the end of the cooking time results in a crunchy layer of fat over the surface of the meat, similar to that of crackling on a pork roast. This, along with the soft, rich meat and the acidity and sweetness of the quinces, makes for a well-balanced assembly of flavours and textures.

SERVES 4

1.35 kg belly pork, boned
oil
1 onion, thickly sliced
1 carrot, roughly chopped
1 stick of celery, roughly chopped
600 ml Brown Stock (see page 452)
300 ml white wine
2 tablespoons Marsala
1 bouquet garni (see page 512)
1 bay leaf

2 cloves
salt and freshly ground black pepper
sprigs of watercress, to garnish

For the caramelized quinces
2 quinces
50 g unsalted butter
2 tablespoon golden caster sugar
2 tablespoons water
2 tablespoons Sauternes

1 Heat the oven to 230°C/450°F/gas mark 8.
2 Using a sharp knife, score the skin of the pork in a cross-hatch pattern, keeping the cuts about 5 mm apart. Take care not to cut right through the fat. Pour a kettleful of boiling water over the pork, then discard the water and pat the pork dry. Brush the skin with a little oil and sprinkle with salt.
3 Place the onion, carrot and celery in a roasting pan and put the pork on top, skin-side up. Pour the stock, wine and Marsala around the meat, add the bouquet garni, bay leaf and cloves and season with salt and pepper. Roast in the middle of the oven for 15–20 minutes, or until the crackling is brown and crisp. Reduce the heat to 140°C/275°F/gas mark 1 and cook for a further 2½ hours. It may be necessary to cover the meat loosely with foil if it gets too brown.
4 For the caramelized quinces, peel the fruit and cut in half. Cut each half into 3 slices and remove the cores.
5 Melt the butter and sugar in a large sauté pan. Place the quince slices in the pan and pour over the water and Sauternes. Cover the pan with a tight-fitting lid and cook very gently for 1½ hours, stirring occasionally, until the quinces are very soft but still holding their shape.
6 Remove the lid from the pan and increase the heat. Cook briskly for 1–2 minutes, or until the quinces are well caramelized and the liquid has evaporated. Keep warm.
7 Transfer the pork to a plate and leave in a warm place to rest.
8 Strain the contents of the roasting pan through a fine sieve into a saucepan, pressing the vegetables gently with the back of a spoon. Place the saucepan on the heat and bring to the boil. Reduce the sauce until it is thick and syrupy. Taste and season if necessary.
9 Carve the meat thickly and arrange in overlapping slices on a warm serving dish. Pour the sauce over the meat and garnish with watercress. Serve with the caramelized quinces.

Drink: Aromatic, fruity white or a good cider

Carolina Pulled Pork

In the southern United States there is an ongoing competition to see who can make the best pulled pork. Family recipes are carefully guarded to be passed from one generation to the next. It is the dish to make for large, informal summertime gatherings, rather like coronation chicken in the UK. Although the preparation is lengthy, it welcomes being made in advance, and can be prepared up to two days before needed. Serve in baps along with side dishes of coleslaw and dill pickles, or with rice.

SERVES 8

1 × 1.8 kg boneless pork shoulder roast
about 750 ml Brown Chicken Stock (see page 454)
½ teaspoon celery salt
½ teaspoon cayenne pepper

For the spice rub
2 tablespoons smoked paprika
2 tablespoons dark muscovado sugar
1 tablespoon mild chilli powder
1 teaspoon cracked black pepper
1 teaspoon dry English mustard
½ teaspoon garlic salt

For the sauce
reserved cooking liquid
150 ml cider vinegar
150 ml tomato ketchup
2 tablespoons dark muscovado sugar
salt, as required

1 Remove the rind and fat from the pork shoulder. If necessary, open it out (like butterflying a leg of lamb, see page 138) so that the meat is of even thickness, about 4 cm.
2 Combine all the ingredients for the spice rub in a bowl. Using your hands, rub the mixture into the meat.
3 Place the meat in a non-corrosive dish, cover with cling film and chill overnight.
4 Heat a barbecue (or grill if absolutely necessary) to a medium heat, then brown the meat on all sides to cook the spices. The meat will not be cooked at this point.
5 Heat the oven to 150°C/300°F/gas mark 2.
6 Place the meat in an ovenproof casserole dish in which it fits snugly. Add enough stock to cover.
7 Place in the oven and cook for 3–4 hours, or until the meat can be shredded with a fork. Although the meat will be a bit dry at this point, it will be rehydrated by the sauce.
8 Remove the meat from the casserole dish and place on a heatproof dish.
9 Skim the fat from the cooking liquid, then add the sauce ingredients. Boil to reduce until just syrupy. Taste and add salt, if necessary.
10 Using two forks, shred the pork into bite-sized chunks. Place in a deep heatproof dish.
11 Pour over the sauce and leave to stand for 1 hour, or chill overnight, so that the meat absorbs it.
12 To serve, reheat gently and serve on baps or with rice.

Wine: Dry white, such as Vouvray sec or Fiano di Avellino

Grilled Pork Quesadillas

Use leftover Carolina Pulled Pork to make as many of these delicious sandwiches as your leftovers permit.

MAKES 1

1 large flour tortilla

1 tablespoon ready-made hot salsa

3 tablespoons pulled pork

2 tablespoons grated Monterey Jack or Cheddar cheese

oil, for brushing

soured cream, to serve

1 Heat the grill to its highest setting.

2 Place the tortilla on the work surface and spread with a half-moon of salsa.

3 Cover with the pork, then the cheese.

4 Fold over the uncovered half of the tortilla to make a 'sandwich'.

5 Place on the grill pan and brush with a little oil.

6 Grill about 7 cm from the heat source until toasted. Turn the tortilla over, brush with a little oil and grill this side until toasted.

7 Cut into wedges to serve, accompanied by soured cream for dipping.

Wine: Full-bodied dry white, such as Californian Chardonnay

Braised Loin of Pork with Prunes

SERVES 4

1 × 1.35 kg loin or leg of pork, skinned and fat removed

oil, for frying

15 g butter

1 onion, finely chopped

300 ml Brown Stock (see page 452)

100 ml red wine

115 g ready-to-eat prunes

1 tablespoon redcurrant jelly

1 bay leaf

2 sprigs of fresh thyme

150 ml whipping cream

1 small bunch of watercress, to garnish

1 Heat the oven to 150°C/300°F/gas mark 2.

2 Bone and tie the loin.

3 Heat the oil in a flameproof casserole. Add the butter and, when foaming, add the pork. Fry until lightly browned all over. Add the onion and fry until golden.

4 Add the stock, wine, one-third of the prunes, the redcurrant jelly, bay leaf and thyme. Bring to the boil, then cover and cook in the oven for 1½ hours.

5 Remove the pork from the casserole and carve neatly. Arrange in overlapping slices on a serving dish and keep warm in the turned-off oven while you make the sauce.

6 Strain the cooking liquor, removing any excess fat. Boil until the sauce has reduced to a syrupy consistency. Add the cream and the remaining prunes.

7 Spoon the sauce over the pork and garnish with watercress to serve.

Wine: Aromatic fruity white or a Saumur-Champigny from the Loire Valley

Cider-braised Pork Chops

SERVES 4

4 pork chops, trimmed of rind and fat

2 tablespoons oil

1 medium onion, finely chopped

1 stick of celery, chopped

2 tablespoons Calvados

150 ml dry cider

150 ml White Chicken Stock (see page 451)

75 ml double cream

1 teaspoon cornflour

lemon juice, to taste

2 tablespoons finely chopped parsley, to garnish

salt and freshly ground black pepper

1 Season the chops with salt and pepper.

2 Heat half the oil in a small saucepan. Add the onion and celery, then cover with a piece of dampened greaseproof paper and sweat until soft.

3 Heat the remaining oil in a sauté pan and brown the chops on both sides.

4 Add the Calvados and set alight. When the flames subside, add the softened vegetables and the cider and stock. Bring to a simmer, then cover and cook for 15 minutes, or until the pork is just cooked through (see The Test of the Thumb, page 20).

5 Using a slotted spoon, remove the pork from the pan and keep warm. Sieve the juices into a small pan. Remove the vegetables from the sieve and divide them between 4 plates. Place a pork chop on top of each mound.

6 Mix together the cream and cornflour and whisk into the juices in the pan. Season to taste with lemon juice, salt and pepper. Pour over the pork and garnish with the parsley.

Drink: Aromatic, fruity white or a good cider

Gruyère-crusted Pork Chops

SERVES 4

2 tablespoons vegetable oil

1 small onion, finely chopped

4 boneless pork loin chops

2 tablespoons Madeira

300 ml White Chicken Stock (see page 451)

50 g breadcrumbs

50 g grated Gruyère cheese

2 teaspoons chopped fresh thyme

2 teaspoons chopped fresh parsley

1 teaspoon cornflour

salt and freshly ground black pepper

1 Place half the oil in a small saucepan over a low heat. Stir in the onion, then cover with a piece of dampened greaseproof paper and a lid. Sweat until softened and golden.

2 Put the remaining oil in a sauté pan. Season the chops with salt and pepper, then brown over a medium heat. Place in a single layer in an ovenproof dish.

3 Mix together the Madeira and stock; use to deglaze the pan. Boil the *déglaçage* until reduced by half. Set aside.

4 Heat the oven to 200°C/400°F/gas mark 6.

5 Combine the breadcrumbs, cheese, thyme, parsley and softened onions.

6 Divide between the chops and press over the surface. Pour the Madeira sauce around the chops, leaving the crumb topping exposed.

7 Bake the chops for 30 minutes, or until cooked through and browned.

8 Using a fish slice, transfer the chops to warmed plates.

9 Sieve the sauce into a small saucepan and bring to the boil. Stir the cornflour into 2 tablespoons cold water and whisk into the boiling sauce. Boil for 1 minute to thicken, then serve with the chops.

Wine: Alsace Pinot Gris or a fine Swiss dry white, such as Dezaley or Fendant

Grilled Pork Chops with Caramelized Apples

SERVES 4

4 × 170 g pork chops
oil, for brushing
3–4 sage leaves, chopped, or pinch of dried sage
freshly ground black pepper

For the caramelized apples

2 eating apples
butter, for frying
1 teaspoon sugar

sprigs of watercress, to garnish

1 Heat the grill to its highest setting.

2 Trim the rind from the chops and make short cuts through the fat, as described on page 192. Brush lightly with oil. Sprinkle with the sage.

3 Season the chops with pepper, then grill for 5–7 minutes on each side, or until cooked through. Keep warm on a warmed serving platter.

4 Cut the apples into eighths and remove the cores.

5 Melt a knob of butter in a frying pan and, when it is foaming, add the apples. Sprinkle with the sugar and fry lightly on both sides until golden brown but not mushy. The sugar will caramelize, giving a toffee-like coating to the apples.

6 Garnish the chops with the caramelized apples and the watercress.

Wine: Aromatic, fruity white, such as Vouvray

Pork with Pumpkin and Pecans

SERVES 4

2 tablespoons oil

1 Spanish onion, finely chopped

½ teaspoon ground cinnamon

½ teaspoon ground cumin

½ teaspoon ground coriander

1 tablespoon soft brown sugar

500 g pumpkin or butternut squash, peeled,
  deseeded and cut into 3 cm chunks

100 ml medium sherry

150 ml White Chicken Stock (see page 451)

500 g lean pork, cut into 3 cm chunks

50 g chopped pecans

30 g fresh thyme, chopped

salt and freshly ground black pepper

To serve

Boiled Rice or Mashed Potatoes
  (see page 494 or 491)

1 Heat 1 tablespoon of the oil in a large non-stick saucepan and cook the onion until soft but not coloured.

2 Add the spices and sugar, turn up the heat and stir until the onion caramelizes. Add the pumpkin and cook for 2 minutes, stirring continuously and adding a little water if necessary to prevent the onions burning. Add the sherry and stock.

3 Heat the remaining oil in a large frying pan. Fry the pork until lightly browned.

4 Add the browned pork to the pumpkin mixture. Bring to the boil, then simmer until the pork and pumpkin are tender, about 15 minutes. Add more water if it becomes too dry.

5 Add the chopped nuts and thyme and season to taste with salt and pepper. Serve with rice or mashed potatoes.

Wine: Dry or aromatic fruity white, perhaps a Pecorino

Java Pork

SERVES 4

600 g trimmed, boneless pork leg or shoulder meat

3 tablespoons oil, for frying

1 medium onion, finely chopped

1 clove of garlic, crushed

4 tablespoons tikka paste

grated zest and juice of 1 orange

200 ml White Chicken Stock (see page 451)

2 teaspoons cornflour

4 tablespoons Greek yoghurt

salt and freshly ground black pepper

2 tablespoons chopped coriander, to garnish

1 Cut the pork into 3 cm cubes, removing any skin and excess fat. Set aside.

2 Heat 1 tablespoon oil, then stir in the onion. Cover with a piece of dampened greaseproof paper and a lid. Cook over a low heat until soft, stirring occasionally. Add the garlic and cook for a further 30 seconds. Set aside.

3 In a sauté pan or flameproof casserole dish, heat the remaining oil over a medium heat. Season the pork with salt and pepper. Brown the pork cubes in the oil, in batches if necessary.

4 Heat the oven to 150°C/300°F/gas mark 2.

5 Return all the pork to the pan or casserole dish and stir in the tikka paste. Place over a medium heat and cook, stirring, for about 2 minutes.

6 Add the orange zest, juice and stock. Bring to a simmer and cover with a lid.

7 Place in the oven for 1½ hours, or until the pork is tender.

8 To serve, remove the pork from the casserole dish and keep warm. Place the casserole dish on the hob over a medium heat. Mix the cornflour with 2 tablespoons water and stir into the sauce.

9 Boil for 2 minutes, then stir in the yoghurt. Heat through, but do not allow to boil. Adjust the seasoning. Pour over the meat and garnish with the coriander to serve.

Wine: Off-dry white, such as Australian Riesling or a Pinot Blanc from Alsace

Thai Basil Pork

SERVES 4

1–2 tablespoons vegetable oil

6 cloves of garlic, finely chopped

3 shallots, finely chopped

450 g pork fillet/tenderloin, trimmed and cut
  into bite-sized pieces

4 Thai red chillies, chopped and pounded into a paste

2 kaffir lime leaves, finely diced

½ teaspoon caster sugar

2 tablespoons dark soy sauce or oyster sauce

2 tablespoons fish sauce

1 bunch of fresh Thai basil, shredded

freshly ground white or black pepper

1 Heat the oil in a wok and add the garlic.

2 Stir in the shallots, then the pork. Cook for 2–3 minutes, or until cooked through.

3 Stir in the chilli paste, kaffir lime leaves, sugar, soy sauce, fish sauce and Thai basil.

4 When the basil has wilted, grind over the pepper and serve.

Wine: New World Chardonnay, Australian Riesling, or New Zealand Pinot Gris

Stir-fried Pork Fillet/Tenderloin

SERVES 4

450 g pork fillet/tenderloin, trimmed

1 tablespoon dry sherry

1 tablespoon soy sauce

1 cm piece of fresh root ginger, peeled and grated

2 tablespoons vegetable oil

100 g baby sweetcorn, blanched

100 g mangetout, topped and tailed

1 bunch of spring onions, sliced

freshly ground black pepper

For the sauce

1 tablespoon dry sherry

1 tablespoon soy sauce

1 Cut the pork into strips the size of your little finger and marinate for at least 1 hour in the sherry, soy sauce, ginger and ground black pepper.

2 In a frying pan or wok, heat the oil over high heat and stir-fry the pork and marinade until cooked through.

3 Add the baby corn, mangetout and sauce ingredients. Cook, stirring, for about 2 more minutes, until the vegetables are warm and the meat is glazed. Sprinkle with the spring onions.

Wine: Aromatic fruity white, especially Alsace Pinot Gris or Gewürztraminer

Pork Fillet/Tenderloin with Bramley Crushed Potatoes and Calvados Sauce

Traditionally, apple sauce is served with pork. Here the sharp flavour of Bramley apples is incorporated into the potatoes and enhanced by the addition of Calvados sauce.

SERVES 4

675 g pork fillet/tenderloin, trimmed
½ tablespoon oil
20 g unsalted butter
2 tablespoons water
3 tablespoons Calvados
75 ml double cream
salt and freshly ground black pepper

For the potatoes

450 g new potatoes
50 g unsalted butter
1 large Bramley apple, peeled,
    cored and cut into small dice
1 tablespoon sugar

1 Season the pork with salt and pepper. Heat the oil in a frying pan. Add the first quantity of butter and, when foaming, add the pork and brown quickly all over. Reduce the heat, then cover the pan with a lid. Cook the pork gently for 20–25 minutes.

2 Meanwhile, cook the potatoes in a pan of boiling salted water until tender, then drain and return to the hot pan. Crush the potatoes roughly with a wooden spoon. Set aside and keep warm.

3 Melt the butter in a frying pan and, when foaming, add the apple. Sprinkle over the sugar and cook briskly until the apple pieces are golden brown and cooked through. Add the apple to the potatoes and pour over the buttery juices. Season with salt and pepper and keep warm while you make the sauce.

4 Transfer the pork to a plate and allow to rest in a warm place. Pour off all the fat from the pan. Add the water and the Calvados, swish it about and bring to the boil. Add the cream and simmer for 2–3 minutes, until the sauce is of a coating consistency. Season with salt and pepper.

5 To serve: cut the pork at an angle into 12 medallions. Place a spoonful of the potatoes on 4 warmed serving plates. Put 3 slices of the pork on top of each mound of potatoes and pour over the sauce.

Drink: Aromatic, fruity white or a good cider

Pan-fried Pork with Warm Mustard, Prune and Watercress Salad

SERVES 4

675 g pork fillet/tenderloin, well trimmed

1 tablespoon oil

110 g ready-to-eat stoned prunes

1½ tablespoons balsamic vinegar

2 large bunches of watercress

1 large bunch of flat leaf parsley

2 tablespoons water

1 tablespoon wholegrain mustard

salt and freshly ground black pepper

1 Season the pork with salt and pepper. Heat the oil in a frying pan and brown the meat on all sides. Reduce the heat and continue to cook gently for 20–25 minutes.

2 Cut the prunes in half, place them in a saucepan with the vinegar and bring to the boil. Leave to stand for 5 minutes.

3 Wash and pick over the watercress and parsley, discarding the stalks. Chop coarsely, then place in a bowl.

4 When the pork is cooked and the juices run clear when pierced with a skewer, remove it from the pan and keep warm.

5 Strain the prunes and pour the vinegar into the hot frying pan. Add the prunes to the watercress. Pour the water into the pan with the strained vinegar and place over the heat, scraping up any sediment. Add the mustard to the pan and season with salt and pepper.

6 Pour the warm dressing over the watercress and prunes and toss lightly to mix. Divide between 4 serving plates.

7 Slice the pork fillet thickly on the diagonal, and arrange on top of the salad. Serve at once.

Wine: New World Chardonnay

Pork Fillet/Tenderloin Sauté with Wholegrain Mustard Sauce

SERVES 4

675 g pork fillet/tenderloin

3 tablespoons vegetable oil

3 tablespoons butter

150 ml apple juice

300 ml White Chicken Stock (see page 451)

1½ tablespoons wholegrain mustard

2 teaspoons cornflour

3 tablespoons double cream or crème fraîche

salt and freshly ground black pepper

1 tablespoon chopped fresh parsley, to garnish

1 Trim the pork fillet of any membrane, then cut on the diagonal into slices 2 cm thick. Place between two sheets of dampened greaseproof paper and beat with a heavy-based saucepan to flatten to 1 cm.

2 Heat half the oil in a large sauté pan and add half the butter.

3 Season the meat with salt and pepper, then fry in batches on both sides until golden brown. Set aside on a plate.

4 Use some of the apple juice to deglaze the pan between batches, reserving the *déglaçage*.

5 Pour the *déglaçage,* any remaining apple juice and the stock into the sauté pan and bring to the boil. Stir in the mustard. Return the meat to the pan, stir into the sauce, then cover and cook through, about 3 minutes.

6 Using a slotted spoon, transfer the meat to a serving dish and keep warm.

7 Stir the cornflour into the cream, then whisk into the sauce. Allow to boil and thicken to a coating consistency. Taste and season.

8 Pour the sauce over the meat and garnish with the parsley.

Wine: Alsace Pinot Gris, white Burgundy or a lighter New World Chardonnay

Cumin Pork Fillet/Tenderloin and Red Pepper Sauté

SERVES 4

450 g pork fillet/tenderloin, trimmed

3 tablespoons vegetable oil

1 red pepper, deseeded and sliced

2 shallots, finely chopped

1 red chilli, deseeded and finely chopped

2 teaspoons peeled and grated fresh root ginger

1 teaspoon cumin seeds, toasted and lightly crushed

1 clove of garlic, crushed

200 ml White Chicken Stock (see page 451)

300 ml coconut milk

2 tablespoons chopped fresh coriander leaves

salt and freshly ground black pepper

To serve

Boiled Rice (see page 494)

To garnish

coriander sprigs

lime wedges

1 Cut the pork at an angle into finger-sized strips. Season with salt and pepper.

2 Heat 2 tablespoons of the oil in a sauté pan over a medium heat and brown a few pieces of pork at a time, transferring them to a dish as they are ready.

3 Lower the heat, then add the remaining oil to the pan and cook the red pepper and shallots until they begin to soften. Add the chilli, ginger, cumin and garlic and cook for a further minute.

4 Add the stock and coconut milk. Return the pork to the pan, then simmer for 15 minutes, or until the pork is firm.

5 Using a slotted spoon, transfer the pork and peppers to a warmed serving dish and keep warm. Boil the sauce until it is the thickness of single cream.

6 Stir in the coriander and season if required.

7 Serve with boiled rice garnished with coriander sprigs and lime wedges.

Wine: Aromatic, fruity white or a dry rosé from Provence or Navarra

Sticky Soy-glazed Pork Fillet/Tenderloin with Coconut Rice

SERVES 4

1 tablespoon oil

675 g pork fillet/tenderloin, trimmed

4 tablespoons water

3 tablespoons dark soy sauce

1 tablespoon clear honey

1 cm piece of fresh root ginger, peeled
  and bruised with a rolling pin

freshly ground black pepper

For the rice

1 tablespoon Clarified Butter (see page xii)

1 kaffir lime leaf

1 medium-hot red Dutch chilli, deseeded and
  finely chopped

285 g Thai jasmine rice

1 × 400 ml can coconut milk

½ teaspoon salt

175 ml boiling water

steamed bok choi, to serve

1 Heat the oil in a heavy-based frying pan. Brown the pork well on all sides.

2 Remove the pork from the pan and set aside. Pour the water into the pan, scraping the bottom to remove any sediment. Add the soy sauce, honey and ginger and season with pepper. Return the pork to the pan and simmer very gently over a low heat for 15–20 minutes, basting occasionally with the sauce.

3 Meanwhile, prepare the rice. Gently heat the clarified butter in a large saucepan. Add the kaffir lime leaf and chilli and cook over a medium heat for a few seconds.

4 Stir in the rice, coconut milk, salt and boiling water. Bring to the boil, then cover, lower the heat and cook for 15 minutes, until all the liquid has been absorbed and the rice is tender.

5 Remove the pork from the pan and discard the ginger. Allow the pork to rest for 5 minutes before slicing into thick medallions. It may be necessary to return the pan to the heat to reduce the sauce to a sticky glaze.

6 Remove the kaffir lime leaf from the rice and fluff up with a fork to separate the grains. Divide the rice between 4 warmed serving bowls. Place the pork slices on top of the rice and pour over the sticky glaze. Serve with steamed bok choi.

Wine: Aromatic, off-dry white or an oaked Chardonnay

Spiced Pork, Sage and Apple Kebabs

SERVES 4

675 g pork fillet/tenderloin, trimmed

2 tablespoons sweet Hungarian paprika

2 eating apples, such as Cox's Orange Pippins

juice and finely grated zest of 1 lime

2 teaspoons sugar

16 sage leaves

2 tablespoons clear honey

salt and freshly ground black pepper

1 Heat the grill to its highest setting.

2 Cut the pork into 16 cubes and rub the paprika into them. Season with salt and pepper.

3 Cut the apples into quarters, remove the cores and cut each quarter into 3 pieces.

4 Toss the apples in the lime juice and zest, then roll in the sugar.

5 Thread 4 pieces of pork on to a metal skewer, alternating with a sage leaf and a piece of apple. Continue with the remaining pork and apple to make 4 kebabs.

6 Put the kebabs on to a grill pan and place under the heat. Cook for 7–10 minutes, turning occasionally, until the pork is brown and cooked through and the apples are lightly caramelized.

7 Remove the kebabs, drizzle with the honey and return to the grill until the honey is bubbling. Serve immediately.

Wine: New World Chardonnay or Australian Riesling

Chinese Spare Ribs

SERVES 4

1.25 kg meaty pork spare ribs

For the marinade

4 tablespoons clear honey

4 tablespoons soy sauce

1 clove of garlic, crushed

juice of 2 lemons

salt and freshly ground black pepper

1 Place the spare ribs in a non-corrosive dish or large plastic bag. Mix the marinade ingredients together. Pour over the ribs, then cover with cling film or seal the bag. Leave to marinate in the refrigerator for at least 1 hour, or up to 48 hours.

2 Heat the oven to 180°C/350°F/gas mark 4.

3 Transfer the spare ribs and marinade to a roasting pan, cover with foil and roast for 1¼ hours.

4 Remove the foil and roast uncovered, basting occasionally, for a further 30–45 minutes, or until the meat is so tender that it falls from the bone and is glazed and sticky.

Drink: Chilled lager with a slice of lime

Bigos

Also called Polish Hunters' Stew, Bigos is widely found in Poland. Each family will have a variation of this stew, which is considered to be the national dish. Some versions include venison and other game, as well as the pork. Serve with baked or boiled potatoes.

SERVES 8

500 g thick-cut pork spare-rib chops

500 g spicy Polish sausage, such as wieska
  or tuchowska

50 g smoked lardons

1 × 1 kg jar sauerkraut

10 g dried porcini mushrooms

2 large onions, chopped

2 tablespoons clear honey

4 tablespoons tomato purée

1 litre Brown Stock (see page 452)

200 g ready-to-eat prunes

2 bay leaves

4 juniper berries

2 whole cloves

salt and freshly ground black pepper

1 Cut the chops and sausage into 3 cm chunks and set aside on separate plates.
2 Place a flameproof casserole over a medium-low heat, add the lardons and cook to render the fat and brown the meat. Remove with a slotted spoon and set aside.
3 Season the pork pieces, then brown a few at a time in the rendered fat. Transfer to a plate when browned.
4 In the meantime, drain and rinse the sauerkraut. Place in a large saucepan with enough stock to cover. Simmer over a low heat.
5 Soak the porcini mushrooms in just enough boiling water to cover. Set aside.
6 Heat the oven to 170°C/325°F/gas mark 3.
7 Fry the onions in the pork fat until golden brown. Stir in the honey and tomato purée.
8 Return the lardons and pork to the pan. Add the sauerkraut and sausages and all the remaining stock.
9 Chop the porcini mushrooms and add to the pan along with their soaking liquid.
10 Add the prunes, bay leaves, juniper berries and cloves. Bring to a simmer, then place in the oven for 2–3 hours, or until the pork is tender enough to cut with a teaspoon.
11 If the stew has not become thick during cooking, transfer the meat to a warmed serving dish, then boil the cooking liquid to reduce.

Drink: Good English bitter

Five-spice Barbecue Pork Ribs

Prepare these ribs a day or two in advance of a barbecue to allow the marinade to flavour the meat.

SERVES 4

4 racks of baby back ribs

1 × 400 g can chopped tomatoes

For the marinade

300 ml pineapple juice

2 tablespoons tomato purée

1 tablespoon peeled and grated fresh root ginger

3 tablespoons dark muscovado sugar

2 teaspoons five-spice powder

¼ teaspoon ground cayenne pepper

2 tablespoons dark soy sauce

¼ teaspoon salt

1 Place the spare ribs in a non-corrosive dish or large plastic bag. Mix the marinade ingredients together. Pour over the ribs, then cover with cling film or seal the bag. Leave to marinate in the refrigerator for at least 2 hours, or overnight.

2 Heat the oven to 170°C/325°F/gas mark 3.

3 Transfer the spare ribs and marinade to a roasting pan, cover with foil and bake in the centre of the oven for 2 hours, or until tender.

4 Allow the ribs to cool in the marinade.

5 Remove the ribs from the marinade and set aside.

6 Place the marinade in a saucepan, add the chopped tomatoes with their juice and boil to reduce to a sauce.

7 Heat a barbecue or grill.

8 Brush the ribs generously with the sauce and grill until browned and slightly charred.

Drink: Chilled lager or beer

Pork Rib and Lentil Potage

SERVES 4

1 kg meaty pork spare ribs or ham bone

1.5 litres water

2 onions, finely sliced

2 large carrots, diced

2 sticks of celery, finely sliced

3 large sprigs of thyme

a few parsley stalks, bruised

3 bay leaves

10 whole cloves, wrapped in a piece of muslin

250 g green or brown lentils, soaked overnight,
   rinsed and drained

salt and freshly ground black pepper

chopped fresh parsley, to garnish

1 Put the spare ribs or ham bone into a large saucepan, cover with cold water and bring to the boil. Discard the water.

2 Pour the measured water over the ribs and add the vegetables, herbs, cloves and lentils to the pan. Season and bring to the boil.

3 Skim any scum from the surface of the pan. Reduce the heat and simmer for 1–1½ hours, or until the lentils are tender and beginning to break up.

4 Lift the ribs from the pan and allow them to cool. When cold enough to handle, remove the meat from the ribs and set aside. Discard the herbs and bag of cloves.

5 Liquidize the lentil stock in batches, adding more water if necessary. The soup should be fairly thick.

6 Return the soup to the pan, add the reserved meat and heat through. Serve garnished with the parsley.

Wine: Dry white or a Côtes-du-Rhône

Pigs' Trotters and Porcini Mushrooms

SERVES 4

55 g dried porcini mushrooms

340 g lean pork

115 g pork fat

1 teaspoon salt

freshly ground white pepper

pinch of ground allspice

1 teaspoon finely chopped fresh sage

4 prepared pigs' trotters (see page 193)

50 g butter, melted

50 g dry white breadcrumbs

To serve

Sauce Robert (see page 465)

Mashed Potatoes (see page 491)

1 Place the mushrooms in a bowl and pour over just enough boiling water to cover. Set aside.

2 Process the pork meat and fat in a food processor, then pass through a sieve.

3 Drain the mushrooms, reserving the liquid. Chop finely and add to the meat.

4 Season with the salt, pepper, allspice and sage. Add 1 tablespoon of the mushroom liquid. Poach a small piece of the mixture to check the seasoning.

5 Stuff the trotters with the mixture, then wrap each one tightly in a square of foil, forming a sausage shape. Refrigerate until firm.

6 Heat the oven to 180°C/350°F/gas mark 4.

7 Place the wrapped trotters on a baking sheet and bake for 45–60 minutes, or until the stuffing is piping hot when tested with a skewer.

8 Heat the grill until hot. Unwrap the trotters.

9 Brush the trotters with the melted butter, then roll in the breadcrumbs. Grill until well browned and crisp. Serve with sauce Robert and mashed potatoes.

Wine: Red Burgundy, Côtes-du-Rhône, or Pinot Noir from California or Oregon

Mu-shu Pork on Little Gem Leaves

These are delicious for canapés, but can also be served as a first course.

MAKES ABOUT 12 CANAPES

SERVES 4 AS A FIRST COURSE

1 tablespoon vegetable or groundnut oil

100 g minced pork

50 g shelled raw prawns, finely chopped

1 small clove of garlic, crushed

1 red chilli, deseeded and finely chopped

2 tablespoons finely chopped carrot

2 spring onions, finely chopped

2 tablespoons soy sauce

1 tablespoon rice wine vinegar

1 tablespoon light brown sugar

pinch of five-spice powder

1 tablespoon chopped fresh coriander leaves

salt

small leaves from 2 heads of little gem lettuce,
   washed and dried, to serve

1 Heat the oil in a sauté pan and cook the pork and chopped prawns until cooked through, about 5 minutes.
2 Stir in the garlic and chilli and cook for a further minute.
3 Stir in the remaining ingredients, except the lettuce.
4 Set aside to cool, then chill until required.
5 To serve, place the lettuce leaves on serving plates, cup-side up, and divide the pork mixture between them. Serve at room temperature.

Wine: Dry white, especially Riesling

Pâté en Croûte

This is a rich meat mixture cooked in a pastry crust.

SERVES 10

15 g butter

1 shallot, very finely chopped

115 g chicken livers, cleaned

2 tablespoons brandy

170 g lean pork, minced

170 g pork fat, minced

170 g lean veal, minced

1 egg, beaten

1 oz fresh white breadcrumbs

1 teaspoon dried mixed herbs

1½ teaspoons ground allspice

1 sheet of pig's caul (see page 513), about
   45 cm square

300 ml Aspic, seasoned with Madeira or
   tarragon vinegar (see page 458)

salt and freshly ground black pepper

For the garnish

115 g lean ham

115 g lean veal

2 tablespoons brandy

1 tablespoon chopped fresh thyme

For the pastry

450 g plain flour

1 teaspoon salt

225 g butter, cubed

1 egg, beaten with 2–3 tablespoons very cold water

beaten egg, for glazing

flour, for rolling

1 Melt the butter in a sauté pan, add the shallot and sweat until soft but not coloured. Add the chicken livers and sauté gently.

2 Warm the brandy in a ladle, set alight with a match, then pour over the chicken livers and allow to flambé until the flames subside.

3 Whizz the mixture in a food processor until smooth, then set aside to cool.

4 Mix the pork and veal with the pork fat, egg, breadcrumbs, herbs, allspice and seasoning. Stir in the liver purée. Cover and leave to marinate overnight in the refrigerator.

5 Meanwhile, prepare the garnish. Cut the ham and veal into strips 1 cm thick. Place in a bowl with the brandy and thyme, cover and marinate overnight in the refrigerator.

6 To make the pastry, sift the flour and salt into a bowl. Rub in the butter until the mixture resembles coarse breadcrumbs.

7 Stir the egg and water mixture into the flour with a knife to form a stiff but not dry dough, adding more water if necessary.

8 On a floured surface, roll the pastry into a large rectangle with the thickness of a £1 coin. Chill for 20 minutes.

9 Cut a strip 10 cm wide off the long edge of the pastry and reserve for the top. Place the remaining rectangle of pastry on a baking sheet.

10 Lay the pig's caul over the pastry to cover it entirely.

11 Take one-third of the meat filling and spread it on the caul in a neat rectangle measuring about 20 × 7.5 cm. Arrange half the garnish strips of ham and veal on top and season with salt and pepper. Repeat this process with another layer of meat and all the remaining garnish. Finish with a final layer of meat.

12 Cut the corners off the pastry, wet the edges and lift the pastry up to the sides of the meat, forming a terrine shape. Seal at the corners and crimp. Cut the reserved strip of pastry down to the exact size and lay over the top. Decorate the edges by crimping. Make 4 steam holes in the pastry.

13 Glaze the pastry all over with beaten egg. Garnish with pastry trimmings cut into decorative shapes. Chill in the refrigerator for 30 minutes.

14 Heat the oven to 220°C/425°F/gas mark 7.

15 Glaze the pastry again with beaten egg. Bake in the top of the oven for 15 minutes, then lower the temperature to 170°C/325°F/gas mark 3 and continue baking at the bottom of the oven for a further 1–1½ hours. The pâté en croûte is cooked when a skewer inserted into the centre comes out hot. Remove from the oven and place on a cooling rack until completely cold.

16 Using a plastic baster, drip the aspic into the steam holes to fill up any air pockets inside the pastry. If there are any holes in the pastry before adding the aspic, block them with softened butter.

17 Chill the pâté en croûte again for at least 1 hour before serving.

Wine: Red Burgundy or red Loire, such as Saumur-Champigny or Bourgueil

Prosciutto-wrapped Wild Boar with Lemon Thyme and Sage Bread Sauce

This recipe uses three different elements of the pig to create a succulent roast. The boneless loin is coated with aromatic herbs and lemon zest, then wrapped in prosciutto to keep it moist and give a good colour and flavour. Finally, it is encased in caul fat or crepinette, which ensures that the pork holds its shape during cooking. As the meat cooks, the caul fat will melt and brown, leaving no visible trace or flavour of its own.

SERVES 4–6

2 tablespoons shredless lemon marmalade, warmed

1 × 1.35 kg boned loin of wild boar, skin and fat removed

1 tablespoon finely chopped fresh lemon thyme

1 tablespoon finely chopped fresh sage

1 tablespoon chopped fresh flat leaf parsley

finely grated zest of 1 large lemon

8–10 slices prosciutto

large sheet of pigs' caul, soaked in cold water (see page 513)

salt and freshly ground black pepper

For the bread sauce

1 large onion

300 ml creamy milk

1 sprig of lemon thyme

1 bay leaf

pinch of freshly grated nutmeg

salt

50 g fresh white breadcrumbs

1 teaspoon finely chopped fresh lemon thyme

½ teaspoon finely chopped fresh sage

finely grated zest of 1 small lemon

50 g unsalted butter

2 tablespoons single cream

1 Heat the oven to 200°C/400°F/gas mark 6.
2 Brush the warm marmalade over the surface of the wild boar.
3 Mix the chopped herbs and lemon zest together. Season with salt and plenty of black pepper and sprinkle evenly over the meat, pressing the mixture firmly on to the marmalade.
4 Wrap the meat in overlapping slices of prosciutto.
5 Spread the caul on to a flat surface, then wrap the meat in it, cutting off any excess. Tuck the ends underneath and place in a roasting pan with the seams facing downwards.
6 Roast in the oven for 50 minutes per kg. Reduce the heat to 170°C/325°F/gas mark 3 and cook for a further 25 minutes.
7 Meanwhile, make the sauce. Cut the onion into quarters and put into a saucepan with the milk, thyme, bay leaf, nutmeg and a good pinch of salt. Bring to the boil very slowly, then remove from the heat and leave to infuse for 30 minutes. Strain.
8 Reheat the milk and add the breadcrumbs, chopped lemon thyme, sage, lemon zest, butter and cream. Simmer gently for 2–3 minutes, until thickened. If it becomes too thick, beat in more hot milk. It should be creamy. Check the seasoning.
9 Once the boar is cooked, remove it from the roasting pan and allow to rest in a warm place.
10 Tip the fat from the pan, reserving as much of the juices as possible and reheat them.
11 Cut the boar into thick slices and serve with the hot pan juices and bread sauce.

Wine: Red from Languedoc or southwest France, such as Cahors or Madiran

Rich Pigs' Cheek Stew with Crisp Pancetta

SERVES 6

2 kg (approx. 4 large) pigs' cheeks, trimmed of fat

seasoned flour

3 tablespoons oil

2 large onions, finely sliced

2 sticks of celery, finely diced

1 large carrot, diced

1 tablespoon sun-dried tomato paste

2 tablespoons cider vinegar

2 tablespoons soft dark brown sugar

600 ml red wine

600 ml Brown Stock (see page 452)

2 large sprigs of thyme

2 bay leaves

45 g unsalted butter

salt and freshly ground black pepper

Crisp Pancetta, to garnish (see below)

1 Dip the pigs' cheeks in the seasoned flour and shake off the excess.

2 Heat 2 tablespoons of the oil in a large casserole and fry the cheeks on both sides until well browned. Remove from the pan and set aside.

3 Heat the remaining oil and fry the onions until beginning to soften. Add the celery and carrot and fry until lightly caramelized. Stir in the tomato paste, vinegar, sugar, wine and stock and bring to the boil.

4 Return the cheeks to the pan. Add the thyme and bay leaves. Season with salt and pepper.

5 Reduce the heat and cover the casserole with a tight-fitting lid. Simmer very gently for 4 hours, or until the meat is very tender and starting to fall apart.

6 Lift the meat out and place in a warmed serving dish. Strain the sauce into a clean saucepan and bring to the boil. Boil rapidly until reduced to a thick, syrupy consistency. Whisk in the butter and season. Pour the sauce over the meat and garnish with the pancetta.

CRISP PANCETTA

MAKES 6 PIECES

6 slices of smoked pancetta

1 Heat the oven to 200°C/400°F/gas mark 6.

2 Lay the pancetta on a baking sheet and place a second baking sheet on top (this keeps it flat and prevents shrinkage). Place in the highest part of the oven for 5–7 minutes.

3 Carefully remove the top baking sheet and transfer the hot pancetta to a sheet of absorbent kitchen paper and allow to cool.

Wine: Southern French red from Gigondas or Pic Saint Loup

Pork Pie

SERVES 4–6

675 g lean pork

1 pig's kidney

1 small onion, finely chopped

1 teaspoon salt

pinch of cayenne pepper

freshly ground black pepper

1 quantity Pâte à Pâte (page 486) or 500 g bought
   shortcrust pastry

beaten egg, for glazing

600 ml Aspic (see page 458)

flour, for rolling and dusting

1 Cut the meats into bite-sized cubes and mix with the onion and seasonings (use plenty of black pepper).

2 Heat the oven to 170°C/325°F/gas mark 3. Lightly grease a 2 kg loose-bottomed pie mould or a 20 cm loose-bottomed cake tin.

3 Roll two-thirds of the pâte à pâte into a circle big enough to cover the base and sides of the pie mould or cake tin. Dust the pastry with a little flour, then fold in half. Place one hand on the fold and with the other gently push and pull the sides to form a bag roughly the shape and size of the mould or tin. Open out the bag and fit inside the prepared mould or tin. Fill with the meat.

4 Roll out the remaining third of the pastry into a circle big enough to cover the top of the pie. Dampen the edge with water, then place over the filling and press on to the pastry case, pinching the edges together. Decorate with pastry trimmings cut into leaves, and make a pea-sized hole in the middle of the top.

5 Brush with egg. Bake in the oven for 1½ hours. After the first hour it might be necessary to cover the pie with a piece of dampened greaseproof paper to prevent it from browning too much.

6 Remove the paper and the sides of the mould or tin. Brush the pastry sides with beaten egg, then return to oven and bake until golden (about 15–20 minutes).

7 Take the pie out of the oven and allow it to get cold. Warm the aspic enough to make it just liquid but not hot. Using a funnel placed in the hole in the pastry lid, pour some aspic into the pie. Add more at roughly 5-minute intervals until you are sure that the pie is completely full. It should take about 600 ml of liquid. Refrigerate the pie for the aspic to set.

Wine: Fruity red, such as Beaujolais, or dry white, such as Alsace, Austrian or Australian Riesling

Ham, Gammon and Bacon

Ham, gammon and bacon are all cuts of pork that have been cured by salting, and often smoking after the salting process. Originally this curing was done to preserve the meat in the absence of refrigeration, though today the curing is done primarily for flavour.

Pigs bred specifically for curing are called 'baconers' and are slightly larger than the pigs bred for pork meat.

Ham

Ham is bacon from the hind leg. The hind leg of the pig is cut from the carcass so that its top is rounded, resulting in a ham weighing as much as 6 kg. It is then salted, often by dry salting, and may be smoked according to local traditions.

Types of ham

Uncooked ham is sold whole, boned and rolled, or thickly sliced. Cooked ham is available on the bone, boned and rolled, or sliced thinly. English hams are generally cooked before eating hot or cold. The most famous are the Bradenham ham and the sweet milk York ham. Paris ham is similar to English York ham. American Virginia hams owe their sweet flavour to the peanuts and peaches on which the hogs are traditionally fed: they are cured in salt and sugar, and smoked over apple and hickory wood for a month. By contrast, Italian Parma ham, German Westphalian ham and French Bayonne ham are salted and smoked but eaten raw, thinly sliced.

Gammon

Like ham, gammon is also the hind leg of a bacon pig, but differs in that it is cured while still attached to the body. The gammon is then cut straight across the top of the leg. A whole gammon can weigh as much as 5 kg, but is usually sold in smaller portions. It is either boiled or roasted.

Choosing ham/gammon

- The ham should be short and thick with a high proportion of meat to fat and a thin rind, indicating that the pig is young.
- The meat should be pale pink and the fat white.

Storing ham/gammon

Both ham and gammon should be stored in the same way as bacon (see below). If the meat is vacuum-packed, it will keep longer. In this case, be guided by the use-by date.

Bacon

To produce bacon, meat of the whole pig is salted in brine or coated with sea salt and vacuum-packed for up to a week, then matured for a further 7–12 days. At this stage it is known as green bacon, which is characteristically deep pink in colour and slightly salty with a white rind. Once bacon has been salted, it may be smoked to increase its shelf life and enhance its flavour. Smoked bacon is hung in cool smoke for up to a month, which gives it a light brown rind and dark pink flesh.

Bacon is available thinly sliced as streaky and back rashers, thickly sliced as steaks for frying or grilling, boned and rolled as a whole joint for boiling or roasting, or on the bone as ham and gammon. Commercially produced bacon is generally mild. Bacon cured at home without the use of chemical preservatives is likely to have more flavour and saltiness, but needs soaking before cooking.

Choosing bacon

Whether the bacon is green or smoked, look out for the following characteristics:
- The flesh should be moist and firm.
- The fat should be white or no darker than cream.
- The bacon should not be dry, hard, dark or patchy in colour.

British bacon varies in price and according to manufacturer, some varieties being saltier than others, so care should be taken if boiling without prior soaking. It is always wise to soak large pieces to be cooked whole, such as gammons or fore hocks. Smaller cuts, steaks and rashers rarely need soaking.

Danish pigs are all cured in the same manner, giving a good-quality, mild-tasting, not very salty bacon. Avoid buying cheap bacon as the meat is often injected with 'smoke' flavouring, as well as a large quantity of water. This becomes clear when the bacon rashers are placed in a hot frying pan, as they boil rather than fry, shrink to half their original length and often taste extremely salty.

Storing bacon

Although bacon is cured, it must be stored in the refrigerator. The shelf life of smoked bacon is longer than unsmoked, but both types should be eaten within 5 days of purchase unless well sealed and oxygen flushed, in which case keep to the use-by date. Bacon may be frozen for up to 1 year.

Cuts of Bacon

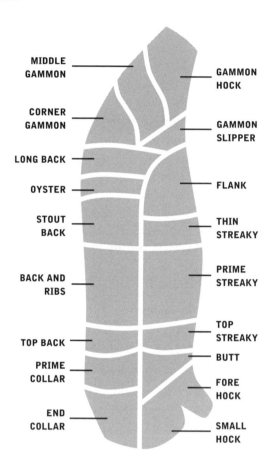

MIDDLE GAMMON
CORNER GAMMON
LONG BACK
OYSTER
STOUT BACK
BACK AND RIBS
TOP BACK
PRIME COLLAR
END COLLAR

GAMMON HOCK
GAMMON SLIPPER
FLANK
THIN STREAKY
PRIME STREAKY
TOP STREAKY
BUTT
FORE HOCK
SMALL HOCK

Cut	Recommended Cooking Methods	Recipe Reference
Back and ribs/Flank/ Prime streaky/Stout back/Thin streaky/ Top back/Top streaky	Frying Grilling	see Frying Bacon (page 224)
Butt/Corner gammon/Gammon slipper/Long back/ Middle gammon/ Oyster/Prime collar	Boiling Baking	see Baked Glazed Ham or Gammon Joint (page 225)
Fore hock/End collar/Gammon hock/Small hock	Soup Stewing	see Pea and Ham Soup (page 231)

Boiling and baking

Most bacon cuts, other than bacon rashers, are suitable for boiling and baking. Due to the density of the meat and the fact that it is salted and maybe smoked, the meat is gently simmered beforehand, with the skin on, in water flavoured with aromatic vegetables, spices and herbs, until just cooked. Roasting or baking the meat from raw would take a long time and would certainly dry it out. After boiling, the meat is baked mainly to improve the appearance of the ham by browning the layer of fat that covers its surface.

Frying

Gammon steaks and chops, streaky and back bacon are suitable for frying.

Gammon steaks or bacon chops: Before grilling or frying gammon steaks or bacon chops (thick rashers from the prime back), trim off the rind and snip into the surrounding thick layer of fat at 1 cm intervals to prevent the chops from curling. Bacon chops are sometimes cooked with the rind left on, but snipping is essential as the fat shrinks and curls during cooking, pulling the chops out of shape. Fry or grill until the meat is firm and loses its translucency.

Streaky bacon: To fry streaky bacon, place it in a cold, dry frying pan. Heat over a medium heat, turning the rashers occasionally until they lose their translucency. For crisp bacon, continue cooking until golden brown. Place on kitchen paper to remove excess fat before serving.

Back bacon: Fry in a sauté pan with just enough oil to coat the surface of the pan until very lightly golden on both sides.

Grilling gammon steaks and bacon

Gammon steaks and rashers of streaky and back bacon are suitable for grilling.

1 Heat the grill to its highest setting until very hot.
2 Place the gammon steaks or bacon on a grill rack over a grill pan.
3 Steaks 5–7.5 cm thick should be grilled for 3–4 minutes per side, until the meat loses its translucency and browns lightly. Streaky or back bacon needs 2–3 minutes per side.

Microwaving bacon

Small numbers of rashers of bacon can be microwaved by placing them in a single layer between two pieces of kitchen paper. Microwave on HIGH for about 2 minutes, depending on the power of the oven.

Baked Glazed Ham or Gammon Joint

When calculating the size of joint needed, allow 170 g meat off the bone or 225 g meat on the bone per person.

1 ham or gammon joint

1 onion

1 carrot

1 bay leaf

fresh parsley stalks

black peppercorns

2 tablespoons demerara sugar

1 teaspoon dry English mustard

1 handful of cloves

To serve

Cumberland Sauce (see page 475)

1 Soak the joint overnight in cold water to remove excess salt. If time does not allow overnight soaking, immerse the joint in cold water and bring to the boil, then simmer for 10 minutes. Drain.

2 Place the joint in a large saucepan of cold water and add the onion, carrot, bay leaf, parsley stalks and peppercorns. Bring slowly to the boil, then turn the heat down to a simmer and cover the pan. Large joints weighing more than 3.5 kg should be simmered for 25 minutes per 450 g. Joints weighing less than 3.5 kg should be simmered for 20 minutes per 450 g. Do not allow the water to boil as the ham may dry out (see page 224).

3 Heat the oven to 220°C/425°F/gas mark 7.

4 Lift the joint out of the poaching liquor and carefully trim off the skin with a sharp knife, leaving a thin coating of fat on the joint. Reserve the liquor for ham stock.

5 Mix the sugar and mustard together and press the mixture evenly all over the fat.

6 Using a sharp knife, cut a diamond lattice pattern across the coated fat. If any sugar falls off, press it back on again. Stick a clove into the centre of each diamond segment, or into the cuts where the lines cross.

7 Stand the joint upright on a roasting rack in a roasting pan, fat side uppermost. Bake the joint for about 20 minutes, or until brown and slightly caramelized.

8 Carve into thick slices and serve with Cumberland sauce.

TO MAKE A HAM FRILL

A ham frill is used to cover the bone sticking out of the end of the ham.

1 Take a piece of greaseproof paper measuring about 20 × 25 cm, fold in half lengthwise, then fold loosely again.

2 Make 4 cm cuts 1 cm apart all along the fold: they should be parallel to the short end of the paper.

3 Open out one fold of the paper and refold it lengthwise in the opposite direction.

4 Wrap the frill around the ham bone and secure with a paste of flour and water.

Wine: Chardonnay from Burgundy or the New World, or a Beaujolais or Merlot

Jambon Persillé

SERVES 6

1 × 900 g piece of middle gammon or
   unsmoked lean bacon
1 slice of onion
1 bay leaf
½ carrot

2 parsley stalks
6 black peppercorns
1 quantity Aspic (see page 458)
3 tablespoons finely chopped fresh parsley

1 Soak the gammon in cold water overnight. Place in a saucepan with the onion, bay leaf, carrot, parsley stalks and peppercorns, cover with fresh cold water and bring to the boil. Simmer for about 1½ hours, or until the gammon is tender. Remove from the heat and leave to cool in the liquid.

2 Cut the gammon into thick slices and then into strips. Arrange a neat layer in the bottom of a mould or soufflé dish that has been rinsed out with cold water or very lightly oiled.

3 Pour in enough almost-cold aspic to hold the gammon in place as it sets. Leave in the refrigerator to set.

4 Mix the chopped parsley into half of the remaining just-liquid aspic and pour a 1 cm depth into the mould. Allow to set. Arrange a second layer of ham on top and set in place with clear aspic.

5 Continue the layers in this way, finishing with clear aspic. Chill well.

6 To turn out, dip the mould into hot water to loosen the aspic. Place a plate over the mould, then invert, giving the mould a slight shake to dislodge the jellied ham.

NOTE: A good but less elegant jambon persillé is made with uncleared veal jelly, chopped parsley and cubes of cooked ham simply combined in a dish and allowed to set.

Wine: Viognier or Cremant de Bourgogne

Gammon Steaks with Bitter Orange Glaze

SERVES 4

4 × 170 g thick-cut gammon steaks
freshly ground black pepper
sprigs of watercress, to garnish

For the glaze
3 tablespoons Seville orange marmalade, chopped
2 teaspoons soft light brown sugar
½ tablespoon wholegrain mustard
¼ teaspoon mixed spice

1 Heat the grill to its highest setting.

2 Season the gammon steaks with black pepper and grill on both sides for 2–3 minutes.

3 Meanwhile, put the glaze ingredients into a small saucepan and heat gently, stirring occasionally. Remove the gammon steaks from the heat. Brush with the orange glaze

and return to the grill for a further 1–2 minutes, or until the glaze is hot and beginning to bubble and caramelize.

4 Garnish with watercress and serve immediately.

Wine: German Riesling, Australian Chardonnay or a Chilean Merlot

Gammon Steaks with Celery and Gorgonzola

SERVES 4

2 celery hearts, trimmed and cut into 2 cm pieces on the diagonal

150 ml White Chicken Stock (see page 451)

15 g unsalted butter

1 large sprig of thyme

4 × 170 g smoked gammon steaks, well trimmed

2 tablespoons crème fraîche

grated zest and juice of ½ a small lemon

140 g Gorgonzola cheese

salt and freshly ground black pepper

1 Heat the oven to 180°C/350°F/gas mark 4.

2 Put the celery into a shallow flameproof casserole dish. Pour over the stock and season with a little salt and plenty of black pepper. Dot with the butter and add the thyme. Cover with a lid or foil and bake for 20–25 minutes, until just tender.

3 Heat the grill to its highest setting. Place the gammon steaks on a baking sheet and grill for 2–3 minutes on each side.

4 Using a slotted spoon, remove the celery from the casserole and drain well. Transfer to a warmed serving dish.

5 Place the casserole over a direct heat, remove the thyme and discard. Bring the liquid to the boil and cook rapidly until reduced to about 4 tablespoons. Stir in the crème fraîche, lemon zest and juice and reduce again until of a thick coating consistency.

6 Spoon the sauce over the celery and top with the gammon steaks. Crumble over the Gorgonzola and return to the grill for 1–2 minutes, or until melted and bubbling.

Wine: Rich, dry Italian white, such as Gavi, Falanghina or Greco di Tufo

Warm Griddled Melon and Parma Ham Salad

SERVES 4

1 medium Galia melon

8 slices of Parma ham

2 tablespoons olive oil

2 teaspoons hazelnut oil

1 tablespoon balsamic vinegar

1 teaspoon wholegrain mustard

finely grated zest of 1 lime

salt and freshly ground black pepper

1 bunch of watercress, washed and trimmed

1 bunch of rocket, washed and trimmed

50 g chervil, roughly chopped

1 Cut the melon into 8 wedges and remove the seeds and skin.

2 Wrap a slice of Parma ham around each melon wedge and set aside.

3 In a small bowl, whisk together 1 tablespoon of the olive oil, the hazelnut oil, vinegar, mustard and lime zest. Season with salt and pepper.

4 Place the salad leaves and half the chervil in a large bowl, pour over the dressing and mix lightly. Divide the salad between 4 plates.

5 Brush a griddle pan with the remaining oil, place over the heat and, when hot, carefully add the wrapped melon. Cook for 30 seconds, or until lightly charred on both sides.

6 Arrange 2 pieces of melon on each plate of salad, sprinkle with the remaining chervil and serve immediately.

Wine: Aromatic dry white or Champagne

Black Forest Ham, Pear and Poppy Seed Pizza

SERVES 4

3 ripe red-skinned pears

3 tablespoons pear or apple juice

8 slices Black Forest ham

1 quantity Pizza Dough (see page 487)

2 tablespoons poppy seeds

flour, for dusting

170 g mascarpone cheese

85 g feta cheese, roughly crumbled

85 g Parmesan cheese, freshly grated

salt and freshly ground black pepper

1 Heat the oven to 200°C/400°F/gas mark 6.

2 Cut the pears into quarters and remove the cores. Cut each quarter into 3 and place the slices in a bowl with the pear or apple juice and toss together.

3 Finely shred 3 slices of the ham, and work into the pizza dough with the poppy seeds until evenly distributed.

4 Lightly flour 2 baking sheets. Cut the dough in half and roll each piece into a circle roughly 22.5 cm in diameter and place on the baking sheets.

5 Spread the mascarpone over each pizza base, leaving a 3 cm border. Season with salt and plenty of black pepper.

6 Lay the pears in overlapping slices on the mascarpone, scatter the feta on top and sprinkle with half the Parmesan.

7 Bake the pizzas on the top shelf of the oven for 25 minutes. Arrange the remaining slices of ham on top, sprinkle with the remaining Parmesan and return to the oven for a further 5–10 minutes, or until the crust is crisp and brown and the cheese bubbling. Serve hot.

Drink: Light ale

Flat Ham Pie

SERVES 4–6

1 quantity Pâte à Pâte (see page 486) or 500g
  bought shortcrust pastry

flour, for dusting

50 g Gruyère cheese, finely grated

30 g Parmesan cheese, finely grated

30 g butter, melted

50 g fresh white breadcrumbs

225 g cooked ham, shredded

2 tablespoons chopped fresh chives

½ clove of garlic, crushed

5 tablespoons soured cream

freshly ground black pepper

beaten egg, to glaze

1 Heat the oven to 200°C/400°F/gas mark 6.

2 Flour a work surface. Roll two-fifths of the pastry into a rectangle about 20 × 15 cm.

3 Place the rectangle on a baking sheet and prick all over with a fork. Refrigerate for 10 minutes, then bake for about 15 minutes, until cooked. Allow to cool.

4 Mix together the cheeses, butter and breadcrumbs. Scatter half the mixture over the baked pastry, leaving a border of 1 cm.

5 Mix together the ham, chives, garlic and soured cream. Season with pepper. Spread the mixture over the crumbs, then top with the remaining crumb mixture.

6 Roll the remaining pastry into a rectangle slightly larger than the first. Dampen the edge of the baked pastry. Place the uncooked pastry on top and trim the edges to fit. Secure the edges by pressing down with a fork.

7 Glaze the pie with the egg. Decorate with thinly rolled pastry trimmings and glaze again. Cut a steam hole in the top of the pie.

8 Bake for about 30 minutes, until golden brown and no grey or damp patches remain on the pastry. Serve hot or cold.

Wine: Dry German, Alsace or Australian Riesling

Linguine with Ham and Peas

SERVES 4

500 g dried linguine pasta

250 g frozen peas

150 ml crème fraîche

170 g honey roast ham, shredded

2 tablespoons fresh basil, roughly torn

salt and freshly ground black pepper

To garnish

Parmesan cheese shavings

fresh basil leaves

1 Cook the linguine in plenty of rapidly boiling salted water.
2 Add the peas to the linguine for the last 2 minutes of its cooking time.
3 Drain the linguine and peas, then return to the saucepan with the crème fraîche, ham and torn basil. Season with salt and pepper and mix together well.
4 Pile on to a warmed serving dish, garnish with the Parmesan and basil leaves, and serve immediately.

Wine: Prosecco or Cava

Warm Rocket and Broad Bean Salad with Crisp Parma Ham

SERVES 4

1 tablespoon olive oil

1 × 80 g packet Parma ham, cut into strips

225 g fresh broad beans, double-podded

1 tablespoon wholegrain mustard

2 tablespoons cider vinegar

170 g rocket, washed and picked over

salt and freshly ground black pepper

hot crusty bread, to serve

1 Heat the oil in a heavy-based frying pan and fry the Parma ham until crisp. Drain on kitchen paper.
2 Meanwhile, cook the broad beans in boiling salted water until tender. Drain well.
3 Mix together the broad beans and Parma ham, then stir in the mustard and vinegar and season to taste with salt and pepper.
4 Add the rocket and stir until just wilted.
5 Serve immediately with chunks of hot bread.

Wine: Aromatic dry white, dry rosé or Champagne/sparkling wine

Pea and Ham Soup

SERVES 4

1 tablespoon vegetable oil

1 onion, thinly sliced

1 stick of celery, chopped

1 ham hock, about 250 g

250 g split peas

1.1 litres water

6 black peppercorns

4 sprigs of fresh thyme

1 bay leaf

1 Heat the oil in deep saucepan over a medium heat, add the onion and celery and cook until softened.

2 Add all the remaining ingredients. Simmer for 1–1½ hours, or until the peas have broken up and the ham is falling from the bone.

3 Discard the peppercorns, thyme and bay leaf.

4 Remove the ham hock. Trim away any fat, then cut the meat into 3 cm pieces. Set aside.

5 Purée the soup in a food processor or liquidizer, then return to the rinsed-out pan.

6 Add the ham and warm through to serve. Do not boil.

Wine: Dry white or a Côtes-du-Rhône

Bacon and Quail's Egg Salad

SERVES 4

2 handfuls of very young spinach or beet leaves

1 handful of lambs' lettuce

1 quantity Vinaigrette (see page 474)

12 raw quails' eggs

3 rashers of rindless streaky smoked bacon

2 tablespoons oil, for frying

1 slice of bread

1 Wash and pick over the spinach and lambs' lettuce, then tear the leaves into small pieces, discarding any stalks or thick ribs. Dry well.

2 Break the quails' eggs carefully on to a plate. Get a frying pan or shallow sauté pan of water bubbling on the heat. Slide the eggs into it. Reduce the heat and poach for 1 minute. Remove the eggs from the pan and slip into a bowl of warm water until ready for use.

3 Cut the bacon crosswise into thin strips. Heat the oil in a frying pan, then brown the bacon rapidly. Transfer to a plate and keep warm.

4 Cut the bread into small dice and fry in the hot fat until evenly browned to make croûtons. Remove with a perforated spoon and drain on kitchen paper.

5 Toss the spinach and lettuce in the vinaigrette and arrange on 6 individual plates.

6 Arrange 3 well-drained eggs per person on the salads. Add a sprinkling of bacon, then the warm croûtons and serve immediately.

Wine: Champagne or an aromatic dry white

Parsnip, Chickpea and Bacon Cakes

MAKES 8

85 g rindless green rashers of bacon
  (see page 222) or smoked streaky
  rashers of bacon, chopped
1 × 400 g can chickpeas, rinsed and drained
250 g cooked Mashed Potatoes (see page 491)
500 g cooked parsnips, lightly mashed
2 tablespoons fresh parsley, finely chopped

1½ teaspoons garam masala
seasoned flour
beaten egg
dried white breadcrumbs
2 tablespoons oil
salt and freshly ground black pepper

1 Place the bacon in a frying pan and fry in its own fat until crisp.
2 In a large bowl, roughly mash the chickpeas with the back of a fork. Add the mashed potato, parsnips, bacon, parsley and garam masala. Season with salt and pepper and mix together well.
3 With lightly floured hands, shape the mixture into 8 balls, then flatten into circles 3 cm thick.
4 Dip the cakes first into seasoned flour, then the beaten egg, then coat thoroughly with the breadcrumbs. Chill for 30 minutes.
5 Heat the oil in a frying pan and, when hot, fry the cakes for 2 minutes on each side, or until brown and crisp and hot in the middle.
6 Lift the cakes from the pan and drain on kitchen paper. Sprinkle with a little salt and serve very hot.

Wine: Aromatic, fruity white, such as Alsace Pinot Gris

Bacon and Tomato Cakes with Poached Eggs

These savoury cakes can be made the day before and then cooked as required, making them perfect for a lazy weekend brunch when topped with a poached or fried egg.

SERVES 4

2 tablespoons oil
200 g bacon lardons
500 g cooked, stiff Mashed Potatoes
  (see page 491)
2 ripe plum tomatoes, deseeded and diced
salt and freshly ground black pepper

2 tablespoons finely chopped chives,
  plus extra for garnish
flour, for shaping and dusting
30 g unsalted butter
4 large fresh eggs, poached to taste

1 Heat ½ tablespoon of the oil in a frying pan. Fry the bacon lardons until crisp and brown. Drain on kitchen paper.

2 Put the mashed potato into a large mixing bowl. Add the tomatoes, chives and bacon lardons. Season with salt and pepper and mix together well.

3 Lightly flour a work surface and your hands, then shape the potato mixture into 4 round cakes about 1 cm thick. Place on a floured tray and chill for 15 minutes.

4 Wipe the frying pan with kitchen paper, then heat the remaining oil in it. Fry the cakes for 1½ minutes. Add the butter to the pan and fry for a further 2–3 minutes, or until nicely browned and hot through. Drain on kitchen paper and sprinkle with a little salt.

5 To serve, place the cakes on 4 warmed serving plates and top each one with a poached egg.

NOTES: Any kind of bacon can be used for this recipe, be it rashers or lardons of green or smoked streaky or back bacon, gammon steaks or pancetta, and in whatever quantity is available. The amount and type given here is a guideline, but the recipe is designed to use up leftovers. Cooked ham works well too.

If using leftover mashed potato, it needs to be quite stiff because a creamy mash won't hold the other ingredients together very well. If you are making mashed potatoes from scratch, do not add any butter, milk or cream to the potatoes.

Wine: Aromatic, fruity white, such as Alsace Pinot Gris

Leek and Bacon Quiche with Mustard

SERVES 4–6

1 quantity Rich Shortcrust Pastry (see page 476)

For the filling

50 g rindless bacon, finely chopped

15 g butter

300 g leeks, white parts only, washed and
    finely chopped

1 egg, beaten

150 ml double cream

3 tablespoons freshly grated Parmesan cheese

salt and freshly ground black pepper

2 tablespoons coarse-grain mustard

1 Roll out the pastry and use to line a 20 cm flan ring. Chill until firm.

2 Heat the oven to 200°C/400°F/gas mark 6. Bake the pastry case blind (see page 478), then set aside. Reduce the oven temperature to 170°C/325°F/gas mark 3.

3 Put the bacon in a frying pan and cook in its own fat until it begins to brown.

4 Add the butter and leeks. Cover with a piece of dampened greaseproof paper and cook over a low heat until the leeks are soft. Drain well and allow to cool.

5 Mix together the egg, cream and cheese. Add the leeks and bacon. Season with salt and pepper.

6 Spread a thin layer of mustard in the bottom of the pastry case, then pour in the filling. Bake in the oven for 40–45 minutes, or until the filling is set.

Wine: Classic match for Alsace or Austrian whites

Spaghetti Carbonara

SERVES 4

450 g spaghetti

salt

1 tablespoon oil

100 g streaky bacon, cut into small strips

4 egg yolks

6 tablespoons single cream

50 g Parmesan cheese, freshly grated

freshly ground black pepper

1 Cook the spaghetti in plenty of rapidly boiling salted water.

2 Heat the oil in a fairly large frying pan, add the bacon and fry lightly over a medium heat until the fat has melted and the bacon has cooked. Remove the pan from the heat and set aside. Keep warm.

3 Meanwhile, whisk the egg yolks in a bowl, then whisk in the cream and half the Parmesan. Season generously with pepper.

4 When the spaghetti is al dente, drain it and transfer to the pan with the bacon and pour the egg mixture over it. Stir quickly and serve immediately, with the remaining Parmesan handed separately.

Wine: Valpolicella

Warm Pink Fir Apple Potato, Smoked Bacon and Tapenade Salad

SERVES 4

675 g Pink Fir Apple potatoes, scrubbed and
    cut in half if large
140 g smoked streaky bacon rashers
2 tablespoons extra virgin lemon olive oil
juice of 1 lemon

4 tablespoons Tapenade (see page 467)
85 g pitted black olives
salt and freshly ground black pepper
sprigs of chervil, to garnish
hot crusty bread, to serve

1 Heat the grill to its highest setting.
2 Cook the potatoes in a large pan of boiling salted water. Drain and allow to cool slightly.
3 Place the bacon on a baking sheet and grill until crisp. Drain on kitchen paper.
4 In a small bowl, mix together the oil, lemon juice and tapenade. Season with salt and black pepper.
5 Put the potatoes into a large bowl and crumble over the bacon. Pour over the dressing and mix gently. Transfer the potato mixture to a serving dish and sprinkle over the black olives.
6 Garnish with sprigs of chervil and serve warm with hot crusty bread.

Wine: Aromatic dry white, such as Grüner Veltliner

Crisp Smoky Bacon with Hot Pineapple Salsa

SERVES 4

4 × 140 g thick-cut rashers of smoked bacon or
    gammon steaks
½ bunch of chives, finely chopped, to garnish
crusty bread, to serve

For the salsa

1 tablespoon oil

1 bunch of spring onions, finely sliced on the diagonal
½ small red chilli, deseeded and diced
1 small fresh pineapple, peeled, cored and
    cut into 1 cm chunks
1 tablespoon sherry vinegar
salt and freshly ground black pepper

1 Heat the grill to its highest setting.
2 Remove the rind from the bacon and snip the fat at intervals. Place the bacon on a wire rack set over a grill pan. Grill until crisp and brown on both sides. Keep warm.
3 Meanwhile, heat the oil in a frying pan and fry the spring onions gently until soft and beginning to brown. Add the chilli and continue to cook for a further 30 seconds.
4 Add the pineapple to the pan, increase the heat and cook for 3–4 minutes. Pour in the vinegar and season. Place a rasher of bacon on each serving plate and place a spoonful of hot salsa on the side. Sprinkle with the chives and serve with crusty bread.

Wine: Aromatic fruity white or a rich New World Chardonnay

Good Bacon Sandwiches with Fresh Tomato Chutney

MAKES 4 SANDWICHES

12 rashers of dry-cured, smoked back bacon, rind removed

85 g unsalted butter

8 thick slices of white country bread

4 tablespoons Fresh Tomato Chutney (see below)

freshly ground black pepper

1 large bunch of watercress, roughly torn

1 Heat a large, heavy-based frying pan over a medium heat until very hot. Carefully lay the bacon in the pan and cook until well browned and crisp, and most of the fat has run from it. Remove the bacon from the pan and keep warm.

2 Return the pan to the heat and add the butter. When foaming, fry the bread slices on one side only until lightly browned.

3 Spread half the bread slices on the unfried side with the tomato chutney, place the hot bacon on top and season with black pepper. Divide the watercress between the sandwiches and top with the remaining bread.

4 Cut the sandwiches in half and serve immediately.

FRESH TOMATO CHUTNEY

This chutney should be stored in the refrigerator and is best used within 2 weeks of making.

MAKES ABOUT 300 ML

1 large onion, finely chopped

1 tablespoon oil

1 clove of garlic, crushed

2 tablespoons soft dark brown sugar

4 tablespoons cider vinegar

2 sprigs of fresh thyme

1 sprig of fresh rosemary

pinch of dried red chilli flakes

675 g baby plum tomatoes

salt and freshly ground black pepper

1 Heat the oil in a frying pan over a low heat. Add the onion and cover with a piece of dampened greaseproof paper and a lid. Cook until softened. Add the garlic and cook for a further minute.

2 Stir in the sugar, vinegar, herbs and chilli flakes, bring to the boil and simmer for 5 minutes.

3 Add the tomatoes to the pan, season with salt and pepper and bring to the boil. Reduce the heat and cook very gently for 30 minutes, stirring occasionally.

4 Allow the mixture to cool slightly before transferring to an airtight container or sterilized jars.

Wine: Barbera d'Asti, Beaujolais-Villages or a dry, aromatic white

Sausages

Sausages are forcemeats stuffed into tube-like skins of pig, sheep or beef intestines, or synthetic collagen. The forcemeat or sausagemeat used to make sausages is made mostly with a mixture of finely minced pork and salted pork fat, flavoured with herbs, aromatic vegetables and spices. Sausages can also be made with other meats, including game, and even with fish or vegetables.

Sausages are available in fresh, smoked, cured and cooked varieties. Provided you have the equipment, both fresh and smoked types are easy to make in the domestic kitchen, as the ingredients are relatively simple to prepare. Cured and cooked sausages are made by specialists, so are not covered in this book. Small sausages, 10–13 cm in length, tend to be eaten for breakfast, while larger ones, up to 15 cm in length, are usually eaten for supper.

Sausage skins

Two types of sausage skin are used to encase forcemeat: natural ones and those manufactured from collagen.

Natural sausage skins are lengths of pig, sheep or beef intestine. They are available in different widths, depending upon the animal or the area of intestine used. Pig intestine is most frequently used, although sheep intestine is considered superior for making small sausages. Beef casings are much wider in diameter and are used mainly for large sausages originating from eastern Europe. Most natural sausage skins are available from good butchers. They are cleaned and salted, so must be rinsed in warm water, then soaked in cold water overnight before they are used.

Collagen sausage skins are manufactured and do not need to be rinsed or soaked prior to use. They are inferior to natural casings in both taste and texture, and should be used only when natural skins are not available.

Sausages are most efficiently made using a stuffing attachment fixed to a mixer, but can also be easily made using a heavy-duty piping bag fitted with a wide nozzle.

Sausagemeat

Belly meat is the best cut of pork to use for sausagemeat, which is also called forcemeat. It is made from finely minced pork and minced salted pork fat, flavoured with herbs and spices. Sausagemeat is used with various seasonings and aromatic vegetables to stuff sausage skins, vegetables, the Christmas turkey and meat or poultry paupiettes, or encased in puff pastry to make sausage rolls.

Pork Sausagemeat

450 g minced fatty pork, such as belly pork
1 medium onion, very finely chopped (optional)
1 egg, beaten
3 fresh sage leaves, chopped, or 1 teaspoon
   dried sage

120 g breadcrumbs
oil, for frying
salt and freshly ground black pepper

1 Mix together the pork and onion, if using.
2 Combine the egg and sage. Stir in the breadcrumbs, plenty of salt and pepper and mix thoroughly into the pork.
3 Heat a little oil and fry a teaspoonful of meat. Taste to check the seasoning.
4 Use the sausagemeat as required.

Forcemeat Balls

Traditionally made to accompany Roast Turkey and Jugged Hare (see pages 344 and 412).

MAKES 20–24

1 quantity Pork Sausagemeat (see above)
1 medium onion, very finely chopped
1 tablespoon finely chopped fresh parsley
grated zest of ¼ lemon

1 tablespoon finely chopped fresh sage or
   1 teaspoon dried sage
30 g fresh white breadcrumbs
salt and freshly ground black pepper

1 Heat the oven to 200°C/400°F/gas mark 6.
2 Mix together the sausagement, onion, parsley, lemon zest, sage and breadcrumbs. Season with salt and pepper.
3 Using wet hands, shape the mixture into spheres the size of a golf ball.
4 Place in a roasting pan and cook in the oven for 30 minutes.

Points to Remember about Cooking Sausages

- Fry sausages over a medium heat in a mixture of butter and oil until they are evenly browned on all sides.
- Sausages will not burst during shallow frying unless they were overfilled.
- Piercing the sausage skin before cooking can cause it to split.
- The fat in sausages escapes through the skin as they cook: they can therefore be grilled to a golden brown, basted in their own juices, under a medium to high heat.

Classic Pork Sausages

MAKES ABOUT 600 G OF SAUSAGES

1 length of washed sausage skin,
about 2 cm in diameter

1 quantity Pork Sausagemeat
(see opposite), chilled

1 Rinse and soak the sausage skin overnight.

2 Cut the skin into 2-metre lengths.

3 Put the sausagemeat into a sausage stuffer or piping bag.

4 Insert the nozzle into one end of the sausage skin. Carefully draw the entire length of sausage skin over the nozzle. Tie a firm knot in the remaining few centimetres of sausage skin and pierce the skin with a skewer a few centimetres from the end to allow trapped air to escape while the skin is stuffed.

5 When using a stuffing attachment, support and guide the casing off the end of the nozzle as the sausagemeat is extruded into the skin. When using a piping bag, squeeze the sausagemeat into the skin with even, consistent pressure, supporting the skin with one hand as it is filled (it's helpful to share this job with another person). Do not overfill the skin or it will burst during cooking.

6 If the skin is unevenly filled, gently squeeze the sausagemeat along to redistribute it. Try not to have any air pockets.

7 Once the skin is filled, twist at regular intervals into individual sausages. Chipolatas (thin sausages) are approximately 10 cm in length; fatter, dinner-style sausages are 12.5–15 cm long. Cumberland sausages are 20–25 cm long and rolled into a flat coil.

NOTE: To ensure that the individual sausages do not untwist, the string of sausages can be twisted together.

Wine: Red from southern France (Languedoc) or Mediterranean Italy, perhaps Sardinia

Venison Sausages

This recipe makes a large quantity of sausages, which is useful for hunters. The sausages freeze well for 6 months.

MAKES ABOUT 80

lengths of sausage skin, 3 cm in diameter

425 ml red wine

4 teaspoons juniper berries, crushed

For the filling

1 clove of garlic, crushed

1.8 kg boned venison (haunch or shoulder)

1 tablespoon ground ginger

900 g rump steak

1½ tablespoons salt

675 g pork fat

1 tablespoon dried sage

225 g canned anchovy fillets

150 ml Jamaica rum

1 teaspoon ground mace

340 g Cox's apples, unpeeled and grated

1 teaspoon mignonette (see Note) or cracked
  black pepper

oil, for frying

1 Mince together the meats, fat and anchovy fillets. Mince again. Mix in all the remaining filling ingredients and beat well.

2 Fry a small amount of the mixture in a little oil to test for seasoning.

3 Following the instructions on page 239, fill the sausage skins with the mixture, but do not pack too tightly or the sausages will burst. Twist every 10–13 cm.

4 Cook as required.

NOTE: Mignonette is coarsely ground black pepper or a 50:50 blend of black and white pepper designed to give the heat of white peppercorns and the pungency of black.

Wine: Full-bodied red, such as Douro, Ribera del Duero or a New World Shiraz

Boudin Blanc

Boudin blanc (white sausage) is bound with cream and breadcrumbs and has a fine texture. It must be poached to firm the sausagemeat before frying.

MAKES ABOUT 10

2-metre length of sausage skin, 3 cm in diameter, soaked in water and drained

15 g butter

1 onion, very finely chopped

100 g fresh white breadcrumbs

150 ml double cream

225 g lean veal

225 g fatty pork

225 g boneless chicken breast or a further 225 g lean veal

3 eggs

½ teaspoon ground allspice

oil, for frying

salt and freshly ground black pepper

slices of sautéd apple, to serve

For poaching

1.5 litres water

750 ml milk

1 Melt the butter in a saucepan and sweat the onion until very soft. Set aside to cool.

2 Place the breadcrumbs in a bowl. Scald the cream in a saucepan by bringing it to a simmer. Pour over the breadcrumbs and leave to cool.

3 Work the veal, pork and chicken twice through the fine blade of a mincer, adding the onion before the second mincing. Alternatively, work the meat and onion a little at a time in a food processor. Put the mixture into a bowl and stir in the soaked breadcrumbs, eggs, allspice and plenty of salt and pepper. Heat a little oil in a sauté pan and sauté a knob of the mixture. Taste to check the seasoning – the mixture should be quite spicy. Beat with a wooden spoon or knead by hand until very smooth.

4 Fill the sausage skin as described on page 239, being careful not to overfill it. Twist into 15 cm sausages and tie together to prevent them untwisting.

5 Pour the water and milk into a large pan and bring to the boil. Lower the string of sausages into the pan. Cover and poach very gently until firm. Do not allow to boil, as this would cause the skins to burst. Remove from the heat and allow the sausages to cool in the liquid until tepid to keep the skins moist. Drain and allow to cool completely. (The sausages can be made a day in advance up to this point and kept covered in the refrigerator.)

6 Reheat by shallow-frying in oil until golden brown and serve with slices of sautéd apple.

Wine: Aromatic, fruity white, perhaps Vouvray or German Riesling

Toad in the Hole

SERVES 4

4 tablespoons beef dripping

8 pork sausages

2 eggs, beaten

150 ml milk, mixed with 150 ml water

For the batter

110 g plain flour

good pinch of salt

To serve

Red Onion Gravy (see page 463)

1 Make the batter: sift the flour and salt into a large, wide bowl. Make a well in the centre and add the eggs.

2 Using a whisk or wooden spoon, mix the eggs to a paste and very gradually draw in the surrounding flour, adding just enough milk and water to keep the central mixture the consistency of single cream. When all the flour is incorporated, stir in the rest of the milk. The batter can be made more speedily by putting all the ingredients in a blender or food processor for a few seconds, but take care not to overwhisk or the mixture will be bubbly. Leave to rest in the refrigerator for 30 minutes before use. This allows the starch cells to swell, giving a lighter, less doughy final product.

3 Heat the oven to 220°C/425°F/gas mark 7.

4 Heat 1 tablespoon of the dripping in a frying pan and fry the sausages until evenly browned all over, but do not cook them through.

5 Heat the remaining dripping in a flameproof shallow dish or roasting pan until smoking hot. Add the sausages and pour in the batter.

6 Bake in the oven for 40 minutes, or until the batter has risen and browned. Serve with the hot gravy.

Drink: Languedoc red or a good IPA (Indian Pale Ale)

Rich Pigs' Cheek Stew with Crisp Pancetta, page 219.

Gammon Steaks with Bitter Orange Glaze, page 226.

Roast Pork with Apple Sauce, page 194.

Making sausages

1 Cutting the sausage casing into two-metre lengths.

2 Filling a piping bag with forcemeat.

3 Filling the sausage casings.

4 Twisting the casings into sausages.

Classic Pork Sausages, page 239.

Toad in the Hole, page 242.

Crisp Smoky Bacon with Hot Pineapple Salsa, page 235.

Bacon and Tomato Cakes with Poached Eggs, page 233.

Cassoulet

SERVES 12

900 g dried haricot beans

225 g salt pork or unsmoked bacon

1 onion, studded with 8 cloves

1 bouquet garni (see page 512)

2 cloves of garlic, crushed

450 g pork blade bone

675 g boned breast of lamb

225 g Toulouse sausage or Cumberland sausage

1 teaspoon tomato purée

8 large tomatoes quartered

2 tablespoons chopped fresh thyme

2 tablespoons chopped fresh parsley

salt and freshly ground black pepper

4 tablespoons fresh white breadcrumbs

1 Wash the beans well, cover in cold water and leave to soak overnight. Drain, then blanch in clean boiling water for 5 minutes.

2 Drain again, rinse well and place in a pan of fresh cold water, making sure the beans are covered. Add the rind of the salt pork or bacon, the onion, bouquet garni and garlic.

3 Bring to the boil, then skim and simmer for 1¾ hours, or until the beans are tender.

4 Meanwhile, heat the oven to 190°C/375°F/gas mark 5.

5 Place the pork blade bone, lamb and sausage in a roasting pan and roast in the oven for 30 minutes, or until the meat is cooked and the sausage brown.

6 Transfer the meat to a chopping board, reserving the cooking fat. Slice the sausages into 1 cm pieces and cut the meat into 3 cm chunks.

7 When the beans are cooked strain them, reserving 600 ml of the cooking liquor. Discard the rind, onion and bouquet garni.

8 Heat the oven to 170°C/325°F/gas mark 3.

9 Place a layer of beans in a deep ovenproof dish. Cover with a layer of the meat, sausage, tomatoes and herbs. Season generously with salt and pepper. Continue to layer up, finishing with a layer of beans. Pour over the cooking liquor and reserved fat, and sprinkle with a layer of breadcrumbs.

10 Place uncovered in the oven for 1½ hours. If the breadcrumbs become dry and crusty, stir them into the cassoulet and add more liquid if necessary. Sprinkle more breadcrumbs on top. At the end of the cooking time the meat and beans should be very tender and creamy and the top crisp and brown.

NOTE: This is delicious if made a couple of days in advance. It is also very good (and traditional) if confit d'oie (preserved goose) is used in place of the pork.

Wine: Languedoc or Roussillon red from Minervois, Fitou, Corbières or Pic Saint Loup

Sausage Cassoulet

SERVES 4

450 g Toulouse sausages or Cumberland sausage

2 slices fat pork belly or rib

2 tablespoons olive oil

1 onion, diced

1 clove of garlic, crushed

1 bay leaf

1 clove

2 × 400 g cans haricot beans, drained

1 × 400 g can chopped tomatoes

1 tablespoon chopped fresh thyme

1 tablespoon chopped fresh parsley

stock or water

8 tablespoons white breadcrumbs

salt and freshly ground black pepper

1 Heat the oven to 200°C/400°F/gas mark 6.

2 Place the sausages and pork belly in a roasting pan and bake until browned. Drain, reserving the fat. Cut the pork belly into bite-sized pieces.

3 Lower the oven temperature to 170°C/325°F/gas mark 3.

4 Heat the oil in a small saucepan and sweat the onion until soft. Add the garlic and cook for a further minute.

5 Add the bay leaf and clove.

6 In a deep casserole dish, layer the beans, onions, tomatoes, sausages, pork belly and herbs, seasoning with salt and pepper as you go.

7 Pour in the reserved fat and cover with stock.

8 Sprinkle with half the breadcrumbs.

9 Bake uncovered in the oven for 2 hours. As the breadcrumbs become dry and crusty, stir them into the cassoulet, adding more liquid if it seems too dry. Sprinkle the remaining crumbs on top. At the end of the cooking time the beans should be creamy and the top crusty.

Wine: Languedoc or Roussillon red from Minervois, Fitou, Corbières or Pic Saint Loup

Three-sausage and Borlotti Bean Soup

Cumberland sausage, black pudding and salami are all big flavours. Combining all three makes for a very full-bodied and substantial soup.

Any kind of canned bean may be used, but borlotti beans have a sweet yet earthy flavour that works well with the richness of the meats.

SERVES 4–6

3 tablespoons extra virgin lemon olive oil

2 Spanish onions, finely sliced

2 medium leeks, finely sliced

2 sticks of celery, finely sliced

1 clove of garlic, crushed

2 × 400 g cans borlotti beans, rinsed and drained

2 teaspoons chopped fresh thyme leaves

finely grated zest of 1 lemon

2 bay leaves

675 ml Brown Chicken Stock (see page 454)

2 Cumberland sausages, cut into 3 cm chunks

140 g black pudding, cut into 3 cm chunks

110 g piece of salami, cut into small dice

salt and freshly ground black pepper

warm crusty bread, to serve

1 Heat 1½ tablespoons of the oil in a large saucepan, add the onions, leeks and celery, cover with a lid and sweat gently for 15 minutes, or until softened.
2 Remove the lid, increase the heat and cook, stirring occasionally, for 5 minutes, or until lightly browned. Add the garlic and cook for a further minute.
3 Add the beans, thyme, lemon zest and bay leaves to the pan, then pour in the stock.
4 Heat the remaining oil in a frying pan and brown the sausages, black pudding and salami on all sides. Add them to the pan and bring to the boil. Season with salt and pepper.
5 Reduce the heat and simmer gently for 5 minutes, or until the sausages are cooked through. Serve in warmed bowls with warm crusty bread.

Wine: Châteauneuf-du-Pape, Languedoc red or Australian Shiraz blend

Hot Sweet Potato and Sausage Stew

SERVES 4

4 tablespoons olive oil

4 large Toulouse sausages or
   1 Cumberland sausage

2 onions, sliced

1 tablespoon yellow mustard seeds

2 green chillies, deseeded and chopped

2 cloves of garlic, crushed

20 g piece of fresh root ginger, peeled and
   finely chopped

225 g orange sweet potatoes, chopped into large dice

1 × 400 g can chopped tomatoes

150 ml water

2 tablespoons chopped fresh coriander or parsley,
   to garnish

1 Place half the oil in a large frying pan over a medium heat. Cook the sausages on all sides, then transfer to a plate and keep warm.
2 Add the remaining oil to the pan and cook the onions over a low heat until soft.
3 Add the mustard seeds, chillies, garlic and ginger and cook for a further minute.
4 Add the sweet potatoes, tomatoes and water. Cover and cook for 10 minutes, or until the sweet potatoes are soft but still hold their shape.
5 In the meantime, cut the sausages on an angle into bite-sized pieces.
6 Add the sausages to the pan and heat through.
7 Serve garnished with the coriander or parsley.

Wine: Languedoc or Côtes-du-Rhône; Chilean Merlot or Pinot Noir

Black Pudding Benedict

SERVES 4

1 tablespoon duck fat

4 × 3 cm slices black pudding

4 English muffins

4 fresh duck eggs

1 × quantity Hollandaise Sauce (see page 476)

1 tablespoon freshly chopped flat leaf parsley

4 slices Serrano ham, folded into 4

1 Heat the grill and bring a large shallow pan of water to the boil.

2 Heat the duck fat in a frying pan and fry the black pudding gently on both sides until crisp and hot through.

3 Toast the muffins without splitting them. Keep warm.

4 Meanwhile, crack the eggs into the pan of barely trembling boiling water and poach for 2–3 minutes, or until set.

5 Place one-third of the hollandaise sauce in a bowl, mix the parsley into it and spread over the muffins.

6 Put a piece of black pudding on each muffin. Cover with a slice of Serrano ham and top with a poached egg. Spoon the remaining hollandaise over the eggs and grill for 30 seconds, or until bubbling and lightly browned. Serve immediately.

Drink: Australian Shiraz or Guinness

Black Pudding and Parsnip Cakes

These savoury cakes are delicious served as a snack with fruit chutney, or for supper with poached or fried duck eggs. They can be made up to a day in advance and kept refrigerated, then fried when needed.

MAKES 8

1 tablespoon oil

340 g black pudding, skinned and roughly
   crumbled

450 g freshly cooked, warm Mashed Potatoes
   (see Note and page 491)

225 g cooked parsnips

1 large, ripe red-skinned pear, cored and diced

2 tablespoons freshly chopped flat leaf parsley

1–2 tablespoons goose fat

salt and freshly ground black pepper

1 Heat the oil in a large frying pan and fry the black pudding briskly until browned and crisp. Allow to cool slightly, then place in a large bowl with the mashed potato.

2 Roughly mash half the parsnips, and cut the remaining half into fine dice. Add to the potato mixture with the pear and chopped parsley. Season well with salt and black pepper.

3 Divide the mixture into 8 equal portions and use wet hands to shape them into patties. Chill for 1 hour.

4 Melt 1 tablespoon of the goose fat in a large, shallow pan. When hot, fry the patties a few at a time on both sides until golden brown and hot through, adding more goose fat

if necessary. Drain the patties on kitchen paper, sprinkle with a little salt and serve very hot.

NOTES: Any variety of pear can be used, and peeled if preferred, but the colour of a red-skinned pear is attractive.

It is important to have freshly made mash for this recipe, as the warm potato starch will bind the mixture together. Cold mashed potato will not bind as effectively.

Frying the black pudding before adding it to the other ingredients gives it a better texture and adds to the overall flavour.

Wine: Crozes-Hermitage or New World Syrah/Shiraz

Open Black Pudding 'Ravioli' with Warm Herb Pesto

SERVES 4

55 g rocket leaves	6 fresh lasagne sheets (see page 83)
1 bunch of chives	1 tablespoon oil
1 large handful of flat leaf parsley	8 × 1 cm slices black pudding
1 large clove of garlic, crushed	3 ripe plum tomatoes, blanched, peeled,
grated zest and juice of 1 small lemon	deseeded and diced
50 g pine nuts	40 g sun-blushed tomatoes, roughly chopped
110 g Parmesan cheese, freshly grated	4 slices prosciutto, cut in half
150 ml olive oil	salt and freshly ground black pepper

1 To make the pesto, put the rocket, chives, parsley, garlic, lemon zest and juice, pine nuts and half the Parmesan in a blender and whizz to combine. Drizzle in 150 ml oil and season with salt and pepper.
2 Cut the pasta sheets in half to make 12 squares. Place in a shallow pan of boiling salted water for 2–3 minutes, then drain. It may be necessary to do this in batches to prevent the squares sticking together.
3 Heat the tablespoon of oil in a frying pan and fry the black pudding for 1 minute on both sides until crisp. Remove and keep warm.
4 Heat the grill to its highest setting.
5 Put the fresh and sun-blushed tomatoes in the hot pan and warm through gently for 1 minute.
6 Put a square of pasta on each warmed serving plate, top with a spoonful of the pesto, some of the tomatoes, a slice of black pudding and a piece of prosciutto.
7 Repeat the layers until all the ingredients are used up, finishing with a piece of pasta.
8 Top the ravioli with the remaining Parmesan and place under the grill until hot and the cheese has browned.

Wine: Châteauneuf-du-Pape or a warming, southern Italian red

Chorizos

This recipe is from Jane Grigson's *Charcuterie and French Pork Cookery*. The sausages are lightly smoked in a food smoker before they are cooked. The smoking, which does not cook the sausages but simply adds flavour, may be omitted.

MAKES 20

1 length of washed sausage skin, 3 cm in diameter

70 ml red wine

1 tablespoon salt

For the filling

¼ teaspoon granulated sugar

450 g lean pork (neck or shoulder)

¼ teaspoon ground mixed spice

225 g pork fat

¼ teaspoon cayenne pepper

1 small red pepper

1 large clove of garlic, crushed

1 small chilli

1 Mince the pork and fat, using the coarse blade of the mincer.
2 Cut the pepper and chilli in half, remove the seeds and stalks, put through the mincer and add to the pork.
3 Add the remaining filling ingredients and mix well.
4 Following the instructions on page239, fill the sausage skins with the mixture, but do not pack too tightly or the sausages will burst. Twist every 13–15 cm.
5 Place the sausages in a smoker and smoke for 20 minutes, if you wish.
6 Cook as required.

Wine: Fino sherry, dry rosé, sparkling wine or fruity red

Spiced Cabbage, Butter Bean and Chorizo Stew

SERVES 4

2 tablespoons olive oil

2 large onions, very finely sliced

2 cloves of garlic, crushed

500 g waxy potatoes, peeled and cut into
  1 cm dice

¼ teaspoon cayenne pepper

2 × 400 g cans butter beans, rinsed and drained

140 g chorizo sausage, cut into 5 mm cubes

600 ml strong Brown Chicken Stock (see
  page 454)

1 medium Savoy cabbage, outer leaves removed
  and cut into 8 wedges

salt and freshly ground black pepper

2 tablespoons roughly chopped flat leaf parsley,
  to garnish

1 Heat the oil in a large saucepan, add the onions and cook gently for 10–25 minutes, or until beginning to soften. Stir in the garlic and cook for a further minute.
2 Add the diced potatoes and cayenne pepper and continue to cook for a further 15 minutes, or until the potatoes are beginning to break up – this will help to thicken the stew.

3 Stir in the butter beans, chorizo and stock and season with salt and pepper. Lay the cabbage wedges on top of the bean mixture, cover with a lid and simmer gently for 10 minutes, or until the cabbage is tender. Adjust the seasoning.

4 Divide the stew between 4 warmed bowls, sprinkle with the parsley and serve.

Wine: Fino sherry, dry rosé, sparkling wine or fruity red

Individual Chorizos in the Hole

SERVES 4

340 g chorizo sausage, thickly sliced

For the batter

110 g plain flour

good pinch of salt

large pinch of paprika

2 eggs, beaten

150 ml milk

150 ml water

To serve

300 ml Gravy (see page 463)

1 Start by making the batter. Sift the flour with the salt and paprika into a large bowl. Make a well in the centre of the flour and add the eggs.

2 Using a wooden spoon, mix the eggs to a paste and very gradually draw in the surrounding flour, adding just enough milk to make a smooth, thin paste. When all the flour is incorporated, stir in the rest of the liquid. Chill for 30 minutes before use.

3 Heat the oven to 220°C/425°F/gas mark 7.

4 Divide the chorizo between an 8-hole, non-stick bun tin. Place in the oven for 4–5 minutes, or until the sausage is lightly browned and the fat is smoking hot.

5 Pour the batter over the chorizo. Bake for 12–15 minutes. Serve with the gravy.

Wine: Fino sherry, dry rosé, sparkling wine or a fruity red

Pizza Kebabs

SERVES 4

1 small ciabatta loaf

3 tablespoons sun-dried tomato oil, from the jar

110 g chorizo sausage, cut into 1 cm dice

8 baby plum tomatoes

1 handful of fresh basil leaves

2 × 125 g balls buffalo mozzarella,
   cut into 1.25 cm cubes

2 kabanos sausages, sliced thickly on the diagonal

6 anchovy fillets, halved lengthwise (optional)

8 Kalamata olives, pitted

3 sun-dried tomatoes in oil, drained and
   cut into quarters

1 tablespoon extra virgin olive oil

salt and freshly ground black pepper

50 g Parmesan cheese, freshly grated, to serve

1 Heat the grill to its highest setting.

2 Cut the ciabatta loaf into 2 cm cubes and drizzle over the sun-dried tomato oil.

3 Thread a piece of the bread on to a long, metal skewer. Follow with a piece of chorizo, a baby plum tomato, 2–3 basil leaves, a cube of mozzarella, a slice of kabanos sausage, a piece of anchovy, an olive and a piece of sun-dried tomato. Repeat until the skewer is filled, finishing with a cube of bread. Fill 4 skewers in this way. Drizzle the olive oil over the kebabs and season with salt and pepper.

4 Grill the kebabs until the bread and mozzarella are lightly browned: they will take about 2 minutes on each side. Serve immediately with the Parmesan handed separately.

Drink: Chilled lager with a slice of lime

Faggots with Pease Pudding and Red Onion Gravy

SERVES 4

250 g pig's liver, skinned, tubes removed

1 pig's heart, tubes removed, roughly chopped

1 pig's kidney, cores removed, roughly chopped

110 g rindless, green streaky bacon
(see page 222), diced

110 g Pork Sausagemeat (see page 238)

50 g pork back fat, diced

115 g coarse oatmeal

4 large fresh sage leaves, finely chopped

½ teaspoon thyme leaves, freshly chopped

2 teaspoons very finely chopped parsley

freshly grated nutmeg

ground allspice

ground mace

1 large sheet of pig's caul, soaked in cold water
and drained (see page 513)

salt and freshly ground black pepper

To serve

Pease Pudding (see below)

Red Onion Gravy (see page 463)

1 Heat the oven to 180°C/350°F/gas mark 4.

2 Place all the meat and fat in the bowl of a food processor and chop coarsely. Turn the mixture into a large bowl and add the oatmeal and herbs. Season with plenty of nutmeg, allspice, mace, salt and pepper and mix well. The meat should be quite spicy.

3 Using wet hands, shape the mixture into 8 balls. Cut the pig's caul into squares large enough to completely encase the balls. Place the wrapped faggots in a roasting pan, seam-side down, and flatten them slightly.

4 Bake in the middle of the oven for about an hour, basting occasionally, until golden brown. Serve with pease pudding and red onion gravy.

PEASE PUDDING

SERVES 4

225 g split yellow peas, soaked in water overnight,
rinsed and drained

30 g butter

1 large egg, beaten

plain flour

salt and freshly ground black pepper

1 Place the peas in a large pan. Cover with cold water and bring to the boil.

2 Drain the peas in a colander, then rinse and return to the pan. Cover with fresh, cold water, return to the boil, then simmer very gently for 1½ hours, or until very tender.

3 Drain the peas, then pass through a sieve into a bowl. Stir in the butter and beaten egg. Season very well with salt and pepper.

4 Flour a clean tea towel or a double layer of butter muslin and turn the pea purée on to it. Tie the cloth up loosely and place the parcel in a basin.

5 Lower the basin into a pan of simmering water and cook gently for 1 hour. Lift the basin out of the pan, untie the cloth and turn the pudding on to a warmed serving plate.

Wine: Rustic, full-bodied red, such as Gigondas or Cannonau

Brawn

Brawn is made from the meat, fat and skin of a pig's head. The cheeks yield most of the meat, but there are plenty of other, possibly less attractive but equally tasty, small pieces of meat on the head too. The easiest way to remove and make use of all the meat is to cook the head whole, submerged in aromatic liquid, until it is so soft that it starts to fall away from the bone. There is a considerable amount of fat on the head too, and this can be mixed in with the meat, in varying proportions, along with the skin, according to taste. Traditionally, rather a lot of the fat and skin would have been used in order to make the meat go further, making the dish a very economical one. Nowadays, most people would probably prefer to use a higher percentage of meat to fat and skin, due in part to changes in taste and the health implications of too high a fat intake. However, omitting too much of the fat will make for a much drier and less tasty brawn. The addition of trotters makes for a particularly gelatinous and tasty stock that sets to a delicious soft jelly.

SERVES 10–12

1 pig's head

2 pig's trotters

3 onions, cut into quarters and studded with 10 cloves

2 carrots, cut into large chunks

2 sticks of celery, cut into large chunks

2 bay leaves

6 sprigs of thyme

1 large handful of parsley stalks, bruised

1 teaspoon coriander seeds

10 black peppercorns, roughly crushed

freshly ground nutmeg

juice of ½ a small lemon

salt and freshly ground black pepper

To serve

Fresh Dill-pickled Cucumbers (see opposite)

1 Cut the pig's head into quarters. Cut off the ears, remove any hairs and scrub well under running water.

2 Place the head quarters, ears and trotters in a very large pan or stockpot. Add the vegetables, bay leaves, thyme, parsley stalks, coriander seeds, peppercorns and a teaspoon of salt. Season with a good grating of nutmeg. Cover with cold water and bring to the boil. Reduce the heat and simmer very gently, uncovered, for 4–4½ hours, until the meat is tender and falling away from the bones. Ensure that the meat is covered with water at all times.

3 Lift the meat from the pan and allow to cool. Remove the skin and fat from the bones and pick off all the meat. Roughly chop the meat, about two-thirds of the skin and fat, and the tongue and place in a large bowl.

4 Stir in the lemon juice and season with salt and freshly ground pepper.

5 Strain the cooking liquor through a sieve lined with fine muslin. Discard the vegetables and herbs.

6 Stir 150 ml of the liquor into the meat and pile the mixture into a 15 cm square cake tin. Press down well and spoon over a little of the remaining liquid. Allow to cool, cover with a large disc of silicone paper and place a weighted plate on top. Chill overnight.

7 To serve, dip the base of the tin briefly into hot water and run a sharp knife around the inside edges. Invert on to a plate and remove the tin. Slice into thin wedges like a cake and serve with the dill-pickled cucumbers.

FRESH DILL-PICKLED CUCUMBERS

Unlike the dill pickled cucumbers or cornichons that are bought in jars, the cucumber in this recipe is lightly cured and used immediately after the curing process. This results in a crisper texture and fresher flavour, with a sweet tanginess. Mini cucumbers can be used, if available, in which case, the seeds may be left in. Here the cucumber skin has been left on, but can be removed if preferred.

SERVES 6–8

1 large cucumber

5 tablespoons white wine vinegar

1 teaspoon salt

2 teaspoons caster sugar

2 tablespoons freshly chopped dill

1 Cut the cucumber in half lengthwise and remove the seeds with a teaspoon.

2 Slice the cucumber finely on the diagonal and place the slices in a large, non-metallic bowl.

3 Pour the vinegar over the cucumber and stir in the salt, sugar and 1½ tablespoons of the dill. Cover and leave to stand for 1 hour.

4 Strain the cucumber through a sieve and discard the liquid. (There may be rather a lot of liquid, as the salt draws the moisture from the cucumber.) Place the drained cucumber in a serving bowl and sprinkle with the remaining dill.

Wine: Mature red Burgundy or Rhône

Poultry

The term 'poultry' refers to all domesticated birds. More poultry is consumed in the UK than any other meat, and the most popular is undoubtedly chicken. Chickens are found throughout the world and are kept for their eggs and bred for their meat. Chicken is tremendously versatile: it can be cooked by every cooking method, from roasting and poaching to deep-frying and stir-frying. The flavour of the meat marries well with a huge range of spices and seasonings.

History

Birds always have been part of man's diet as they are plentiful and easy to capture. The ancestor of today's chicken is the Red Jungle Fowl, which can still be found running wild in Southeast Asia. It is thought that domestication of chickens occurred before 5000 BC in China, and somewhat later in Thailand and India – later than the domestication of cattle and sheep. Until chickens became mass-produced, the birds were more prized for their egg-laying ability than their meat. Hens were cooked only once their laying days were over, whilst cocks were grown until they were rather old and tough compared to today's tender chickens.

Common Breeds

Almost all the chickens bred in the UK are of the Ross Cobb breed. This breed is known for its ability to gain weight quickly. Although hormones were at one time used to promote growth, their use is no longer allowed. Chickens of this breed that are fed high-protein food are ready for slaughter at about 6 weeks of age, rather than the 18–20 weeks needed for a free-range chicken.

There is a great deal of controversy over the rearing of chickens. The popularity of chicken meat has placed huge pressure on farmers to produce the meat more cheaply. This has led to intensive rearing methods, where the chickens are kept inside in extremely overcrowded conditions. These poor conditions have led to an increase in disease and mortality. To counteract disease some chickens are routinely given antibiotics along with their high-protein feed. This has resulted in some bacteria commonly found on chickens becoming antibiotic resistant.

In most countries it is prohibited for the meat of chickens that have died prior to slaughter to enter the food chain, but this is not true for all countries. There is an enormous world market for chicken meat, both fresh and frozen. The consumer should be aware that not all countries have the same regulations as the UK.

Overbreeding and intensive farming methods have resulted in chickens that have huge breasts and weak skeletons, so by the time they are nearly ready for slaughter, their legs are too weak to support their weight. Their legs collapse, leaving them kneeling for the latter part of their short lives. The kneeling produces 'hock burn', which can be seen in some supermarket chickens by discoloration and redness around the knees.

The most naturally reared chickens are labelled 'organic and free-range'. These birds should be antibiotic-free and have lived a more natural existence than their intensively reared counterparts. It's often said that 'You get what you pay for', and this is certainly the case when buying chicken.

Choosing Poultry

- Choose a bird with plump breasts, dry skin and no bruising or blood spots.
- A pliable breastbone is an indication of a young bird.
- If the legs are attached, they should be smooth and flexible.

Storing Poultry

Uncooked

If you buy a bird with giblets, remove them as soon as you get home and store them separately in the bottom of the refrigerator. Unwrap the bird and cover loosely with greaseproof paper so that air can circulate over the skin. When poultry is wrapped in plastic, moisture tends to condense beneath, creating perfect conditions for bacterial growth (see Meat Storage and Hygiene, page 4). Store poultry at the bottom of the refrigerator for not more than 2 days.

Cooked

Cooked poultry may be stored near the top of the refrigerator for up to 2 days provided it is wrapped in cling film to prevent it from drying out or being tainted by other items stored nearby.

Defrosting Poultry

Frozen poultry needs to be defrosted slowly and carefully to avoid the risk of salmonella contamination. At temperatures above 5°C salmonella bacteria can multiply. When defrosting, place the poultry in its wrapper at the bottom of the refrigerator on a wire rack placed on a plate to catch any juices or blood that might run from the meat. The bottom of the refrigerator is the coldest part, and to avoid the risk of cross-contamination raw meat should never be placed above or near any other food. Large pieces of poultry and whole birds can take a day or more to defrost (see tables on pages 262 and 263).

Chicken

Chickens are available in a range of sizes determined by their age. They are usually sold oven-ready, meaning that they are plucked, drawn and often trussed. The more you spend on a chicken, the better it is likely to taste. A frozen supermarket bird, raised on a battery farm and fed fishmeal, is unlikely to taste as good as a free-range bird, however well cooked.

Poussin

Poussins (very young chickens) come in two sizes – single and double. Single poussins are 4–6 weeks old, weigh approximately 250 g and serve one person. They look attractive on the plate, but have very little meat or flavour. To make them more interesting they may be stuffed and/or served with a piquant sauce. Single poussins are suitable for oven-roasting and spit-roasting, or may be flattened (see Spatchcocking, page 319).

Double poussins are 6–12 weeks old, weigh approximately 350 g, serve two people and have a little more flavour than single poussins. Double poussins are often stuffed and roasted, then split in half to serve to two people. They are also suitable for spit-roasting, or may be spatchcocked and grilled.

Spring Chicken

Spring chickens are 10–12 weeks old and weigh approximately 450 g. They serve two people and have a similar flavour to that of double poussins. They are best roasted.

Roasting Chicken

Roasters are usually over 3 months old and weigh 1.2–1.8 kg. They can have an excellent flavour as long as they have been raised in reasonable conditions. Allow 450 g (on the bone weight) per serving. Whole chickens are suited to oven-roasting, braising, pot-roasting and poaching. If jointed, they can be grilled, baked, fried or stewed.

Corn-fed Chicken

This is a free-range chicken fed on corn, which colours its fat yellow and gives it a distinctive, rich flavour. French corn-fed chickens generally seem to have a slightly gamier flavour than English ones.

Poulet Noir

This is a French black-legged chicken. When plucked, it looks more like a guinea fowl, with larger legs and a narrower breast than a standard chicken. The texture of the cooked meat is firmer than that of standard chicken. Poulet noir is more expensive than a conventional chicken as it is reared on pasture from a month old, and fed on corn and dairy products in addition to its free-range diet.

Capon

This bird was originally a castrated cockerel, which, having lost its interest in sex, ate voraciously and became very plump and tender, weighing as much as 4 kg. They are no longer available.

Duck

Duck is more expensive than chicken because it is unsuited to intensive battery farming and yields a small proportion of meat, despite its weight and size. Ducks have a large carcass, and farmed ducks contain a high quantity of fat.

Most ducks sold today are ducklings aged 7–9 weeks old. A 1.8 kg duck feeds only 2–3 people due to its large carcass and high proportion of subcutaneous fat. Look for a plump breast and skin that is dry, soft and smooth. The duck should not be slimy and should not smell strongly.

Aylesbury and Gressingham ducks are considered to be the best. Because of their fat content, whole ducks are best oven-roasted, jointed duck is often baked or made into *confit*, and duck breasts are usually pan-fried. The rich meat stands up to strongly flavoured sauces that often contain fruit.

Goose

Goose is at its best when it weighs about 4.5 kg at around 6–9 months of age. A bird of this size will serve 4–6 people. Goose is more expensive than duck, and has an even larger carcass relative to the quantity of meat, and a great deal of subcutaneous fat. As a result, it became less popular at Christmas than it was previously, and the more economical turkey became prevalent.

Goose can be delicious, but make sure you choose a young bird as old geese can be very tough. Fresh goose has a clean white skin, which is soft and dry to the touch. The flesh is a cream colour, but becomes light brown with a gamy flavour when cooked. Its high fat content means that goose is best roasted.

Today goose is bred specially for the Christmas season, so birds are more readily available in December.

Choosing a Goose

Follow the same rules as for turkey (see opposite).

Storing Goose

Follow the same rules as for turkey (see page 260).

Guinea Fowl

Usually a little smaller than the average-sized chicken, the guinea fowl weighs 1–1.5 kg and has a slightly scrawny appearance. Although traditionally a game bird, and supermarkets often treat it as such, selling it only in the winter months, it is now widely farmed all year round. The taste is that of a very delicious, slightly gamy chicken. Guinea fowl is most suitable for oven-roasting or pot-roasting, braising or stewing. As the meat is very lean, it must be cooked with great care to prevent it from drying out.

Turkey

The wild turkey originated in the New World and was brought back to Europe by the Spanish conquistadors. The first record of a turkey in England dates to 1524. The bird took well to domestication and was raised extensively in East Anglia. From the early 1700s turkey (and goose) flocks were herded to London, beginning in August, for the Christmas festivities.

In the UK turkey is most associated with Christmas. Although roast goose is also popular on the British Christmas table, the turkey gained dominance in the last century, and retains it still.

While turkey is still a traditional part of the Christmas celebration meal in the USA, it is also very popular throughout the year, and is made into smaller roasts, cut into steaks, or minced for burgers. The meat is low in fat and high in protein, making it an excellent choice for year-round eating.

Common Breeds

A wild turkey is distinguished by having bronze-coloured feathers. It has fairly dark, gamy-flavoured meat, which is not dissimilar to chicken thigh meat.

By the mid-20th century turkeys called Broad-breasted Whites were being intensively farmed, and throughout the 1960s turkeys were bred to have bigger breasts. These farmed turkeys were bred to have white feathers because dark feathers gave the turkey an unpleasant 'stubble' effect after plucking.

In recent years there has been a revival of the wild breed, the bronze turkey. When kept free range and allowed to live to a greater age of about 6 months, it develops an exceptional flavour, which can be enhanced if allowed to hang for 2–4 weeks. When cooked properly, the flesh remains moist.

Another popular breed is the Norfolk Black, which has a flavour and texture somewhere between the mass-produced supermarket birds and the free-range organic bronze turkey.

Mass-produced birds are slaughtered at about 14 weeks and are plucked in a water bath, which is faster and cheaper than other methods. Look for turkey that has been 'dry-processed' (plucked by hand). It will have more flavour and a better texture.

Choosing a Turkey

Turkeys are available in many sizes, frozen and fresh, whole or in portions. The giblets are usually included in a bag packed inside the bird. These are used to flavour stocks and gravy, and can be included in stuffings and pâtés.

Fresh turkey will normally be of better quality than frozen turkey, and will have better flavour and texture. The size of a turkey will depend to some extent on its age, but also on the size of the stock from which it has been bred.

When calculating servings, allow 450 g of the bird's weight per person to take into account the weight of the carcass.

- Look for skin that is firm and dry.
- Avoid birds with blood spots or bruising.
- The flesh should be pale pink or white.

Storing Turkey

Whole: Place on a plate to collect any juices, cover with greaseproof paper and store in the bottom of the refrigerator for up to 3 days.

Pieces: Discard the plastic wrapping. Place the meat on a plate, cover with greaseproof paper and store in the bottom of the refrigerator for up to 2 days.

Mince: Store well wrapped in the coldest part of the refrigerator. Use within 24 hours.

Giblets: Remove all the giblets from the bird as soon as possible and store in the same way as poultry livers (see page 360). Use within 24 hours.

Freezing: Turkey portions and mince can be frozen and stored for up to 3 months. It is not advised to freeze a whole turkey in a home freezer, although a bird that is purchased frozen can be stored in one.

Defrosting Turkey

Their large size means that frozen turkeys can take a long time to defrost. They should be defrosted slowly to reduce loss of moisture in the meat (see page 262). Thawing turkey in a warm room (over 18°C/65°F) or under warm water is not recommended, as warmth will encourage the growth of micro-organisms, which might result in food poisoning. It is best to thaw a turkey in the bottom of the refrigerator.

Methods of Cooking Poultry

Roasting

All types of poultry are good for roasting. For instructions on plucking and drawing poultry see Preparing Feathered Game for Cooking (page 375).

Stuffing whole birds: Roasting chickens and other medium-sized birds can be stuffed in both the neck and body cavity. Turkeys are generally stuffed only in the neck end because the body cavity is large and it takes too long to become hot enough to kill any salmonella bacteria. For this reason it is recommended that the body cavity of large birds is not stuffed.

Smaller birds, such as poussins, are stuffed in the larger body cavity. Do not pack the stuffing in too firmly as it swells with cooking, which may cause it to push its way out of the bird. When the neck end of a bird is filled, the flap of neck skin is folded over the stuffing and secured with thread or a skewer.

Stuffing birds under the skin: Chickens and smaller birds can be stuffed between the skin and the breast flesh with flavoured butters, herbs or soft-textured stuffing to provide flavour and to help prevent the lean flesh from drying out.

Before the bird can be stuffed in this way, the skin must be loosened away from the flesh. This is done by inserting the first two fingers under the skin at the neck end and sweeping them back and forth to loosen the skin covering the breasts. The stuffing is then inserted, using a piping bag or your fingers. Distribute the stuffing evenly under the skin by moving it about over the breasts, stroking the skin lightly with the fingertips. Only a very thin layer of stuffing should be inserted under the skin or it will cause the skin to split when the bird is cooked.

Trussing: Birds are trussed to maintain a neat, compact shape during roasting. Trussing large birds is not done as it prevents the inside of the thigh from being cooked through by the time the breast is ready. Small birds, especially game birds where underdone thighs are desirable (to prevent toughness), are trussed with their feet left on. The feet may simply be tied together for neatness and the pinions (wing tips) skewered under the bird. Or they may be trussed in other ways, one of which is described below. If the bird is to be stuffed, it is best done before trussing.

1   Arrange the bird so that the neck flap is folded over the neck hole, and the pinions turned under and tucked in tightly. If folded correctly, they will hold the neck flap in place, but if the bird is well stuffed the neck flap may have to be skewered or sewn into place.
2   Press the legs down and towards the bird to force the breast into a plumped-up position.
3   Thread a long trussing needle with thin string and push it through the wing joint, right through the body and through the other wing joint.
4   Push the needle through the body again, this time through the thighs.
5   Tie the two loose ends of string together in a bow to facilitate removal later.
6   Thread a shorter piece of string through the knobbly ends of the two drumsticks and tie them together, winding the string around the parson's nose at the same time to close the vent. Sometimes a small slit is cut in the skin just below the end of the breastbone, and the parson's nose is pushed through it.

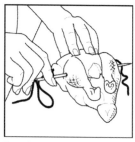

Trussing a bird

Points to Remember about Roasting Poultry

- Chicken and turkey must be roasted until thoroughly cooked to prevent the risk of food poisoning, in contrast to duck, goose and feathered game, all of which are better roasted until lightly pink to ensure that the meat remains tender and moist.
- Birds for roasting are often stuffed at the neck end. Make sure the weight of the stuffing is taken into account when calculating the cooking time.
- Poultry liable to dry out during cooking can be barded by tying fatty bacon or rindless pork back fat strips over the body of the bird. The barding is removed towards the end of cooking to allow the breasts to brown.
- Fatty birds, such as duck and goose, should be placed on a wire rack above the roasting pan to allow the large quantity of melted fat to collect below.
- Place the bird breast-side down for the first 30 minutes to encourage the juices to run into the breasts and keep them moist.

Defrosting and Roasting Times for Chicken, Duck, Goose and Guinea Fowl

Bird	Weight	Defrosting time in refrigerator at 5°C/40°F	Oven temperature			Cooking time per kg	Internal temperature	
			°C	°F	Gas mark		°C	°F
Chicken	1.35 kg 2.25 kg 4.5 kg 6.75 kg 9 kg	24 hours 24 hours 36 hours 48 hours 64 hours	200°	400°	6	35–45 mins	82°	185°
Duck	1.3–2.5 kg	As chicken	200°	400°	6	45 mins	82°C/185°F or 65°C/150°F for pink duck	
Goose	2.5–8 kg	As chicken	190°	375°	5	35 mins	82°	185°
Guinea fowl	1–1.5 kg	As chicken	200°	400°	6	35–45 mins	82°	185°

NOTE: Few birds, however small, will be cooked in much under 1 hour.

Defrosting and Roasting Times for Turkey

The cooking times given opposite depend on an accurate oven. For safety's sake, plan the timing so that the bird will be ready 1 hour before dinner. This will give you leeway if necessary. When the bird is cooked, open the oven door to cool the oven, then put the turkey on a serving dish and put it back in the oven to keep warm.

Weight of oven-ready turkey, including any stuffing	Defrosting time in refrigerator at 5°C/40°F	Cooking time at 200°C/400°F/gas mark 6	Cooking time at 180°C/350°C/gas mark 4	Internal temperature
4–5 kg	65 hours	2½–3 hours	–	
5–6 kg	70 hours	3–3¾ hours	–	
6–7 kg	75 hours	30 mins then >	3¼–4 hours	82°C/185°F for turkeys of every size
8–9 kg	80 hours	30 mins then >	4–4½ hours	
9–11 kg	86 hours	1 hour then >	4–4½ hours	

Grilling

This technique is described in Methods of Cooking Meat (Grilling, page 18).

As poultry is prone to drying out, it is important that the meat is regularly basted with melted butter or oil during cooking. The grill must be very hot to brown the surface of the meat sufficiently before or just as the centre of the meat is cooked. Poultry for grilling is often marinated in liquids containing oil, which penetrates the flesh and helps to keep the meat moist during cooking. Although poultry joints may be browned and crisped further under the grill, this cooking method is used mostly for tender cuts of meat from the breast or the thigh, and very young birds, such as spatchcocked poussin, which is flattened for grilling (see page 319).

It is important that the chicken is cooked thoroughly. It is recommended that thicker chicken pieces, such as the breast with the bone, are poached (see Poaching, page 265) before grilling or barbecuing.

Small whole birds, such as poussin and spring chicken, can be cut in half or spatchcocked (see page 319) and grilled. To grill a small bird, heat the grill or barbecue to its highest setting. Brush the bird with oil, then grill until brown.

Pan-frying and Sautéing

These techniques are described in Methods of Cooking Meat (see Frying, page 16).

Jointed poultry is often fried to brown and partially cook it before completing the cooking in liquid (see Coq au Vin and Chicken Sauté Normande, pages 286 and 287). The skin is browned to give colour and flavour to the dish, and is left on during cooking to prevent the meat from drying out. The heat under the pan should be adjusted to medium-low so that the fat melts from the skin in the time it takes to brown. If the chicken is cooked over a high heat, only the surface of the skin will brown, leaving a thick layer of fat underneath. Thoroughly browned, well-seasoned and crisp skin will also enhance the appearance and flavour of the cooked meat.

Thin pieces of chicken can be browned without the skin, but care must be taken not to cook them for too long or over too high a heat or the meat will dry out (see Stir-frying, page 264). Boned chicken is unsuitable for stewing, as the meat tends to become tough, dry or stringy with prolonged cooking.

Pan-frying and Sautéing: What has gone wrong when...

The chicken skin is pale and flabby.
• The chicken skin was not browned thoroughly enough.

Deep-frying

Due to their delicately flavoured, tender flesh, chicken and turkey breast or thigh meat are most suitable for deep-frying. The meat is often cut into strips called goujons and protected with a breadcrumb coating, or left whole and partially boned, as in a supreme (see below). For deep-frying techniques and safety information, see page 53.

Making a supreme
A supreme is a whole breast with the first joint of the wing attached. The wing is cut off at the middle joint, then the small bone is trimmed by scraping it clean with a paring knife. Chicken supremes are used to make Chicken Kiev (see page 298).

Stir-frying

This method is described in detail in Methods of Cooking Meat, page 18.

Poultry meat cut into dice or thickish strips must be fried quickly to brown the surface of the meat before the centre of the meat is overcooked. Use fat or oil with a high smoke point, such as sunflower or grapeseed, so that the fat may be heated and maintained at a high temperature while the poultry is cooking. Very thin slices or strips of poultry, however, can be browned and cooked briefly in fats such as whole butter as they require very little cooking.

Season poultry just before pan-frying, sautéing or stir-frying, otherwise the salt will cause juices to leach from the meat, making the surface damp and difficult to brown.

Stir-frying Chicken: What has gone wrong when...

The chicken is dry.
• The chicken was overcooked.

The chicken is pale.
• The fat was not heated sufficiently before the chicken was added.

Braising and Stewing

These techniques are described in Methods of Cooking Meat (pages 24 and 25).

Poaching

Poaching is a very gentle cooking technique, suitable for birds of any age. Young birds need just cooking through so that they remain tender and do not dry out, whereas older birds require longer poaching, until the meat starts to fall away from the bone. Amongst poultry, chicken is most frequently chosen for poaching. It is poached whole, either boned or unboned, and a whole boned bird may also be stuffed. Whole poached chicken is used as the basis for a number of classic dishes, such as Chicken Elizabeth (see page 280).

Poaching is also a perfect cooking method for tender pieces of poultry, such as the breast, which is often stuffed and firmly wrapped in cling film or foil to set its shape while it gently cooks through (see Stuffing a Chicken Breast, page 290). The tender breast meat must be cooked very gently in barely simmering water to avoid overcooking and drying out. Cook the breasts until they are just firm (see The Test of the Thumb, page 20).

For further information about poaching, see Methods of Cooking Meat, page 22.

Poaching Chicken: What has gone wrong when...

The chicken is dry.
- The poaching liquor was allowed to boil.

The meat is tender but falling off the bone.
- The chicken is overcooked.

Jointing a Chicken

A medium-sized bird (about 1.8 kg) can be jointed into eight pieces to serve four people, providing each person with a piece of dark meat and a piece of white breast meat. Before jointing, remove any trussing strings, then singe the bird if necessary to remove any stubble. Wipe clean with kitchen paper to remove any hairs and pin feathers. Use a cook's knife to cut through the flesh, and poultry shears or kitchen scissors to cut the bones and cartilage.

1 Place the bird breast-side down on a board with the parson's nose facing you.
2 Using a large cook's knife, make a cut through the skin along the backbone from one end to the other. (a)
3 Locate the soft pockets of flesh called the oysters on either side of the backbone at the top of the legs. Cut around them with the tip of the knife, then loosen them with the fingertips and thumbs so that they come away freely from the bone. This way the oysters will remain intact with the legs as they are pulled from the carcass. (b)
4 Turn the bird over so that it is breast-side up. Pull the skin covering the breast meat towards the breastbone, then cut through the skin between the breast and the leg, cutting as close to the leg as possible, using the blade of the knife, not the tip. (c)
5 Continue cutting the skin around the leg to make a cut perpendicular to the backbone next to the loosened oyster. Bend the leg out from the body and down towards the chopping board to release it from the socket. (d)
6 Use a small knife to cut the cartilage and tendons around the ball joint.
7 Remove the leg by grasping it firmly and pulling it towards the back of the chicken. Provided the oyster piece is completely loosened, it should come away with the leg.
8 Repeat the process with the other leg.
9 Using the cook's knife, cut cleanly through the skin and flesh between the breasts slightly to one side of the breastbone. (e)
10 Using poultry shears or kitchen scissors, cut along the length of the breastbone and through the wishbone at the neck end. (f)
11 Still using shears, cut along the fat line running along the edge of each breast, cutting through the ribs then around and underneath the wings to the neck of the chicken. (g) Do not separate the meat from the breastbone, as the bone will help to keep the meat moist during cooking. Cut out the wishbone in each piece. Save the carcass for stock.
12 Tuck the wings behind the breasts in the 'sunbathing position', so called because it resembles a person lying on their back with their arms supporting their head. Place the breasts next to each other to form a heart shape. Using the cook's knife, cut through the meat on a slant, from the cleavage of the heart to the elbow joint of the wing, then use the shears to cut through any bone. (h) You now have two wing-breast portions and two larger triangular-shaped breast portions. Leave the wing tips (pinions) intact as they help to hold the wing in position while the chicken cooks. They are trimmed off once the chicken is cooked.
13 Place the legs skin-side up on the board. Locate the joint between the drumstick and thigh by pressing against the meat with your finger to find the notch of the joint.
14 Using a large knife, cut down through the joint on both legs. The knife should do this easily. If it does not, you have hit the bone and are cutting in the wrong place. (i)
15 You now have eight portions of chicken, four with white meat and four with dark meat. (j)

Jointing a chicken

Cutting through the skin
along the backbone (a)

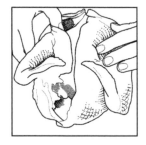

Loosening the oysters (b)

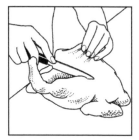

Cutting alongside
the leg (c)

Bending the leg back (d)

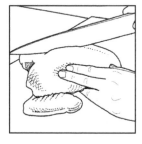

Cutting through the
skin and breast (e)

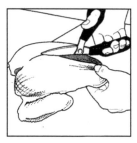

Cutting through the
breastbone (f)

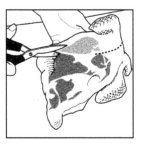

Cutting along the
fat line (g)

Dividing the breast
in two (h)

Dividing the thigh
and drumstick (i)

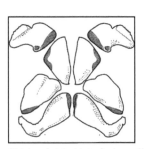

Chicken jointed into 8 pieces (j)

Cutting Small Birds into Portions

Small to medium-sized birds, such as spring chickens and guinea fowl, are often cut into four pieces for cooking. To joint a small bird into four pieces, follow steps 1–12 above, then use a knife to cut off the wing tip through the wing joint on each breast.

Trimming Poultry Joints after Cooking

As the jointed bird cooks, the flesh shrinks, exposing unsightly bone. This should be trimmed off before serving using poultry shears or kitchen scissors.

1   Cut the pinion (wing tip) from each wing by cutting through the middle joint.
2   Remove the end joint of the drumsticks by grasping the end with kitchen paper, then cutting the skin around the end of the bone just above the joint with a knife. Using kitchen scissors, push the skin back, then cut through and remove the bone.

Splitting a Small Bird in Half

1   Place the bird, breastbone uppermost, on a board.
2   Using a sharp knife, cut through the breast meat as close to the breastbone as possible, from one end of the bird to the other. (a)
3   Using poultry shears or kitchen scissors, cut through the exposed breastbone and the wishbone located at the neck end of the bird. (b)
4   Open out the bird and cut along the length of the backbone on the same side. (c)
5   Cut the backbone away from the other half of the bird.
6   The knobbly ends of the drumsticks and the fleshless tips of the pinions can be cut off before or after cooking.

Cutting the meat close to
the breastbone (a)

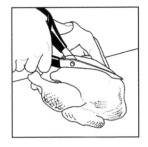

Cutting through the
breastbone (b)

Cutting down one side of
the backbone (c)

Boning a Whole Bird

Small to medium-sized birds are often boned and stuffed to serve hot or cold, cut into slices.

1   Put the bird breast-side down on a board. Cut through the skin to the backbone along the length of the bird.
2   Feel for the fleshy oyster at the top of each thigh and cut round it against the bone, loosening further with the fingers and thumb (see Jointing a Chicken, page 266).
3   Working down one side of the bird, cut and scrape the flesh from the carcass with a small sharp knife held as close as possible to the bone. Take care not to cut through the skin.
4   Cut the flesh from each side of the shoulder blade, then, using scissors or poultry shears, cut through the bone at the base of the wing next to the body of the bird.
5   Continue cutting along one side of the body until the ribcage is exposed. Once you have reached the centre of the breastbone, start again on the other side of the bird from step 3 above. (a)
6   When the flesh has been scraped from the carcass on both sides, hold the bird by the carcass, allowing the meat to hang down off the breastbone, and carefully cut the flesh away from the tip of the breastbone. (b) Avoid puncturing the skin.
7   Lay the boned bird skin-side down on the board.
8   Using a heavy knife, cut through the skin just above the feet joints to remove the knuckle end of the drumsticks.
9   Working from the inside thigh end, scrape one leg bone clean (c), pushing the flesh down towards the end of the drumstick until you can pull the thigh bone through and remove it. Push the boned skin and flesh of the legs inside the bird. Repeat on the other leg.
10 To bone the wings, cut them off at the elbow joint with a heavy knife.
11 Scrape the wing bones clean from the inside as you did for the leg bones.
12 Trim away any excess fat and any remaining bone from inside the bird with a sharp knife.
13 Keep the neck flap of skin intact to fold over the end once the bird is stuffed.

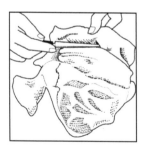

Scraping the meat
from the carcass (a)

Cutting the carcass from
the breastbone (b)

Scraping the thighbone (c)

Boning Poultry Legs

Legs of poultry, especially chicken and turkey, can be boned, stuffed and shaped to resemble a miniature gammon, as in Chicken Jambonneaux Stuffed with Wild Mushrooms (see page 305).

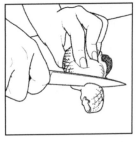

Cutting the knobbly end
from the drumstick (a)

Scraping the bone (b)

Spatchcocking a Bird

See page 319.

Ballotines

A ballotine is made from boned poultry (see page 269) or game birds stuffed with forcemeat, and either poached, braised with vegetables or roasted. It is usually served hot with a sauce made from the cooking juices.

The forcemeat is rolled tightly inside the boned bird and the whole is wrapped securely inside a muslin cloth tied with string for poaching or roasting (see pages 278–9).

Galantines

The Old French word *galantine* means 'jelly', and refers to the aspic used to decorate the dish (see page 485). A classic galantine is made with boned chicken stuffed with chicken-based forcemeat to return the bird roughly to its original shape, or it may be rolled into a cylindrical shape. The galantine is then poached in stock and served cold, sliced and glazed with aspic.

Preparing a Galantine

A galantine can be made with any bird, game, veal or fish, but here we use chicken as an example.

1   Bone the chicken as instructed on page 269.
2   Prepare the stuffing, e.g. the pistachio and apricot mixture used in Boned Stuffed Duck (see page 328).

3 Stuff the boned bird and roll into a sausage shape.
4 Wrap in muslin and tie securely.
5 Submerge in a pan of stock, court-bouillon (see page 457) or water and poach for about 1½ hours, until a skewer inserted into the middle of the stuffing comes out piping hot.
6 Remove from the poaching liquid and allow to cool.
7 Chill well, then unwrap. Remove the skin from the bird and discard.
8 Cut into 1 cm slices.

English Roast Chicken

1 × 1.35 kg roasting chicken
15 g butter, softened

For the stuffing

30 g butter
1 onion, finely chopped
50 g fresh white breadcrumbs
1 small cooking apple, grated
2 teaspoons chopped fresh herbs
grated zest of ½ a lemon
½ egg, beaten
salt and freshly ground black pepper

To garnish

4 chipolata sausages
4 rashers of rindless streaky bacon

For the gravy

1 scant tablespoon plain flour
300 ml White Chicken Stock (see page 451)

To serve

Bread Sauce (see page 475)

1 Heat the oven to 200°C/400°F/gas mark 6.
2 To make the stuffing, melt the butter in a saucepan and sweat the onion until soft but not coloured. Allow to cool.
3 Mix the breadcrumbs, apple, herbs and lemon zest together in a bowl.
4 Add the softened onion and enough beaten egg to bind the mixture together. Do not make it too wet. Season to taste with salt and pepper.
5 Stuff the chicken from the neck end, making sure the breast is well plumped. Draw the neck skin flap down to cover the stuffing. Secure with a skewer if necessary. Place in a roasting pan.
6 Smear a little butter all over the chicken and season with salt and pepper. Roast in the oven for about 1½ hours, or until the juices run clear when the thigh is pierced with a skewer.
7 Meanwhile, make the chipolatas into cocktail-sized sausages by twisting gently in the middle. Cut each bacon rasher in half and roll up.
8 After the chicken has been roasting for 1 hour, put the sausages and bacon rolls into the roasting pan, wedging the rolls together so that they cannot come undone.
9 Baste occasionally and check that the sausages and bacon are not sticking to the side of the pan and getting burnt.
10 When the chicken is cooked, transfer it to a warmed serving dish. Trim off the wing tips and tops of the drumsticks, surround with the bacon rolls and sausages and keep warm while you make the gravy.
11 Slowly pour off all but 1 tablespoon of the fat from the roasting pan, taking care to keep any juices. Add the flour and cook until straw coloured. Add the stock and stir until the sauce boils. Simmer for 3 minutes. Check the seasoning. Strain into a warmed gravy boat.
12 Serve the chicken with the bread sauce and gravy.

1 First cut off the legs. Cut through the skin between the breast and the leg and press the thighs down towards the carving dish to expose the hip joint. Cut through the joint and continue to bend the leg back to remove it from the body with the oyster intact. If the bird is very small, the thigh and drumstick are served together.

2 With larger birds, cut through the knee joint to separate the thigh from the drumstick.

3 Remove the wings by cutting diagonally, using the top of the wishbone as a guide, straight through the shoulder joint.

4 With small birds, the breast can be prised from the breastbone in one piece. Larger breasts are sliced thickly diagonally downwards from both sides of the breastbone. Or carve thin slices from each breast by cutting from the top of the breastbone down across the breast towards the leg joint.

Wine: Red or white Burgundy, or New World Pinot Noir (apart from the very strong ones)

Roasting Chicken: What has gone wrong when...

The breast meat is dry.
- The bird was not basted regularly.
- The bird should have been barded to protect the delicate breast meat.
- The bird was small and should have been roasted breast-side down for half of the roasting time.
- The bird was cooked for too long.

French Roast Chicken

Unlike its English counterpart, French roast chicken is baked partially covered in stock, which gives the meat a moister texture.

SERVES 4

butter, softened

1 × 1.35 kg roasting chicken with giblets

1 slice of onion

1 bay leaf

a few parsley stalks

300 ml White Chicken Stock (see page 451) or
vegetable water

salt and freshly ground black pepper

For the gravy

1 scant tablespoon plain flour

300 ml White Chicken Stock (see page 451)
or vegetable water

1 Heat the oven to 200°C/400°F/gas mark 6.

2 Smear a little butter all over the chicken. Season inside and out with pepper only. Put the bird, breast-side down, in a roasting pan.

3 Put all the chicken giblets (except the liver) and the neck into the pan with the chicken. Add the onion, bay leaf and parsley stalks. Pour in the stock. Roast in the oven for 30 minutes.

4 Remove from the oven, season all over with salt, turn the chicken breast side up and baste it with the fat and juices from the pan. Return to the oven.

5 Check periodically to see how the chicken is doing. It will take 60–80 minutes, and is cooked when the leg bones wobble loosely and independently from the body and the juices are not bloody. Baste occasionally as it cooks, and cover with foil or greaseproof paper if it is browning too much. Transfer the cooked chicken to a warmed serving dish and keep warm while making the gravy.

6 Place the roasting pan with its juices over a low heat. Skim off most of the fat.

7 Whisk in enough flour to absorb the remaining fat.

8 Add the stock or vegetable water and stir until the sauce boils. Simmer for 2–3 minutes. Check the seasoning. Strain into a warmed gravy boat and serve with the chicken.

Wine: Red or white Burgundy, or New World Pinot Noir (apart from the very strong ones)

Greek Lemon Chicken

SERVES 4

1.8 kg chicken

1 lemon, cut into quarters

4 cloves of garlic, unpeeled and bruised

250 ml chicken stock

100 ml olive oil

ground paprika

400 g baby new potatoes

2 tablespoons crème fraîche or double cream

salt and freshly ground black pepper

1 Heat the oven to 200°C/400°F/gas mark 6.

2 Rinse the chicken and place in a deep roasting pan or ovenproof lasagne dish breast-side down.

3 Squeeze the lemon quarters over and inside the chicken, then add the lemon quarters to the pan. Place 1 piece of lemon inside the chicken.

4 Place 1 clove of garlic inside the chicken and the remaining garlic around the chicken.

5 Pour over the chicken stock and half of the oil.

6 Sprinkle the paprika, salt and pepper over the chicken, taking care not to over-season.

7 Place in the centre of the oven and roast for 30 minutes, basting the inside of the chicken every 10 minutes.

8 Turn the chicken breast-side up. Place the potatoes around the chicken.

9 Pour the remaining oil over the chicken and the potatoes. Season the breast-side of the chicken and the potatoes with paprika, salt and pepper.

10 Roast for a further 45 minutes. Baste the inside of the chicken with the stock every 10 minutes.

11 When the chicken is cooked through, so no bloody juices run from the thick part of the thigh when pierced, remove the chicken to a warmed serving platter.

12 Remove the potatoes, lemon wedges and garlic from the stock and place on a baking sheet. Return to the oven to roast for a further 15 minutes.

13 Tip the stock into a saucepan and boil to reduce to thicken and to concentrate the flavour. Whisk in the crème fraîche or cream. Pour into a warmed sauceboat.

14 Joint the chicken into 8 pieces (see page 266) and arrange on a serving platter. Surround with the potatoes, roasted lemon wedges and garlic to serve.

Wine: Retsina

Chicken with Prunes

SERVES 4

1 × 1.35 kg roasting chicken with giblets
30 g butter, softened
a few slices of onion
1 slice of lemon
1 bay leaf
a few slices of carrot
salt and freshly ground black pepper
1 bunch of watercress, to garnish

For the sauce
15 g butter
12 shallots, peeled
12 cooked prunes, stoned
1 tablespoon sugar
1 tablespoon wine vinegar

1 Heat the oven to 200°C/400°F/gas mark 6.

2 Wipe the chicken inside and out. Place half the butter, half the onion and the lemon in the breast cavity. Place breast-side down in a roasting pan with 5 mm water. Spread the remaining butter over the chicken and season with salt and pepper. Add the giblets (except the liver), the bay leaf, remaining onion and the carrot to the water.

3 Roast in the oven for 1–1¼ hours, basting 3 or 4 times and turning the bird over halfway through. The chicken is cooked when the juices run clear from the thigh when pierced with a skewer.

4 Meanwhile, prepare the sauce. Melt the butter and, when foaming, add the shallots. Season with salt and pepper. Cover and cook slowly, shaking the pan occasionally to prevent them from burning, but allowing them to brown all over. Add the prunes to the pan and reduce the heat to a minimum.

5 Slowly melt the sugar in a heavy-based saucepan, tilting and turning it as necessary to get an even pale caramel colour. Add the vinegar, taking care to stand back as it will hiss and splutter. Add 2 tablespoons of the chicken stock from the bottom of the roasting pan. Simmer until the caramel has dissolved. Check the seasoning.

6 Joint the chicken and arrange on a warmed serving dish. Spoon over the prunes and shallots and glaze with the caramel sauce. Garnish with watercress.

Wine: Rich Pinot Noir from Chile, New Zealand or Oregon

Chicken Paprika

SERVES 4

1 × 1.35 kg chicken

1 tablespoon oil

15 g butter

1 onion, thinly sliced

2 tablespoons paprika

1 × 200 g can tomatoes

100 ml dry white wine

600 ml White Chicken Stock (see page 451)

1 bay leaf

2 slices of lemon

1 parsley stalk

150 ml White Sauce (see page 460)

salt and freshly ground black pepper

To garnish

1 tablespoon soured cream

chopped fresh parsley

1 Wash the chicken and wipe dry. Heat the oven to 200°C/400°F/gas mark 6.

2 Heat the oil in a frying pan. When hot, add the butter. When the butter is foaming, add the chicken and brown it well all over. Transfer to a casserole.

3 Fry the onion in the oil and butter and when just beginning to brown, reduce the heat and add the paprika. Cook for 2–3 minutes. Stir in the tomatoes, wine and stock. Add the bay leaf, lemon slices and parsley stalk. Season well with salt and pepper. When boiling, pour over the chicken.

4 Cover and bake in the oven for about 1 hour, or until the chicken is cooked.

5 When the chicken is tender, transfer to a plate and keep warm. Remove the bay leaf, parsley stalk and lemon slices from the sauce. Carefully skim off the fat with a spoon, or soak it up by laying kitchen paper on the surface. Whizz the sauce in a blender, then push it through a sieve.

6 Beat the paprika sauce into the prepared white sauce until completely incorporated and smooth.

7 Joint the chicken neatly into 8 pieces and arrange on a warmed serving dish. Heat the sauce and spoon it over the chicken. Trickle over the soured cream and sprinkle with parsley.

Wine: Red Burgundy, Rioja or a warming Languedoc red from Pic Saint Loup

Tarragon Chicken

SERVES 4

1 × 1.35 kg chicken with giblets

50 g Clarified Butter (see page xii)

1 slice of lemon

4 sprigs of fresh tarragon

150 ml White Chicken Stock (see page 451)

20 g plain flour

150 ml double cream

a squeeze of lemon juice

salt and freshly ground black pepper

1 Heat the oven to 200°C/400°F/gas mark 6.

2 Wipe the chicken inside and out. Place a small knob of the butter, the lemon slice and half the tarragon leaves inside the cavity. Season inside and out with salt and pepper.

3 Melt the remaining butter in a flameproof casserole the size of the chicken and brown the bird on all sides. Place the giblets (except the liver) in the casserole and pour over the stock. Cover with a lid and cook in the oven for 1¼ hours, or until the juices run clear when the thigh is pierced with a skewer.

4 Remove the chicken, draining the juices back into the casserole. Joint the chicken neatly into 8 pieces and place in a covered dish. Keep warm.

5 Skim all the fat from the stock. Put 1 tablespoon of this fat into a cup and mix in the flour. When thoroughly blended, pour some stock into the cup and mix well. Return this liquid to the casserole and stir over direct heat until boiling. Simmer for 5 minutes.

6 Strain into a clean saucepan. Chop the remaining tarragon and add to the pan. Simmer for 1–2 minutes, then stir in the cream. Taste and season with salt, pepper and lemon juice.

7 Spoon the sauce over the chicken pieces and serve.

Wine: Red or white Burgundy, New World Pinot Noir, or even Barolo or Barbaresco

Ballotine of Chicken Stuffed with Ricotta and Sun-dried Tomatoes

A ballotine is a boned bird that is stuffed and then roasted. It can be served hot or cold.

SERVES 6

1 × 1.8 kg chicken

50 g butter, melted

salt and freshly ground black pepper

fresh basil leaves, to garnish

For the stuffing

170 g ricotta cheese

50 g grated Parmesan cheese

1 egg, beaten

85 g fresh white breadcrumbs

50 g sun-dried tomatoes, cut into slivers

30 g black olives, pitted

1 tablespoon roughly chopped fresh basil

1 Bone the chicken, including the legs and wings (see page 269).

2 Heat the oven to 200°C/400°F/gas mark 6.

3 To make the stuffing, beat together the ricotta and Parmesan. Add the egg and beat again. Add the breadcrumbs, tomatoes, olives and chopped basil. Season to taste with salt and pepper.

4 Prepare a square of muslin or a clean J-cloth about 10 cm bigger all round than the bird by dipping the cloth in the melted butter: when wrapped around the bird, this will help the skin to brown evenly. Spread the cloth on a work surface and season generously with salt and pepper.

5 Lay the boned chicken flat, skin-side down, on the buttered cloth. Open out the bird and arrange it in a rectangular shape. Separate the false fillets from the breasts and place them on the skin between the leg and breast so that the skin is evenly covered with meat.

6 Press the stuffing into a cylindrical shape and place in the centre of the chicken.

7 Firmly fold the surrounding chicken over it, trimming off any skin overlapped by flesh along the seam, as it will not become crisp during cooking.

8 Secure the ballotine by drawing opposite edges of the cloth together, then folding them down until the cloth holds the ballotine together tightly. Twist the open ends of the cloth to form a cracker shape and tie each end with a short length of string.

9 Place the wrapped bird, seam-side down, on a wire rack in a roasting pan. The rack raises the bird above the cooking juices, thus enabling it to brown evenly on all sides.

10 Roast in the oven for 1 hour. To test that the chicken is cooked, insert a skewer into the centre and leave it there for 10 seconds. Draw the skewer out and place the pointed end on your wrist. If the skewer is too hot to hold against the skin, the stuffing is cooked. If the skewer can be held on the wrist comfortably, return the ballotine to the oven for a further 15 minutes and test again.

11 Remove the cloth from the chicken immediately otherwise it might stick to the skin. Using a pair of kitchen scissors, carefully cut the cloth away from the bird, taking care not to damage the crisp, brown skin.

12 Cut the ballotine into thick slices and serve garnished with basil leaves. To serve cold, wrap the bird tightly in foil to set the shape and make it easier to slice. Allow to cool completely before unwrapping. Once cold, cut into 1 cm slices and serve.

Wine: Italian red, such as Barbera d'Asti or Montepulciano d'Abruzzo, or a less aromatic dry white, such as Gavi

Ballotine: What has gone wrong when...

The ballotine does not hold together.

• The ballotine was not wrapped tightly enough when cooked and/or when cooling before serving cold.

The cloth has stuck to the chicken skin.

• The cloth was not buttered sufficiently.

• The cloth sticks to the chicken if it is not removed immediately after cooking.

Chicken Elizabeth

The Cordon Bleu School devised this dish for the celebration of Elizabeth II's coronation in 1953.

SERVES 4

1 × 1.35 kg chicken	1 slice of lemon
1 bay leaf	2 teaspoons fresh thyme leaves
6 peppercorns	225 ml Elizabeth Sauce (see below)
1 teaspoon salt	1 bunch of watercress, to garnish
2 parsley stalks	rice salad, to serve

1 First poach the chicken. Place the chicken, breast-side up, in a large saucepan and add the herbs and flavourings. Pour enough cold water into the pan to leave the breasts standing slightly proud of the water to steam. Cover with greaseproof paper and a lid.

2 Bring to a simmer, then adjust the heat so that the occasional bubble rises to the surface. Cook gently for 1¼–1½ hours, or until the juices run clear when the flesh is pierced, and the drumsticks feel loose. Remove the chicken from the pan and set aside to cool.

3 Remove the meat from the chicken bones, and when quite cold, mix together with all but 4 tablespoons of the sauce. Pile the chicken into the middle of a serving dish and coat with the reserved sauce. Garnish with watercress and serve with rice salad.

NOTE: It is easier to remove the meat from the bones while the chicken is still lukewarm. But on no account should the sauce be added to the meat until the meat is completely cold as it is mayonnaise-based and contains raw eggs. If the sauce is allowed to warm beyond 4°C/40°F for any length of time, there could be a danger of food poisoning. We recommend using bought mayonnaise made with pasteurized egg yolks and/or Greek yoghurt if there is a chance that the dish might sit at room temperature for any length of time.

ELIZABETH SAUCE

2 teaspoons oil	2 teaspoons apricot jam
1 small onion, chopped	1 slice of lemon
2 teaspoons curry powder	1 teaspoon lemon juice
½ teaspoon tomato purée	1 quantity Mayonnaise (see page 466) or
3 tablespoons water	1 × 300 ml jar mayonnaise
1 small bay leaf	2 tablespoons double cream
4 tablespoons red wine	salt and freshly ground black pepper

1 Heat the oil in a frying pan and cook the onion gently for 10 minutes.

2 Add the curry powder and fry gently for 1 minute. Add the tomato purée, water, bay leaf, wine, salt, pepper, jam, lemon slice and juice and simmer for 8 minutes.

3 Strain the mixture, pushing as much as possible through the sieve. Leave to cool.

4 When cold, use this sauce to flavour the mayonnaise to the desired strength.

5 Half-whip the cream and stir into the sauce.

Wine: Viognier or New World Chardonnay; off-dry or dry rosé

Quick Coronation Chicken

SERVES 6

1 slice of onion

1 slice of lemon

1 stick of celery, chopped

1 × 1.8 kg chicken

½ teaspoon salt

3 parsley stalks

1 bay leaf

½ teaspoon peppercorns

For the sauce

about 3 tablespoons good-quality chicken tikka paste

200 g mayonnaise

150 g Greek yoghurt (0% fat is fine)

1 tablespoon mango chutney

1 Place the onion, lemon and celery in a saucepan large enough to hold the chicken.

2 Place the chicken, breast-side up, in the saucepan. Cover with cold water.

3 Add the salt, parsley stalks, bay leaf, and peppercorns.

4 Place over a medium heat and bring to the 'poach', where the water just trembles and a few bubbles come to the surface. Do not boil the chicken or this will make it tough. Cook for 1¼ hours, skimming occasionally. The meat fibres in the thighs will be firm and legs will be loose in their sockets

5 Remove the chicken and set aside until cold enough to handle.

6 Pull the chicken into bite-sized pieces and allow to cool completely.

7 Mix together the sauce ingredients and fold into the chicken.

8 The dish will keep for up to 2 days if refrigerated. Do not freeze.

Wine: Viognier or New World Chardonnay; off-dry or dry rosé

Chicken Breasts Stuffed with Red Pepper Mousseline

Wrapping the chicken breasts tightly in cling film or foil before poaching helps them to keep their shape, but they may also be wrapped in bacon or Parma ham and roasted.

SERVES 4

1 red pepper
½ tablespoon chopped fresh basil
1 teaspoon finely chopped fresh parsley
4 boneless, skinless chicken breasts
1 egg white
75 ml double cream

¼ teaspoon ground mace
1 tablespoon Tapenade (see page 467)
salt and freshly ground white pepper

To serve
Tomato Sauce I (see page 469)

1 Grill or roast the red pepper until the skin blackens and blisters. Place in a plastic bag to allow the pepper to cool and the skin to loosen. When cool enough to handle, remove the skin, membrane and seeds. Cut the flesh into medium dice. Place in a chilled food processor bowl with the basil and parsley.
2 Remove the false fillet from the chicken breasts. Chop roughly and add to the food processor.
3 Whizz the mixture briefly, then add the egg white and cream while the machine is still running. The mixture should be smooth, but be careful not to overprocess to prevent it from warming and splitting.
4 Season well with the mace, salt and pepper. Refrigerate until ready to use.
5 Cut a small pocket in the side of each chicken breast (see Stuffing a Chicken Breast, page 290) and spread a little tapenade inside it. Put a spoonful of the red pepper mousseline mixture into the pocket and pull the edges together to seal.
6 Wrap the breasts in cling film and place in a large, shallow saucepan or roasting pan. Pour boiling water over the chicken, then poach for about 15 minutes, or until the meat is firm to the touch. Remove from the pan and allow to set for 10 minutes.
7 Cut the chicken breasts into thick slices and serve with the warm tomato sauce.

Wine: Plump red from Côtes-du-Rhône, Languedoc or the New World

Chicken Breasts with Parma Ham and Spinach

SERVES 4

4 boneless, skinless chicken breasts, fat removed

4 thin slices of best-quality Parma ham

8 large spinach leaves, blanched and refreshed

600 ml White Chicken Stock (see page 451)

1 tablespoon chopped fresh parsley

1 tablespoon chopped fresh dill

1 teaspoon coarse-grain mustard

salt and freshly ground black pepper

For the dressing

4 tablespoons good-quality olive oil

4 tablespoons salad oil

2 tablespoons tarragon vinegar

To garnish

cherry tomatoes, halved

pine nuts, toasted

chopped fresh basil

1 Wrap each chicken breast in a slice of Parma ham and then in 2 spinach leaves.

2 Place the chicken breasts in a saucepan side by side, not on top of each other, and pour over the stock.

3 Cover the saucepan and bring back to the boil, then turn down the heat and poach gently for 18–20 minutes, or until the breasts feel just firm to the touch.

4 Meanwhile, make the dressing. Place all the ingredients in a liquidizer or food processor and whizz to a green purée.

5 Flood 4 plates with some of the dressing, then lift the chicken breasts out of the saucepan and drain. Slice each chicken breast on the diagonal and arrange the overlapping slices in a semi-circle on the dressing. Garnish with the cherry tomatoes, pine nuts and basil.

NOTE: This dish can be served hot or cold.

Wine: Aromatic dry white, such as Fiano di Avellino, or a dry rosé

Chicken Breasts with Leek and Watercress Sauce

SERVES 4

4 boneless, skinless chicken breasts, fat removed

30 g truffle, thinly sliced (optional)

15 g butter

85 g white parts of leeks, finely chopped

1 small shallot, finely chopped

1 small bunch of watercress, carefully picked over

2 tablespoons port

300 ml White Chicken Stock (see page 451)

2 egg yolks

75 ml double cream

1 Using a sharp knife, make a horizontal incision in the thickest part of each chicken breast and insert slices of truffle, if using.

2 Melt the butter, add the leeks and shallot and cook slowly until soft but not brown. Add all but 2 sprigs of the watercress, the port and stock and simmer for 10 minutes.

3 Add the chicken breasts. Cover and poach for 12 minutes, turning the chicken over halfway through the cooking time. Remove from the pan, returning any watercress or leeks stuck to the breasts to the saucepan. Keep warm while you make the sauce.

4 Chop the remaining watercress very finely.

5 Reduce the poaching liquid to 200 ml by boiling rapidly. Liquidize in a blender until very smooth. Pour into a clean saucepan and heat to just below boiling point.

6 Mix the egg yolks with the cream, add a little of the hot sauce, then add the mixture to the saucepan. Stir over a medium heat until thickened. It is essential that the sauce does not boil or it will curdle. Stir in the remaining watercress to improve the colour.

7 Arrange the chicken breasts, split in 2 if liked, on warmed serving plates. Spoon over the sauce.

Wine: Aromatic dry white, such as Grüner Veltliner

Mustard-grilled Chicken

Although this is called grilled chicken, it is partially baked to ensure that the meat is cooked without becoming burnt.

SERVES 4

30 g butter, softened
2 tablespoons Dijon mustard
1 × 2 kg chicken
juice of 1 lemon

1 teaspoon sugar
1 teaspoon paprika
freshly ground black pepper
sprigs of watercress, to garnish

1 Mix together the butter and mustard.
2 Heat the oven to 200°C/400°F/gas mark 6.
3 Joint the chicken into 8 pieces (see page 266). Cut off the wing tips and the knuckles. Remove any small feathers.
4 Spread the underside of each chicken joint with half the mustard mixture. Place in a roasting pan in a single layer. Sprinkle with half the lemon juice, sugar and paprika. Season with pepper. Bake for 20 minutes.
5 Turn the chicken over and spread with the remaining mustard mixture. Sprinkle with the rest of the lemon juice, sugar and paprika. Season with pepper. Bake for a further 10 minutes.
6 Heat the grill to its highest setting.
7 Arrange the chicken under the grill in such a way that the larger pieces are closest to the strongest heat and the breast joints are near the edges.
8 Grill until dark and crisp, but be very careful not to let the pieces burn.
9 Arrange the chicken neatly on a flat serving dish. Pour over the juices from the pan and garnish with watercress.

Wine: Red or white Burgundy, or a New World Pinot Noir

Coq au Vin

SERVES 4

1 x 1.35 kg chicken, jointed into 8 pieces
   (see page 266)

300 ml red wine

1 small clove of garlic, bruised

1 bouquet garni (see page 512)

115 g rindless bacon, cut into 20 lardons 5 x 5 mm

50 g Clarified Butter (see page xii)

8 button onions

12 button mushrooms

600 ml White Chicken Stock (see page 451)

1 clove of garlic, crushed

20 g plain flour

salt and freshly ground black pepper

1 tablespoon finely chopped fresh parsley, to garnish

1 Place the chicken pieces in a large plastic bag with the wine, bruised garlic and bouquet garni. Tie the top and marinate in the refrigerator for a few hours or overnight.

2 Blanch the bacon in boiling water for 30 seconds to remove the excess salt. Drain and dry well.

3 Melt half the butter in a large, heavy-based saucepan and brown the onions, bacon and mushrooms. Remove and reserve.

4 Remove the chicken from the bag, reserving the marinade and the bouquet garni, but discarding the garlic. Pat the chicken dry and season with salt and pepper.

5 Melt the remaining butter in the pan and brown the skin side of the chicken over a medium-low heat. Tip off and reserve all the fat.

6 Return the vegetables and bacon pieces to the pan. Add the reserved marinade and enough stock nearly to cover the chicken pieces.

7 Add the crushed garlic and reserved bouquet garni.

8 Cover with a piece of dampened greaseproof paper and a tightly fitting lid, and simmer slowly for about 45 minutes, until the onions and chicken are tender. Test each piece of chicken by cutting into the underside near the bone and pressing the meat to make sure the juices run clear.

9 Discard the bouquet garni. Using a slotted spoon, transfer the vegetables and bacon pieces to a warmed serving dish. Keep warm while you make the sauce.

10 Place the cooking liquid in a jug and reserve.

11 Mix the flour with enough of the reserved fat to make a roux (see page 459). Cook the roux in a small pan over a medium heat until light brown.

12 Use a bulb baster to remove the reserved cooking liquid from the bottom of the jug, leaving the fat behind. Add the liquid to the roux off the heat, stirring to make a smooth sauce.

13 Return to the heat, bring to the boil and boil for 2 minutes. Adjust the thickness of the sauce to a coating consistency either by boiling further or by adding water, as required. Taste and adjust the seasoning.

14 Trim the chicken pieces (page 268), arrange in a warmed, deep serving platter and spoon the sauce over them. Garnish with the parsley.

Wine: Red Burgundy

Chicken Sauté Normande

SERVES 4

45 g Clarified Butter (see page xii)

1 × 1.35 kg chicken, jointed into 8 pieces
  (see page 266)

1 tablespoon Calvados or brandy

1 shallot, finely chopped

2 teaspoons plain flour

225 ml dry cider

150 ml White Chicken Stock (see page 451)

1 bouquet garni (see page 512)

2 tablespoons double cream

salt and freshly ground black pepper

For the garnish

15 g butter

1 tablespoon caster sugar

2 eating apples, cored and cut into 8 wedges

1 tablespoon chopped fresh parsley

1 Heat the butter in a large sauté pan. Season the chicken skin with salt, and brown over a medium heat on the skin side only. Pour off and reserve the excess fat.

2 With a lid or baking sheet close at hand in case the flames flare up, flambé the chicken. Heat the Calvados in a ladle over a gas flame and set alight. (If using an electric cooker, pour the Calvados into the hot pan and set alight with a match.) Pour over the hot chicken, pouring it away from you. Shake the pan and allow the flames to subside.

3 Remove the chicken and set aside. Add 1 tablespoon of the reserved fat to the pan. Add the shallot and cook for 2–3 minutes.

4 Add the flour and cook until pale straw-coloured. Slowly mix in the cider to make a smooth sauce. Add the stock. Bring to the boil and boil for 2 minutes.

5 Return the chicken to the pan with the bouquet garni, cover with a piece of dampened greaseproof paper and a lid and simmer for 30–45 minutes, until the chicken is cooked through. Check each piece by cutting on the underside down to the bone and pressing the meat to make sure the juices are clear.

6 Lift out the chicken and trim as described on page 268. Place on a warmed serving dish and keep warm.

7 Sieve the sauce into a clean saucepan and reduce to a coating consistency by boiling rapidly.

8 Add the cream to the sauce and season to taste with salt and pepper.

9 For the garnish, heat the butter and sugar in a small pan until lightly caramelized. Stir in the apple and cook until just tender when pierced with a sharp knife.

10 Pour the sauce over the chicken and garnish with the caramelized apple and the parsley.

Drink: Riesling from Alsace, Germany or Australia, or a good Normandy cider

Chicken with Cranberry-orange Sauce

SERVES 4

1 × 1.8 kg chicken, jointed into 8 pieces
  (see page 266)

flour

2 tablespoons vegetable oil

15 g butter

1 small onion, finely chopped

¼ teaspoon ground cinnamon

¼ teaspoon ground ginger

100 g fresh or defrosted cranberries

50 g caster sugar

1 teaspoon grated orange zest

150 ml orange juice

salt and freshly ground black pepper

2 tablespoons chopped fresh parsley, to garnish

1 Heat the oven to 180°C/350°F/gas mark 4.

2 Season the chicken pieces with salt and pepper, then dredge with the flour.

3 Heat the oil in a sauté pan over a medium heat. Add the butter. When it starts to sizzle, brown the chicken pieces on all sides, taking care not to overcrowd the pan.

4 Place the browned chicken pieces in a single layer in a large ovenproof dish.

5 Reduce the heat to low and add the onion and sauté until translucent.

6 Stir in the cinnamon and ginger and cook for a further minute.

7 Add the cranberries, caster sugar, orange zest and juice. Bring to the boil, then pour over the chicken.

8 Cover the dish tightly with foil, then place in the centre of the oven and cook for 45 minutes, or until the chicken is cooked through. Check each piece by cutting on the underside down to the bone and pressing the meat to make sure the juices run clear.

9 Transfer the chicken to a serving platter. Boil the sauce and cooking juices to thicken slightly, then pour over the chicken. Sprinkle with the parsley.

Wine: Red Burgundy or a lighter New World Pinot Noir (Chile, South Africa)

Chicken with Tomato and Coriander

SERVES 4

1 × 1.35 kg chicken, jointed into 8 pieces
  (see page 266)

seasoned flour

2 tablespoons oil

2 onions, finely chopped

1 clove of garlic, crushed

1 teaspoon ground coriander

1 × 400 g can tomatoes

1 bay leaf

2 teaspoons tomato purée

2 tablespoons roughly chopped fresh coriander

salt and freshly ground black pepper

1 Dip the chicken pieces in the seasoned flour.

2 Heat the oil in a large sauté pan and brown the chicken all over. Using a slotted spoon, transfer the pieces to a roasting dish or casserole.

3 Heat the oven to 180°C/350°F/gas mark 4.

4 Add the onions to the sauté pan and cook over a low heat for 10 minutes, or until beginning to soften. Add the garlic and ground coriander and cook for 1 further minute. Add the tomatoes, bay leaf and tomato purée. Season to taste with salt and pepper. Bring slowly to the boil, stirring continuously.

5 Pour the mixture over the chicken pieces. Add 100 ml water to the sauce, then cover and cook in the oven for 45–50 minutes, or until the chicken is tender.

6 Lift the chicken pieces out of the sauce. Trim them as described on page 268, then arrange on a warmed serving dish. Keep warm in the turned-off oven.

7 Skim any fat off the sauce, then boil rapidly to a syrupy consistency, stirring continuously to prevent the sauce from catching. Add three-quarters of the coriander. Check the seasoning and pour the sauce over the chicken. Garnish with the remaining coriander.

Wine: Sauvignon Blanc from the Loire or New Zealand, or Alsace Riesling

Chicken in Creamy Garlic Sauce

SERVES 4

30 g Clarified Butter (see page xii)
1 x 1.35 kg chicken, jointed into 8 pieces
  (see page 266)
5 large cloves of garlic, unpeeled
5 tablespoons wine vinegar
300 ml dry white wine

2 tablespoons brandy
2 teaspoons Dijon mustard
1 heaped teaspoon tomato purée
300 ml double cream
2 tomatoes, blanched, peeled and deseeded
salt and freshly ground black pepper

1 Heat the butter in a large sauté pan and brown the chicken pieces on the skin side. Add the garlic and cover the pan. Cook over a low heat for 20 minutes, or until the chicken is cooked and tender. Remove the chicken and keep warm. Pour off all the fat from the pan.

2 Add the vinegar to the pan with the garlic, stirring well and scraping any sediment from the bottom. Boil rapidly until the liquid is reduced to about 2 tablespoons.

3 Add the wine, brandy, mustard and tomato purée, mix well and boil to a thick sauce (about 5 minutes at a fast boil).

4 In a large, heavy saucepan boil the cream until reduced by half, stirring frequently to prevent burning. Remove from the heat and fit a small wire sieve over the saucepan. Push the vinegar sauce through this, pressing the garlic cloves well to extract their pulp.

5 Stir the sauce and season to taste with salt and pepper. Cut the tomato into thin strips and stir into the sauce. Arrange the chicken on a hot serving dish and spoon over the sauce.

NOTES: The deliciousness of this dish – and it is delicious – depends on the vigorous reduction of the vinegar and wine. If the acids are not properly boiled down, the sauce will be too sharp.

Five cloves of garlic might seem a lot, but the resulting sauce does not taste strongly of garlic.

Wine: Pinot Noir or Reisling

Pan-cooked Chicken Breasts

SERVES 4

1 tablespoon oil

4 chicken breasts, with skin and rib bones

salt and freshly ground black pepper

1 Heat the oil in a heavy-based sauté pan over a medium-low heat.

2 Season the skin of the chicken breasts with salt and pepper and place them skin-side down in the pan in a single layer.

3 Cover the pan with a tightly fitting lid and cook for 30 minutes.

4 Check the chicken by cutting next to the bone to see if the juices run clear. If not, return to the pan and cook for a further 5 minutes before checking again.

5 Serve basted with the pan juices.

Wine: Red or white Burgundy, or New World Pinot Noir (apart from the very strong ones)

Stuffing a Chicken Breast

The breasts of poultry and feathered game are often stuffed with a soft-textured filling or strong-flavoured ingredients such as truffles. For Chicken Kiev (see page 298) the chicken is stuffed with garlic butter. The stuffing provides added flavour and a contrast in texture. It also enhances the appearance of the sliced breast once it is cooked. Soft stuffing is spooned into a shallow pocket made by cutting into the side of the chicken breasts.

1 Remove the false fillet, the tapered flap of meat on the back of the breast that runs along its length. It is usually only partially attached to the breast and can be removed easily by cutting or pulling.

2 Make a shallow pocket by cutting into the side of the chicken breast. (a)

3 Spoon the stuffing into the pocket.

4 Tuck both ends of the false fillet into the ends of the pocket so that the stuffing is secured. (b)

Cutting a pocket in
a breast fillet (a)

Securing the stuffing
with the false fillet (b)

Tapenade-stuffed Chicken Breasts with Slow-roasted Mediterranean Vegetables and Capers

SERVES 4

4 tablespoons Tapenade (see page 467)

finely grated zest of ½ a lemon

1 teaspoon thyme leaves, finely chopped

4 chicken breasts, boned, with skin

1 tablespoon oil

For the vegetables

2 red peppers

1 yellow pepper

1 orange pepper

4 vine-ripened tomatoes, blanched and
   peeled if desired

2 cloves of garlic, crushed

8 pitted black olives, sliced

8 large basil leaves, shredded

8 tablespoons extra virgin olive oil

1 × 400 g can artichoke hearts, rinsed and drained

2 tablespoons capers, rinsed and dried

flaky sea salt and freshly ground black pepper

fresh basil leaves, to garnish

1 Heat the oven to 180°C/350°F/gas mark 4.

2 Start by preparing the vegetables. Cut the peppers in half through the stalks. Remove the pith and seeds, but leave the stalks in place. Lay the peppers cut-side up in a large, shallow baking dish.

3 Cut each tomato into 6 wedges and place 3 inside each pepper half. Add some garlic, olives and shredded basil. Pour 1 tablespoon oil into each pepper half and season well with salt and pepper. Bake in the oven for 40 minutes.

4 Meanwhile, prepare the chicken. In a small bowl, mix the tapenade with the lemon zest and thyme leaves. Push a tablespoon of the mixture under the skin of each chicken breast, smoothing the skin over the stuffing to secure it. Season the skin with salt and pepper.

5 Heat the oil in a frying pan and brown the chicken well, skin-side down. Reduce the heat and brown lightly on the other side for 1 minute.

6 Remove the chicken from the pan, and place in between the peppers. Add the artichokes and capers to the dish and return to the oven for a further 15–20 minutes, or until the chicken juices run clear when the flesh is pierced with a skewer and the vegetables are very soft. Garnish with fresh basil leaves and serve from the baking dish.

Wine: Red Burgundy, Rioja or a warming Languedoc red from Pic Saint Loup

Chicken Breasts with Red Pepper Sauce

SERVES 4

4 boneless, skinless chicken breasts

3 tablespoons finely shredded white of
  leek

2 tablespoons finely shredded carrot

salt and freshly ground black pepper

watercress leaves, to garnish

For the red pepper sauce

1 tablespoon sunflower oil

1 onion, finely chopped

2 tomatoes, chopped

1 red pepper, peeled (by grilling or singeing
  over a flame), deseeded and cut into strips

1 clove of garlic, crushed

1 bouquet garni (see page 512)

6 tablespoons water

salt and freshly ground black pepper

1 Start by making the sauce. Heat the oil in a saucepan and cook the onion until just beginning to soften.
2 Add the tomatoes, red pepper, garlic and bouquet garni. Pour in the water and season lightly. Cover and cook slowly for 20 minutes.
3 Liquidize the sauce until smooth and push through a sieve. Chill.
4 Remove any fat from the chicken breasts.
5 Mix the leek and carrot together and season with salt and pepper.
6 Stuff the leek mixture between the main part of the chicken breasts and the false fillet. Wrap each breast in a piece of cling film.
7 Poach the chicken breasts in barely trembling boiling water for 15 minutes. Remove from the pan, unwrap and leave to get completely cold.
8 Flood 4 dinner plates with the red pepper sauce.
9 Put a chicken breast on each plate and garnish with watercress leaves.

Wine: New World Pinot Noir

Baked Stuffed Chicken Breasts with Sun-dried Tomatoes and Parma Ham

SERVES 4

2 slices Parma ham

3 sun-dried tomatoes in olive oil, drained,
  oil retained

8 large sage leaves

1 tablespoon freshly grated Parmesan cheese

2 tablespoons sun-dried tomato oil, from the jar

4 chicken breasts, boned, with skin

100 ml dry white wine or vermouth

salt and freshly ground black pepper

sprigs of watercress, to garnish

1 Heat the oven to 200°C/400°F/gas mark 6.
2 Shred the Parma ham. Finely chop the sun-dried tomatoes and sage.
3 Mix together with the Parmesan, salt and freshly ground black pepper and ½ tablespoon of the sun-dried tomato oil.

4 Push equal amounts of the mixture under the skin of each chicken breast, smoothing the skin over it to keep it secure.

5 Put the chicken pieces into a roasting pan and season with salt and pepper. Pour the remaining oil over them and bake on the top shelf of the oven for 20–25 minutes. Pour the wine over the chicken and continue to cook for a further 5 minutes, or until the meat juices run clear when pierced with a skewer and the skin is brown and crisp.

6 Serve the chicken with the pan juices poured over it. Garnish with watercress.

Wine: Dry Italian red, such as Barbera d'Asti, or a dry rosé

Chicken Breasts with Ginger

SERVES 4

4 boneless, skinless chicken breasts

1 large onion, very finely chopped

2 cloves of garlic, crushed

5 cm piece of fresh root ginger,
  peeled and very finely chopped

5 cardamom pods, cracked

1 teaspoon ground turmeric

2 tablespoons light soy sauce

2 tablespoons dry sherry (optional)

1 Place the chicken breasts in a bowl with all the other ingredients. Cover and chill for about 2 hours so that the meat can absorb the flavours. Turn the chicken once or twice.

2 Heat the oven to 200°C/400°F/gas mark 6.

3 Line a shallow baking dish with foil, leaving 15–20 cm hanging over the sides. Arrange the chicken in a single layer on the foil. Pour over the marinade, then fold the surrounding foil over the chicken, sealing it tightly so that none of the liquid can escape.

4 Bake in the oven for 30 minutes.

Wine: Chardonnay or Pinot Noir from Burgundy or the New World

Chicken with Mushrooms and Coriander

SERVES 4

4 boneless, skinless chicken breasts

15 g cornflour

1–2 tablespoons sunflower oil

1 large onion, thinly sliced

2 teaspoons coriander seeds, very well crushed

225 g flat mushrooms, sliced

150 ml White Chicken Stock (see page 451)

2 tablespoons medium sherry

salt and freshly ground black pepper

fresh coriander leaves, to garnish

1 Trim any fat from the chicken breasts and cut the meat into large cubes. Toss in the cornflour and set aside.

2 Heat 1 tablespoon of the oil in a pan and fry the onion. When beginning to soften, add the coriander seeds, increase the heat and allow the onion to brown and the seeds to toast (1–2 minutes).

3 Add the chicken and fry for 3 minutes. Remove the chicken and set aside.

4 Add the remaining oil to the pan, stir in the mushrooms and cook until beginning to soften.

5 Return the chicken to the pan. Add the stock and season with salt and pepper. Stir well and simmer for 4–5 minutes.

6 Add the sherry and boil for 30 seconds. Pile the chicken into a warmed serving dish and garnish with coriander leaves.

Wine: Red Burgundy or Oregon Pinot Noir; if white is preferred, try Alsace Riesling

Chicken Curry with Almonds

This is a fairly mild curry. Extra spices can be added if you wish.

SERVES 8

8 boneless, skinless chicken breasts

6 tablespoons sunflower oil

85 g blanched almonds

2 teaspoons ground cardamom

1 teaspoon ground cloves

1 teaspoon ground chilli

4 teaspoons ground cumin

4 teaspoons ground coriander

2 teaspoons ground turmeric

2 onions, finely chopped

3 cm piece of fresh root ginger,
  peeled and finely chopped

2 cloves of garlic, crushed

1 × 400 g can chopped tomatoes

150 ml water

2 tablespoons Greek yoghurt

salt and freshly ground black pepper

fresh coriander leaves, to garnish

1 Heat the oven to 190°C/375°F/gas mark 5.
2 Remove any fat or gristle from the chicken breasts. Set aside.
3 Put 1 tablespoon of the oil into a saucepan and fry the almonds until golden brown but not burnt. Set aside.
4 Add 3 tablespoons oil to the pan and slowly cook the spices for 1 minute.
5 Put the almonds and cooked spices in a blender, add a little water and whizz to make a smooth paste.
6 Rinse out the saucepan, heat 2 more tablespoons oil, then fry the onions and ginger until the onions are golden brown. Add the garlic and cook for a further minute.
7 Reduce the heat and add the tomatoes and almond paste, seasoning and 150 ml water. Stir well and simmer for 2–3 minutes.
8 Pour the sauce into an ovenproof dish. Add the chicken breasts and spoon some of the sauce over them. Cover with foil and bake for 40 minutes, or until the chicken is cooked.
9 Transfer the chicken to a warm serving dish. Swirl the yoghurt into the sauce. Pour over the chicken breasts and garnish with fresh coriander.

Wine: Aromatic fruity white or a Viognier

Thai Green Chicken Curry

SERVES 4

1 tablespoon oil

2 cloves of garlic, sliced

2 tablespoons Green Curry Paste (see below)

300 ml thick coconut milk

2 tablespoons nam pla (Thai fish sauce)

1 teaspoon sugar

3 small green Thai aubergines, quartered if large, or 1 medium purple aubergine, diced

4 boneless, skinless chicken breasts

3 lime leaves, shredded

20 horapa (sweet basil) leaves

1 Heat the oil and fry the garlic until it is golden brown. Add the green curry paste, then gradually blend in the coconut milk, fish sauce and sugar.

2 Add the aubergines and cook for 7 minutes.

3 Cut the chicken into strips and add to the aubergines. Cook for a further 5 minutes, until the chicken feels firm and is cooked. You might need to add extra water if it begins to dry out.

4 When the chicken and aubergines are cooked stir in the lime leaves and sweet basil.

GREEN CURRY PASTE

15 green chillies, deseeded and roughly chopped

2 sticks of lemon grass, chopped

4 shallots

1 piece of galangal/laos

1 piece of krachai (optional, see Note)

2–3 roots of coriander

2 teaspoons ground cumin

3 kaffir lime leaves, chopped

1 teaspoon shrimp paste

6 whole black peppercorns

1 Pound or blend all the ingredients to a paste. Use as required.

NOTES: There is no English common name for krachai (*Kaempferia pandurata*). The tubers of this member of the ginger family look like a bunch of yellow-brown fingers. Krachai is always added to Thai fish curries, and peeled and served as a raw vegetable with the popular summer rice dish khao chae. Galangal is similar to ginger, but slightly more aromatic and considerably more expensive.

Various brands of Thai green curry paste can now be found in all large supermarkets. The intensity of flavour tends to be less than in home-made paste. Use according to personal taste.

Wine: Aromatic fruity white or a Viognier

Thai Chicken Soup

SERVES 4

1 litre White Chicken Stock (see page 451)

2 cm piece of fresh root ginger, peeled and grated

1 bunch of spring onions, finely sliced diagonally

½ clove of garlic, crushed

1 stick of lemon grass, crushed

4 boneless, skinless chicken breasts, finely sliced

2½ tablespoons nam pla (Thai fish sauce)

1 tablespoon light soy sauce

1 tablespoon rice wine

30 g creamed coconut, chopped

2 kaffir lime leaves

1 Dutch red chilli, very finely chopped

juice of 2 limes

50 g beansprouts

1 large handful of chopped fresh coriander

1 Place the stock in a large saucepan and bring to the boil. Add the ginger, spring onions, garlic and lemon grass and simmer for 2 minutes.

2 Add the chicken to the pan and stir in the fish sauce, soy sauce, rice wine, creamed coconut, lime leaves and chilli and lime juice. Return to the boil, then reduce the heat and simmer gently for 5–7 minutes, or until the chicken is tender and cooked through.

3 Stir in the beansprouts and coriander. Ladle into warmed bowls and serve immediately.

Wine: Amontillado or dry Amontillado sherry, according to taste

Chicken and Mango Wonton Ravioli

SERVES 4

225 g cooked, boneless chicken, cut into 2 cm dice

2 tablespoons mango chutney

1½ teaspoons Madras curry paste

2 spring onions, finely sliced

grated zest of 1 lime

grated zest of ½ a lemon

3 cm piece of fresh root ginger, peeled and grated

2 tablespoons coriander, roughly chopped

20 × 10 cm square wonton wrappers

1 egg white

oil, for frying

salt and freshly ground black pepper

1 Put all the ingredients, except the wonton wrappers, egg white and oil, into a food processor, and whizz briefly until the mixture is coarsely chopped. Set aside.

2 Lay half the wrappers on to a flat work surface and brush the edges with egg white.

3 Divide the chicken mixture between the wrappers, then cover with a second wrapper. Press the edges together to seal well.

4 Heat 5 cm oil in a heavy-based pan and heat until a cube of bread browns and sizzles in 30 seconds (see Warning, page 53).

5 Cook batches of the wonton parcels in the hot oil for 7–8 seconds on each side, or until brown, crisp and hot through. Remove from the pan with a slotted spoon, drain on kitchen paper and sprinkle with salt. Serve very hot.

Wine: Riesling or Pinot Gris from Alsace or the New World

Chicken Kiev

Chicken supremes are traditionally used for this recipe, but the small wing bone at the shoulder end of the breast can be removed if desired. The flavoured butter sealed in the centre melts on cooking to moisten and enhance the flavour of the meat.

SERVES 4

115 g butter, softened	seasoned flour
1 clove of garlic, crushed	1 large egg, beaten
1 tablespoon chopped fresh parsley	dried white breadcrumbs
squeeze of lemon juice	oil, for deep-frying
4 chicken supremes (see page 264)	salt and freshly ground black pepper

1 Mix the butter with the garlic, parsley, lemon juice, salt and pepper. Divide into 4 equal pieces, shape into rectangles and chill well in the refrigerator. (Chilled butter will melt more slowly during cooking, allowing the meat to set and any potential cracks to seal before the butter is liquid and likely to leak away.)

2 Remove the skin and breastbone from the chicken breasts. Remove the false fillet and cut into the breast on either side to make a large, horizontal central pocket (see page 290).

3 Insert a piece of butter into each pocket, then enclose it by replacing the false fillet, tucking each side of it into the horizontal cuts along the length of the breast. When the breast is cooked and sliced across, the butter should be perfectly in the centre of the meat.

4 To seal the chicken breasts, dust lightly with seasoned flour, dip into beaten egg, then roll carefully in breadcrumbs. Refrigerate for 30 minutes to set the shape.

5 Brush the Kievs with more beaten egg and roll again in breadcrumbs. Refrigerate for a further 30 minutes. The second covering of egg and crumbs is to ensure that the chicken is properly sealed to prevent melting butter escaping while the chicken is frying, and also to create a crust that becomes firm and crisp.

6 Heat some oil in a deep-fat fryer until a cube of bread sizzles vigorously in it (see Warning, page 53). Fry the chicken pieces in the oil for 12 minutes. Drain on kitchen paper, sprinkle with salt and serve.

Wine: White Burgundy or Alsace Riesling; if red is preferred, try a light one, such as Beaujolais

Chicken Kiev: What has gone wrong when...

Most of the butter has disappeared from the centre of the chicken.

• The butter was not chilled sufficiently, so melted and escaped before the meat started to set.
• The butter was not encased correctly.

The chicken breast is still rare in the middle and the crust is only lightly coloured.

• The oil was not hot enough. The chicken must not be added until the oil is heated sufficiently to fry a cube of bread quickly to golden brown.
• The chicken was not cooked long enough.

Barbecued Chicken Breasts with Peach and Mint Salsa

This recipe calls for the chicken breasts to be brined before marinating. Both the brining and marinating will help the keep the chicken moist during barbecuing.

SERVES 4

4 boneless chicken breasts, skin on
600 ml water
4 tablespoons fine sea salt

2 tablespoons clear honey
150 ml natural yoghurt
freshly ground black pepper

For the marinade

1 teaspoon paprika
pinch of chilli powder
1 tablespoon tomato purée
1 teaspoon Dijon mustard
1 clove of garlic, crushed

For the salsa

½ red onion, finely chopped
grated zest and juice of 1 lime
2 ripe yellow peaches
1 green chilli, deseeded and finely chopped
15 g fresh mint, leaves only, finely chopped

1 Place the chicken breasts in a pan just large enough to contain them in a single layer.

2 In a separate pan heat 200 ml of the water and dissolve the salt. Add the remaining cold water to cool the brine. Pour over the chicken to cover. Refrigerate for 1 hour.

3 Meanwhile, mix together the marinade ingredients. Refrigerate until required.

4 For the salsa, place the onion, lime zest and juice in a small dish. Set aside for 30 minutes.

5 To peel the peaches, place them in boiling water for 30 seconds, then transfer to cold water.

6 Remove the stones from the peaches and cut the flesh into rough 5 mm dice. Place in a bowl. Stir in the onion mixture, chilli and mint. Chill until required, or up to 24 hours.

7 Remove the chicken breasts from the brine and pat dry. Place in the marinade and turn to coat. Refrigerate for 1 further hour.

8 Heat the barbecue to its highest setting. Scrape any excess marinade from the meat.

9 Cook the chicken, turning every 2 minutes and basting with marinade during the first half of cooking only, until cooked through, about 12–14 minutes. The chicken will be firm to the touch when done. Serve garnished with salsa.

Wine: Pinot Grigio

Chicken Breasts with Caramelized Red Onions

SERVES 6

560 g red onions, thinly sliced

2 tablespoons sunflower oil

6 boneless, skinless chicken breasts

2 cloves of garlic, crushed

2 teaspoons finely chopped fresh rosemary

2 teaspoons clear honey

grated zest and juice of 2 oranges

salt and freshly ground black pepper

1 tablespoon chopped fresh parsley, to garnish

1 Put the onions and the oil in a large saucepan over a low heat, place a piece of dampened greaseproof paper over them, cover with a lid and cook for about 15 minutes, or until soft.

2 Heat the oven to 180°C/350°F/gas mark 4. Place the chicken breasts in a shallow ovenproof dish and season well.

3 Uncover the onions, increase the heat to medium and continue to cook until they are just beginning to brown (about 30 minutes more). Add the garlic, rosemary, honey, orange zest and juice and cook, stirring, for a further 2 minutes.

4 Pile the onion mixture on top of the chicken breasts, spreading it evenly.

5 Bake for 40 minutes on the top shelf of the oven and serve sprinkled with parsley.

Wine: Oaked New World Chardonnay, Viognier, or an off-dry Riesling or Pinot Gris

Parmesan Chicken Breasts with Cherry Tomato Salsa

SERVES 4

4 boneless, skinless chicken breasts

4 slices wholemeal bread, crusts removed

6 tablespoons freshly grated Parmesan cheese

2 eggs, beaten

100 g plain flour

salt and freshly ground black pepper

For the salsa

200 g cherry tomatoes, halved

½ cucumber, deseeded and diced

50 g pitted black olives, roughly chopped

1 tablespoon balsamic vinegar

4 tablespoons olive oil

3 sprigs of basil, shredded

1 Heat the oven to 200°C/400°F/gas mark 6.

2 Place the chicken breasts between 2 sheets of slightly dampened greaseproof paper and beat them with a heavy-based pan to flatten them slightly. Chill.

3 Place the bread in a food processor or blender and whizz to make crumbs. Turn on to a dinner plate and stir in the Parmesan.

4 Sieve the eggs into a wide, shallow bowl or lipped dinner plate.

5 Sift the flour on to a third dinner plate and season well with salt and pepper.

6 Dip the chicken breasts one at a time first into the flour, then the egg, then the crumbs. Place in a single layer on a baking sheet.

7 Place in the top third of the oven for 20–25 minutes, or until the chicken is golden brown and feels firm when pressed with your finger.

8 Meanwhile, mix all the salsa ingredients together. Season with salt and pepper, then chill.

9 To serve, slice each chicken breast in half across its width and top with a spoonful of salsa.

NOTE: Sieving eggs makes the texture of them smooth and liquid, which gives a more even and thorough coating when dipping into breadcrumbs. Otherwise, the coating can become thick and claggy, as the viscous egg clings to the meat in clumps. Sieving also removes the thick, white chalaza, which is the thread that attaches the egg to its shell.

Wine: An Italian red, such as Barbera d'Asti or Montepulciano d'Abruzzo

Chicken Goujons with Caramelized Lemons

Goujons are finger-sized strips of meat.

SERVES 4

4 boneless, skinless chicken breasts	2 lemons, cut into wedges
2 tablespoons clear honey, warmed	4 teaspoons caster sugar
juice and grated zest of 1 lemon	15 g unsalted butter
1½ tablespoons oil	salt and freshly ground black pepper
2 tablespoons sesame seeds	

1 Heat the oven to 200°C/400°F/gas mark 6.

2 Cut the chicken into 1 cm strips and place in a large bowl.

3 Pour over the honey, lemon juice and zest. Season with salt and pepper. Toss to coat well.

4 Heat the oil in a roasting pan and add the chicken. Bake for 15 minutes. Sprinkle over the sesame seeds and bake for a further 5 minutes, or until the chicken is cooked through and the sesame seeds are nicely browned.

5 Meanwhile, place the lemon wedges in a separate roasting pan and sprinkle over the sugar. Dot with the butter and bake alongside the chicken, basting occasionally, until well caramelized.

6 Pile the chicken goujons on to a warmed serving dish and surround with the lemon wedges.

Wine: Whites with high acidity, such as Sancerre or Alsace/German Riesling

Chicken and Chorizo Pasta

SERVES 4

3 boneless, skinless chicken breasts

3 tablespoons olive oil

1 clove of garlic, crushed

1 tablespoon salt

400 g bow-tie pasta (farfalle)

100 g chorizo, diced

1 red pepper, deseeded and diced

4 small tomatoes, quartered

salt and freshly ground black pepper

4 sprigs of basil, shredded

4 tablespoons grated Parmesan cheese

4 sprigs of basil, to garnish

1 Cut the chicken into bite-sized pieces and place in a bowl. Pour over the olive oil and stir in the garlic. Leave to marinate while preparing the other ingredients.

2 Bring a large saucepan of water to the boil. Add the salt, then cook the pasta until al dente.

3 Meanwhile, sauté the chorizo and red pepper over medium heat until just starting to brown, about 5 minutes. Add the chicken, garlic and oil. Brown lightly.

4 Stir in the tomatoes and cook for a further 5 minutes, or until the chicken is cooked through and the tomatoes have started to break down.

5 Drain the pasta, return to the pan and stir in the sauce and shredded basil.

6 Pile into warmed serving dishes. Sprinkle with Parmesan and garnish with the basil sprigs.

Wine: Dry rosé or less aromatic dry white

Chicken with Harissa and Apricots

Harissa is a fiery-hot paste used in North African cooking. It is made from red chillies, garlic, cumin, coriander and mint. Rabbit makes a tasty substitute for chicken. Serve with rice or couscous (see page 494 or 495).

SERVES 6

2 tablespoons olive oil

12 chicken thighs, with skin

225 g onion, chopped

2 sticks of celery, chopped

2 cloves of garlic, crushed

½ teaspoon ground cinnamon

1 tablespoon ground cumin

3 tablespoons harissa paste

2 × 400 g cans chopped tomatoes

140 g dried apricots, shredded

1 tablespoon lemon juice

salt and ground black pepper

2 tablespoons chopped fresh coriander, to garnish

1 Heat the oil in a sauté pan. Add the chicken thighs and brown the skin over a medium-low heat. When they have browned, transfer them to an ovenproof dish large enough to hold them in a single layer. Set aside.

2 Pour off all but 1 tablespoon of fat from the sauté pan and add the onion and celery. Cover the pan with dampened greaseproof paper and a lid and cook over a medium-low heat for about 15 minutes, until the vegetables are soft.

3 Heat the oven to 180°C/350°F/gas mark 4. Remove the lid and paper from the pan, add the garlic, cinnamon, cumin and harissa paste and cook for 1 minute. Add the tomatoes, apricots and lemon juice. Heat gently and season with salt and pepper. Pour the mixture over the chicken, then bake in the oven for 1 hour.

4 Sprinkle the chicken with chopped coriander before serving.

Wine: Dry rosé, Viognier or a Roussanne from Languedoc-Roussillon

Balti Chicken

A *balti* is a flat-bottomed, wok-shaped pan with two handles. The name originates from northern Pakistan and is also used to describe the food cooked in the pan.

SERVES 4

4 tablespoons vegetable oil

1 onion, chopped

115 g new potatoes, diced into 1 cm cubes

1 green pepper, deseeded and diced into
  1 cm cubes

1 × 400 g can chopped tomatoes

4 tablespoons Balti curry paste

450 g boneless, skinless chicken breasts,
  cut into 3 cm pieces

To garnish

4 tablespoons Greek yoghurt

2 tablespoons chopped fresh coriander

1 Heat half the oil in a frying pan, then fry the onion until soft, about 10 minutes.

2 Add the potato cubes and green pepper and fry to brown lightly.

3 Place these vegetables in a saucepan and add the tomatoes. Bring to a simmer.

4 Heat the remaining oil in the frying pan and lightly brown the chicken. Stir in the Balti paste and cook for 30 seconds. Stir in 2 tablespoons water, then add the chicken and sauce to the vegetables.

5 Simmer for about 15 minutes, or until the chicken is cooked through.

6 Serve garnished with the yoghurt and coriander.

Wine: Viognier, German Riesling or Pinot Blanc/Pinot Gris from Alsace

Yakitori Chicken with Ginger and Lime Dipping Sauce

These Japanese kebabs require 16 skewers. If using bamboo skewers, they should be soaked in water for at least 15 minutes before use to help prevent them burning as the chicken cooks.

SERVES 4

4 large boneless, skinless chicken breasts, cut into 3 cm cubes

2 tablespoons toasted sesame seeds, to garnish

For the marinade

125 ml dark soy sauce

5 tablespoons mirin

5 tablespoons sake

1½ tablespoons peanut oil

1 tablespoons clear honey

3 tablespoons soft light brown sugar

3 cm piece of fresh root ginger, peeled and grated

2 cloves of garlic, crushed

To serve

Ginger and Lime Dipping Sauce (see below)

1 Place the chicken in a large, non-metallic bowl.

2 Add the marinade ingredients, stir thoroughly, then cover and place in the refrigerator for 1 hour or overnight.

3 Using a slotted spoon, transfer the chicken to a plate. Pour the marinade into a small saucepan and set aside.

4 Heat a griddle pan or heavy-based frying pan.

5 Thread the pieces of chicken on to the skewers and cook in the hot pan for 1½–2 minutes on each side, until cooked through.

6 Meanwhile, bring the marinade to the boil, reduce the heat and simmer until it has reduced to about a third of its original volume or is a thick, sticky glaze.

7 Place the yakitori skewers on 4 warmed serving plates, brush with the glaze and sprinkle with the sesame seeds. Serve with the dipping sauce.

GINGER AND LIME DIPPING SAUCE

SERVES 4

6 tablespoons mirin

finely grated zest of 1 lime

2 tablespoons lime juice

1½ tablespoons fish sauce

1 tablespoon soft palm sugar or soft light brown sugar

1 cm piece of fresh root ginger, peeled and grated

½ red chilli, finely chopped

1 In a small bowl, mix together the mirin, lime zest and juice, and fish sauce.

2 Whisk in the palm sugar until it has dissolved.

3 Stir in the ginger and chilli and serve.

Wine: Riesling or Pinot Gris from Alsace or the New World

Chicken Jambonneaux Stuffed with Wild Mushrooms

Jambonneaux are boned legs of poultry that have been stuffed and shaped to resemble hams.

SERVES 4

30 g Clarified Butter (see page xii)

4 chicken drumsticks, thighs still attached

6 tablespoons dry sherry or Madeira

300 ml White Chicken Stock (see page 451)

For the stuffing

30 g butter

1 onion, very finely chopped

1 rindless rasher of streaky bacon, finely chopped

50 g fresh wild mushrooms, finely chopped

85 g shiitake mushrooms, finely chopped

30 g fresh white breadcrumbs

1 tablespoon finely chopped parsley

1 teaspoon chopped fresh thyme

1 teaspoon dry sherry or Madeira

salt and freshly ground black pepper

small sprigs of watercress, to garnish

To serve

Madeira Sauce (see page 464)

1 First make the stuffing. Melt half the butter in a small pan, add the onion, then cover with a piece of dampened greaseproof paper and a lid. Cook until soft but not brown. Remove the paper, add the bacon and stir over a medium heat until cooked. Transfer to a bowl.

2 Melt the remaining butter in a frying pan and cook the mushrooms until all the liquid released from them has evaporated. Add to the bowl of onion and leave to cool. Stir in the breadcrumbs, parsley, thyme and sherry or Madeira.

3 Bone the drumsticks as described on page 270. The skin can be removed if you wish. Season with salt and pepper.

4 Stuff the chicken pieces with the mushroom mixture, then fold over the chicken meat and tie to secure.

5 Heat the oven to 200°C/400°F/gas mark 6.

6 Heat the clarified butter in a sauté pan over a medium heat. If the chicken has the skin on, brown it well on all sides. If the chicken is skinned, brown very lightly, taking care not to scorch the meat.

7 Place the chicken in an ovenproof dish and pour over the sherry and stock. Cover and bake for 30 minutes, or until the juices run clear from the chicken when it is pierced with a skewer. Remove the string.

8 Place the chicken on a warmed serving dish. Add the cooking juices to the Madeira sauce and reduce to a coating consistency. Spoon a little of the sauce over the chicken and garnish with watercress. Hand the remaining sauce separately.

Wine: Red Burgundy, Barolo or Barbaresco

Chicken, Sage and Onion Burgers

SERVES 4

8 chicken thighs, skinned and boned

4 tablespoons oil

2 bunches spring onions, finely chopped

4 slices of smoked pancetta, chopped

8 sage leaves, finely chopped

½ egg, beaten

salt and freshly ground black pepper

sprigs of watercress, to garnish

To serve

Potato Wedges (see below)

1 Cut the thigh meat into small pieces and either chop very finely with a large knife or whizz in a food processor using a mincing blade. Chill for 15 minutes.

2 Heat 2 tablespoons of oil in a frying pan and sweat the onions over a low heat for 12–15 minutes, or until soft but not coloured.

3 Increase the heat and add the pancetta to the pan. Fry for 2–3 minutes, then remove from the heat, stir in the sage and allow to cool completely.

4 In a large bowl, mix the chilled meat with the cooked onion mixture. Add the beaten egg and season with salt and pepper. Mix thoroughly.

5 Divide the mixture into 8 equal pieces and, with wet hands, shape them into flattish rounds. Chill for 5–10 minutes.

6 Heat the remaining 2 tablespoons of oil in a large frying pan and brown the chicken burgers on both sides. Reduce the heat and continue to cook for 8–10 minutes, or until cooked through and the juices run clear when pierced with a skewer. Drain on kitchen paper and sprinkle with a little salt.

7 Garnish with sprigs of watercress and serve with potato wedges.

POTATO WEDGES

Rosemary, thyme and sage are all good with potato dishes, and any one of them, or even a mixture, can be used in this recipe, depending on preference or availability. As the stalks of all herbs contain a lot of flavour, the sprigs can be chopped roughly and removed before serving.

Sweet potatoes are a good alternative to baking potatoes. However, the cooking time will be shorter as they contain a lot of water and generally cook much faster. An average-sized, orange-fleshed sweet potato, cut into eight wedges, will cook in around 30–45 minutes.

SERVES 4

4 large baking potatoes, scrubbed

2 tablespoons oil

2 sprigs of rosemary, roughly chopped

flaky sea salt and freshly ground black pepper

1 Heat the oven to 200°C/400°F/gas mark 6.

2 Cut the potatoes in half lengthwise, and cut each half into 4 wedges.

3 Place the wedges in a large bowl and pour in the oil. Add the rosemary and season well with salt and pepper. Toss to coat them thoroughly.

4 Transfer the potato wedges to a large roasting pan, making sure that there is space between them. If they are too close or touching, they will not take on a good colour.

5 Place the roasting pan on the top shelf of the oven and cook for 45–60 minutes, or until the potatoes are crisp and brown, and tender when pierced with a knife. Remove the sprigs of rosemary before serving.

Wine: Light, fruity red, such as Beaujolais

Stir-fried Chicken with Cashew Nuts

SERVES 4

4 boneless, skinless chicken breasts

3 cm piece of fresh root ginger, peeled and sliced

2 small cloves of garlic, sliced

2 teaspoons cornflour

1 tablespoon soy sauce

1 tablespoon dry sherry

150 ml White Chicken Stock (see page 451)

1 tablespoon sunflower oil or grapeseed oil

50 g unsalted cashew nuts

2 spring onions, sliced diagonally

salt

1 Trim the chicken of all fat and cut into finger-sized strips.

2 Put into a bowl with the ginger and garlic, cover and leave to stand.

3 Mix the cornflour with soy sauce, sherry and stock and set aside.

4 Heat the oil in a wok. Add the cashew nuts and stir-fry until lightly browned. Remove with a slotted spoon and place on kitchen paper.

5 Add the chicken mixture to the wok and stir-fry for 4–5 minutes, until the chicken is cooked and tender. Discard the ginger and garlic.

6 Add the cornflour mixture and stir until well blended and thickened. Add a little water if the sauce seems too thick. Check the seasoning. Pile into a warmed serving dish and sprinkle with the cashew nuts and spring onions.

Wine: Riesling from Alsace, Germany or Austria

Warm Chicken and Peanut Salad with Bok Choi

SERVES 4

8 chicken thighs, skinned and boned

3 teaspoons cornflour

2 tablespoons peanut oil

1 cm piece of fresh root ginger, peeled and grated

85 g roasted and salted peanuts, lightly crushed

2 small heads bok choi, finely shredded

110 g beansprouts

grated zest and juice of 1 small lime

1 tablespoon oyster sauce

1 tablespoon light soy sauce

salt and freshly ground black pepper

1 Trim the chicken of all fat and cut into 3 cm chunks.

2 Put the chicken into a bowl with the cornflour and season with salt and pepper. Toss to coat the pieces well, shaking off the excess.

3 Heat the oil in a wok and stir-fry the chicken for 4–5 minutes, or until it is browned, crisp and cooked through.

4 Lift from the wok with a slotted spoon and drain on kitchen paper. Keep warm.

5 Add the ginger, peanuts, bok choi, beansprouts and lime zest to the wok and cook for 30 seconds. Pour in the liquid ingredients and cook for a further 30 seconds. Taste and season if necessary.

6 Transfer to a warmed serving dish and top with chicken.

Wine: Champagne, a less aromatic dry white or a dry rosé

Warm Chicken Salad

This salad can be adapted according to whatever salad ingredients you have in the refrigerator. It can easily be made into a complete meal with the addition of hot new potatoes. The essential ingredients (other than the chicken) are the rocket, chives, walnut oil and balsamic vinegar. It is also very good made with breast of pheasant instead of chicken.

SERVES 4

4 chicken breasts, skinned

seasoned flour

rocket and salad leaves, such as frisée,
  lambs' lettuce, gem lettuce

110 g baby sweetcorn

110 g broccoli, cut into florets

sunflower oil

110 g shiitake or chestnut mushrooms

1 bunch of fresh chives, chopped

4 tablespoons walnut oil

1 tablespoon balsamic vinegar

salt and freshly ground black pepper

1 Remove any fat from the chicken breasts, cut the meat into bite-sized pieces and coat them lightly with seasoned flour. Put them on to a plate, making sure that the pieces are not touching.

2 Put the rocket and salad leaves into a large salad bowl.

3 Cook the sweetcorn and broccoli in a small amount of boiling salted water. Drain.

4 Heat a little sunflower oil in a frying pan and fry the chicken pieces for about 5 minutes, until browned on both sides. Reduce the heat and continue to fry until the chicken is completely cooked. Meanwhile, heat a little more oil in a second pan and fry the mushrooms.

5 Using a slotted spoon, place the chicken pieces on kitchen paper.

6 Transfer all the ingredients to the salad bowl, mix together, season well with salt and pepper and serve immediately.

Wine: German Riesling or an off-dry white from Alsace

Smoked Chicken and Watercress Salad with Sour Cherry and Hazelnut Dressing

SERVES 4

40 g dried cherries

1 smoked chicken

170 g watercress, washed and trimmed

110 g beansprouts

85 g hazelnuts, toasted, skinned and
roughly chopped

2 tablespoons olive oil

2 teaspoons hazelnut oil

1½ tablespoons sherry vinegar

1 teaspoon clear honey

salt and freshly ground black pepper

1 Put the dried cherries into a small bowl, cover with boiling water and leave to soak for 15 minutes. Drain and pat dry.

2 Meanwhile, remove the skin and bones from the chicken and cut the meat into large pieces.

3 Put the watercress, beansprouts, cherries and hazelnuts into a bowl and add the chicken pieces.

4 In a separate bowl, whisk together the olive and hazelnut oils, the vinegar and honey. Season very well with salt and pepper. Pour the dressing over the chicken mixture and toss to coat thoroughly. Serve immediately.

Wine: Oaked Chardonnay from Europe or the New World

Smoked Chicken and Chorizo Salad

SERVES 4

450 g smoked chicken breast, cut into thick strips

100 g watercress, washed and picked over

1 small head of radicchio, roughly shredded

85 g pitted black olives

140 g chorizo, sliced diagonally

For the dressing

2 tablespoons balsamic vinegar

1½ tablespoons water

2 tablespoons salad oil

1 teaspoon honey

salt and freshly ground black pepper

1 Put the chicken, watercress, radicchio and olives into a large bowl.

2 Heat a heavy-based frying pan and fry the chorizo gently until brown and crisp. Using a slotted spoon, transfer it to the bowl.

3 Pour the vinegar, water, oil and honey into the hot pan, bring to the boil and simmer for 30 seconds. Season with salt and pepper, then pour into the bowl.

4 Mix the ingredients together lightly and divide between 4 serving plates. Serve immediately.

Wine: Oaked Chardonnay from Europe or the New World

Curried Chicken and Mango Naan Sandwich

SERVES 4

1 tablespoon medium curry paste

3 tablespoons mango chutney, chopped

2 tablespoons Greek yoghurt

finely grated zest of 1 lime

1 little gem lettuce heart, shredded

½ bunch of spring onions, finely sliced

50 g coriander leaves, roughly chopped

2 plain naan breads

285 g cooked chicken, shredded

salt and freshly ground black pepper

1 Heat the oven to 200°C/400°F/gas mark 6.

2 Mix the curry paste, chutney and yoghurt together in a small bowl. Add the lime zest and season with salt and pepper. Stir in the shredded lettuce, spring onions and coriander leaves. Set aside.

3 Cut the naan breads in half and place on a baking sheet. Heat in the oven for 5 minutes, or until puffed up.

4 Divide the chicken between the warm naan pockets along with the lettuce and onion mixture. Serve immediately.

Wine: Aromatic, fruity white, such as New Zealand Pinot Gris

Chicken and Avocado Sandwich with Lime and Pine Nut Butter

SERVES 4

50 g unsalted butter, softened

85 g pine nuts, toasted

finely grated zest of 1 lime

1 large or 2 small avocados

juice of ½ lime

4 cooked chicken thighs, skinned and boned

1 large handful of watercress, washed, trimmed
    and roughly chopped

sunflower oil

8 slices walnut bread

salt and freshly ground black pepper

1 Beat the butter, pine nuts and lime zest together in a small bowl.

2 Cut the avocado in half, discard the stone, peel, and slice the flesh thickly. Put the slices in a bowl and sprinkle over the lime juice.

3 Shred the chicken roughly and add to the bowl with the watercress. Season with salt and pepper and toss everything together.

4 Lightly oil a griddle pan and place over a high heat until smoking. Lay 2 slices of bread on the pan and char slightly on one side. Repeat with the remaining bread.

5 Spread the reserved butter mixture over the uncharred sides of the bread and pile the chicken mixture on to 4 of them. Sandwich with the remaining bread and press down firmly. Cut each sandwich into 4 and serve immediately.

Wine: Quality Riesling from Alsace, Germany or Australia

Chicken and Coriander Filo Pie

This pie is based on a delicious dish from Morocco, the b'stilla. It goes well with tzatziki.

SERVES 6

50 g fresh coriander

5 eggs, beaten

30 ml single cream

50 ml White Chicken Stock (see page 451)

olive oil, for brushing

4 boneless, skinless chicken breasts

lemon juice, to taste

½ teaspoon ground cumin

¼ teaspoon ground coriander

pinch of ground cinnamon

1 × 400 g packet filo pastry, defrosted if frozen

30 g flaked almonds

salt and freshly ground black pepper

To serve

Tzatziki (see page 164)

1 Finely chop the leaves and thin stems of the coriander. Mix with the eggs, cream and chicken stock.

2 Brush a thin coating of olive oil in the bottom of a sauté pan and place over a medium heat. When hot, cook the egg mixture, stirring constantly, until it thickens to the consistency of Greek yoghurt. Do not allow it to overcook or it will separate into lumpy egg in runny liquid. Transfer to a large bowl to cool.

3 Cut the chicken into finger-sized strips and place in a bowl. Sprinkle with a little lemon juice and the spices. Season with salt and pepper.

4 Heat the oven to 190°C/375°F/gas mark 5.

5 Line an oblong ovenproof dish with 5 layers of filo, brushing between each sheet with a little oil and allowing it to hang over the edges by 3 cm. Keep the remaining filo covered with cling film to prevent it drying out.

6 Place half the cooled egg mixture in the bottom of the filo case, then top with the chicken. Cover with the remaining egg mixture.

7 Fold back the overhanging filo pastry. Cover the pie with 4 sheets of filo, brush with oil and cut them to fit with scissors.

8 Brush the top of the pie with olive oil and sprinkle over the almonds.

9 Bake in the centre of the oven for 40 minutes, or until the pastry is golden brown. If you insert a skewer into the centre of the pie for 10 seconds, it should come out hot.

10 Serve warm or at room temperature with the tzatziki.

Wine: Aromatic dry white, such as Albarino or Grüner Veltliner

Curried Chicken and Ham Pie

SERVES 4

1 × 1.35 kg chicken, poached (see page 280),
   stock reserved
50 g butter
1 onion, chopped
2 teaspoons mild curry paste
½ teaspoon ground turmeric
45 g plain flour, plus extra for dusting
150 ml creamy milk
1 teaspoon chopped fresh parsley
1 teaspoon chopped fresh mint

pinch of crushed cardamom seeds
pinch of dry English mustard
squeeze of lemon juice
2 hardboiled eggs, chopped
115 g ham, cut into 1 cm dice
1 quantity Wholemeal Pastry (see page 477)
1 egg, beaten with a pinch of salt and 1 teaspoon
   water, to glaze
salt and freshly ground black pepper

1 Remove the skin and bones from the chicken and cut the meat into bite-sized pieces.
2 Melt the butter in a saucepan and add the onion. Cover with a piece of dampened greaseproof paper and a lid. Cook gently until soft but not coloured.
3 Stir in the curry paste and turmeric and cook for 1 minute. Remove from the heat.
4 Add the flour, then return to the hob and cook over a low heat for 1 minute. Remove the pan from the heat. Gradually add 300 ml of the reserved stock and stir well. Return to the heat and bring slowly to the boil, stirring continuously until the sauce is thick and shiny.
5 Add the milk and stir again until the sauce returns to the boil.
6 Add the parsley, mint, cardamom seeds, mustard, salt and pepper. Simmer for 2–3 minutes.
7 Taste, adding more salt if necessary, then add the lemon juice. Allow to cool.
8 Stir in the hardboiled eggs, the ham and chicken. Pour the mixture into a pie dish.
9 Flour a work surface and roll out the pastry to a rectangle about 5 mm thick.
10 Cut a strip of pastry slightly wider than the edge of the pie dish. Brush the rim of the dish with water and press the pastry strip around it. Brush with a little beaten egg or water and lay the pastry lid over the pie. Trim away any surplus pastry.
11 Press the pie edges together and mark a pattern with the point of a small knife, or pinch with the fingers into a raised border. Shape the pastry trimmings into leaves for decoration. Make a small hole in the pastry to allow the steam to escape. Chill until firm – about 30 minutes.
12 Heat the oven to 200°C/400°F/gas mark 6.
13 Brush the pie with beaten egg and decorate with the pastry leaves. Glaze again.
14 Bake for 30–35 minutes, until golden brown.

Wine: New World Chardonnay, or Viognier or Gewürztraminer from France or the New World

Chicken and Mushroom Pies with Vermicelli Topping

SERVES 4

45 g butter

3 shallots, very finely chopped

170 g button mushrooms, stalks trimmed and
   quartered

45 g plain flour

425 ml milk

2 teaspoons finely chopped fresh sage

500 g cooked chicken, cut into large pieces

salt and freshly ground black pepper

20 g melted butter, to glaze

For the topping

2 × 140 g egg vermicelli nests

2 slices Parma ham, roughly chopped

2 teaspoons finely chopped fresh sage

1 Melt the butter in a saucepan, add the shallots and cook over a gentle heat until softened but not coloured.

2 Add the mushrooms to the pan and increase the heat. Cook briskly for 3–4 minutes, or until nicely browned. Stir in the flour and cook for a further minute.

3 Reduce the heat and slowly add the milk. Bring to the boil and simmer for 1 minute. Stir in the sage and season with salt and pepper. Allow to cool.

4 Meanwhile, make the topping. Cook the vermicelli according to the packet instructions. Drain, then combine with the Parma ham and sage. Season with salt and pepper.

5 Heat the oven to 200°C/400°F/gas mark 6.

6 Stir the chicken into the cooled mushroom sauce and mix well. Divide the mixture between 4 individual pie dishes.

7 Loosely pile the vermicelli on top of each dish and place on a baking sheet. Brush with the melted butter and bake in the centre of the oven for 20–25 minutes, or until the pies are hot and bubbling and the vermicelli is crisp and brown.

Wine: Cru Beaujolais, Côtes-du-Rhône or Alsace Riesling

Chicken and Golden Vegetable Paprika Pie

SERVES 4–6

2 small carrots, cut into 1 cm cubes

1 small swede, cut into 1 cm cubes

½ butternut squash, cut into 1 cm cubes

1 large sweet potato, cut into 2 cm cubes

45 g unsalted butter

2 teaspoons sweet Hungarian paprika

60 g Cheddar cheese, coarsely grated

675 g cooked chicken thighs, skinned and boned, cut into 3 cm cubes

425 ml Béchamel Sauce (see page 460)

2 tablespoons flat leaf parsley, finely chopped

45 g Parmesan cheese, freshly grated

salt and freshly ground black pepper

1 Bring a large pan of salted water to the boil. Cook the vegetables until tender. Drain in a colander and place in a large bowl with the butter, paprika and Cheddar. Season with salt and pepper and set aside.

2 Heat the oven to 200°C/400°F/gas mark 6.

3 Mix the chicken and the Béchamel sauce together, stir in the parsley and season with salt and pepper. Place the mixture in a large ovenproof dish.

4 Pile the vegetables on top of the chicken and sprinkle over the Parmesan.

5 Place the pie on the top shelf of the oven and bake for 20 minutes, or until the cheese is brown and bubbling and the centre is piping hot.

Wine: Viognier or an aromatic, fruity white

Rechauffé Dishes

Cooked poultry is often cut into bite-sized pieces and reheated (*rechauffé*) in a sauce to serve. Poached or roasted meat (see pages 265 and 260) is the best to use for rechauffé poultry dishes.

Chicken and Mushroom Gougère

A gougère is a large ring of choux pastry with no central base, which is filled with cooked poultry or fish and/or vegetables, reheated and bound in a sauce.

SERVES 4

1 quantity Choux Pastry (see page 482), with a little cayenne pepper added to the flour

50 g strong Cheddar cheese, cut into 5 mm cubes

30 g butter

1 medium onion, thinly sliced

115 g mushrooms, sliced

20 g plain flour

300 ml White Chicken Stock (see page 451)

2 teaspoons chopped fresh parsley

340 g cooked chicken, shredded

2 teaspoons breadcrumbs

1 tablespoon grated Parmesan cheese

salt and freshly ground black pepper

1 Heat the oven to 200°C/400°F/gas mark 6.
2 First make the choux pastry for the gougère. When it is dropping consistency, stir in the diced cheese.
3 Spoon the mixture around the edge of a 30 cm shallow greased ovenproof dish. Bake for 25 minutes, or until golden brown and firm to the touch.
4 To make the filling, melt the butter in a saucepan and soften the onion over a low heat. Add the mushrooms and cook until soft, about 3–4 minutes.
5 Stir in the flour and cook for 1 minute.
6 Remove the pan from the heat and stir in the stock. Return to the heat and bring to the boil, stirring continuously. Season to taste with salt and pepper. Simmer for 2 minutes. If the dish is not going to be baked immediately, let the sauce cool down before adding the chicken.
7 Add the parsley and chicken.
8 Pile the filling into the centre of the gougère and sprinkle with the breadcrumbs and grated cheese. Return to the oven and bake for about 15 minutes, until the filling is hot.

Wine: Aromatic dry white or light, fruity red (Beaujolais style)

Chicken and Bacon Risotto Cakes

This recipe makes good use of leftover chicken, transforming it into a delicious dish that can be served hot with a salad for lunch or supper, or cold as a snack or for a picnic. Leftover grilled or fried bacon or pancetta can also be used in place of freshly cooked bacon. The cakes can be shallow-fried in a little vegetable oil if a deep-fat fryer is not available.

MAKES 8

1 tablespoon sunflower oil

1 bunch of spring onions, very finely sliced

¼ teaspoon cayenne pepper

250 g Arborio rice

4 tablespoons white wine

425 ml hot White Chicken Stock (see page 451)

1 egg, beaten

2 tablespoons flat leaf parsley, roughly chopped

juice of ½ a lemon

170 g cooked chicken, shredded

6 rashers of smoked streaky bacon, grilled until very crisp and finely chopped

seasoned flour

beaten egg

panko breadcrumbs (see Note below)

oil, for deep-frying

salt and freshly ground black pepper

1 Heat the sunflower oil in a deep-sided pan. Add the spring onions and cook slowly until softened but not coloured. Stir in the cayenne pepper and cook for a further 30 seconds.

2 Add the rice to the pan and fry for 1 minute, or until it begins to turn opaque. Pour in the wine and stir to coat the rice thoroughly.

3 Pour a ladleful of the hot stock into the pan and stir constantly over a low heat until the liquid has been absorbed. Repeat until all the stock has been used. The rice should be firm and fairly dry.

4 Tip the mixture on to a plate and allow to cool completely.

5 When cold, transfer the rice to a bowl, then beat in the egg, parsley and lemon juice. Stir in the chicken and bacon and season with salt and pepper.

6 Divide the mixture into 8 equal pieces and shape into round patties about 1 cm thick.

7 Dip the cakes first into the seasoned flour, then the beaten egg and finally the breadcrumbs. Chill for 30 minutes.

8 Heat the oil in a deep-fat fryer until a cube of bread sizzles vigorously (see Warning, page 53). Fry the risotto cakes for 2–3 minutes, or until golden brown and hot through. Drain on kitchen paper and sprinkle lightly with salt.

NOTE: Panko breadcrumbs have a coarse, very crisp texture and sweetish flavour. They can be found in Japanese food shops and some of the larger supermarkets. If unavailable, use dried white breadcrumbs instead.

Wine: Aromatic dry white, dry rosé or light, fruity red

Chicken Croquettes

SERVES 4

50 g butter

1 small onion, chopped

30 g mushrooms, chopped

50 g plain flour

300 ml milk, or milk mixed 50:50 with
   White Chicken Stock (see page 451)

1 teaspoon chopped fresh parsley

1 egg yolk

lemon juice

285 g cooked chicken, finely diced or minced

seasoned flour

1 egg, beaten

dried white breadcrumbs

oil, for deep-frying

salt and freshly ground black pepper

1 Melt the butter in a saucepan and add the onion. Cook until soft but not coloured, then add the mushrooms and cook for 1 further minute.

2 Add the flour and cook, stirring, for 1 minute. Remove the pan from the heat and stir in the milk. Return to the heat and bring slowly to the boil, stirring continuously. Simmer for 2–3 minutes, season to taste with salt and pepper and add the parsley. Remove from the heat and allow to get completely cold. The sauce should be very thick.

3 When the sauce is cold, beat in the egg yolk, add a squeeze of lemon juice and stir in the chicken.

4 With floured hands, roll the mixture into croquette shapes about 3.5 cm long.

5 Coat in the beaten egg, then roll in the breadcrumbs. Chill until firm – about 30 minutes.

6 Heat the oil in a deep-fat fryer until a cube of bread will sizzle in it (see Warning, page 53).

7 Deep-fry the croquettes until golden brown. Drain well on kitchen paper, sprinkle with salt and serve immediately.

Wine: Riesling, Sauvignon Blanc or a light, fruity red

Spatchcocking a Bird

Spatchcocking is a method of flattening a small bird, such as poussin or quail, before cooking so that it can be grilled or barbecued quickly and evenly. Small birds can be served as a single portion. Spatchcocked birds are often marinated or flavoured with herbs and spices, then grilled or char-grilled (see Methods of Cooking Meat, page 18).

1 Place the bird breast-side down on a board.
2 Using poultry shears or a knife, cut the bird down one side of the backbone. (a)
3 Cut down the other side of the backbone to remove it.
4 Open out the bird and flatten well on a board by pressing along the breastbone with the heel of your hand. (b)
5 Skewer the bird in position, i.e. flat and open. (c)

Cutting the bird alongside the backbone (a)

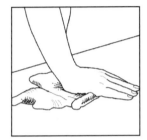

Flattening the bird (b)

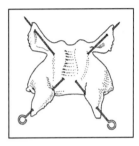

Securing with skewers (c)

Spatchcocked Chutney-grilled Poussins

SERVES 4

4 single poussins
pinch of cayenne pepper
lemon juice

4 tablespoons oil
4 tablespoons mango chutney
salt and freshly ground black pepper

1 Spatchcock the poussins as described above.
2 Season with salt, pepper and cayenne, and sprinkle with lemon juice. Chill for 1 hour.
3 Heat the grill to its highest setting. Brush the underside of the poussins with oil. Grill the birds about 5 cm away from the heat source until browned, then turn them over, brush with oil and grill until browned. Move the birds further from the heat to finish cooking through.
4 Grill for about 12 minutes, or until golden brown, brushing frequently with the pan juices. When the thickest part is pierced with a skewer the juices should run clear.
5 Spread the skin side of the birds with the chutney. Grill until golden brown and crisp.

Wine: Aromatic, fruity white or a rich, Languedoc red

Poussins with Apricot and Pistachio Stuffing

SERVES 4

30 g butter

½ onion, finely chopped

2 double poussins, chest cavity boned, legs intact
  (see page 269)

2 boneless, skinless chicken breasts

50 g dried apricots, roughly chopped

30 g shelled pistachios, roughly chopped

zest of 1 lemon

2 tablespoons chopped fresh herbs
  (thyme, parsley and chives)

1 carrot, chopped

1 stick of celery, chopped

2 bay leaves

300 ml White Chicken Stock (see page 451)

30 g dried apricots or 4 fresh apricots in season,
  sliced

2 teaspoons cornflour

salt and freshly ground black pepper

1 Melt the butter in a small saucepan. Add the onion and sweat over a low heat until soft and translucent.

2 Roughly chop the chicken breasts and put in a food processor. Pulse to a smooth paste. Add the apricots, pistachios, lemon zest and herbs. Process to combine. Season with salt and pepper.

3 Heat the oven to 200°C/400°F/gas mark 6. Wipe the poussins with damp kitchen paper inside and out.

4 Place the birds skin-side down on a chopping board and place half the stuffing down the centre of the breasts. Bring the sides up to enclose the stuffing with a 1 cm overlap of skin. Secure with a skewer or cocktail stick. Set aside to chill.

5 Place the carrot, celery and bay leaves in a roasting pan and pour over the stock. Place the stuffed poussins in the pan, breast-side down, and cover with a tight-fitting lid. Roast for approximately 20 minutes.

6 Remove the lid and turn the birds over. Return to the oven and cook uncovered for another 20 minutes.

7 Remove the poussins from the pan and keep warm. Strain the cooking juices into a saucepan and remove any excess fat. Add the sliced apricots and simmer until soft.

8 Slake the cornflour with a tablespoon of water and stir into the apricot sauce. Simmer for 2 minutes.

9 Cut each poussin in half and serve with the warm apricot sauce.

Wine: Viognier or a dry rosé

Spanish Poussins

SERVES 4

2 double poussins or 4 single poussins

2 tablespoons olive oil

12 shallots, peeled

4 cloves of garlic

150 ml sherry vinegar

425 ml amontillado sherry

2 tablespoons chopped fresh tarragon

2 teaspoons cornflour

2 tablespoons full fat crème fraîche or
   double cream

salt and freshly ground black pepper

sprigs of fresh tarragon, to garnish

1 Divide each poussin into 4 pieces, removing the backbone (see page 268).

2 Heat the oil in a sauté pan. Season the poussin pieces, then brown well on the skin side. Place in a roasting pan.

3 Heat the oven to 190°C/375°F/gas mark 5.

4 Fry the shallots until brown, then add the garlic and cook for a further minute.

5 Place the shallots and garlic around the poussin.

6 Remove the excess fat from the pan, then pour in the vinegar and the sherry. Bring to the boil and boil for 2 minutes Pour over the poussin. Add the chopped tarragon and bake in the oven for 30 minutes, or until the meat juices run clear.

7 Arrange the poussin and shallots on a serving dish.

8 Place the cooking juices in a sauté pan. Bring to the boil and reduce until almost syrupy.

9 Stir the cornflour into the crème fraîche, then whisk into the boiling sauce. Boil for 1 minute. If the sauce becomes too thick, add water as necessary to make it a light coating consistency. Sieve over the poussin. Garnish with the tarragon sprigs.

Wine: Oloroso sherry

Roast Poussins Stuffed with Fig and Shallot Chutney

SERVES 4

2 double poussins, chest cavity boned
  (see page 269)
60 g unsalted butter
150 ml red wine
4 tablespoons water
1 bay leaf
3 sprigs of thyme
sprigs of chervil, to garnish

For the chutney

1 tablespoon sunflower oil
3 shallots, very finely chopped
170 g semi-dried figs, roughly chopped
4 tablespoons water
2 tablespoons red wine vinegar
salt and freshly ground black pepper

1 Heat the oven to 200°C/400°F/gas mark 6.

2 First make the chutney. Heat the oil in a medium-sized saucepan. Add the shallots and cook very gently for 10 minutes, until beginning to soften.

3 Add the figs, water and vinegar and continue to cook slowly until the figs are very soft and most of the liquid has been absorbed. Season with salt and pepper and allow to cool completely.

4 Lay the poussins on a work surface, skin-side down. Season with salt and pepper. Place the fig chutney in the breast cavity of the birds and sew up the poussins with fine string. Shape them back into their original form and place in a roasting pan.

5 Season the skin with salt and pepper, dot with half of the butter and roast for 30 minutes.

6 Reduce the heat to 180°C/350°F/gas mark 4. Pour the wine and water over the birds, and add the bay leaf and thyme to the pan. Return to the oven and roast for a further 30–45 minutes, or until the juices run clear when the thigh is pierced with a skewer.

7 Lift the poussins from the roasting pan, remove the string and keep the birds warm.

8 Skim the fat from the pan and strain the liquid into a clean saucepan. Boil rapidly until it has a syrupy consistency. Whisk in the remaining butter and season with salt and pepper.

9 Cut the birds in half lengthwise and arrange on a warmed serving plate. Pour over the sauce and garnish with sprigs of chervil.

Wine: Aromatic, fruity white or a rich Languedoc red

Boned Stuffed Poussins with Porcini and Wild Rice

SERVES 4

4 single poussins, chest cavity
  boned (see page 269)
oil, for frying
15 g butter
1 small onion, finely chopped
1 small carrot, finely chopped
1 stick of celery, finely chopped
300 ml White Chicken Stock (see page 451)
1 bay leaf
salt and freshly ground black pepper
1 bunch of watercress, to garnish

For the stuffing

30 g butter
85 g fresh porcini mushrooms, sliced
4 spring onions, chopped
85 g rice, cooked
30 g wild rice, cooked
30 g pistachio nuts, roughly chopped
1 egg, beaten

1 Bone the poussins without removing the legs or wings (see page 269).
2 To make the stuffing, melt the butter in a frying pan and slowly cook the mushrooms and spring onions for 3 minutes. Add to the rices with the pistachio nuts. Bind with the beaten egg and season to taste with salt and pepper.
3 Lay the poussins flat on a work surface, skin-side down. Divide the stuffing between them and sew them up, using cotton or very fine string. Try to shape them back into their original form. Truss the poussins (see page 261).
4 Heat a little oil in a large flameproof casserole. Add the butter and, when foaming, add the poussins, 2 at a time. Brown lightly all over, then transfer to a plate.
5 Add the onion, carrot and celery to the pan and fry until lightly browned. Set the poussins on top of the vegetables. Add the stock, bay leaf and salt and pepper. Bring to the boil, then cover and simmer for 40–50 minutes.
6 When the poussins are cooked, transfer them to a warmed serving plate and remove the stitching and the trussing string.
7 Meanwhile, make the sauce. Skim the fat from the cooking juices. Strain the liquid into a clean saucepan, adding a small amount of the vegetables. Boil rapidly to a syrupy consistency. Check that the sauce is not too strong – if necessary, it can be thickened with a little beurre manié (see Cookery Terms and Kitchen French, page 512) and need not be reduced. Taste and season. Pour into a warm sauceboat.
8 Garnish the poussins with watercress and serve with the sauce.

Wine: Mature red Burgundy, Barolo or Barbaresco

Guinea Fowl Braised with Caramel and Oranges

SERVES 4

2 guinea fowl

2 teaspoons sunflower oil

50 g shallots, finely chopped

30 g granulated sugar

1 tablespoon wine vinegar

175 ml White Chicken Stock (see page 451)

juice of 2 oranges, strained

salt and freshly ground black pepper

To garnish

1 orange, segmented

1 small bunch of watercress

1 Heat the oven to 190°C/375°F/gas mark 5.

2 Remove any feathers from the guinea fowl and wipe clean inside with a damp cloth.

3 Heat the oil in a flameproof casserole. Add the guinea fowl and brown them all over. Transfer them to a plate.

4 Reduce the heat, add the shallots to the casserole and cook for 2 minutes. Remove from the pan. Add the sugar and vinegar, dissolving the sugar over a low heat, then boil the liquid until the sugar caramelizes. Carefully pour in the stock – it will hiss and splutter – and stir over a low heat until the caramel lumps disappear. Add the orange juice. Season well with salt and pepper. Return the guinea fowl and the shallots to the casserole and bring the cooking liquor to the boil.

5 Cover the casserole and place in the oven for 1 hour.

6 Remove the guinea fowl and joint them as you would a chicken. Arrange the pieces on a warmed serving plate. Skim as much fat as possible from the cooking liquor. Strain it into a clean saucepan, skim it again and boil rapidly for 3 minutes. Add the orange segments to warm through.

7 Garnish the guinea fowl with the orange segments and the watercress, and serve the sauce separately in a warmed gravy boat.

Wine: Viognier

Soy-braised Guinea Fowl with Shiitake Mushrooms

SERVES 4

20 g dried shiitake mushrooms

250 ml boiling water

2 tablespoons sunflower oil

2 guinea fowl, each jointed into 8 pieces
   (see page 266)

2 cloves of garlic, crushed

15 g piece of fresh root ginger, peeled and
   sliced

100 ml dry Madeira or sherry

240 g vacuum-packed whole peeled chestnuts

1 tablespoon clear honey

8 tablespoons dark soy sauce

500 ml White Chicken Stock (see page 451)

2 teaspoons cornflour

2 tablespoons water

1 Cover the shiitake with the boiling water and leave for 20–30 minutes.
2 Heat the oil in a frying pan and brown the guinea fowl, skin-side down, over a medium heat – about 8 minutes. Remove from the pan and set aside.
3 Add the garlic and ginger to the pan and cook for 1 minute. Pour in the Madeira or sherry, scraping the sediment from the bottom of the pan. Boil to reduce by half.
4 Return the guinea fowl to the pan with the chestnuts, honey, soy sauce, stock and the mushrooms with their soaking liquid. Bring to simmering point, then cover and cook over a low heat for 45 minutes, or until the guinea fowl is cooked through (the juices should run clear when the meat is pierced with a skewer).
5 Arrange the guinea fowl on warmed plates with the chestnuts and mushrooms. Bring the pan juices to the boil over a medium heat. Slake the cornflour with the water, then whisk the paste into the pan juices to thicken. Bring to the boil, stirring, then spoon over the guinea fowl and serve immediately.

Wine: Gewürztraminer

Guinea Fowl Wrapped in Pancetta

SERVES 4

4 boneless guinea fowl breasts
30 g butter
1 small carrot, shredded
½ leek, white part only, julienned

4 sprigs of tarragon chopped
8 slices of thin pancetta
salt and freshly ground black pepper

1 Heat the oven to 190°C/375°F/gas mark 5.
2 Cut a horizontal pocket in each guinea fowl breast. Season with salt and pepper.
3 Melt the butter in a saucepan and stir in the carrot and leek. Sweat until soft.
4 Stir in the tarragon, then season with salt and pepper. Spread on a plate to cool.
5 Divide the carrot mixture between the guinea fowl pockets.
6 Wrap 2 pieces of pancetta around each breast. Place in a single layer on a baking sheet. Bake for 30 minutes, or until firm to the touch and cooked through.

Wine: Chardonnay or Pinot Noir

Roast Duck

SERVES 3

1 × 1.8 kg oven-ready duck
1 small onion, halved
1 small orange, halved
1 tablespoon plain flour
salt and freshly ground black pepper

300 ml duck stock or strong White Chicken Stock
 (see page 451)

To serve
Apple Sauce (see page 194)

1 Heat the oven to 200°C/400°F/gas mark 6.
2 Wipe the duck clean inside and out. Season the cavity well with salt and pepper. Place the onion and orange inside the duck. Prick the duck skin all over and sprinkle with salt to release the fat and crisp the skin.
3 Put the duck breast-side down on a rack in a roasting pan and place in the oven for 30 minutes (placing the duck breast-side down helps to protect the breast meat from overcooking and drying out). Pour off the fat. Turn the duck over and continue roasting for about 1 hour, until cooked. Test by piercing the thigh with a skewer. If the juices run out dark pink, the duck needs further cooking; if the juices are light pink, the duck is ready.
4 Tip the juices from the cavity into a bowl and reserve them. Joint the duck into 6 pieces (see below) and arrange on a serving dish. Alternatively, leave the duck whole for carving at the table (see below). In any event, keep warm without covering, as this would soften the crisp skin.
5 To make the gravy, pour off all but 1 tablespoon of the fat in the roasting pan. Stir over a low heat, scraping the bottom of the pan to loosen all the sediment. Whisk in the flour, then add the stock and reserved juices. Whisk until smooth. Simmer, stirring, for 2 minutes. Season to taste with salt and pepper.
6 Strain the gravy into a warmed gravy boat. Fill a second gravy boat with hot or cold apple sauce and serve with the duck.

Carving a duck
1 Remove the wings at the shoulder joints.
2 Carve the breast in slices, starting from the wing and working up towards the breastbone.
3 Once the breast meat is carved, slice the leg meat thinly along the length of the bones. Place the meat on a serving dish and discard the bones.

Jointing a cooked duck into six portions
1 Gather your equipment together while the duck is resting. You will need a board, a tray large enough to hold the board (optional), kitchen scissors, a cook's knife and gloves (optional).
2 Place the board over the tray to catch any juices while jointing the duck.
3 Place the duck breast-side down on the board. Using a pair of scissors, cut out and discard the backbone. (a)
4 Turn the duck breast-side up and cut lengthwise down the breast, halfway between the breastbone and the wing on both sides. (b)

5 There are now three pieces of duck: one breast and two wing-and-leg/thigh pieces. (c)

6 Take the breast piece – you will see that the meat is thicker at one end, almost a wedge shape. From the thin end of the breast measure two-thirds of the way up the breast and cut through so that the thicker end of the breast is the smaller piece. (d)

7 Take the wing-and-leg/thigh pieces and cut each piece in two between the wing and the leg/thigh to ensure that each portion has the same amount of meat. (e)

8 There are now six portions of duck: two breast pieces, two wing-and-breast pieces, and two thigh/leg pieces. (f)

9 Trim off any unsightly bones, fat and skin.

Jointing a cooked duck

Removing the backbone (a)

Cutting through
the breast (b)

Three pieces of duck (c)

Dividing the breast (d)

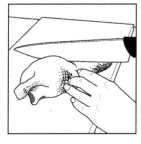
Dividing the leg
and wing (e)

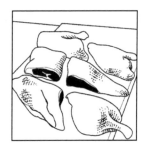
Duck jointed into
6 pieces (f)

Wine: Medium- to full-bodied reds, including Bordeaux and Hermitage, and Shiraz from Australia and South Africa

Boned Stuffed Duck

Duck is boned and made into a ballotine in the same way as chicken. The stuffing used here is also delicious in a boned chicken.

SERVES 4

1 duck, boned (see page 269)

For the stuffing
1 large boneless, skinless chicken breast
½ small onion, chopped
115 g dried apricots, sliced

1 tablespoon mixed chopped fresh tarragon and parsley
30 g unsalted pistachio nuts, skinned
salt and freshly ground black pepper

To serve
Cumberland Sauce (see page 475)

1 Heat the oven to 200°C/400°F/gas mark 6.
2 Remove any excess fat from the duck, especially from the vent end.
3 To make the stuffing put the chicken breast and onion in a food processor and whizz briefly. Add the apricots, herbs and pistachio nuts. Mix well and season with salt and pepper.
4 Assemble the ballotine as described on page 279, salting the cloth before wrapping up the bird.
5 Prick the wrapped bird lightly all over and place on a wire rack in a roasting pan (this keeps it above the cooking juices, thus enabling it to brown evenly on all sides).
6 Roast in the oven for 1¼ hours. To test that the duck is cooked, insert a skewer into the centre and leave it there for 10 seconds. Draw the skewer out and place the pointed end on your wrist. If the skewer is too hot to hold against the skin, the stuffing is cooked. If the skewer can be held on the wrist comfortably, return to the oven for a further 15 minutes and test again.
7 Using a pair of kitchen scissors, remove the muslin immediately from the cooked bird or it might stick. Take care not to damage the crisp, brown skin.
8 Slice the ballotine thickly and serve with the Cumberland sauce. To serve cold, wrap the bird (muslin removed) tightly in cling film or foil to set the shape and make it easier to slice. Allow to cool completely before unwrapping. Once cold, slice thinly and serve with salad.

Wine: Medium- to full-bodied reds, including Bordeaux and Hermitage, and Shiraz from Australia and South Africa

Leiths Roast Duckling

SERVES 3

1 × 1.8 kg oven-ready duckling

30 g granulated sugar

1 tablespoon wine vinegar

150 ml duck stock or strong White Chicken Stock
  (see page 451)

grated zest and juice of 1 orange

2 teaspoons brandy

1 stick of celery, finely chopped

1 small onion, finely chopped

salt and freshly ground black pepper

To garnish

1 whole orange, segmented

45 g flaked almonds, toasted

1 bunch of watercress

1 Heat the oven to 200°C/400°F/gas mark 6.

2 Wipe the duckling clean inside and out. Season the cavity well with salt and pepper. Place on a wire rack in a roasting pan, prick all over with a fork and sprinkle lightly with salt. Place breast-side down for the first 30 minutes of roasting, then turn it right-side up for a further 30 minutes.

3 Remove the duckling from the oven, drain well and joint it (see page 327). Put the pieces into a clean roasting pan, skin-side up. Reserve the roasting juices.

4 Put the sugar and vinegar into a heavy-based saucepan over a low heat until the sugar dissolves. Turn up the heat and boil until the sugar caramelizes: it will go dark brown and bubbly, with large slow bubbles. Pour in the stock; it will hiss and splutter, so take care that it does not splash your skin. Stir until the caramel lumps disappear. Add the orange zest and juice, the reserved roasting juices (skimmed of fat) and the brandy. Pour around the duck.

5 Return to the oven and continue cooking until the joints are cooked through (a further 20 minutes or so). Do not baste. Remove the duck joints to an ovenproof plate and keep warm. If the skin is not truly crisp, the duck can be returned to the oven for 10 minutes without the sauce.

6 Skim the sauce to remove any fat, and strain into a saucepan. Add the celery and onion, and boil until the celery is just beginning to soften but is still a little crunchy (about 5 minutes). Check the sauce for seasoning. You should have a thin, fairly clear liquid with plenty of chopped celery and onion in it.

7 Serve the sauce separately or poured around, not over, the duck. Surround the bird with the orange segments, scatter over the almonds and garnish with watercress.

Wine: Full-bodied red, such as Pomerol, Côte-Rôtie or Australian Shiraz

Cooking Duck Breasts

Roasting

Due to their substantial covering of fat, duck breasts are well suited to roasting. They can be served whole or sliced in hot dishes, or cold and thinly sliced in salads. Before they can be roasted, the subcutaneous fat must be rendered by frying them in a dry pan.

1 Heat the oven to 200°C/400°F/gas mark 6.
2 Score the skin with a sharp knife and rub with salt and pepper. Lightly season the flesh side.
3 Place the breasts, skin-side down, in a dry pan over a medium heat. Brown the skin, pouring off the excess fat. This will take 10–15 minutes.
4 Place the breasts in a roasting pan and roast in the oven for 10 minutes, or until the meat is medium-rare (see The Test of the Thumb, page 20).
5 If serving hot, allow the breasts to rest for 5 minutes, then serve whole, thinly or thickly sliced, or cut in half on the diagonal. If serving cold, allow to cool before slicing to ensure that the meat remains moist and pink.

Duck Breasts à la Muse

The length of cooking time will be determined by how well done you would like the duck. If the duck breasts are small and you like rare duck, just fry them and omit cooking in the oven.

SERVES 4

4 duck breasts, about 225 g each
salt and freshly ground black pepper

For the sauce

3 ripe plums, stoned and cut into eighths
4 tablespoons sherry vinegar
4 tablespoons good-quality cherry jam
100 ml orange juice

1 Heat the oven to 170°C/325°F/gas mark 3.
2 Score the skin on the duck breasts in lines 5 mm apart, cutting through the fat but not into the meat. Rub with salt.
3 Place the breasts in a large frying pan, skin-side down, over a medium-low heat. Cook for about 6 minutes, or until the skin is golden brown. Pour off the excess fat during cooking, reserving it for the sauce and for making roast potatoes.
4 Turn the breasts over and brown the flesh – about 5 minutes. Place in a roasting pan and cook in the oven for a further 5–10 minutes if desired (see The Test of the Thumb, page 20).
5 Transfer the duck to a warmed plate and leave to stand at room temperature for 10 minutes. Reserve the pan juices.
6 To make the sauce, heat 1 tablespoon reserved duck fat in the frying pan. Sauté the plum wedges on each side to brown lightly. Transfer to a plate.
7 Deglaze the frying pan with the vinegar, scraping up the sediment. Boil to reduce by half.

8 Add the cherry jam and orange juice and boil until a light syrup. Return the plums to the pan to warm though. Add the reserved pan juices and adjust the seasoning.

9 Slice the duck breasts and arrange on warmed plates. Spoon the sauce and plums over the sliced duck.

Wine: New Zealand Pinot Noir, Amarone della Valpolicella, Australian Shiraz, or possibly even sparkling Shiraz

Duck Breasts with Green Peppercorn Sauce

Duck breasts can also be pan-fried without the skin, as in this recipe.

SERVES 4

4 large duck breasts, skinned
45 g unsalted butter

For the sauce
150 ml dry white wine
3 tablespoons brandy
120 ml White Chicken Stock (see page 451)
300 ml double cream
2 tablespoons wine vinegar
1 teaspoon sugar

1 tablespoon port
20 g canned green peppercorns, well rinsed
20 g red pimento, cut into tiny dice
salt and freshly ground black pepper

For the garnish
30 g unsalted butter
a little caster sugar
2 firm eating apples, cored and cut into eighths

1 To make the sauce, put the wine and brandy into a large saucepan and boil gently for about 5 minutes, or until reduced by two-thirds.

2 Add the stock and boil for a further 5 minutes. Add the cream and boil for about another 5 minutes, stirring occasionally so that the mixture does not catch on the bottom of the pan, until the sauce has reduced by about a third and is of a pouring consistency about as thick as single cream.

3 Put the vinegar and sugar into a small saucepan. Boil until the mixture is caramelized and has reduced to about 1 tablespoon. Add to the reduced cream sauce. It might be necessary to replace the pan over the heat to remelt the caramel. Stir well. Add the port, peppercorns and pimento. Season with salt and pepper. Set aside.

4 To cook the duck breasts, melt the 45 g butter in a large, heavy frying pan. When it stops foaming, add the duck breasts and fry quickly on both sides to brown the surface. Reduce the heat and fry slowly for 8–10 minutes, or until the meat is medium-done in the centre (see The Test of the Thumb, page 20). Remove from the pan and allow to stand for 10 minutes.

5 Melt the 30 g butter in a second frying pan and add the sugar. Cook until starting to brown, then fry the apples until golden brown.

6 Serve the duck breasts garnished with the apples and hand the sauce separately.

Wine: Weighty red, such as Châteauneuf-du-Pape, Primitivo, Zinfandel, Australian Shiraz or Pinotage

Warm Duck and Pink Grapefruit Salad with Potato Croûtons

SERVES 4

4 × 225 g duck breasts, skinned

zest of 1 pink grapefruit

6 tablespoons olive oil

3 large potatoes

4 spring onions, finely chopped

2 pink grapefruit, segmented or sliced (make sure
   that all pith and membrane are removed)

2 bunches of watercress, coarse stalks removed

flaky sea salt and freshly ground black pepper

For the dressing

juice of 1 pink grapefruit, approx. 300 ml

1 teaspoon honey

4 tablespoons olive oil

1 Heat the oven to 200°C/400°F/gas mark 6.

2 Place the duck breasts in a bowl with the grapefruit zest and 2 tablespoons of the oil. Stir, making sure the zest coats the breasts, and leave for at least 15 minutes.

3 Peel the potatoes and cut into 2 cm cubes. Place them in a bowl and stir in 2 tablespoons of the oil and 1 tablespoon sea salt flakes. Spread out on a baking sheet and bake for 30 minutes, or until brown and crisp, turning occasionally.

4 Meanwhile, in a large frying pan, heat the remaining 2 tablespoons of oil. Season the duck breasts with salt and pepper. When the pan is hot, fry for 2 minutes each side, or until lightly browned. Reduce the heat and continue to cook for 3 minutes each side, or until the duck is still pink inside. Remove from the pan and leave to rest.

5 Stir-fry the onions in the same frying pan for 30 seconds, or until just beginning to soften. Remove from the pan and keep warm.

6 Make the dressing. Pour the oil out of the frying pan and add the grapefruit juice and honey. Boil rapidly until reduced by two-thirds. Remove from the heat and liquidize with the 4 tablespoons of olive oil until well combined. Season to taste with salt and pepper.

7 Toss the watercress, spring onions and grapefruit segments with the dressing. Pile on to plates.

8 Slice the duck breasts thinly. Arrange in overlapping slices on top of the salad. Sprinkle with the potato croûtons and serve immediately.

NOTE: The potatoes can be made in advance and reheated when assembling the salad.

Wine: Aromatic, dry whites, such as Alsace Riesling, or a rosé Champagne

Duck Breasts with Blackberry and Apple Sauce

Serve this delicious dish with mashed potato or crushed new potatoes.

SERVES 4

4 large duck breasts

1 small eating apple, peeled, cored and
  cut into 2 cm chunks

1 tablespoon port

1½ tablespoons water

finely grated zest of ½ a lemon

sugar, to taste

110 g blackberries

oil, for frying

salt and freshly ground black pepper

1 bunch of watercress, to garnish

1 Using a sharp knife, score a lattice pattern on the duck skin, cutting through the fat, but not into the meat. Sprinkle with salt.

2 Heat the oven to 220°/425°F/gas mark 7.

3 Place the apple in a small saucepan with the port, water, lemon zest and about 20 g sugar (less if the blackberries are very ripe) and heat very gently until the apples begin to soften and the juices are thick and syrupy.

4 Wash the blackberries and stir into the apples. Heat for a further 2 minutes to warm the berries. Taste, season with black pepper and add more sugar if the sauce is very tart (don't add too much as the final sauce should be a little sharp).

5 Heat a little oil in a heavy-based frying pan. When hot, add the duck breasts, skin-side down, and fry until evenly browned (about the colour of roast chicken). Drain the fat from the pan 2 or 3 times during this process.

6 Transfer the duck to a roasting pan, skin-side up, and place in the oven for 8–10 minutes, or until the duck is cooked but still pink (see The Test of the Thumb, page 20).

7 Remove from the oven and rest for 10 minutes, then cut the meat into slices on the diagonal. Garnish with watercress and serve with the warm blackberry and apple sauce.

Wine: Rosé Champagne or Pinot Noir from New Zealand or Chile

Five-spiced Duck Breasts with Bok Choi

SERVES 4

2 tablespoons groundnut oil, for frying

4 × 225 g duck breasts, skinned

For the marinade

1 tablespoon sesame oil

1 tablespoon Chinese five-spice powder

1 teaspoon mild chilli powder

2 tablespoons soy sauce

For the vegetables

2 tablespoons groundnut oil

1 clove of garlic, crushed

1 cm piece of fresh root ginger, peeled and chopped

340 g bok choi, torn into bite-sized pieces

200 g mangetout

1 Mix together the marinade ingredients, then rub into the duck breasts. Chill for 1 hour or overnight.

2 Heat the oven to 200°C/400°F/gas mark 6.

3 Heat the groundnut oil in a large frying pan. Fry the duck breasts over a medium heat for 2 minutes on each side to brown.

4 Transfer to a baking sheet and cook at the top of the oven for 10 minutes: the meat will be pink.

5 Remove from the oven and leave to stand for 10 minutes.

6 Meanwhile, prepare the vegetables. Heat the groundnut oil in a wok or large frying pan. Add the garlic and ginger and stir-fry for 20 seconds.

7 Add the bok choi and mangetout and cook for a further 2 minutes. Divide between 4 dinner plates.

8 Carve each duck breast on the angle into 1 cm slices and arrange on top of the vegetables.

Wine: Gewürztraminer

Duck Breasts with Whole Baked Caramelized Oranges

SERVES 4

4 large duck breasts

1 tablespoon oil

5 tablespoons Brown Chicken Stock
  (see page 454)

2 tablespoons sherry vinegar

salt and freshly ground black pepper

sprigs of chervil, to garnish

For the caramelized oranges

4 small oranges, peeled and all pith removed

4 tablespoons granulated sugar

1 Heat the oven to 200°C/400°F/gas mark 6.

2 Make 5–6 diagonal slashes through the duck skin and season with salt and pepper.

3 Heat the oil in a frying pan. When hot, reduce the heat and fry the duck breasts, skin-side down, very gently until crisp and well browned.

4 Transfer the breasts to a wire rack set over a roasting pan. Bake for 7–10 minutes, or until pink and juicy in the middle (see The Test of the Thumb, page 20).

5 Place the oranges in a separate roasting pan and sprinkle a tablespoon of sugar over each of them. Put them on the top shelf of the oven and bake for 10–15 minutes, or until nicely caramelized.

6 Remove the duck from the pan and leave to stand for 10 minutes. Pour off any excess fat and place the pan over direct heat. Add the stock and bring to the boil, scraping the bottom of the pan to remove any sediment. Add the vinegar and simmer until syrupy, skimming off any fat. Season with salt and pepper.

7 Slice the duck breasts on the diagonal and serve each with a whole caramelized orange. Pour the sauce over the duck and garnish with sprigs of chervil.

Wine: Full-bodied red, such as Pomerol, Côte-Rôtie or Australian Shiraz; or an adventurous Auslese from Germany

Duck Wellington

SERVES 4

4 small duck breasts, skinned

½ tablespoon duck or goose fat

1 portobello mushroom, finely chopped

85 g pâté de foie gras

225 g flour quantity Pâte à Pâte (see page 486)

salt and freshly ground black pepper

beaten egg, to glaze

sprigs of watercress, to garnish

To serve

300 ml Wild Mushroom Sauce (see page 468)

1 Trim any fat and membranes from the duck breasts. Season with salt and pepper.

2 Heat the fat in a frying pan and fry the duck breasts on both sides. Reduce the heat and continue to cook for a further 5 minutes. Transfer the meat to a wire rack to cool.

3 Cook the mushroom in the pan until lightly browned, and then allow to cool. Place the mushroom into a bowl and add the foie gras. Beat together, then season with salt and pepper.

4 Spread one side of each duck breast with the foie gras mixture.

5 On a floured work surface, roll out the pastry until it is about the thickness of a £1 coin. Cut into 4 × 18 cm squares.

6 Place each duck breast, foie-gras-side down, on a piece of pastry. Brush the edges with water and draw them together over the duck breasts, making neat, well-sealed parcels. Place them on a baking sheet, foie-gras-side up, and brush with beaten egg.

7 Make a small slit in the top of each parcel to allow the steam to escape. Decorate with leaves cut from the pastry trimmings. Brush these with egg too. Place in the refrigerator for 30 minutes to allow the pastry to become firm.

8 Heat the oven to 200°C/400°F/gas mark 6. Brush the parcels with a little more egg. Bake for 15 minutes, or until the pastry is golden brown. (The duck will be pink.) Meanwhile, reheat the sauce.

9 Serve the duck breasts on warmed dinner plates, garnished with watercress. Offer the sauce separately.

Wine: Australian Shiraz from McLaren Vale, Syrah from Apalta in Chile, or Pinotage

Duck Breast and Pine Nut Salad

SERVES 4 AS A FIRST COURSE

2 handfuls of bitter salad leaves, such as
   lambs' lettuce, watercress, chicory, radicchio

2 tablespoons Vinaigrette, made with walnut oil
   (see page 474)

15 g unsalted butter

2 duck breasts, skinned and halved horizontally

50 g pine nuts

1 Pick over the salad leaves and pull them into small pieces. Toss in the vinaigrette and arrange on 4 dinner plates.

2 Heat the butter in a frying pan until it has ceased to foam. Add the duck breast pieces and fry fairly fast to brown on both sides – about 3 minutes in all. They are done when they feel firm to the touch and are pink, not blue, when cut. Transfer to a chopping board.

3 Put the pine nuts into the frying pan and shake over the heat until pale brown and crisp.

4 Cut the duck diagonally into thin slices and scatter over the salad with the pine nuts. Serve immediately.

Wine: Medium-bodied dry red, such as Burgundy, Ribera del Duero, Rioja or Chianti Classico

Duck Breast and Walnut Salad

SERVES 4 AS A FIRST COURSE

6 salad potatoes (Charlotte or Belle de Fontenay)
1–2 tablespoons walnut oil
1 large or 2 small duck breasts
100 g smoked lardons
1 tablespoon red wine vinegar
200 g lambs' lettuce or mixed leaf salad
salt and freshly ground black pepper

For the garnish

2 shallots, peeled and thinly sliced
6 tablespoons chopped walnuts

1 Boil the potatoes in salted water until tender. Drain. When they are cool enough to handle, slice thickly. Drizzle with a little walnut oil, season and keep warm.

2 Heat the oven to 200°C/400°F/gas mark 6.

3 Score a lattice pattern into the skin of the duck breasts. Place in a sauté pan, skin-side down, and fry until beginning to brown.

4 Add the lardons and cook until they are crisp, but not dry. The duck skin should be brown and crisp.

5 Scatter the lardons over the potatoes and keep warm. Place the duck breast on a rack set over a roasting pan in the oven for 10 minutes or until cooked to pink in the middle (see The Test of the Thumb, page 20).

6 Remove all but 3 tablespoons of duck fat from the sauté pan. Stir in the vinegar, then toss with the salad leaves.

7 Divide the salad between 6 plates and top with the warm potatoes and lardons. Remove the skin from the duck breasts and cut into strips. Slice the duck breasts thinly and arrange over the potatoes. Garnish with the duck skin, shallots and walnuts. Serve warm.

Wine: Dry red from Languedoc or southern Italy, or a New Zealand Pinot Noir

Smoked Duck Breasts with Crisp Potato Skins and Pomegranate Salsa

SERVES 4

3 smoked duck breasts, skinned and sliced
    into 1 cm strips
sprigs of fresh coriander, to garnish

For the potato skins

4 × 340 g baking potatoes
sunflower oil, for deep-frying

For the pomegranate salsa

½ red onion, very finely chopped
1 tablespoon olive oil
1 tablespoon hazelnut oil
1 tablespoon sherry vinegar
1 tablespoon pomegranate molasses (see Note)
juice of ½ a lime
seeds from 1 pomegranate
15 g fresh coriander, chopped
salt and freshly ground black pepper

1 Heat the oven to 200°C/400°F/gas mark 6.
2 Prick the potatoes all over with a fork, place on a baking tray and bake for 1¼ hours, until tender.
3 Meanwhile, make the salsa. Place the onion in a bowl and pour over the oils, vinegar, pomegranate molasses and lime juice. Stir in the pomegranate seeds and season with salt and pepper. Cover and leave to marinate for 1 hour.
4 Heat the sunflower oil in a deep-fat fryer to 190°C/375°F (see Warning, page 53). Remove the potatoes from the oven and cut them into quarters lengthwise. Scoop away most of the cooked potato with a spoon to leave the skins about 1 cm thick. Deep-fry the potato skins in batches for 1½–2 minutes, until crisp and golden. Lift out with a slotted spoon and dry briefly on kitchen paper. Sprinkle with a little salt.
5 Lay the strips of duck breast on a baking sheet and place in the hot oven for 5 minutes to warm through. Transfer to a warmed serving dish and mix with the potato skins.
6 Stir the chopped coriander into the pomegranate salsa and pour into a small bowl. Serve with the duck and potatoes, garnished with coriander sprigs.

NOTE: Pomegranate molasses is a thick, sour-tasting syrup that adds a deep, tangy flavour to savoury dishes. It can be found in Middle Eastern food stores and many large supermarkets.

Wine: Châteauneuf-du-Pape, Douro red or Australian Shiraz; or sparkling wine with fresh pomegranate juice

Smoked Duck with Creamed Haricots Blancs and Garlic

SERVES 4–6

1 small head of garlic

1 tablespoon oil

1 onion, very finely chopped

3 × 400 g cans haricots blancs, rinsed and drained

425 ml Brown Chicken Stock (see page 454)

1 bouquet garni (see page 512)

3 teaspoons freshly chopped thyme leaves

3 smoked duck breasts, skinned and all fat removed

salt and freshly ground black pepper

warm crusty bread, to serve

1 Heat the oven to 170°C/325°F/gas mark 3.

2 Place the garlic in the middle of the oven and bake for 20 minutes.

3 Meanwhile, heat the oil in a large saucepan and sweat the onion until soft but not coloured.

4 Add all but half a can of beans to the pan and cover with the stock.

5 Add the bouquet garni and thyme, season with salt and pepper and cover with a lid. Bring to the boil, then simmer for 20–25 minutes, or until the beans are very soft and almost a purée.

6 Remove the garlic from the oven and allow to cool. Squeeze the soft garlic from its papery skin, add to the beans and discard the bouquet garni.

7 Slice the duck breasts into strips. Add to the pan with the remaining beans and heat through.

8 Serve in warmed bowls with plenty of crusty bread.

Wine: Something spicy, such as Crozes-Hermitage or Syrah/Shiraz-based wines

Duck Confit

Confit, a traditional dish from southwest France, is made with goose or duck and takes two days to prepare. The fat will preserve the meat for up to a month if the confit is kept refrigerated.

SERVES 4

4 duck legs or 1 whole duck, jointed
   (see page 269)

For the marinade

4 tablespoons brandy

30 g sea salt

1 tablespoon black peppercorns, cracked

2 cloves, crushed

4 sprigs of fresh rosemary, chopped

2 bay leaves, crushed

For the confit

675 g goose fat

1 head of garlic, divided into cloves, unpeeled

15 g sprigs of fresh thyme

1 Place the duck pieces fat-side down in a single layer in a non-corrosive dish. Sprinkle with the brandy.

2 Mix together the remaining marinade ingredients. Sprinkle over the duck.

3 Cover with cling film and place a weight on top. Refrigerate for 24 hours.

4 Heat the oven to 150°C/300°F/gas mark 2.

5 Pour off any liquid from the duck and scrape off the marinade.

6 Heat the fat over a low heat in a heavy flameproof casserole.

7 Layer the duck with the garlic and thyme in the casserole. The duck should be entirely submerged in the fat.

8 Bake for 3½–4 hours, or until the meat is very tender when pierced with a skewer and the fat in the skin is totally rendered.

9 Remove from the oven and allow to cool uncovered.

10 Remove the duck from the fat and trim off any exposed bone.

11 Strain a little of the cooking fat into the bottom of a clean ceramic dish. Refrigerate to set.

12 Place the duck pieces in the dish, making sure they do not touch the sides. Strain over the liquid fat to cover. Allow to cool. Refrigerate until required. Scrape the fat from the duck before using either cold or reheated.

NOTE: Confit can be reheated in the oven or under the grill to crisp the skin. Heat the oven to 200°C/400°F/ gas mark 6. Scrape the fat from the duck, place the meat in a roasting pan and bake for 20 minutes, or until heated through.

Wine: Classic red Bordeaux; also well matched to Rioja, Ribera del Duero and New World Syrah/Shiraz

Confit of Duck with Hot Sautéd Plums

SERVES 4

1 quantity Duck Confit (see page 340)

1 small ciabatta loaf

flaky sea salt

2 bunches of watercress, to garnish

To serve

Hot Sautéd Plums (see below)

1 Wipe the fat from the duck. Melt 3 tablespoons of it in a large frying pan.
2 Add the duck pieces and cook very gently until hot through.
3 Heat the grill. Slice the bread thickly and spread each slice with some of the duck fat. Place under the grill and toast on both sides.
4 Pile the duck on to the toast and top with the watercress. Sprinkle with sea salt flakes and serve with the sautéd plums.

HOT SAUTÉD PLUMS

SERVES 4

500 g plums, halved and stoned

1 tablespoon water

3 tablespoons cider vinegar

2 tablespoons soft light brown sugar

1 star anise

2 cloves

½ cinnamon stick

1 strip of orange zest

1 Cut each plum half into 3–4 pieces. Place them in a sauté pan with the water, vinegar, sugar, spices and orange zest. Bring to the boil, then reduce the heat and cover the pan with a lid.
2 Cook the plums very gently for 15 minutes, or until they are very soft, but still holding their shape.
3 Remove the lid from the pan, increase the heat and cook briskly for 1 minute, until the excess liquid has evaporated. Discard the spices and orange zest before serving.

Wine: Full-bodied New World Syrah/Shiraz or Amarone della Valpolicella

Confit of Duck Gizzards

The gizzard is a small organ that is found in the digestive tract of all birds and some toothless animals, such as reptiles and fish. It has thick, muscular walls that are used for grinding up food. Some birds swallow small stones or grit that further aid the grinding of food within the gizzard. The word itself comes from the Middle Eastern *giser*, which in turn derives from the Latin *gigeria*, meaning 'giblets'. The flavour is rich and meaty, like that of strong-tasting offal, such as chicken livers.

Poultry gizzards are used in cuisines around the world. Those from chicken are popular throughout Southeast Asia, whilst pickled turkey gizzards are traditional in parts of the USA. In Pakistan they are served in curries or barbecued, and throughout France and Europe they are preserved in duck or goose fat before being fried and served in salads or with mashed potatoes. In European Jewish cuisine they are often cooked at Passover, along with the necks and feet of the chicken.

Before use, gizzards must be split open and the thick, inner membrane peeled away before washing thoroughly.

SERVES 4

900 g duck gizzards, split open, cleaned and rinsed
225 g rock salt
3 cloves of garlic, bruised
6 sprigs of fresh thyme
1 sprig of rosemary, bruised

4 sage leaves, roughly torn
3 juniper berries, lightly crushed
3 allspice berries, lightly crushed
freshly ground black pepper
1.35 kg duck fat

1 Place the prepared gizzards in a plastic bag with the salt, garlic, herbs, spices and plenty of black pepper. Mix thoroughly and refrigerate for 3 hours.
2 Remove the gizzards from the bag and discard the salt and seasonings.
3 Rinse the gizzards in plenty of cold, running water, and pat dry with kitchen paper.
4 Melt the fat in a large pan over a low heat. When liquid, add the gizzards and cook very gently for 1½–2 hours. If possible, check the temperature of the oil with a thermometer. It should remain at a constant 80°C/175°F. The gizzards must not deep-fry.
5 Lift the gizzards from the fat and store in sterilized jars, covered in the strained, liquid fat. Keep in the refrigerator and use as required. They will keep for several weeks.

Wine: Châteauneuf-du-Pape

Duck Gizzard and Three-pea Salad

SERVES 4 AS A FIRST COURSE

1 quantity Confit of Duck Gizzards (see page 342)
110 g frozen peas
110 g sugarsnap peas, finely sliced diagonally
2 large handfuls of pea shoots
1 head of frisée lettuce, picked into small pieces
50 g sun-blushed tomatoes, finely chopped
chopped flat leaf parsley, to garnish

For the dressing
2 tablespoons oil
1 tablespoon cider vinegar
1 teaspoon clear honey
1 teaspoon wholegrain mustard
salt and freshly ground black pepper

1 Wipe the fat off the gizzards, then cut into quarters and set aside.
2 Bring a pan of salted water to the boil and cook the peas for 1 minute. Add the sugarsnaps and cook for a further 30 seconds. Drain and rinse under cold running water. Pat dry with kitchen paper.
3 Place the pea shoots, lettuce and tomatoes in a bowl.
4 Mix the dressing ingredients together, season with salt and pepper and pour over the salad. Toss lightly and arrange on a serving dish.
5 Place the prepared gizzards on top of the salad, sprinkle over the parsley and serve.

Wine: Cru Beaujolais or Chianti Classico; if white is preferred, try Alsace or German Riesling

Roast Turkey

A large sheet of fine muslin about 1 metre square is needed for this recipe. It is saturated in melted butter and wrapped around the bird before roasting, which does away with the need for basting during cooking. When the muslin is removed the bird will be brown and crisp.

SERVES 12

1 × 5.35 kg oven-ready turkey, with giblets
170 g butter
½ onion
2 bay leaves
a few parsley stalks
300 ml water
salt and freshly ground black pepper

For the stuffing

30 g butter
1 onion, finely chopped
450 g Pork Sausagemeat (see page 238)
225 g fresh white breadcrumbs
1 large egg, beaten
grated zest of 1 lemon
2 teaspoons chopped fresh thyme

1 tablespoon chopped fresh parsley
½ teaspoon salt

For the garnishes

24 chipolata sausages
24 rashers of rindless streaky bacon

For the gravy

4 tablespoons plain flour
600 ml Turkey Stock I (see page 456)
  or vegetable water

To serve

Cranberry Sauce (see opposite)
Bread Sauce (see page 475)

1 To make the stuffing, melt the 30 g of butter in a saucepan. Add the onion, cover with a piece of dampened greaseproof paper and a lid, and sweat over a low heat until soft. Allow to cool, then tip into a bowl and mix together with the remaining stuffing ingredients.

2 Just before cooking the turkey, stuff the neck end, making sure that the breast is well plumped. Draw the skin flap down to cover the stuffing, and secure with a skewer. Shape any remaining stuffing into balls about the size of a golf ball and refrigerate until required.

3 Heat the oven to 200°C/400°F/gas mark 6.

4 Weigh the turkey, then calculate the cooking time according to the table on page 263.

5 Melt the 170 g of butter and soak a very large piece of butter muslin (about 4 times the size of the turkey) in it until all the butter has been absorbed.

6 Season the turkey well with salt and pepper. Fold the buttered muslin in half and completely cover the bird with it. Place it in a large roasting pan with the giblets (except the liver) and neck. Add the onion, bay leaves and parsley stalks and pour in the water. Roast in the oven breast-side down for the first hour of the calculated time, then turn the bird over for the remaining time.

7 One hour before the turkey is ready, place the stuffing balls in a baking tin and cook in the oven with the turkey, turning occasionally.

8 Meanwhile, prepare the garnishes. Make each chipolata into a cocktail-sized sausage by twisting gently in the middle and cutting them apart. Stretch each bacon rasher slightly with the back of a knife, then cut in half lengthwise and roll up. Place the sausages and bacon rolls in a second roasting pan, with the bacon rolls wedged in so that they cannot unravel. (Alternatively, the sausages can be wrapped in the bacon before roasting.) Place in the oven 30 minutes before the turkey is ready.

9 The turkey is cooked when the thigh is pierced with a skewer and the juices run clear. Lift the bird on to a serving dish and remove the muslin. Surround with the bacon rolls, sausages and stuffing balls. Keep warm while making the gravy.

10 Place the roasting pan with 4 tablespoons of fat back on the hob. Whisk in the flour and cook, stirring, until a deep straw colour. Remove from the heat.

11 Stir gradually into the flour mixture and return to the hob.

12 Bring to the boil. Simmer until a light coating consistency, then adjust the seasoning. Strain into a warmed gravy boat.

13 Serve the turkey with the gravy, cranberry sauce and bread sauce.

CRANBERRY SAUCE

SERVES 8

100 g caster sugar

150 ml water

5 cm strip of lemon zest

5 cm piece of cinnamon stick

350 g fresh or frozen and defrosted cranberries

1 Place the caster sugar and water in a deep saucepan over a medium-low heat. Add the lemon zest and cinnamon stick. Heat, stirring, until the sugar dissolves.

2 Add the cranberries and turn up the heat to medium–high. Bring to the boil.

3 Boil until the cranberries have softened and started to 'pop', about 5–10 minutes.

4 Remove from the heat and allow to cool. Discard the lemon zest and cinnamon stick. The sauce will thicken as it cools.

Carving a turkey

The bird can be carved either in the kitchen on to a warmed serving dish, or at the table on to warmed plates. If carving in the kitchen, be sure to cover the carved meat with a large piece of foil to keep it warm.

Method 1
Simply follow the directions for carving a chicken (see page 273). This method is most suitable for carving at the table.

Method 2
This method is most suitable for carving in the kitchen, and is the easier method to use for large birds.

1 Remove the legs by slicing between them and the body of the bird. Twist to separate the joint.
2 Slice the leg meat thinly along the length of the bones. Place the meat on the serving dish and discard the bones.
3 Clip the wing pinions and discard.
4 Sever the wings at the body through the joints. Place on the serving dish.
5 Using a large knife (20 cm at least), remove the breasts from the bird by cutting down from the centre along the keel (breast) bone following the ribcage.
6 Place the breast meat on the chopping board and cut into 5 mm slices across its width. Place on the serving dish.
7 Turn the turkey carcass over and, using a small knife, remove the oyster pieces. If they are particularly large, they can be sliced in half, otherwise place on the serving dish whole.

Wine: Burgundy, red or white, according to taste

Christmas Turkey Stuffed with Ham

This turkey is also delicious served cold with a herby mayonnaise.

SERVES 20

1 × 6.7 kg turkey, boned (see page 269)
1 × 2.3 kg long, thin piece of boiled ham or bacon, skinned
50 g butter, softened
1 onion, sliced
3 bay leaves
2 parsley stalks
425 ml water
1 bunch of watercress, to garnish

For the stuffing

30 g butter
1 large onion, finely chopped

900 g pork belly, minced
450 g unsweetened canned chestnut purée or mashed cooked fresh chestnuts
225 g fresh white breadcrumbs
2 eggs, lightly beaten
1 teaspoon dried sage
2 tablespoons chopped fresh parsley
salt and freshly ground black pepper

For the gravy

4 tablespoons plain flour
600 ml Turkey Stock I (see page 456)

1 Start by making the stuffing. Melt the butter in a saucepan, add the onion and cook until soft but not coloured. Set aside to cool.
2 When the onion is cold, mix it with all the other stuffing ingredients.
3 Heat the oven to 200°C/400°F/gas mark 6.
4 Open the turkey out flat on a board, skin-side down. Spread with the stuffing and put the ham on top.
5 Draw up the edges of the turkey and sew together with fine string. Turn the bird right-side up and push it into an even, rounded shape.

6 Smear the butter all over the turkey and put it into a roasting pan. Add the onion, bay leaves and parsley stalks. Pour in the water. If the turkey looks too flat, wedge the sides with loaf tins to hold it in shape.

7 Roast in the oven for 1 hour, then lower the temperature to 180°C/350°F/gas mark 4 and roast for a further 3 hours. Baste occasionally as the turkey cooks, and cover with foil or greaseproof paper if it is browning too much.

8 When the turkey is cooked, the juices from the thigh will not be bloody. Transfer to a serving dish and keep warm while you make the gravy.

9 Place the roasting pan on the hob. Skim off as much fat as possible from the turkey juices.

10 Using a wooden spoon or wire whisk, stir in enough flour to absorb the remaining fat. Add the stock and stir until it boils. Check the seasoning. Strain into a warmed gravy boat.

11 Garnish the turkey with the watercress and serve the gravy separately.

NOTES: If you wish, the turkey-wrapped ham can be cooked within butter-saturated muslin, as in the previous recipe.

Wine: Best Burgundy, red or white, according to taste

Turkey Tonnato

Tonnato is an Italian tuna sauce, classically used for poached veal, but it also works tremendously well with turkey breast. It is an elegant dish for a summer lunch party, served with other cold salads.

SERVES 8

1 × 1.5 kg boneless turkey breast
300 ml white wine
1 stick of celery, sliced
1 carrot, sliced
1 small onion, sliced
1 clove of garlic, sliced
1 teaspoon peppercorns
4 parsley stalks
1 teaspoon salt
1 bay leaf

For the sauce

1 × 170 g can tuna in olive oil
5 anchovy fillets, rinsed
2 cloves of garlic, crushed
250 ml mayonnaise
lemon juice, to taste (about ½–1 lemon)
freshly ground black pepper

To garnish

4 tablespoons small capers, rinsed
3 tablespoons chopped flat leaf parsley
1 lemon, cut into 8 wedges

1 Tie the turkey breast together with string at 2 cm intervals to make a log shape.

2 Place the wine, celery, carrot, onion, garlic, peppercorns, parsley stalks, salt and bay leaf in a saucepan large enough to hold the turkey.

3 Place the turkey on top, then add enough water to cover. Bring to the poach, where just a few bubbles rise to the surface around the turkey. Do not boil.

4 Poach for about 1 hour, or until the internal temperature of the turkey reaches 70°C/150°F.

5 Turn off the heat and allow to cool to a warm room temperature. Transfer the turkey to a plate and the stock to a bowl, cover and chill overnight.

6 To make the sauce, place the tuna and its oil in a food processor with the anchovies and garlic. Blend to a smooth paste.

7 Add the mayonnaise and process briefly. Add lemon juice and pepper to taste. Let the mixture down with a little of the poaching liquid so that it reaches a coating consistency the thickness of double cream.

8 To serve, spread a 1 cm thick layer of sauce on a serving platter.

9 Remove the string from the turkey, then carve on the angle into slices 5 mm thick. Reassemble the turkey, using the sauce to stick the pieces together. Coat with the remaining sauce.

10 Garnish with the capers and parsley, placing the lemon wedges alongside.

Wine: Viognier

Turkey Escalopes with Baby Leeks, Mushrooms and Tarragon

SERVES 4

4 turkey escalopes (about 500 g in total)

45 g butter

seasoned flour

50 ml dry white wine

150 ml White Chicken or Turkey Stock
(see page 451 or 456)

175 g baby leeks, trimmed

100 g button mushrooms, sliced

1 teaspoon cornflour

2 tablespoons crème fraîche

salt and freshly ground black pepper

1 tablespoon chopped fresh tarragon, to garnish

1 Place the turkey slices between two pieces of dampened greaseproof paper. Beat with a heavy-based saucepan to a thickness of 5 mm.

2 Melt the butter in a large frying pan. Dredge the turkey slices in the seasoned flour, then brown on both sides in the butter. Set aside on a warmed plate.

3 Add the wine and stock to the hot pan and stir to deglaze.

4 Add the leeks and mushrooms, then arrange the escalopes on top in a single layer.

5 Adjust the heat so that the mixture just simmers, then cover and cook for 20 minutes, or until the leeks and turkey are cooked through.

6 Using a slotted spoon, transfer the turkey, leeks and mushrooms to a serving dish and keep warm.

7 To make the sauce, mix the cornflour with the crème fraîche, then stir into the pan juices. Allow to boil and become syrupy, then season with salt and pepper.

8 Pour the sauce over the escalopes and garnish with the tarragon.

Wine: Well-chilled Cava

Turkey and Pine Nut Kofta

Kofta are small, flattened meatballs that are served as a *meze*, one of several Middle Eastern appetizers. They make a good first course when garnished with a small salad, or can be served on cocktail sticks as canapés with a yoghurt and mint dipping sauce (see Tzatziki, page 164).

SERVES 4

250 g minced turkey

1 clove of garlic, crushed

½ teaspoon salt

½ teaspoon ground cumin

¼ teaspoon mild chilli powder

15 g fresh breadcrumbs

2 tablespoons milk

2 tablespoons toasted pine nuts

3 tablespoons chopped fresh coriander

freshly ground black pepper

4 tablespoons Greek yoghurt

1 Place the turkey in a large bowl and add the garlic, salt, cumin and chilli powder.

2 Combine the breadcrumbs and milk in a small bowl, then add to the turkey.

3 Add the pine nuts and coriander and season with black pepper. Mix with a fork to combine.

4 Dampen your hands with a little water and divide the turkey mixture into 12 equal pieces. Shape into flattened ovals about 1 cm thick. Place on a plate in a single layer and cover with cling film. Chill for at least 30 minutes.

5 Heat a barbecue or grill until it is very hot.

6 Spread half the yoghurt over the koftas, then grill yoghurt-side towards the heat for 5 minutes. Spread the remaining yoghurt over the other side of the koftas and grill for a further 5 minutes, or until they are cooked through. Serve warm.

Wine: Fruity Côtes-du-Rhône

Oriental Turkey with Sesame Seeds

Use this quick recipe to spice up leftover turkey.

SERVES 4–6

340 g cooked turkey

1 × 200 g packet egg noodles

1 tablespoon sesame oil

1 tablespoon vegetable oil

1 tablespoon sesame seeds, toasted

2 tablespoons chopped fresh coriander,
   to garnish (optional)

For the marinade

1 clove of garlic, crushed

1 cm piece of fresh root ginger, peeled and grated

3 tablespoons soy sauce

1 tablespoon sesame oil

½ tablespoon honey

½ tablespoon wine vinegar or sherry

pinch of ground turmeric

1 teaspoon tomato purée

For the vegetables

1 tablespoon vegetable oil

50 g mangetout

50 g baby sweetcorn

50 g button mushrooms, sliced

1 red pepper, deseeded and thinly sliced

1 orange pepper, deseeded and thinly sliced

1 Cut the turkey into chunks and place in a bowl.

2 Mix together the marinade ingredients and toss with the turkey. Chill for 1 hour.

3 Heat the vegetable oil in a wok and stir-fry the vegetables. Place in a dish and keep warm.

4 Cook the noodles according to the packet instructions. Drain and toss with the sesame oil. Place on a serving platter and keep warm.

5 Heat the vegetable oil in the wok and stir-fry the turkey to heat through. Add to the vegetables.

6 Place the turkey and vegetables on the noodles. Sprinkle with the sesame seeds and coriander, if using. Serve immediately.

Drink: Chilled beer or sake

Turkey and Apricot Pie

Leftover turkey, chicken or ham from the bone can be used in this recipe.

SERVES 6

500 g bought puff pastry or 1 quantity Rough
   Puff Pastry (see page 479)
2 tablespoons oil
1 large onion, finely chopped
225 g mushrooms, sliced
1 tablespoon finely chopped fresh lemon thyme
50 g butter
50 g plain flour

450 ml milk
450 ml Turkey Stock (see page 456)
700 g cooked turkey, shredded
170 g dried apricots, sliced
salt and freshly ground black pepper
beaten egg, to glaze

1 On a floured surface roll out the pastry so that is about 7.5 cm larger than a 2.2 litre pie dish. Cut a strip of pastry about 3 cm wide. Wet the lip of the dish and press the strip on to it. Cut out some leaves or other decorative shapes from the pastry trimmings. Put the pastry and the prepared dish on to a baking sheet, cover and refrigerate.

2 Heat the oven to 200°C/400°F/gas mark 6.

3 Heat the oil in a large, heavy-based pan. Add the onion, cover with dampened greaseproof paper and a lid, and sweat until soft but not coloured. Add the mushrooms and cook until soft and any liquid has been driven off. Stir in the thyme.

4 Add the butter to the pan and melt, then add the flour and cook, stirring, for 1 minute. Remove from the heat and gradually add the milk a little at a time, stirring well. Return to the heat and bring to the boil. Add the stock, stir well and simmer for 2–3 minutes. Season with salt and pepper.

5 Add the turkey and apricots to the sauce, season to taste and transfer to the pie dish.

6 Brush the pastry lip with a little beaten egg. Put the pastry lid on top, press around the edge and trim off any excess. Make a hole or a couple of slits in the top and arrange the leaves on the surface. Brush the pastry with the beaten egg.

7 Bake on the top shelf of the oven for 30–40 minutes, or until the pastry is golden brown and the filling piping hot.

NOTE: If you want to make this pie in advance, make sure the sauce is completely cold before adding the other ingredients and topping with the pastry. The pie can be refrigerated or frozen, but should not be glazed until just before baking. If frozen, the pie must be thoroughly defrosted in the refrigerator before cooking.

Wine: Aromatic, fruity white, such as German Riesling Kabinett or Viognier

Turkey Tetrazzini

'Tetrazzini' denotes chicken or turkey with pasta in a casserole with a cream sauce. The combination here contains mushrooms and peas, and is a popular post-Christmas supper.

SERVES 6

100 g butter

2 small shallots, finely chopped

200 g button mushrooms, sliced

45 g plain flour

pinch of cayenne pepper

500 ml Turkey or White Chicken Stock
  (see page 456 or 451)

30 ml sherry

50 ml double cream

300 g cooked turkey, cut into bite-sized pieces

200 g bow-tie pasta (farfalle) or similar, cooked

100 g petits pois, cooked

salt and freshly ground black pepper

For the topping

50 g dried breadcrumbs

50 g finely grated fresh Parmesan cheese

1 Heat the oven to 190°C/375°F/gas mark 5. Butter a baking dish.

2 Melt half the butter in a large frying pan. Add the shallots and mushrooms and cook over a medium heat, stirring, until the mushrooms have given up their juices and are starting to fry. Transfer to a plate and set aside.

3 Add the remaining butter to the frying pan. When it has melted stir in the flour and cayenne pepper. Cook over a medium heat until pale golden, then remove from the heat.

4 Gradually stir in the stock to make a smooth sauce. Return to the heat and bring to the boil.

5 Add the sherry. Boil for 2 minutes.

6 Add the cream and season to taste with salt and pepper. (If making ahead, allow the sauce to cool before adding the turkey.)

7 Place the turkey, pasta, peas, mushrooms and shallots in the prepared dish. Pour over the sauce and stir to combine. Taste and adjust the seasoning.

8 For the topping, combine the breadcrumbs and Parmesan and sprinkle over the pasta.

9 Bake for 30–40 minutes, or until the top is golden brown and the food is piping hot in the centre.

Drink: Chilled Fino sherry or light beer

Salad of Turkey Confit

Turkey legs are low in fat and have a tendency to be dry. Making them into confit keeps the meat moist and succulent.

SERVES 4

1 kg sea salt or coarse salt

2 small turkey legs, about 500 g each

2 large cloves of garlic, thinly sliced

2 tablespoons chopped fresh thyme

4 whole cloves

freshly ground black pepper

1 litre goose fat

For the salad

2 large handfuls of lambs' lettuce

4 tablespoons Vinaigrette (see page 474)

8 dried apricots, shredded

4 tablespoons toasted almonds

1 Place a 1 cm layer of salt in the bottom of a non-corrosive container just large enough to hold the turkey legs.

2 Place the legs on top of the salt and sprinkle with the garlic, thyme, cloves and black pepper.

3 Pour the remaining salt over the turkey to cover it.

4 Cover the container and place in the refrigerator overnight.

5 Heat the oven to 150°C/300°F/gas mark 2.

6 Remove the turkey from the container and brush off as much salt as possible.

7 Place the turkey in an ovenproof casserole dish.

8 Melt the goose fat and pour over the turkey legs. It should be just enough to cover them.

9 Cover the casserole dish and place in the oven for 3 hours, or until the turkey pulls easily from the bone.

10 Remove the dish from the oven and allow the turkey to cool in the fat.

11 To serve, lift the turkey out of the fat and scrape off as much fat as possible. Remove and discard the skin and bones. Shred the turkey meat.

12 Toss the lambs' lettuce with the vinaigrette and divide between 4 plates. Scatter over the turkey confit, apricots and almonds.

Wine: Chilled Beaujolais

Turkey Sandwiches

This recipe assumes that you have the leftovers from a turkey roast, and makes use of the flavoursome dripping and stuffing. Mix the tasty dripping jelly with a little of the fat to make a spreadable paste, or just use the jelly if preferred. If dripping is not available, use good unsalted butter.

SERVES 4

8 slices rye bread

turkey dripping

500 g brown and white turkey meat

100 g turkey stuffing

45 g Cranberry Sauce (see page 345)

2 bunches of watercress, washed and trimmed

2 tablespoons Vinaigrette (see page 474)

salt and freshly ground black pepper

1 Spread one side of each slice of bread with a little turkey dripping. Top 4 of the slices with a mixture of the brown and white turkey meat.

2 Crumble over the stuffing and spoon over the cranberry sauce. Season well with salt and black pepper.

3 Dip the watercress in the vinaigrette, shake off the excess, and arrange on top of the other ingredients.

4 Cover with the remaining slices of bread and press gently to seal. Cut the sandwiches into quarters and serve.

Drink: Light ale or lager

Roast Goose Mary-Claire

A 4.5 kg goose might sound huge for six people, but most of the bird is carcass. Be careful not to overcook the goose or it will become dry and tough.

SERVES 6

1 × 4.5 kg oven-ready goose
½ a lemon
salt and freshly ground black pepper

For the stuffing

30 g butter
1 onion, finely chopped
285 g chicken breast, minced
1 tablespoon chopped fresh sage
340 g eating apples, peeled and chopped
10 dried apricots, soaked for 2 hours,
   drained and chopped

50 g unsalted pistachio nuts, lightly chopped
50 g shredded beef suet
85 g fresh white breadcrumbs
1 egg
1 tablespoon clear honey, to glaze
1 bunch of watercress, to garnish

For the gravy

2 tablespoons flour
600 ml potato water or goose stock
2 tablespoons Calvados

1 Wipe the goose all over. Season the inside with salt and pepper and rub with the lemon.
2 To make the stuffing, melt the butter in a saucepan, add the onion and cook for about 10 minutes, until soft but not coloured. Mix together the chicken, onion, sage, apples, apricots, pistachio nuts and suet. Add enough of the breadcrumbs to make a firm but not solid stuffing. Season to taste with salt and pepper. Add the egg and beat really well. You can make the stuffing in a food processor, but leave out the pistachios and stir them in at the end.
3 Fill the goose cavity with the stuffing. Weigh the stuffed goose, then calculate the cooking time: 35 minutes per kg, plus an extra 15 minutes.
4 Heat the oven to 190°C/375°F/gas mark 5.
5 Prick the goose all over with a fork and sprinkle with salt. Place on a wire rack over a roasting pan. Roast in the oven, basting occasionally. Every so often you will have to remove fat from the roasting pan with a baster. If the goose gets too dark, cover it with kitchen foil.
6 Ten minutes before the bird is cooked, brush the honey evenly over the skin. This will help to make it crisp. When the goose is cooked, place on a serving plate and return to the turned-off oven.
7 To make the gravy, carefully spoon off all the fat in the roasting pan, leaving the cooking juices behind. Scrape off and discard any burnt pieces stuck to the bottom of the pan. Stir the flour into the roasting pan. Cook over a medium heat until the flour is a deep golden brown. Add the potato water or stock and, if you can, a little of the stuffing. Bring to the boil, whisk well and simmer for about 15 minutes. Increase the heat and boil until syrupy, then add the Calvados, season to taste and boil for 30 seconds. Taste and strain into a warmed gravy boat.
8 Garnish the goose with watercress.

Wine: New World Pinot Noir or Shiraz blend

Honey-glazed Goose with Kumquat Sauce

SERVES 6-8

1 × 5 kg oven-ready goose

2 eating apples, quartered

1 onion, sliced

3 tablespoons clear honey

juice of ½ an orange

2 teaspoons dry English mustard

1 bunch of watercress, to garnish

salt and freshly ground black pepper

For the kumquat sauce

170 g golden caster sugar

250 g fresh kumquats, quartered

250 g cranberries, fresh or defrosted

6 whole cloves

1 stick of cinnamon

1 bay leaf

4 tablespoons port

For the gravy

4 tablespoons flour

150 ml white wine

425 ml White Chicken Stock (see page 451)

1 Heat the oven to 190°C/375°F/gas mark 5. Weigh the goose to establish the correct cooking time: 35 minutes per kg, plus 20 minutes resting time.

2 Pull out any pin feathers and remove any lumps of fat from the body cavity. Rinse the cavity and place the apples inside.

3 Place the goose on a wire rack set over a large roasting pan. Tie the legs together with string. Pierce all over with a knitting needle or skewer, rub with salt and place in the oven. After an hour, drain the excess fat from the pan to use for roast potatoes. Cover the goose with foil if it is becoming too dark.

4 About 30 minutes before the goose is cooked, remove all but 4 tablespoons fat from the pan. Add the onion to the pan and return to the oven.

5 Ten minutes before the goose is cooked, mix together the honey, orange juice and mustard. Glaze the goose with the mixture, then return to the oven.

6 For the sauce, place the sugar in a small saucepan with 4 tablespoons water. Dissolve over a low heat.

7 Add the kumquats, cranberries, cloves, cinnamon stick and bay leaf. Bring to the boil and cook, stirring, for 5 minutes.

8 Stir in the port. Discard the cinnamon stick, cloves and bay leaf. Set the sauce aside.

9 Remove the goose from the oven and allow to rest for 20 minutes before serving

10 To make the gravy, stir the flour into the remaining fat in the roasting pan. Cook over a medium heat until the flour is a deep golden brown.

11 Remove from the heat and gradually stir in the wine and the stock. Return to the heat, bring to the boil, then simmer for 10 minutes or until syrupy. Check the seasoning. Sieve into a warmed gravy boat.

12 Carve the goose in the same way as chicken (see page 273) and serve with the kumquat sauce and gravy.

Wine: Gewürztraminer or Chenin Blanc

Smoked Goose Breast and Winter Vegetable Stew

SERVES 4–6

2 tablespoons goose or duck fat

4 small onions, cut into 6 wedges

2 sticks of celery, cut diagonally into 3 cm lengths

2 carrots, cut diagonally into 3 cm lengths

2 parsnips, cut into chunks

1 small swede, cut into chunks

1 sweet potato, scrubbed and cut into chunks

20 g flour

600 ml strong Brown Chicken Stock
   (see page 454)

2 bay leaves

4 sprigs of thyme

170 g Puy lentils

½ tablespoon sun-dried tomato paste

1 × 400 g can chopped plum tomatoes

1 teaspoon sugar

3 smoked goose breasts, skinned,
   and meat cut into 3 cm cubes

salt and freshly ground black pepper

To serve

Soda Bread (see page 497), or crusty
   wholemeal bread

1 Heat the fat in a very large saucepan or casserole. Add the onions and celery, then cover with a tight-fitting lid and sweat over a gentle heat for 15 minutes, or until beginning to soften.

2 Add the carrots, parsnips, swede and sweet potato and cook for a further 10 minutes. It might be necessary to add a little of the stock to prevent the vegetables from catching.

3 Stir in the flour to coat the vegetables and cook for 1 minute. Pour in the stock. Add the bay leaves and thyme and season with salt and pepper.

4 Bring to the boil and simmer, uncovered, for 10–15 minutes, or until the vegetables are beginning to soften.

5 Add the lentils, sun-dried tomato paste, tomatoes and sugar to the pan and simmer for 10 minutes.

6 Stir in the smoked goose meat and continue to cook for a further 5–10 minutes, or until the vegetables and lentils are very tender, and the goose is heated through. It may be necessary to add a little more stock or water, but the consistency should be quite thick. Taste and reseason if necessary.

7 Serve very hot in warmed bowls with crusty wholemeal or soda bread.

Wine: Rich red Burgundy, Rioja or Douro red; if white is preferred, an oaked Chardonnay from California or Chile

Smoked Goose with Christmas Bubble and Squeaks and Date and Fig Chutney

This is a perfect way of using up seasonal fruit and vegetables. Leftover roast goose can be used if smoked goose breast is not available. The bubble and squeak and chutney go equally well with turkey, chicken or ham.

SERVES 4

2 smoked goose breasts, skinned and thinly sliced

sprigs of watercress, to garnish

For the bubble and squeak

500 g Mashed Potatoes (see page 491)

170 g cooked parsnips, diced

170 g cooked Brussels sprouts, roughly chopped

1 small Bramley apple, peeled and grated

50 g cooked chestnuts (vacuum packed)

1½ tablespoons goose or duck fat

salt and freshly ground black pepper

To serve

Date and Fig Chutney (see below)

1 To make the bubble and squeaks put the mashed potato, parsnips, sprouts, grated apple and chestnuts in a large bowl and mix well. Season with salt and pepper.
2 With floured hands, divide the mixture into 8 and shape roughly into rounds.
3 Heat the goose fat in a heavy-based frying pan and fry the bubble and squeaks until well browned. Reduce the heat and cook for a further 5–7 minutes, or until hot through.
4 Place 2 bubble and squeak cakes on each of 4 serving plates.
5 Top with the sliced goose breast and place a spoonful of the chutney on the side.
6 Garnish with watercress and serve.

DATE AND FIG CHUTNEY

MAKES APPROX. 450 G

225 g soft dark brown sugar

300 ml cider vinegar

3 shallots, very finely diced

170 g dried dates, stoned and chopped

170 g dried figs, chopped

2 Cox's Orange Pippin apples, cored and diced

finely grated zest of 2 lemons

¼ teaspoon ground ginger

salt and freshly ground black pepper

1 Place the sugar and vinegar together in a large saucepan and heat gently, stirring occasionally, until the sugar has dissolved.
2 Add the shallots and dried fruit to the pan, bring to the boil and cook rapidly for 5–10 minutes, or until the liquid is syrupy.
3 Stir in the apples, lemon zest and ginger. Season with salt and pepper and continue to cook over a low heat for a further 5–10 minutes.
4 Ladle the hot mixture into warm sterilized jars, or cool and transfer to an airtight plastic container. The chutney will keep for 2 weeks if refrigerated.

Wine: Southern French red or New World Pinot Noir

Poultry Livers

The poultry livers most often used in a wide variety of hot and cold dishes include chicken, duck and sometimes goose. Chicken livers are more widely available than duck or goose and are by far the cheapest. Of the three types, goose liver is the largest, most richly flavoured and most expensive, followed by duck and then chicken, but are all sweetly flavoured and have a rich, creamy texture when cooked and served pink. Ducks and geese are force-fed in France to produce the grossly enlarged livers that are used for making the delicacy foie gras (see opposite).

Both chicken and duck livers are sautéd alone or with other flavouring ingredients, and served hot, often in warm salads. They are also vital flavouring and texture-improving ingredients in forcemeats for terrines, pâtés and meat pies. In addition, they are used to make savoury mousses and canapés, such as chicken livers wrapped in bacon.

Choosing Poultry Livers

Goose, duck and chicken livers may be included with the bird, or may be sold with the giblets or in larger numbers in packs. Chicken livers are sold in most supermarkets and butchers. Duck and goose liver have to be specially ordered from a butcher.

Livers must be brought absolutely fresh. Look for:
- A deep red colour. They will become brown, then grey as they age.
- The livers should be moist but not bloody. They tend to dry out if stored uncovered.
- The two halves of each liver should be intact and holding their shape firmly. If they are mushy and shapeless, this is a sign that they are deteriorating.

Storing Poultry Livers

Poultry livers must be stored in the refrigerator and used within 24 hours of purchase. As they contain a great deal of blood and other fluids which might drip or leak on to other ingredients, store them in the bottom of the refrigerator, well covered in cling film to prevent them from drying out. Poultry livers may also be frozen in a sealed airtight container for up to 3 months.

Preparing Poultry Livers

The livers are surrounded and connected by tough membrane and blood vessels that must be removed before cooking. They may also show traces of discoloration where the bitter-tasting, greenish-yellow bile contained in the gall bladder (often left attached) has leaked into them. If the gall bladder is still present, it must be removed, together with any surrounding discoloured tissue. Once the livers are trimmed, they are left whole or cut into bite-sized pieces for sautéing, or roughly chopped, or puréed by pushing through a drum sieve, for use in terrines, pâtés, forcemeats and savoury mousses.

Sautéing Poultry Livers

Livers are sautéd either for serving hot or before puréeing to make smooth pâtés and savoury mousses. It is important to sauté the livers as quickly as possible in hot fat or oil so that the surface is lightly browned before the centre loses its pink colour and creamy texture. Overcooked liver becomes dull brown, dry, grainy in texture and unpleasant to eat. It will also fail to form a smooth, creamy purée that is important for making smooth pâtés.

Foie Gras

Foie gras, meaning 'fattened liver', is the grossly enlarged liver of a goose or duck methodically fattened on a diet of corn. There is a general misconception that foie gras means goose liver, perhaps because *oie* is French for 'goose'. However, fattened duck liver is preferred over goose liver. During the process of fattening, a goose liver reaches an average weight of 675–900 g, while a duck liver will reach 300–400 g.

Foie gras is served cold in thin slices, or used to make terrines, mousses and fine pâtés, encased in brioche for pâté en croûte, sliced and glazed in aspic, or potted and preserved in goose fat. Foie gras may also be served hot, sliced and fried in butter, poached or baked.

Classic garnishes include cornichons, toasted brioche, caramelized orange segments, truffles, Muscat grapes and seafood, such as scallops, oysters and lobster. Foie gras may also be coated in aspic or served with a well-flavoured diced aspic jelly made from its poaching liquor (see Aspic, page 458).

Although both goose and duck foie gras are considered delicacies, duck foie gras is often preferred as its flavour is more delicate. Raw foie gras should have well-developed lobes that are firm and intact, smooth, putty-coloured and rounded. Do not select over-large foie gras as it may contain an excessive quantity of fat in relation to the liver. Also avoid foie gras that is yellowish in colour, as it tends to be grainy in texture.

Preparing foie gras

1 Chilled raw foie gras is hard and brittle, so remove it from the refrigerator and leave covered until it reaches room temperature and is soft and pliable.
2 Carefully part the two lobes so that the artery and veins become visible. Using a long, thin pointed knife, pull the veins away, taking care not to break the liver or break the lobes in two. Remove any green parts.
3 Remove any skin covering the liver.
4 The flavour of the foie gras can be enhanced by seasoning the opened lobes with finely ground salt and pepper, then closing and wrapping them tightly in cling film before refrigerating overnight, and/or marinating the liver for 48 hours in port mixed with 10 per cent armagnac.

Cooking foie gras

Foie gras can be poached or baked, but whatever the method, it is essential that the recipe is followed very accurately. If overcooked, the foie gras simply melts away, leaving a much smaller liver with an unappealing, soggy texture. If undercooked, the liver will taste raw.

Cook the foie gras very gently at a constant temperature until the centre of the liver reaches 60°C/140°F. Ideally, use a thermometer to achieve this.

Poaching foie gras in stock or goose fat

1   Remove the foie gras from the marinade or wipe any excess seasoning from its surface.
2   Weigh the foie gras and calculate the cooking time at 4 minutes per 115 g.
3   Heat the stock or fat in a pan to 60°C/140°F, using a thermometer to guarantee the temperature. Add the foie gras to the pan and continue to heat until the stock reaches 65°C/150°F.
4   Poach the liver for the calculated time, constantly regulating the heat source to ensure that the poaching liquor remains at a constant temperature.
5   To check if the liver is cooked, part the lobes: the centre should be warm, slightly pink and have the consistency of lightly set egg white.
6   Using 2 large slotted spoons, carefully lift out the liver and lay it on a large sheet of cling film. Reserve the stock or fat in the pan. Wrap the liver firmly to retain its shape, place in a terrine mould, or roll it into a cylindrical shape and cool on a wire rack, then refrigerate overnight.
7   Reduce and clear the stock for jelly to accompany slices of poached foie gras. The fat can be used for sealing the foie gras in the terrine mould, or for roasting potatoes, or mixed with butter to enrich sauces, meat and vegetables.
8   Serve the foie gras sliced, with toasted brioche.

Cooking foie gras at a high temperature

Foie gras can be sautéd at a very high temperature in a heavy sauté pan or frying pan. Alternatively, it can be baked briefly. The oven needs to be turned to its highest setting and heated thoroughly. The sliced foie gras should be seasoned and placed in a roasting pan, and baked on the top shelf for 2–2½ minutes, or until springy to the touch.

Slicing foie gras

Slice foie gras with a hot, thin-bladed knife to obtain a clean finish. Clean and reheat the knife in hot water between each slice.

Salade Tiède

The word *tiède* is French for 'warm', and refers to the toppings for the salad leaves.

SERVES 4

150 ml olive oil

115 g rindless bacon lardons

4 slices of white bread, cut into 1 cm cubes

salt

225 g chicken livers, cleaned (see page 360)

5 spring onions, sliced on the diagonal

1 tablespoon tarragon vinegar

For the salad

1 small frisée lettuce

1 bunch of watercress

1 small head of radicchio

Vinaigrette (see page 474)

1 bunch of chervil, roughly chopped, to garnish

1 To make the salad, wash the leaves and dry well. Tear into bite-sized pieces. Place in a large bowl and set aside. Heat the oven to 150°C/300°F/gas mark 2.

2 Heat a tablespoon of the oil in a frying pan and cook the bacon until it is evenly browned all over. Lift it out with a slotted spoon and keep warm in a low oven.

3 Heat the remaining oil in another frying pan and cook the bread cubes until golden brown (see Warning, page 53). Drain well and sprinkle with a little salt. Keep warm in the oven.

4 Tip most of the oil out of the frying pan and cook the livers over a medium heat until slightly stiffened and fairly firm but not hard to the touch. They should be golden brown and crisp on the outside and pink in the middle. Add the spring onions and fry for 30 seconds.

5 Add the vinegar and shake the pan for 10 seconds to combine.

6 Toss the salad with enough vinaigrette to lightly coat the leaves.

7 Divide the salad between 4 plates. Top with the chicken livers and bacon mixture and garnish with the croûtons and chervil.

Wine: Chilled Beaujolais

Chicken Liver Pâté

SERVES 6

450 g chicken livers

85 g butter

1 large onion

1 clove of garlic, crushed (optional)

2 tablespoons brandy

4 tablespoons crème fraîche

salt and freshly ground black pepper

1 Wash the chicken livers and discard any green or discoloured parts and connective membranes.

2 Melt half the butter in a large, heavy-based frying pan and gently fry the onion until soft and transparent.

3 Add the garlic, if using, and continue cooking for a further minute.

4 Add the livers to the pan and fry, turning to brown them lightly on all sides, until cooked. Flame the brandy and add to the livers.

5 When the flames subside, add salt and plenty of pepper.

6 Add the crème fraîche, then transfer to a blender or food processor and whizz with the remaining butter. Place the pâté in an earthenware dish or pot to serve.

Wine: Vendange Tardive from Alsace, or Spätlese/Auslese from Germany

Balsamic-glazed Chicken Livers on Coriander Toasted Brioche

SERVES 4

50 g unsalted butter

30 g coriander leaves, finely chopped

1 teaspoon lemon juice

4 thick slices of Savoury Brioche
  (see page 487)

1 bunch of spring onions, trimmed and very finely
  sliced on the diagonal

340 g chicken livers, washed and picked over

2 tablespoons water

2 tablespoons good-quality balsamic
  vinegar

salt and freshly ground black pepper

whole coriander leaves, to garnish

1 Heat the grill.

2 Soften 40 g of the butter in a small bowl; beat in the coriander leaves and season with salt, pepper and the lemon juice.

3 Toast the brioche on both sides, then spread the coriander butter on each slice and keep warm.

4 Melt the remaining butter in a frying pan and fry the spring onions for 1–2 minutes, or until softened. Add the chicken livers and fry briskly for 2–3 minutes, until browned on the outside but still pink in the middle.

5 Pour the water and balsamic vinegar into the pan, bring to the boil and simmer for 1 minute. Season with salt and pepper.

6 Spoon the chicken livers on to the hot coriander toast and pour the balsamic glaze over the top. Garnish with coriander leaves and serve immediately.

Wine: Vendange Tardive from Alsace, or Spätlese/Auslese from Germany

Mi-cuit Foie Gras Terrine

To make this terrine the liver must be left at room temperature until it is soft. A thermometer is required to monitor the temperature during cooking.

SERVES 15–20

2 fattened duck livers (foie gras), total
  weight about 1.5 kg
milk
30 g coarse sea salt (you need 15–20 g salt
  for every kilo of foie gras)

pinch of caster sugar
1 glass of white port
1 glass of cognac or armagnac
freshly ground white pepper

1 When the duck livers are soft and pliable, remove as many veins as you can without breaking up the lobes. Soak the livers in just enough milk to cover. Refrigerate overnight.
2 Drain the livers well and place in a roasting pan. Sprinkle with the salt, sugar and pepper. Pour over the port and cognac. Turn the livers so that they are evenly seasoned. Leave to marinate at room temperature for 1 hour.
3 Heat the oven to 170°/325°F/gas mark 3.
4 Place the livers in the oven for 10–12 minutes, or until they reach an internal temperature of 45°C/113°F. It might be necessary to remove pieces of liver from the pan as they reach the required temperature. If the foie gras gets too hot, it is ruined.
5 Remove from the oven. Lay the lobes on a clean kitchen cloth. Reserve the pan juices.
6 Press the lobes into a terrine and refrigerate for 24 hours. Serve as required.

NOTES: Tip all the pan juices into a bowl and place in the refrigerator. When set, lift off the fat. Discard the pan juices (they will be bitter, salty and alcoholic). Let the fat reach room temperature. It can then be whizzed with room-temperature unsalted butter and used to enhance the meat flavour of different sauces.

  If the terrine is to be kept for any length of time, the livers should reach an internal temperature of 55°C/131°F. The final terrine will have a coarser, slightly more granular texture.

Wine: Sauternes or Champagne

Chicken Liver and Foie Gras Parfait

This recipe has been adapted from one by Marco Pierre White. It must be made 24 hours in advance.

SERVES 15

400 g fresh foie gras

400 g fresh chicken livers, picked over

sel rose (pink sea salt)

white sea salt

200 ml ruby port

200 ml Madeira

100 ml brandy

300 g shallots, blanched, peeled and finely sliced

3 cloves of garlic, finely sliced

2 large sprigs of thyme

8 eggs, at room temperature

800 g unsalted butter, melted and just
   above blood temperature

150 g unsalted butter

To serve

Sauternes Jelly (see opposite)

Savoury Brioche, sliced and toasted
   (see page 487)

coarsely ground white pepper

1 Slice the foie gras and chop the chicken livers. Sprinkle over 1 dessertspoon of sel rose and 1 tablespoon of white sea salt, and leave out at room temperature.

2 Heat the oven to 150°C/300°F/gas mark 2 and have ready a terrine or pâté mould 30 × 11 cm and 10 cm deep.

3 Pour the port, Madeira and brandy into a pan and add the shallots, garlic and thyme. Place over the heat and boil until there is very little liquid left. Remove the thyme.

4 Place the port mixture and the livers in a liquidizer and blend until fully liquidized. (You might need to do this in batches.)

5 Add the eggs and mix well.

6 Mix in the warm melted butter, then, working quickly, push through a chinois sieve into a warm container. Transfer to the terrine and cover tightly with a piece of greaseproof paper and then a piece of foil.

7 Place in a bain-marie and cook in the preheated oven for 1 hour, 10 minutes.

8 Remove from the bain-marie, cool and then refrigerate for 24 hours.

9 To finish: melt a quarter of the butter and soften the remainder. Emulsify together by whisking (this lightens the butter).

10 Spread a thin layer of this light butter on top of the parfait, then chill to set. Run a hot knife around the edges of the parfait and turn out on to a board. (If it is difficult to get out, it may be sticking on the bottom. In this case, put a tea towel over the base and pour some boiling water over to loosen it.) Butter the other sides of the parfait in the same way as the top, then chill until set.

11 Meanwhile, pour a little liquid Sauternes jelly (either warmed or used before the bulk of the jelly has set) on to the chosen serving plates and allow to set.

12 To serve, slice the parfait with a hot knife and place a slice just below the centre of the plate on top of the set jelly. Sprinkle with a little sea salt and coarsely ground white pepper. Offer slices of toasted brioche as accompaniment.

NOTE: The sel rose helps retain the colour of the livers; the white salt is the seasoning. To gild the lily, you could include a chopped black truffle in the parfait mixture before cooking. This recipe might seem expensive, but in fact the only thing that costs anything worth mentioning is the foie gras itself.

SAUTERNES JELLY

Setting the wine softly with gelatine makes a delicious accompaniment to a foie gras parfait or terrine, adding another dimension of texture, as well as flavour, to the finished dish. Sauternes can be a very expensive wine, but there are numerous delicious and less expensive sweet wines available, such as a pale Muscat, that would work equally well. A sweet sparkling wine could also be used as an alternative, resulting in a slightly fizzy finish on the palate, although this is probably not one for purists.

MAKES ABOUT 300 ML

150 ml White Chicken Stock, fat free (see page 451)
2 eggshells, crushed
1 egg white

3 leaves of gelatine, soaked in cold water
150 ml Sauternes
salt and freshly ground black pepper

1 Season the stock well with salt and pepper.
2 Put the stock into a saucepan, add the eggshells and egg white, then place over the heat and whisk steadily with a balloon whisk until the mixture begins to boil. Stop whisking immediately and remove the pan from the heat. Allow to subside, then bring back to the boil and remove from the heat. Do not stir.
3 Fix a double layer of fine muslin over a clean saucepan and carefully strain the stock into it. Add the gelatine and allow to dissolve completely. Stir in the wine.
4 Pour into a clean shallow tray and allow to set. Serve, carefully diced, as a garnish for terrines and pâtés.

Wine: Sauternes

Foie Gras with Yorkshire Puddings and Muscat Gravy

SERVES 4

340 g foie gras lobe, cut into 1 cm pieces

2 tablespoons goose fat or good beef dripping

1 quantity Yorkshire Pudding batter (see page 496)

30 g unsalted butter

1 bunch of watercress, picked over and
   coarse stalks removed

salt and freshly ground white pepper

For the caramel marinade

110 g caster sugar

2 tablespoons red wine vinegar

2 tablespoons orange Muscat wine

To serve

Muscat Gravy (see below)

1 Make the marinade: place the sugar in a heavy-based saucepan and dissolve slowly without stirring.

2 Once the sugar has dissolved, turn up the heat and cook until it is a good caramel colour.

3 Tip in the vinegar and wine (it will fizz dangerously, so stand back). Stir until any lumps have dissolved, then remove from the heat and allow to cool.

4 Place the foie gras in a plastic bag or non-metallic bowl and pour in the cold marinade. Leave in a cool place to marinate for 1 hour, or cover and chill overnight.

5 Heat the oven to 200°C/400°F/gas mark 6.

6 Put dabs of the goose fat into an 8-hole non-stick Yorkshire pudding tin and heat until very hot. Ladle the batter into the tin. Bake for 15 minutes or until well risen and golden.

7 Meanwhile, drain the foie gras and pat lightly with kitchen paper. Season the pieces with salt and white pepper. Discard the marinade.

8 Heat the butter in a frying pan and, when foaming, quickly fry the foie gras on all sides until just coloured. Take care not to overcook; it should be just lightly seared.

9 Remove the Yorkshire puddings from the oven and divide the watercress between them. Top with the foie gras and spoon around a little of the hot gravy.

MUSCAT GRAVY

20 g unsalted butter

2 banana shallots, very finely chopped

1 sprig of thyme

scant ½ teaspoon flour

150 ml orange Muscat wine

200 ml Brown Stock (see page 452)

1 teaspoon balsamic vinegar

salt and freshly ground black pepper

1 Melt half the butter in a small saucepan and add the shallots and thyme. Cover with a piece of dampened greaseproof paper and a tight-fitting lid. Cook over a low heat until the shallots are very soft and greatly reduced in quantity.

2 Stir in the flour and cook until a good golden brown. Add the wine and stock and bring to the boil. Reduce the heat and simmer gently until reduced by half.

3 Pour in the vinegar and whisk in the remaining butter. Season with salt and pepper.

Wine: A classic match for Sauternes, Côteaux du Layon, Tokaji or other sweet white

Individual Foie Gras and Ham Hock Terrines with Potato Galettes

SERVES 4

1 very small ham hock, soaked in water overnight
1 onion, roughly chopped
1 small carrot, roughly chopped
1 stick of celery, roughly chopped
a few parsley stalks
1 bay leaf
6 black peppercorns
150 g foie gras lobe

oil
cayenne pepper
flaky sea salt and freshly ground black pepper
4 small sprigs of chervil
1 teaspoon finely chopped chervil

To serve
Potato Galettes (see overleaf)

1 Place the ham hock in a large saucepan of cold water and add the onion, carrot, celery, parsley, bay leaf and peppercorns. Bring slowly to the boil, then cover and simmer gently for 1–1½ hours, or until the meat is falling off the bone.

2 Remove the ham hock from the pan and allow to cool. Strain the liquid through a fine sieve into a bowl and set aside.

3 Cut the foie gras into 1 cm cubes and season with cayenne pepper and sea salt flakes.

4 Heat a little oil in a frying pan and fry the foie gras briskly for about 30 seconds, or until lightly browned. Remove from the pan and drain on kitchen paper.

5 Line 4 espresso cups with cling film and place a sprig of chervil in the bottom of each.

6 Using 2 forks, finely shred the ham and place about 340 g of it in a bowl with the foie gras and chopped chervil and 3 tablespoons of the reserved cooking liquor. Mix everything together, trying not to break up the foie gras. Season with salt and pepper.

7 Divide the mixture between the espresso cups, packing it down firmly. Spoon some of the cooking liquor over the top of the meat and allow to settle for a few minutes. Add a little more of the liquor if possible.

8 Place a small disc of cardboard covered with cling film on top of each cup and press it down gently (don't worry if a little of the liquid spills over the sides). Put a small weight on top of each disc and refrigerate overnight to set.

9 Remove the weights and carefully unmould the terrines. Allow to come to room temperature before serving with the warm potato galettes.

NOTES: There may be some ham left over for sandwiches, as even the smallest ham hock will probably yield more meat than is required for this recipe.

The terrines can be served on the same day, but the mixture will be a much softer set and might not turn out of the moulds cleanly. However, they can be served straight from the cups, each guest spooning out the mixture to pile on to warm toast or brioche spread with good unsalted butter. In this case, omit the lining of the cups and the sprig of chervil in the bottom.

POTATO GALETTES

Potato galettes are not unlike big, tasty crisps. The potatoes need to be very finely sliced and almost see-through. Galettes are most often used as a crisp base or garnish for steaks and similar cuts of meat, and are delicious served warm with terrines or pâtés, instead of bread, providing a contrasting texture. They also make good 'lids' when placed on top of individual casseroles and stews instead of pastry, for a different kind of pie topping. Any variety of root vegetable can be used, such as parsnips and sweet potatoes, but the high level of starch in an ordinary potato gives the crispest result. Whether or not the potatoes are peeled is a matter of personal taste.

MAKES 4 LARGE OR 8 SMALL GALETTES

1 very large white potato, such as Marfona or
   Desiree, scrubbed
30 g unsalted butter, melted

freshly grated nutmeg
salt and freshly ground black pepper

1 Heat the oven to 200°C/400°F/gas mark 6.
2 Slice the potatoes very thinly using a mandolin or very sharp knife.
3 Season the butter with salt, pepper and a little nutmeg.
4 Dip the potato slices into the butter and arrange 5–6 slices in a circle on a baking sheet, overlapping them to ensure they stick together. Continue with the remaining potato and brush any leftover butter over the galettes.
5 Bake on the top shelf of the oven for 12–15 minutes, or until brown, crisp and tender when tested with the tip of a knife.

Wine: Champagne, possibly demi-sec, or German Auslese

Roast Turkey, page 344.

Yakitori Chicken with Ginger and Lime Dipping Sauce, page 304.

Chicken and Chorizo Pasta, page 302.

Thai Chicken Soup, page 297.

Duck Breasts à la Muse, page 330.

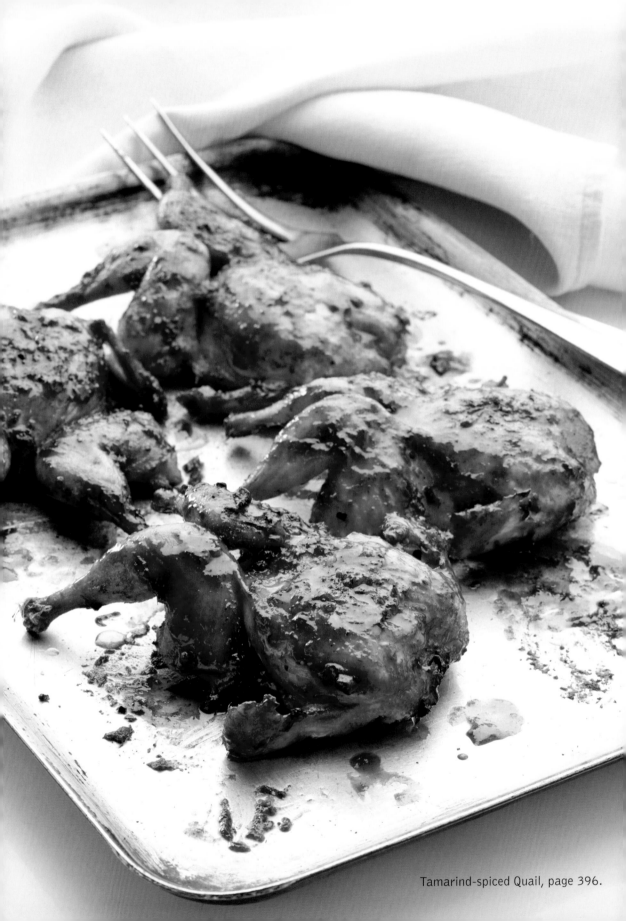

Tamarind-spiced Quail, page 396.

Pan-fried Alligator Tail Steaks with Lime Butter, page 424.

Chambord-glazed Kangaroo Medallions with Warm Red Chicory
and Blackberry Salad, page 435.

Autumn Terrine with Kumquat Syrup and Hazelnut Salad, page 390.

Game

The term 'game' refers to all wild animals and birds hunted for sport and cooked for the table. Due to an active life in the wild, game tends to be lean, often darkly coloured, and has a stronger flavour than farmed animals or birds.

For cooking purposes, game is divided into two major groups: furred and feathered. Furred game is subdivided into large game, including deer, roebuck and wild boar, and small game, such as wild rabbit and hare. Feathered game includes a wide variety of bird species, such as woodcock, grouse, pheasant, partridge, duck and wild pigeon.

Being low in fat, game must be cooked carefully to prevent it from becoming dry and tough. The meat is often marinated to help tenderize it. Tender cuts of larger game, such as haunches, saddles and loins of venison, and of hare and rabbit are roasted; noisettes and cutlets are either fried or sautéd. Tougher cuts containing more connective tissue, such as the breast, shoulder and neck, are slow-cooked in casseroles and braised dishes.

Feathered game is generally cooked by the same methods used for poultry (see page 260). Due to the strong flavour of furred and feathered game, both are usually accompanied with highly flavoured sauces often containing fruit and nuts. Game is also used to make terrines, pâtés and game pies.

Game Seasons

The game season for furred and feathered game is determined by breeding season. For purposes of conservation, it is important that each species should breed uninterrupted and that their offspring grow to a sufficient size to enable them to breed or at least to be worth hunting and eating (see table below).

Seasonal Table for Game

Feathered Game

Grouse	12 August – 10 December
Partridge	1 September – 1 February
Pheasant	1 October – 1 February
Pigeon and squab	In season all year round
Quail	Available all year round
Snipe	August – January
Wild duck, teal and wigeon	Various, starting September and finishing 20 February
Woodcock (Scotland)	1 September – 31 January
Woodcock (England and Wales)	1 October – 31 January

Furred Game

Venison seasons are complicated (see close seasons table below), but frozen wild venison is often available all year round, and farmed venison is available throughout the year.

Hunting Seasons

Autumn stags	early August – end October
Hinds	1 November – end February
Spring stags	March – mid April
Rabbit	Wild or farmed available all year
Hare	September – March

Statutory Close Seasons for Deer

Species	M/F	England and Wales	Scotland
Fallow	Bucks	1 May – 31 July	1 May – 31 July
	Does	1 March – 31 October	16 February – 20 October
Red	Stags	1 May – 31 July	21 October – 30 June
	Hinds	1 March – 31 October	16 February – 20 October
Roe	Bucks	1 May – 31 July	21 October – 31 March
	Does	1 March – 31 October	1 April – 20 October
Sika	Stags	1 May – 31 July	21 October – 30 June
	Hinds	1 March – 31 October	16 February – 20 October

Muntjac and Chinese water deer have no statutory close seasons. The British Deer Society recommends that to avoid orphaning muntjac fawns dependent upon their mother's milk, only immature and heavily pregnant females (at which time a previous fawn will be independent) should be culled.

Hanging and Storing Game

Game is usually matured or 'hung' to tenderize the muscle fibres and strengthen the meat's characteristic flavour (see page 3). Furred game is hung by the hind legs to give the haunches a good shape, and feathered game is hung by the neck. Game is not skinned or plucked before hanging as this would encourage deterioration. During hanging, the flavour of the meat develops from 'mild' to 'gamy' to 'high'. It is important not to overhang game in order to prevent the risk of food poisoning. It is also worth knowing that the fresher the bird, the easier it is to pluck and draw as the skin and flesh are firmer and less likely to tear (see Plucking and Drawing, page 375).

The period of time for which game is hung is determined by a number of factors:

Age and size: Older and larger game requires longer hanging than young or small game as the muscle fibres are coarser and take longer to tenderize. Younger, smaller game will be reasonably tender without hanging, so is hung for a short period of time mainly to develop its flavour.

Variety: Feathered game generally requires less hanging than furred game.

Storage facilities: The hanging room should be dry, cool and well ventilated. In warm, humid weather game will reach the required maturity in half the time it would take to mature in cold, dry conditions.

Personal taste: Many people are unused to the flavour of well-hung meat.

If the game is already prepared, i.e. drawn, skinned or plucked, it should be stored loosely wrapped in the bottom of the refrigerator.

Further Tenderizing Game after Hanging

Larger and older game is often marinated to partially break down the meat fibres, using acidic ingredients such as wine, lemon juice and vinegar. Marinades also contain oil to prevent the lean meat from drying out as it cooks. Young animals and birds rarely require marinating, as they are relatively tender after hanging. If a marinade is used, be careful that it enhances rather than overpowers the flavour of the meat (see Factors Affecting the Tenderness of Meat, page 6).

Tougher cuts of venison, such as flank and neck, may be tenderized by mincing, which breaks up the meat fibres and connective tissue. Venison mince may be used to make venison burgers and sausages, or combined with pork mince in forcemeats for terrines, coarse pâtés and raised pies.

Feathered Game

Type	Hanging time	Number per person	Notes
Grouse	2–10 days	1	After 2 days grouse does not have a strong flavour, but after 10 days it will be very gamy. Red or Scottish grouse is best.
Partridge	3–4 days	1	The grey British partridge is considered by many to be best of all the game birds.
Pheasant	3–4 days	Allow 1 pheasant for 2 people	As with most game birds, the hen is juicier than the cock. Pheasant is fairly mild in terms of gaminess.
Pigeon and squab	Eat fresh	1 whole bird or 2 breasts	These are in season all year round. Squab are fledgling pigeon. Pigeon breast meat should be moist and a glistening dark red. It is hard to judge the age of pigeon by its appearance, so you need to buy it from a reliable game dealer.
Quail	Eat fresh	2	Most quail today are farmed and look plump for their size. They have a slightly gamy flavour.
Snipe	4 days	2	Snipe is a small bird with a long bill that is sometimes pushed into the body of the bird like a skewer, drawing the head through the legs, before roasting. It is traditionally roasted ungutted and served on a croûte.
Wild duck Teal Wigeon	Eat fresh Eat fresh Eat fresh	1 2 3–4	Wild duck varies in size from the large mallard to the tiny teal. It tends to be dry and can have a fishy flavour. This can be overcome by stuffing the cavity with an orange, by marinating, or by parboiling the plucked bird.
Woodcock	2 days	1–2	Like snipe, woodcock is roasted undrawn. It is very rarely available in shops.

Furred Game

Type	Hanging time	Number per person	Notes
Rabbit	24 hours	A 1 kg rabbit feeds 2–3	Wild and farmed rabbit are available all year round. Rabbit must be paunched (gutted) as soon as it is killed.
Hare	5–6 days	A good-sized hare feeds 4, a leveret 3	Unlike rabbit, hare is hung unpaunched.
Venison	3–10 days	See Venison, page 414	Unlike wild venison, which has strictly controlled seasons (see above), farmed venison is available all year round. It is not as strongly flavoured as its wild counterpart.

Feathered Game

Choosing

As with poultry, when choosing feathered game it is important to be able to distinguish young from old birds.
- Young birds have soft, pliable feet and a flexible breastbone and beak.
- Older birds have a hard breastbone and hard, scaly feet with pronounced spurs.

Preparing Feathered Game for Cooking

Plucking

Some birds are harder to pluck than others, ducks being notoriously tedious. All birds are easier to pluck if still warm, as the feathers pull out more easily and cleanly without tearing the skin.

1 Place a chopping board supporting the bird in a bin liner and work away from draughts to help prevent the feathers from flying about while plucking. Rub some washing-up liquid around the opening of the bin bag: it will attract small feathers.
2 Tug the feathers, working from the tail to the head, pulling against the direction of growth.
3 At the breast, however, pluck the feathers in the direction of the growth, supporting the skin with the fingers of your other hand to avoid tearing the flesh. Do not pluck the wings. Cut them off at the first joint from the body.
4 Cut off the head next to the body and remove the neck. Watch out for the swollen pouch in the neck called the 'crop'. It often contains recently ingested corn and is messy if cut into.
5 Singe the bird over a flame to remove any down, hairs and parts of feathers still attached to the skin. This can be done directly over a burning taper or gas flame. Take care to singe only the down and small feathers and not to blacken the flesh.
6 If any quills remain embedded in the skin, they can be removed with tweezers after singeing.
7 Rub the bird clean with kitchen paper to remove any remaining stubble.

Drawing Birds

The cooking time for feathered game is little affected by the removal of the innards. Birds actually keep better if they are hung with their innards intact as they are less likely to attract flies. However, woodcock and snipe are not drawn. Their gizzards are removed before cooking, then the cooked innards are spread on toasted bread (croûtes) and served with the roasted bird. Once eviscerated, they must be cooked within 1–2 days. When you are ready to cook the bird, take it down and proceed as follows.

1 Pluck the bird as described above.
2 Cut around the feet at the drumstick joint, but do not cut right through the tendons.

3 Pull the feet off the bird, drawing the tendons with them. If the bird is small, this is easy enough – just bend the foot back over the edge of a table until it snaps, and pull. Turkeys are more difficult; snap the feet at the drumstick joint by bending them over the edge of the table, then hang the bird up by its feet from a stout hook, and pull on the bird. The feet plus tendons will be left on the hook. All too often birds are sold with the tendons still in the legs, making the drumsticks tough when cooked.

4 Put a finger into the neck hole, to the side of the stump of neck left on the bird. Move the finger right round, loosening the innards from the neck. If you do not do this, you will find them difficult to pull out from the other end.

5 Using a sharp knife, slit the bird open from the vent to the parson's nose (where the tail feathers were attached), making a hole just large enough to get your hand in. Covering the gutting hand with a cloth or wearing a rubber glove helps extract the intestines in one piece. Insert your hand (or the first two fingers if the bird is small), working so that the back of the hand is up against the arch of the breastbone, and carefully loosen the entrails from the sides of the body cavity all the way around. Pull them out, taking care not to break the gall bladder, the contents of which would make any flesh they touch taste bitter. The first time you do this it is unlikely that you will get everything out in one motion, so check that the lungs and kidneys come too. Once the bird is empty, wipe off any traces of blood with a clean, damp cloth.

The neck and feet can be used with the heart and cleaned gizzard to make stock. To clean the gizzard, carefully cut the outside wall along the natural seam so that you can peel it away from the inner bag of grit. Throw the grit bag away, along with the intestines and the gall bladder.

Do not include the liver when making stock: it can make it taste bitter. Instead, it may be trimmed of membranes and any bitter-tasting discoloured areas where it lay against the gall bladder, then cut into small pieces to fry and add to a sauce or gravy. Alternatively, it may be frozen until enough poultry liver has been collected to make a pâté.

Cooking Feathered Game

The rules and procedures for preparing and cooking feathered game are much the same as for poultry (see page 260). Feathered game contains very little subcutaneous fat and must be cooked carefully to prevent the meat from drying out. Provided the bird is cooked correctly, the breast meat is always tender, but the legs are often very tough. For this reason, they are frequently not eaten. Long, slow cooking is needed to tenderize legs, so remove them from the body and continue cooking at a low temperature until tender.

Young feathered game is sufficiently tender for roasting, grilling, sautéing and serving pink. The exception to the rule is guinea fowl, which must be cooked through to prevent the risk of salmonella poisoning. Tougher, older birds are often marinated to tenderize the flesh, then casseroled or braised until the meat is beginning to fall away from the bone.

Roasting

Roast the bird upside down or on its side to protect the tender breast meat from the fierce heat of the oven. Alternatively, the bird may be barded (see page 262) with strips of streaky bacon. A soft stuffing or flavoured softened butter can be stuffed under the skin to keep the breasts moist, or a quartered apple placed in the body cavity will help to prevent the bird from drying out. The bird should also be basted regularly while roasting.

Roast game birds are traditionally served with Game Chips and Bread Sauce or Fried Crumbs (see pages 381, 475 and 380). Smaller birds, such as woodcock and snipe, are served on a croûte, a circular piece of toasted bread spread with the birds' innards or 'trails'.

Larger birds, such as pheasant and grouse, are drawn before roasting as the innards are not suitable for eating, but the liver may be returned to the body cavity to cook with the bird. This, plus any scrapings from the inside of the bird, is spread on the uncooked side of the croûte, which is then cut in half on the diagonal, and served as a garnish with the whole roast bird.

Grilling and Pan-frying

These techniques are described in Methods of Cooking Meat (see Frying, page 16).

As with roasting, it is best to use young birds to ensure that the meat is tender. The breasts are most suited to grilling or pan-frying, and are best served pink in the centre to prevent the meat from being dry. They are often separated from the carcass, which is used to make stock for an accompanying sauce. The tender meat must be grilled under or pan-fried over a high heat to allow the surface of the meat to brown before the centre of it overcooks. The breasts are served whole, sliced in half diagonally or sliced thinly and fanned on the plate.

Roasting Table for Game Birds

Bird	Oven temperature			Cooking time	Internal temperature (all game birds)	
	°C	°F	Gas mark		°C	°F
Grouse	190	375	5	20–30 mins		
Guinea Fowl	190	375	5	70 mins		
Partridge	190	375	5	20–25 mins		
Pheasant	190	375	5	45–60 mins		
Pigeon	200	400	6	25–35 mins	71°	160° for pink meat
Quail	180	350	4	20 mins	82°	180° for well-done meat
Snipe	190	375	5	15–20 mins		
Wild duck	200	400	6	40 mins		
Woodcock	190	375	5	20–30 mins		

Roast Grouse with Pears and Pine Nuts

SERVES 4

knob of unsalted butter, softened

2 oven-ready grouse, feet removed,
    neck and giblets reserved

4 rashers of green streaky bacon (see page 222)

75 ml white port

150 ml Brown Chicken Stock (see page 454)

2 sprigs of thyme

15 g unsalted butter

salt and freshly ground black pepper

sprigs of watercress, to garnish

For the pears

2 large ripe pears

50 g unsalted butter

1½ tablespoons soft light brown sugar

1 tablespoon water

1 teaspoon honey

finely grated zest and juice of ½ a lemon

30 g pine nuts, lightly toasted

1 Heat the oven to 230°C/450°F/gas mark 8.

2 Smear the butter over the grouse and season. Lay the bacon over the breasts of the birds. Place in a roasting pan with the neck and giblets. Roast for 10 minutes.

3 Remove the bacon from the grouse and discard the bacon. Pour the port and stock around the grouse, add the sprigs of thyme and return to the oven for a further 15 minutes.

4 Peel the pears and cut into quarters. Remove the cores and cut each quarter into 3 slices.

5 Melt the butter in a large shallow pan and, when foaming, add the sugar, water, honey, lemon juice and zest. Stir gently to dissolve the sugar. Lay the slices of pear in the pan and spoon the buttery sauce over them. Increase the heat slightly and cook the pears until they are caramelized on both sides and the sauce is very thick and sticky. Stir in the pine nuts and keep warm.

6 Remove the grouse from the oven and allow to rest in a warm place. Strain the cooking liquor into a saucepan. Discard the neck, giblets and thyme and bring the liquid to the boil. Cook rapidly until it is reduced to half its original volume. Whisk in the butter, season with salt and pepper and pass the sauce through a fine sieve.

7 To serve, cut the grouse in half through the breastbone and place on warmed plates with the sauce poured over them. Put pears on each plate and garnish with watercress.

Wine: New World Chardonnay, Pinot Gris or a New Zealand Pinot Noir

Roast Partridges with Muscat Cream Sauce

SERVES 4

4 small oven-ready partridges

1 eating apple, quartered

4 slices of smoked pancetta

1 shallot, very finely chopped

3 tablespoons stock or water

75 ml Muscat wine

75 ml double cream

salt and freshly ground black pepper

1 Heat the oven to 220°C/425°F/gas mark 7.

2 Remove any remaining feathers from the partridges. Put a quarter of the apple inside each one. Cover each bird with a slice of pancetta and season with salt and pepper.

3 Place in a roasting pan with the chopped shallot, pour in the stock and roast for 5 minutes.

4 Reduce the temperature to 180°C/350°F/gas mark 4 and continue to cook for a further 20 minutes, removing the pancetta halfway through to allow the breasts to brown.

5 Remove from the oven. Discard the apple, and tip any meat juices from the partridges back into the roasting pan. Transfer the birds to a warmed serving platter and keep warm.

6 Skim any excess fat from the pan, add the Muscat and cook on the hob for 1 minute, scraping up any sediment.

7 Add the cream to the pan and return to the boil. Boil rapidly to reduce to a coating consistency. Strain into a warmed gravy boat and serve with the partridges.

Wine: Condrieu or Roussanne/Marsanne from Roussillon

Partridges with Lentils

SERVES 2

2 oven-ready partridges, trussed and larded
  (see page 108)
30 g lard or 2 tablespoons oil
30 g rindless unsmoked bacon, chopped
30 g onion, chopped
115 g Puy lentils, soaked in cold water for
  1 hour and drained
grated zest of ½ a lemon

1 bay leaf
115 g Gyula sausage or similar dried, smoked
  pork sausage (such as chorizo)
300 ml White Chicken Stock (see page 451)
85 ml crème fraîche
salt

1 Heat the oven to 170°C/325°F/gas mark 3.

2 Sprinkle the partridges with salt. Melt the lard or place the oil in a large frying pan and fry the birds until they are golden brown all over. Remove from the pan.

3 Fry the bacon and onion in the same pan until golden brown.

4 Put the lentils into a large casserole with the lemon zest and bay leaf. Add the partridges, sausage, bacon and onion. Pour over enough stock to cover the ingredients. Cover with a lid and cook in the oven until the partridges are tender, about 45 minutes. If the birds are ready before the lentils, remove them and the sausages from the pan and continue to cook the lentils.

5 When the lentils are tender, remove and discard the bay leaf. Pour over the crème fraîche and bring the liquid to the boil.

6 Carve the partridges and cut the sausages into thin slices. Place the lentils in a deep serving dish, put the partridge pieces on top and garnish with the sliced sausage.

Wine: Red or white Burgundy

Roast Pheasant

Young birds are best for roasting. Fried crumbs and game chips are the traditional accompaniments.

SERVES 4

2 medium oven-ready pheasants

4 rashers of streaky bacon

salt and freshly ground black pepper

For the gravy

1 tablespoon plain flour

1 tablespoon ruby port

1 tablespoon redcurrant jelly

To serve

Fried Crumbs (see below)

Game Chips (see opposite)

1 Wipe the pheasants and remove any remaining feathers.
2 Heat the oven to 200°C/400°F/gas mark 6.
3 Season the birds inside with salt and pepper.
4 Tie the bacon over the breasts with string to prevent drying out during cooking. Season with salt and pepper.
5 Place the pheasants in a roasting pan and pour in a 5 mm depth of water. Roast for 40–50 minutes, basting frequently.
6 Check if the pheasants are cooked by cutting into the thickest part of the thigh with the point of a sharp knife. The juices can be slightly pink but should not be bloody. The fibres of the meat should be set. Lift the birds out of the pan and keep warm.
7 Sprinkle the flour into the roasting juices and add the port and jelly. Bring to the boil, stirring. Boil for 2 minutes, then sieve into a warmed gravy boat and serve with the pheasant and accompaniments.

FRIED CRUMBS

SERVES 4

50 g butter

2 tablespoons dried white breadcrumbs

1 Melt the butter in a frying pan and fry the crumbs very slowly until they have absorbed most of it and are golden and crisp.
2 Serve in a warmed bowl, handed with any sauce(s).

NOTE: Fresh white breadcrumbs can also be used, but rather more butter will be needed as they are very absorbent. Great care should be taken to fry slowly so that the crumbs become crisp as well as brown.

GAME CHIPS

SERVES 4

500 g potatoes (each potato should be
  roughly the same size)

oil, for deep-frying
salt

1 Peel the potatoes and shape them into cylinders of similar diameter.

2 Slice very thinly into rounds using a mandolin or very sharp cook's knife.

3 Soak the potato slices in cold water for 10 minutes to remove some of the surface starch, as this will improve their crispness.

4 Dry thoroughly in a clean tea towel because water will cause the fat to spit as the potato slices fry.

5 Heat the oil in a deep-fryer (see Warning, page 53) and test the temperature with a couple of potato slices: if they rise to the surface within a minute or so, the oil is ready.

6 Lower the first batch of potato slices into the hot oil and gently move them around with a metal slotted spoon to prevent them from sticking to one another. As the slices cook and dry out, they will rise to the surface. Allow them to cook a little longer until they are crisp and light golden.

7 Using a metal slotted spoon, place the cooked potato slices on kitchen paper and allow to drain. Sprinkle lightly with salt.

8 The game chips should be served immediately, or placed in a warm oven to remain crisp until they are to be served.

Wine: Red Burgundy, Chianti Classico, Chilean Pinot Noir, Alsace or German Riesling

Salmis of Pheasant with Dried Cranberries and Thyme

A salmis is a method of cooking game in which it is partially roasted, then jointed before being casseroled in a wine-based sauce. It is a particularly good way of cooking older game birds.

SERVES 4

2 oven-ready pheasants

4 rashers of streaky bacon

2 bay leaves

4 large shallots

150 ml white wine

300 ml White Chicken Stock (see page 451)

4 sprigs of thyme

50 g dried cranberries

salt and freshly ground black pepper

2 tablespoons flat leaf parsley, chopped, to garnish

For the sauce

2 tablespoons plain flour

2–4 tablespoons double cream

1 Heat the oven to 200°C/400°F/gas mark 6.

2 Wipe the birds and remove any remaining feathers. Season inside with salt and pepper.

3 Tie 2 rashers of bacon over the breast of each bird with string to prevent drying out during cooking. Season with salt and pepper. Tuck the bay leaves inside the birds.

4 Place the pheasants on a rack in a roasting pan breast-side up.

5 Halve the shallots lengthwise, then peel. Place on the rack with the pheasants. Roast for about 30–40 minutes. The pheasants should be browned but only half-cooked.

6 Remove the pheasants from the oven and allow to stand for 10 minutes to cool a little. Turn the oven down to 150°C/300°F/gas mark 2. Reserve the fat from the roasting pan.

7 Wearing rubber gloves to protect your hands from the heat of the birds, joint the pheasants into 4 pieces. Place in an ovenproof casserole along with the shallots, bacon and bay leaves.

8 Pour over the wine and stock, then add the thyme and cranberries.

9 Bring to a simmer on top of the stove, then cover the casserole with a lid and place in the oven and cook for a further 35–40 minutes.

10 Remove the casserole from the oven. Place the pheasant pieces, shallots, bacon, thyme and cranberries in a serving dish. Keep warm if serving immediately, otherwise allow to cool. Skim any fat from the surface of the cooking liquid.

11 Add the flour to the fat from the roasting pan to make a smooth paste. Cook over a medium heat until a russet brown, then whisk in the liquid from the casserole. Boil until syrupy.

12 Stir in the cream and season to taste. Pour over the pheasant and serve garnished with the parsley.

Wine: Rosé Champagne, or a dry rosé or aromatic dry white, or a Merlot

Whiskied Pheasant

SERVES 4

85 g butter

2 oven-ready pheasants

1 onion, finely chopped

60 ml whisky

300 ml double cream

1–2 tablespoons Dijon mustard

juice of 1 lemon

salt and freshly ground black pepper

1 bunch of watercress, to garnish

1 Heat the oven to 190°C/375°F/gas mark 5. Wipe the pheasants and remove any remaining feathers.

2 Melt the butter in a flameproof casserole and gently fry the onion until golden; add the pheasants and brown on all sides.

3 Pour over the whisky and set alight, shaking the pan until the flames subside. Season with salt and pepper, then cover the casserole tightly and cook in the oven for 40–50 minutes, until the pheasants are tender.

4 Remove and joint the birds; keep warm.

5 Place the pan over a high heat and boil the juices to reduce to 2–3 tablespoons, stirring. Gradually add the cream, boiling down the mixture until you have a coating sauce.

6 Remove the pan from the heat, add the mustard and season to taste with salt and pepper. Add the lemon juice, then pour the sauce over the birds and serve garnished with the watercress.

Wine: Rioja, red Burgundy or Chianti Classico

Pheasant Breasts with Pancetta and Rosemary

At Leiths this is served on top of Carrot and Courgette 'Pappardelle' (see page 499), but it is also good with mashed potatoes.

SERVES 4

4 boneless, skinless pheasant breasts

4 sprigs of fresh rosemary, finely chopped

125 g pancetta or dry-cured streaky bacon, thinly sliced

salt and freshly ground black pepper

1 small bunch of watercress, to garnish

1 Heat the oven to 200°C/400°F/gas mark 6.

2 Wipe the pheasant breasts and season lightly with salt and pepper.

3 Sprinkle the rosemary on each breast and cover with the pancetta slices, folding the overlap underneath.

4 Place the breasts on an oiled baking sheet, cover tightly with foil and bake for 5 minutes. Remove the foil and cook for a further 10 minutes, or until the pheasant is cooked (see The Test of the Thumb, page 20) and the pancetta is lightly browned.

5 Transfer to a warmed serving dish, garnish with the watercress and serve.

Wine: Dry white, such as Fiano di Avellino

Griddled Pheasant Breasts with Marsala and Prune Sauce and Creamed Cavolo Nero

SERVES 4

4 boneless, skinless pheasant breasts

2 tablespoons olive oil

2 teaspoons lemon thyme leaves

For the sauce

110 g mi-cuit prunes, roughly chopped (see Note)

200 ml hot tea

30 g unsalted butter

1 large onion, very finely sliced

½ tablespoon soft light brown sugar

100 ml Marsala

100 ml Brown Stock (see page 452)

salt and freshly ground black pepper

For the cavolo nero

15 g unsalted butter

1 head of cavolo nero, very finely shredded, blanched and refreshed

finely grated zest of ½ a lemon

50 ml mascarpone cheese

50 ml double cream

1 Place the pheasant breasts in a shallow dish, pour over the oil and sprinkle with the thyme leaves. Cover and leave to marinate in a cool place for 30 minutes.

2 Put the prunes into a bowl and pour over the hot tea. Leave to soak for 15 minutes.

3 Heat the butter in a frying pan and sweat the onion until soft but not coloured. Stir in the sugar, increase the heat and cook for a further minute, until the onions are lightly caramelized.

4 Strain the prunes, reserving the tea, and set aside.

5 Add the Marsala to the pan, along with the stock and reserved tea, and season with salt and pepper. Bring to the boil, reduce the heat and simmer gently for 20 minutes, or until reduced by half and the liquid is thick and syrupy. Stir in the prunes.

6 Heat a griddle pan and, when very hot, place the pheasant breasts on it. Brown well on both sides. Reduce the heat and cook for a further 1½ minutes on each side, or until pink in the middle. Allow to rest for 5 minutes before carving into thick slices.

7 Meanwhile, prepare the cavolo nero: heat the butter in a large saucepan, then add the cavolo nero and lemon zest. Stir in the mascarpone and cream, bring to the boil and cook for 2–3 minutes, or until the cavolo nero is hot and the cream has thickened to a light coating consistency. Season with salt and pepper.

8 To serve, place a spoonful of the creamed cavolo nero on warmed serving plates. Sit the sliced pheasant breasts on top and spoon the prunes around. Pour over the sauce and serve immediately.

NOTE: If mi-cuit or semi-dried prunes are not available, use dried prunes, soaking them in hot tea (an Earl Grey infusion, if you wish) for 5–10 minutes before draining and using as instructed above.

Wine: Red Burgundy or Montepulciano d'Abruzzo

Warm Pheasant Breast with Walnut and Pomegranate Salad

SERVES 4

1½ tablespoons oil

4 boneless, skinless pheasant breasts

2 pomegranates

1 tablespoon water

1½ tablespoons raspberry vinegar

½ teaspoon clear honey

2 tablespoons walnut oil

1 head of radicchio, finely sliced

50 g walnuts, lightly toasted

salt and freshly ground black pepper

1 Heat the oil in a large frying pan. Season the pheasant breasts with salt and pepper and fry until browned on both sides.

2 Reduce the heat and continue to cook for a further 5 minutes, or until pink and juicy in the middle.

3 Meanwhile, cut the pomegranates in half and remove the seeds, discarding the tough white membrane.

4 Remove the pheasant breasts from the pan and allow to rest for 5 minutes.

5 Return the pan to the heat and add the water, scraping the bottom to remove any sediment. Add the vinegar and honey. Season with salt and pepper and bring to the boil. Remove from the heat and whisk in the walnut oil.

6 Put the radicchio leaves, walnuts and pomegranate seeds into a bowl, add the warm dressing and mix lightly. Divide between 4 large plates.

7 Slice the warm pheasant breasts into 4 thick slices and place on top of the salad. Serve immediately.

Wine: Dry rosé or Alsace Pinot Blanc

Cider-casseroled Pheasants

SERVES 4

4 tablespoons vegetable oil

1 large onion, chopped

2 oven-ready pheasants

2 cloves of garlic, thinly sliced

850 ml dry cider

300 ml White Chicken Stock (see page 451)

30 g butter

250 g chestnut or cap mushrooms, quartered

2 teaspoons cornflour

50 ml double cream or crème fraîche

1 tablespoon finely chopped fresh parsley

salt and freshly ground black pepper

1 Wipe the pheasants and remove any remaining feathers.

2 Place half the oil in a small saucepan and stir in the onion. Cover with a piece of dampened greaseproof paper and a lid and cook over low heat for 10–15 minutes, or until softened.

3 Heat the oven to 150°C/300°F/gas mark 2.

4 Place the remaining oil in a large flameproof casserole over a medium heat.

5 Season the pheasants with salt and pepper. Brown well on all sides, then transfer to a plate.

6 Stir the softened onions into the casserole and add the garlic. Cook for 1 minute.

7 Add the cider and allow to boil for 1 minute, scraping any sediment from the bottom of the pan.

8 Return the pheasants to the casserole and add the stock. Bring to a simmer, then cover and place in the oven for 1½ hours.

9 In the meantime, melt the butter in a frying pan and sauté the mushrooms for about 10 minutes, or until cooked through. Set aside.

10 When the pheasants are tender remove them from the casserole. Wearing rubber gloves to protect your hands, joint each bird into 6 pieces (this is done in the same way as chicken, but without dividing the breasts, see page 266). Place in a serving dish and keep warm.

11 Boil the sauce until the flavour is good but the consistency is still a little too runny. Add the mushrooms.

12 Mix the cornflour into the cream, then whisk into the sauce. Boil for 1 minute. Taste and add salt or pepper if required. Pour the sauce over the pheasants and serve.

Drink: Red or white Burgundy, or dry cider

Pheasant and Pistachio Terrine

This terrine needs to be made at least one day in advance of serving. It can be frozen for up to one month.

MAKES 12 SLICES

650 g strips of skinless, boneless
  pheasant (or duck)
4 tablespoons brandy or port
12 rashers of streaky bacon
225 g pork back fat
250 g chicken livers, cleaned
1 teaspoon salt
freshly ground black pepper
2 shallots, peeled and chopped
1 clove of garlic, crushed (optional)

1 teaspoon juniper berries, crushed
pinch of ground cloves
1 tablespoon chopped parsley
50 g shelled pistachio nuts
3 bay leaves
salad leaves, to garnish

To serve
chutney or Cumberland Sauce (see page 475)

1 Place the strips of pheasant in a non-corrosive dish and pour over the brandy. Cover with cling film and leave to marinate for at least 2 hours, or overnight in the refrigerator.
2 Stretch the bacon with the back of a knife and use all but 3 or 4 rashers to line a 1.1 litre terrine or loaf tin.
3 Put the pork back fat, chicken livers, salt, pepper, shallots, garlic, juniper berries, cloves and parsley in a food processor and whizz to a purée.
4 Heat the oven to 170°C/325°F/gas mark 3. Place a roasting pan half-filled with water (bain-marie) in the centre of the oven.
5 Spread a thin layer of the chicken liver mixture over the bottom of the terrine. Cover with a layer of marinated pheasant and sprinkle with some of the pistachio nuts. Continue layering until these ingredients are used up.
6 Cover the top of the terrine with the remaining bacon and place the bay leaves on top. Cover with a piece of greaseproof paper and a lid.
7 Place the terrine in the bain-marie and bake for about 1¼ hours, or until a metal skewer inserted in the centre comes out hot.
8 Remove from the bain-marie, take off the lid and allow to cool for about 10 minutes, then place a weight on top of the terrine to compress the meat. When completely cold, refrigerate overnight.
9 Turn out the terrine and discard the bay leaves. Serve sliced with chutney or Cumberland sauce and a salad garnish.

Wine: Aromatic, fruity white, such as Alsace Vendange Tardive or German Auslese

Pheasant and Duck Liver Terrine with Morello Cherry Relish

This rich terrine can be made two or three days in advance, and stored in the refrigerator, wrapped in a double layer of greaseproof paper, to keep it moist. It can be thinly sliced and served with melba toast for a dinner party, or cut into thick slices and served with salad and a large chunk of warm soda bread for lunch.

MAKES 10–12 SLICES

1 oven-ready pheasant
60 g unsalted butter, plus extra for greasing
675 g belly of pork, skin removed, cut into
  small cubes
110 g duck livers, cleaned and picked over
4 juniper berries, crushed
125 ml ruby port
2 tablespoons armagnac

1 large egg, beaten
20 slices of pancetta
flaky sea salt and freshly ground black pepper

To serve
Morello Cherry Relish (see opposite)
Melba Toast or Soda Bread
  (see page 496 or 497)

1 Heat the oven to 200°C/400°F/gas mark 6.
2 Place the pheasant in a roasting pan and smear with the butter. Roast for 20 minutes.
3 Allow to cool, then pick off the meat. Discard the skin and bones.
4 Roughly chop the pheasant meat, belly pork and duck livers in a food processor, or by hand for a coarser finish.
5 Add the crushed juniper berries, port, armagnac and beaten egg, and season with salt and pepper. Mix well.
6 Cover and leave to rest in a cool place for 1–1½ hours.
7 Heat the oven again to 170°C/325°F/gas mark 3.
8 Line a 1.1 litre terrine or loaf tin with two-thirds of the pancetta. Press the pheasant mixture into the lined terrine and cover with the remaining pancetta.
9 Cover the terrine with buttered greaseproof paper and a double layer of foil. Seal well.
10 Place the terrine in a bain-marie (see page 387) and cook for 1¾–2 hours. Remove from the bain-marie, place a small weight on top and allow to cool. When completely cold, refrigerate overnight.
11 To serve, unmould the terrine and cut into slices. Serve with the cherry relish and melba toast or warm soda bread.

MORELLO CHERRY RELISH

Although the fresh cherries in this recipe need to be stoned, a cherry stoner is not essential as the fruit breaks down and loses its shape during the cooking process. The cherries can therefore be cut in half at this point for the stones to be extracted. The relish works well with most types of game and poultry, and is particularly good in turkey sandwiches.

MAKES ABOUT 450 G

1 tablespoon oil

1 large onion, finely chopped

140 g dried morello cherries

50 g soft dark brown sugar

1 star anise

good pinch of ground allspice

340 g fresh cherries, stoned

2 tablespoons balsamic vinegar

flaky sea salt and freshly ground black pepper

1 Heat the oil in a saucepan. Add the onion and cover with a piece of dampened greaseproof paper and a lid. Cook very gently over a low heat for 10–15 minutes, or until very soft but not coloured.

2 Place the dried cherries in a bowl and pour over enough boiling water to cover. Leave to stand whilst the onions are cooking.

3 Drain the dried cherries, reserving a little of the liquid, and add them to the softened onions with the sugar, star anise and allspice. Season with salt and black pepper, and stir until the sugar dissolves.

4 Add the fresh cherries to the pan and bring to the boil. Reduce the heat and cover the pan. Simmer gently for about 10 minutes, or until the fruit is very soft, stirring occasionally. If the mixture looks dry, stir in a little of the reserved soaking liquid. This will prevent the fruit from catching at the bottom of the pan before the cherries begin to release their juices.

5 Stir in the vinegar and bring to the boil. Cook rapidly for 3–4 minutes, or until the mixture is bubbling and has a soft, jammy consistency. Allow to cool slightly and adjust the seasoning. Cool completely before using.

Wine: Alsace Pinot Gris, or a young Australian Shiraz

Autumn Terrine with Kumquat Syrup and Hazelnut Salad

This is quintessentially an autumn dish, combining game, hazelnuts and kumquats, which are at their best during this season. Fresh hazelnuts are both crisp and sweet, and have a flavour that is quite superior to those ready shelled and bought in packets.

MAKES 10–12 SLICES

1 oven-ready pheasant

60 g unsalted butter, plus extra for greasing

675 g belly of pork, skin removed, cut into
    small cubes

110 g duck livers, cleaned and picked over

4 juniper berries, crushed

125 ml ruby port

2 tablespoons armagnac

1 large egg, beaten

20 slices of pancetta

flaky sea salt and freshly ground black pepper

To serve

Kumquat Syrup (see opposite)

Hazelnut Salad (see opposite)

hot crusty bread

unsalted butter

1 Heat the oven to 200°C/400°F/gas mark 6.
2 Place the bird in a roasting pan and smear with the butter. Roast for 20 minutes.
3 Allow to cool, then pick off the meat. Discard the skin and bones.
4 Roughly chop the pheasant meat, belly pork and duck livers in a food processor, or by hand for a coarser finish. Transfer to a large, non-metallic bowl.
5 Add the juniper berries, port, armagnac and beaten egg, and season well with salt and pepper. Mix thoroughly.
6 Cover and leave to rest in a cool place for 1–1½ hours.
7 Reduce the oven temperature to 170°C/325°F/gas mark 3.
8 Line a 1.1 litre terrine with two-thirds of the pancetta. Press the pheasant mixture into the lined terrine and cover with the remaining pancetta.
9 Cover the terrine with buttered greaseproof paper and a double layer of foil to seal well.
10 Place the terrine in a bain-marie (see page 387) and cook for 1¾–2 hours. Remove from the water, place a heavy weight on top and allow to cool overnight.
11 Serve the terrine in thick slices with the kumquat syrup and hazelnut salad, plus hot bread and unsalted butter.

KUMQUAT SYRUP

SERVES 10–12

1 kg kumquats, cut into quarters

3 cm piece of fresh root ginger, peeled and grated

175 g granulated sugar

75 ml white wine vinegar

75 ml water

1 star anise

½ cinnamon stick

1 Place all the ingredients in a large saucepan and bring to the boil.
2 Reduce the heat and simmer gently for 30–45 minutes, or until the kumquats are very tender.
3 Strain the mixture through a sieve into a clean saucepan, pressing gently to extract the juices. Discard the pulp and spices.
4 Place the pan over a high heat and boil rapidly for 5 minutes, until thick and syrupy. Allow to cool completely.

HAZELNUT SALAD

SERVES 4

140 g blanched hazelnuts

1 tablespoon hazelnut oil

1 tablespoon sherry vinegar

2 bunches of watercress, washed and trimmed

salt and freshly ground black pepper

1 Heat the oven to 200°C/400°F/gas mark 6.
2 Put the hazelnuts on a baking sheet and place on the top shelf of the oven for 5–7 minutes, or until a pale golden brown.
3 Crush the nuts roughly with a rolling pan or a heavy-based saucepan. Transfer to a bowl and, whilst still warm, pour over the oil and vinegar.
4 Place the watercress in a bowl, add the hazelnuts, season with salt and pepper and toss lightly.

Wine: Aromatic, fruity white such as Alsace Vendange Tardive or German Auslese

Moroccan B'stilla

B'stilla is a Moroccan meat pie traditionally made using filo pastry and pigeon. It contains fragrant spices, such as cinnamon and cardamom, and can be served sprinkled with icing sugar to give a sweet/savoury/spicy flavour combination.

MAKES 8–10 SLICES

675 g cooked pigeon breasts, skinned and boned
50 g unsalted butter
4 spring onions, finely chopped
4 eggs, beaten
1 tablespoon ground cinnamon
2 tablespoons sugar
16–20 sheets filo pastry
melted butter
85 g blanched almonds

3 tablespoons flat leaf parsley, roughly chopped
salt and freshly ground black pepper
1 tablespoon icing sugar, to finish

For the spice mixture
¼ teaspoon ground ginger
¼ teaspoon ground cardamom
¼ teaspoon ground cumin
¼ teaspoon ground black pepper

1 Cut the pigeon meat into 5 cm chunks, season with salt and pepper and set aside.
2 Melt the butter in a small saucepan, add the spring onions and cook gently for 5 minutes, until soft and lightly browned. Reduce the heat and add the beaten eggs. Stir gently over the heat until creamy and just set. Season and allow to cool.
3 Mix together the cinnamon and sugar.
4 Heat the oven to 180°C/350°F/gas mark 4. Place a baking sheet in the oven.
5 Line the sides and base of a loose-bottomed, 14 cm diameter cake tin with overlapping sheets of the pastry. Brush with some of the melted butter, sprinkle with half the cinnamon and sugar mixture and cover with a second layer of pastry.
6 Carefully spread half the egg mixture over the pastry and cover with half the diced pigeon.
7 Mix the spices together and sprinkle evenly over the pigeon layer. Cover with the almonds and chopped parsley.
8 Top with another layer of buttered pastry and the remaining sugar and cinnamon.
9 Repeat the egg and pigeon layers.
10 Butter the remaining pastry, then scrunch it up and place on top.
11 Place the cake tin on the hot baking sheet in the centre of the oven for 25–30 minutes. Increase the temperature to 200°C/400°F/gas mark 6 and cook for a further 5 minutes, until well browned and crisp. Allow to cool slightly before removing from the tin. Dust lightly with icing sugar and serve sliced in thick wedges.

NOTE: Cooked skinned chicken breasts can be used in place of the pigeon if preferred.

Wine: A dry rosé or light, fruity red, such as Tarrango from Australia

Warm Pigeon Breasts and Cracked Wheat Salad

Pigeon is a dark purple-coloured meat and should be sautéed or grilled until 'blue' (rare) or, at most, pink (medium-rare) as the meat will toughen with overcooking. In this recipe the pigeon breasts are marinated to enhance their flavour rather than tenderize them. Four boneless, skinless chicken or duck breasts can be substituted for the pigeon breasts, if desired.

SERVES 4

8 pigeon breasts, skinned

115 g bulghar or cracked wheat

2 tablespoons sesame oil

½ red chilli, deseeded and finely chopped

2 cm piece of fresh root ginger, peeled and grated

115 g shiitake mushrooms, sliced

115 g Parma ham, sliced

140 g plum jam

5 spring onions, sliced on the diagonal

50 g sun-dried tomatoes in oil, drained and sliced

lemon juice, to taste

30 g pine nuts, toasted

½ cucumber, deseeded and finely chopped

2 tablespoons oil, for frying

salt and freshly ground black pepper

2 tablespoons chopped fresh chives, to garnish

For the marinade

2 tablespoons Chinese five-spice powder

1 tablespoon light soy sauce

1 Mix together the marinade ingredients and coat the pigeon breasts on both sides. Place in a shallow dish, cover and leave to marinate for at least 30 minutes, or overnight in the refrigerator.

2 Put the cracked wheat into a bowl and cover with boiling water. Leave to stand for 15 minutes. Drain thoroughly, squeeze out any remaining water and spread out to dry on kitchen paper.

3 Heat the sesame oil in a wok or large frying pan, add the chilli, ginger, mushrooms and Parma ham and stir-fry over a high heat for 2–3 minutes. Add the jam, spring onions and sun-dried tomatoes and bring to the boil. Add the cracked wheat and season to taste with salt, pepper and lemon juice. Heat thoroughly and stir in the pine nuts and cucumber. Keep warm.

4 Heat the oil in a frying pan. Season the pigeon breasts with salt, then add to the pan in batches and fry for 3 minutes. Turn and cook for a further 2 minutes, until browned but pink inside.

5 To serve, place 2 pigeon breasts on each of 4 dinner plates and spoon a portion of the cracked wheat salad beside them. Sprinkle with the chives.

Wine: Aromatic dry white or a light red, such as Dolcetto

Warm Pigeon Breasts and Bitter Leaf Salad

SERVES 4

8 pigeon breasts, skinned

oil

salt and freshly ground black pepper

For the salad

1 head of fennel

2 large handfuls of mixed bitter salad leaves, such
   as dandelion, radicchio and frisée, washed
   and torn into bite-sized pieces

85 g hazelnuts, toasted, skinned and roughly chopped

1 tablespoon groundnut oil

1 tablespoon hazelnut oil

1 tablespoon raspberry vinegar

1 Rub the pigeon breasts with a little oil and season with salt and pepper.

2 Heat a griddle pan until it is beginning to smoke. Brown the pigeon breasts quickly on both sides. Reduce the heat and continue to cook for a further minute, or until pink in the middle. Turn off the heat and allow the pigeon to rest on the warm griddle pan while you make the salad.

3 Trim the fennel and reserve the feathery fronds. Slice the fennel as finely as possible and place it in a bowl with the salad leaves and hazelnuts.

4 Whisk together the oils and vinegar and season with salt and pepper. Pour the dressing into the bowl and toss everything together lightly. Divide the salad between 4 serving plates.

5 Cut each of the pigeon breasts in half on an angle and arrange 4 pieces on top of each salad. Garnish with the reserved fennel tops and serve immediately.

Wine: Vouvray or Frascati

Pigeon Pâté on Toasted Brioche with Moscato Jelly and Chicory Salad

SERVES 8–10

1½ tablespoons oil

3 large shallots, finely chopped

1 clove of garlic, crushed

50 g unsalted butter

10 plump wood pigeon breasts, cut into 4–5 pieces

110 g chicken livers, washed and trimmed
   (see page 360)

75 ml tawny port

85 g Pork Sausagemeat (see page 238)

1 large egg, beaten

1 teaspoon thyme leaves

ground allspice

ground mace

12–16 rashers of thin, smoked streaky
   bacon or pancetta

3 bay leaves

salt and freshly ground black pepper

To serve

thick slices of Savoury Brioche (see page 457)

Moscato Jelly (see opposite)

Chicory Salad (see opposite)

1 Heat the oil in a frying pan and sweat the shallots gently until soft but not coloured. Add the garlic and continue to cook for a further minute. Tip the mixture into a bowl.

2 Add half the butter to the pan, increase the heat and, when foaming, fry the pigeon breasts quickly until lightly browned. Add them to the bowl with the shallots.

3 Heat the remaining butter and cook the chicken livers in the same way. Pour the port into the pan and bring to the boil, scraping up any sediment. Add the livers to the pigeon and shallots and allow to cool completely.

4 Heat the oven to 180°C/350°F/gas mark 4.

5 Place the sausagemeat in the bowl of a food processor and add the cooled meat mixture. Add the egg and thyme and season well with allspice, mace, salt and pepper. Process until the mixture comes together but is of a fairly coarse texture.

6 Line a 450–675 g terrine or loaf tin with the bacon. Pile the meat mixture into it. Fold the loose ends of the bacon over the pâté and press the bay leaves firmly on the top. Cover with a piece of greased greaseproof paper, then cover with foil.

7 Stand the terrine in a roasting pan half-filled with hot water and bake in the middle of the oven for 1–1¼ hours. The pâté should feel fairly firm to the touch and be just shrinking away from the sides of the dish. Remove from the pan, place a weight on top and allow to cool. Refrigerate overnight and turn out on to a plate.

8 To serve, toast the brioche on both sides, cut off the crusts and place on serving plates. Slice the pâté thickly and put a piece on top of each slice of brioche. Spoon some of the Moscato jelly on to each plate and serve with the chicory salad.

MOSCATO JELLY

SERVES 8–10

1½ leaves gelatine

150 ml cold water

300 ml Moscato wine

1 Place the gelatine in a bowl with the cold water and leave to soak for 10 minutes.

2 Put 75 ml of the wine into a small saucepan and heat gently. Remove the pan from the heat.

3 Squeeze the excess water from the gelatine and discard the water. Add the softened gelatine to the warm wine, stir until melted, then add to the remaining wine.

4 Pour the wine mixture into a container and place in the refrigerator until set. The jelly should be very soft.

CHICORY SALAD

SERVES 8–10 AS AN ACCOMPANIMENT

1 head of chicory

2 teaspoons mirin

½ teaspoon sunflower oil

flaky sea salt

pinch of paprika

¼ teaspoon poppy seeds

1 Cut the chicory lengthwise into 4 pieces and remove the core. Shred the leaves as finely as possible and place in a bowl with the mirin and oil.

2 Season with salt and a small pinch of paprika. Add the poppy seeds and toss together.

Wine: Aromatic, fruity white or an Austrian or Hungarian Muscat/Muskateller

Tamarind-spiced Quail

The tamarind tree, which is native to Africa, produces fruit that is both sweet and sour, making it a perfect ingredient in dishes that are either rich or spicy, as its sharp, tangy flavour cuts through either fat or heat. It is also referred to as the 'Indian date'. In parts of Asia the seedpods and flowers are pickled and served as side dishes. The Egyptians use it to make refreshing drinks, and the Mexicans use it as an ingredient in confectionery. In this recipe it is used with a mixture of spices to create a crust for quail. The mixture would work equally well with all kinds of game birds, guinea fowl or duck.

SERVES 4

4 oven-ready quail
1 small bunch of watercress, to garnish

For the spice mix

½ teaspoon cayenne
½ teaspoon ground ginger
good pinch of ground cloves
salt and freshly ground black pepper

For the tamarind paste

75 ml pineapple juice
1 tablespoon soft palm sugar
½ tablespoon light soy sauce
3 cm piece of fresh root ginger, peeled and grated
1 tablespoon tamarind paste

1 Split the quail down one side of the backbone with a pair of poultry shears or kitchen scissors (see Spatchcocking, page 319). Cut down the other side of the backbone to remove it. Open out the quail and flatten well on a board by pressing with the heel of your hand.

2 Mix the spices together and rub into the quail on both sides. Leave for 1 hour.

3 Meanwhile, make the tamarind paste. Put all the paste ingredients into a small saucepan and bring to the boil. Reduce the heat and simmer until reduced by half.

4 Heat the grill to its highest setting.

5 Put the quail on to a baking sheet, cut-side uppermost, and brush with half the tamarind paste. Grill for about 10 minutes, brushing frequently with the pan juices. Turn over, brush with the remaining paste and grill for a further 8–10 minutes, or until the quail are cooked. The skin should be crisp and the meat just pink in the middle.

6 Arrange the quail neatly on a warmed serving dish. Pour over the juices from the pan and garnish with watercress.

Wine: Alsace whites, especially Gewürztraminer

Roast Woodcock

SERVES 4

4 woodcock

4 rashers of bacon

4 rounds of white bread 13 cm in diameter,
  toasted on one side

1 teaspoon flour

150 ml stock

squeeze of lemon juice

salt and freshly ground black pepper

watercress, to garnish

1 Pluck the woodcock. Remove the heads and draw the gizzards through the neck openings, but do not draw the entrails. Truss neatly.

2 Heat the oven to 180°C/350°F/gas mark 4.

3 Cover the birds with the bacon and season well. Place in a roasting pan and roast for about 25 minutes, removing the bacon after 20 minutes to allow the breasts to brown thoroughly. Discard the bacon.

4 Spoon out the entrails and spread on the untoasted side of the bread. Place a bird on top of each and keep warm while you prepare the gravy.

5 Tip off all except a scant tablespoon of the fat from the roasting pan.

6 Add the flour and cook until a russet brown.

7 Gradually stir in the stock and bring to the boil, stirring continuously and scraping up any sediment.

8 Season with salt, pepper and lemon juice. Strain into a warmed gravy boat.

9 Place the woodcock on a serving dish and garnish with watercress.

Wine: Rioja, red or white Burgundy, or Chianti Classico

Blackcurrant Tea-smoked Woodcock

Woodcock is traditionally served whole and undrawn, with the head and beak on and the eyes removed. As it is the smallest of the game birds, it is difficult to shoot and therefore rarely available. Given that one whole woodcock is served per head, it makes it especially hard to put them on the menu. If you can get them, this recipe calls for woodcock that are oven ready, that is, without the head and entrails. As the birds freeze well, you can store them until you have the required amount. They must be thoroughly defrosted before smoking.

Smoking the meat makes for a very distinctive and rich flavour, which means it needs to be served only in small portions, which is perfect for a first course or supper dish. The smoking technique used here is straightforward, and works well for other small game birds, or individual portions of meat, such as duck breasts. Other fruit teas, such as raspberry and fruits of the forest, work well too.

SERVES 4 AS PART OF A SALAD

4 blackcurrant-flavoured fruit tea bags
85 g long-grain rice
2 cardamom pods, crushed

2–3 woodcock, drawn and split in 2
along the backbone
salt and freshly ground black pepper

1 Season the woodcock on both sides with salt and pepper.
2 If a home smoker is available, smoke the birds for 15 minutes. Alternatively, use a large roasting pan: sprinkle the contents of the tea bags plus the rice and cardamom pods in the bottom and sit a ramekin of water on top.
3 Place a wire rack on top of the pan and put the prepared woodcock on this. Cover the pan securely with a tent of foil that will allow the smoke generated in the next step to circulate around the birds.
4 Place the pan directly over a low heat for 15–20 minutes. Avoid removing the foil or smoke will escape and the cooking time will be increased. Turn off the heat and allow to cool under the tent. The meat should be pink in the middle.
5 When cool enough to handle, remove the flesh from the woodcock and use as required.

Wine: Red Burgundy, Pinot Noir or a Rioja Reserva

Smoked Woodcock and Broad Bean Salad

SERVES 4

110 g fresh or frozen broad beans, double-podded

30 g unsalted butter

2 tablespoons crème fraîche

squeeze of lemon juice

1 tablespoon salad oil

1 tablespoon raspberry vinegar

2 small handfuls of lambs' lettuce

4 slices of Savoury Brioche, toasted
 (see page 487)

1 quantity Blackcurrant Tea-smoked Woodcock
 (see opposite), cut into bite-sized pieces

salt and freshly ground black pepper

1 Bring a large pan of salted water to the boil and cook the broad beans until they are just tender. Drain and refresh under cold running water.

2 Melt the butter in a pan and add the broad beans. Cook for 1 minute, add the crème fraîche and continue to cook for a further minute. Season to taste with the lemon juice, salt and pepper.

3 Mix the oil and vinegar together in a bowl and season with salt and pepper. Add the lambs' lettuce and toss lightly to coat the leaves, shaking off the excess.

4 Put a piece of hot brioche on each serving plate and divide the broad beans between them. Place some lambs' lettuce on the beans and top with the smoked woodcock. Drizzle the remaining dressing around the plate and serve immediately.

Wine: Châteauneuf-du-Pape or Sangiovese

Roast Snipe with Rosehip Jelly and Pancetta Scratchings

SERVES 4

4 oven-ready snipe

4 teaspoons unsalted butter

4 small sprigs of thyme

2 bay leaves

4 slices of smoked pancetta

2 shallots, finely sliced

1 stick of celery, diced

4 tablespoons Rosehip Jelly (see opposite)

300 ml White Chicken Stock (see page 451)

1 teaspoon cornflour

salt and freshly ground black pepper

1 Heat the oven to 190°C/375°F/gas mark 5.

2 Season the cavities of the snipe with salt and pepper. Place a teaspoon of butter, a sprig of thyme and half a bay leaf inside each of them and cover with a slice of pancetta.

3 Put the shallot and celery into a large roasting pan and set the snipe on top. Roast on the top shelf of the oven for 15 minutes.

4 Remove the pancetta from the snipe and reserve. Spread 1 tablespoon of rosehip jelly over each of the birds and pour the stock around them. Return to the oven for a further 10 minutes.

5 Lift the birds from the roasting pan and leave to rest in a warm place. Strain the stock through a fine sieve into a bowl. Discard the vegetables.

6 Place the roasting pan directly over a low heat and add the cornflour. Cook for 1 minute, scraping up any sediment. Gradually add the strained stock to the pan, stirring constantly. Bring to the boil and simmer gently for 5 minutes, or until syrupy. Season to taste.

7 Meanwhile, heat the grill to its highest setting and grill the reserved pancetta on both sides until brown and very crisp.

8 Cut each snipe in half and discard the herbs. Arrange the birds on a warmed serving platter and spoon the gravy over and around them. Garnish with the crumbled pancetta.

ROSEHIP JELLY

This luxurious, clear, fragrant jelly is a perfect and unusual accompaniment to rich, strongly flavoured or fatty meats. It can be used as a glaze, being brushed on to the skin or flesh of meat in the final stages of cooking, or can be added to sauces and gravies to enhance their flavour and give added consistency and shine. A softer set and therefore more acidic jelly can be achieved by reducing the amount of sugar added to the purée before boiling.

Feathered game is particularly well suited to the aromatic qualities of rosehips, and a perfect match in terms of seasonality, being synonymous with autumn and the start of the game season. However, as they are not available for sale, they need either to be foraged from hedgerows, or picked from the garden once rose bushes or shrubs have finished flowering. If neither of these is an option, or the harvest is too small to make a reasonable quantity of jelly, the hips can be mixed with or replaced by other fruits, such as blackberries, blackcurrants, redcurrants, sloes, hawthorn berries, elderberries or crab apples, as all of these contain sufficient pectin to ensure that the jelly sets, and can be found during the autumn.

rosehips water

golden granulated sugar

1 Put the rosehips into a large saucepan and add enough water to cover three-quarters of the fruit. Bring to the boil, then reduce the heat and simmer gently until the fruit is tender, mashing occasionally to extract as much of the juice and flavour as possible.
2 Suspend a scalded jelly bag or several layers of muslin over a large bowl, and carefully ladle in the hot fruit pulp and juices. Allow to drip for several hours or overnight. Do not squeeze the bag.
3 Measure the juice and pour into a large pan. Add 450 g sugar to each 600 ml of juice.
4 Bring to the boil slowly, stirring constantly, ensuring that the sugar has dissolved before the juice has boiled.
5 Boil briskly, uncovered, for about 10 minutes, skimming frequently. Test for setting point (see Note).
6 When this has been reached, pour into warm, sterilized jars and cover.

NOTE: Setting point can be tested by placing a small amount of the jelly on a very cold small plate or saucer. If the mixture wrinkles when gently pushed with a finger, it is ready.

Wine: Riesling or Gewürztraminer from Alsace, Chile or elsewhere

Preparing and Cooking Furred Game

Drawing Game

Most large game, such as venison, is drawn, which means the innards are removed. This is done as soon as the animal is killed to allow the carcass to cool down quickly and delay the onset of deterioration. Rabbits, though much smaller, are given the same treatment because their digestive juices quickly cause the surrounding meat to deteriorate. In this case, drawing is referred to as 'paunching'.

Rabbit

Rabbits are herbivores that graze on grass, small plants and weeds. They are able to reproduce at a very young age and, with a gestation period of just 28–31 days, can produce litters of up to seven kittens four or five times a year. They produce exceptionally nutritious milk, and the kittens are usually weaned within a month. A doe may become pregnant again in as little as four days after the birth of a litter.

Native to Morocco and the Iberian peninsular, rabbits are now found throughout the world, largely due to the actions of sailors who introduced them to new habitats so they would have a supply of meat when they next visited. In 14th-century England rabbit was a highly prized meat.

The flesh of wild rabbit is gamier and less tender than farmed, which has pale flesh rather like chicken. If the rabbit has not been skinned, look for smooth, sharp claws and delicate, soft ears. The meat is lean and tender, low in fat and high in protein, and suitable for roasting, grilling, sautéing or cooking slowly by braising and stewing. However, a wild rabbit weighing more than 1 kg is likely to be tough, and therefore always better suited to long, slow methods of cooking.

Rabbit meat should be cooked through and is often served with sauces flavoured with mustard. When roasted, rabbit may be stuffed with any stuffings suitable for poultry, and must be basted well to prevent the lean meat from drying out. Before cooking, rabbit is often soaked – in cold salted water, with a little vinegar added, or milk – to whiten the flesh.

Skinning a rabbit
1 Cut off the four feet above the knee.
2 Place the rabbit on a work surface with the tail nearest to you.
3 Make a 3 cm cut across the belly to the width of the thighs.
4 Pull the skin towards the tail, turning the thighs out as you might turn a glove inside out.
5 Continue pulling the skin towards the tail, until the whole lower body is skinned.
6 Turn the body over so that the head is nearest you and firmly pull the skin towards the head. Turn out the legs, working on one at a time. Pull the skin off towards the head end.
7 Cut off the head with the skin.

Jointing a rabbit
1 Remove the hind legs by cutting through the joint between the legs and the body. Cut the fore legs away from the ribs.

2 Chop the saddle across the width into 2 pieces.

3 If you want 8 pieces rather than 6, separate the thighs from the drumsticks.

Boning a saddle of rabbit or hare

A saddle of rabbit is very similar in shape to a saddle of lamb (see page 152). However, the rib bones of furred game are very fine and brittle, and boning out the saddle can be a fiddly business.

1 Place the rabbit saddle, underside uppermost, on a chopping board.

2 With a sharp, fine-bladed knife, and starting at the chump end, run the blade between the meat and the rib bones using a gentle scraping action. It is important to keep the knife angled towards the rib bones in order to prevent cutting into the meat.

3 Repeat on the other side. Once the meat is released, lift the whole saddle in one piece.

Roasting Times for Furred Game

Venison is cooked in the same way as beef (see Beef Roasting Table, page 33) and rabbit and hare the same way as chicken (see page 262).

Flavouring with Fruit and Alcohol

The addition of dried fruit in meat dishes, specifically in a stew, serves to enrich and sweeten a sauce or gravy. Prunes, for example, can be added at the beginning of cooking in order for them to break down completely and give a syrupy quality to the dish, acting rather like a thickening ingredient. If added towards the end of cooking, they will plump up as they absorb some of the cooking liquor, but remain whole and act as a garnish to the pieces of meat.

The combination of rabbit with prunes is classic. The gamy flavour of rabbit meat, particularly that of wild rabbit, demands the rich, full-bodied, winey quality that prunes deliver. They in themselves have a 'meaty' texture and depth of flavour that is upheld in a strong meat sauce, whereas a less powerful fruit, such as the dried apricot, lends itself to the softer-textured, sweeter meat of lamb.

If steeped in alcohol before being added to a recipe, the prunes will absorb the liquid, swell and take on an even more powerful flavour. Fortified wines, such as Madeira and Marsala, are excellent partners for prunes as they add some extra sweetness, with an almost burnt caramel edge. Those looking for the richness and body of a macerated prune with a less sweet flavour will find armagnac or port to be good choices. This method of soaking the fruit first, especially if heated and then left to stand for a few minutes, means that very little alcohol will go a long way: the flavour is enhanced during the 'brewing'.

Cider, either apple or pear, also complements rabbit dishes well, but gives a much lighter result in both the colour and flavour of the finished dish. In this case, dried apple rings or pear halves could be added to the sauce in place of prunes. The addition of a little Calvados or Poire William would make for a real sense of occasion.

The experienced or experimental cook might choose to draw upon some of the following rabbit recipes in terms of ingredient quantities, but ring the changes using some of the ideas outlined here.

Provençal Rabbit with Prunes, Artichokes and Olives

This recipe is also delicious made with chicken thighs.

SERVES 4

1 large oven-ready rabbit, jointed into 8 pieces
  (see page 402)

milk

2 cloves of garlic, crushed

½ tablespoon dried Herbes de Provence

2 tablespoons sherry vinegar

3 tablespoons olive oil

1 tablespoon capers, rinsed

10 stoned prunes

100 g baby artichokes in oil

10 large, pitted green olives

1 lemon, cut into 8 wedges

1 tablespoon brown sugar

salt and freshly ground black pepper

2 tablespoons chopped fresh parsley, to garnish

salt and freshly ground black pepper

1 Heat the oven to 180°C/350°F/gas mark 4.
2 If the rabbit is at all bloody, soak it in milk for 10 minutes, then discard the milk. Rinse the rabbit and pat dry.
3 Rub the garlic into the rabbit pieces and place in a single layer in an ovenproof dish.
4 Sprinkle over the herbs, vinegar, olive oil and capers.
5 Tuck the prunes, artichokes, olives and lemon wedges around the rabbit pieces.
6 Sprinkle with the brown sugar, salt and pepper.
7 Cover with foil and bake for 50 minutes. Remove the foil and bake for a further 15 minutes, or until the rabbit is cooked through and lightly browned. Test for doneness in the same way as chicken pieces (see Testing Roast Meat for Doneness, page 14).
8 Sprinkle with the parsley to serve.

Wine: Sancerre

Rabbit with Mustard and Tarragon Sauce

The preparation of this dish begins a day in advance.

SERVES 4

1 oven-ready rabbit

2½ tablespoons Dijon mustard

1 teaspoon chopped fresh tarragon

45 g butter or bacon dripping

85 g bacon or salt pork, diced

1 onion, finely chopped

1 clove of garlic, crushed

1 teaspoon plain flour

600 ml White Chicken Stock (see page 451)

2 tablespoons chopped fresh parsley, to garnish

salt and freshly ground black pepper

1 If the rabbit's head has not been removed, cut it off with a sharp, heavy knife. Joint the rabbit into 6 pieces, following the instructions on page 402.

2 If the rabbit is at all bloody, soak it in cold salted water for 1 hour.

3 Combine 2 tablespoons of the mustard with the tarragon, then spread over the rabbit pieces. Cover and refrigerate overnight.

4 The following day, heat the oven to 170°C/325°F/gas mark 3.

5 Heat the butter or dripping in a frying pan. Pat the rabbit pieces dry, season with salt and pepper, then brown them all over. Using a slotted spoon, transfer them to a casserole.

6 Add the bacon or salt pork and onion to the pan and cook over a low heat until the onions are soft and just browned. Add the garlic and cook for 1 minute. Stir in the flour and cook for 1 minute.

7 Remove the pan from the heat and stir in the stock. Return to the heat and bring the sauce to the boil, stirring continuously.

8 Pour the sauce over the rabbit. Cook in the oven for 1½ hours, or until the rabbit is tender.

9 Lift the rabbit on to a warmed serving dish. Add the remaining ½ tablespoon of mustard to the sauce. Reduce it by boiling rapidly until it is shiny and rich in appearance. Check the seasoning. Pour the sauce over the rabbit pieces.

10 Sprinkle with the parsley and serve.

Wine: White Burgundy or other less aromatic dry white

Wild Rabbit Stew with Cider and Prunes

SERVES 6–8

2 rashers of green streaky bacon (see page 222), chopped

2 wild rabbits, skinned and jointed (see page 404)

1 large onion, finely sliced

2 tablespoons Calvados

300 ml medium cider

300 ml Brown Stock (see page 452)

16 prunes, pitted

2 sprigs of thyme

2 bay leaves

salt and freshly ground black pepper

1 Gently fry the bacon in a frying pan until the fat runs.

2 Discard the bacon and fry the rabbit pieces, a few at a time, until nicely browned. Transfer to a casserole.

3 Add the onion to the pan and cook gently, covered with a piece of dampened greaseproof paper, until softened. Increase the heat and cook for a further minute until well browned. Add to the casserole.

4 Warm the Calvados and carefully set alight. Pour over the rabbit. When the flames subside, add the cider, stock, prunes, thyme and bay leaves. Season with salt and pepper and bring to the boil.

5 Cover with a tight-fitting lid and simmer for 1¼ hours, or until the meat is very tender and falling from the bone. Discard the thyme and bay leaves.

6 Using a slotted spoon, transfer the meat to a warmed serving dish. Keep warm.

7 Boil the sauce to a syrupy consistency and pour over the meat.

Drink: Red Burgundy, New World Pinot Noir or Chilean Merlot; or a dry cider

Rabbit Ravioli

SERVES 4

225 g flour weight Egg Pasta (see page 488)

For the filling

450 g rabbit

1 tablespoon oil

3 onions, finely chopped

1 teaspoon soft dark brown sugar

1 tablespoon balsamic vinegar

300 ml White Chicken Stock (see page 451)

3 tablespoons finely chopped fresh thyme

juice of ½ a lemon

pinch of cayenne pepper

salt and freshly ground black pepper

For the sauce

150 ml dry white wine

150 ml White Chicken Stock (see page 451)

1 tablespoon dry sherry

200 ml double cream

1 tablespoon grainy mustard

salt and freshly ground white pepper

1 Make the pasta, then wrap in cling film and leave to relax in a cool place for 1 hour.

2 Skin, bone and mince the rabbit finely. Set aside.

3 Heat the oil in a heavy-based frying pan and sweat the onions until soft and translucent.

4 Add the sugar, increase the heat and stir until the onions are a dark golden brown. Add the vinegar, then remove the mixture from the pan.

5 Add more oil to the pan if it seems dry and brown the minced rabbit meat thoroughly.

6 Return the onion mixture to the pan with the stock, thyme, lemon juice, cayenne and salt and pepper. Simmer for about 45 minutes, or until all the liquid has evaporated and the rabbit is tender. Taste and add extra salt and pepper if necessary. Leave to cool.

7 Roll out the pasta as thinly as possible and stamp out circles using a 7.5 cm round cutter.

8 Put a heaped teaspoon of the rabbit mixture in the centre of half the circles. Wet the edges and cover with the remaining pasta circles. Press the edges together firmly to seal and eliminate any air bubbles. Leave to dry on a wire rack for 30 minutes.

9 To make the sauce, put the wine into a saucepan and boil rapidly to reduce by one-third. Add the stock and sherry and boil again to reduce by half.

10 Add the cream and reduce again by about half, or until the sauce coats the back of a spoon. Add the mustard and season to taste with salt and white pepper.

11 Cook the pasta in a large pan of boiling salted water until tender (about 4–6 minutes).

12 To serve, drain the pasta well, arrange on 4 warm serving plates and pour over the sauce.

Wine: A buttery white Burgundy

Warm Pan-fried Rabbit and Black Pudding Salad with Marsala Prunes

SERVES 4 AS A FIRST COURSE

85 g mi-cuit pitted prunes (see page 384)

1½ tablespoons Marsala

1 tablespoon oil

4 slices of smoked pancetta

2 saddles of rabbit, boned (see page 403)

4 × 1 cm thick slices black pudding

1 tablespoon water

2 tablespoons olive oil

1 tablespoon sherry vinegar

½ small head of fennel, sliced very finely on a mandolin

juice of ½ a small lemon

1 large bunch of flat leaf parsley, roughly chopped

salt and freshly ground black pepper

1 Place the prunes in a small saucepan and cover with water, bring to the boil, then drain. Put the hot prunes into a small bowl and pour over the Marsala. Leave to macerate for 30 minutes, stirring occasionally, then chop roughly.

2 Heat ½ tablespoon of the oil in a frying pan and fry the pancetta until very crisp and brown. Using a slotted spoon, transfer the pancetta to kitchen paper to drain, and set aside. Reserve the unwashed pan.

3 Season the rabbit with salt and pepper and fry in the pan until golden brown. Lower the heat and continue to cook for a further 25–30 minutes, or until cooked through. Remove the rabbit from the pan and slice thickly. Keep warm.

4 Heat the remaining oil in the pan and fry the black pudding for 1 minute on each side. Remove from the pan and drain on kitchen paper. Keep warm.

5 Pour the water, olive oil and vinegar into the hot pan and bring to the boil. Season with salt and pepper and turn off the heat.

6 To assemble the salad, place the fennel in a large bowl and sprinkle over the lemon juice. Add the rabbit, chopped prunes and parsley to the bowl. Crumble over the pancetta and pour in the hot dressing. Toss everything together very gently and divide between 4 serving plates. Top each plate with a slice of black pudding and serve immediately.

Wine: Côtes-du-Rhône or less aromatic dry white

Pan-fried Rabbit with Fresh Peas, Broad Beans and Monbazillac Sauce

SERVES 4

1 tablespoon oil

2 saddles of rabbit, boned (see page 403)

1 large shallot, finely chopped

75 ml Monbazillac wine

75 ml Brown Stock (see page 452)

140 g fresh peas, blanched

140 g fresh broad beans, blanched and double-podded

30 g unsalted butter

flaky sea salt and freshly ground black pepper

warm crusty bread, to serve

1 Heat the oil in a sauté pan and brown the rabbit well on both sides. Reduce the heat and fry gently until just cooked through. Transfer to a plate and keep warm.

2 Add the shallot to the pan and fry gently until browned.

3 Pour the wine and stock into the pan and bring to the boil. Boil rapidly until reduced by half.

4 Return the rabbit to the pan along with the peas and broad beans. Simmer gently for 2–3 minutes, or until the peas and beans are cooked through.

5 Whisk in the butter and season with sea salt flakes and pepper. Serve with warm crusty bread.

Wine: Light, fruity red or aromatic dry white, such as Riesling

Pan-fried Saddle of Rabbit with Mustard Cream Sauce

SERVES 4

1½ tablespoons clear honey

½ teaspoon very finely chopped thyme leaves

¼ teaspoon paprika

2 tablespoons wholegrain mustard

2 saddles of rabbit, boned (see page 403)

4 slices of Parma ham

1 tablespoon oil

75 ml dry white wine

2 tablespoons Muscat wine

300 ml White Chicken Stock (see page 451)

75 ml double cream

salt and freshly ground black pepper

sprigs of flat leaf parsley, to garnish

1 Mix together the honey, thyme leaves, paprika and 1½ tablespoons of the mustard in a small bowl. Season with salt and pepper.

2 Spread the mixture over the rabbit saddles and wrap each of them in 2 slices of Parma ham.

3 Heat the oil in a heavy-based frying pan and brown the parcels very gently on both sides. Reduce the heat, then cover the pan with a lid and cook very gently for 30–35 minutes, or until the rabbit is cooked through.

4 Lift the rabbit from the pan with a slotted spoon and keep warm. Return the pan to the heat and pour in the wine, Muscat and stock. Bring to the boil, scraping up the sediment, and reduce the liquid to about half of its original volume.

5 Pour the cream into the pan and simmer for 1–2 minutes, or until the sauce is of a light coating consistency. Season with salt and pepper.

6 Cut each of the rabbit saddles into thick slices and place on warmed serving plates. Pour over the sauce and garnish with the parsley. Serve immediately.

Wine: Red or white Burgundy, or a less aromatic dry white

Mustard Rabbit Liver and Bacon Salad

MAKES 4 SMALL FIRST-COURSE PORTIONS

2–3 tablespoons oil

4 slices of smoked pancetta

340 g cooked Anya or baby new potatoes, cut in half

225–250 g rabbit livers, washed and picked over

½ tablespoon wholegrain mustard

1 tablespoon sherry vinegar

30 g sun-blushed tomatoes, roughly chopped

2 punnets mixed leaf micro-cress or mustard and cress, washed and trimmed

salt and freshly ground black pepper

1 Heat 1 tablespoon of the oil in a frying pan and fry the pancetta on both sides until very crisp. Drain on kitchen paper and set aside.

2 Add a further tablespoon of oil to the pan and mix with the fat that has run from the pancetta, scraping up any crusty sediment. Add the potatoes and fry briskly until brown, very crisp and hot through. Remove from the pan and keep warm.

3 If necessary, add the remaining oil, and fry the livers over a high heat until browned but still pink in the middle.

4 Add the mustard and vinegar to the pan and season with salt and pepper. Stir in the tomatoes.

5 Gently stir the mixed cresses and potatoes together and arrange on warmed serving plates.

6 Spoon over the liver and tomatoes and serve with the pancetta crumbled over the top.

NOTES: It is important to cook the livers quickly and keep them pink in the middle as they will dry out and become tough if overcooked.

An average rabbit liver weighs 45–55 g, so this recipe makes four small first-course portions. If you are lucky enough to find a butcher who will supply you with larger quantities, double up the ingredients for a more substantial lunch dish.

Wine: Sauvignon Blanc

Creamed Devilled Rabbits' Kidneys

As the flavour of the kidney is so delicate, it is important not to over-season the sauce or make it too spicy. A pastry cutter can be used to cut rounds of toasted brioche for an elegant dinner-party first course.

MAKES 4 SMALL FIRST-COURSE PORTIONS

225 g rabbits' kidneys

30 g unsalted butter

½ teaspoon Worcestershire sauce

½ teaspoon tomato purée

¼ teaspoon English mustard powder

4 tablespoons crème fraîche

squeeze of lemon juice

4 small slices Savoury Brioche, toasted
   (see page 487)

salt and freshly ground black pepper

1 Pick over the kidneys and remove any membranes.
2 Heat the butter in a pan and, when foaming, add the kidneys and fry briskly until nicely browned.
3 Stir in the Worcestershire sauce, tomato purée, mustard powder and crème fraîche. Season to taste with lemon juice, salt and pepper. Pile on to the toasted brioche and serve immediately.

Wine: Alsace Riesling or off-dry German Riesling Kabinett or Spätlese

Hare

If the hare has not been skinned, look for smooth, sharp claws and delicate, soft ears. Dry, ragged ears and blunt claws are signs of age. A leveret (young hare) has a hardly noticeable harelip – this becomes deeper and more pronounced in an older animal. Once the hare has been hung, skin it, collecting any blood, as this is used to thicken the gravy or sauce when the hare is roasted or jugged. If the hare has been skinned, look for deep claret-coloured flesh.

Skinning a hare

Skin the hare in the same way as described for rabbit (see page 402).

Jointing a hare

1 Cut off the hind legs at the hip joint and chop them in two at the knee.
2 Cut off the fore legs at the shoulder joint and chop them in two at the knee.
3 The back (saddle) can be left intact for roasting, or may be cut into 4–6 pieces for slow cooking.
4 Trim off any surplus fat.

Boning a hare

Bone the hare in the same way as a saddle of rabbit (see page 403).

To flavour and tenderize the meat, hare is often marinated for up to 2 days before roasting or stewing. Roast hare is often stuffed and served with gravy thickened with its blood and flavoured with redcurrant jelly.

Jugged Hare

This is a traditional English dish where the hare is slow-cooked in brown stock. The stock is made into a sauce, flavoured with port and redcurrant jelly, and thickened with the hare's blood at the end of cooking. If very little blood (less than 150 ml) comes with the hare, the basic stock must be thickened with a little beurre manié (see page 512). This must be done before the addition of the blood, which curdles if boiled.

SERVES 6

1 hare, jointed (see page 411), blood reserved

1 teaspoon white wine vinegar

60 g plain flour

¼ teaspoon freshly ground nutmeg

¼ teaspoon ground allspice

¼ teaspoon ground mace

2 tablespoons vegetable oil

600 ml Brown Chicken Stock (see page 454)

1 large onion, roughly chopped

1 large carrot, roughly chopped

1 stick of celery, trimmed and roughly chopped

1 bouquet garni (see page 512)

125 ml red wine

3 tablespoons port

2 tablespoons redcurrant jelly

salt and freshly ground black pepper

1 Heat the oven to 150°C/300°F/gas mark 2.
2 Wipe the hare with a damp cloth and place in a large plastic bag.
3 Stir the vinegar into the blood to prevent it from curdling. Set aside.
4 Mix the flour with the spices and season well with salt and pepper. Tip into the bag with the hare, and shake well to coat the pieces.
5 Heat 1 tablespoon of the oil in a large pan and fry the meat until well browned all over. Transfer to a casserole.
6 Pour the stock into the pan and bring to the boil, scraping up any sediment. Pour over the meat.
7 Heat the remaining oil and brown the vegetables. Add to the casserole along with the bouquet garni.
8 Cover the casserole with a tight-fitting lid and put in the middle of the oven for 3 hours, or until the meat is very tender. Using a slotted spoon, transfer the meat to a warm serving dish.
9 Strain the juices into a clean saucepan, discarding the vegetables and bouquet garni.
10 Add the wine, port and redcurrant jelly to the saucepan and bring to the boil. Reduce the liquid to two-thirds of its original volume.
11 Mix a little of the hot liquid into the blood, reduce the heat, and stir the blood into the pan. Do not let it boil or it will curdle. Taste and season with salt and pepper.
12 Pour the gravy over the meat and serve immediately.

Wine: Crozes-Hermitage, Languedoc red or New World Syrah/Shiraz

Hare Rillettes

Rillettes are similar to a coarse pâté, made from meat cooked in fat until very tender. This cooking method can be used to preserve the meat for up to a week if it is sealed with a covering of the fat and kept in the refrigerator.

SERVES 4

500 g hare meat

150 g goose or duck fat

50 ml water

2 large sprigs of thyme

1 bay leaf

2 cloves

ground mixed spice

freshly grated nutmeg

cayenne pepper

salt and freshly ground black pepper

To serve

warm crusty bread

cornichons

piccalilli

1 Heat the oven to 110°C/225°F/gas mark ½.

2 Cut the meat along the grain into 1 cm strips.

3 Put the fat and water into a large, shallow, flameproof dish or casserole and heat gently until liquid. Add the meat, thyme, bay leaf and cloves.

4 Cover the dish and place in the oven for 4–4½ hours, or until the meat is very soft and just falling apart, stirring occasionally.

5 Remove from the oven and allow the meat to stand for about 30 minutes, or until it cools to blood temperature.

6 Strain the meat and discard the thyme sprigs and bay leaves. Reserve the fat and juices. Shred the meat quite finely with 2 forks. Season with salt, pepper, plenty of mixed spice, nutmeg and a little cayenne pepper.

7 Divide the mixture between 4 ramekins and pour over the fat and juices. Cover each dish with a disc of greased silicone paper and refrigerate for 24–36 hours.

8 Serve with warm crusty bread, cornichons and piccalilli.

Wine: Crozes-Hermitage, Languedoc red or New World Syrah/Shiraz

Venison

Venison, the meat of deer, used to be available only during hunting seasons. Since the 1960s, venison has been farmed successfully for all-year-round availability. The animals are fed on a diet of grass, hay, potatoes and apples, and are slaughtered at around 18 months old. Farmed venison is usually sold ready-prepared for cooking.

Being exceptionally lean meat, venison often requires a relatively lengthy hanging period to tenderize it and develop the flavour. It is hung for 3–10 days, depending on the hanging conditions and the required gaminess. Venison hung for 3 days tastes rather like beef that has been hung for 3 weeks. Venison hung for 10 days becomes very gamy. As with all game, older venison will be tougher and more strongly flavoured than young venison and will require a longer period of hanging to tenderize the tough muscle fibres.

Choosing venison

The meat should be dark red, with a firm texture and fine grain. It should be moist but not slimy or gelatinous, and with very little fat.

The small amount of fat under the skin should be firm and white. Unlike in beef, fat does not marble venison meat.

Preparing venison for cooking

When preparing venison, remove as much of the membrane surrounding the meat as possible because this will toughen on cooking and distort the shape of the meat. Tougher, older venison, despite being hung for a relatively long time, may require marinating to tenderize the meat fibres further.

Methods of Cooking Venison

The tenderest cut of venison is from the loin and is suitable for grilling, frying and roasting. It is best served pink. The other cuts benefit from marinating and slow cooking so that the meat fibres start to fall apart. Venison is traditionally accompanied by redcurrant jelly, Poivrade Sauce (see page 465), cranberries and braised chestnuts. Bitter chocolate is sometimes added to sauces served with venison to enhance the rich flavour of the meat.

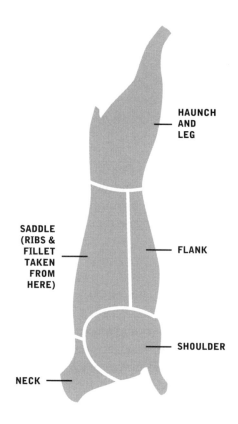

HAUNCH
AND
LEG

SADDLE
(RIBS &
FILLET
TAKEN
FROM
HERE)

FLANK

SHOULDER

NECK

Venison Cooking Table

Cut	Recommended cooking methods	Recipe reference
Haunch/leg	Roasting Braising (haunch of older animal)	Braised Haunch of Venison (page 421)
Whole saddle	Roasting Frying	(see overleaf)
Saddle chops	Grilling	(see overleaf)
Fillet	Roasting	(see overleaf)
Fillet steaks	Frying Grilling	Peppered Venison Steak (page 420)
Shoulder	Braising Stewing	Venison Casserole (page 422)
Neck	Stewing Mincing	Venison Casserole (page 422)
Flank	Stewing Mincing	Venison Casserole (page 422)

Roasting venison

The whole haunch, saddle and the fillet are the best cuts of venison for roasting. To protect the lean meat during this process, large joints of venison (weighing more than 3.5 kg) are often barded with streaky bacon (see page 262) or larded with strips of pork fat (see page 108).

Season the venison with salt and freshly ground black pepper. Brown in a little oil, then place in an oven preheated to 200°C/400°F/gas mark 6 and roast for 35–40 minutes per kg. (For further roasting information, see the Beef Roasting Table, page 33.)

To ensure the venison remains moist and juicy it is best eaten pink. A large joint of venison also benefits from resting for up to 30 minutes before carving. This resting period allows the meat to reabsorb some of the free-running juices released during cooking.

Grilling and frying venison

These techniques are described in Methods of Cooking Meat (page 11).

Although venison steaks and chops are suitable for both grilling and frying, the meat is so lean that it becomes dry if cooked beyond medium-rare. If less pink meat is required, it should be browned well until medium-rare, then transferred to a low oven (150°C/300°F/gas mark 2), which will allow the meat to continue cooking very slowly for a few more minutes. This way, the meat is able to relax and will remain tender and juicy.

Roast Venison with Chanterelles

Although farmed venison can be bought at any time of year, using venison that is in season (see page 372), along with autumnal wild mushrooms, makes for a very rich and earthy dish.

SERVES 6

1 × 1.35–2 kg haunch of venison
2 red onions, finely sliced
1 large sprig of rosemary
2 large sprigs of thyme
1 tablespoon oil
150 ml red wine

425 ml Veal Stock (see page 454)
1 teaspoon mushroom ketchup
50 g unsalted butter
225 g chanterelle mushrooms
salt and freshly ground black pepper

1 Weigh the venison to calculate the cooking time. Heat the oven to 220°C/425°F/gas mark 7.

2 Put the onions, rosemary and thyme in the bottom of a large roasting pan. Place the venison on top and pour over the oil. Season with salt and pepper.

3 Roast for 20 minutes on the top shelf of the oven.

4 Pour the wine around the meat and lower the temperature to 170°C/325°F/gas mark 3. Continue to cook for a further 20 minutes per kg.

5 Remove the venison from the pan, and allow to rest in a warm place. Discard the rosemary and thyme and place the roasting pan on the hob. Add the stock and bring to the boil, scraping the bottom of the pan. Add the mushroom ketchup and simmer the sauce until thick and syrupy.

6 Melt the butter in a frying pan and fry the chanterelles briskly for 1 minute, or until nicely browned. Add them to the sauce and season with salt and pepper. Serve with the venison.

NOTE: To carve a haunch of venison, follow the instructions for a leg of lamb on page 145.

Wine: Saumur Champigny or chilled Madeira

Venison Steaks with Sour Cherries and Port

SERVES 6

4 x 170 g venison steaks

6 tablespoons sunflower oil

425 ml Brown Stock (see page 452)

1 bay leaf

115 g dried sour cherries

3 tablespoons port

salt and freshly ground black pepper

3 tablespoons chopped fresh parsley, to garnish

For the marinade

425 ml orange juice

250 m full-bodied red wine

170 g onions, finely sliced

8 juniper berries, roughly crushed

2 cloves of garlic, sliced

2 tablespoons sunflower oil

1 Trim the fat and membrane from the venison, then cut the steaks into 7 × 5 cm pieces.

2 Combine the marinade ingredients in a large plastic bag or non-corrosive dish, then add the venison. Refrigerate overnight.

3 Using a slotted spoon, lift out the meat, pat dry with kitchen paper and season with salt and pepper.

4 Strain the marinade, reserving the liquid and the onion. Discard everything else.

5 Heat a little of the oil in a large sauté pan and brown batches of the meat on all sides. Pour a little of the marinade into the pan between batches in order to scrape up the sediment. Place these pan juices in a large flameproof casserole with the browned meat. After deglazing, add a little oil to the sauté pan to fry the next batch of meat. When all the meat has been browned and placed in the casserole, add the marinade and stock.

6 Heat the oven to 150°C/300°F/gas mark 2.

7 Brown the onions from the marinade in the remaining oil, then add them to the casserole along with the bay leaf.

8 Bring the casserole to a simmer, then cover and place in the oven for 2 hours. Meanwhile, soak the cherries in the port.

9 Using a slotted spoon, transfer the meat to a warmed serving dish. Remove the bay leaf from the casserole, then liquidize the remaining contents.

10 Add the cherries and port to the sauce. Simmer for 5 minutes. Season to taste, then pour over the meat. Garnish with the parsley.

Wine: Languedoc red, Douro red or Amarone della Valpolicella

Venison Steaks with Lemon and Redcurrant Sauce

SERVES 4

4 × 170 g venison steaks, cut from the leg or loin

1 tablespoon juniper berries, crushed

50 g butter

2 tablespoons olive oil

4 tablespoons port

salt and freshly ground black pepper

1 small bunch of watercress, to garnish

For the sauce

1 lemon

110 g redcurrant jelly

1 cinnamon stick

2 tablespoons port

45 g butter, chilled and cut into small pieces

1 First prepare the sauce: pare the zest from the lemon and cut into fine needle shreds. Cut the lemon in half, squeeze the juice and reserve.

2 Heat the redcurrant jelly gently with the cinnamon stick, port and lemon shreds. Simmer for 10 minutes, then add the strained lemon juice. Keep warm.

3 Trim the venison steaks of any tough membranes and season them with salt, pepper and juniper berries.

4 Heat the butter and oil in a heavy-based frying pan and cook the steaks over a high heat to brown on both sides. Reduce the heat and cook for a total of about 8 minutes, depending on size.

5 Transfer the steaks to a warmed serving dish. Pour the fat out of the frying pan and deglaze with the port. Pour over the steaks. Garnish the steaks with watercress.

6 Beat the butter into the warm lemon and redcurrant sauce. Pour into a warmed gravy boat and serve separately.

Wine: Red Burgundy, Vino Nobile di Montepulciano or Rioja

Peppered Venison Steak

If the venison is very fresh and you want a gamier taste, marinate it for two days in equal quantities of red wine and oil flavoured with sliced onion, six juniper berries and a bay leaf. Dry well with kitchen paper before frying.

SERVES 4

4 × 140 g venison collops (round steaks),
   cut from the fillet

2 tablespoons black peppercorns

1 tablespoon olive oil

30 g unsalted butter

2 tablespoons brandy

150 ml double cream

pinch of salt

1 Wipe the venison steaks and trim off any gristle and membranes.

2 Crush the peppercorns coarsely in a mortar or under a rolling pin and press them into the surface of the meat on both sides.

3 Cover the steaks and refrigerate for 2 hours so that the flavour penetrates the meat.

4 Heat the oil in a heavy-based pan, add the butter and, when it is foaming, fry the steaks as fast as possible until done to your liking (about 2 minutes per side for blue, 3 minutes for rare, 3½ minutes for medium and 4 minutes for well done).

5 Pour in the brandy and carefully set alight. When the flames have died down, add the cream and salt. Mix the contents of the pan thoroughly, scraping up any sediment stuck to the bottom.

6 Place the steaks on a warmed serving platter.

7 Boil the sauce to a syrupy consistency and pour over the meat. Serve immediately.

Wine: New World Syrah/Shiraz or Pinotage

Braised Haunch of Venison

The shoulder and haunch of venison are the best cuts for braising. Before cooking these tougher cuts, remove as much gristle as possible because it will not soften during cooking.

SERVES 6–8

1 × 2.7 kg haunch of venison	1 tablespoon chopped fresh thyme
1 teaspoon oil	1 teaspoon chopped fresh sage
60 g butter	300 ml red wine
2 onions, sliced	425 ml Brown Stock (see page 452)
225 g carrots, sliced	30 g flour
4 sticks of celery, sliced	1 tablespoon cranberry jelly
1 bay leaf	salt and freshly ground black pepper

1 Heat the oven to 150°C/300°F/gas mark 2.
2 Prepare the venison by trimming away any tough membranes, sinews and gristle. Season with salt and pepper.
3 Heat the oil and half the butter in a large, flameproof casserole and brown the venison well on all sides. Remove from the casserole.
4 Add the onions, carrots and celery, and fry until lightly browned.
5 Stir in the bay leaf, thyme and sage. Lay the venison on top of the vegetables. Add the wine and enough stock to come about a quarter of the way up the meat.
6 Bring to simmering point, then cover tightly and cook in the oven for 1½ hours, or until tender. Check the meat after 1 hour to ensure there is still liquid in the casserole. If not, add 300 ml water.
7 When cooked, lift out the meat, carve it neatly and place on a warmed serving dish. Keep warm, covered with foil or a lid.
8 Strain the liquid from the vegetables into a saucepan. Skim any fat from the surface.
9 Mix the flour with the remaining 30 g butter to make a beurre manié. Add this to the liquid bit by bit, stirring, and bring to the boil. Boil until syrupy. Stir in the cranberry jelly and check the seasoning.
10 To serve, spoon a thin layer of the sauce over the venison to make it look shiny and appetizing; serve the remaining sauce in a warmed gravy boat.

Wine: Red Burgundy, Rioja or Chianti Classico

Venison Casserole with Chestnuts and Cranberries

SERVES 4

675 g shoulder, neck or flank of venison

1 tablespoon sunflower oil

30 g butter

115 g button onions

1 clove of garlic, crushed

115 g whole button mushrooms

1 teaspoon plain flour

150 ml Brown Stock (see page 452)

1 tablespoon cranberry jelly

50 g fresh cranberries

15 g sugar

115 g cooked whole chestnuts

salt and freshly ground black pepper

chopped flat leaf parsley, to garnish

For the marinade

5 tablespoons sunflower oil

1 onion, sliced

1 carrot, sliced

1 stick of celery, sliced

1 clove of garlic, crushed

6 juniper berries

1 slice of lemon

1 bay leaf

300 ml red wine

2 tablespoons red wine vinegar

6 black peppercorns

1 Cut the venison into 5 cm cubes, trimming away any tough membranes, sinews or gristle.

2 Combine the ingredients for the marinade in a non-corrosive bowl or large plastic bag and add the venison. Mix well, then cover and refrigerate overnight.

3 Heat the oven to 170°C/325°F/gas mark 3.

4 Remove the venison from the marinade and pat dry with kitchen paper. Strain the marinade and reserve.

5 Heat half the oil in a heavy-based frying pan and brown the venison cubes a few at a time. Place them in a casserole. If the bottom of the pan becomes brown or too dry, pour in a little of the strained marinade to deglaze it, then pour the *déglaçage* over the browned meat. Heat a little more oil and brown the remaining meat.

6 When all the venison has been browned, do a final deglazing with a little of the remaining marinade and add to the casserole.

7 Melt the butter in a saucepan and fry the onions until golden brown. Add the garlic and cook for a further minute. Add the mushrooms and continue cooking for 2 minutes.

8 Stir in the flour and cook for 1 minute. Remove from the heat and stir in the stock until boiling. Return to the heat and stir, again scraping the bottom of the pan.

9 Add the cranberry jelly to the sauce. Season to taste. Pour the sauce over the meat.

10 Cover the casserole and cook for about 2 hours, or until the venison is very tender.

11 Meanwhile, cook the cranberries briefly with the sugar in 2–3 tablespoons water until just soft but not crushed. Strain off the liquid.

12 Using a slotted spoon, lift the venison, mushrooms and onions into a warmed serving dish.

13 Boil the sauce fast until reduced to a shiny, almost syrupy consistency. Add the cranberries and chestnuts and simmer gently for 5 minutes.

14 Pour the sauce over the venison and serve garnished with chopped parsley.

Wine: Red Burgundy, Vino Nobile di Montepulciano, Rioja or Rhône red

Exotic Meats

In this section there are recipes for rather more unusual and rare types of meat. They have been included in recognition of constantly changing and developing food trends and the increased availability of exciting produce and ingredients.

The media may, in part, be responsible for this, with innovative food and cookery programmes on television and a vast number of magazines, food publications and newspaper articles, all serving to whet the appetite, enhance the knowledge and boost the confidence of the home cook.

Travel plays a part too, with exotic holiday destinations and trips abroad exposing us to a wealth of new culinary experiences with unfamiliar dishes, ingredients and flavours, giving us the inspiration to experiment back home.

Our multicultural society also encourages diversity, as specialist shops, selling delicious and unusual foodstuffs, readily present us with the opportunity to source and cook with new ingredients. And for those of us with the desire to cook with something really different and exceptionally exotic, the internet makes it possible to obtain items, such as crickets, ants and locusts. Even worms are available at the click of a button.

This section aims to tempt the adventurous cook by providing recipes for unusual types and cuts of meat. Whilst it is unlikely that most of these dishes would make a regular appearance on the weekly family menu, and the majority of us wouldn't necessarily think of having python or rattlesnake for a quick mid-week supper, they would certainly be the talking point of any dinner party. And for those just wanting something with a little more edge than the traditional joint of roast beef or venison, there is a haunch of meltingly soft and tender wildebeest, or an antelope fillet and chips instead of steak.

Some of the of red meat species, such as kangaroo, can now be found in larger supermarkets, and for some years, wild boar and bison have been fairly widely available. Other, perhaps less familiar, species need to be sourced from specialist suppliers. These include the various members of the antelope family – kudu, springbok, impala and eland – which originate from South Africa, Namibia, Botswana and Angola (Zimbabwe is said to have more impalas than people), and are usually imported frozen. A list of specialist suppliers can be found on page 529.

The protein content in the majority of these meats is much higher than that of beef or lamb, and the fat content is considerably lower. Therefore, the structure of the meat differs, resulting in a finer grain that is very tender, but prone to drying out in the cooking process. Overcooking is impossible to rectify, with the meat quickly becoming dry and fibrous, as there is none of the 'internal basting' that takes place within the structure of fattier meats as the fat renders and becomes moist and gelatinous. Quick cooking methods, such as pan-frying or grilling, are advised for small cuts, such as leg or fillet steaks. Baking en papillotte, so that the meat cooks in steam and its own juices, is another good method for individual portions.

Larger cuts can be roasted at a high temperature for a relatively short period of time, or cut into large chunks and submerged in liquid for a casserole. In any event, it is advised that all these meats are served medium-rare in order to retain their moisture and juiciness and to enjoy them at their best.

Alligator and Crocodile

Probably the most familiar of the exotic white meats, alligator and crocodile have increased in both popularity and availability over the last few years. The most likely reason for this trend is their low fat content, as people become increasingly health-conscious. The skinless, white meat is an excellent source of protein, and as it cooks quickly, can be considered somewhat a convenience health food.

The majority of crocodile meat is imported from Australia, New Zealand and parts of Africa, while alligator comes from South America. Although alligators are hunted because they are not an endangered species, they are most often raised in captivity for the meat market.

Both crocodile and alligator have a delicate, fishy flavour, with a colour and texture similar to that of chicken or even a tender loin of rabbit. They are best prepared as for chicken and pork dishes. They are good mediums for aromatic flavours, working well in marinated dishes. The white loin and tail meat are more tender than the darker body meat. Any fat should be trimmed as this has a rather unpleasant taste.

The meat is usually bought frozen, and it is advisable to cook it from frozen, as much of the moisture is lost after defrosting. As with anything cooked from frozen, the internal temperature should be checked with a meat thermometer. In this case, it should register 75°C/165°F in the centre.

Pan-fried Alligator Tail Steaks with Lime Butter

Soaking the alligator in milk before cooking produces a more delicate favour.

SERVES 4

4 × 170 g alligator tail steaks	50 g unsalted butter
300 ml milk	juice of 2 limes
cayenne pepper	flaky sea salt and freshly ground black pepper
1 tablespoon oil	sprigs of watercress, to garnish

1 Place the alligator steaks in a shallow bowl and pour over the milk. Cover and leave in the refrigerator for 1 hour.
2 Drain the steaks, discarding the milk, and pat dry with kitchen paper. Season with salt and cayenne pepper.
3 Heat the oil in a heavy-based frying pan and fry the steaks for 1 minute on each side, or until nicely browned. Reduce the heat and continue to cook for a further 2–3 minutes, or until just cooked through.
4 Remove the steaks from the pan and allow to rest. Return the pan to the heat, add the butter and, when foaming, add the lime juice, scraping up any sediment.
5 Season with salt and black pepper, pour over the steaks and serve immediately garnished with sprigs of watercress.

Wine: Dry Riesling from Alsace, Germany, Austria or Australia

Cajun Alligator

SERVES 4

675 g alligator tail, cut into 5 cm pieces

oil, for deep-frying

1 egg white, beaten

seasoned cornflour

salt and freshly ground black pepper

1 teaspoon Worcestershire sauce

1 teaspoon tamarind pulp

1 teaspoon tomato ketchup

½ teaspoon chilli powder

dash of Tabasco sauce

½ small clove of garlic, crushed

For the marinade

grated zest and juice of 1 lime

2 tablespoons white wine vinegar

1 tablespoon soft light brown sugar

To garnish

flat leaf parsley

lime wedges

1 Place all the marinade ingredients in a large, non-metallic bowl or plastic bag. Add the alligator and season with black pepper. Marinate in the refrigerator for 2–3 hours, turning the meat in the mixture occasionally.

2 Heat the oil in a large pan until a cube of bread will brown in 20 seconds (see Warning, page 53).

3 Drain the alligator, discarding the marinade. Dip into the beaten egg white, then toss in the cornflour to coat the pieces thoroughly.

4 Deep-fry in batches until golden brown. Drain on kitchen paper and sprinkle with salt.

5 Garnish with the parsley and lime wedges, and serve immediately.

Wine: Alsace or northern Italian Pinot Gris/Grigio or Pinot Blanc/Bianco, or Gavi

Crisp Crocodile Wontons with Sweet and Sour Dipping Sauce

SERVES 4

1 packet 5 × 5 cm square wonton wrappers

1 egg white, beaten

oil, for deep-frying

For the wonton filling

340 g crocodile tail meat, minced or shredded

1 small carrot, cut into julienne strips

1 × 3 cm piece mouli, grated (see Note)

½ small red chilli, finely diced

1 × 5 cm piece of fresh root ginger, peeled and grated

50 g sugarsnap peas, finely shredded

1 tablespoon very finely chopped fresh coriander

salt and freshly ground black pepper

For the sweet and sour sauce

50 g soft palm sugar

4 tablespoons white wine vinegar

½ tablespoon light soy sauce

½ teaspoon shrimp paste

1 teaspoon sesame oil

½ red pepper, very finely diced

½ green pepper, very finely diced

1 Mix together all the filling ingredients and season with salt and pepper.

2 Lay half the wonton wrappers on a flat surface and divide the filling mixture between them. Brush the edges of the wrappers with beaten egg white and carefully place another wonton wrapper on top. Press the edges together firmly.

3 Half-fill a large pan with oil and heat until a cube of bread browns in 20 seconds (see Warning, page 53).

4 Fry the wonton parcels a few at a time, until crisp and brown. Remove from the pan with a slotted spoon and sprinkle with a little salt. Keep warm.

5 To make the sauce, place the palm sugar, vinegar, soy sauce and shrimp paste in a small saucepan and heat very gently until the sugar has dissolved. Simmer gently for 2 minutes. Stir in the sesame oil and diced peppers. Pour into a small bowl and serve with the wontons.

NOTE: Mouli is a large, white root vegetable, and is often referred to as daikon or white radish. It has a flavour similar to that of the more familiar red radish.

Wine: Alsace or northern Italian Pinot Gris/Grigio or Pinot Blanc/Bianco, or Gavi

Antelope

The lifestyle and diet of the many members of the antelope family are reflected in the flavour and texture of the meat. The animals are herbivores, eating a varied grass and herbal diet. This, along with them being very athletic creatures, results in an exceptionally sweet flavour and lean texture to the meat. Most antelopes for the meat industry would be older males. Their meat can be used interchangeably in the recipes that follow.

Blesbok is mainly a leaf-eater, and this is reflected in its delicate flavour. The leg muscles are particularly tender.

Eland is the largest of the antelope family, growing to around 600–700 kg. It has a diet of fruit, grass and leaves, so contains six times less fat than beef and half the calories. It provides cuts that are good for roasting and pan-frying.

Gnu is very lean, making it suitable only for cooking rare or medium. It is comparable in texture to good-quality beef, but with a lighter colour. The black gnu, having at one point been near extinction, has been farmed and reintroduced back into the wild. Stags are hunted for their meat, but only when rejected from the herd. Does and calves are never hunted.

Impala is a deep red, very lean meat with no visible fat and is very low in cholesterol.

Kudu is very similar to blesbok. It has a slightly gamier flavour than venison, and the haunch is good for roasting.

Springbok is one of the smallest of the antelope family, an average adult weighing only about 30 kg, and has perhaps the finest texture of all.

Pan-fried Blesbok Steaks with Pink Peppercorn Sauce

SERVES 4

4 × 225 g blesbok leg steaks
oil
2 tablespoons brandy
4 tablespoons crème fraîche

1½ tablespoons pink peppercorns in brine, rinsed and dried
salt and freshly ground black pepper
sprigs of watercress, to garnish

1 Season the steaks with salt and pepper. Brush a frying pan with oil and heat until beginning to smoke.

2 Brown the steaks quickly on both sides. Reduce the heat and continue cooking for a further 2–3 minutes, or until the steaks are pink and juicy in the middle.

3 Pour in the brandy and set alight. When the flames subside, remove the steaks from the pan and allow to rest on a warmed serving dish.

4 Add the peppercorns and crème fraîche to the pan and mix well, scraping up any sediment. Bring to the boil, season with salt and pepper and pour over the steaks.

5 Garnish with watercress and serve immediately.

Wine: Dry rosé, less aromatic dry white, or light, fruity red (Beaujolais style)

Impala Fillet with Ginger and Lemon Grass

Banana leaves, which are used to wrap the meat in this recipe, can be found in some of the bigger supermarkets, where they are sold singly, folded and wrapped in plastic, rather like a sheet of wrapping paper. However, they are more likely to be found in Asian grocery shops or street markets, where they would probably be sold by the box. They freeze well, and can be kept for up to 4 weeks. Thereafter, they might start to turn a little brown around the edges. As this doesn't affect the flavour or texture of the leaves, they can still be used for cooking. However, if they are just to be used for presentation, a freshly bought leaf would be preferable.

It is not imperative to cook the impala in a banana leaf, but it does impart a delicate aroma, and is visually pleasing if the parcel is unwrapped at the table. In the absence of banana leaves, a double layer of baking parchment or aluminium foil can be used instead.

SERVES 4

1 tablespoon oil
1 × 700 g impala fillet, trimmed
20 g unsalted butter
2 banana shallots, very finely sliced
1 clove of garlic, crushed
2 cm piece of fresh root ginger, peeled and grated

1 stick of lemon grass, outer leaves discarded and very finely chopped
1 small red chilli, deseeded and finely chopped
4 tablespoons White Chicken Stock (see page 451)
4 tablespoons Noilly Prat
1 large banana leaf
salt and freshly ground black pepper

1 Heat the oven to 200°C/400°F/gas mark 6.
2 Heat the oil in a large frying pan. Season the impala fillet with salt and pepper and brown well on all sides. Remove from the pan and set aside.
3 Add the butter to the pan and gently sweat the shallots without colouring for 5 minutes, or until beginning to soften.
4 Add the garlic, ginger, lemon grass and red chilli to the shallots and continue to cook gently for a further 5 minutes.
5 Pour the stock and Noilly Prat into the pan and bring to the boil. Reduce the heat and simmer for 1 minute.
6 Lay the banana leaf shiny side down on a work surface and place the impala fillet in the centre of it. Spoon the shallot mixture over the meat.
7 Wrap the fillet up in the banana leaf and secure with cocktail sticks. Place the parcel on a baking sheet and put on the top shelf of the oven for 15 minutes.
8 Remove the parcel from the oven and allow to rest for 5 minutes. Carefully open the parcel and slice the meat thickly. Serve with the juices poured over.

Wine: Dry rosé, less aromatic dry white, or light, fruity red (Beaujolais style)

Butterflied Roast Haunch of Springbok

SERVES 8–10

1 × 3 kg haunch of springbok, butterfly-boned
  (see page 138, or ask your butcher to
  do this)
2 tablespoons olive oil
2 sprigs of rosemary, bruised

2 cloves of garlic, unpeeled
600 ml Veal Stock (see page 454)
75 ml Muscat wine
30 g unsalted butter
salt and freshly ground black pepper

1 Heat the oven to 230°C/450°F/gas mark 8.

2 Rub the springbok with the oil and season with salt and pepper.

3 Place the rosemary and garlic in a large roasting pan and place the meat, cut-side down, on top. Place on the top shelf of the oven and cook for 30 minutes, until the meat is well browned. Reduce the heat to 170°C/325°F/gas mark 3 and continue to cook for a further 30–45 minutes, or until medium rare.

4 Transfer the meat to a warm serving plate, cover loosely with foil and leave to rest for 15–20 minutes.

5 Discard the rosemary from the pan. Gently squeeze out the softened garlic, then discard the papery skin. Place the pan on the hob and add the stock and wine. Bring to the boil, scraping up any sediment. Reduce the heat and allow to simmer until reduced by half, or until glossy and strongly flavoured.

6 Strain the sauce through a fine sieve or chinois into a clean pan. Bring to the boil and whisk in the butter. Taste and season with salt and pepper.

7 Serve the meat in thick slices and hand the sauce separately.

Wine: Dry rosé, light fruity red, red Burgundy or South African Pinot Noir

Bison/Buffalo

'Bison' is a Greek word, meaning 'ox-like animal'. It is a domesticated ruminant, belonging to the Bovidae family, and is grass-fed and organically raised without hormones. The meat is very lean and resembles well-flavoured beef. Indigenous to North America, where they are often called 'buffalo', bison are now farmed throughout Europe, with France being the leading exporter. Breeding started at the beginning of the 21st century, when it was realized that bison were near extinction, with numbers down to only double figures. Although they are no longer a threatened species, there are no true wild bison left.

Larger than domestic cattle, bison are able to go without water for days, and can endure sub-zero temperatures, making them very self-sufficient. Although regarded as game, there is no true breeding season, the meat being available year round. Only bulls are slaughtered for the meat market. Females are used for breeding and providing milk for products such as mozzarella cheese.

Bison Medallions with Caper Sauce and Salsify Chips

SERVES 4

1 tablespoon oil

4 × 170 g bison medallions

For the sauce

30 g unsalted butter

1 banana shallot, blanched, peeled and finely sliced

100 ml white wine

1 tablespoon capers, rinsed and roughly chopped

4 tablespoons crème fraîche

squeeze of lemon juice

salt and freshly ground black pepper

To serve

Salsify Chips (see opposite)

1 First make the sauce. Melt the butter in a saucepan and add the shallot. Cover with a piece of dampened greaseproof paper and a lid, and cook over a low heat until soft but not coloured.

2 Pour the wine into the pan and bring to the boil. Simmer for 5 minutes, or until reduced to half its original volume.

3 Add the chopped capers and stir in the crème fraîche. Season with salt, pepper and a squeeze of lemon juice and set aside.

4 Heat the oil in a frying pan. Season the bison steaks and fry on both sides until a good golden brown colour. Reduce the heat and continue to cook for a further 2½–3 minutes.

5 Reheat the sauce and serve with the bison steaks and salsify chips.

NOTE: The timing above assumes that the steaks will be eaten medium rare. If a less or more well done steak is required, see the frying times for steak (page 35). As the fat content of bison is lower than that of beef, a well-done steak might be a little dry.

SALSIFY CHIPS

Salsify, also known as scorzonera, is a root vegetable that belongs to the dandelion family. It is long, thin and stick-like in appearance with creamy white flesh. It can be boiled, mashed or fried. It is also a tasty addition to soups and casseroles. The roots need to be scrubbed well, under cold running water, before being peeled. The peeled roots tend to discolour quickly, but this can be prevented if they are placed in a bowl of cold water to which a squeeze of lemon juice or a dash of vinegar has been added. Likewise, adding lemon juice or vinegar to the cooking water will ensure that they keep a good colour. Parsnips are a good alternative for this recipe if salsify cannot be found.

SERVES 4

675 g salsify, scrubbed	seasoned flour
juice of 1 lemon	1 egg, beaten
85 g fresh white breadcrumbs	oil, for deep-frying
45 g freshly grated Parmesan cheese	flaky sea salt

1 Peel the salsify and cut them into approximately 10 cm pieces. Place them in a bowl of cold water with half of the lemon juice.

2 Bring a large pan of salted water to the boil and add the remaining lemon juice. Simmer the salsify for 5 minutes, or until just tender. Drain and pat dry, and allow to cool slightly.

3 Mix the breadcrumbs with the Parmesan.

4 Dip the cooled salsify into the seasoned flour, shaking off the excess. Dip them into the beaten egg, then toss in the breadcrumb mixture, ensuring that they are coated thoroughly.

5 Heat about 8 cm of oil in a heavy-based saucepan until a cube of bread sizzles and browns in about 30 seconds (see Warning, page 53). Fry the salsify, a few at a time, for 2–3 minutes, or until nicely browned. Remove them from the pan with a slotted spoon and drain on kitchen paper. Sprinkle with a little salt and serve.

Wine: Pinot Noir

Bison and Blue Cheese Burgers

These burgers are made in the conventional way, but with the delicious addition of a soft, creamy blue cheese centre. Any combination of cheese can be used as long as it includes something soft that will melt well. The addition of Stilton makes for a fairly strong flavour, but using a mixture of a soft, young goat's cheese and blue Brie would result in a much milder flavour. This recipe is also a good excuse to use up the remnants on a cheese board: just keep to the total weight, using whatever combination you like.

SERVES 4

85 g Cambozola cheese

85 g Stilton cheese

500 g bison mince, preferably from the shoulder

30 g flat leaf parsley, finely chopped

1 egg, beaten

oil, for frying

salt and freshly ground black pepper

4 soft white rolls, warmed, to serve

1 Place the Cambozola in a small bowl and mash with a fork until creamy. Crumble the Stilton into the bowl and mix the cheeses together. Divide into 4 portions and chill.

2 Put the minced bison, parsley and beaten egg into a bowl and season with salt and pepper. Mix together thoroughly.

3 Divide the bison mixture into 4 equal portions and roll each piece into a ball. Using your thumb, make a deep well in the centre of each ball and push a portion of the cheese mixture inside. Cover with the meat to seal completely, then flatten the burgers slightly with the palm of your hand. Chill for 20 minutes.

4 Heat a little oil in a heavy-based frying pan and brown the cheese burgers on both sides. Reduce the heat and continue to cook for a further 3–4 minutes on each side.

5 Serve inside the warmed soft rolls.

VARIATION: For a total change of flavour, the burgers can be made from minced lamb instead of bison, with a centre of crumbled feta and cream or curd cheese. The addition of fresh oregano or marjoram, along with a few chopped black olives, would be reminiscent of Greece.

Drink: Full-bodied red, such as a Zinfandel or Chilean Cabernet, or a good ale

Camel

Camel has been eaten for centuries, primarily in northern Africa, although there are ancient Greek references to camel meat being part of feasts. The loin, ribs, brisket and hump are eaten, with the hump being considered a delicacy. Although similar in texture to mutton, camel meat is sweeter in flavour.

An Arabian male dromedary weighs on average around 400 kg. An Asian male bactrian can weigh up to 650 kg, whereas females are usually 250–350 kg. The camel is a cud-chewer, and whilst it has a foot that is split into two toe-like structures, it is not classed as a cloven hoof. As most of the fat is stored in the hump, camel is a very lean meat. It needs careful cooking or it will be come dry and inedible. Both the fat and protein content are lower than that of beef.

It is said that in the Middle East a whole roast camel is a cooked for special occasions. After being boned out, it is stuffed with a whole boned sheep that has been stuffed with several boned chickens. Whilst it would provide around 100 good-sized portions, it is perhaps a little on the large size for the average domestic barbecue.

Camel Fillet with Châteauneuf-du-Pape and Butter Jus

The deeply flavoured wine in this dish has a rich spiciness that stands up well to the density of camel meat without overpowering it. If Châteauneuf-du-Pape is not available, any similar, well-bodied red wine, such as a Shiraz or Rioja, may be used instead.

SERVES 4–6

oil

1 × 1 kg camel fillet, trimmed

1 onion, roughly chopped

1 carrot, roughly chopped

1 stick of celery, roughly chopped

300 ml gelatinous Brown Stock (see page 452)

300 ml Châteauneuf-du-Pape or similar full-bodied red wine

4 sprigs of thyme

1 handful of parsley stalks, lightly bruised

45 g butter

salt and freshly ground black pepper

1 Heat 1 tablespoon of oil in a heavy-based casserole dish.

2 Season the meat with salt and pepper and brown well on all sides. Remove and set aside.

3 Add the chopped vegetables to the pan and brown well, adding more oil if necessary.

4 Pour the wine and stock into the pan and bring to the boil. Simmer for 3–4 minutes.

5 Set the meat on top of the vegetables, add the thyme and parsley stalks, and cover tightly with a tight-fitting lid. Reduce the heat and simmer very gently for 1–1¼ hours, or until very tender.

6 Remove the meat from the dish and allow to rest in a warm place while you make the sauce.

7 Strain the liquid through a sieve into a clean saucepan and discard the vegetables. Bring to the boil and reduce by two-thirds, or until thick and syrupy. Whisk in the butter, then taste and season if necessary.

8 Slice the camel fillet thickly and arrange in overlapping slices on a warm serving plate. Pour over the sauce and serve immediately.

Wine: Châteauneuf-du-Pape or quality red Bordeaux

Elk

While elk is the sweetest of the deer meats, it is a little harder to find than red and roe deer, which are commonly available in butchers' shops. It is well worth the effort, however, as it has the advantage of a distinctively rich, full flavour, similar to that of beef, but with less fat and cholesterol than skinless chicken. Its lean texture and gamy flavour make it a good choice for roasting, and it works well with winter vegetables in casseroles. The leg muscles, when minced, make an excellent choice for home-made sausages and burgers.

Elk Scallopini

SERVES 4

100 ml soured cream

85 g grated Parmesan cheese

85 g panko breadcrumbs (see Note, page 317)

2 tablespoons chopped fresh flat leaf parsley

675 g elk fillet, cut into 8 × 1 cm slices

2 tablespoons seasoned flour

1 tablespoon oil

100 ml Veal Stock (see page 454)

75 ml Marsala

salt and freshly ground black pepper

1 Heat the oven to 200°C/400°F/gas mark 6.

2 Mix together the soured cream, Parmesan, breadcrumbs and parsley in a bowl. Season with salt and pepper and set aside.

3 Place the meat between 2 sheets of dampened greaseproof paper and pound with a meat mallet or a heavy-based pan until 5 mm thick.

4 Dip the slices in the seasoned flour. Heat the oil in a frying pan and fry the meat until browned on both sides.

5 Remove the meat from the pan and spread the cream mixture on one side of each slice. Place the slices in a very shallow baking dish and pour the stock and Marsala around, not over, the slices.

6 Place the dish in the oven and bake for 7–10 minutes, or until the meat is pink and the topping is well browned and crisp. Serve immediately with the pan juices poured around.

Wine: Syrah/Shiraz or Cabernet Sauvignon

Kangaroo

Kangaroo meat is very lean and has a gamy flavour, which varies somewhat depending on the region in which it was raised. As the animal is a herbivore, the flavour of the meat is affected by its diet, which varies from area to area, depending on the plant and grass species available. Kangaroo is a sustainable meat as by law, only 15–20 per cent of the population is harvested each year.

It is a high-protein, low-fat meat. When trimmed of visible fat, it has a typical fat content of just 1–2 per cent, compared with an identical cut of lamb at 5–7 per cent. It is also high in iron, containing only slightly less than beef. As with all lean game meats, the cooking method and times need careful consideration in accordance with the chosen cut in order to prevent it overcooking and drying out.

When butchered, the resulting cuts of kangaroo meat are much the same as from a carcass of beef or lamb. These include loin, fillet, saddle, leg, topside, shank and tail. However, the most readily available and commonly used cuts in the UK tend to be fillet and leg steaks, along with diced or cubed meat. Ready-prepared meat products, such as burgers and sausages, come from cheaper cuts and the residual meat on the carcass once the primal muscles have been removed. However, these still have a good nutritional value because of the overall low fat content of the animal.

Chambord-glazed Kangaroo Medallions with Warm Red Chicory and Blackberry Salad

SERVES 4

4 × 170 g kangaroo medallions
oil
3 tablespoons Chambord liqueur
150 ml Veal Stock (see page 454)

1 teaspoon red wine vinegar
salt and freshly ground black pepper

To serve
Warm Red Chicory and Blackberry Salad
(see overleaf)

1 Season the kangaroo medallions with salt and pepper.
2 Brush a frying pan with a little oil and, when very hot, brown the steaks quickly on both sides. Reduce the temperature and continue to cook for a further 2 minutes.
3 Pour in the Chambord and set alight. When the flames subside transfer the steaks to a warmed serving dish.
4 Pour the stock and vinegar into the pan and mix well, scraping up any sediment. Bring to the boil and cook until reduced to about 5–6 tablespoons. Pour over the steaks and serve with the salad.

WARM RED CHICORY AND BLACKBERRY SALAD

The combination of bitter leaves and fruit is a good one. Grilling the chicory intensifies the bitterness of the leaf, and lightly cooking the berries brings out their juices, which, mixed with the warm dressing and fresh fruit, intensify the overall flavour of the dish.

Although cultivated blackberries can be found all year round, wild ones, which can be picked from August to the end of September, are infinitely plumper, juicier and tastier, and should be used for this salad where possible.

SERVES 4

2 small heads of red chicory

1½ tablespoons oil

1 tablespoon raspberry vinegar

125 g blackberries

salt and freshly ground black pepper

1 Heat the grill to its highest setting.

2 Cut the chicory in half lengthwise and carefully cut out the central core. Cut each half into 3 so that you have 6 long wedges, and lay them on a baking sheet, cut side facing uppermost.

3 Mix the oil and vinegar together and season with salt and pepper.

4 Brush or spoon the dressing over the chicory and place under the grill for 1 minute.

5 Add half the blackberries to the baking sheet and grill for a further minute, or until the chicory is just beginning to brown at the edges and the blackberries are starting to burst and release their juices.

6 Lift the chicory and blackberries on to a serving dish and scatter over the remaining fruit. Pour over any juices from the baking sheet and serve immediately.

Wine: McLaren Vale Shiraz or Coonawarra Cabernet from Australia

Kangaroo and Peanut Sambal Salad

SERVES 4

4 × 170 g kangaroo fillet steaks

oil

salt and freshly ground black pepper

For the dressing

3 tablespoons smooth peanut butter

1½ tablespoons soft light brown sugar

5 tablespoons water

finely grated zest and juice of 2 limes

1 teaspoon tamarind paste

1 teaspoon fish sauce

½ large red chilli, deseeded and very finely chopped

85 g roasted salted peanuts, roughly chopped

2 hearts of little gem lettuce, shredded

1 tablespoon chopped fresh coriander

sprigs of coriander, to garnish

1 Season the kangaroo steaks with salt and pepper.

2 Brush a heavy-based frying pan with a little oil and, when very hot, brown the steaks on both sides over a high heat.

3 Reduce the heat and continue cooking for a further 2–3 minutes, or until done to your liking. Transfer the steaks to a plate and leave to rest in a warm place.

4 To make the dressing, place the peanut butter, brown sugar and water in a small saucepan and bring to the boil, stirring to dissolve the sugar. Add the lime juice and zest, tamarind, fish sauce and chilli and simmer for 1 minute. Stir the peanuts into the sauce and allow to cool.

5 Divide the lettuce between 4 serving plates. Cut the kangaroo steaks into 3–4 thick slices and place them on top of the lettuce.

6 Stir the coriander into the sauce. If the sauce is too thick, add a spoonful or so of water. It should be the consistency of mayonnaise. Adjust the seasoning.

7 Spoon the sauce over and around the kangaroo and lettuce, and serve garnished with sprigs of coriander.

Wine: Light, fruity red (Beaujolais style) or aromatic, fruity white

Kangaroo, Pomegranate and Macadamia Nut Stir-fry

SERVES 4

1 × 500 g kangaroo fillet, cut into thin,
finger-length strips

1½ tablespoons cornflour

about 500 ml peanut oil, for deep-frying, plus an
extra tablespoon for stir-frying

1 large head of bok choi, shredded

110 g beansprouts

2 mini cucumbers, cut diagonally into thin, long ovals

50 g roasted, salted macadamia nuts, roughly chopped

seeds from 1 pomegranate

3 tablespoons mirin

1 tablespoon pomegranate molasses (see page 338)

½ tablespoon fish sauce

1 small bunch of coriander, roughly chopped

salt and freshly ground black pepper

1 Coat the kangaroo evenly with the cornflour and shake off the excess.

2 Heat the peanut oil in a deep-fat fryer or heavy-based saucepan until very hot (see Warning, page 53). Tip the kangaroo gently into the oil and deep-fry for 2–3 minutes, or until brown and crisp. Turn off the heat, remove the kangaroo with a slotted spoon and drain on kitchen paper.

3 Heat a wok or large frying pan and add 1 tablespoon of the peanut oil. When very hot, add the bok choi and stir-fry for 30 seconds. Add the beansprouts, cucumber, macadamia nuts and pomegranate seeds and cook for a further 30 seconds.

4 Return the kangaroo to the pan. Pour over the mirin, pomegranate molasses and fish sauce. Sprinkle over the coriander, season with salt and pepper and gently stir everything together. Serve immediately.

Wine: Australian or New Zealand Pinot Noir

Llama

The llama's natural habitat is high in the mountains of Peru and Chile. It has been used for its wool, milk and meat for centuries, and is perhaps the earliest domesticated animal. Although the meat is similar in appearance and texture to lamb, the camel is the llama's closest relation. Fillet and haunch meat are the most commonly imported cuts of llama. The meat is usually dark red, but this can vary, depending on the age of the animal. The meat from older animals is often dried to make *charqui* (jerky). Despite these uses, llamas were, and still are, kept as pets too.

Currently, llama meat is difficult to obtain outside South America, but that is likely to change over the next few years.

Alpaca, like most other species of llama, is farmed primarily for its wool, and is the largest producer of it. Its meat is also the type most commonly available

Guanaco is a species of wild llama, and the hunting season for it is during the summer months, mainly due to the freezing temperatures and inaccessibility of its terrain, whereas farmed llama meat is available all year round.

Vicuna is another type of wild llama, and is a protected species.

Llama Stew

SERVES 4

675 g llama meat, cut into 3 cm cubes
½ teaspoon paprika
½ teaspoon ground cumin
½ teaspoon ground allspice
3 tablespoons oil
200 g baby button onions, blanched and peeled

200 g button mushrooms, trimmed
1 bouquet garni (see page 512)
150 ml red wine
600 ml Veal Stock (see page 454)
salt and freshly ground black pepper

1 Toss the meat in the spices and season well with salt and pepper.
2 Heat 1½ tablespoons of the oil in a large sauté pan and fry the meat in batches until well browned, deglazing the pan as necessary. Using a slotted spoon, transfer the meat to a bowl.
3 Heat the remaining oil in the pan and add the onions and mushrooms. Cook for 5 minutes, or until well browned.
4 Add the bouquet garni to the pan and pour over the red wine. Bring to the boil and cook for 1 minute. Add the stock and return to the boil. Reduce the heat, return the meat to the pan and cover with a tight-fitting lid. Simmer gently for 1–1½ hours, or until the meat is tender.
5 Remove the meat from the pan with a slotted spoon and set aside. Discard the bouquet garni. Bring the sauce to the boil and reduce until it is thick and syrupy. Taste, and season if necessary. Return the meat to the pan and reheat gently. Serve immediately.

Wine: Chianti or Cabernet Franc

Muscox

Also known as musk ox, this animal's shaggy coat and bearded face make it look somewhat like a throwback from the ice age. It is related to the Tibetan yak and very heavily built, with a fully grown adult weighing up to 300 kg. Being native to Greenland and the polar circle of Canada, it has long been hunted by the Inuit people, who make use of the entire animal, eating the meat and making warm clothing from the skin. Extinction threatened the species at one time, due to large numbers being shot by European whale hunters to sustain them whilst on hunts.

Today muscox are bred for their meat, but not farmed in the traditional manner. They live in the wild, so the meat is free range, and only stags that are rejected by the herd and live by themselves are shot at the end of the mating season. This ensures that the numbers are protected.

Although the meat is similar in both structure and flavour to that of beef and lamb, it is exceptionally lean and tender, despite the fact that young animals are never shot. It is this leanness that allows the meat to be served raw – either minced, as in tartare, or very thinly sliced, as in carpaccio. By the same token, it can overcook very easily, so great care must be taken to ensure that it does not dry out.

Muscox Carpaccio

SERVES 6 AS A FIRST COURSE

1 × 500 g muscox fillet, cut across the grain into very thin slices

olive oil

1 tablespoon chopped fresh chervil

fresh lime juice

salt and freshly ground black pepper

For the sauce

5 tablespoons crème fraîche

2 tablespoons Mayonnaise (see page 466)

1 teaspoon wasabi paste

To garnish

mizuna leaves

dandelion leaves

shavings of pecorino cheese

1 Place the slices of muscox between 2 sheets of silicone paper and use a meat mallet or rolling pin to beat them as flat and thin as possible.
2 Arrange the meat on a large platter and pour over a little olive oil.
3 Mix together the crème fraîche, mayonnaise and wasabi. Stir in the chervil and season to taste with lime juice, salt and pepper.
4 Garnish the meat with the mizuna, dandelion and pecorino. Serve the sauce separately.

Wine: Red Burgundy, Cru Beaujolais or good, unoaked South African Chenin Blanc

Muscox and Sour Cherry Ragout

SERVES 4–6

1 kg muscox, preferably from the shoulder	**For the marinade**
1 tablespoon oil	300 ml red wine
2 onions, finely sliced	1 onion, roughly chopped
150 ml Veal Stock (see page 454)	1 clove of garlic, crushed
85 g dried cherries	1 bay leaf
1 bouquet garni (see page 512)	2 sprigs of fresh thyme
salt and freshly ground black pepper	1 sprig of fresh rosemary
2 tablespoons chopped fresh flat leaf parsley, to garnish	

1 Trim the muscox and cut into large pieces.
2 Mix all the marinade ingredients together in a non-metallic bowl. Add the meat, cover and leave overnight in the refrigerator.
3 Heat the oven to 170°C/325°F/gas mark 3.
4 Drain the meat, reserving the marinade, and pat dry.
5 Heat the oil in a heavy-based frying pan and brown the onions. Lift out with a slotted spoon and place in a casserole.
6 Brown the meat in the same pan in small batches and add it to the casserole.
7 Strain the marinade into the empty frying pan. Add the stock and bring to the boil, scraping up any sediment. Pour over the meat and season with salt and pepper.
8 Add the cherries to the casserole and immerse the bouquet garni in the liquid.
9 Cook in the oven for 45–60 minutes, until tender. Remove the bouquet garni.
10 Transfer the meat to a warmed serving dish and keep warm.
11 Boil the sauce to a syrupy consistency and pour over the meat. Sprinkle over the parsley and serve.

Wine: Crozes-Hermitage, New World Pinot Noir or Pinotage

Ostrich/Rhea

Originally from South Africa, ostriches are now farmed and bred worldwide. There are even some small producers in parts of the UK. Wild ostrich is a protected species, so there is no trade for it.

Although ostrich farming began 150 years ago, it was for the animals' highly prized skins and plumes. In the last 20 years, however, demand for ostrich meat has grown.

Typically, birds are slaughtered at 12–18 months, with the meat being considered at its peak around 14 months. As they are flightless, the bulk of the meat comes from the well-developed leg muscles. There is no breast meat, so this distinguishes ostrich from other types of poultry. There is no true fillet meat either, the term being used to describe the more tender and succulent parts of the leg, for example, the 'fan fillet'.

In nutritional terms, ostrich compares favourably with more traditional red meats, such as beef or lamb, because it lacks intramuscular fat. The removal of visible, external fat results in a fine-grained, very lean meat, which is high in protein and with similar levels of iron to that found in beef. In addition, raw ostrich meat contains roughly half the fat of raw chicken breast.

Ostrich is normally sold vacuum-packed. This prolongs its shelf life, as the meat, being low in fat, deteriorates quite quickly. Once removed from the vacuum-packaging and exposed to the air, its haemoglobin, which gives it a deep red colour, breaks down, causing the meat to turn an unappetizing brown colour. Although this is not harmful and does not affect the flavour, most people would probably prefer to buy it as needed and use it quickly whilst it looks its best.

Like the ostrich, the rhea is a flightless bird and is similar in appearance, though smaller in stature. It originated in South America and is now farmed throughout the world. The meat is dark in colour, rather like venison, and most similar in flavour and texture to beef. As both ostrich and rhea meat are low in fat, they should be cooked quickly over a high heat to brown the outside whilst keeping the centre pink. Rhea benefits particularly from strong-flavoured marinades, and is best when cooked quickly over a high heat so that it remains pink on the inside. It is particularly good in teriyaki and satay.

Ostrich Steaks with Wasabi and Ginger

SERVES 4

4 × 170 g ostrich steaks

oil

salt and freshly ground black pepper

For the marinade

2 tablespoons mirin

½ tablespoon light soy sauce

1 teaspoon clear honey

1 teaspoon wasabi paste

1.5 cm piece of fresh root ginger,
  peeled and finely grated

½ stalk of lemon grass, bruised

To serve

Hot Ginger Dressing (see below)

1 Place the ostrich steaks in a dish. Combine the marinade ingredients and pour over the steaks. Cover and refrigerate for 1 hour or overnight, turning them occasionally.

2 Discard the lemon grass from the marinade. Season the steaks with salt and pepper.

3 Brush a griddle pan with a little oil and place over a high heat until very hot.

4 Brown the ostrich steaks on both sides. Reduce the heat and continue to cook for a further 3–4 minutes, or until pink and juicy in the middle. Serve with the hot ginger dressing.

HOT GINGER DRESSING

SERVES 4

1 tablespoon soft palm sugar

1 cm piece of fresh root ginger,
  peeled and finely grated

½ teaspoon wasabi paste

finely grated zest and juice of 1 lime

1 tablespoon rice wine vinegar

½ small red chilli, very finely diced

pinch of salt

1 Put all the ingredients into a small saucepan and bring to the boil, stirring to dissolve the sugar.

2 Reduce the heat and simmer for 1 minute. Turn off the heat and allow to cool.

Wine: Pinot Gris/Grigio from Alsace or New Zealand

Snake

The majority of snakes are hunted for their skin, the meat being something of a by-product. However, the popularity of snake meat has increased in recent years, so they are now hunted specifically for the food industry too. Snakes are skinned, gutted and cleaned after slaughter, before being frozen. They are usually sold whole in the UK, portions rarely being available. However, those parts of America from where the bulk of snake meat is imported do sell snake fillets. Care is needed not to overcook the meat as it quickly becomes tough and dry.

Python is now the most popular type of snake as the meat to bone ratio is much higher than rattlesnake. Although usually frozen, it can also be bought dried, but often only in bulk. The dried meat features in Chinese delicacies, and is also used as a health tonic in Chinese medicine, with the desiccated gall bladder being prescribed as an aphrodisiac.

Rattlesnake was once the most popular snake meat, particularly in Australia and the southern hemisphere, and until recently was the only type available.

Python Nuggets

SERVES 6 AS A FIRST COURSE, OR 4 AS A MAIN COURSE

1 × 500 g python fillet, cut into 5 cm cubes

juice of ½ a lemon

oil, for deep-frying

panko breadcrumbs (see Note, page 317)

finely grated zest of 1 lemon

seasoned flour

1 egg, beaten

salt and freshly ground black pepper

To garnish

flat leaf parsley

lemon wedges

1 Place the snake pieces on a board. Sprinkle the lemon juice over them and season with salt and pepper.
2 Heat the oil in a deep-fryer until a cube of bread will brown in 20 seconds (see Warning, page 53).
3 Mix the panko breadcrumbs with the lemon zest.
4 Dip the snake in seasoned flour, then in the beaten egg, and finally in the lemon breadcrumbs, turning carefully to coat thoroughly. Lower into the hot oil and deep-fry until golden brown. Drain on kitchen paper and sprinkle with salt.
5 Garnish with the parsley and lemon wedges and serve immediately.

Wine: Light, fruity red (Beaujolais style) or less aromatic dry white

Griddled Python with Baby Fennel Tempura and Pernod Sauce

SERVES 4

500 g boneless python, cut into 5 cm cubes
oil
2 bunches of baby fennel, trimmed and
    cut into quarters, lengthwise
salt and freshly ground black pepper

For the tempura batter
110 g plain flour
110 g cornflour
2 small egg yolks
340 ml ice-cold soda water
pinch of fennel seeds, crushed
pinch of salt

For the sauce
1 shallot, finely chopped
2½ tablespoons Pernod
2½ tablespoons water
225 g unsalted butter, cut into small
    cubes and chilled
1 tablespoon finely chopped fresh tarragon leaves
freshly ground white pepper
squeeze of lime juice
lime wedges, to serve

1 Season the python with salt and pepper. Brush a griddle pan with a little oil and, when very hot, cook the python in batches until brown on all sides and cooked through. Keep warm.

2 Fill a deep-fryer with oil and heat until a cube of bread will sizzle vigorously in it (see Warning, page 53).

3 When the oil is hot, mix the batter ingredients together – the mixture should not be smooth.

4 Dip the prepared fennel into the batter and deep-fry in small batches. Drain well on kitchen paper and sprinkle lightly with salt.

5 To make the sauce, put the shallot, Pernod and water into a small, heavy-based pan and boil slowly until reduced to 2 tablespoons. Strain and return to the pan.

6 Lower the heat under the pan. Whisking continuously with a wire whisk, gradually add the butter, piece by piece. The sauce should be thick, creamy and pale. Stir in the tarragon and season to taste with salt, white pepper and lime juice.

7 Arrange the python and fennel tempura on a warmed serving platter. Garnish with lime wedges and hand the sauce separately.

Wine: Light, fruity red (Beaujolais style) or less aromatic dry white

Zebra

The Burchell's zebra is the only species that is hunted for meat, and it is easily distinguished from other zebras by its brown as well as black stripes. The meat is very lean and intensely red, being similar in appearance to the more expensive cuts of beef, and has a sweet, slightly gamy flavour. The fillet, loin and haunch are the main cuts imported into Europe. The neck, shoulders and other parts are rarely offered.

Zebra are hunted mainly in South Africa (where their skins are valued, but their meat is not popular), Tanzania, Kenya, Ethiopia and even in the Sudan. They are not bred for meat, but hunted from game farms, and the bulk of the meat comes from stallions.

Zebra Saltimbocca

Saltimbocca means literally 'jump in the mouth'. It's appropriate here because the combination of zebra meat, salty Parma ham and aromatic sage is a powerful one.

SERVES 4

4 × 170 g zebra fillet steaks	30 g unsalted butter
4 large sage leaves	1½ tablespoons Calvados
8 slices Parma ham	100 ml double cream
1 tablespoon oil	salt and freshly ground black pepper

1 Wipe the steaks and trim off any gristle or fat. Season with salt and pepper.
2 Lay a sage leaf on top of each steak, then wrap in a slice of Parma ham.
3 Heat the oil in a heavy-based frying pan, add the butter and, when foaming, fry the steaks for 3½ minutes on each side, starting with the seam facing uppermost. Remove any excess fat from the pan.
4 Pour in the Calvados and set it alight. Once the flames have subsided, remove the steaks from the pan and allow to rest on a warm serving platter.
5 Pour the cream into the pan and mix the contents thoroughly, scraping up any sediment stuck to the bottom. Bring the sauce to the boil and simmer to a syrupy consistency. If the sauce is too thick, add a little water. Season to taste and pour over the meat. Serve immediately.

Wine: Medium-bodied dry red, such as Chianti Classico

Zebra Stew

This casserole is best eaten on the day it is made as the low fat content of the meat is likely to make it a little dry on reheating.

SERVES 4–6

1 × 1 kg haunch of zebra

seasoned flour

oil

30 g unsalted butter

2 red onions, finely sliced

2 sticks of celery, finely sliced

300 ml brown ale

300 ml Brown Stock (see page 452)

1 tablespoon redcurrant jelly

2 bay leaves

1 tablespoon chopped fresh thyme

50 g fresh blueberries

salt and freshly ground black pepper

chopped fresh parsley, to garnish

1 Heat the oven to 150°C/300°F/gas mark 2.

2 Prepare the zebra by trimming away any membranes, sinews and fat, and cut into 5 cm pieces. Toss in the seasoned flour and shake off the excess.

3 Heat 1 tablespoon of oil in a large flameproof casserole and brown the zebra in small batches. Transfer the meat to a large bowl. If the casserole becomes too dry between batches, pour in a little of the stock, scrape up any sediment stuck to the bottom and pour over the zebra pieces. Heat a little more oil in the deglazed pan and continue browning the meat.

4 When all the meat has been browned and set aside, add the butter to the pan and cook the onions and celery over a low heat until softened and lightly browned.

5 Pour the ale and stock into the pan and bring to the boil. Simmer for 2 minutes.

6 Return the zebra to the pan and stir in the redcurrant jelly. Add the bay leaves and thyme and season with salt and pepper.

7 Cover the casserole and cook in the oven for 1½ hours, or until the meat is very tender.

8 Using a slotted spoon, transfer the zebra, onions and celery to a serving dish.

9 Boil the sauce fast until reduced to a shiny, syrupy consistency. Add the blueberries and simmer gently for 2 minutes.

10 Pour the sauce over the zebra and serve garnished with parsley.

Wine: Medium-bodied dry red, such as a Stellenbosch Bordeaux blend from the Cape

Basic Recipes

The making of stocks, sauces, pastries and pasta is a skill in its own right. Therefore, this section of the book is dedicated to recipes and techniques to ensure their successful execution.

Stocks and sauces play a major role in meat cookery. Stocks are the basis of a good gravy, and sauces are either a further accompaniment to meat that is served with gravy, or the only one, in the case of, say, a fried or grilled piece of meat.

Pastry has one of the earliest links to meat cookery, originally being used as a crust to protect and preserve its content, whereas nowadays it is served as a delicious addition in its own right.

Pasta is an integral part of many meat sauce dishes, such as cannelloni and lasagne, and although it is good in its shop-bought dried or fresh forms, home-made pasta is perhaps the most delicious, and relatively simple to make.

Stocks

Stock is flavoured liquid, and the basic flavour can be poultry, meat, fish or vegetable. Many of the recipes in this book suggest a particular type of stock to use, such as brown chicken stock or veal stock. These suggestions are designed to give an appropriate depth of flavour to the meat being used in the dish, for example, brown chicken stock for a richly flavoured red meat dish, or white chicken stock for a milder flavoured white meat dish. However, it is not essential to adhere strictly to these suggestions: any good, well-flavoured stock is better than no stock at all. Similar results can be achieved by adding just a little brown stock to a lightly flavoured meat and diluting it. By the same token, a white stock can be boiled and reduced, to concentrate the flavour, where more strength is required. Not everyone will always be fortunate enough to have the best, tasty, specific type of home-made stock to hand all the time, and it is important not to feel daunted by this.

On occasion, a type of stock that differs greatly from the type of meat being used is suggested – for example, white chicken stock in a pork dish. This is because pork bones don't make good stock: it is invariably fatty and strongly flavoured, and overpowers the meat.

The advantage of using stock made from scratch at home means that the cook can be in control of the seasoning and strength of the finished product. When using a commercial cube or bouillon, the flavour can be quite overpowering and often rather salty. Check the labels carefully to ensure the product is made using meat bones and vegetables and does not contain monosodium glutamate (MSG). Commercial, fresh liquid stocks are generally very tasty and well seasoned, making them a good alternative to home-made.

Making a Stock

The secret of stocks is slow, gentle poaching. If the liquid is the slightest bit greasy, vigorous boiling will produce a murky, fatty stock. Skimming, especially for meat stocks, is vital: as fat and scum rise to the surface, they should be lifted off with a perforated spoon, perhaps every 10–15 minutes.

Rich, brown stocks are made by first frying or baking the bones, vegetables and scraps of meat until a good, dark, even brown. Only then does the cook proceed with the gentle poaching. Care must be taken not to burn the bones or vegetables: just one burnt carrot can ruin several litres of stock. Brown stocks are usually made from the bones of red meats or veal, but can also be made from browned chicken carcasses and wings. These stocks are best simmered for 6–8 hours.

White stocks are more delicate and are made by simmering only. They are usually based on white poultry or vegetables and are simmered for only 3–4 hours.

The bones: Most households rarely have anything other than the cooked bones from a roast available for stocks. These will make good stock, but it will be weaker than that made with raw bones. Very often raw bones can be had free or bought very cheaply from the butcher. Get them chopped into manageable small pieces in the shop. A little raw meat, the bloodier the better, gives a rich, very clear liquid.

Water: The water must be cold; if it is hot, the fat in the bones will melt immediately into the stock. The stock will then be murky, have an unattractive smell and a nasty flavour. Cold water encourages the fat to rise to the surface; it can then be skimmed.

Jellied stock: Veal bones produce a particularly good stock that will set to a jelly. A calf's foot added to any stock will have the same jellifying effect. Jellied stock will keep longer than liquid stock, but in any event, stocks should be reboiled every 2 or 3 days if kept refrigerated, or every day if kept in a larder, to prevent them going bad.

Salt: Do not add salt to stock. It may be used later for something that is already salty, or boiled down to a concentrated glaze (glace de viande, see page 455), in which case the glaze would be over-salted if the stock contained salt. (Salt does not boil off with the water, but remains in the pan.)

Storage: A good way of storing a large batch of stock is to boil it down to double strength, and to add water only when using. Alternatively, stock can be boiled down to a thick, syrupy glaze, which can be used like stock cubes. The glaze can be frozen in ice-cube trays, then turn the frozen cubes into a plastic box in the freezer. They will keep for at least a year if fat-free.

Points to Remember about Making Stocks

- Do not use salt.
- Use fresh ingredients and raw bones where possible (cooked bones can be used but may result in a cloudier stock).
- Cover the ingredients with cold water.
- Skim frequently. Stock that is not skimmed properly will be greasy.
- Dépouiller – add cold water to the stock. Bring to the poach again to bring scum to the surface. Skim with a ladle.
- Heat so that the surface just trembles: do not allow to boil. Boiling will make the stock cloudy.
- Use *non*-starchy vegetables, such as carrot, onion and celery.
- Cook for the recommended time; do not overcook.

White Chicken Stock

2 chicken carcasses, broken up

1 veal knuckle bone

about 2 litres cold water

2 onions, cut into 3 cm pieces

1 medium carrot, cut into 3 cm pieces

2 sticks of celery, cut into 3 cm chunks

1 leek, green leaves removed, cut into 3 cm pieces

50 g button mushrooms

1 handful of fresh parsley stalks

1 bay leaf

1 sprig of fresh thyme

½ teaspoon black peppercorns

1 Trim any excess fat from the bones.

2 Place the prepared bones in a deep, narrow pot. Cover with cold water and slowly bring to a poach.

3 Using a ladle, skim off the scum and fat that rise to the surface.

4 When the water starts to boil, pour cold water into the pan to solidify the fat and scum. Skim well to remove the fat and scum, ensuring that the remaining liquid is clear.

5 Add the vegetables, herbs and peppercorns to the pot and cover all the ingredients with the cold water.

6 Bring back to a poach, then regulate the heat so that the stock poaches gently throughout the cooking time of 2–3 hours. Skim occasionally.

7 Make sure the ingredients remain covered with water. As the liquid evaporates, top up the pot with cold water as this helps to draw any remaining fat and scum to the surface.

8 Once the stock is cooked, strain carefully through a fine sieve into a storage container or a clean, wide pan for reducing. Do not force the liquid through the sieve by pressing the ingredients as this may result in a cloudy stock.

9 Reduce the stock to the required strength, skimming regularly to remove any further impurities on the surface. To store the stock, continue to reduce it to a glace (see page 455), then cool.

Brown Stock

Lamb bones can be substituted for the beef bones when stock is required for a lamb recipe. Using lamb stock with give a stronger lamb flavour to the finished dish. Ensure the stock is dépouillered (see page 514) and skimmed thoroughly to remove any excess fat. Stock made with lamb bones should be cooked for 2–3 hours, then strained from the bones and reduced, if required.

1 kg beef and veal marrow bones
2 tablespoons vegetable oil
2 onions, unpeeled and cut into eighths
   through the root
2 carrots, peeled and cut into large pieces
2 sticks of celery, cut into large pieces
½ small celeriac, peeled and cut into 3 cm pieces
1 head of fennel, cut into large pieces

110 g button mushrooms
1 scant tablespoon tomato purée
about 2 litres cold water
1 handful of fresh parsley stalks
1 bay leaf
½ teaspoon black peppercorns
1 sprig of fresh thyme

1 Heat the oven to 220°C/425°F/gas mark 7.
2 Trim any excess fat from the bones. Place in a roasting pan and roast in the oven for about 1 hour, until a rich russet brown. Turn the bones occasionally to ensure that they roast and brown evenly on all sides. During the browning process most of the fat will melt and collect in the roasting tray. Discard any burnt bones.
3 Place the oil and vegetables, except for the mushrooms, in a frying pan and fry until they are caramelized to a rich golden brown. It is essential they do not burn.
4 Add the tomato purée to the vegetables just before they are fully browned to caramelize them to a deeper red-brown colour.
5 Place the bones and browned vegetables in a deep, narrow pot and cover with cold water. Bring slowly to the boil, skimming off any scum as it rises to the surface. There should be little fat as most of it was rendered down during the roasting and browning process.
6 Pour cold water into the pan to solidify the fat and scum, then skim well to remove it, ensuring that the remaining liquid is as clear as possible.
7 Add the remaining ingredients, add more cold water to cover, and bring back to the boil. Poach the ingredients for 5–6 hours, skimming occasionally.
8 Strain the stock, but do not press the vegetables in the sieve as this could make the stock cloudy.
9 Reduce the stock to the required strength by boiling rapidly, and skim regularly.
10 To store the stock, reduce to a glace (see page 455), then cool.

Beef Bouillon (Broth)

1 veal bone

50 g fatty bacon, chopped

3 carrots

2 turnips

2 leeks

stick of celery

1 small parsnip

1 onion

900 g shin of beef, cut into cubes

3.5 litres cold water

½ teaspoon salt

2 bay leaves

3 cloves

1 good handful of parsley stalks

2 sprigs of thyme

1 Heat the oven to 200°C/400°F/gas mark 6.
2 Put the veal bone and bacon into a roasting pan and brown in the oven for 1 hour.
3 Cut the vegetables up roughly, reserving the onion skin.
4 Put the vegetables and the meat in the pan with the bones, then place on the hob and fry until well browned, stirring occasionally to prevent sticking or burning.
5 Drain off the fat. Put the bones, vegetables and reserved onion skin in a large saucepan with the water and salt. Bring slowly to the boil, skimming off the scum and fat as it rises to the surface. When the water is boiling, pour in a glass of cold water and immediately skim off the fat. Repeat the process once the liquid is boiling again.
6 Add the flavourings. Turn down the heat, cover and allow the stock to poach for a good 3 hours. Inspect it occasionally and repeat the skimming process if necessary. You should now have about 1.45 litres of stock.
7 Strain and allow to cool, then chill so that any remaining fat sets on top. Lift off the fat. The bouillon should be jellied, but will of course melt on reheating.

Veal Stock

900 g beef and veal bones
1 onion, chopped, skin reserved
1 carrot, roughly chopped
1 stick of celery, chopped
2 leeks, green parts only, chopped (optional)
oil

about 2 litres cold water
parsley stalks
a few mushroom peelings (optional)
2 bay leaves
6 black peppercorns

1 Heat the oven to 220°C/425°F/gas mark 7.
2 Put the bones into a roasting pan and brown in the oven (up to 1 hour).
3 Brown the onion, carrot, celery and leeks (if using), in a little oil in a large stockpot. It is essential that they do not burn.
4 When the bones are well browned add them to the vegetables with the onion skin, parsley stalks, mushroom peelings (if using), bay leaves and peppercorns. Cover with cold water and bring to the boil slowly, skimming off any scum as it rises to the surface.
5 When clear of scum, poach gently for 6–8 hours, or even longer, skimming off the fat as necessary and topping up with water if the level gets very low. The longer it poaches, and the more liquid reduces by evaporation, the stronger the stock will be.
6 Strain, cool, and lift off any remaining fat.

Brown Chicken Stock

2 kg chicken carcasses
oil
1 onion, chopped, skins reserved
1 carrot, roughly chopped
1 stick of celery, chopped
green parts of 2 leeks, chopped (optional)

parsley stalks
a few mushroom peelings (optional)
2 bay leaves
6 black peppercorns
about 2 litres cold water

1 Heat the oven to 220°C/425°F/gas mark 7.
2 Put the chicken carcasses into a roasting pan and brown in the oven for up to 1 hour.
3 Place the oil in a large stockpot and brown the onion, carrot, celery and leeks, if using. It is essential that they do not burn.
4 When the carcasses are well browned, add them to the vegetables together with the onion skins, parsley stalks, mushroom peelings, if using, bay leaves and peppercorns. Cover with cold water and bring to the boil slowly, skimming off any scum as it rises to the surface.
5 When clear of scum, poach gently for 6–8 hours, or even longer, skimming off the fat as necessary and topping up with water if the level gets very low. The longer it poaches and the more the liquid reduces by evaporation, the stronger the stock will be.
6 Strain, cool, and lift off any remaining fat.

Glace de Viande

600 ml Brown Stock (see page 452), absolutely free of fat

1 Place the stock in a heavy-based saucepan and reduce by boiling over a steady heat until thick, clear and syrupy.
2 Pour into small pots. When cold, cover with cling film or jam covers and secure with rubber bands.
3 Keep in the refrigerator until ready for use.

NOTE: Glace de viande keeps for several weeks and is very useful for enriching sauces.

Ham Stock

The best-flavoured ham stock is generally the well-skimmed liquor from boiling a ham or gammon (see page 221), but this recipe works well with a cooked ham bone.

1 cooked ham bone	1 bay leaf
1 onion, chopped	fresh parsley stalks
1 carrot, chopped	black peppercorns

1 Place all the ingredients in a large saucepan. Cover with cold water and bring slowly to the boil. Skim off any fat and/or scum. Poach for 2–3 hours, skimming frequently and topping up the water level if necessary.
2 Strain and use as required.

NOTE: Ham stock is usually salty, so should not be reduced.

Turkey Stock I

Ideally, all stocks should be made from raw bones, but no one is likely to have raw turkey bones. If you are making stock before Christmas, you will have to make it from the giblets – but never add the liver as it will make the stock taste bitter. This recipe can also be used for making goose, pheasant or chicken stock.

1 turkey neck
turkey giblets, well washed, without the liver
1 onion, sliced
1 stick of celery, sliced
1 carrot, sliced

1 parsley stalk, bruised
1 sprig of fresh thyme
2 bay leaves
10 black peppercorns

1 Put all the ingredients into a large saucepan. Cover generously with cold water and bring slowly to the boil. Skim off any fat or scum.
2 Poach slowly for 2–3 hours, skimming frequently and topping up the water level if necessary. The liquid should reduce to half the original quantity.
3 Strain and cool.

Turkey Stock II

This recipe for making stock uses the cooked turkey bones. It is important that the water is very cold; if it is hot, the fat in the turkey skin will melt immediately and much of it will bubble into the stock. This stock can also be used in any of the recipes that call for chicken stock.

cooked turkey bones
1 onion, sliced
1 stick of celery, sliced
1 carrot, sliced

1 parsley stalk, bruised
1 sprig of fresh thyme
2 bay leaves
10 black peppercorns

1 Put all the ingredients into a large saucepan. Cover generously with cold water and bring slowly to the boil. Skim off any fat and/or scum.
2 Poach slowly for 2–3 hours, skimming frequently and topping up the water level if necessary. The liquid should reduce to half the original quantity.
3 Strain and cool.

Court-bouillon

1 litre water
150 ml white wine vinegar
1 carrot, sliced
1 onion, sliced

1 stick of celery
12 black peppercorns
2 bay leaves
salt

1 Place half the water with all the remaining ingredients in a large saucepan. Bring to the boil, then simmer for 20 minutes.

2 Add the remaining water, then allow to cool before straining.

Stock: What has gone wrong when...

The stock is greasy.
- The stock was not skimmed thoroughly.
- The stock was allowed to boil.
- The meat was not well trimmed of fat.
- Too much oil has been used to brown the vegetables (brown stocks).

The stock is cloudy.
- The stock was allowed to boil.
- Starchy vegetables were included in the stock.
- The stock has fermented.
- The stock was not skimmed regularly.

The stock has a weak, insipid flavour.
- The stock has not been cooked for long enough.
- The stock needs to be strained and reduced.
- Insufficient bones and flavouring ingredients were added to the stock.
- If a brown stock, the bones and vegetables were not browned enough.

The stock tastes bitter.
- The stock is overcooked.
- Bitter vegetables were used in the stock.
- Bones and/or vegetables were burnt during browning.

The stock tastes too sweet.
- Too high a ratio of vegetables to bones/carcasses has been used.

Aspic

1 litre well-flavoured White Chicken Stock
  (see page 451)

15–30 g powdered gelatine, as necessary

2 eggshells, crushed

2 egg whites

1 Lift or skim any fat from the stock.
2 Put the stock into a large saucepan. If it is liquid when chilled, sprinkle 30 g gelatine over it; if it is set when chilled, gelatine will not be necessary. Dissolve over a low heat, then allow to cool.
3 Put the shells and egg whites into the stock. Place over the heat and whisk steadily with a balloon whisk until the mixture begins to boil. Stop whisking immediately and remove the pan from the heat. Allow the mixture to subside. Take care not to break the crust formed by the egg white.
4 Bring the aspic just to the boil again, and again allow to subside. Repeat this once more (the egg white will trap the sediment in the stock and clear the aspic). Allow to cool for 2 minutes.
5 Fix a double layer of fine muslin over a clean basin and carefully strain the aspic through it, taking care to hold back the egg-white crust. When all the liquid is through (or almost all of it) allow the egg white to slip into the muslin. Then strain the aspic again – this time through both egg white crust and cloth. Do not try to hurry the process by squeezing the cloth, or murky aspic will result.

NOTE: The saucepan, sieve and whisk used for clearing the aspic should be scalded before use.

VARIATIONS
Brown Stock Aspic: Use Brown Chicken Stock (see page 454) in place of White Chicken Stock.
Madeira Aspic: Add 45 ml Madeira to 600 ml aspic.
Tarragon Aspic: Per 600 ml aspic add 1½–2 tablespoons tarragon vinegar, or 1 tablespoon fresh chopped tarragon.

Aspic: What has gone wrong when...

The aspic is cloudy.
- The stock contained fat that was dispersed in the stock when the stock was boiled.
- Whisking continued after the stock began to steam and the crust was beaten into the stock.
- The bowl and/or other equipment was not sterilized properly.

The aspic has a lot of bubbles in it.
- The aspic was stirred vigorously during cooling.
- Bubbles were not removed with a cocktail stick before the aspic set.

The aspic splits into layers after it has set.
- The first layer of aspic was set too firmly before the second later was added.

Sauces

Larousse Gastronomique defines a sauce as a 'liquid seasoning for food', and this covers anything from juices in a frying pan to complicated and sophisticated emulsions.

Flour-thickened sauces

The commonest English sauces are those thickened with flour, and these are undoubtedly the most practical for the home cook. The secret is not to make them too thick (by not adding too much flour), to beat them well and to give them a good boil after they have thickened to make them shine. They will also look professionally shiny if they are finished by whizzing in a blender, or if they are 'mounted' with a little extra butter, gradually incorporated as dice, at the end.

The butter and flour base of a sauce is called a 'roux'. In a white roux, the butter and flour are mixed over a gentle heat without browning; in a blond roux, they are allowed to cook to a biscuit colour; and in a brown roux, they are cooked until distinctly brown.

Another way of thickening a sauce with flour is to make a beurre manié. Equal quantities of softened butter and flour are kneaded to a smooth paste and whisked gradually into a boiling liquid. As the butter melts, the flour is evenly distributed throughout the sauce, thickening the liquid without allowing lumps to form.

Cornflour and arrowroot are also useful thickeners. They are 'slaked' (mixed to a paste with cold water, stock or milk), added to a hot liquid and allowed to boil for a couple of minutes to thicken it.

Emulsions

These are liquids that contain tiny droplets of oil or fat evenly distributed in suspension.

Cold and stable emulsions: Mayonnaise (see page 466) is the best known of the cold and stable emulsion sauces, in which oil is beaten into egg yolks and held in suspension. If the oil is added too fast the sauce will curdle.

Warm and stable emulsions: The most stable warm emulsions, like cold emulsions, are based on egg yolks and butter. The best known is hollandaise. Great care has to be taken not to allow the sauce to curdle.

Eggless emulsions: These have become the more fashionable butter sauces. The classic is Beurre Blanc (see page 473). Eggless emulsions split very easily, so great care should be taken to follow the recipe precisely.

Unstable emulsions: French dressing or vinaigrette will emulsify if whizzed or whisked together, but will separate back to its component parts after about 15 minutes.

Liaisons

Egg yolk can be mixed with cream to form a liaison. It is then used to thicken and enrich sauces. The yolks must not boil or the sauce will curdle.

White Sauce

This is a quick and easy basic white sauce.

MAKES APPROXIMATELY 300 ML

20 g butter

20 g plain flour

pinch of dry English mustard

300 ml creamy milk

salt and freshly ground white pepper

1 Melt the butter in a heavy-based saucepan.
2 Add the flour and mustard and stir over the heat for 1 minute. Remove the pan from the heat, gradually pour in the milk and mix to a smooth sauce.
3 Return the sauce to the heat and stir continuously until boiling.
4 Simmer for 2–3 minutes and season with salt and white pepper.

Béchamel Sauce

Unlike the basic white sauce, Béchamel uses milk infused with onion and flavourings that give it a richer flavour.

MAKES APPROXIMATELY 300 ML

300 ml creamy milk

1 slice of onion

1 blade of mace

a few fresh parsley stalks

4 white peppercorns

1 bay leaf

30 g butter

20 g plain flour

salt and freshly ground white pepper

1 Place the milk in a saucepan with the onion, mace, parsley, peppercorns and bay leaf and slowly bring to simmering point.
2 Remove from heat and set aside for 8–10 minutes so that the flavours infuse.
3 Melt 20 g of the butter in a heavy-based saucepan, mix in the flour and stir over the heat for 1 minute.
4 Remove from the heat. Strain the infused milk and stir in gradually.
5 Return the sauce to the heat and stir or whisk continuously until boiling. Add the remaining butter and beat very well (this will help to make the sauce shiny).
6 Simmer, stirring well, for 3 minutes.
7 Season to taste with salt and white pepper.

NOTE: To make a professionally shiny Béchamel sauce, pass through a tammy strainer before use, or whizz in a blender.

Mornay Sauce

MAKES APPROXIMATELY 300 ML

20 g butter

20 g plain flour

pinch of dry English mustard

pinch of cayenne pepper

300 ml milk

50 g Gruyère or strong Cheddar cheese, grated

15 g Parmesan cheese, freshly grated (optional)

salt and freshly ground black pepper

1 Melt the butter in a heavy-based saucepan and stir in the flour, mustard and cayenne pepper. Cook, stirring, for 1 minute. Remove the pan from the heat. Gradually stir in the milk and mix until smooth.

2 Return the pan to the heat and stir until boiling. Simmer, stirring well, for 2 minutes.

3 Add all the cheese and mix well, but do not reboil or the cheese will become greasy.

4 Season to taste with salt and pepper.

Parsley Sauce

This sauce is very good with ham.

MAKES APPROXIMATELY 300 ML

300 ml creamy milk

1 slice of onion

1 good handful of fresh parsley

4 black peppercorns

1 bay leaf

20 g butter

20 g plain flour

salt and freshly ground black pepper

1 Put the milk, onion, parsley stalks (but not leaves), peppercorns and bay leaf into a saucepan and slowly bring to simmering point.

2 Remove from heat and leave for about 10 minutes so that the flavours infuse.

3 Melt the butter in a heavy-based saucepan, stir in the flour and cook, stirring, for 1 minute.

4 Remove from the heat. Strain in the infused milk and gradually stir into the roux.

5 Return the sauce to the heat and stir continuously until boiling, then simmer for 2–3 minutes. Season to taste with salt and pepper.

6 Chop the parsley leaves very finely and stir into the hot sauce. Serve immediately.

Soubise Sauce

30 g butter
225 g onions, very finely chopped
4 tablespoons double cream

For the béchamel sauce
20 g butter
1 bay leaf
20 g plain flour
300 ml milk

1 Melt the first quantity of butter in a heavy-based saucepan. Add the onions and cook over a very low heat, preferably covered with a lid to create a steamy atmosphere. The onions should become very soft and transparent, but on no account brown. Add the cream.

2 Now prepare the béchamel: melt the butter in a saucepan, add the bay leaf and flour and cook, stirring, for 1 minute. Remove from the heat and gradually stir in the milk. Return to the heat and bring slowly to the boil, stirring continuously. Simmer for 2 minutes. Remove the bay leaf and mix with the soubise.

NOTE: This sauce can be liquidized in a blender or pushed through a sieve if a smooth texture is desired.

Velouté Sauce

20 g butter
20 g plain flour
300 ml White Chicken Stock, strained and
  well skimmed (see page 451)

2 tablespoons double cream
a few drops of lemon juice
salt and freshly ground white pepper

1 Melt the butter in a heavy-based saucepan. Add the flour and cook, stirring, over a low heat until straw-coloured. Remove from the heat. Add the stock and mix well.

2 Return to the heat and bring to the boil, stirring, then simmer until slightly syrupy and opaque. Stir in the cream. Season to taste with salt, pepper and lemon juice.

Gravy

This recipe for thickened gravy be can used with any dish that might require it.

MAKES ABOUT 600 ML

2 tablespoons flour

1 bay leaf

2 sprigs of thyme

600 ml stock

salt and freshly ground black pepper

1 Pour off the fat and juices from the roasting pan.
2 Return 2 tablespoons of fat to the pan.
3 Add the 2 tablespoons flour to the fat and stir over the heat until the flour has browned and any sediment from the bottom of the pan has loosened.
4 Add the bay leaf and thyme, and up to 600 ml stock and any juices from the roasting pan. Stir or whisk until boiling. Season to taste with salt and pepper. Simmer for 2–3 minutes. Remove the bay leaf and thyme before serving.

Red Onion Gravy

MAKES 200–350 ML, DEPENDING ON REDUCTION

675 g red onions, finely sliced

2 tablespoons oil

1½ tablespoons soft dark brown sugar

1 tablespoon balsamic vinegar

750 ml Brown Chicken Stock (see page 454)

1 bouquet garni (see page 512)

salt and freshly ground black pepper

1 Place the onions and oil in a large pan and sweat for 15–20 minute over a low heat, until very soft and reduced by half of their original volume.
2 Stir the sugar and vinegar into the pan, increase the heat and cook for a further 5 minutes, or until nicely browned.
3 Pour over the stock and bring to the boil.
4 Add the bouquet garni, reduce the heat and simmer until reduced by half.
5 Remove the bouquet garni, taste and season with salt and pepper.

Sauce Espagnole

4 tablespoons oil

1 small carrot, diced

1 small onion, diced

1 stick of celery, diced

2 teaspoons plain flour, browned (see Note)

600 ml Brown Stock (see page 452)

½ teaspoon tomato purée

a few mushroom stalks

1 bouquet garni (see page 512)

1 Heat the oil in a heavy-based saucepan, add the vegetables and fry until they begin to soften.
2 Stir in the flour and continue to cook slowly, stirring occasionally and scraping up any sediment. Cook to a good russet brown.
3 Remove from the heat, add three-quarters of the stock, the tomato purée, mushroom stalks and bouquet garni.
4 Return to the heat and bring to the boil, then simmer for 30 minutes.
5 Skim twice to remove any scum and fat: adding a splash of cold stock to the boiling liquid helps bring the scum and fat to the surface. Tilting the pan slightly, skim with a large metal spoon. Strain.

NOTE: The flour can be browned in the oven (200°C/400°F/gas mark 6). This gives the sauce a good colour.

Demi-glace Sauce

Demi-glace sauce is a refined sauce espagnole.

1 quantity Sauce Espagnole (see above)
Brown Stock (see page 452)

salt and freshly ground black pepper

1 Place the sauce and an equal quantity of stock in a heavy-based saucepan. Bring to a simmer, then reduce by boiling to half the original quantity. Skim off any impurities as they rise to the surface.
2 Pass through a fine chinois (conical strainer), reboil and check the seasoning.

Madeira Sauce

3 tablespoons Madeira

1 teaspoon Glace de Viande (see page 455)

300 ml Sauce Espagnole (see above)

1 knob of butter

1 Place the Madeira and glace de viande together in a small, heavy-based saucepan. Boil until reduced by half.

2 Add the sauce espagnole and warm, but do not boil.

3 Beat in the knob of butter.

Sauce Robert

a little butter

1 tablespoon chopped onion

150 ml wine vinegar

300 ml Demi-glace Sauce (see opposite)

3 gherkins, chopped

1 teaspoon Dijon mustard

1 teaspoon chopped fresh parsley

1 Melt the butter in a heavy-based saucepan and soften the onion over a low heat. Add the vinegar and boil until the liquid has reduced to 1 tablespoon. Pour in the demi-glace sauce, stir, and simmer for 15 minutes.

2 Immediately before serving, add the gherkins, mustard and parsley.

Poivrade Sauce

50 g butter

4 shallots, blanched, peeled and very finely chopped

3 teaspoons cracked black peppercorns

300 ml red wine

600 ml Veal Stock (see page 454)

2 tablespoons freshly chopped parsley

salt and freshly ground black pepper

1 Melt the butter in a saucepan and add the shallots. Cover with a piece of dampened greaseproof paper and a lid and sweat until soft but not coloured.

2 Stir the peppercorns into the shallots, add the wine and bring to the boil. Reduce the heat and simmer until reduced by half of its original volume.

3 Add the stock and return to the boil. Simmer the sauce until it is thick and syrupy.

4 Stir in the parsley and season with salt and pepper.

NOTE: Canned green peppercorns can be used as an alternative to black ones. Rinse them well before using to remove the brine.

Mayonnaise

2 egg yolks

1 teaspoon dry English mustard

300 ml olive oil, or 150 ml each olive oil and salad oil

a squeeze of lemon juice

1 tablespoon white wine vinegar

salt and freshly ground white pepper

1 Put the yolks into a bowl with a pinch of salt and the mustard and beat well with a wooden spoon.
2 Add half the oil, literally drop by drop, beating all the time. The mixture should become very thick.
3 Beat in the lemon juice.
4 Resume pouring in the oil, going more quickly now, but alternating the dribbles of oil with small quantities of vinegar.
5 Season to taste with salt and pepper.

NOTE: If the mixture curdles, another egg yolk should be beaten in a separate bowl, and the curdled mixture beaten into it drop by drop.

VARIATIONS: To make green mayonnaise, pick over a bunch of watercress to remove the stalks and any yellowed leaves. Blanch and refresh. Dry thoroughly and chop very finely. Add to the basic mayonnaise mixture and season to taste with salt and pepper. If you prefer, cooked and very well-drained spinach can be used instead of watercress.

Aïoli

This is a speciality of Provence.

6 cloves of garlic, crushed

3 egg yolks

3 tablespoons fresh white breadcrumbs

2 tablespoons white wine vinegar

300 ml good-quality olive oil

1 tablespoon boiling water

salt and freshly ground white pepper

1 Put the garlic, egg yolks, breadcrumbs, salt, pepper and vinegar into a food processor. Whizz to a paste.
2 With the motor running, slowly add the oil to make a thick, emulsified sauce. Add the boiling water. Season to taste and use as required.

Rémoulade Sauce

150 ml Mayonnaise (see page 466)
1 teaspoon Dijon mustard
½ tablespoon finely chopped capers

½ tablespoon finely chopped gherkin
½ tablespoon finely chopped fresh tarragon or chervil
1 anchovy fillet, finely chopped

1 Mix all the ingredients together.

NOTE: Rémoulade sauce is a mayonnaise with a predominantly mustard flavour. The other ingredients, though good, are not always present.

Tapenade

110 g pitted black olives
2 tablespoons capers, rinsed
1 medium clove of garlic, chopped

75 ml olive oil
freshly ground black pepper

1 Put the olives, capers and garlic into a food processor and process until smooth.
2 While the motor is still running, pour in the oil. Season with pepper.

Pesto Sauce

2 cloves of garlic
2 bunches of fresh basil leaves
50 g pine nuts

50 g Parmesan cheese, freshly grated
150 ml olive oil
salt

1 In a blender or mortar, grind the garlic and basil together to a paste. Add the pine nuts, cheese, oil and plenty of salt. Keep in a covered jar in a cool place.

VARIATION: Pesto is sometimes made with walnuts instead of pine nuts, and the nuts may be pounded with the other ingredients to give a smooth paste.

Wild Mushroom Sauce

30 g butter

2 shallots, chopped

110 g wild mushrooms, such as horn of plenty, chanterelles, etc.

50 g flat mushrooms, sliced

425 ml Brown Stock (see page 452)

100 ml dry white wine

170 g unsalted butter, chilled and cut into small pieces

salt and freshly ground black pepper

1 Melt the butter in a sauté pan, add the shallots and cook until soft. Increase the heat and cook until golden brown.

2 Add all the mushrooms and cook for 1–2 minutes.

3 Add the stock and wine. Remove the mushrooms with a perforated spoon and reserve. Boil the liquid until reduced to about 150 ml. Lower the heat under the pan.

4 Using a small wire whisk and plenty of vigorous, continuous whisking, gradually add the butter piece by piece. This process takes about 5 minutes and the sauce should become thick and creamy. Check the seasoning.

5 Return the mushrooms to the sauce and serve.

Mushroom Herb Sauce

2 handfuls of mixed fresh herbs, such as tarragon, parsley, chervil

150 ml White Chicken Stock (see page 451)

220 ml double cream

30 g butter

110 g button mushrooms

110 g oyster mushrooms

salt and freshly ground black pepper

1 Drop the herbs into a saucepan of boiling salted water. Bring back to the boil, then strain through a sieve. Pour cold water on to the herbs and squeeze out any excess moisture. Put into a blender.

2 Put the stock and cream into a saucepan, bring up to the boil, then simmer until a coating consistency is achieved. Pour into the blender and liquidize with the herbs until smooth and green.

3 Melt the butter in a sauté pan and cook the mushrooms until soft and any liquid has evaporated. Add the herb sauce to the pan and reheat. Season to taste with salt and pepper.

Tomato Sauce I

1 large onion, finely chopped
3 tablespoons oil
10 tomatoes, roughly chopped
pinch of caster sugar

150 ml White Chicken Stock (see page 451)
1 teaspoon fresh thyme leaves
salt and freshly ground black pepper

1 Sweat the onion in the oil in a saucepan. Add the tomatoes, salt, pepper and sugar, and cook for a further 25 minutes. Add the stock and cook for 5 minutes.
2 Liquidize the sauce and push through a sieve. If it is too thin, boil rapidly to reduce to the desired consistency. Take care: it will spit and has a tendency to catch.
3 Add the thyme. Check the seasoning.

Tomato Sauce II

1 × 400 g can tomatoes
1 small onion, chopped
1 small carrot, chopped
1 stick of celery, chopped
½ clove of garlic, crushed
1 bay leaf

parsley stalks
juice of ½ a lemon
a dash of Worcestershire sauce
1 teaspoon caster sugar
1 teaspoon chopped fresh basil or thyme
salt and freshly ground black pepper

1 Put all the ingredients in a heavy-based saucepan, cover and simmer over a medium heat for 30 minutes.
2 Liquidize and sieve the sauce, then return it to the pan.
3 If it is too thin, reduce by boiling rapidly. Check the seasoning, adding more salt or sugar if necessary.

Barbecue Sauce

This sauce is particularly suitable for fried, barbecued, grilled or roasted pork. Brush some of the sauce on the meat, and heat the remainder to serve separately.

50 g unsalted butter

4 spring onions, white part only, thinly sliced

1 teaspoon finely grated lime zest

1 teaspoon peeled and finely grated
   fresh root ginger

juice of 2 oranges, strained

75 ml soy sauce

30 g soft light brown sugar

75 ml water

2 teaspoons cornflour

1 Melt the butter in a saucepan and add the spring onions. Sweat for 3 minutes, or until soft.

2 Add the lime zest, ginger, orange juice, soy sauce and sugar and simmer for 5 minutes.

3 Mix the water with the cornflour and stir into the glaze mixture off the heat. Return to the heat and bring to the boil, stirring continuously, then simmer gently for 4 minutes.

Tomato and Mint Salsa

This sauce is very good with grilled lamb chops.

1 shallot, finely diced

1 tablespoon wine vinegar

3 tablespoons extra virgin olive oil

1 clove of garlic, crushed

4 tomatoes, blanched, peeled,
   deseeded and finely chopped

1 tablespoon chopped fresh mint

salt and freshly ground black pepper

1 Mix together the shallot, vinegar and oil and allow to stand for 10 minutes.

2 Add the tomatoes, garlic and mint and season to taste with salt and pepper.

Warm Red Salsa

SERVES 10

2 red peppers

2 large tomatoes, blanched, peeled,
   deseeded and finely diced

1 tablespoon chopped fresh basil

1 tablespoon olive oil

juice of ½ a lemon

juice of ½ an orange

salt and freshly ground black pepper

1 Heat the oven to 180°C/350°F/gas mark 4.

2 Place the peppers on a baking sheet and roast in the oven for about 30 minutes, or until soft and the skin will come off easily.

3 Leave the peppers until cold, then cut them in half, discard the seeds and membrane, and peel off the skin. Dice the flesh finely and mix with the remaining ingredients. Season to taste with salt and pepper. Just before serving, heat through very gently until just warm.

Exotic Sauce

This sauce has been adapted from a recipe by Josceline Dimbleby. It is a useful accompaniment to chicken or veal.

2 large green chillies, finely chopped

450 g tomatoes, blanched, peeled and chopped

2–3 cloves of garlic, crushed

1 teaspoon ground cardamom

2 teaspoons caster sugar

1 tablespoon tomato purée

juice of ½ a lemon

1 tablespoon chopped fresh coriander

110 g button mushrooms, thinly sliced

salt and freshly ground black pepper

1 Put the chillies, tomatoes, garlic, cardamom, sugar, tomato purée and lemon juice into a saucepan. Bring to the boil, then simmer for 10 minutes.

2 Add the coriander and mushrooms. Season to taste with salt and pepper.

NOTE: If this sauce is too thick, it can be thinned to the required consistency with water.

Hollandaise Sauce

3 tablespoons wine vinegar

6 black peppercorns

1 bay leaf

1 blade of mace

2 egg yolks

110 g cold unsalted butter

lemon juice

salt

1 Place the vinegar, peppercorns, bay leaf and mace in a small, heavy-based saucepan and reduce by simmering to 1 tablespoon.

2 Cream the egg yolks with a pinch of salt and a knob of the butter in a small heatproof bowl. Set over, not in, a saucepan of gently simmering water. Using a wooden spoon, beat the mixture until slightly thickened, taking care that the water immediately around the bowl does not boil.

3 Strain the reduced vinegar into the egg mixture. Mix well and stir over the heat until slightly thickened.

4 Beat in the cold butter bit by bit, increasing the temperature as the sauce thickens and you add more butter, but take care that the water does not boil.

5 When the sauce has become light and thick remove from the heat and beat or whisk for 1 minute. Check the seasoning, adding lemon juice and salt if necessary. Keep warm by standing the bowl in hot water. Serve warm.

NOTE: Hollandaise sauce will set too firmly if allowed to get cold, and will curdle if overheated. It can be made in larger quantities in either a blender or food processor: simply put the eggs and salt into the blender and blend lightly. With the machine running, add the hot vinegar reduction and allow to thicken slightly. Set aside. When ready to serve, pour in warm melted butter, slowly allowing the sauce to thicken as you pour.

Béarnaise Sauce

3 tablespoons white wine vinegar

6 black peppercorns

1 bay leaf

1 small shallot, chopped

1 sprig of fresh tarragon

1 sprig of fresh chervil

2 egg yolks

110 g cold unsalted butter

1 teaspoon chopped fresh tarragon

1 teaspoon chopped fresh chervil

a nut of Glace de Viande (see page 455)

salt and freshly ground black pepper

1 Place the vinegar, peppercorns, bay leaf, shallot, tarragon and chervil in a heavy-based saucepan and reduce over a medium heat to 1 tablespoon.

2 In a small heatproof bowl cream the egg yolks with a pinch of salt and a knob of cold butter. Set the bowl over, not in, a saucepan of gently simmering water and beat the mixture with a wooden spoon until slightly thickened.

3 Strain the reduced vinegar into the bowl. Mix well and beat until thickened.

4 Beat in the remaining butter bit by bit, increasing the temperature as the sauce thickens and you add more butter, but take care that the water does not boil.

5 Stir in the tarragon, chervil and glace de viande. Taste and adjust the seasoning.

Hollandaise and Béarnaise Sauce: What has gone wrong when...

The sauce has curdled.

• The sauce has got too hot. Beat in a splash of cold water and turn the sauce into a cold bowl. If the sauce has split only slightly, place a new yolk in a clean bowl over a bain-marie and slowly add the sauce to form an emulsion.

The sauce has not thickened.

• The sauce was not beaten vigorously enough.

• The mixture was not heated enough.

• Too much liquid has been added. If the sauce is too cool, reheat it gently in a bain-marie.

The sauce looks oily.

• Not enough liquid was added.

• The sauce is too hot. To correct, beat in a few drops of cold water.

Beurre Blanc

225 g unsalted butter, chilled	3 tablespoons water
1 tablespoon chopped shallot	a squeeze of lemon juice
3 tablespoons white wine vinegar	salt and freshly ground white pepper

1 Cut the butter in 3 lengthwise, then across into thin slices. Keep cold.

2 Put the shallot, vinegar and water into a heavy-based stainless steel or galvanized copper sauté pan or small, shallow saucepan. Boil until reduced to about 2 tablespoons. Strain and return to the saucepan.

3 Lower the heat under the pan. Using a wire whisk and plenty of vigorous continuous whisking, gradually add the butter piece by piece. The process should take about 5 minutes and the sauce should become thick, creamy and pale – rather like a thin hollandaise. Season to taste with salt, pepper and lemon juice.

Beurre Blanc: What has gone wrong when...

The sauce has turned grey.

• The sauce was made in an aluminium pan. The pan reacts with the vinegar reduction and discolours the sauce. Use a heavy-based stainless steel or galvanized copper pan that distributes the heat well.

The sauce has separated into an oily and liquid layer.

• The sauce has overheated. To correct, add a small amount of cold water and beat vigorously.

The sauce tastes sweet.

• Too much reduction was used.
• Too much shallot was used in the reduction. To correct, add lemon juice and/or salt.

Chicken Beurre Blanc

225 g unsalted butter, chilled	1 tablespoon white wine vinegar
1 shallot, finely chopped	a squeeze of lemon juice
5 tablespoons very strong White Chicken Stock	salt and freshly ground white pepper
(see page 451)	

1 Cut the butter in 3 lengthwise, then across into thin slices. Keep cold.

2 Put the shallot, stock and vinegar into a small, heavy-based saucepan and boil until reduced to 2 tablespoons. Strain and return to the pan.

3 Keep the stock hot but not boiling. Using a wire whisk and plenty of vigorous continuous whisking, gradually add the butter piece by piece. The process should take about 5 minutes and the sauce should become thick, creamy and pale, rather like a thin hollandaise. Season to taste with salt, pepper and lemon juice.

Maître d'Hôtel Butter

50 g butter
2 teaspoons lemon juice

1 teaspoon finely chopped parsley
salt and freshly ground black pepper

1 Cream the butter. Stir in the lemon juice and parsley and season to taste. Mix well. Wrap in cling film in a sausage shape and chill until firm.

Vinaigrette

3 tablespoons salad oil
1 tablespoon wine vinegar

salt and freshly ground black pepper

1 Put all the ingredients into a screw-top jar. Before using, shake until well emulsified.

NOTES: This dressing can be flavoured with crushed garlic, mustard, a pinch of sugar, chopped fresh herbs, etc., as desired.

If kept refrigerated, the dressing will more easily form an emulsion when whisked or shaken, and have a slightly thicker consistency.

Tomato Dressing

1 tomato
4 tablespoons oil
1 tablespoon water

1 tablespoon tarragon vinegar
a small pinch of dry English mustard
a small pinch of caster sugar

1 Chop the tomato and whizz in a blender with the remaining ingredients.
2 When well emulsified, push through a sieve. If the dressing looks as though it might separate, add a little very cold water.

Soy, Garlic and Olive Dressing

This dressing is delicious with cold meats, and particularly good with cold Butterflied Leg of Lamb (see page 148). Scatter the olives and rosemary over the meat and hand the sauce separately.

1 small clove of garlic, unpeeled
2 teaspoons olive oil
300 ml natural yoghurt
1 tablespoon light soy sauce
2 teaspoons sesame oil

salt and freshly ground black pepper

To serve
50 g pitted black olives
1 tablespoon roughly chopped fresh rosemary

1 Heat the oven to 200°C/400°F/gas mark 6.
2 Brush the clove of garlic with a little of the olive oil, place on a baking sheet and bake for 15 minutes. Peel the garlic and mash well.
3 Mix together the mashed garlic, yoghurt, soy sauce, sesame oil and remaining olive oil. Season to taste with salt and pepper. Serve with the olives and rosemary as required.

Cumberland Sauce

2 oranges	150 ml port
1 lemon	½ teaspoon Dijon mustard
225 g redcurrant jelly	pinch of cayenne pepper
1 shallot, chopped	pinch of ground ginger

1 Peel 1 orange and the lemon, removing only the outer skin. Cut the zest into fine shreds.
2 Squeeze the juice from the peeled fruit and the remaining orange and strain into a pan. Add the remaining ingredients with the needleshreds. Simmer for 10 minutes and cool.

Bread Sauce

This very rich sauce is served with roast chicken and roast turkey. For a lighter sauce, reduce the quantity of butter and omit the cream.

1 small onion	pinch of freshly grated nutmeg
6 whole cloves	50 g fresh white breadcrumbs
300 ml full-fat milk	50 g butter
1 bay leaf	2 tablespoons single cream (optional)
10 peppercorns	salt

1 Cut the onion in half, then stud the 2 halves with the cloves.
2 Place the milk in a saucepan and add the onion, bay leaf, peppercorns, nutmeg and a pinch of salt. Heat over a medium heat until the milk steams, then set aside and leave to infuse for 30 minutes. Strain.
3 Reheat the milk. Sieve the breadcrumbs and stir into the milk with the butter and cream, if using.
4 Heat the sauce gently to thicken. If it becomes too thick, add more warm milk to adjust the mixture to a thick coating consistency. Season to taste.
5 If not using immediately, dot the surface with butter to prevent a skin forming. Stir in the butter when reheating.

Pastry

Pastry comes in many forms. All of them are made from a mixture of flour and liquid, and usually contain fat. Variations in quantities and the ingredients themselves give each type its distinctive texture and taste. The three most common types of pastry are short, flaky and choux, all of which have variations. The degree of shortness (crisp crumbliness) depends on the amount and type of fat (the shortening factor) incorporated into the flour and the way in which the uncooked pastry, or paste, is handled.

The recipes in this book usually stipulate a certain flour quantity of the pastry required. If using ready-made pastry instead, you will need double the weight of the flour quantity specified.

Shortcrust Pastry (Pâte Brisée)

170 g plain flour
pinch of salt
30 g lard

50 g butter
very cold water, to mix

1 Sift the flour with the salt into a large bowl.
2 Rub in the fats until the mixture resembles coarse breadcrumbs.
3 Add 2 tablespoons water to the mixture. Mix to a firm dough, first with a knife, and then with one hand. It may be necessary to add more water, but the pastry should not be too damp. Although crumbly pastry is more difficult to handle, it produces a shorter, lighter result.
4 Wrap the dough in cling film and chill for 30 minutes before using.

Rich Shortcrust Pastry

170 g plain flour
pinch of salt
100 g butter

1 egg yolk
very cold water, to mix

1 Sift the flour with the salt into a large bowl.
2 Rub in the butter until the mixture resembles breadcrumbs.
3 Mix the egg yolk with 2 tablespoons water and add to the mixture.
4 Mix to a firm dough, first with a knife, and then with one hand. It may be necessary to add more water, but the pastry should not be too damp. (Although crumbly pastry is more difficult to handle, it produces a shorter, lighter result.)
5 Wrap the dough in cling film and chill for 30 minutes before using.

Wholemeal Pastry

110 g wholemeal flour
110 g plain flour
pinch of salt

140 g butter
very cold water, to mix

1 Sift the flours with the salt into a large bowl and add the bran from the sieve. Rub in the butter until the mixture looks like coarse breadcrumbs.

2 Add 2 tablespoons water and mix to a firm dough, first with a knife and then with one hand. It might be necessary to add more water, but the pastry should not be too damp. (Although crumbly pastry is more difficult to handle, it produces a shorter, lighter result.)

3 Wrap in cling film and chill for at least 30 minutes before using.

VARIATION: All wholemeal flour may be used if preferred.

Lining a Flan Ring or Tart Tin with Pastry

Metal flan rings or tart tins produce crisper pastry than ceramic dishes. To line a flan ring or tin, place the ring on a baking sheet, then drape the rolled pastry over a rolling pin. Gently lower the pastry into the ring, placing the side that was against the work surface uppermost. Allow the pastry to drape over the sides of the ring. With the side of your finger, ease the pastry into the edges of the ring, then gently press it against the side, taking care to avoid creasing or stretching the pastry.

Use the rolling pin to remove the excess pastry by rolling from the centre of the ring to the edge. The sharp edge will cut through the pastry.

Run the side of your thumb along the top edge of the pastry and the ring to straighten the sides of the pastry case and ease it away from the edge. If the pastry overlaps the edge of the ring, it will be impossible to remove after it is baked without breaking it.

Refrigerate the pastry case until it is firm. This will take up to 30 minutes if the pastry is very soft and the kitchen is warm.

Very soft pastry can be rolled between cling film. After rolling, chill the pastry. When firm enough to handle, remove the film from one side of the pastry and use the other side to guide the pastry into place.

Baking Blind

If a recipe calls for baking the pastry blind, this means that the pastry needs to be baked completely before the filling is added. Heat the oven to the required temperature, usually 200°C/400°F/gas mark 6, and place a shelf in the top third of the oven. Make a cartouche (see page 512). Crumple the paper to make it more pliable, then use it to line the pastry case. Fill with enough baking beans to support the sides of the pastry until they are completely baked. (Baking beans are either small ceramic beans or dried haricot beans used exclusively for the purpose of baking pastry cases blind.) The base of the pastry case needs only a thin layer of beans (about 1 cm) in order to stop it puffing up.

Place the pastry case on a baking sheet near the top of the oven and bake for about 15 minutes, or until the sides of the pastry have cooked through. The pastry will lose its grey tinge and become opaque and sand-coloured when cooked.

Using a large spoon, remove the beans from the pastry case and transfer them to a bowl to cool. Remove the greaseproof paper and return the case to the oven, placing it on the middle shelf. Continue to bake for 5–10 minutes, until the base is a pale golden brown and feels sandy to the touch.

If the pastry base forms a hump, it means that some air was trapped underneath when the ring was lined. Gently press the hump with the back of a spoon to flatten it.

Shortcrust Pastry: What has gone wrong when...

The pastry has shrunk.
- It has been over-handled and stretched too much during rolling.
- It was not sufficiently chilled.
- It was not cooked on the top shelf of the oven.

The pastry is tough.
- Too much water was added.
- It was over-handled.
- The rolling was too heavy-handed.

The pastry looks greasy.
- The pastry was overworked.
- Your hands were too hot.
- It was cooked at too low a temperature.

The pastry looks grey.
- It was not baked blind for long enough.
- It was not covered well enough in the refrigerator.

Rough Puff Pastry

225 g plain flour
pinch of salt

140 g butter
120–150 ml very cold water, to mix

1 Sift the flour with the salt into a chilled bowl. Cut the butter into knobs about the size of a sugar lump and add to the flour. Do not rub in, but add just enough water to bind the paste together. Mix first with a knife, then with one hand. Knead very lightly.

2 Wrap in cling film and chill for 10 minutes.

3 On a floured surface, roll the pastry into a rectangle measuring about 30 × 10 cm. This must be done carefully: with a heavy rolling pin, press firmly on the pastry and give short, sharp rolls until it has reached the required size. Take care not to overstretch and break the surface of the pastry.

4 Fold the rectangle into 3 and turn so that the folded edge (like the spine of a closed book) is to your left.

5 Roll out again into a rectangle about 1 cm thick. Fold in 3 again, wrap in cling film and chill for 15 minutes.

6 Roll and fold the pastry as before, then wrap and chill again for 15 minutes.

7 Roll and fold the pastry again: by this time it should be ready for use, with no signs of streakiness. If it is still streaky, roll and fold once more.

8 Finally, roll into the required shape and chill again before baking.

Puff Pastry

225 g plain flour

pinch of salt

30 g lard

85–130 ml iced water

140–200 g unsalted butter

1 If you have never made puff pastry before, use the smaller amount of butter: it is easier. If you have some experience, more butter will produce a lighter, very rich pastry.

2 Sift the flour with the salt into a large bowl. Rub in the lard. Add 6 tablespoons water and mix to a doughy consistency with a knife, adding more water if too dry. Turn on to a floured board and knead quickly until just smooth. Wrap in cling film and chill for 30 minutes.

3 Lightly flour the work surface and roll the dough into a rectangle about 15 × 30 cm.

4 Tap the butter lightly with a floured rolling pin to shape it into a flattened block slightly less than half the size of the pastry. Put the butter on the lower half of the pastry and fold the edges over to enclose it. Fold over the top half of the pastry.

5 Tap the pastry parcel with the rolling pin to flatten the butter a little, then roll out, quickly and lightly, until the pastry is 3 times as long as it is wide. Fold it very evenly in 3, first folding over the third closest to you, then bringing the top third down. Give it a 90-degree anti-clockwise turn so that the folded, closed edge is on your left. Press the edges firmly with the rolling pin, then roll out again to form a rectangle as before.

6 Now the pastry has had 2 rolls and folds. It should be put to rest in a cool place for 10–20 minutes. The rolling and folding must be repeated twice more, the pastry again rested, and then again given 2 more turns. This makes a total of 6 turns. If the pastry is still very streaky with butter, roll and fold it once more.

Vol-au-vents

1 quantity Puff Pastry (see above)

beaten egg, to glaze

1 Heat the oven to 220°C/425°F/gas mark 7.

2 Roll out the pastry to a thickness of 2 cm and cut into 4 circles about 5 cm in diameter. Place on a damp baking sheet. Using a cutter half the size of the pastry circle, cut into the centre of the pastry, but take care not to cut right through to the baking sheet.

3 Use a small, sharp knife to knock up the sides of the pastry, slightly separating the leaves horizontally so that the edge flakes readily when baking. This also counteracts the squashing effect of the cutter, which may have pressed the edges together, making it more difficult for the pastry to rise in even layers.

4 Brush the pastry carefully with the beaten egg, avoiding the knocked-up sides (if they are covered with egg, the pastry will not rise).

5 Using the back of the knife blade (so as not to cut into the pastry), make a star pattern on the borders of the vol-au-vent cases and mark a lattice pattern on the inner circles.

6 Bake for 30 minutes, then carefully lift off the top of the inner circles. Keep these to use

as lids for the cases when filled. Pull out and discard any partially cooked pastry from the centre of the cases.

7 Return the cases to the oven for 5 minutes to dry out. The vol-au-vents are now ready for filling, ideally with something hot. Top with their lids and serve straight away.

NOTE: Rough puff pastry is also suitable for making vol-au-vents, but the method of cutting is different: cut the pastry into 2 rounds the size of a side plate. Stamp a circle right out of the centre of one of them. Brush the uncut round with egg and place the ring of pastry on top. Bake the middle small round of pastry too, and use it for the vol-au-vent lid.

Layered Pastry: What has gone wrong when...

The pastry is tough.
- Too much water was used.
- The pastry was over-handled.
- The fat used was not cold enough.
- The pastry was not allowed to rest for long enough between rolls and folds.

The pastry is leaking fat.
- The fat was not incorporated correctly.
- The fat was not cold enough.
- The pastry was not chilled enough.
- The pastry has been overbaked.

The pastry has risen poorly.
- The butter broke through during rolling and folding, so the layers have been lost.
- The fat was rubbed in too much at the beginning.
- The pastry was incorrectly rolled and folded.
- The final pastry was rolled and folded too many times and the layers have been lost.

The layers are visible in the pastry, but it has not risen very much.
- The pastry was removed from the oven before the sides had baked enough to hold its shape.
- The oven door was opened during the first 15 minutes of baking.

The pastry has risen unevenly.
- Uneven pressure was used during rolling.

Choux Pastry

85 g butter, cut into 1 cm cubes
200 ml water
105 g plain flour, well sifted

pinch of salt
3 eggs

1 Put the butter and water into a heavy-based saucepan. Bring slowly to the boil so that by the time the water is boiling the butter has completely melted.

2 As soon as the mixture is boiling really fast, tip in all the flour with the salt and remove the pan from the heat.

3 Working as fast as you can, beat the mixture hard with a wooden spoon: it will soon become thick and smooth and leave the sides of the pan.

4 Turn the panada (flour mixture) on to a large plate to cool to tepid.

5 Return the panada to the pan and beat in the eggs a little at a time, until it is soft, shiny and smooth. If the eggs are large, it may not be necessary to add all of them. The mixture should be of a dropping consistency, which means that it will fall off a spoon rather reluctantly and all in a blob; if it runs off, it is too wet, and if it will not fall even when the spoon is jerked slightly, it is too thick.

6 Bake as required in the recipe. Alternatively, to make choux buns, bake on a lightly greased baking sheet in an oven heated to 200°C/400°F/gas mark 6 until well risen, browned and firm to the touch.

Choux Pastry: What has gone wrong when...

The pastry is badly risen.
- The oven door was opened before the pastry was set.
- The pastry was removed from the oven too soon.
- Not enough egg was beaten into the pastry.
- The panada was too warm when the egg was added.

The pastry is flat and cracked.
- The panada was beaten too much when the flour was added.

Suet Pastry

As suet pastry is most often used for steamed puddings, instructions for lining a pudding basin are included here. Use the pastry as soon as it is made.

butter, for greasing
340 g self-raising flour
salt

170 g shredded beef suet
very cold water, to mix

1 Grease a 1.1 litre pudding basin.
2 Sift the flour with a good pinch of salt into a large bowl. Stir in the suet and add enough water to mix to a soft dough, mixing first with a knife, and then with one hand.
3 On a floured surface, roll out two-thirds of the pastry into a circle about 1 cm thick. Sprinkle the pastry evenly with flour.
4 Fold the circle in half, with the open curved sides towards you.
5 Shape the pastry by rolling the straight edge away from you and gently pushing the middle and pulling the sides to form a bag that, when spread out, will fit the pudding basin.
6 With a dry pastry brush, remove all excess flour, and place the bag in the prepared basin.
7 Fill the pastry bag with the desired mixture.
8 Roll out the reserved piece of pastry and use it as a lid, damping the edges and pressing them firmly together.
9 Cover the basin with buttered greaseproof paper, pleated in the centre, and a layer of pleated kitchen foil. (Pleating the paper and foil allows the pastry to expand slightly without bursting the wrappings.) Tie down firmly to prevent water or steam getting in during cooking.

NOTE: Occasionally suet pastry is used for dishes other than steamed puddings, in which case it should be mixed as above and then handled like any other pastry, except that it does not need to relax before cooking.

Suet Pastry: What has gone wrong when...

The pastry is grey, oily and has not risen.
• The water has not been boiling throughout the cooking time.

The pastry has a tough, heavy texture.
• It has been over-handled.
• Too much liquid has been added.

Filo or Strudel Pastry

285 g plain flour

pinch of salt

1 egg

150 ml water

1 teaspoon oil

1 Sift the flour with the salt into a large bowl.

2 Beat the egg and add the water and oil. First with a knife and then with one hand, mix the water and egg into the flour, adding more water if necessary to make a soft dough.

3 The dough now has to be beaten: lift the whole mixture up in one hand and then, with a flick of the wrist, slap it on to a lightly floured board. Continue doing this until the dough no longer sticks to your fingers, and the whole mixture is smooth and very elastic. Put it into a clean floured bowl. Wrap in cling film and leave on the counter for at least 30 minutes.

4 The pastry is now ready for rolling and pulling. To do this, flour a tea towel or large cloth on a work surface and roll out the pastry on it as thinly as possible. Now put your well-floured hands under the pastry and, keeping your hands fairly flat, gently stretch and pull the pastry, gradually and carefully working your way around until the pastry is paper thin (a). (You should be able to see through it easily.) Trim off the thick edges.

5 Use immediately, as filo/strudel pastry dries out and cracks very quickly. Brushing with melted butter or oil helps to prevent this (b). Alternatively, the pastry sheets may be kept covered with a damp cloth.

NOTE: If the pastry is not for immediate use, wrap it well and freeze, or wrap and keep refrigerated (for up to 3 days). Flour the pastry surfaces before folding up; this will prevent sticking.

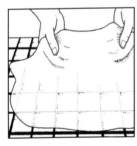

Stretching strudel
pastry (a)

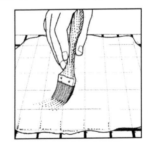

Brushing strudel pastry
with melted butter (b)

Hot Watercrust Pastry

This pastry is used for raised pies, such as pork pie and game pie.

450 g plain flour	200 ml water
1 teaspoon salt	80 g butter
2 eggs, beaten	80 g lard

1 Wrap a piece of paper around the outside of a small soufflé dish or straight-sided saucepan. Fold it over the lip of the dish or pan and place upside down to keep it in place.

2 Sift the flour with the salt into a large bowl. Make a well in the middle, add the eggs into it and toss a liberal covering of flour over it.

3 Put the water, butter and lard into a saucepan and bring slowly to the boil.

4 Once the liquid is boiling, pour it on to the flour, mixing with a knife as you do so. Using the fingertips of one hand, knead until all the egg streaks have gone and the pastry is smooth.

5 Wrap the pastry in cling film and chill for 10 minutes.

6 Reserve about a third of the pastry for a pie lid, keeping it covered or wrapped in a warm place. Roll out the remaining pastry into a circle and drape it over the upside-down dish or saucepan. (a) Working fast, shape it to cover the dish or pan to a depth of about 7 cm. Leave to chill, uncovered, in the refrigerator. As the pastry cools it will harden.

7 When the pastry is hard, turn the dish or saucepan upright and carefully remove it, leaving the paper inside the pastry case. Carefully draw the paper away from the pastry and, when it is all loosened, take it out. (b) Stand the pastry case on a baking sheet and fill as required. Use the reserved third of the pastry to make the lid, wetting the rim of the pie case to make it stick down firmly. Crimp the edges (c), then bake as required.

Shaping a raised pie

  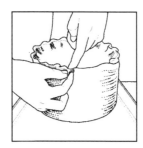

Draping pastry over the
prepared dish (a)

Drawing out the paper
after the dish has been
removed (b)

Crimping the edges
of the pie (c)

Pâte à Pâte

225 g plain flour
½ teaspoon salt
165 g butter, softened

2 small egg yolks
3–4 tablespoons water

1 Sift the flour with the salt on to a work surface. Make a large well in the centre and put the butter and egg yolks in it. Using the fingers of one hand, work the yolks and butter together, drawing in the surrounding flour and adding the water to give a soft, malleable, but not sticky paste.
2 Wrap in cling film and chill for 30 minutes. Use as required.

Dumplings

These dumplings can be flavoured with chopped fresh herbs or grated fresh horseradish, if desired.

SERVES 4

200 g plain flour
3 teaspoons baking powder
½ teaspoon dry English mustard
¼ teaspoon cayenne pepper

½ teaspoon salt
50 g lard, suet or solid vegetable shortening
about 150 ml iced water

1 Sift the flour, baking powder, mustard, cayenne and salt into a large bowl. Add the fat.
2 Using 2 table knives scissor-fashion, cut the fat into the flour until each piece is no bigger than a small pea. Rub in lightly. Mix in the herbs or horseradish, if using.
3 Stir in enough water to make a soft dough, taking care not to overwork the mixture.
4 Divide the dough into 8 pieces and place on the hot stew or soup, spacing them evenly. Cover and simmer for about 15 minutes. Do not lift the lid during cooking or the dumplings will be heavy.
5 When the dumplings feel firm to the touch, remove the lid and cook for a further 5 minutes to dry the surface of the dumplings. Break one open to check that it is cooked through. There should not be any uncooked, doughy mixture left in the centre.

VARIATION: For soured cream and chive dumplings, add 2 tablespoons finely chopped chives at the end of step 2. Substitute 150 ml soured cream for the iced water.

NOTE: Dumplings are always a little soggy when cooked on the hob. For a drier version, they can be baked in the oven at 220°C/425°F/gas mark 7 for 15–20 minutes.

Pizza Dough

30 g fresh yeast
pinch of sugar
300 ml lukewarm water

450 g plain flour
1 teaspoon salt
1 tablespoon olive oil

1 Cream the yeast with the sugar and 2 tablespoons of the water.

2 Sift the flour with the salt and make a well in the centre. Pour in the yeast mixture, the remaining water and the oil. Mix together until it forms a soft but not wet dough. Add more water or flour if necessary.

3 Turn on to a floured surface and knead well for about 10 minutes, until the dough is smooth. Place in a clean, oiled bowl and cover with a greased cling film. Leave in a warm place until the dough has doubled in bulk. Use as required.

Savoury Brioche

MAKES 12 SMALL BRIOCHES OR 1 LARGE ONE

10 g fresh yeast
3 teaspoons caster sugar
2 tablespoons warm water
225 g flour
pinch of salt

2 eggs, beaten
50 g melted butter, cooled

For the glaze
1 egg mixed with 1 tablespoon water
    and 1 teaspoon sugar

1 Grease a large brioche mould or 12 small brioche tins.

2 Mix the yeast with 1 teaspoon of the sugar and the water.

3 Sift the flour with the salt into a bowl. Sprinkle with the remaining 2 teaspoons of sugar. Make a well in the centre. Drop in the eggs, yeast mixture and melted butter and mix with the fingers of one hand to a soft but not sloppy paste. Knead on an unfloured work surface for 5 minutes or until smooth. Put into a clean bowl, cover with a damp cloth or greased cling film and leave to rise in a warm place until doubled in bulk (about 1 hour).

4 Turn out and knead again on an unfloured work surface for 2 minutes.

5 Place the dough in the brioche mould (it should not come more than halfway up the mould). If making individual brioches, divide the dough into 12 pieces. Using three-quarters of each piece, roll them into small balls and put them in the brioche tins. Make a dip on top of each brioche. Roll the remaining paste into 12 tiny balls and press them into the prepared dents. Push a pencil, or thin spoon handle, right through each small ball into the brioche base as this will anchor the balls in place when baking.

6 Cover with greased cling film and leave in a warm place until risen to the top of the tin(s). The large one will take about 30 minutes, the individual ones 15 minutes.

7 Heat the oven to 200°C/400°F/gas mark 6. Brush the egg glaze over the brioches. Bake the large one for 20–25 minutes, and the small ones for 10 minutes.

NOTE: 1 teaspoon of easy-blend yeast can be used in place of fresh yeast.

Pasta

For all pasta recipes use strong 'oo' pasta flour, or strong bread flour if pasta flour is not available. Pasta should always be cooked al dente (firm to the bite). Remember that fresh or home-made pasta, which already contains moisture, cooks much faster than the dried commercial equivalents. If the pasta is very fresh it will be cooked in under 2 minutes.

To cook pasta

Both fresh and home-made should be boiled in a large quantity of salted water until al dente. The water should boil vigorously to help keep the pasta from sticking together. Fresh pasta, if very thin, will usually cook in 1–2 minutes, but purchased dried pasta will take 10–15 minutes. Cook bought pasta according to the manufacturer's directions. Drain it in a colander, leaving some water still adhering to the pasta. Toss in sauce immediately.

Egg Pasta

450 g strong 'oo' flour   1 tablespoon oil
4 large eggs, beaten

1 Sift the flour on to a wooden board. Make a well in the centre and put in the eggs and oil.
2 Using the fingers of one hand, mix together the eggs and oil, gradually drawing in the flour to make a dough that is not sticky.
3 Knead until smooth and elastic (about 15 minutes). Wrap in cling film and leave to relax in a cool place for 1 hour.
4 Roll out one small piece of dough at a time until paper thin. Cut into the required shape.
5 Allow to dry (unless making ravioli), hanging long noodles over a chair back and laying smaller shapes on a wire rack or dry tea towel, for at least 30 minutes before cooking. Ravioli is dried after stuffing.

NOTE: If more or less pasta is required, the recipe can be altered on a pro-rata basis. For example, a 340 g quantity of flour calls for 3 eggs and 1 scant tablespoon of oil.

VARIATION: For herb pasta, add plenty of fresh chopped herbs, such as parsley, thyme or tarragon, according to taste.

Green Pasta

225 g spinach, cooked

340 g strong '00' flour

2 eggs

1 tablespoon double cream

1 Chop or liquidize the spinach and push it through a sieve to get a fairly dry paste.
2 Sift the flour on to a work surface. Make a well in the centre, put in the eggs, spinach and cream and mix together using the fingers of one hand, gradually drawing in the flour to make a dough that is not sticky.
3 Knead until smooth and elastic (about 15 minutes). Wrap in cling film and leave to relax in a cool place for at least 30 minutes.
4 Roll out one small piece of dough at a time until paper thin. Cut into the required shape.
5 Allow to dry (unless making ravioli), hanging long noodles over a chair back and laying smaller shapes on a wire rack or dry tea towel, for at least 30 minutes before cooking. Ravioli is dried after stuffing.

Accompaniments

Mashed Potatoes

SERVES 6–8

900 g old floury potatoes, such as Maris Piper
50 g butter

100–150 ml warm milk
salt and freshly ground black pepper

1 Wash and peel the potatoes. Cut into evenly sized 3 cm chunks.
2 Place in a large saucepan and cover with cold water. Add 1 teaspoon salt. Cover and bring to the boil.
3 Turn the heat down a bit so that the potatoes just simmer. Tilt the lid so it is only half-covering the pan.
4 Cook until the potatoes can be pierced easily with a sharp knife.
5 Drain in a colander, then return to the pan over a low heat for 1 minute to dry out.
6 Add the butter and mash into the potatoes using a potato masher or fork.
7 Heat the milk, then stir enough into the mash to get the desired consistency. Push the mixture through a sieve using a wooden spoon, or process through a mouli. Adjust the seasoning.

VARIATIONS
Mustard Mash: Stir 2 tablespoons wholegrain mustard into the potatoes when adding the milk.
Olive Oil and Garlic Mash: Add 2 cloves of peeled garlic to the boiling water and process with the potatoes. Substitute olive oil for the butter.

Mashed Potatoes: What has gone wrong when...

The mash is gluey.
It has been overstirred, or cold milk was added, or the potatoes cooled down before they were mashed.

The mash is watery.
The potatoes were overcooked, or were not drained thoroughly, or were boiled too hard.

Sage and Bacon Fondant Potatoes

SERVES 4

sage leaves

675 g small new potatoes

170 g rindless, smoked streaky bacon,
    cut into short lengths

1 clove of garlic, crushed

85 g unsalted butter, diced

500 ml hot Brown Chicken Stock
    (see page 454)

salt and freshly ground black pepper

1 Heat the oven to 200°C/400°F/gas mark 6.
2 Wrap a sage leaf around each potato, followed by a piece of bacon. Secure with a cocktail stick.
3 Put the potatoes in a small roasting pan so they are just touching each other. Add the garlic and butter.
4 Pour over the hot stock and season with a little salt and plenty of black pepper.
5 Put the potatoes on to the top shelf of the oven and cook for 1½ hours, turning occasionally, or until they are very tender, the bacon is crisp and the liquid has almost completely evaporated.
6 Remove the cocktail sticks from the potatoes, transfer to a warmed serving dish and pour over the remaining concentrated stock. Serve hot.

Boiled New Potatoes

SERVES 4

600 g new potatoes, scrubbed and halved

1 Cook the potatoes in boiling salted water until tender (about 10–15 minutes). Drain well and serve.

NOTE: The potatoes may be tossed in a little unsalted butter and chopped seasonal herbs.

Baked Potato with Soured Cream and Chives

SERVES 1

1 medium potato, well scrubbed

2 tablespoons soured cream

1 teaspoon chopped fresh chives

salt and freshly ground black pepper

1 Heat the oven to 200°C/400°F/gas mark 6.
2 Prick the potato with a fork several times to prevent it from bursting in the oven.
3 Bake for 1 hour, or until a skewer glides easily through the potato.
4 Mix together the soured cream and chives. Season with salt and pepper.

5 Split the potato without quite cutting it in half and fill with the soured cream mixture. Serve immediately.

NOTE: There is some controversy about preparing potatoes for baking: oiling and wrapping them in foil gives a soft, shiny skin; wetting them with water and sprinkling them with salt gives a dull but very crisp skin.

Roast Potatoes

SERVES 4
900g floury potatoes
salt and freshly ground pepper
4 tablespoons dripping, oil or goose fat

1 Heat the oven to 200°C/400°F/gas mark 6.
2 Wash and peel the potatoes and, if they are large, cut them into 5 cm pieces.
3 Bring them to the boil in salted water. Simmer for 5 minutes. Drain well, return to the pan and shake the potatoes to roughen their surfaces.
4 Melt the dripping, oil or goose fat in a roasting pan and when hot add the potatoes, turning them so that they are coated all over. Season with salt and pepper.
5 Roast, basting occasionally, and turning the potatoes over halfway through cooking.

NOTES: Potatoes can be roasted at almost any temperature, usually taking 1 hour in a hot oven, or 1½ hours in a moderate one. They should be basted and turned over once or twice during cooking, and they are done when a skewer glides easily into them. Potatoes roasted in the same pan as meat have the best flavour, but will not be as crisp as potatoes roasted only in fat.

The water in which the potatoes were parboiled can be saved and used for making gravy if no stock is available.

We recommend King Edward potatoes as the best for roasting.

Boiled Rice

50 g long-grain rice per person, rinsed   salt

1 Fill a large saucepan with salted water (4 servings, or 200 g rice, will need at least 1½ litres of water, but the exact quantities do not matter as long as there is plenty of water).
2 Tip in the rice and stir until the water returns to the boil.
3 Simmer for 10 minutes, then test: the rice should be neither hard nor mushy, but firm to the bite (al dente).
4 Drain the rice in a colander or sieve. Rinse briefly with cold water to stop the cooking. Place the colander or sieve over the saucepan and cover with the lid. Allow to steam for 5 minutes. This allows the rice to steam dry and separates the grains.

Basmati Rice

This recipe cooks the rice by the absorption method.

SERVES 4–6

250 g basmati rice   400 ml water
20 g butter or 2 tablespoons salad oil   ½ teaspoon salt

1 Wash the rice in 3–4 changes of cold water by swirling it around in a bowl, then draining through a sieve to remove excess starch.
2 Melt the butter or heat the oil in a saucepan over a medium heat.
3 Add the rice and stir to coat in the fat for about 1 minute.
4 Add the water and salt. Turn up the heat and bring to the boil.
5 Reduce the heat so that the mixture just simmers. Cover with a lid and cook for 10 minutes.
6 Remove from the heat. Wrap a clean tea towel around the lid and replace it on the pan to form a good seal. Let stand for 5 minutes. The tea towel will help to dry the rice as it steams.
7 Fork the rice into a warmed serving bowl.

VARIATIONS
Saffron Rice: Add a large pinch of saffron stamens to the rice when the water is added in step 4.
Spiced Rice: Add 4 cardamom pods, a 5 cm stick of cinnamon and 6 black peppercorns to the butter or oil in step 2.

Soft Polenta

Polenta is a classic dish of northern Italy. It can be eaten as soon as it is cooked, served with roasts, grills, casseroles or poultry, or it can be left to cool, sliced and then grilled or fried.

The cooking time for polenta varies according to whether it is coarse, fine or pre-cooked. For best results, follow the manufacturer's instructions.

SERVES 4–6

2 litres White Chicken Stock (see page 451)
1 teaspoon salt

285 g polenta (coarse cornmeal)

1 Put the stock and salt into a large saucepan and bring to the boil.
2 Remove from the heat and sprinkle on the polenta, whisking quickly to prevent lumps from forming.
3 Return the pan to the heat and cover it as the mixture will bubble and spatter.
4 Continue cooking until the polenta is very thick (about 35–40 minutes), stirring often to prevent sticking and burning. Pre-cooked polenta will take 8–10 minutes to cook.
5 Pile high on a plate and serve immediately.

Lemon Buttered Couscous

Couscous is made from wheat. It is similar to semolina, but coarser.

SERVES 4

500 g couscous
grated zest and juice of 1 lemon
450 ml hot White Chicken Stock (see page 451)
  or water

50 g butter
pinch of cayenne pepper
salt

1 Place the couscous in a large bowl and stir in the lemon zest.
2 Add the lemon juice to the stock or water, then stir into the couscous.
3 Leave to soak for about 15 minutes, occasionally fluffing the couscous with a fork.
4 Chop the butter into small dice and stir into the couscous with the seasoning.

NOTE: Different brands of couscous require varying amounts of liquid, so check the liquid quantity with the manufacturer's instructions.

The couscous will be warm, but if you want it hotter, you can cook it for 20 seconds in the microwave.

Yorkshire Pudding

SERVES 4

110 g plain flour

good pinch of salt

2 eggs, beaten

300 ml milk, or 200 ml milk plus 90 ml water

4 tablespoons good beef dripping

or 2 tablespoons oil

1 Sift the flour and salt into a bowl. Make a well in the centre and pour the eggs into it.

2 Beat the eggs with a wooden spoon, gradually drawing in more flour to the centre.

3 Beat in the milk little by little until the batter is smooth. Leave for 30 minutes before use.

4 Heat the oven to 200°C/400°F/gas mark 6.

5 Put the dripping or oil in a roasting pan, flameproof dish or Yorkshire pudding tin and heat until very hot.

6 Pour in the batter. Bake a large pudding in the oven for 40 minutes, or until it is risen and golden. Individual Yorkshire puddings take about 15 minutes.

NOTES: If the pudding is to be served with roast beef, you can place it in the roasting pan, under an open rack holding the beef. In this way any dripping juices from the beef will fall on to the pudding and improve its flavour. However, this makes for a slightly flat pudding.

Alternatively, roast the beef directly in the pan (not on a wire rack) and 30 minutes before it is ready, increase the oven temperature to 200°C/400°F/gas mark 6 and pour the batter around the beef. If the pudding is not quite cooked when the beef is ready, keep the beef warm and increase the oven temperature to 220°C/425°F/gas mark 7. Continue cooking the pudding until well risen and golden brown.

Melba Toast

MAKES 12 PIECES

6 slices of white bread

1 Heat the grill to its highest setting. Heat the oven to 150°C/300°F/gas mark 2.

2 Grill the bread on both sides until lightly browned.

3 While still hot, quickly cut off the crusts and split the bread in half horizontally.

4 Put the bread in the oven untoasted-side up and bake until golden brown.

NOTE: Melba toast can be kept for a day or two in an airtight container, but will lose its flavour if kept longer. It is undoubtedly best served straight from the oven.

Soda Bread

MAKES 1 LOAF

225 g wholemeal flour

225 g plain white flour

1½ teaspoons salt

2 teaspoons bicarbonate of soda

45 g butter

1 tablespoon caster sugar

280–425 ml buttermilk

1 Heat the oven to 190°C/375°F/gas mark 5. Lightly flour a baking sheet.
2 Sift the flours, salt and bicarbonate of soda together 3 times. Add most of the bran left in the sieve and stir through the flour. Reserve the rest for the topping.
3 Cut the butter into small pieces, then rub into the flour using your fingertips.
4 Stir in the sugar.
5 Make a well in the centre. Stir in enough buttermilk to make a soft dough.
6 Knead lightly to bring together into a round.
7 Place on the prepared baking sheet and sprinkle with the reserved bran.
8 Using a wooden spoon handle, make a deep cross in the centre of the bread, pressing nearly all the way down to the baking sheet.
9 Bake in the oven for about 40 minutes, or until well risen and browned. The cross in the centre of the bread should not seem damp.
10 Transfer the loaf to a wire rack and leave to cool.

NOTE: If you are unable to obtain buttermilk, use regular milk and add 2 teaspoons cream of tartar to the flour in step 2.

Wilted Spinach

SERVES 4

50 g unsalted butter

1 kg baby leaf spinach, washed

freshly grated nutmeg

salt and freshly ground black pepper

1 Heat the butter in a large frying pan and, when foaming, add the spinach.
2 Cover the pan with a lid and cook over a medium heat for 1–2 minutes, or until the spinach is just beginning to wilt.
3 Season with freshly grated nutmeg, salt and pepper. Serve immediately.

Savoy Cabbage with Pancetta and Sesame Seeds

This makes an excellent accompaniment to a roast dish; it is particularly good with chicken.

SERVES 4

1 tablespoon sunflower oil

170 g pancetta, chopped

1 bunch of spring onions, finely sliced

1 Savoy cabbage, outer leaves removed, finely shredded

1 tablespoon sesame seeds

salt and freshly ground black pepper

1 Heat the oil in a frying pan, add the pancetta and fry until lightly browned.
2 Add the spring onions and cook until just beginning to brown. Remove the pan from the heat.
3 Bring a large pan of salted water to the boil and cook the cabbage until just tender. Drain well.
4 Mix the cabbage with the pancetta and spring onions, stir in the sesame seeds and season to taste with salt and pepper. Serve very hot.

Glazed Carrots

SERVES 4

450 g carrots

2 teaspoons butter

½ teaspoon salt

1 teaspoon caster sugar

1 teaspoon each chopped fresh mint and parsley

freshly ground black pepper

1 Peel the carrots and cut them into sticks or even-sized barrel shapes; or if they are very young, leave them whole.
2 Put them in a saucepan with all the remaining ingredients, except the pepper and herbs, half-cover them with water and boil until the water has almost evaporated and the carrots are tender.
3 Lower the heat and allow the carrots to glaze in the butter and sugar remaining in the pan, making sure they do not burn.
4 Season with pepper and mix in the herbs.

NOTE: It is important not to oversalt the water. When the water has evaporated the entire quantity of salt used will remain with the carrots.

Courgette and Carrot 'Pappardelle'

SERVES 2

2 medium courgettes

2 medium carrots

butter

salt and freshly ground black pepper

1 Wash and trim the courgettes. Peel the carrots.

2 Using a potato peeler, peel strips off the vegetables to make long thin slices or 'pappardelle'.

3 Steam or stir-fry the vegetables for about 2 minutes, or until just cooked. Toss in a little butter and season with salt and pepper before serving.

Caramelized Shallots

SERVES 4

85 g unsalted butter

1 kg small shallots, blanched and peeled

½ teaspoon salt

1½ tablespoons soft dark brown sugar

1 tablespoon balsamic vinegar

salt and freshly ground black pepper

1 Melt the butter in a large sauté pan and, when foaming, add the shallots and sprinkle over the salt. Reduce the heat, cover with a lid and cook very gently, turning occasionally, for 30 minutes, or until the shallots are very tender and beginning to lose their shape.

2 Remove the lid and increase the heat. Sprinkle over the sugar and cook briskly, stirring frequently, until the shallots are a deep golden brown. Add the vinegar and cook for a further minute. Season with salt and pepper and serve immediately.

NOTE: Adding salt at the beginning of cooking helps to draw the moisture from the shallots and will help to prevent them from burning. The cooking time may vary, depending on their size and the pan they are cooked in. It is important that they are meltingly tender and have a very sticky caramel coating: this might take a little more or less time than suggested in the recipe.

Red Onion Marmalade

MAKES ABOUT 340 g

oil, for frying

3 medium red onions, diced

1 clove of garlic, crushed

3 tablespoons soft dark brown sugar

300 ml red wine

1 tablespoon honey

salt and freshly ground black pepper

1 Sweat the onions in the oil until very soft. Stir through the garlic for 30 seconds.

2 Add the sugar whilst stirring, then turn up the heat and allow the onions to caramelize.

3 Add the wine and reduce until there is almost no liquid left in the pan.

4 Stir in the honey, then season to taste. This marmalade can be served hot or cold.

Matching Wine with Food

by Richard Bampfield MW

Taste in wine is as individual as taste in food, so when you put the two together, the chances of pleasing everyone all the time are remote. But that is no excuse not to try, so in *Leiths Meat Bible* you will find wine recommendations with most of the recipes. (The exceptions are breakfast dishes and certain family dishes, such as pizza.)

The wine selections are based on some simple principles that, over the years at Leiths School of Food and Wine, we have found to be a useful guide:

- Match the weight of the wine to the weight of the dish. Rich dishes, especially rich sauces, require rich styles of wine.
- The acidity that fruit brings to a recipe tends to reduce the perceived acidity in a wine. This means that if you wish the wine still to refresh, it is best to choose one that is naturally higher in acidity.
- Fattiness and creaminess in food soften the tannins in a red wine, so dishes with these characteristics tend to be friendly to higher tannin wines, such as young red Bordeaux.
- Pepper and spice in food are not always complemented by a rich, spicy wine. Often a rounder, fruitier style is more refreshing.
- Dishes that have blended ingredients, such as stews and casseroles, often work better with blended wines (blends of different grape varieties).
- Premium ingredients and premium cuts of meat demand premium wines. Similarly, glassware should be of a quality to match the context of the meal.

We make no apologies for selecting wines that, where possible, have the same geographical origins as the dish. Both aesthetically and from a gustatory point of view, these are often the most natural match. The majority of wine recommendations come, in fact, from Europe. This is partly because the majority of the recipes are also Europe-influenced and partly because the lower alcohol levels and pronounced freshness of European wines tend to make them more appetizing accompaniments to food.

The term 'New World' is used to refer to wines produced in North America and countries of the southern hemisphere.

The charts that follow grade many of the most familiar wine types by weight, style and level of dryness/sweetness. Wine drinkers will know that not all Saint-Emilions taste the same, any more than all lamb chops taste the same. Consequently, the chart should be seen as a general guide rather than a fail-safe reference.

We hope that you will have as much fun exploring the wine recommendations as you will experimenting with the different recipes.

Wine Categories

White Wine and Rosé

Aromatic dry whites	Less aromatic dry whites	Aromatic, fruity whites	Fuller-bodied whites (sometimes oaked)	Sweet whites	Dry rosés
France					
Sancerre (Loire)	Chablis	Alsace Pinot Gris	Corton-Charlemagne (France – Burgundy)	Sauternes	Sancerre Rosé
Pouilly-Fumé, Menetou-Salon (Loire)	White Burgundy (Meursault, Puligny-Montrachet, Chassagne-Montrachet, Saint-Véran, Pouilly-Fuissé)	Alsace Gewürz-traminer	White Hermitage and Châteauneuf-du-Pape	Coteaux-du-Layon	Côtes de Provence Rosé
Alsace Riesling		Alsace Pinot Blanc		Muscat de Rivesaltes/ Beaumes-de-Venise	Tavel Rosé
Viognier					Rosé de Marsannay
Condrieu (Rhône)		Alsace Sylvaner	Roussanne/ Marsanne (Southern France)	Alsace – Sélection de Grains Nobles	Bergerac Rosé
Alsace Muscat	Muscadet de Sèvre-et-Maine (Loire)	Vouvray demi-sec			Bordeaux Clairet
Bordeaux Sauvignon	Vouvray sec (Loire)				
Vin de Pays Sauvignon	Graves sec, Pessac-Léognan (Bordeaux)				
	Côtes de Gascogne				

Aromatic dry whites	Less aromatic dry whites	Aromatic, fruity whites	Fuller-bodied whites (sometimes oaked)	Sweet whites	Dry rosés
Rest of the World					
Cortese (Italy)	Fiano di Avellino (Italy)	German Riesling Kabinett	Australian Chardonnay	Vin Santo (Italy)	Navarra Rosado (Spain)
Riesling Kabinett Trocken/ Halbtrocken	Gavi (Italy) Soave (Italy)	Australian Chenin Blanc	Californian Chardonnay	Moscato d'Asti (Italy)	Rioja Rosado (Spain)
Albarino (Spain)	Pecorino (Italy)		White Rioja (traditional) (Spain)	Late-harvested wines from the New World	
Verdejo (Spain)	Frascati (Italy)	Torres Vina Esmeralda (Spain)		Tokaji (Hungary)	
Grüner Veltliner (Austria)	Greco di Tufo (Italy)	New World Gewürz- traminer	Australian Semillon	Beerenauslese and Trocken- beerenauslese (Germany and Austria)	
Australian Riesling	Verdicchio (Italy)	New Zealand Pinot Gris			
New Zealand Sauvignon	Falanghina (Italy)			Icewine (Canada)	
Chile Sauvignon	Dezaley (Switzerland)	Torrontes (Argentina)			
South Africa Sauvignon	Fendant (Switzerland)	Bacchus (England)			
Vinho Verde (Portugal)	Assyrtiko (Greece)				
	Chenin Blanc (South Africa)				
	Semillon/ Chardonnay (Australia)				
	Rueda (Spain)				

Red Wine

Dry reds – medium body	Dry reds – full body	Lighter, fruitier reds
France	France	France
Red Burgundy	Châteauneuf-du-Pape (Rhône)	Beaujolais
Cru Beaujolais (Fleurie, Brouilly, Morgon, Moulin-a-Vent, etc.)	Roussillon	Saumur-Champigny
	Hermitage (Rhône)	
Red Bordeaux, including Saint-Emilion, Médoc, Côtes de Castillon, Bourg and Blaye	Crozes-Hermitage (Rhône)	Rest of the World
	Madiran	Valpolicella (Italy)
St Nicolas de Bourgueil (Loire)	Côte-Rôtie (Rhône)	Bardolino (Italy)
Chinon (Loire)	Gigondas (Rhône)	Dolcetto (Italy)
Côtes-du-Rhône	Pic Saint-Loup (Languedoc)	Blaufrankisch (Austria)
Minervois (Languedoc)	Pomerol (Bordeaux)	Tarrango (Australia)
Corbières (Languedoc)		Dole (Switzerland)
Fitou (Languedoc)	Rest of the World	
Côtes du Ventoux	Aglianico (Italy)	
Bergerac	Brunello di Montalcino, and the less expensive Rosso di Montalcino (Italy)	
Vin de Pays d'Oc Merlot and Cabernet	Salice Salentino (Italy)	
Cahors	Amarone della Valpolicella (Italy)	
	Cannonau (Sardinia)	
Rest of the World	Primitivo (Italy)	
Chianti Classico (Italy)	Priorato/Montsant (Spain)	
Vino Nobile di Montepulciano (Italy)	Ribera del Duero (Spain)	
Barbera d'Asti (Italy)	Douro Red (Portugal)	
Barolo (Italy)	Argentina Malbec	
Barbaresco (Italy)	New Zealand Pinot Noir	
Montepulciano d'Abruzzo (Italy)	South Africa Pinotage	
Negroamaro (Italy)	Australian Shiraz	
Rioja (Spain)	Zinfandel (California)	
Bairrada (Portugal)	Californian Cabernet and Merlot	
Naoussa (Greece)	Chilean Cabernet Sauvignon and Syrah	
Oregon Pinot Noir	Australian Cabernet	
Chile Merlot and Carmenère	Tannat (Uruguay)	
Chile Pinot Noir		
Tasmanian Pinot Noir (Australia)		

Menu Planning

Designing a menu that is nutritious and exciting to eat is often a daunting task. There are certain criteria any menu must satisfy in order to make a successful meal. To help decide what to cook, ask yourself the following questions:

- **What is the occasion?** Special occasions will require more expensive, elaborate food than, say, a simple family lunch. The style of the food should complement the style of the occasion.
- **Who is the menu designed to feed?** The food should be suitable for the diners' needs. How hungry are they likely to be? A light summer lunch, for example, will be quite different from a rugby club supper. The age group and nationality of the diners will also influence your menu choice.
- **Are there any special diets to be catered for?** It is advisable to ask in advance to avoid any last-minute menu changes.
- **What is the season?** Seasonal produce will usually taste better and be less expensive than food that is out of season. People naturally prefer lighter food in hot weather and warming food when it is cold outside.
- **How many people are you cooking for?** With large numbers, the logistics are critical. Do you have the oven, hob and refrigerator space to prepare the food? Do you have the required pots and pans?

It is often easiest to choose a main course first, as this is the focal point or the foundation of the meal. Once you have decided on that, try to imagine what you would like to have for the first course. It should complement the main course as well as whet the appetite, and should not be more strongly flavoured than the main course.

The dessert can be decided upon once the first course and the main course have been chosen. Imagine eating the meal: what would you choose for dessert? Keep the points above in mind when choosing both the first course and the dessert.

When you have decided upon your menu, review it against the following criteria:

- **Is there any repetition of ingredients?** For example, do cheese, fruit or pastry appear more than once? That would be undesirable.
- **Is the menu too rich or light?** Does it contain too much cream or fat? Serving a salad is recommended with any rich meal.
- **Does the menu have a variety of textures?** Often texture can be added with the addition of a garnish.
- **Does the menu have a variety of colour?** Food can often be too brown or too pale. Colour is visually exciting and will make the food seem more attractive. Add colour with garnish and vegetables.
- **Does the menu skip from one continent to another?** It is usually best to keep within the same cultural realm to avoid culinary culture clashes. Try not to include too many exotic tastes in the same menu.

- **Does the menu stay in style throughout?** Does it feature sophisticated, restaurant-style food, or is it based on simple home cooking?
- **Is the menu nutritionally balanced?** It should contain a variety of food from a range of food groups.
- **Is it possible to cook and serve the menu easily?** This means taking into account any limitations imposed by the kitchen, equipment, dining room, cook, and/or any time constraints.
- **How will you present and garnish the food?** Remember to include garnish in your menu planning when writing your shopping list.

At Leiths there is always much discussion about the order of a meal. In the UK we conventionally serve dessert followed by cheese. In France it is more usual to serve cheese before the dessert so that the dinner wine may accompany the cheese, and a dessert wine is then served with the dessert. In the United States cheese is often served as an appetizer with pre-dinner drinks and the salad is often part of the first course. If cooking commercially, check the order of the courses with the host/hostess.

Once the menu has been decided, make a time plan detailing when each component of the menu will be made. If you are cooking for a large number of people, a time plan is vital as the preparation time will often span several days. Be sure to include time for shopping and putting away the food.

Catering Quantities

As a general rule, the more people you are catering for, the less food per head you need to provide, e.g. 250 g stewing beef per head is essential for four people, but 170 g per head would feed 60 people.

Soup

Allow 300 ml soup a head, depending on the size of the bowl.

Beef

Stewed: 225 g boneless trimmed meat per person.
Roast off the bone: If serving men only, 225 g per person; if serving men and women, 200 g per person.
Roast on the bone: 340 g per person.
Roast whole fillet: 1.8 kg piece for 8–10 people.
Grilled steaks: 170–225 g per person, depending on appetite.

Minced Meat

Cannelloni, lasagne, etc: 85 g per person.
Hamburgers, shepherd's pie, etc: 170 g per person.
Moussaka: 110 g per person.
Spaghetti: 50 g per person.
Steak tartare: 110 g per person

Veal

Stews or pies: 225 g pie veal per person.
Fried: 1 × 170 g escalope per person.

Lamb or Mutton

Casseroled: 225 g per person (boneless, with fat trimmed away).
Roast leg: 1.35 kg for 3–4 people; 1.8 kg for 4–5 people; 2.7 kg for 7–8 people.
Roast shoulder: 1.8 kg shoulder for 5–6 people; 2.7 kg shoulder for 7–8 people.
Grilled best end cutlets: 3–4 per person.
Grilled loin chops: 2–3 per person.

Pork

Casseroled: 170 g per person.
Roast leg or loin off the bone: 200 g per person.
Roast leg or loin on the bone: 340 g per person.
Fillet: 340 g will feed 2–4 people.
Grilled: 1 × 170 g chop or cutlet per person.

Poultry

Chicken and turkey: Allow 340 g per person, weighed when plucked and drawn. An average chicken serves 4 people on the bone and 6 people off the bone.
Duck: A 2.7 kg bird will feed 3–4 people; a 1.8 kg bird will feed 2 people. A duck makes enough pâté for 6 people.
Goose: Allow 3.6 kg for 4 people; 6.9 kg for 8 people.

Game

Pheasant: Allow 1 bird (roast) for 2 people; 1 bird (casseroled) for 3 people.
Pigeon: Allow 1 bird per person.
Grouse: Allow 1 young grouse (roast) per person; 2 birds (casseroled) for 3 people.
Quail: Allow 2 small birds per person or 1 large boned stuffed bird served on a croûton.
Partridge: Allow 1 bird per person.
Venison: Allow 170 g lean meat per person; 1.8 kg cut of haunch weighed on the bone for 8–9 people.
Steaks: Allow 170 g per person.

Essential Equipment

When buying kitchen equipment, the basic rule for standard items is to buy the best you can possibly afford. Good kitchen equipment will probably last for 15 years and is worth the investment. When buying small or specialist equipment that may be used only once, be as economical or extravagant as your purse dictates.

The following is not intended to be a complete list of the kitchen equipment available, but includes all the utensils that the home cook could possibly want, while excluding certain specialist items, such as preserving equipment, barbecues, smokers and storage items.

Utensils

The following items of equipment are essential for any cook:

1 cook's knife with 20 cm blade
1 cook's knife with 7.5 cm blade
1 filleting knife with 14 cm blade
1 fruit knife
1 serrated bread knife
1 palette knife
1 stockpot
1 large saucepan 21 cm diameter with lid
1 medium saucepan 19 cm diameter with lid
1 small saucepan 12 cm diameter base
1 frying pan with 25 cm diameter base
1 sauté pan with 25 cm diameter base
1 colander
2 wooden spoons
1 fish slice
1 rubber spatula
1 sieve (bowl strainer)
1 chinois (conical strainer)
1 vegetable peeler

1 set of scales
1 measuring jug
1 pair kitchen scissors
3 gradated pudding basins
1 cheese grater
2 wooden or plastic chopping boards
   (1 for raw meat, 1 for cooked)
1 rolling pin
1 pastry brush
1 set of measuring spoons
2 roasting tins: 1 small, 1 large
1 salad bowl
1 whisk
2 baking sheets
1 wire rack
2 large stainless steel bowls
20 cm flan ring
20 cm cake tin
450 g loaf tin

Cookery Terms and Kitchen French

À point: French, meaning 'cooked perfectly'; also used to describe a steak cooked rare.

Abats: French for 'offal' (hearts, livers, brains, tripe, etc.). Americans call them 'variety meats'.

Acidulate: To turn cooking liquor or a dish slightly acid or piquant by adding acid, such as lemon juice or vinegar.

Al dente: Italian for 'firm to the tooth', which describes the degree to which pasta should be cooked. Sometimes used to describe the degree of 'doneness' in vegetables.

Aromatic ingredients: Leaves, flowers, seeds, fruits, stems, roots and bulbs of fragrant plants, such as herbs, parsley, thyme, chervil and tarragon and vegetables such as onions, garlic, carrots and celery used to flavour stocks, sauces and stews.

Bain-marie: A roasting pan half-filled with hot water in which terrines, custards, etc. stand while cooking. The food is protected from direct fierce heat and cooks in a gentle, steamy atmosphere. Also a large container that will hold a number of pans standing in hot water, used to keep soups, sauces, etc. hot without further cooking. A cold bain-marie is also used to cool hot food.

Bake blind: To bake a pastry case while empty. In order to prevent the sides falling in or the base bubbling up, the pastry is usually lined with paper and filled with 'blind beans' (see page 512).

Ballotine: Boned stuffed meat, poultry or game birds. A ballotine is normally poached or braised and served hot. Often the term is used interchangeably with 'galantine' (see page 270).

Barbecue: Used originally to describe roasting over an open fire, but now applied to cooking food on a grill over burning charcoal, hot coals, wood embers or gas flames in the outdoors.

Bard: To tie bacon or pork fat over a joint of meat, game bird or poultry to be roasted. This helps to prevent the flesh from drying out.

Bark: The thin pink membrane often found over part of the fat layer in cuts of lamb. It can be removed by pulling/peeling back and/or by cutting.

Baste: To spoon over liquid (sometimes stock, sometimes fat) during cooking to prevent drying out and to promote flavour.

Beurre manié: Butter and flour in equal quantities worked together to a soft paste, and used as a liaison or thickening for liquids. Small pieces are whisked into boiling liquid. As the butter melts, it disperses the flour evenly through the liquid, thereby thickening it without causing lumps.

Beurre noisette: Browned butter (see Noisette).

Blanch: Originally, to whiten by boiling, e.g. to boil sweetbreads or brains briefly to remove traces of blood (and strong flavours), or to boil almonds to make the brown skin easy to remove, leaving the nuts white. Now commonly used to mean parboiling, as in blanching vegetables prior to freezing, or as in precooking them so that they have only to be reheated before serving.

Blanching is also a good technique to make the peeling of shallots, button onions and tomatoes easier: simply immerse shallots and onions in boiling water for 30 seconds, and tomatoes for 10 seconds, refresh in cold water, then peel off the skins.

Blanquette: A stew made without prior frying of the meat. Usually used for lamb, chicken or veal. The sauce is often thickened with an egg and cream liaison.

Blind beans: Dried beans, peas, rice or pasta used to fill pastry cases temporarily during baking.

Bouchées: Small puff pastry cases like miniature vol-au-vents.

Bouillon: Broth or uncleared stock.

Bouquet garni: Parsley stalks, small bay leaf, fresh thyme, celery stalk, sometimes with a blade of mace, tied together with string and used to flavour stews, etc. Removed before serving.

Braise: To bake or stew slowly on a bed of vegetables with a small amount of liquid in a tightly covered pan.

Brine: A salt solution used to cure meat (ham and bacon) or to add moisture and flavour to meat, as in brining (see page 9).

Brochette: A large, slightly flattened skewer on which small pieces of meat are threaded for cooking on a barbecue or chargrill.

Brunoise: Vegetables cut into very small dice and slowly cooked in butter; used to flavour sauces and stews.

Canapé: A small bread or biscuit base, sometimes fried, spread or covered with savoury paste, egg, etc., used for cocktail titbits or as an accompaniment to meat dishes. Sometimes used to denote the base only, as in champignons sur canapé.

Caramel: Sugar cooked to a toffee.

Cartouche: Piece of greaseproof paper dampened and placed directly on top of vegetables when sweating, or used dry for baking blind.

Casserole: A heavy dish made of metal, enamelware, pottery or earthenware with a close-fitting lid. Also the name for the food cooked and served in a casserole dish.

Caul/crépinette: A fatty membrane that surrounds the internal organs of animals. It has a lacy structure and can be used to encase meat before cooking in order to keep its shape, or to hold component parts together, such as a chicken breast wrapped in Parma ham. When heated, the fat softens and melts, and all but disappears.

If the meat is cooked immersed in liquid, or in a steamy environment such as a bain-marie, the caul will dissipate and be barely visible at the end of the cooking time. If a dry method of cooking is used, such as baking or frying, the caul will first start to render down, before caramelizing and creating a flavoursome outside layer.

Chargrill: To grill food on a metal grid over intense heat provided by burning charcoal or gas flames, or to cook on a ridged heavy pan.

Chateaubriand: Roast fillet steak from the thick end for two or more people.

Chiffonade: Shredded leaves, such as lettuce and soft herbs.

Chine: To remove the backbone from a rack of ribs. Carving is almost impossible if the butcher has not chined the meat.

Chinois: Fine conical sieve.

Clarified butter: Butter that has been separated from the milk solids and salt that cause it to look cloudy when melted, and to burn easily when heated (see page xii).

Clarify or clear: To make a cloudy liquid clear by using fine filters or coagulated protein. The process, called 'clarification', is used to purify stocks used for consommé and aspic.

Coating consistency: The point at which a sauce has thickened enough to coat the back of a spoon; often likened to the consistency of single cream.

Collops: Small slices of meat taken from a tender cut, such as loin of lamb.

Concassé: Tomatoes cut into small even squares or diamonds.

Concasser: To chop roughly.

Confit: Traditionally, pork, duck or goose cooked and preserved in its own fat.

Consommé: Clear soup.

Court-bouillon: Acidulated liquid used for poaching delicate meats and offal, and also for cooking white ingredients in order to keep them white.

Crêpes: Thin French pancakes.

Crépin or crépinette: See Caul.

Croquettes: Balls or patties made of stiff mashed potato and possibly puréed poultry, fish or meat; they are coated in egg and breadcrumbs and deep-fried.

Croustade: Bread case dipped in butter and baked until crisp. Used to contain hot savoury mixtures for a canapé, savoury or as a garnish.

Croûte: Literally 'crust'. Sometimes a pastry case, as in Fillet of Beef en Croûte (see page 40), sometimes toasted or fried bread, as in scrambled eggs on toast.

Croûtons: Small, evenly sized cubes of fried bread used as a soup garnish and occasionally in other dishes.

Dariole: Small castle-shaped mould.

Daube: Classic French stew, traditionally cooked in a very deep casserole with a tight-fitting lid to keep in the moisture. In France the casserole dish is called a *daubière*. If a tight-fitting lid is not available, a *repère* paste (see page 518) can be made up and placed around the edge of the dish to create a seal. This is chipped off and discarded when the stew is ready.

Déglaçage: The liquid produced by the process of deglazing.

Déglacer: To loosen and liquefy fat, sediment and browned juices stuck at the bottom of a frying pan or saucepan by adding liquid (usually stock, water or wine) and stirring while boiling.

Deglaze: See Déglacer.

Dégorger: To extract the juices from meat, fish or vegetables, generally by salting, then soaking or washing. Usually done to remove indigestible or strong-tasting juices.

Dépouiller: To skim off the scum from a sauce or stock. A splash of cold water or stock added to the boiling liquid helps to bring scum and fat to the surface, allowing it to be skimmed more easily.

Dripping: The melted fat and juices that run from a roasting joint of meat. Rendered and sieved meat fat.

Dropping consistency: The consistency at which a mixture will drop reluctantly from a spoon, neither pouring off nor obstinately adhering.

Duxelles: Finely chopped raw mushrooms, sometimes with chopped shallots or chopped ham, often used as a stuffing.

Egg wash: Beaten raw egg, sometimes with salt, used for glazing pastry to give it a shine when baked.

Emulsion: A stable suspension of fat and other liquid, e.g. mayonnaise, hollandaise, vinaigrette dressing.

Entrecôte: Sirloin steak.

Entrée: Traditionally, a dish served before the main course, but usually served as a main course today.

Escalope: A thin slice of meat, sometimes beaten out flat to make it thinner and larger.

Farce: Stuffing or forcemeat.

Fécule: Farinaceous thickening, usually arrowroot or cornflour.

Finish: To complete the preparation of a dish by adjusting the seasoning, consistency or appearance.

Flamber: To set alcohol alight, usually to burn it off, but frequently performed for dramatic effect. (Past tense flambé or flambée.)

Flame: See Flamber.

Fold: To mix with a gentle lifting motion, rather than to stir vigorously. The aim is to avoid beating out air while mixing.

Forcemeat: A seasoned mixture of raw or cooked ingredients, chopped or minced, used to stuff meats or vegetables or cooked on its own, such as Forcemeat Balls (see page 238).

French-trim: To remove the fat and scrape the bones clean of any sinew and/or membrane, usually on a rack of lamb or chops (see page 141).

Fricassée: White stew made with cooked or raw poultry meat or rabbit and a velouté sauce, sometimes thickened with cream and egg yolks.

Galantine: Boned poultry or meat that is stuffed, roasted and served cold.

Game chips: Thinly sliced potatoes fried in oil and used to garnish roast game birds (see page 381).

Gastrique: Sugar dissolved in vinegar, then caramelized to form a brown liquid used to enhance the colour and flavour of sauces, usually tomato or fruit-based.

Glace de viande: Reduced brown stock, very strong in flavour, used for adding body and colour to sauces (see page 455).

Glaze: To cover with a thin layer of shiny jellied meat juices (for roast turkey), melted jam (for fruit flans) or syrup (for rum baba) or beaten egg (bread and pastries).

Goujons: Finger-sized strips of poultry or fish that are often coated with flour, egg and crumbs before deep-frying.

Gratiner: To brown under a grill after the surface of the dish has been sprinkled with breadcrumbs and butter and, sometimes, cheese. Dishes finished like this are sometimes called gratinée or au gratin.

Hang: To store a whole animal or bird carcass for a length of time in order for bacterial action to soften the fibres of the meat and develop flavour.

Hors d'oeuvre: Usually means the first course. Sometimes used to denote a variety or selection of many savoury titbits served with drinks, or a mixed first course (hors d'oeuvres variés).

Infuse: To steep or heat gently to extract flavour, as when infusing milk with onion slices.

Joint: To cut meat, game or poultry into portions.

Julienne: Vegetables or citrus rind cut in thin matchstick shapes or very fine shreds.

Jus or jus de viande: God's gravy, i.e. juices that occur naturally in cooking, not a made-up sauce. Used in restaurants to denote a thin but intense sauce.

Jus lié: Thickened gravy.

Knock down/back: To punch or knead out the air in risen dough so that it resumes its pre-risen bulk.

Knock up: To separate slightly the layers of raw puff pastry with the blade of a knife to facilitate rising during cooking.

Lard: To thread strips of bacon fat (or sometimes anchovy) through meat to give it flavour, and, in the case of fat, to moisturize very lean meat.

Lardons: Lardons are strips of either smoked or unsmoked streaky bacon cut from a whole piece into 20 × 5 × 5 mm pieces. They are used to add flavour to stews and casseroles.

Liaison: Ingredients for binding together and thickening sauce, soup or other liquid, e.g. roux, beurre manié or blood, but usually denotes the use of egg yolk and cream.

Luting paste: See Repère.

Macédoine: A selection of cut fruits that have been soaked in liqueur, or small diced, cooked mixed vegetables, usually containing some root vegetables.

Macerate: To soak food in a syrup or liquid to allow flavours to mix.

Mandolin: Frame of metal or wood with adjustable blades set in it for thinly slicing cucumbers, potatoes, etc.

Marinade: A liquid containing oil, aromatic vegetables, herbs and spices, and an acid such as wine, lemon juice or vinegar.

Marinate: To soak meat, fish or vegetables before cooking in acidulated liquid containing flavourings and herbs; this gives flavour and tenderizes meat.

Marmite: French for a tall, covered earthenware container in which a soup or stew is both cooked and served.

Medallions: Small rounds of meat, evenly cut. Occasionally used of vegetables if cut in flat, round discs.

Mirepoix: The bed of diced vegetables, mentioned in Braise (page 512).

Mortifier: To hang meat, poultry or game.

Napper: To coat, mask or cover.

Needleshreds: Fine, evenly cut shreds of citrus zest, generally used as a garnish. The French term is 'julienne' (see above).

Noisette: Literally 'hazelnut'. Usually means nut-brown, as in beurre noisette, i.e. butter browned over heat to a nut colour. Noisettes are also the neat rounds cut from a boneless, rolled and tied rack of lamb.

Nouvelle cuisine: Style of cooking that promotes light and delicate dishes, often using unusual combinations of very fresh ingredients attractively arranged.

Oyster: Small piece of meat found on either side of the backbone of a chicken. Said to be the best-flavoured flesh. Also a bivalve mollusc.

Panade or panada: The term used for choux pastry base.

Paner: To flour, egg and crumb ingredients before deep-frying.

Pan-fry: To quickly cook small, thin, tender pieces of meat and other foods in up to 5 mm of oil or fat in the base of a wide, shallow pan over medium to high heat.

Papillote: A wrapping of paper in which fish or meat is cooked to contain the aroma and flavour. The dish is brought to the table still wrapped up. Foil is sometimes used, but as it does not puff up dramatically, it is less satisfactory.

Parboil: To half-boil or partially soften by boiling.

Parisienne: Potato (sometimes with other ingredients) scooped into small balls with a melon baller and usually fried.

Pass: To strain or push through a sieve.

Pâte: The basic mixture or paste, often used of uncooked pastry, dough, etc.

Pâté: A savoury paste of liver, pork, game, etc.

Paupiette: Beef (or pork or veal) olive, i.e. a thin layer of meat, spread with a soft farce, rolled up, tied with string and cooked slowly.

Piquer: To insert in meats or poultry a large julienne of fat, bacon, ham, truffle, etc.

Potage or pottage: Originally a 'potted dish'. A thick stew or soup, often with chunks of meat or vegetables in it (see page 214).

Poussin: Young chicken.

Prove: To put dough or a yeasted mixture to rise before baking.

Purée: Liquidized, sieved or finely mashed vegetables.

Quenelles: A finely minced mixture shaped into small oval portions and poached. Served in a sauce, or as a garnish to other dishes.

Ragoût: A stew.

Rechauffé: A reheated dish made with previously cooked food.

Reduce: To decrease the amount of liquid by rapid boiling, causing evaporation and a consequent strengthening of flavour in the remaining liquid.

Refresh: To hold boiled food under cold running water, or to immerse it immediately in cold water to prevent it cooking further, and to set the colour.

Relax or rest: To set aside after removing from the oven; allows the fibres of meat to unwind and reabsorb some of the juices, and make carving easier.

Render: To melt solid meat fat (e.g. beef, pork) slowly in the oven.

Repère: Flour mixed with water or white of egg and used to seal pans when cooking a dish slowly, such as lamb daube. Sometimes called 'luting paste'.

Revenir: To fry meat or vegetables quickly in hot fat in order to warm them through.

Rouille: Garlic and oil emulsion used as flavouring.

Roux: A basic liaison or thickening for a sauce or soup. Melted butter to which flour has been added to form a smooth paste.

Salamander: A hot oven or grill used for browning or glazing the tops of cooked dishes, or a hot iron or poker for branding the top with lines or a criss-cross pattern.

Salmis: A game stew sometimes made with cooked game, or partially roasted game.

Salsa: Chunky sauce made from chopped, uncooked vegetables, usually including tomatoes, chillies and onions.

Sauter: Method of frying in a deep frying pan or sautoir. The food is continually tossed or shaken so that it browns quickly and evenly.

Sautoir: Deep frying pan with a lid used for recipes that require fast frying and then slower cooking (with the lid on).

Scald: Of milk – to heat until just below the point of boiling, when some movement can be seen at the edges of the pan but there is no overall bubbling. Of muslin, cloths, etc. – to immerse in clean boiling water, generally to sterilize.

Score: To make long, shallow cuts along the surface of meat to assist flavouring with marinades, to help render fat, and for decoration; for example, the skin and fat on a joint of pork is scored to make crackling.

Sear: To brown meat rapidly, usually in fat, for flavour and colour.

Season: Of food – to flavour, generally with salt and pepper. Of iron frying pans, griddles, etc. – to prepare new equipment for use by placing it over a high heat, generally having coated it first with oil and a sprinkling of salt. This prevents subsequent rusting and sticking.

Singe: To burn the pin feathers off a bird before cooking by rotating it over a flame.

Slake: To mix flour, arrowroot or cornflour to a thin paste with a small quantity of cold water.

Smoke point: The temperature at which the molecular structure of fat or oil begins to break down and smoke.

Soubise: See page 521.

Spatchcock: A small chicken or other bird flattened along the breastbone and secured with skewers for grilling or barbecuing (see page 319).

Stew: To slowly cook meat and possibly vegetables immersed in liquid in a pot with a tight-fitting lid, either on the hob or in the oven.

Supreme: Choice piece of poultry (usually from the breast). See also Making a Supreme, page 264.

Sweat: To cook gently, usually in butter or oil, but sometimes in the food's own juices, without frying or browning.

Tammy: A fine muslin cloth through which sauces are sometimes forced. After this treatment they look beautifully smooth and shiny. Tammy cloths have generally been replaced by blenders or liquidizers, which give much the same effect.

Terrine: Pâté or minced mixture baked or steamed in a loaf tin or earthenware container.

Timbale: A dish that has been cooked in a castle-shaped mould.

Tournedos: Fillet steak. Usually refers to a one-portion piece of grilled fillet.

Turn vegetables: To cut carrots or turnips into small barrel shapes. To cut the surface of mushrooms into a decorative spiral pattern.

Velouté: See page 462.

Vol-au-vent: A puff pastry case with high raised sides and a deep hollow centre into which a savoury mixture is put.

Well: A hollow or dip made in a pile or bowlful of flour, exposing the work surface or the bottom of the bowl, into which other ingredients are placed prior to mixing.

Wilt: To cook leaves, such as spinach, briefly until they lose their original volume and texture.

Zest: The outermost skin of any citrus fruit. It is very thinly pared without any of the bitter white pith, and used to give flavour.

Classic Garnishes

Anglaise: Braised vegetables, such as carrots, turnips and quartered celery hearts, used to garnish boiled salted beef.

Bolognese: A rich sauce made from chicken livers and/or minced beef flavoured with mushrooms and tomatoes. Usually served with pasta.

Bonne femme: To cook in a simple way. Usually of chicken – sautéd and served with white wine gravy, bacon cubes, button onions and garnished with croquette potatoes. Of soup – a simple purée of vegetables with stock.

Boulangère: Potatoes and onions sliced and cooked in the oven in stock.

Bouquetière: Groups of very small carrots, turnips, French beans, cauliflower florets, button onions, asparagus tips, etc. Sometimes served with a thin demi-glace or gravy. Usually accompanies beef or lamb entrées.

Bourgeoise: Fried diced bacon, glazed carrots and button onions. Sometimes red wine is used in the sauce. Used for beef and liver dishes.

Bourguignonne: Button mushrooms and small onions in a sauce made with red wine (Burgundy). Used for beef and egg dishes.

Bretonne: Haricot beans whole or in a purée. Sometimes a purée of root vegetables. Usually served with a gigot (leg) of lamb.

Chasseur: Sautéd mushrooms added to a sauté of chicken or veal.

Chiffonnade: Chopped lettuce or sorrel cooked in butter to garnish soup.

DuBarry: Denotes the use of cauliflower; potage DuBarry is cauliflower soup. Also, cooked cauliflower florets coated with Mornay sauce and browned under the grill. Used for meat entrées.

Flamande: Red cabbage and glazed small onions; used with pork and beef.

Florentine: In the manner of Florence, a dish including spinach. Also a 16th-century name for a pie.

Hongroise: Usually implies the addition of paprika.

Indienne: Flavoured with curry powder.

Jardinière: Garnished with fresh vegetables.

Lyonnaise: Denotes the use of onions as a garnish; the onions are frequently sliced and fried.

Milanese: With a tomato sauce, sometimes including shredded ham, tongue and mushrooms. Frequently served with pasta.

Minute: Food quickly cooked, either fried or grilled; usually applied to a thin entrecôte steak.

Mornay: With a cheese sauce.

Napolitana: Tomato sauce and Parmesan cheese (for pasta).

Normande: A creamy sauce containing cider or Calvados, and sometimes apples.

Parmentier: Denotes the use of potato as a base or garnish.

Paysanne: Literally 'peasant'; usually denotes the use of carrots and turnips sliced across in rounds.

Portugaise: Denotes the use of tomatoes or tomato purée.

Princesse: Denotes the use of asparagus (usually on breast of chicken).

Printanière: Early spring vegetables cooked and used as a garnish, usually in separate groups.

Provençal: Denotes the use of garlic, and sometimes tomatoes and/or olives.

Rossini: With collops of foie gras and truffles tossed in butter, served with a rich meat glaze.

St Germain: Denotes the use of peas, sometimes with pommes Parisienne (see page 517).

Soubise: Onion purée, frequently mixed with a Béchamel sauce.

Vichy: Garnish of small glazed carrots.

Conversion Tables

This book specifies metric measurements only. To be strictly accurate, 1 oz = 28 g, but it is easier to weigh out 25 g or 30 g. With many recipes a few grams here and there does not make too much of a difference, with the exception of baking recipes, where the ingredients should be weighed accurately. The following conversion table gives a range of grams for the equivalent in ounces.

Weight

Metric	Imperial
15–20 g	½ oz
25–30 g	1 oz
50–60 g	2 oz
80–90 g	3 oz
100–120 g	4 oz
130–150 g	5 oz
160–180 g	6 oz
200 g	7 oz
220–230 g	8 oz
250–260 g	9 oz
280–290 g	10 oz
300–320 g	11 oz
330–340 g	12 oz
360–380 g	13 oz
400 g	14 oz
410–430 g	15 oz
450 g	16 oz/1 lb
1 kg	2 lb 4 oz
1.5 kg	3 lb 5 oz

Liquids

Metric	Imperial
15 ml	1 tablespoon or ½ fl oz
30 ml	2 tablespoons or 1 fl oz
150 ml	¼ pint or 5 fl oz
280–300 ml	½ pint
425–450 ml	¾ pint
570–600 ml	1 pint or 20 fl oz
1 litre	1¾ pints
1.2 litres	2 pints

Useful conversions

1 tablespoon = 3 teaspoons

1 level tablespoon = approx. 15 g or ½ oz

1 heaped tablespoon = approx. 30 g or 1 oz

1 glass of wine = 100–150 ml

1 egg = 55 ml/55 g/2 fl oz

1 lime gives about 30 ml or 2 tablespoons juice

1 lemon gives about 120 ml or 8 tablespoons juice

Length

Metric	Imperial
1 cm	½ inch
2.5 cm	1 inch
5 cm	2 inches
15 cm	6 inches
20 cm	8 inches
30 cm	12 inches

American Conversions

1 cup liquid = 8 fl oz = 225 ml

1 American pint = 16 fl oz = 450 ml

2 American pints = approx. 1 litre (1000 ml)

Ingredient	US	Metric	Imperial
Butter/margarine/lard	1 cup/2 sticks	225 g	8 oz
Cheese, grated	1 cup	110 g	4 oz
Currants/raisins/sultanas	1 cup	140 g	5 oz
Flour	1 cup	125 g	4½ oz
Nuts, chopped	1 cup	100 g	3½ oz
Rice, uncooked	1 cup	170 g	6 oz
Sugar, brown	1 cup	170 g	6 oz
Sugar, granulated/caster	1 cup	170 g	6 oz

Australian Conversions

5 ml/5 g = 1 teaspoon

20 ml/20 g = 1 tablespoon

250 ml = 1 cup

Ingredient	Metric	Imperial
1 cup butter	225 g	8 oz
1 cup fresh breadcrumbs	55 g	2 oz
1 cup flour	140 g	5 oz
1 cup chopped nuts	110 g	3 oz
1 cup rice, uncooked	200 g	7 oz
1 cup sugar, crystal/caster	225 g	8 oz
1 cup sugar, brown, firmly packed	170 g	6 oz

Oven temperatures

°C	°F	Gas mark	US
70	150	¼	COOL
80	175	¼	
100	200	½	
110	225	½	
130	250	1	VERY LOW
140	275	1	
150	300	2	LOW
170	325	3	MODERATE
180	350	4	
190	375	5	MODERATELY HOT
200	400	6	FAIRLY HOT
220	425	7	HOT
230	450	8	VERY HOT
240	475	8	
250	500	9	EXTREMELY HOT
270	525	9	
290	550	9	

Bibliography

Bissell, Francis, *The Real Meat Cookbook* (Chatto & Windus, 1992)

Culinary Institute of America, *The Professional Chef* (John Wiley, 2006)

Davidson, Alan, *The Penguin Companion to Food* (Penguin, 2002)

Herbst, Sharon Tyler and Herbst, Ron, *Food Lover's Companion* (Barron's Educational Series, 2007)

Leith, Prue and Waldegrave, Caroline, *Leiths Cookery Bible* (Bloomsbury, 2003)

McGee, Harold, *On Food and Cooking* (Hodder & Stoughton, 2004)

Spaull, Susan and Bruce-Gardyne, Lucinda, *Leiths Techniques Bible* (Bloomsbury, 2003)

Time-Life Books, *The Time-Life Good Cook Series* (Time-Life Books)

Wrangham, Richard, *Catching Fire: How Cooking Made Us Human* (Basic Books, 2009)

Suppliers

Dried Herbs and Spices

Seasoned Pioneers
0800 06822348
www.seasonedpioneers.co.uk

Exotic Meats

Alternative Meats Ltd
0844 545 6070
www.alternativemeats.com

C & K Meats
01379 870939
www.ckmeats.co.uk

Freedown Food
020 7720 4520
www.freedownfood.com

The Original Pig
01308 863680
www.theoriginalpig.com

Osgrow
0117 973 0300
www.osgrow.com

Ostriches Online
01625 432462
www.ostrichesonline.co.uk

River Wood Ostrich Farm
0118 973 1702
www.ostrich-meat.co.uk

Woldsway Foods Ltd
0800 298 5000
www.woldsway.co.uk

Ham and Bacon

Emmetts Store
01728 660250
www.emmettsham.co.uk

Pyrenees Milk-fed Lamb

London Fine Foods
0845 643 9121
www.londonfinefoods.com

Turkeys

Kelly Bronze Turkeys
01245 223581
www.kelly-turkeys.com

About Leiths
and the Authors

Prue Leith was the founder of the prestigious Leiths Restaurant, Leiths School of Food and Wine, and Leiths Ltd, a catering company founded in 1961. She has been a prolific contributor to the press, TV and radio, and is the author of many cookbooks. In 1989 she was awarded the OBE for services to good food, and in 1991 she won the Veuve Clicquot Award for Businesswoman of the Year.

Caroline Waldegrave joined Prue's catering company in 1971 and helped set up the school in 1975. Caroline was the principal and managing director until 1993, when she became the co-owner with Christopher Bland. Caroline has written numerous cookery books. Formerly a member of the Health Education Authority (1983–7) and ex-chair of the Guild of Food Writers, she is also a qualified instructor in wine. In June 2000 she was awarded the OBE for services to the catering industry.

Max Clark worked in veterinary medicine for 12 years before completing the Diploma in Food and Wine at Leiths School in 1988. After graduating, she worked as a chef for the Roux Brothers and Covent Garden's Sanctuary spa. She has worked as a caterer and makes wedding and special occasion cakes. She joined Leiths School as a teacher in 1989, and taught there for 10 years before becoming the Buyer. She has written for Leiths *Daily Mail* recipe column, contributed to *Leiths Cookery Bible*, and is a co-author of *Leiths Vegetarian Bible*. Max lives in London.

Susan Spaull is a freelance cookery writer, food stylist and recipe development consultant. She is the author of the award-winning *Leiths Techniques Bible* and co-author of *Leiths Baking Bible*, as well as *Ideal Home Entertaining*. Having trained at Cordon Bleu and Leiths School of Food and Wine in London, she ran her own catering business before returning to Leiths, where she taught for 10 years. Susan currently divides her time between London and the USA.

If you would like details of the courses at the school, please contact:

Leiths School of Food and Wine
16–20 Wendell Road
London W12 9RT
Tel. 020 8749 6400
www.leiths.com

General Index

See Recipe Index for individual recipes

freezing 5, 7
  defrosting poultry 256, 260, 262
  stocks 450
French terms 511–21
frying 11, 16–18
  see also **deep-frying**
  see also specific types of meat

G
galantines 270–1
game 371–422
  catering quantities 508
  choosing 375
  drawing 375–6, 402
  feathered game 375–401
  furred game 402–22
  hanging 373–4
  plucking game birds 375
  recipes, game birds **376–7**
  seasons 371–2
  storing 373
  tenderizing 373
  see also **hare; pheasant; rabbit; venison**
gammon 221–7
  choosing 221
  cooking methods 224
  recipes **224–7**
  storing 222
  see also **bacon; ham**
gelatine 2
ghee xii
giblets 256
gizzards 342–3
  duck 342
  game 375, 376
glace de viande 455
gnu 427
goat 181
goose 258
  catering quantities 508
  choosing 258
  recipes **356–7**
  roasting 262
  storing 258
goose fat xii
goose liver 360
  foie gras 361–2
grain of meat 2
gravy, see sauces
grilling 11, 18–21
  see also specific types of meat
grouse
  catering quantities 508
  hanging 374
  recipes **378**
  roasting 377
  season 371

guanaco 439
guinea fowl 259
  cutting into portions 266–7
  recipes **324–5**
  roasting 262, 377

H
ham
  choosing 221
  cooking methods 224
  recipes **225–31**
  storing 222
  types of 221
ham frills 225
hanging meat 3–4
  see also specific types of meat
hare 411
  boning 403
  hanging 374
  jointing 411
  recipes **412–3**
  season 372
  skinning 411
hearts
  lambs' **187**
hygiene 4–5

I
impala 427

J
jointing
  chicken 266–7
  duck 326–7
  hare 411
  rabbit 402–3

K
kangaroo 423
  recipes **435–8**
kidneys
  lambs' 183
    recipes **184–5**
  ox and calves' 95
    choosing 95
    sautéing 95
    storing 95
    recipes **96–7**
kudu 427

L
lamb 131–87
  boning 136–8
  breeds 131–2
  butterfly joint 138
  carving 145, 152
  catering quantities 507
  choosing 132–3
  cooking methods 135–6

crown roast of lamb, preparation 142
  cuts 133–4
  French-trimmed cutlets 141
  guard of honour, preparation 142
  hanging 132
  history 131
  noisettes, preparing 143
  Pyrenean milk fed lamb 132
  rack of lamb, preparation 140–2
  recipes **146–87**
  saddle of lamb 143
  salt marsh lamb 132
  storing 133
  stuffing boned shoulder of lamb 139
lambs' kidneys 183
  recipes **183–5**
larding veal 108
liaisons 459
liver
  calves' 92
    recipes **93–4**
  see also **chicken livers; foie gras**
llama 439

M
marbling 2
marinating meat 8–9
marrow 129
meat
  choosing 4
  colour 3, 11, 30
  cooking methods 11–27
  hanging 3–4
  hygiene 4–5
  storage 4, 5–6, 7
  structure 1–3
  tenderizing 7–9
  tenderness 6–7
  see also specific types of meat
menu planning 505–6
microwaving bacon 224
muscle fibres 1–2
muscox 440–1
mutton 131
  catering quantities 507
  choosing 133
  recipes **178–80**

N
noisettes of lamb, preparing 143

O
oil xii–xiii
olive oil xii–xiii

organic meat 6, 256
ostrich 442–3
ox kidneys 95
  choosing 95
  recipes **96–7**
  storing 95

P
pan-frying, *see* **frying**
partridge 371
  catering quantities 508
  hanging 374
  recipes **378–9**
  roasting 377
  season 371
pasta 488–9
pastry 476–86
paunching rabbit 402
pheasant
  catering quantities 508
  hanging 374
  recipes **380–90**
  roasting 377
  season 371
pigeon
  catering quantities 508
  hanging 374
  recipes **392–4**
  roasting 377
  season 371
pig's head, offal 251–2
poaching 22
pork 189–220
  breeds 189–90
  carving 195
  catering quantities 508
  choosing 190
  cooking methods 191–2
  crackling 192, 195
  cuts 190–1
  history 189
  preparation 192–3
  recipes **194–220**
  roasting 191–3
  storing 190
  see also **bacon**; **ham**;
    gammon; **pig's head**;
    sausages
pork trotters, preparation 193
pot-roasting 12, 23–4
poulet noir 257
poultry 255–369
  ballotines 270
  boning 269–70
  breeds 255
  catering quantities 508
  choosing 256
  cooking methods 260–4
  cutting into portions 268

defrosting 256, 262
giblets 256
gizzards 342
history 255
livers 360–9
spatchcocking 319
splitting small birds in half 268
storing 256
trussing 261
see also **chicken**; **duck**;
  goose; **guinea fowl**;
  turkey
poussins 257
  cooking methods 263
  recipes **319–23**
  spatchcocking 319
proteins 1, 3, 11, 423
python 444

Q
quail
  catering quantities 508
  hanging 374
  recipes **396**
  roasting 377
  season 371
  spatchcocking 319
quantities, catering 507–8

R
rabbit 402–3
  boning, saddle of 403
  hanging 373–4
  jointing 402–3
  paunching 402
  recipes 402–11
  roasting 403
  season 372
  skinning 402
rack of lamb, preparing 140–1
rattlesnake 444
rearing methods 6
refrigerators 5, 6
religious customs 1
resting roast meat 14
reticulin 2
rhea 442
roasting 11, 12–15
  see also specific types of meat

S
safety, deep-frying 53
salad oil xiii
salmonella 256
salt xiii
  brining meat 9
saturated fat 3–4, 6
sauces
  recipes **459–75**

sausagemeat 237, 238
sausages 237–53
  cooking 238
  recipes **239–45**
  skins 237
  see also **black pudding**
sautéing 17
  see also specific types of meat
sea salt xiii
seasons, game 371–2
skewer test, roasting meat 14
skinning
  hare 411
  rabbit 402
skins, sausages 237
snake 444–5
snipe 371, 374, 377
soups
  catering quantities 507
  see recipe index
spatchcocking 270, 319
spit-roasting 16
spring chicken 257
  cutting into portions 268
  grilling 263
springbok 427
  recipe **429**
squabs *see* **pigeon**
stewing 12, 25–7
  see also specific types of meat
  see also **curries**
stir-frying 18, 264
  see also recipe index
stocks 449–57
  recipes **451–7**
  storing 450
storage 4, 5–6, 7
  see also specific types of meat
supremes, chicken 264
sweetbreads 123
  see also **veal**; **lamb**
  see also recipe index

T
temperatures
  cooking meat 11
  oven temperatures 525
  thermometers 33
  see also specific meat roasting
    charts
tenderizing meat 7–9, 373
tenderloin, pork, preparation 191
tenderness 6–7
terrines
  see recipe index
testing for doneness 14, 20
thermometers 33
tongue
  see recipe index

Recipe Index

pan-fried sweetbreads on
toasted brioche 123
sweetbread terrine 125
sweetbread ravioli with chervil
crème fraîche sauce 124
veal escalopes with ragoût fin
117
veal offal stew 126

T
tagine, lamb with prunes and
almonds 166
tamarind-spiced quail 396
tapenade 467
tapenade-stuffed chicken
breasts 291
warm Pink Fir Apple potato,
smoked bacon and
tapenade salad 235
teal 371, 374
tempura, griddled python with
baby fennel 445
**teriyaki beef with mushrooms
and noodles** 61
terrines
autumn terrine 390
brawn 252
chicken liver and foie gras
parfait 366–7
individual foie gras and ham
hock terrines 369
mi-cuit foie gras terrine 365
pheasant and duck liver terrine
388
pheasant and pistachio terrine
387
sweetbread terrine 125
Thai basil pork 206
Thai green chicken curry 296
Thai stir-fried beef 58
toad in the hole 242
toast
marrow on toast with French
radish salad 129
Melba toast 496
pan-fried sweetbreads on
toasted brioche 123
tomatoes
bacon and tomato cakes with
poached eggs 233
cherry tomato salsa 300–1
chicken with tomato and
coriander 288–9
exotic sauce 471
fresh tomato chutney 236
lamb steaks with roast butter
beans and tomatoes 161
Mediterranean veal knuckle
stew 112

moussaka 176
osso bucco 111
spaghetti Bolognese 82
tomato and mint salsa 470
tomato dressing 474
tomato sauce 469
warm red salsa 470
tortillas
grilled pork quesadillas 201
Toulouse sausages
cassoulet 243
hot sweet potato and sausage
stew 245
sausage cassoulet 244
tripe, deep-fried tripe and onions
102–3
trotters, pigs' trotters and
porcini mushrooms 215
tsimmes 69
tuna, turkey tonnato 348
turkey
confit
salad of turkey confit 354
escalopes
turkey escalopes with baby
leeks, mushrooms and
tarragon 349
minced
turkey and pine nut kofta
350
poached
turkey tonnato 348
rechauffé dishes
oriental turkey with sesame
seeds 351
turkey and apricot pie 352
turkey tetrazzini 353
roast
Christmas turkey stuffed
with ham 346–7
roast turkey 344–5
sandwiches
turkey sandwiches 355
stock
turkey stock 456

V
veal
braised
osso bucco 111
veal fricandeau 110
minced
veal spring rolls 122
pies
pâté en croûte 216-7
veal and ham raised pie 121
roast
veal fricandeau 110
roast loin of veal 109

sausages
boudin blanc 241
sauté
Hungarian veal medallions
with aubergine 119
veal escalopes with ragoût
fin 117
veal escalopes with rosemary
115
veal Florentine 118
veal Marsala 115
veal Martini 116
veal medallions and grilled
vegetables with aïoli 120
veal medallions with wild
mushrooms 118–19
veal piccata 116–17
stew
blanquette de veau 114
Mediterranean veal knuckle
stew 112
osso bucco 111
veal knuckle and black-eyed
bean stew 113
stock
brown stock 452
jellied stock 450
veal stock 454
veal kidneys
feuilletées 128
veal kidneys Robert 127
veal kidneys with wholegrain
mustard and leek cream
127
veal offal stew 126
veal marrow 129
marrow on toast with French
radish salad 129
veal offal stew 126
veal sweetbreads, *see*
sweetbreads
vegetables
braising 24–5
court-bouillon 457
smoked goose breast and
winter vegetable stew 358
see also **peppers**; **tomatoes**
etc
venison
braised
braised haunch of venison
421
roast
roast venison with
chanterelles 417
sausages
venison sausages 240
steaks
peppered venison steak 420